OTHER A TO ...
THE SCARECROW PRESS, INC.

1. *The A to Z of Buddhism* by Charles S. Prebish, 2001.
2. *The A to Z of Catholicism* by William J. Collinge, 2001.
3. *The A to Z of Hinduism* by Bruce M. Sullivan, 2001.
4. *The A to Z of Islam* by Ludwig W. Adamec, 2002.
5. *The A to Z of Slavery & Abolition* by Martin A. Klein, 2002.
6. *Terrorism: Assassins to Zealots* by Sean Kendall Anderson and Stephen Sloan, 2003.
7. *The A to Z of the Korean War* by Paul M. Edwards, 2005.
8. *The A to Z of the Cold War* by Joseph Smith and Simon Davis, 2005.
9. *The A to Z of the Vietnam War* by Edwin E. Moise, 2005.
10. *The A to Z of Science Fiction Literature* by Brian Stableford, 2005.
11. *The A to Z of the Holocaust* by Jack R. Fischel, 2005.
12. *The A to Z of Washington, D.C.* by Robert Benedetto, Jane Donovan, and Kathleen DuVall, 2005.
13. *The A to Z of Taoism* by Julian F. Pas, 2006.
14. *The A to Z of the Renaissance* by Charles G. Nauert, 2006.
15. *The A to Z of Shinto* by Stuart D. B. Picken, 2006.
16. *The A to Z of Byzantium* by John H. Rosser, 2006.
17. *The A to Z of the Civil War* by Terry L. Jones, 2006.
18. *The A to Z of the Friends (Quakers)* by Margery Post Abbott, Mary Ellen Chijioke, Pink Dandelion, and John William Oliver Jr., 2006
19. *The A to Z of Feminism* by Janet K. Boles and Diane Long Hoeveler, 2006.
20. *The A to Z of New Religious Movements* by George D. Chryssides, 2006.
21. *The A to Z of Multinational Peacekeeping* by Terry M. Mays, 2006.
22. *The A to Z of Lutheranism* by Günther Gassmann with Duane H. Larson and Mark W. Oldenburg, 2007.
23. *The A to Z of the French Revolution* by Paul R. Hanson, 2007.
24. *The A to Z of the Persian Gulf War 1990–1991* by Clayton R. Newell, 2007.
25. *The A to Z of Revolutionary America* by Terry M. Mays, 2007.
26. *The A to Z of the Olympic Movement* by Bill Mallon with Ian Buchanan, 2007.

The A to Z of African American Theater

Anthony D. Hill
with
Douglas Q. Barnett

The A to Z Guide Series, No. 111

The Scarecrow Press, Inc.
Lanham • Toronto • Plymouth, UK
2009

Published by Scarecrow Press, Inc.
A wholly owned subsidiary of
The Rowman & Littlefield Publishing Group, Inc.
4501 Forbes Boulevard, Suite 200, Lanham, Maryland 20706
http://www.scarecrowpress.com

Estover Road, Plymouth PL6 7PY, United Kingdom

British Library Cataloguing in Publication Information Available

Library of Congress Cataloging-in-Publication Data

The hardback version of this book was cataloged by the Library of Congress as
follows:

Hill, Anthony D., 1947–
   Historical dictionary of African American theater / Anthony D. Hill with
Douglas Q. Barnett.
      p. cm. — (Historical dictionaries of literature and the arts ; no. 31)
   Includes bibliographical references.
   1. African American theater–Dictionaries. I. Barnett, Douglas Q. II. Title.
PN2270.A35H53 2009
792.089'96073–dc22   2008027154

ISBN 978-0-8108-6898-4 (pbk. : alk. paper)
ISBN 978-0-8108-7061-1 (ebook)

⊗™ The paper used in this publication meets the minimum requirements of
American National Standard for Information Sciences—Permanence of Paper
for Printed Library Materials, ANSI/NISO Z39.48-1992.

Printed in the United States of America

I dedicate this book to my mother, Flavor Bell Booker, the essence of my existence, and to all my family members, loved ones, and friends who inspired and encouraged me. — ADH

I thank my mother and father, who showed me the way, my loving family for supporting me, and Roberta Byrd Barr for encouraging me to follow my dreams. Last, I thank the women in my life, whose magic I will always treasure. — DQB

Contents

Editor's Foreword

African American theatre does not have a very long history, and this is certainly less the fault of African Americans than their fellow citizens. Initially, the very idea of such a theatre seemed ludicrous, and it was only about the time of the African Grove Theatre (1821–23) that the first actors appeared, the first play was written, and the first theatre was opened. Early on, blacks usually had just minor—and frequently demeaning—roles, and even "minstrels" were white. But over the past century, things have changed, very slowly and painfully at first and more recently with amazing speed and verve. Today, there are countless actors, a plethora of playwrights, and theaters of all sorts in large cities and increasingly small as well. While many of the plays grapple with specific themes, others tackle universal problems and issues. They partake in all the genres, comedy and tragedy and farce, straight and musical shows, from 1 act to 3 to even a cycle of 10. Most impressive, the audience is no longer only African American but far broader, as many of their fellow citizens also appreciate this theater, which has been successfully exported as well, while the more outstanding actors, producers, directors, playwrights, and others are widely recognized and win prestigious awards.

Yet, while this branch of theater is increasingly familiar to many African Americans, there are others for whom it is not even on the radar. And most other Americans, let alone foreigners, still find it a bit strange and exotic. This feeling, rooted in a lack of knowledge, can only be overcome by providing more information, and fortunately, this latest historical dictionary is a treasure chest of information. The dictionary section, the core of the book, has well over 600 entries on, in order of emphasis, playwrights, actors, theater-producing organizations, directors, plays, musicals, and themes. It does not have everything, but it certainly has more than can be found anywhere else, and it conveys this information with the insight of insiders. The chronology tracks the progress, from the exceedingly hesitant steps of a century and a half ago to the fast-paced changes of recent decades. Alas, it is hard to follow any of this without a knowledge of acronyms, which explains the abundance of its list. The introduction does just that, introducing and also explaining the emergence of African American theater. The bibliography provides precious hints on where to go for further information, although, alas, there is not all that much literature on the topic, which only enhances the importance of this book.

The A to Z of African American Theater was written by two insiders, Anthony D. Hill and Douglas Q. Barnett. Both are writers, theater administrators, and play directors, and the former is also an academic. Dr. Hill, who has written widely on African American theater in the past, has advanced degrees in theater and performance studies and is presently associate professor of drama in the Department of Theatre at Ohio State University. On the practical side, he has been associated with the National Black Theatre Network, the National Conference of African American Theatre, and other theater organizations. Barnett was the founding director of Black Arts/West in Seattle, WA, where he produced many plays and—almost more important—has trained a large number of students who have since become professionals. He has also worked with the Negro Ensemble Company, Seattle Arts Commission, and GeVa Theatre; directed plays; and written a few plays of his own in addition to acting in over 30 productions. This experience and the combined abilities of these two authors were essential in creating this exceptional tool for all those interested in African American theater, whether creating it, performing it, or just enjoying it.

Jon Woronoff
Series Editor

Preface

The A to Z of African American Theater celebrates nearly 200 years of black theater in the United States. It is a cross-section of the thousands of black theater artists across the country. It identifies representative African American theater-producing organizations, playwrights, and selected works by these playwrights, actors, and directors. It also chronicles their contributions to the field, from its birth in 1816 to the present. The dictionary includes the editor's foreword, preface, acknowledgments, acronyms and abbreviations, chronology, introduction, dictionary, bibliography, and information about the writers.

More than 600 selected entries are comprised in this collection. The criteria for each are as follows: African American theater-producing organizations are included whose primary intent was to present plays of relevance to the African American community with an ongoing record of production accomplishments. Information on playwrights includes the date of birth and death only if the writer is deceased; a brief biographical sketch (if available); the person's name or names (including pseudonyms, nicknames, and married names); place of birth; career highlights; family background or relationships if pertinent to the profile; theatrical training or education; a brief synopsis of one or two notable plays with subtitles; dates of publication; location of production; significance of work if applicable; a brief list of other plays; and honors, awards, grants, fellowships, and honorary degrees. The writer must be of African American ancestry even if he or she is only partly black (or a white writer who has made exceptional contributions to the field), be an American citizen (including expatriates), and have written more than one notable play that has been produced at a professional venue. The actors, plays, and musicals are representative samplings from each decade. The inclusion of directors is based on the number of plays mounted at their own theater companies, professional regional theaters, and off and on-Broadway venues. While we tried to make this collection as inclusive as possible, the omission of other important entries was unavoidable.

The dictionary represents the ongoing research and collection of materials at major archives in New York City, the Hatch-Billops Collection, Schomburg Center for Research in Black Culture of the New York Public Library, Theatre Collection of the New York Public Library at Lincoln Center, and the James Weldon Johnson Memorial Collection at Yale University in New Haven, Connecticut. The search was expanded to include the personal collections in the archives at the Research Center for the Federal Theatre Project at George Mason University in Fairfax, VA; the repositories of the federal government, such as the National Archives and the Library of Congress in Washington, DC, and the Moorland-Spingarn Research Center at Howard University; the Los Angeles Public Library; and archives in Chicago, Seattle, and Fairfax, VA. The research material was examined extensively for information on various aspects of African American theater. The searches included published and unpublished sources, anthologies, periodicals, newspapers, bibliographies, dissertations and theses, play manuscripts, programs advertisements, the World Wide Web, announcements, and personal collections. Information was acquired from e-mails, interviews, questionnaires, and telephone calls to hundreds of theater founders and artistic directors, playwrights, performers, directors, and others in the field.

We hope that this dictionary will be of value to librarians; teachers; high school, graduate, and undergraduate students; theater owners; performers; directors; dramaturges; theater critics; historians; scholars; and all others in need of information on black theater and black-authored plays. It may lead to more detailed studies by researchers in the fields of black studies, literature, and drama and by playwrights, as well as producers, directors, actors, and theatrical organizations. It will be a valuable resource to serious theater scholars who would otherwise have to travel to archives and libraries outside their educational institutions.

Acknowledgments

I thank my editor, Jon Woronoff, for keeping me on track; Ruthmarie Mitsch for the proofreading and editing; the playwrights for the scripts; the black theater–producing organization heads for providing venues for the plays; and theater pioneers, researchers, educators, and scholars for sharing their research and keeping African American theater alive and in the eye of the theater world.

I thank all the librarians and curators of archives, repositories, and personal collections for their generous assistance, in particular James V. Hatch, the Hatch-Billops Collection in New York City; Richard H. Engleman, Sayer-Carkeek Collection, special collection and preservation division; Liz Fugate; and Theatre Arts at the University of Washington. Other collections I found useful were the Schomburg Center for Research in Black Culture of the New York Public Library; the James Weldon Johnson Memorial Collection; Federal Theatre Project at George Mason University in Fairfax, VA; National Archives and the Library of Congress in Washington, DC; Moorland-Spingarn Research Center at Howard University; and the collections in Chicago and Los Angeles.

I thank the actors, directors, and theater practitioners for the personal correspondence, telephone conversations, interviews, and talks. I also thank the sponsors of symposiums at such conferences as Black Theatre Network and the National Black Theatre Festival in Winston-Salem, NC.

I especially thank Douglas Q. Barnett for agreeing to work with me on this project. He has been a student of black theater since his stage debut in *A Raisin in the Sun* in 1961. His vast knowledge of theater both locally and nationally has contributed immeasurably to the final product of this book. He thanks in particular the librarians and curators of the Seattle Public Library system for their assistance. He extends kudos especially to Carletta Wilson at the central downtown branch; Samuel Jackson at the Douglass-Truth branch; and Kathy Harvey, Theatre and Performance, Sayre-Carkeek Collection.

Acronyms and Abbreviations

AADC	African American Drama Company
AASAS	African American Studio for Acting and Speech
AASC	African American Shakespeare Company
ACT	American Community Theatre (New York City), American Conservatory Theatre (San Francisco), A Contemporary Theatre (Seattle)
ACTF	American College Theatre Festival
AEA	Actors Equity Association (a union)
AETA	American Educational Theatre Association
AGIA	African Grove Institute for the Arts
ANT	American Negro Theatre
ANTA	American National Theatre and Academy
ATRA	African Theatre and the Related Arts
Audelco	Audience Development Committee
BARTS	Black Arts Repertory Theatre School
BA/W	Black Arts/West (Seattle, WA)
BET	Black Ensemble Theatre
BSTC	Black Spectrum Theatre Company
BTA	Black Theatre Alliance
BTN	Black Theatre Network (an annual conference)
BTT	Black Theatre Troupe
BWPG	Black Women Playwright Group
CAMP	Central Area Motivation Program
CART	Caribbean American Repertory Theatre
CAT	Community Actors Theatre
CAU	Colored Actors Union
CBTC	Cincinnati Black Theatre Company
CCLA	City College of Los Angeles
CCNY	City College of New York

CET	Concept East Theatre
CETA	Comprehensive Employment Training Act
CNA	Committee for the Negro in the Arts
CSTC	Congo Square Theatre Company
CTC	Chicago Theatre Company
CUNY	City University of New York
DPT	Dashiki Project Theatre
DRT	Dunbar Repertory Theatre
FST	Free Southern Theatre
FSWW	Frank Silvera Writers' Workshop
FTP	Federal Theatre Project
HADLEY	Harlem Artistic Developmental League Especially for You
HARYOU	Harlem Youth Opportunities Unlimited, Inc., and Associated Community Teams
HBCU	Historically Black Colleges and Universities
HCTC	Harlem Children's Theatre Company
HET	Harlem Experimental Theatre
HP	The Hansberry Project
HRT	Harlem Repertory Theatre
HST	Harlem Showcase Theatre, Harlem Suitcase Theatre
HTC	Harlem Theatre Company
ICCC	Inner-City Cultural Center
IRT	Impact Repertory Theatre
JLT	Juneteenth Legacy Theatre
KRIGWA	Crisis Guild of Writers and Actors
KRT	Kuntu Repertory Theatre
LHT	Lorraine Hansberry Theatre
LORT	League of Resident Theatres
MET	Metropolitan Ebony Theatre
MPAACT	Ma'at Production Association of Afrikan-Centered Theatre
NAACP	National Association for the Advancement of Colored People
NADSA	National Association of Dramatic and Speech Arts
NAG	Negro Actors Guild
NBAF	National Black Arts Festival
NBTC	National Black Touring Circuit

NBTF	National Black Theatre Festival
NCATT	National Conference on African American Theatre
NCBRT	North Carolina Black Repertory Theatre
NEA	National Endowment for the Arts
NEA/TCG	National Endowment for the Arts/Theatre Communications Group
NEC	Negro Ensemble Company
NEH	National Endowment for the Humanities
NFT	New Federal Theatre
NHRT	New Heritage Repertory Theatre
NHT	New Horizon Theatre
NLT	New Lafayette Theatre
NTC	Nubian Theatre Company
NYPL	New York Public Library
NYSCA	New York State Council on the Arts
NYSF/ Public Theatre	New York Shakespeare Festival/Public Theatre
NYU	New York University
OBIE	Off-Broadway award for excellence in theatre
OET	Oakland Ensemble Theatre
PASLA	Performing Arts Society of Los Angeles
PBRT	Providence Black Repertory Theatre
PEW	Pew Charitable Trusts
RACCA	Richard Allen Center for Culture and Art
RRP	Ripe and Ready Players
SADSA	Southern Association of Dramatic and Speech Arts
SAG	Screen Actors Guild
SCLC	Southern Christian Leadership Conference
SLBRT	St. Louis Black Repertory Theatre
SNCC	Student Nonviolent Coordinating Committee
STC	Shadow Theatre Company
SUNY	State University of New York
TBS	Turner Broadcasting System
TCG	Theatre Communications Group
TOBA	Theatre Owners Booking Association ("tough on black actors")

TONY	Antoinette Perry Awards for excellence in a Broadway show
UAC	Urban Arts Corps
UCLA	University of California at Los Angeles
UPET	Unity Players Ensemble Theatre Company
USC	University of Southern California
WPA	Works Progress Administration

Chronology

17th–18th Century Blacks are depicted in farces and melodramas as glorified minstrels; servants/maids; comic "raccoons"; "fools"; ignorant West Indians; and shuffling, cackling, singing, and dancing "darkies."

1789 Josiah Henson, an escaped slave and reputed model for Uncle Tom in *Uncle Tom's Cabin*, is born in Charles County, MD. In 1849, Henson publishes *The Life of Josiah Henson, Formerly a Slave, Now an Inhabitant of Canada as Narrated by Himself.*

1821 On Mercer Street in New York City, William Alexander Brown forms the African Grove Theatre and the first known all-black acting troupe. James Hewlett and Ira Aldridge, the principal actors, perform Shakespearean dramas, the classics, and lighter popular melodramas.

1825 Ira Aldridge (1807–65) arrives in London from the United States to begin his professional acting career. He performs for 42 years throughout Europe, Russia, and the British Isles.

1829 Thomas "Daddy" Rice, a white delineator, first performs on a Washington, DC, stage in blackface. He influences the minstrelsy performance tradition (whites imitating negative portrayals of blacks) that lasts over 100 years.

1844 Le Théâtre Français produces Victor Séjour's first play, *Diegareas*, which inaugurates a brilliant career for Séjour. He is one of the more commercially successful black dramatists of the 19th century in Paris.

1846 Ira Aldridge's play *The Black Doctor* opens in London.

1850 The Federal Fugitive Slave Law allows any claimant of a runaway black slave to take possession of his slave upon establishing proof of ownership before a federal commissioner. The ramifications of this law on escaped slaves are explored in plays with abolitionist themes.

1852 Harriet Beecher Stowe's novel *Uncle Tom's Cabin* is published. It portrays the plight of the black slave in highly emotional language. The novel becomes America's greatest hit by a white writer for the next 80 years. Later, George L. Aiken adapts it into play form.

1856 *The Escape; or, Leap to Freedom* by William Wells Brown is reportedly the first play written by an escaped black slave. It is read frequently at abolitionist society meetings but never produced.

1858 Victor Séjour writes *The Brown Overcoat*. It is produced the following year.

1865 The Ku Klux Klan is formed in Tennessee after the Civil War to terrorize blacks and keep them in check.

1867 Howard University, chartered by the federal government, is established in Washington, DC.

1878 B. J. Ford and J. A. Arneaux are the leading black Shakespearean actors of the period. They perform in their own black companies, such as the Astor Place Colored Tragedy Company. Arneaux publishes an edited version of *Richard III* in 1886.

1891–1900 In a multipronged attack, black theatrical pioneers set out to destroy the minstrel pattern that seriously distorts their image. Sam T. Jack's *The Creole Show* opens in Boston. It is among the first black productions that break from the minstrel pattern by allowing black women to perform in a musical revue and to be featured as singing women.

1895 John W. Isham's *The Octoroons*, a musical, breaks further from the minstrel pattern. His next play, *Oriental America*, makes an even greater break from this form. Bob Cole organizes the Worth's Museum All-Star Stock Company in New York City and begins the first training school for black performers.

1896 Sissieretta Jones, a black opera singer, is nicknamed "Black Patti" after the Italian soprano Adelina Patti. She is the first known black singer to appear at Wallach's Theater in Boston. She organizes Black Patti's Troubadours. Bill "Bojangles" Robinson, vaudevillian and movie star, first appears in vaudeville on the Keith circuit.

1898 Black colleges begin to encourage play production among their students. Tuskegee Institute in Alabama appoints Charles Wood, a classical actor, as a professor of drama and elocution. *A Trip to Coontown*, a musical operetta by Bob Cole and William Johnson, is the first known musical comedy presented by blacks for blacks. Paul Laurence Dunbar and Will Marion Cook's *Clorindy, the Origin of the Cakewalk*, more than any other work, bridges the gap between minstrel shows and musicals.

1899 Bert Williams and George Walker produce their first musical show on Broadway, *The Sons of Ham*, at the Grand Opera House. The show further bridges the gap between minstrelsy and musical comedy. It also initiates a 12-year collaboration that lasts until Walker's death in 1911.

1900 Bob Cole wrote the highly successful *A Shoo Fly Regiment*, a musical about blacks in the U.S. forces in the Spanish–American War.

1902 **2 September:** Bert Williams and George Walker's *In Dahomey*, with lyrics by Paul Laurence Dunbar and music by Will Marion Cook, opens to enthusiastic notices at the Globe Theater in Boston. It becomes the most artistically and financially successful black musical of its time.

1905 Atlanta University initiates the custom of presenting a Shakespearean play by the graduating class. W. E. B. DuBois and others found the Niagara Movement, which is later known as the National Association for the Advancement of Colored People (NAACP).

1906 Robert T. Motts forms the Pekin Stock Company in Chicago and includes drama on the bill. Bert Williams and George Walker star in *Abyssinia* by Alex Rogers, Jesse Shipp, and Will Marion Cook. The next year, the same authors produce *Bandana Land*. Henrietta Vinton Davis produces William Edgar Easton's play about the Haitian revolution, *Dessalines*, in Chicago. The Louisville, KY, poet Joseph C. Cotter publishes the drama *Caleb the Degenerate*, which is concerned with the racial theories of Booker T. Washington.

1911 S. H. Dudley, a black actor and entrepreneur, buys theaters in Washington, DC, and Virginia and organizes his own chain of black theaters, the S. H. Dudley Theatrical Enterprise. This is the first black theatrical circuit of record that became known as the "Chitlin' Circuit."

1912 Henrietta Vinton Davis performs in a production of an original tragedy, *Christophe*, by William Edgar Easton at the Lenox Casino in New York City.

1913 **13 October:** *The Star of Ethiopia*, W. E. B. DuBois's monumental drama commemorating the 50th anniversary of the Emancipation Proclamation, premiers at the Armory in New York City.

1914 The Lincoln Theatre in Harlem presents its first known black play, *The Odd Man's Boy* by Henry Cramer. S. H. Dudley also writes and produces several shows there. The Lafayette Stock Company is formed in Harlem for the promotion of black theater.

1915 Anita Bush assembles the Lafayette Players (1915–32) at the Lafayette Theatre in Harlem. Russell and Rowena Jellifes (both white) organize the Karamu Theatre in Cleveland, OH, as part of a private philanthropic social welfare center. The Jellifes encourage blacks to engage in their drama and theater productions. Charles Gilpin forms a stock company, the Gilpin Players, which produces and writes plays especially for the Karamu house.

1916–25 African American female playwrights begin to emerge, such as Angelina Weld Grimké, Georgia Douglas Johnson, Alice Dunbar-Nelson, Mary Burrill, Myrtle Smith Livingston, Ruth Gaines-Shelton, Eulalie Spence, Marita Odette Bonner, and May Miller. The National Association for the Advancement of Colored People unsuccessfully tries to prevent the showing of D. W. Griffith's *Birth of a Nation*. Griffith bases the film on Thomas Dixon's violently antiblack book *The Klansman*. Black nationalist and reformer Marcus Garvey (1887–1940) arrives in New York City and establishes the newspaper *The Negro World*. He gains tremendous support for the Universal Negro Improvement Association (UNIA), his "back to Africa" movement.

1917 On Broadway at the Old Garden Theatre, white playwright Ridgeley Torrence uses black life as subject matter in *Three Plays for the Negro Theatre*: *Simon the Cyrenian*, *The Rider of Dreams*, and *Granny Maumee*. These nonmusical shows are greeted with great success. It marks the first time on the American stage that black actors perform in a drama and command the serious attention of critics, the general public, and audiences. It also reintroduces black actors to the legitimate Broadway professional stage.

1919 February: W. E. B. DuBois organizes the first pan-African congress in Paris, France. **17 February:** The 369th Regiment marches up Fifth Avenue to Harlem. Blacks, upon returning home from World War I, are denied equal employment opportunities. **June to December:** A period that becomes known as the "Red Summer" because of the number of blacks who are killed during the race riots throughout the country. There are 25 race riots in such cities as Washington, DC; Chicago; Charleston, SC; Knoxville, TN; and Omaha, NE. **September:** The Race Relations Commission is founded. **15 December:** Charles Gilpin makes his Broadway debut as William Custis, the black clergyman in the American production of John Drinkwater's *Abraham Lincoln*. Marcus Garvey forms the Black Star Shipping Line. Benjamin Brawley publishes *The Negro in Literature and Art in the United States*.

1920 August: Marcus Garvey's UNIA Convention is held at Madison Square Garden. **1 November:** Charles Gilpin plays Brutus Jones to great acclaim in Eugene O'Neill's *The Emperor Jones* at the Provincetown Playhouse on MacDougal Street in New York City. It runs for 399 performances. Gilpin receives the Drama League Award and the NAACP Spingarn Medal. James Weldon Johnson is elected its first black officer (secretary).

1921 22 May: *Shuffle Along* by Noble Sissle and Eubie Blake (lyrics by Flournoy Miller and Aubrey Lyles) opens at Broadway's David Belasco Theater. It is the first record of a musical revue written and performed by African Americans. Professor Montgomery Gregory, a Harvard graduate, begins offering college credit at Howard University toward a degree for production work. **September:** Marcus Garvey founds the African Orthodox Church. The Colored Players Guild of New York is formed.

1922 The House of Representatives approve the first antilynching legislation.

1923 Marcus Garvey is arrested for mail fraud and sentenced to five years in prison. Jean Toomer's *Cane* is published. Willis Richardson becomes the first African America to have a serious one-act dramatic play produced on Broadway, *The Chip Woman's Fortune.*

1924   21 March: The Civic Club Dinner, sponsored by *Opportunity*, brings black writers and white publishers together. This event is considered the formal launching of the New Negro Movement. **15 May:** Paul Robeson stars in Eugene O'Neill's *All God's Chillun' Got Wings.*

1925   March: Alain Locke and Charles Johnson edit the *Survey Graphic* issue "Harlem: Mecca of the New Negro," which is devoted entirely to black arts and letters. **13 October:** *Appearances* by Garland Anderson opens on Broadway. It is the first full-length serious drama to play Broadway.

1926   30 December: *In Abraham's Bosom*, an antilynching play by Paul Green (white) and starring Rose McClendon, opens on Broadway. It is the recipient of the Pulitzer Prize for Drama.

1935   24 October: *Mulatto*, a play about miscegenation in the Deep South by Langston Hughes, opens on Broadway. It becomes the longest running drama (373 performances) on "The Great White Way" of its time.

1935–39   President Franklin D. Roosevelt launches the Federal Works Progress Administration Program that establishes Negro Units in key cities throughout the United States.

1940   Abram Hill and Fred O'Neal form the American Negro Theatre. Theodore Ward's *Our Lan'* opens off Broadway at the Henry Street Playhouse and moves to the Royale Theatre on Broadway for a limited run.

1943   *Othello*, starring Paul Robeson, Uta Hagen, and Jose Ferrer, opens at the Shubert Theatre on Broadway. It sets a record for the run of a Shakespearean play (296 performances).

1953   24 September: *Take a Giant Step* by Louis Peterson about the urban flight of middle-class blacks opens to critical acclaim on Broadway.

1954   26 October: *In Splendid Error* by William Branch about the meeting between Frederick Douglass and John Brown opens at Greenwich Mews Theatre in New York City. Harry Belafonte becomes the first African American to receive the Tony Award for supporting or featured role in the musical *John Murray Anderson's Almanac*.

1955   November: Alice Childress's *Trouble in Mind*, a play within a play addressing the representation of black actors on Broadway, opens off Broadway at the Greenwich Mews Theatre in New York City. It receives the Obie Award for best play.

1957   28 March: Loften Mitchell's *A Land beyond the River* opens at the Greenwich Mews Theatre in New York City. It confronts a pressing issue of its time—public school desegregation.

1959   11 March: The decade of the 1950s reached its zenith with *A Raisin in the Sun*, Lorraine Hansberry's masterpiece about a black family purchasing a new home in an all-white neighborhood in Chicago. Hansberry's first play opens on Broadway to wide critical and popular acclaim under Lloyd Richards's direction. Aside from attracting the interest of white playgoers, the play also helps to lure black audiences to professional Broadway theater.

1960s–70s   Over 600 community and university black theater organizations flourish with the works of Ben Caldwell, Sonia Sanchez, Martie Charles, Kalamu Ya Salaam, Barbara and Carlton Molette, Ted Shine, and dozens of others. Among the college and university theater teachers who lead the development of black playwrights during the summer at the University of California at Santa Barbara are Owen Dodson at Howard University, Tom Pawley at Lincoln University, Randolph Edmonds at Florida A&M, Ted Shine at Prairie View, George Bass at Brown University, and William R. Reardon at the University of California at Santa Barbara.

1960   4 May: Gene Frankel's (white) production of Jean Genet's *The Blacks: A Clown Show* begins its long successful run off Broadway at the St. Mark's Playhouse, giving center stage to James Earl Jones, Roscoe Lee Browne, Louis Gossett Jr., and many other rising black actors.

1961   28 September: The comedy *Purlie Victorious* by Ossie Davis opens at the Cort Theatre on Broadway. The cast includes Davis, Ruby Dee, Godfrey Cambridge, Alan Alda, Beah Richards, and Sorrell Brooke.

11 December: *Black Nativity* by Langston Hughes opens at the Forty-first Street Theatre on Broadway. It becomes a Christmas holiday classic.

1963 Approximately 200,000 civil rights activists march on Washington, DC, resulting in the passage of the landmark Civil Rights Act of 1964 by Congress.

1964 24 March: *Dutchman* by LeRoi Jones (Amiri Baraka) opens at the Cherry Lane Theatre off Broadway. Jones's manifesto "The Revolutionary Theatre" heralds the black revolutionary drama of the 1960s. Claudia McNeill receives the Tony Award as dramatic actress for *Tiger Tiger Burning Bright*.

1967–87 A resurgence of black community theater groups takes place around the country, most notably in Boston; Buffalo, NY; Chicago; Cleveland, OH; Detroit; Los Angeles; New Orleans; Harlem; Philadelphia; and Washington, DC.

1967 Douglas Turner Ward, Robert Hooks, and Gerald Krone organize the Negro Ensemble Company at the St. Mark's Playhouse in Greenwich Village, New York City.

1968 The New Lafayette Theatre is founded by Robert MacBeth. **2 January:** The Negro Ensemble Company premiers its first production, *Song of the Lusitanian Bogey*. Barbara Ann Teer launches the National Black Theatre in Harlem. She concentrates on black communal ritual theater as advocated by writers like Carlton Molette and Paul Carter Harrison.

1969 James Earl Jones is awarded the Tony Award for his performance as Jack Johnson in Howard Sackler's (white) play *The Great White Hope*. Professional theater ensembles emerge throughout the country: in New York City the Frank Silvera Writers' Workshop, Negro Ensemble, Richard Allen Center, AMAS Theatre, New Federal Theatre, New Lafayette Theatre, and National Black Theatre; in Los Angeles the Inner-City Cultural Center; and in Seattle Black Arts/West. With the advent of black female playwrights, they depict an empowered and multidimensional image of women. Adrienne Kennedy wins the Obie Award for her avant-garde play *Funnyhouse of a Negro*.

1970 The 1970s were rife with the success of musicals—*Purlie*, *Ain't Supposed to Die a Natural Death*, *Don't Bother Me, I Can't Cope*, *The*

Wiz, Bubbling Brown Sugar, Ain't Misbehavin', and *Eubie*. Charles Gordone becomes the first African American playwright to win the coveted Pulitzer Prize for *No Place to Be Somebody*. *Ceremonies in Dark Old Men* by Lonnie Elder III was also nominated. Black dramas invade the "Great White Way" (Broadway)—Joseph Walker's *The River Niger*, Melvin Van Peebles's *Don't Play Us Cheap*, Phillip Hayes Dean's *Paul Robeson*, Samm-Art Williams's *Home*, A. Marcus Hemphill's *Inacent Black* (starring Melba Moore), and Richard Wesley's *The Mighty Gents* (with Morgan Freeman). There is a rapid increase in the number of black people in the audiences, but by the mid 1970s, the momentum of community black theater dwindles.

1971 **14 March:** The Negro Ensemble Company produces Derek Walcott's *Dream on Monkey Mountain* at the St. Marks Playhouse off Broadway. It receives an Obie Award. **29 November:** Ernie McClintock directs N. R. Davidson's play *El Hajj Malik* about Malcolm X at his Afro-American Studio Theatre in Harlem. It typifies the best of the sociopolitical theater presented throughout the country.

1972 The New Lafayette Theatre disbands. This is where Ed Bullins is discovered as a promising playwright, along with Richard Wesley.

1973 Vivian Robinson forms the Audience Development Committee (Audelco), an organization that awards excellence for off-Broadway black theater productions. *My Sister, My Sister* by Ray Aranha receives a Drama Desk Award for playwriting, and Seret Scott wins for best actress. Barbara Montgomery wins both the Audelco and Obie Award as the mother.

1974 *The River Niger* by Joseph A. Walker receives the Tony Award for drama. This is the first play the Negro Ensemble Company takes to Broadway.

1976 **November:** Steve Carter's *Eden* is the winner of the Audelco Award for best play of the year.

1977 Ntozake Shange utilizes poetry, dance, and color symbolism in her play *For Colored Girls Who Have Considered Suicide When the Rainbow Is Enuf'* to popularize a new form she calls a "choreopoem." It receives the Outer Critics Circle Award, a Grammy, an Emmy, and three Obie Awards for the playwright, the producers (Joseph Papp and

Woodie King Jr.), and actress Trazana Beverly, who also won a Tony Award and a Theatre World Award.

1978   Phillip Hayes Dean's play *Paul Robeson* opens on Broadway at the Lunt-Fontainne Theatre amid criticism for Dean's depiction of the title character played by James Earl Jones.

1981   Laurence Holder receives an Audelco Award for best playwright for *When the Chickens Came Home to Roost* (1981) starring Denzel Washington and Kirk Kirksey under the direction of Allie Woods, Jr. It is about a fictitious meeting between Elijah Muhammad and Malcolm X.

1982   Charles Fuller receives the Pulitzer Prize award in drama for *A Soldier's Play*.

1984   August Wilson makes his Broadway debut with *Ma Rainey's Black Bottom*. It wins the New York Drama Critics' Circle best play award. This is the first play in Wilson's 10-play cycle about black existence in America set in every decade of the 20th century.

1985   Alice Childress receives the Audelco Pioneer Award.

1986   George C. Wolfe takes theater audiences by storm with his satirical revue *The Colored Museum*, which opens at the NYSF/Public Theatre in New York City. *Woza Africa!* is the Lucile Lortel Award winner for outstanding musical/play.

1987   August Wilson's *Fences*, a play about family life, is awarded the Pulitzer Prize for drama, the Drama Critics' Circle Award, the Tony Award, and the American Theatre Critics/Steinberg New Play Awards and Citations. Douglass Turner Ward, founder of the Negro Ensemble Company, relinquishes the artistic directorship after 20 years of service.

1988   *Joe Turner's Come and Gone* by August Wilson wins the New York Drama Critics' Circle Award.

1989   Larry Leon Hamlin organizes the first National Black Theatre Festival held in Winston-Salem, NC. Barbara Ann Teer's National Black Theatre production of *Song of Sheba* premiers in Harlem and wins eight Audelco awards.

1990   August Wilson is awarded his second Pulitzer Prize for *The Piano Lesson* and receives the American Theatre Critics/Steinberg New Play Awards and Citations.

1991   *Two Trains Running* by August Wilson wins the American Theatre Critics/Steinberg New Play Awards and Citations.

1992   August Wilson is named "Pittsburgher of the Year" by *Pittsburgh Magazine*.

1993   George C. Wolfe is appointed director of Joseph Papp's NYSF/Public Theatre in New York (its first black director).

1996   June: August Wilson gives his "The Ground on Which I Stand" speech before the National Convention of the Theatre Communications Group, advocating black theater for black people, that sends reverberations throughout the theater community. **16 October:** Distinguished theater and movie veteran Jason Bernard dies of a heart attack at age 58 at the height of his creative potential.

1997   In a national setting at New York's Town Hall with Anna Deveare Smith moderating, Robert Brustein and August Wilson debate the pros and cons of black theater versus white theater.

1998   The first meeting of the African Grove Institute, a gathering of black theater professionals, is held on the campus of Dartmouth University. It is headed by August Wilson, Victor Walker II, and 43 other professional theater practitioners.

1999   August Wilson's *King Hedley* premieres at the Pittsburgh Public Theatre.

2000   Tyler Perry first appears in drag as the Madea persona in his play *Woman, Thou Art Loosed*. He begins renting theaters on the "Urban Circuit," formerly known as the "Chitlin' Circuit," to great success.

2001   Martha Jackson Randolph, cofounder and coartistic director at Atlanta's Jomandi Productions for over 22 years, abruptly resigns to accept the artistic directorship at the Ensemble Theatre in Houston, TX, her hometown.

2002   The Classical Theatre of Harlem produces a revival of *The Blacks*. *Jitney* by August Wilson wins the New York Drama Critics' Circle Award. Suzan-Lori Parks becomes the first African American woman to win the coveted Pulitzer Prize for drama with her play *Top Dog/Underdog*. George C. Wolfe receives an Obie Award for best direction, and Jeffrey Wright wins for best performance for *Topdog/Underdog*.

2003   August Wilson receives the New Dramatists Lifetime Achievement Award for his outstanding artistic contribution to American theatre. **17 March:** Rob Penny, Pittsburgh playwright and confidant to August Wilson, dies. **May:** The world premiere of *Gem of the Ocean* by Wilson takes place at the Goodman Theatre in Chicago and is directed by Marion McClinton. **19 May:** Mos Def receives the 48th annual Village Voice Obie Award for outstanding achievement in *Fucking A*. **2 June:** Whoopi Goldberg coproduces a revival of *Ma Rainey's Black Bottom* by August Wilson at the Royale Theatre on Broadway. Goldberg assumes the title role opposite Charles Dutton.

2004   The revival of the black Broadway classic *A Raisin in the Sun* by Lorraine Hansberry returns to Broadway 45 years later with a cast of television and movie stars and a rock mogul. Audra McDonald (Ruth) and Phylicia Rashad (Mama) are Tony Award winners. Rashad is the first black woman to receive the award for best dramatic performance by an actress in a play. Sanaa Latham (Beneatha) is nominated for a Tony Award. Sean "Puffy" Combs plays Walter Lee. **September:** Charles Weldon, a member of the Negro Ensemble Company since 1970, is chosen to become its new artistic director. He replaces artistic director O. L. Duke, who tragically lost his life in an automobile accident.

2005   **29 June:** Lloyd Richards dies after a prolonged illness. He is director of the epical Broadway production of Lorraine Hansberry's *A Raisin in the Sun* (1959), the Eugene O'Neill Playwrights Center, and the Yale Repertory Theatre and the mentor of August Wilson, whose plays Lloyd eventually directed. **2 October:** August Wilson dies. Two months later, the Virginia Theatre is renamed the August Wilson Theatre. **21 November:** S. Epatha Merkerson wins an Audelco Award for outstanding performer in the musical/female lead actress category for Cheryl L. West's *Birdie Blue*.

2006   The Signature Theatre in New York City dedicates its entire season to the plays of August Wilson.

2007   The resurrected Negro Ensemble Company under Charles Weldon produces Samm-Art Williams's *In the Waiting Room* in New York City. **20 April:** August Wilson's *Radio Golf* opens on Broadway, the 10th and final play of his 10-play cycle. It is nominated for four Tony Awards. **8 June:** Larry Leon Hamlin dies. He was the force behind the National Black Theatre Festival in Winston-Salem, NC. Four years after Phylicia Rashad played the matriarch (Aunt Ester) in the Broadway production of *Gem of the Ocean*, she directs the Seattle Repertory Theatre production, one of the first women to do so. **October:** Tim Bond is appointed chair of the drama department at the University of Syracuse and artistic director of Syracuse Stage in upstate New York. He joins the handful of African Americans who have become artistic directors at white regional theaters. The others are Sheldon Epps, Kenny Leon, Tazewell Thompson, Harold Scott, and George C. Wolfe. **19 November:** The Audelco Awards celebrates its 35th anniversary at City College in New York City.

2008   **21 July:** Barbara Ann Teer, founder of the National Black Theatre, dies.

Introduction

BLACK THEATER: FROM BIRTH TO REBIRTH TO SURVIVAL

African American theater is a vibrant and unique entity enriched by ancient Egyptian rituals, West African folklore, and European theatrical practices. A continuum of African folk traditions, it combines storytelling, mythology, rituals, music, song, and dance with ancestor worship from ancient times to the present. It has afforded black artists a cultural gold mine to celebrate what it had been like to be an African American in the New World.

Black theater began its quest for legitimacy emulating mainstream American theatrical traditions at the African Grove in 1821 and from there to Minstrelsy, to William Wells Brown's play *Escape; or, a Leap to Freedom*, to the musical comedies at the turn of the century, to the Harlem Renaissance of the 1920s, to the Negro Unit of the Federal Theatre Project of the 1930s, to the American Negro Theatre and social dramas and musicals of the 1940s, to the avant-garde and off-Broadway movement of the 1950s, to the new Renaissance and Black Power Movement of the 1960s, to the feminist movement of the 1970s, to August Wilson's 10-play cycle for every decade of the 20th century, and to the array of plays presented at Larry Leon Hamlin's National Black Theatre Festival (NBTF).

Black theater boasts award-winning playwrights, actors, directors, choreographers, designers, and theater companies. It refined the popular minstrel tradition—America's first pure form of entertainment. It helped to originate and shape America's musical comedy format. It brought to the American stage a rich theatrical history and cultural practice and captivated American as well as European audiences with its Charleston dance craze and rhythms. Due to social restrictions that created major barriers to its development, it took the fledgling African

American theater a few centuries longer to find its place among American theater and popular entertainment.

Africans, as history bears witness, were brought to America in chains as slaves and remained in servitude for another 244 years until ostensibly being "freed" with the Emancipation Proclamation (1863). This involuntary servitude established a racial divide between blacks and whites that has never been completely resolved despite the civil rights movement of the 1960s. Over the years, measurable advancements have been made in many areas of commerce and industry, but only minimal progress has been made in regard to total acceptance of African Americans as human beings with the same foibles, weaknesses, strengths, and intelligence as their white counterparts. This has colored efforts by African Americans to integrate the theater of America. Numerous attempts to do so have been rebuffed, but with blacks becoming more educated, more economically dependent, and with a growing pride in their own history and culture, fewer attempts at integrating theater are being made.

The black theater movement, however, that started in the civil rights revolution during the middle of the 20th century, after a few faltering steps, has regained its direction and has grown immeasurably. Theater artists founded their own theaters and companies; performed in black minstrel shows and musical comedies; and wrote protest, comedy, and folk plays. It evolved into a theatrical tradition with a sense of pride, struggle, history, community, purpose, and achievement that became a rich and vital entity with its own set of characteristics.

FROM THE 1810s TO 1940s

Contemporary African American theater owes a debt of gratitude to the pioneering efforts of early African American theater practitioners. The formal groundwork for this cultural and artistic movement began on the Lower West Side of Manhattan in 1816. William Alexander Brown welcomed guests from the five boroughs to his home, where he provided an assortment of entertainment by local artists. By 1821, Brown had assembled the first known black theater troupe and founded the African Grove Theatre. Brown mounted white classics ranging from Shakespeare to pantomime to farce. He also wrote and staged the first known

African American play, *The Drama of King Shotaway* (1823), a historical drama based on the Black Carib War in St. Vincent in 1796 against both English and French settlers. At that time, dramas by and about African American life were practically nonexistent. The company's principal actors were James Hewlett (1778–1836), the first acknowledged African American Shakespearean actor, and a young teenager, Ira Aldridge (1807–65), later acclaimed internationally in the capitals of Europe. It would be another 30-odd years after *King Shotaway* before a black playwright would dramatize the problems of slavery in America. William Wells Brown, a self-educated man with no formal training in playwriting technique, documented his life experience in his semiautobiographical play *Escape; or, a Leap to Freedom* (1856). It is the first extant play by an African American playwright to be published in the United States.

After the American Civil War (1860–65), Jim Crow laws were enforced in the southern and border states of the United States mandating that public schools, public spaces, and public transportation have separate facilities for blacks and whites in practically every part of American life. This kind of rampant discrimination denied blacks equal access to theaters and popular entertainment. Not to be deterred, S. H. Dudley, a black actor and entrepreneur, bought theaters in Washington, DC, and Virginia and organized his own chain of black theaters in 1911—the S. H. Dudley Theatrical Enterprise. Of the nine theaters on the chain, Dudley owned six. By 1916, this number of theaters more than tripled to 28, with the additional locations in the Midwest, the East, and the South. This was the first black theatrical circuit of record. It became known as the Chitlin' Circuit—a string of small black nightclubs, music venues, juke joints, eating establishments, and theaters that catered to African American audiences. The name *Chitlin'* derived from the bill of fare usually served in the venues—chitlins (hog intestines), a soul food delicacy that originated in the South during slavery time. The circuit became the life blood of black entertainers and offered a kaleidoscope of entertainment featuring vaudevillians, musicians, comedians, minstrel shows, and playlets. Blacks now had their own circuit entertaining black audiences, and for the first time, some were able to secure contracts for an eight-month season through Dudley's office. After Dudley's death in 1935, the circuit continued to gain momentum well into the late 1960s and the early 1970s. Such entertainers as Bill "Bojangles" Robinson,

Duke Ellington, Billie Holiday, B. B. King, Jackie Wilson, Ike and Tina Turner, Moms Mabley, Etta James, James Brown, and Jimi Hendrix all regularly toured on the circuit. Over time, new civil rights legislation and the overturning of Jim Crow laws forced the Chitlin' Circuit to give way to social integration—and disco.

During the early decades of the 20th century, Harlem became the site for the rebirth of African American culture and creative activity that flourished with the advent of the Harlem Renaissance (1915–29)—also known elsewhere as the Negro Renaissance in the United States. It was a time of ragtime and jazz, the black bottom and the Charleston, and bootleg whiskey. It was a time of change and creativity in Harlem, the black entertainment capital of America. Whites and blacks who lived "uptown" were living in the midst of the Renaissance, and those who lived "downtown" came uptown. With the influx of ex-slaves from the South converging on Harlem after the Civil War and the rental of property to African Americans by black realtor Philip Peyton, performing artists and playwrights readily followed. The names of show business folk of that time have become bywords in the history of black entertainment: Bert Williams, Charles Gilpin, Ethel Waters, W. C. Handy, Bessie Smith, Ma Rainey, Fats Waller, Rose McClendon, Paul Robeson, and Josephine Baker.

This period also saw African American female playwrights assert their right to be heard as part of the creative and artistic pulse of the Renaissance. Angelina Weld Grimké, Mary Burill, Georgia Douglass Johnson, Marita Bonner, Ruth Gaines Shelton, and Alice Dunbar Nelson wrote plays unlike their black male counterparts. They explored issues that impacted the lives of black people—the military, lynching, sanctity of family, absentee fathers, miscegenation, marriage, racism, disparity between religious ideology and practice, and the depiction of heroes. They produced most of their plays in churches, lodges, and local schools.

As these playwrights were establishing theatrical traditions unique to women, a pioneer theatrical phenomenon, the little theater movement, was gaining momentum throughout Harlem with the advent of such amateur theater groups as the Krigwa Players, the Acme Players, the National Ethiopian Art Theatre, Players' Guild, and the Sekondi Players. Many of these companies thrived for one or two years before fading from sight. Some of the theaters adapted Dr. W. E. B. DuBois's manifesto he set for the Krigwa Theatre, declaring black theater should be by, for, about, and near the black community. New theater houses and professional companies were also started. Among them were the Harlem Experimental Theatre, New Negro Art Theatre, Aldridge Players, Alhambra Theatre and Alhambra Players, Ida Anderson Players, and National Colored Players at the West End Theatre. Former vaudeville houses also revitalized a once thriving industry by offering dramatic presentations at the Lafayette Theatre, the Lincoln Theatre, and the Apollo Theatre. Even though some of these professional and community theaters were short lived, they provided an outlet for the fledgling stage performers and a place for writers to develop their craft and stimulate the growth of African American theater.

In the middle of the Great Depression that began in 1929, President Franklin Delano Roosevelt implemented the Works Progress Administration Federal Theatre Project as part of the New Deal, an economic recovery program. Black units, also called the Negro Theatre Project, were set up in 23 cities throughout the United States. This short-lived (1935–39) project provided much-needed employment and apprenticeships to hundreds of black actors, directors, theater technicians, and playwrights. It was a major boost for African American theater during an economically depressed era.

In 1940, Abram Hill, Frederick O'Neal, and others founded the American Negro Theatre (ANT) in Harlem. This community-based company, active between 1940 and 1949, was an outgrowth of the Negro Unit of the Federal Theatre Project in Harlem. Among its illustrious alumni were Alice Childress, Sidney Poitier, Harry Belafonte, Ruby Dee, Ossie Davis, Alvin Childress, Maxwell Granville, Hilda Simms, Earle Hyman, Clarice Taylor, Gordon Heath, Isabel Sanford, Roger Furman, and Rosetta LeNoire. ANT produced at least 20 plays, as well as original plays—*On Striver's Row*, *Natural Man*, *Three Is a Family*, *Anna Lucasta*, *Garden of Time*, *Henri Christophe*, *Home Is the Hunter*, *Angel Street*, *Juno and the Paycock*, *You Can't Take It with You*, *The Peacemaker*, *Tin Top Valley*, *The Later Christopher Bean*, *Rope*, *The Show Off*, *Rain*, *The Washington Years*, *Sojourner Truth*, *Almost Faithful*, *Riders to the Sea*, and *Freight*. ANT's most significant and successful play was Hill's *On Striver's Row*. It also adapted theater classics by white playwrights, such as *Anna Lucasta* by Philip Yordan, which was moved from ANT in Harlem to Broadway, where it played for 957 performances. Later it toured throughout the country and abroad in London. While *Lucasta* garnered the most recognition for ANT, its success on Broadway had a twofold effect on the company: the demise of ANT because it departed from the company's community roots and the loss of its founder Hill, who resigned due to the shift in goals and ideology.

These theatrical venues of the 1920s, 1930s, and 1940s provided outlets for performing artists and honed the playwriting talents of such notables as Willis Richardson, Randolph Edmonds, Langston Hughes, Ted Ward, and Abram Hill. Prior to the 1950s, black theater existed peripherally in the psyche of black America. Splintered as they were, they laid the groundwork for a black cultural aesthetic. Jealousy, artistic differences, social restrictions, and an inability to agree on what constituted black theater limited its effectiveness. An ongoing issue had been nontraditional or "color-blind casting" or whether black theater would be inclusive or noninclusive. For those involved, it was a labor of love and a triumph of the times in which they lived. This was a period of rampant discrimination and oppression and almost daily lynching and a time when just to get through the day was an accomplishment. So, these theater workers did what they had to do but nevertheless left a legacy upon which to build an African American theatrical tradition. A look back on this time period is reflective of Melvin B. Tolson's commentary in *The Harlem Gallery* (1965) on the plight of the black artist:

> The Negro is a dish in the white man's kitchen —
> a potpourri,
>> an ola-podidra,
>> a mixie-maxie,
>> a hotchpotch of lineal ingredients;
>> with UN guests at his table,
> the host finds himself a Hamlet on the spot,
> for, in spite of his catholic pose,
> the Negro dish is a dish nobody knows:
> to some . . . . tasty,
> like an exotic condiment —
>> to others . . . . . unsavory,
>> and inelegant.

FROM THE 1950s TO 1960s

By the 1950s, the wind of change in the African American culture was blowing. In 1955, Rosa Parks, a day worker, refused to relinquish her seat to a white passenger on a bus that was almost empty. This sparked the Montgomery bus boycott, and the civil rights movement, a slow, lumbering whale, roared to life with a new energy, bringing with it a new generation of young, bright, black intellectuals who saw the arts, particularly theater, as a way to communicate the message of the movement. The black arts movement was born, and their efforts over the next 20 years would dwarf the accomplishments of the previous 150 years.

The civil rights movement that had been brewing since the first slave ship arrived on these shores at Jamestown, VA, in 1619 was on. It was joined across the country by millions of people who were tired of being denied basic human rights, whose families had been broken apart and sold, and whose past had been erased from the history books. While the Greensboro, NC, lunch-counter sit-ins, the Alabama freedom rides, and the riots in Philadelphia; Watts, CA; and Harlem raged on, black America became a boiling cauldron of cultural inspiration and expression. Young people born in the 1930s and 1940s led the charge. They ignored their elders, who cautioned them to "go slow" and "don't rock the boat." Instead, they put themselves in harm's way and somehow endured the water hoses, pistol whippings, and police dogs sent their way when protesting for human dignity and civil rights.

As the civil rights movement was taking hold in the early 1950s, a technological revolution was also afoot that provided much-needed exposure to the American public. Television was introduced, and now people could witness the ugly side of a country's racial divide—one they previously only heard about. Aside from the news however, black faces were missing. So scarce was the sighting of a black person on television that when one was seen, it was a cause for celebration. People would call their friends and relatives and say, "Turn on channel 5. They got a show with some Negroes in it!" Television at that time was a sea of whiteness in its formative stage and still trying to find its way. The volatile and dramatic civil rights movement was alive, vivid, and in living color. It captivated television audiences and made headline news with its marches, sit-ins, demonstrations, beatings, and occasional murders. This depiction of blacks shown in homes throughout the country awakened the conscience of a nation to the plight of African Americans and showed up close what it was really like to be black in America.

The first significant television show featuring black actors was *Amos 'n Andy* in 1951, produced by the Columbia Broadcasting System. Two years later, the National Association for the Advancement of Colored People (NAACP) and other concerned blacks pressured the network to cancel the show, which it did. Although the network assembled the talented and funny cast of black actors Tim Moore, Spencer Williams Jr., Ernestine Wade, Nick Stewart, and Alvin Childress, the NAACP protested the show's depiction of stereotypical, lazy, shiftless blacks with questionable ethics. Thereafter, blacks essentially disappeared from the television screen except for an occasional appearance by a major entertainer. As television grew from three networks and a few affiliates with limited air time to four networks with hundreds of affiliates and unlimited air time, the demand for product grew exponentially. But it was not until the 1960s that blacks began to appear with some regularity on television. Two other developments of note played out as a backdrop during these tumultuous times. One was the Vietnam War that began as a festering sore in the early 1960s but developed into a 15-year conflict that eventually claimed over 58,000 American lives and 1.1 million Vietnamese. The other was the advent of the women's liberation movement, followed closely by the black feminist movement. This development radically altered the relationship dynamics between the sexes.

The civil rights movement also coincided with the paperback revolution to reveal that the vast historical contributions of blacks altered the thinking of many blacks. They had been proselytized socially as a race into believing that they were worthless as a people because the hegemonic society had erased most of their contributions from history books. But the paperback revolution changed all that. Black people began to read and learn of the great African kingdoms of Kush and Benin; the early fighters for civil rights like Harriett Tubman, Denmark Vesey, and Nat Turner; and the contributions of doctors and inventors like George Washington Carver, William Just, and Daniel Hale Williams. They learned that a third of the cowboys who roamed the west with Doc Holiday and Wyatt Earp were black. People like Isom Dart, Deadwood Dick, Stagecoach Mary, and Ben Hodges rode horses, strapped on guns, ate chewing tobacco, spit, and made love like other cowboys.

Along with a new pride came resentment toward white society for emasculating its history of a proud people. The arts, specifically theater people, turned inward in celebration of the kingdoms and contributions Afrocentric peoples had carried with them from Africa to the New World. They no longer saw heroes of western theater, like Joan of Arc, Richard III, and Willy Loman, as their role models. They found their own heroes, like Toussaint L'Ouverture, Cleopatra, Alexander Pushkin, Publius Terentius Afer, and kings and queens. Thus began a process of search and discovery to unearth details of African American culture theater history traditions for incorporation into the working literature of black America and especially theater. This cultural revolution began to surface in the work of Ossie Davis, Adrienne Kennedy, Joseph Walker, Charles Fuller, Paul Carter Harrison, and August Wilson. Wilson, for example, skillfully interwove African cultural practices of storytelling, the juba dance, ritual, and the conjure man into his plays, such as *Joe Turner's Come and Gone*, *The Piano Lesson*, and *Gem of the Ocean*, to show the relationship between the African past and its impact on African Americans in the presence.

During the civil rights movement, paperback technology, stalled by World War II, became a powerful tool in the dissemination of information. People could now buy books at a reasonable price, and with the civil rights movement in full swing, publishers reaped a bonanza in producing books that shed new light on the history of a once enslaved people. Blacks also ventured into the publishing arena. John Johnson established *Ebony Magazine*, a high-gloss magazine of the black world published monthly. He followed with *Negro Digest*, also known as *Black World*. Hoyt Fuller, editor of *Black World*, saw theater of such importance that every April he devoted a special edition exclusively to coverage of the black theater world. Small black presses began to appear, like *Liberator*, *Freedomways*, *Umbra*, *Third World Press*, and *The Black Scholar*, carrying the writings of a new generation of writers deeply involved in both the civil rights movement and the arts. Their writings reflected a black aesthetic in plays and poetry. It mirrored a new, more militant tone that challenged cultural hegemony and called for a new black nationalism. This was also the call of a new generation of poets and playwrights, like Don L. Lee, Amiri Baraka (LeRoi Jones), Sonia Sanchez, Clarence Major, Amus Moore, Nikki Giovanni, Gylan Kain, Conyuhs, Rosa Guy, Gwendolyn Brooks, and others who embraced different aspects of black nationalism. Jones called their efforts black arts to differentiate between black and white America. He was in the spotlight, but the words he uttered were strongly influenced by Larry Neal, a brilliant writer and scholar whom many credit with being the philosophical architect of the black arts movement. Neal and Baraka jointly wrote the anthology *Black Fire* in 1968, which is widely recognized as the bible of the black arts movement. These young poets and playwrights saw theater as a communicating tool and began using it not only as a venue for community meetings and study groups but also as a vehicle to present their own plays, usually in a one-act agitprop form. Some even used the old commedia dell'arte form, with white masks to illustrate the oppressors.

What happened in New York City began to emerge in San Francisco, Baltimore, Seattle, Detroit and throughout the country, even in Jackson County, MS, where the Free Southern Theatre was born. In the past, playwrights had made powerful statements about the black experience in America in such plays as Langston Hughes's *Mulatto* and in the handful of original plays written for the Negro Unit of the Federal Theatre Project. The black community, however, did not fully embrace black theater as an art form until the arrival of the black arts movement. Theatre was becoming relevant again to black people. It was the vehicle of choice to redress the wrongs of white America, whether it was *The First Militant Preacher* by Ben Caldwell, *Black Girl* by J. E. Franklin, or *A Son Come Home* by Ed Bullins. Black theater as an art form was being revitalized, however the rabid militancy of the movement made the production of anything but black plays a dicey proposition. The word was out—black was in and white was out.

The dreams of a multitude of African Americans began to be realized with the passing of the Civil Rights Act of 1964. Congress passed legislation that banned racial discrimination and practices. The following year, the Voting Rights Act was passed, giving minorities the right to vote without harassment. Open housing legislation was also either passed or strengthened in various municipalities, and most blacks now had the freedom to live where they preferred, governed only by their economic circumstances. However, it all came at a price. Over a five-year period, many advocates who championed the cause for civil rights were killed systematically, one by one: Medgar Evers, John F. Kennedy, Malcolm X, Dr. Martin Luther King Jr., and Robert Kennedy.

Kennedy's death marked the end of an era of unprecedented overhaul of the nation's laws governing the civil rights of people in interstate commerce, housing, voting, and employment. The net effect was a leveling of the playing field for all Americans, not just black ones. After 14 years of demonstrations, marches, sit-ins, freedom rides, beatings, disappearances, and killings during which thousands of people died, the civil rights movement had run out of steam. Many of its leaders, supporters, and innocent victims as mentioned had been killed, as well as Viola Liuzzo, Michael Schwerner, James Chaney, Andrew Goodman, the four little girls of Birmingham, and countless others who had lost their lives to the cause so that others might live a better life. The climate of fear that engulfed the country after these killings was palpable. Disillusion, confusion, and fear reigned. Those who were in a position to lead chose not to. The energy and urgency that marked the civil rights movement had dissipated. Although efforts continued through the years to address civil rights concerns with minimal success, the assassination of Martin Luther King Jr. and Robert Kennedy marked the end of the activist phase of the civil rights movement.

In the face of this, Jesse Jackson tried but was unable to fill the void, while Stokely Carmichael took his black power movement to Africa. But reform legislation and the make-work programs like the Office of Equal Opportunity, the Haryou Act Program, and eventually the Comprehensive Employment Training Act were in place, and blacks took advantage of these organizations. Black theaters appeared in great numbers across the country in practically every major and midsize city. In a remarkable period between 1961 and 1982, over 600 black theaters sprouted in the United States. What many believe to be the golden age of black theater began with the establishment of such theaters as Roger Furman's New Heritage Theatre, Woodie King Jr.'s New Federal Theatre in New York City, the Dashiki Project Theatre in New Orleans, the Kuumba Theatre in Chicago, and Black Arts/West in Seattle.

This was the flowering of the black arts movement, when seemingly every city had its own form of theatrical expression. The starting point of this movement, some believe, began with the award-winning 1959 production of Lorraine Hansberry's play *A Raisin in the Sun*. Others believe it had to do with the ascendancy of poet/playwright LeRoi Jones and specifically with his acerbic 1964 Obie-winning play *Dutchman*. Black America exploded with approbation at Clay's big speech, when he excoriated the white woman Lula (a symbol of hegemony) with death as a recipe for all the wrongs America had visited on black people. The pent-up fury and frustration of a people who had been denied for so long erupted in approval for this new kind of play that expressed what they were thinking but were afraid to say. *Dutchman* had hit a nerve.

Clearly the apogee of the black arts movement was the establishment of the Negro Ensemble Company (NEC) in 1968. The theater came into being as a result of funding from the Ford Foundation. Artistic director Douglas Turner Ward and his associates used the money to initiate a black version of the historical Berliner Ensemble, complete with a full training program. Over a three-year period, they were the toast of New York City and the world theatrical community. Productions like Peter Weiss's *Song of the Lusitanian Bogey* and Derek Walcott's *Dream on Monkey Mountain* sparkled with a sheen seldom seen on any stage, performed by a world-class group of actors. When Ford cut the funding, however, the NEC ceased to be a continuing producing entity, concentrating instead on training.

An equally promising venture was the New Lafayette Theatre (NLT). It started producing in 1966, funded by the Rockefeller Foundation. The charismatic Robert Macbeth guided the enterprise, which was centered in Harlem. After the NLT was firebombed, it regrouped and reopened but never fully recovered. Although short lived, it was at the NLT that Ed Bullins began to earn a reputation as one of the leading playwrights of the era and also the equally promising Richard Wesley, who eventually turned to screenwriting.

Crossroads Theatre in Brunswick, NJ, was another black theater that blazed across the firmament during the late 1970s. It was founded by two Rutgers graduates, Ricardo Khan and L. Kenneth Richardson, who achieved what no black theater had before: membership in the League of Resident Theatres, the governing entity of regional theater in the United States. But the bubble of depending on "soft" money burst. The theater retrenched and then closed. It has since reorganized and reopened. At the time of this writing it remains a producing entity.

Any recounting of black theater would be remiss without mention of the prodigious accomplishments of the indefatigable Woodie King Jr., whose achievements over the last 40 years dwarf many others. As the founder/director of the New Federal Theatre (NFT), he has produced

over 200 productions, some of them prize-winning plays like *For Colored Girls Who Have Considered Suicide When the Rainbow Is Enuf*,
The Taking of Miss Janie, and *When the Chickens Came Home to Roost*.
King has functioned as a producer, director, and writer at universities,
regional theaters, and off Broadway. He continues to be a dominant
force and trendsetter, both for the NFT and for the National Black Touring Circuit that he established in 1976.

FROM THE 1970s TO 1980s

The 1970s also produced two admirable attempts to deal with the age-
old issue of color-blind or nontraditional casting. The Renaissance man
of American theater, Joseph Papp (white), producing director of the
New York Shakespeare Festival, led the way. Papp's initial effort was
the 1972 all-black production of Anton Chekhov's *The Cherry Orchard*,
featuring James Earl Jones in the lead role of Lopahin. The cast of classically trained actors featured Ellen Holly, Gloria Foster, and Earle Hyman. The results were inconclusive, with proponents on both sides
claiming victory. Undeterred, Papp continued to prime the pump, and
by 1979, he had raised considerable money toward the establishment of
an African American/Hispanic troupe devoted entirely to producing the
works of Shakespeare. Auditions were held, and the company under-
went three months of intensive Shakespearean training, including voice
production, diction, movement, stage fighting, and other exercises.
Papp had brought in the esteemed English director Michael Langham to
oversee the company and direct the first production, *Julius Caesar*.
Among the actors chosen for the company were Morgan Freeman,
Miriam Colon, C. C. H. Pounder, and Gloria Foster. Despite weeks of
intensive work, the results were catastrophic. The production of *Caesar*
was panned. The second production, *Coriolanus*, did not fare any better
with the critics, aside from the work of Morgan Freeman and Gloria
Foster. The reasons most people gave were the failure of the acting
troupe to master the rudiments of Shakespearean speech and iambic
pentameter. To compound matters, Papp came under attack by the Asian
American community for not providing a forum for Asian actors and by
black theaters for siphoning off money that would otherwise go to black
theater–producing organizations. Amid all of this chaos and criticism,

the African American/Hispanic Shakespeare project was shelved. In spite of the difficulties, Papp introduced and pushed further than any individual in introducing the concept of color-blind casting into the psyche of American theater.

The issue was also spurred by the pioneering efforts of the legendary actress, dancer, and producer Rosette LeNoire, founder of the Amas Repertory Theatre. LeNoire had appeared in the celebrated all-black production of *MacBeth* directed by Orson Welles (white) in 1936 and later in the Broadway production of *Anna Lucasta* that also toured overseas. The Actors Equity Association recognized LeNoire's work in this area in 1989 when it established the annual Rosetta LeNoire Award. LeNoire's and Papp's vision may have inspired such companies as the African American Shakespeare Company in San Francisco and the Classical Theatre of Harlem to follow this lead; both are quite active as of this writing.

The 1970s were also rife with the success of musicals—*Purlie* (1970), *Ain't Supposed to Die a Natural Death* (1971), *Don't Bother Me, I Can't Cope* (1972), *The Wiz* (1975), *Bubbling Brown Sugar* (1976), *Ain't Misbehavin'* (1978), and *Eubie* (1979)—that dominated the Broadway stage. They lay to rest the myth that black people would not support a Broadway show. Even the staid *New York Times* acknowledged as much with a Sunday entertainment headline that read "Broadway! The Great Black Way!" Many of these shows emanated from the work done by actors, writers, musicians, and technicians connected with the black theater movement.

The number of black actors in the American film industry also changed. Despite intense lobbying by the NAACP and other black leaders, the film industry continued ignoring black actors or casting them in stereotyped, demeaning roles. This all changed, however, once independent black filmmaker Melvin Van Peebles made *Sweet Sweetback's Badasssss Song* in 1971, in which a black hero outwits the white establishment. Van Peebles wrote, produced, and directed the film outside the Hollywood system, bankrolled by him and a few friends. The film was a huge success, making over $1 million from mostly black audiences who were starved to see themselves depicted on the silver screen. Having seen the evidence, Hollywood began cranking out low-budget B movies with black casts during the 1970s. This was a boon for black actors working in the black theater movement, many of whom felt they had no place to be somebody, but now the door was open to possible fame and fortune. But Hollywood still controlled the product, and for the most part, the movies were shallow in nature, exploring the seamier side of black life and focusing on drugs, pimps, gangsters, and ghetto life. Very few films of a redemptive and affirming life were made. Black leaders and others concerned by the negative depiction of blacks lobbied for change, and by the end of the decade, "blaxploitation" movies slowly faded away. It was a huge crack in the door of racism and discrimination that had existed in Hollywood. By the 1990s and heading into the millennium, black actors and directors had established themselves as major players in the film industry, led by two veterans of the black theater movement, Samuel L. Jackson and Morgan Freeman.

The 1970s ended on a high note with a stunning 1979 television production of *Roots*, a 12-hour miniseries adapted from Alex Haley's book of the same name, documenting the slave trade and the beginning of slavery in America. The show was a huge ratings success, scoring higher than any previous television program in history. *Roots* generally had a positive effect on race relations and exposed a cadre of new black actors to the public at large. After a slow beginning, television was beginning to look more and more like the America it represented: multicolored with an attitude!

From the writings of such early playwrights as Georgia Douglas Johnson to contemporary writers like Laurie Carlos, black women have played key and seminal roles in black theater. One cannot overlook Lorraine Hansberry's award-winning Broadway production of *A Raisin in the Sun* or Ntozake Shange's long-running "choreopoem" *For Colored Girls Who Have Considered Suicide When the Rainbow Is Enuf*. Some members of the black theater movement took umbrage at Shange's message in the play, perceiving it as an attack on black males. The issue had overtones of the message in Sonia Sanchez's play *Sister Sonji*, excoriating the actions of the black male leadership in the movement. Nevertheless, such theater pioneers as Jackie Taylor, Barbara Ann Teer, Val Gray Ward, Adrienne Kennedy, Abena Joan Brown, and others have greatly advanced the field. In addition, the contributions of performers, writers, and directors like Pearl Cleague, Aishah Rahman, Shauneille Perry, Regina Taylor, Ifa Bayeza, and Phylicia Rashad—to name just a few—loom as large as any in the pantheon of black theater.

An offshoot of the black arts movement that renewed interest and vigor as a theater component was the Chitlin' Circuit. Heretofore, this type of theater was a mere dot on the radar screen, but some enterprising producers took advantage of the demand for black product that the black arts movement had created and began producing this type of play in large urban cities like New York, Philadelphia, Chicago, and Detroit. Hence, a new name of Urban Circuit evolved to describe this kind of play. Vy Higgenson's *Mama, I Want to Sing* grossed over $1 million in a year, and *Beauty Shop* by entrepreneur Shelly Garrett grossed over $30 million during a four-year period. This type of theater gained popularity with black people with strong ties to the church and those who just wished to be entertained. Conversely, many traditional black theatergoers lamented this type of theater as being lowbrow, an *Amos 'n Andy* type of theater that presented black people in the worst light possible. Meantime, current-day advocates like Tyler Perry and Billy Talbert earn millions of dollars while making television and movie deals to expose their Urban Circuit efforts to an ever-expanding audience.

While the black arts movement spawned an amazing array of new theaters across the country, in a startling development, a parallel theater movement came into being. Broadway had been looked upon as the promised land almost from the time America began with the arrival of Europeans. There was just a small handful of what could be called professional theaters spread out across America. But in the 1960s, white regional theaters were founded as well as funded throughout the country. In 1947, Margo Jones started the phenomenon with her Theater 47 in Dallas, TX. She also originated the concept of developing nonprofit status with broad community support to undergird the theater. Nina Vance followed with the Alley Theatre in Houston, as did Zelda Fichlander with the Arena Stage in Washington, DC. Theaters were also developed in New Haven, CT; San Francisco; Providence, RI; and Seattle. One of the most prestigious was the Tyrone Guthrie Theatre in St. Paul, MN, named after the famed English director who was its first artistic director. For the most part, regional theater was mostly white and seldom hired blacks or produced black plays. A federal suit, however, was filed in 1965 under Title VI of the 1964 Civil Rights Act (denial of federal monies to institutions that discriminated) against the Seattle Repertory Theatre. Within months, the theater hired three black actors for their 1965 resident company, and the suit was dropped. Other regional theatres fell in line and changed their hiring practices. By 1970, there were over 60 regional theaters across the country. The National Endowment for the Arts (NEA) also came into being in 1965 as a legacy of the late President Kennedy. For the first time since the Federal Theatre era of the 1930s, the government started funding the arts. Enchanted by the prospect of decentralizing the arts from its eastern base and possibly of building a long-dreamed-of national theater, the NEA awarded millions of dollars to these new regional theaters. If nothing else, theater as we knew it was being decentralized. The NEA also set quantifiable funding benchmarks that favored large, stable, established organizations and effectively excluded black cultural organizations.

Funding for black organizations did not materialize until 1971, when NEA director Nancy Hanks tapped black theater veteran Vantile Whitfield to head the newly formed Expansion Arts Division (EAD) of the NEA. When Ronald Reagan was elected president in 1980, one of the first departments to fall was the EAD. By then, the black theater movement that had started out so promisingly began sputtering and falling back to its previous levels. Of the 600 black theaters that were created between 1961 and 1982, only about 40 survived for more than 10 years. They died for a variety of reasons—poor management, dwindling community support, a reliance on soft money, decreasing donations, lack of support from foundations, departures of original leaders, changes in the original mission, competing theaters siphoning off their audience, plays not being reflective of the community, and no long-range planning. Another contributing factor was the blaxploitation filmmaking explosion of the 1970s, when many actors raced to make quick, easy money, leaving the theaters that they had helped create. For these and other reasons, theaters like the Dashiki Project Theatre in New Orleans, Black Arts/ West in Seattle, Theatre Black in New York, the Free Southern Theatre in Mississippi, and the X Bag in Chicago, among others, withered and died.

In a development little noted at the time, in 1981, Lloyd Richards of the Eugene O'Neil Theatre Center culled a script from the hundreds submitted for a possible staged reading at the center—*Ma Rainey's Black Bottom*. This was the sixth time the aspiring playwright, August Wilson, had submitted a script for consideration. He had been encouraged to do so by his friend, director Claude Purdy. On a hot, humid July night in 1982, *Ma Rainey's Black Bottom* was given a staged reading by professional actors at the center. Little did anyone know at the time that those four hours would change the face of American theater—forever. The play subsequently premiered at the Yale Repertory Theatre and opened on Broadway in 1984, winning the New York Drama Critics' Circle Award for best play. Wilson would go on to become the nonpareil African American playwright of his generation and possibly of all time.

The 1980s ended on a high note with the establishment of the NBTF by Larry Leon Hamlin of the North Carolina Black Repertory Theatre in 1989. It was conceived as a vehicle to unite black theaters across the country as a unified whole to ensure their survival into the 21st century. He succeeded beyond his wildest dreams, as the festival grew from a five-day event that drew some 10,000 people to one that now draws 60,000 people over a six-day span. The festival has proven to be a windfall for the city of Winston-Salem, generating revenues exceeding $10 million dollars for the week. More to the point, the festival has proved to be a unifying force for black theater workers, as people from all over the country convene every odd year to see new plays, meet their fellow actors and technicians, and study new trends in the theater industry. The festival continues to attract celebrity performers and personalities from across the entertainment world, like Sidney Poitier, Oprah Winfrey, Maya Angelou, Quincy Jones, Ruby Dee, Samuel L. Jackson, and others. New plays from the pens of Daniel Beaty, Sarah Jones, Ted Lange, Lorey Hayes, Ella Joyce, Leslie Lee, Layon Gray, and others are performed and evaluated. Overall, the festival has become a highlight of the black theater movement and has galvanized and strengthened the movement in America.

FROM THE 1990s TO THE PRESENT

The 1990s was a decade dominated by playwright August Wilson, who wrote 5 of his 10 plays during that period and won a second Pulitzer Prize for *The Piano Lesson*. Other significant developments were the founding of several new black theaters, the appointment of George C. Wolfe as artistic director of the New York Shakespeare Festival Public Theatre (NYSF/PT), greater opportunities in the film industry, and the rise of playwright Suzan-Lori Parks to the top rank of American playwrights.

During this decade, Wilson captured the attention of the world. He was halfway through his 10-play cycle, and his every move was chronicled by the press. He had breathed new life into the movement with plays that crossed racial lines and put a human face on black America. Regional theaters across the land not only embraced his work wholeheartedly but also began producing the works of new black playwrights, like Lynn Nottage, Carlyle Brown, Tanya Barfield, Ifa Bayeza, and Charles Randolph Wright. Wilson brought an excitement and a much-needed acceptance of the black theater movement to the nation as a whole. The establishment of five regional theaters to produce his plays prior to any Broadway opening allowed for rewrites, a slow seasoning of the play, and at least five months of continued work for the acting company. He also challenged the theatrical establishment to change its funding priorities in his groundbreaking manifesto, "The Ground on Which I Stand" speech, at the 1996 Theatre Communications Group national conference. Wilson won almost every theatrical award possible, including two Pulitzer Prizes for best play in *Fences* and *The Piano Lesson*. His plays provided work for hundreds of black actors who otherwise would have been unemployed or underemployed.

The founding of the new black theaters was especially important from a geographical standpoint. The Providence Black Repertory Theatre (1996) in Providence, RI, and the African Continuum Theatre Coalition (1996) in Washington, DC, combined with the Robey Theatre (1994) in Los Angeles and the African American Shakespeare Company (1994) in San Francisco bookended the United States, while the Congo Square Theatre Company (1999) in Chicago and the Shadow Theatre (1997) in Denver, CO, gave middle America a chance to witness black theater.

The charismatic, multitalented George C. Wolfe was appointed producing director of the NYSF/PT in March 1993. Wolfe had previously directed Tony Kushner's award-winning play *Angels in America* and written his own play satirizing the black experience in *The Colored Museum*. After a rocky beginning, Wolfe went on to establish himself as a director of the first rank and the NYSF/PT as one of the most ingenious and vital producing entities in the country, building on the previous record of the legendary Joseph Papp. During Wolfe's 12-year reign, the theater had a series of successful ventures, including the musical *Harlem Song* and the memorable *Bring in 'da Noise, Bring in 'da Funk* that Wolfe both conceived and directed. The musical had a three-year Broadway run from 1996 to 1999, a total of 1,135 performances. The show won nine Tony Awards, including best musical, book, music, and director. Wolfe resigned after 12 years on the job, choosing to concentrate on film projects, though he remains somewhat active in theater.

Actors love to act, no matter where; the bigger the platform, the better. But the black actor has historically been denied access to one of the most glamorous and lucrative platforms of them all: the silver screen. A movement in film of accessibility that started in the 1980s exploded in the 1990s and became a fait accompli in the 21st century. Hollywood moved away from earmarking, a practice specifying which ethnicity should play the part. Although racism is still prevalent, the record shows that since 1980, there have been changes in Hollywood. For example, since 1980, blacks have been nominated 37 times in four different acting categories and won 11 Oscars, contrasted with only 2 Oscars since the awards began in 1929. Black actors now play roles previously the exclusive province of white actors. Examples include U.S. presidents, CIA agents, bank presidents, action heroes, heroic cowboys, wealthy patrons, detectives, doctors, lawyers, and creatures from other planets, to name a few. Of all the actors and actresses starring in Hollywood films today, most of the major celebrities got their start in black theater. Such is the case with Ruby Dee, James Earl Jones, Claudia McNeill, Denzel Washington, Samuel L. Jackson, Mary Alice, Delroy Lindo, S. Epatha Merkerson, Laurence Fishburne, Rosalind Cash, and Morgan Freeman, all of whom worked in black theater for years before heading to Hollywood. They serve as examples of the hard work and training that exemplifies black theater and are an incentive for young people considering a career in the theater.

The 21st century started out with yet another resurgence in plays modeled after those in the Urban Circuit. The surge was led by Tyler Perry, a self-taught writer and actor who had failed miserably during the early 1990s but finally struck pay dirt in 1998 with his play *House of Blues*. His adaptation of the T. D. Jakes novel *Woman, Thou Art Loosed!* for the stage was also successful, and Perry was on his way. In 2002, he rendered one of his plays, *Diary of a Mad Black Woman*, to film, and it was a raging success, grossing over $50 million off a production budget of $5,500. Since then, Perry has opened his own Tyler Perry Production Studio in Atlanta and has begun filming his own movies. His most recent film, *Why Did I Get Married* (2007), opened number one at the box office to over $21 million (first weekend). In 2006, Perry inked a multiyear deal with TBS worth an estimated $200 million, and the resulting sitcom, *House of Payne*, began airing in June 2007. The success of Tyler Perry and the Urban Theatre format of plays raises the question as to what black theater should be. It is a question that has plagued black theater since its inception and still needs to be resolved.

Another playwright on the rise in the realm of a Samuel Beckett or Adrienne Kennedy is the perky, peripatetic Suzan-Lori Parks. An army brat, Parks began writing in the 1980s after taking a class from novelist/playwright James Baldwin. Parks showed a lot of promise in her early plays, like *The Death of the Last Black Man in the Whole World*, *In the Blood*, and *Fucking A*. She put it all together, however, in 2001, when she wrote *Topdog/Underdog*, a play about two brothers in a sibling rivalry revolving around a hustler game of three-card monte. The play was first mounted at the NYSF/PT that year under the direction of George C. Wolfe. It opened on Broadway (April 2002) with Wolfe directing. The two brothers were played by Jeffrey Wright and Mos Def. The play ran for 144 performances and earned Drama Desk and Tony awards for best play. *Topdog/Underdog* also won the Pulitzer Prize for drama. Parks became the first African American woman to win the prize since its inception in 1917 and the fourth African American playwright since 1975 to win the honor, joining Charles Gordone, Charles Fuller, and August Wilson. Parks is but another example of the rich diversity of talent that resides in American theater, whether it be black or white.

On 8 October 2005, the theatrical community and the world at large was devastated when the inimitable August Wilson succumbed to liver cancer at the relatively young age of 60. He died in Seattle shortly after finishing the 10th and last play of the "Pittsburgh Cycle," *Radio Golf*. Wilson was a giant among humankind, whose prodigious talents had dominated the American theatrical landscape for almost two decades.

In August 2007, many theater artists and luminaries attended the NBTF held in Winston-Salem, NC. Though the founder of the festival, Larry Leon Hamlin, had died a few months earlier, the festival planners had decided the festival would go forward as a tribute to Hamlin and his boundless enthusiasm and to pay homage to the late August Wilson. A series of symposia were held examining various aspects of Wilson's plays, with a panel of scholars and experts on each panel. Nobel Prize winner Wole Soyinka gave the keynote address and chaired the opening panel. The six-day festival turned out to be an exuberant, joyful celebration attended by visitors from all over the planet. From noon to 2:00 a.m. over the course of six days, there were over 130 performances of some 37 diverse plays, mostly new with a sprinkling of old favorites, presented in 12 separate venues.

There was Layon Gray's searing ensemble piece *WEBEIME*, Endesha Mae Holland's semiautobiographical play *From the Mississippi Delta*, Herb Newsome's Shakespearean hip-hop rendering of *Revenge of the King*, actor/cowboy Glynn Turmans autobiographical piece *Movin' Man*, Ella Joyce and her Rosa Parks biopic *A Rose among Thorns*, August Wilson's *Gem of the Ocean*, and Carl Clay's rollicking resurrection of the *Amos 'n Andy* show in *Kingfish, Amos 'n Andy*. Many veterans of the theater were there, but one could not fail to be impressed by the presence of so many young actors of a new generation who were present as well. They were there with their cell phones, laptop computers, BlackBerrys, résumés, and business cards networking, looking for work, and making themselves available for play readings and other possibilities that might give them visibility. It was amazing to see how much detail they had absorbed about the entertainment industry. They cited the names of casting agents, upcoming plays, schedules, sitcom and movie opportunities, casting calls, the dos and don'ts of auditioning, and a myriad of details regarding theater.

On the second floor of the Marriott Hotel and at the Embassy Suites Hotel across the street, play readings were held from noon until after midnight every day. It was bubbling with activity: the scheduling of plays to be read in different rooms, the matching of actors with the right play and character, and the covering of emergencies that would arise. Free buses would convene daily at 2:30 and 7:30 to transport theatergoers to outlying venues within 10 minutes, where plays were performed. Many of the theaters were in walking distance. Sitting in the lobby of the Marriott Hotel—the official headquarters of the festival—one could see all the movers and shakers of black theater stroll by. There was theatrical guru and legend Woodie King Jr., composer/vocalist Micki Grant, playwright Ed Bullins, director Shauneille Perry, actor Glynn Turman, Nobel Prize winner Wole Soyinka, actress Barbara Montgomery, artistic director Lou Bellamy, playwrights Barbara and Carlton Molette, Adella Adella the Storyteller, actor/playwright Ted

Lange, administrator Eileen Morris, showman Rome Neal, and actress Stephanie Berry, to name a few. Everywhere, no matter the time of day or night, there was an infectious, friendly enthusiasm that permeated the festival. This was the first festival held after the death of August Wilson in 2005, and one wondered what the mood would be combined with the death of festival founder Hamlin. The overall impression was that of an unflagging enthusiasm for black theater, especially as a stepping-stone for entrée into the television and movie industries.

It is in the traditional role that theater has always provided a training ground where one learns the craft of acting before moving on to the next level. And yes, while the funding for black theater is not where it should be and the deaths of Wilson and Hamlin dealt a body blow to black theater, the industry as a whole seems to be stronger and more enthusiastic than ever. The overall impression from absorbing six days of black theater, hobnobbing with artistic directors, playwrights, actors, technicians, university, and theater scholars, the powerful and the novice, the young and the old, is that black theater is very much alive and well, thank you. It is an industry that has created playwrights from Marita Bonner to August Wilson, actors from Charles Gilpin to S. Epatha Merkerson, and plays and musicals from *Big White Fog* to *Eubie* and from *A Raisin in the Sun* to *The Color Purple*.

Geographically, black theater is no longer centered in New York City but in major cities across the American landscape. Many of the young people involved in black theater are college educated. Still others have received training at some of the most prestigious theatrical institutions here and abroad, including New York University's Tisch School of the Performing Arts, the Yale School of Drama, the Royal Academy of Dramatic Arts in London, and Rites and Reason Theatre at Brown University—people like actor/director Charles Randolph-Wright, Pulitzer Prize winner and playwright Suzan-Lori Parks, actor/playwright David Barr III, actor Lorey Hayes, Obie Award winner Daniel Beaty, actor/playwright Javon Johnson, administrator/playwright Ifa Bayesza, and, yes, Urban Circuit playwright Tyler Perry. And thanks to Victor Walker II's African Grove Institute, there is now a working relationship between black theaters and the Tuck School of Business, where blacks receive training in the business side of theater.

We are now in the 21st century with over 100 black theaters stretched across the American landscape from north to south, east to west. Black theater has evolved from being a clone of western theater to its retention of the richness and fullness of African American folklore from the mother country, Africa, to their frenetic existence in search of its history and culture while pursuing the elusive American dream. It has gone from a sporadic, hit-and-run affair operating from whatever venue blacks could find to producing plays on a regular basis at permanent facilities. It has also built a substantial body of quality literature to draw from where there was very little before. More importantly, there is greater communication among theater artists realizing that what benefits one benefits all.

There is a lesser sense of isolation and a greater sense of cooperation thanks to the NBTF. Black theater has grown from a pale imitation of white western culture to a vital, vibrant piece of the American landscape, incorporating key elements of African folklore with the reality of the black experience in America. It is now in the middle phase of development, buoyed by the work of August Wilson, who explored the everyday joys, torments, and dreams of the working class, overlaid with African American rituals of totemic carvings, ring shouts, and the blues. It is not institutionalized as yet, but that will come in time. Efforts to do just that materialized in the wild, halcyon days of the civil rights movement. Universities across the land were importuned to make black theater a part of the basic theater curriculum. The effort was successful to a degree, but many universities have recanted since then, and only a few remain, like Rites and Reason at Brown University and components at the Universities of Louisville and Iowa. Some of the largest universities have only token representation in their theater departments and seldom, if ever, produce a black play other than a one-person performance piece.

This is likewise in the book industry. Your local bookstore does not always carry African American plays, and if it does, you may find a few by August Wilson. This is because black theater has not yet been recognized as a legitimate piece of the American theatrical landscape by publishers and many institutions of higher education. But it will happen. The power, magic, beauty, and style of black theater will overcome this naïve, insecure attempt to ignore it and will, in the end, be recognized for what it is—a vibrant, powerful voice of theatrical expression second to none. In the near future, drama students will sit down and explore black theater in the course curriculum along with Italian theater, Greek theater, Noh theater, and German and Russian theater. It just hasn't happened yet. The progress made, especially over the latter part of the 20th century, augurs well for the future. The best days of black theater are ahead. One is reminded of that old jazz standard, "The Best Is Yet to Come."

This collection of African American theater includes selected playwrights; their plays, musicals, and themes; theaters and companies; actors; producers; directors; designers; composers; and theater awards; as well as the major theatrical and cultural movements and its ideology. It is in exaltation of black theater and in recognition of its major contributions to the advancement of its own genre as well as to American theater.

The Dictionary

115TH STREET LIBRARY THEATRE (115TH STREET PEO-PLE'S THEATRE). This theater was founded by librarian **Regina Andrews** and **Loften Mitchell** at the 115th Street Library in New York City around 1945. They produced a variety of plays on a somewhat erratic basis, two of which were by Mitchell, in 1947. Among them were *The Cellar* and *The Bancroft Dynasty*. The last known production was *The Shame of a Nation*, also written by Mitchell in 1952. The theater then moved to 290 Lenox Avenue in **Harlem** and changed its name to the **Harlem Showcase Theater**. The theater closed its doors forever in 1956.

– A –

AAKHU, SHEPSU (REGINALD LAWRENCE). Born Reginald Lawrence in Illinois, the playwright, musician, and producer changed his name to Shepsu Aakhu. He holds a B.S. in kinesiology and an M.S. in physiology from the University of Illinois. It was there in the late 1980s that he became involved with a group of students clamoring for a more African-based curriculum. What began then at the university was realized in 1991, when they formed the **Ma'at Production Association of Afrikan-Centered Theatre (MPAACT)**, a multidisciplinary theater dedicated to original concepts in addressing the contemporary African American scene. At this point, several events took place. Lawrence was elected executive director, he became the first resident playwright, and he changed his name to Shepsu Aakhu. Though it is a collective, Aakhu emerged as the spokesperson for the group.

Aakhu has been successful as a playwright. In 1999, he won the esteemed **Theodore Ward** Prize for African American playwriting for *Kiwi Black*, a story about a father and son on a train ride of discovery. His plays have been produced at the Body Politic Theatre, the Storefront Theatre, Victory Gardens, **Plowshares Theatre Company**, and other venues, including several universities. A list of some of his plays include *SOST*, about three Ethiopian female travelers on a journey to America; *The Abesha Conspiracy*; *The Glow of Reflected Light*; *Relevant Hearsay . . . Stories from 57* (2001); *Softly Blue*, a romantic comedy (2003); *Kosi Dasa*; *Beneath a Dark Sky*; *Gabriel's Threshold*; and *A Kwanzaa Caro*. Aakhu is the 1999 recipient of the **Ira Aldridge** Award.

ACADEMY AWARDS (OSCARS). Founded in May 1927 as a nonprofit corporation, the Academy of Motion Picture Arts and Sciences is an honorary organization of motion picture professionals that gives out annual awards, "Oscars." Its original 36 members included production executives and film luminaries of the era. In time, membership grew to over 2,000. The stated mission of the academy is to advance the arts and sciences of motion pictures; foster cooperation among creative leaders for cultural, educational, and technological progress; recognize outstanding achievements; cooperate on technical research and improvement of methods and equipment; provide a common forum and meeting ground for various film-related crafts; represent the viewpoints of actual creators of motion pictures; and foster educational activities between the professional community and the public.

The first African American to receive an Oscar was Hattie McDaniel in the best supporting actress category for *Gone with the Wind* (1939). The second winner of this category was Whoopi Goldberg for *Ghosts* (1990), and the third was Jennifer Hudson for *Dreamgirls* (2007). Halle Berry became the first African American woman to win the best actress award for *Monster's Ball* (2001) and **Sidney Poitier** the first African American male to garner the best actor award for *Lilies of the Field* (1963), followed by **Denzel Washington** for *Training Day* (2001), Jamie Foxx for *Ray* (2004), and Forest Whitaker for *The Last King of Scotland* (2007). In the best supporting actor category, Louis Gossett Jr. became the first African American male performer to win this honor for *An Officer and a Gentlemen* (1982), succeeded by Denzel Washington for *Glory* (1989), Cuba Gooding Jr., for *Jerry McGuire* (1996), and **Morgan Freeman** for *Million Dollar Baby* (2003).

ADKINS, KEITH JOSEF. Playwright and screenwriter, Adkins was born in Cincinnati, OH. He is a graduate of Wright State University and the University of Iowa, from which he graduated with an M.F.A. in 1996. He divided his time writing for the stage and screen while living and working in Los Angeles, where he spent three years writing for the television series *Girlfriends*. His work for theater has been impressive. He received commissions from the Alabama Shakespeare Festival, Louisville Actors Theatre, Mark Taper Forum, and the NYSF/ Public Theatre. This enabled him to develop over 10 plays. His works have been performed at the Cleveland Public Theatre, the Black Dahlia, the Hartford Stage, and others. Among them are *On the Hills of Black America*, *The Patron Saint of Peanuts*, *Farewell Miss Cotton*, *Cobra Neck*, *Crossing America*, *Sketches of Yucca*, *Grey Haired Smoochie with Rufus*, *Wilberforce*, *Hollis Mugley's Only Wish*, and *Salt on Sugar Hill*. During his brief career, Adkins has been honored with a Van Lier fellowship, EST/Sloan Science Foundation playwriting grant, Sherwood Distinguished Emerging Artist Award, and the first **August Wilson** Memorial Commission.

AFRICAN AMERICAN DRAMA COMPANY (AADC). Based in San Francisco, the AADC is among the oldest black theater–producing entities in the United States. Founded in 1977, it is the only known theater dedicated to telling the story of African American history from Africa to the present. The administrators are two highly acclaimed practitioners in black theater. Dr. Ethel Pitts Walker and her husband, **Phillip E. Walker**, function as executive director and artistic director, respectively. Dr. Walker is a full professor of television, radio, film, and theater at San Jose State University, a position held since 1989. Philip Walker holds an M.A. from the University of Illinois and an M.F.A. from the University of California at Davis. A working actor, director, and playwright, he has also taught at the American Conservatory Theatre, San Jose State University, Lincoln University, and Santa Clara University and has chaired the Dramatics and Speech Department at Fisk University.

During its 30-year history, the AADC has visited each of the 50 states in the United States. The repertoire of produced plays is minimal, but the company is popular and slips in and of the repertory as needed. Some of the shows presented are *Can I Sing for You, Brother?* by Lewis G. Tucker; *The Highland Avenue Trilogy* by Arlene D. Washington; *Love Machine*, a 1970s rhythm-and-blues operetta by Travis D. Walker; *History of Kwanzaa*; *Being Black Is Being Smart*; *Sister, Can We Speak for You*; and *The Black/Green Room*. Philip Walker authored the latter four plays. As part of the touring program, the AADC has also put together a package aimed at children as well as one for students at the collegiate level. These consist not only of productions but also lectures and workshops that focus on African American history. The AADC was the second African American theater to perform at the prestigious **National Black Theatre Festival** in Winston-Salem, NC.

AFRICAN AMERICAN FOLKLORE. The continuum of African American folk traditions was retained in the South during the antebellum and postslavery era (*see* SLAVERY THEME). It thrived from that period to the present through the rich oral traditions of storytelling, music, dance, song, mythology, signifying, rituals, trickster tales, ancestor worship, and the dozens. During the Black Power Movement of the 1960s, some black playwrights drew from this subject matter for their plays. A few adapted **Paul Carter Harrison**'s notion of Kuntu drama that called upon these traditions to seek ultimate truths about African American history and traditions. It provided these writers the freedom to break from linear forms, to juxtapose images and ideas relating to their own culture, and to convey greater meaning.

Harrison's Obie Award–winning play *The Great MacDaddy* (1973) is a ritualized, episodic, imagistic African American event in two acts. It is based on African storyteller Amos Tutuola's mythic novel *The Palm Wine Drinkard*. The play is set at the wake of the elder MacDaddy in Los Angeles. The son is heir to his father's lucrative bootlegging operation, however Wine, the protector of the race, is the only one who knows the formula for the home brew—and he disappears into the spirit world. The son, with his African juju stick as protection, begins a journey eastward toward the motherland, Africa, in pursuit of Wine. Along the way, he encounters an array of emblematic folk characters in various disguises, such as Scag, Spirit of Woe, Shine, and Signifying Baby. When the son finally finds Wine, whom he was unaware had guided him throughout his journey, the son is rewarded with something much greater than what he had set out to find—the essence of life. The play is a spiritual odyssey through African American folk traditions in which the son gains force by encountering manifestations of the oppression and spiritual resistance of blacks throughout American history before he can become the Great MacDaddy and savior of his people.

In William Wells Brown's *The Escape; or, a Leap for Freedom* (1856), the black heroine successfully wards off the plantation owner after she threatens to "fix" or put a curse on him if he rapes her. In **Zora Neale Hurston** and **Langston Hughes**'s *Mule Bone: A Comedy of Negro Life* (1930), African American folk traditions drive the central action in the play. The story depicts black rural life as experienced by Hurston as a child growing up in the all-black town of Eatonville, FL, at the turn of the 20th century. She and Hughes capture the rich, vibrant, ridiculously funny, and amusing folkways of black people without sensationalizing stereotypical behavior that was prevalent in the literature of mainstream American writers.

In **Adrienne Kennedy**'s Obie-winning play *Funnyhouse of a Negro* (1963), Sara, the central character, is in denial of her African past and folkways. This episodic, abstract, and surrealistic drama utilizes Harrison's Kuntu theory of drama. Props in the play represent ideas. Sara transforms into various personalities, sometimes simultaneously, creating the effect of a nightmare. She is a biracial woman torn between the paradoxes of her African and Anglo ancestry, past and present, flesh and spirit. In her surrealistic rooming house, she is visited by various historical figures that represent facets of her divided self. Repulsed by her blackness, she is attracted to her whiteness, whose culture rejects her. Unable to rectify her black–white psychological conflict, Sara descends into insanity. By refusing to acknowledge her African past and folkways, Sara does not embrace important truths about her ancestry and cultural traditions that could provide spiritual sustenance.

AFRICAN AMERICAN SHAKESPEARE COMPANY (AASC). This San Francisco theater company was created in 1994 to provide an opportunity for blacks to study classical theater and to embrace their cultural identity and aesthetic. Sherri Young, a four-year graduate of American Conservatory Theatre's Training Program, found that after graduation, she was all dressed up for the ball with no place to dance because most American theaters still had major problems with color-blind casting. In response to her desire for classical roles, she funded AASC with an initial investment of $1,500. It took two years, but AASC debuted in 1996 with a production of *Oedipus the King* by Sophocles.

Since then AASC, has been performing in the bay area, presenting classics like *Much Ado about Nothing* and *Lysistrata*. To give these classics more relevancies to African American culture, Young set *The Importance of Being Earnest*, for example, in **Harlem** against the backdrop of the Harlem Renaissance, with music by Duke Ellington. *Julius Caesar* was set in the tumultuous 1960s in the Unites States. The factions vying for power were the Nation of Islam and the Black Panthers. *Romeo and Juliet* was set in Cuba during its carnival. Purists railed, but Young defended the idea of incorporating an African American aesthetic into the play as long as no lines are changed. Young developed a three-pronged program to attract more people to the classics. It includes the Summer Youth Troupe, the after-school program for students 9 to 13, in which excerpts from Shakespearean plays are performed and followed by a question-and-answer period, and the Summer Youth Program, in which students are taught to perform Shakespeare.

The AASC has no theater of its own. Its plays are produced at various venues in the bay area. It employs on average 30 actors and 20 designers every year, while barely making its budget. Despite this, Young has plans for a world tour with the company playing Europe, Asia, and, of course, Africa. She also muses about changing the name to the more accurate designation of the African American Classical Company.

AFRICAN COMPANY (AC)/AFRICAN GROVE THEATRE (AGT). The AC was the first known black theater troupe. In 1816, William Alexander Brown (?–1884), a retired West Indian steamship steward, acquired a house on Thomas Street in lower Manhattan. He offered a variety of instrumental and vocal entertainments on Sunday afternoons in the tea garden at the rear of his house, attracting a sizeable audience from the five boroughs (Manhattan, Brooklyn, Queens, Bronx, and Staten Island) of New York City. Owing to the growing popularity of this novel theatrical activity, Brown moved his venture to Mercer and Bleeker Street in 1821 to the vacated African Grove Hospital, a two-story house with a spacious tea garden. He converted the second floor into a 300-seat theater and renamed the enterprise the AGT.

The company opened the season with a performance of *Richard III* (September 1821) and thereafter mounted productions ranging from Shakespeare to pantomime to farce. Brown followed with *Tom and Jerry; or, Life in London*; *The Poor Soldier*; *Othello*; *Don Juan*; and *Obi; or, Three-Finger'd Jack*. Brown also wrote and staged perhaps the first African American play, *The Drama of King Shotaway* (1823), a historical drama based on the Black Carib War in St. Vincent in 1796 against both English and French settlers. Dramas about African American life were practically nonexistent at that time. The company's principal actors were **James Hewlett** (1778–1836), the first African American Shakespearean actor, and a young teenager, **Ira Aldridge** (1807–67), later acclaimed internationally in the capitals of Europe. They learned their craft while sitting in the balcony of Stephen Price's landmark Park Theatre (New York City), observing the acting styles of European transports in Shakespearean plays.

In 1823, the company presented two benefits for Brown. The date of the first performance is unknown; the second consisted of two parts highlighted by Hewlett performing excerpts from *King Shotaway* as the chief of the Black Caribs. As AGT's popularity grew, it also became a diversion and meeting place for white patrons. The company lasted three years before it was burned down in 1823 under questionable circumstances. Shortly thereafter, Aldridge sailed to London, where he was free to practice his craft as a respected professional. He reached the pinnacle of acclaim as a stage actor for over 42 years throughout Europe, Russia, and the British Isles.

AFRICAN CONTINUUM THEATRE COALITION (ACTCO).
Located in Washington, DC, ACTCo emerged as a producing entity from a service organization that had been promoting African American theater for over five years. They began operations in 1996 and

since then have mounted over 30 plays of distinction and merit under the helm of producing artistic director Jennifer Nelson, who recently left the company but continues in a directing capacity. The theater's goals of presenting new plays and old favorites grounded in an African American aesthetic have been realized in productions like *Spunk* by **George C. Wolfe**, *The Oracle* by Ed Shockley, *The Gingham Dog* by Lanford Wilson, *A Night with Bessie and Tess* by **Caleen Sinette Jennings**, *Buffalo Hair* by **Carlyle Brown**, *The Story* by **Tracey Scott Wilson**, and *The Hip Hop Nightmares of Jujube Brown* by Nelson and Toni Blackman.

Nelson worked in professional theater for over 30 years as an actress, administrator, director, playwright, and educator. Under her directorship, the company established a permanent residency status at the Atlas Performing Arts Center and a new play development initiative with the Fresh Flavas Program and generated a $500,000 annual budget, which is still in the black. ACTCo has received support from the Meyer Foundation, the Ford Foundation, the National Endowment for the Arts, and other corporate entities.

AFRICAN GROVE INSTITUTE FOR THE ARTS (AGIA). The AGIA was born in March 1997 at a conference of theater professionals and practitioners at Dartmouth University. The meeting stemmed from playwright **August Wilson**'s famous "The Ground on Which I Stand" speech at the Theatre Communication Group's national conference in 1996. Wilson had called for a summit meeting of black theater people in his speech, and this was the result. It was arranged and organized by Wilson and two Dartmouth University professors, Victor Leo Walker II and William W. Smith. The conference, dubbed "On Golden Pond," was funded by the Ford and Rockefeller Foundations and by Dartmouth University. There were 45 selected participants who labored over five days in examining the many problems of black theater. Over 300 people attended the conference on the sixth day, when it was announced that an arrangement had been made with the Amos Tuck School of Business at Dartmouth for training in business management and that Dartmouth University would help establish the AGIA as a vehicle to promote black theater and artists both locally and globally. The AGIA was founded in 1998 with the late Wilson serving as its first chairman. It was named in honor of the African Grove, generally acknowledged as the first African American theater, founded in New York City by blacks in 1821.

Since then, the organization has broadened its scope and now serves as a national arts service organization for the entire African American cultural community in the United States. It has worked with the Getty Research Institute and the National Council of Teachers of English in setting up programs of residency, teacher training, and workshops in poetry and drama to broaden the scope of high school curricula. The AGIA was also instrumental in producing a groundbreaking anthology of literary and performance criticism in the 2003 book *Black Theatre: Ritual Performance in the African Diaspora*. That work was authored by playwrights **Paul Carter Harrison**, **Gus Edwards**, and Walker. Presently, the AGIA is working on a nationwide *Directory of Black Cultural Organizations in the United States* and a companion report, *The State of Black Cultural Organizations in the United States*. Both are scheduled for publication in 2008. Recently, the organization relocated to Los Angeles, where Walker serves as president and CEO.

AFRO-AMERICAN STUDIO FOR ACTING AND SPEECH (AASAS). In 1966, Ernie McClintock formed and incorporated the AASAS in **Harlem**. He trained his actors in theatrical technique and scene study, with an emphasis on discipline. His goal was to form a school and ensemble theater troupe to teach actors to observe and study black life to recreate a more realistic portrayal onstage of their experiences. McClintock was inspired to start his own company by the experience he gained as an actor and artistic director at Louis Gossett's Academy of Dramatic Arts and while studying with Edward Albee at the Playwrights Workshop at the Circle in the Square in New York City. McClintock's pedagogy for actor training encompassed the in-depth study of black history and culture, the study of African dance, African American music and folklore, theater history, and black aesthetics. He wanted students to become more flexible and versatile in developing their craft to create any role from a wide repertory ranging from William Shakespeare and Anton Chekhov to **Ed Bullins** and **Amiri Baraka (LeRoi Jones)**.

McClintock and company members also developed three original plays he directed. By 1968, the company expanded to a 100-seat theater on 15 West 126th Street, where it remained for four productive years. By then, their training program had increased to over 200 participants. McClintock hired a professional staff of 12 to teach courses as diversified as karate and voice and diction. During the summer of 1970, he took his company to the streets of New York City, rigging two portable stages together to present impressions of city life in the company's original production of *Where It's At—70.* The theme of black pride was realized through poetry, pantomime, songs, and sketches. The troupe also gave lectures on negative elements eroding the cultural fabric of the black community. The company's in-depth training program prepared them to establish a common ground with street theater audiences as a form of identification. It was not uncommon for audience members to interact verbally with the actors onstage. The following year, the number of productions had increased to nine per season. The studio expanded its basic Actor Training Program to consist of four to six sessions per week for 10 weeks at a cost of $125 per term. Growing pains mandated the company to relocate a year later to a more spacious venue at 415 West 127th Street.

The studio used a variety of methods to finance their productions and programs. They sponsored and took part in community-related concerts, movies, variety shows, and workshop presentations. The source of major funding came from public and private benefactors and donors. Although McClintock was committed to doing black plays, he also wanted to diversify the season. Beginning in 1968, he did just that with *Clandestine on the Morning Line* by Josh Greenfield; *Fortune in Men's Eyes* by John Herbert, a depiction of homosexuality in prison; *Moon on a Rainbow Shawl* by Caribbean playwright Errol John; and *Black Nativity*, a Christmas pageant by **Langston Hughes**. The next year, McClintock resumed his interest in works by black playwrights. The season was comprised of Ed Bullins's *Clara's Ole Man*, **Douglas Turner Ward**'s *Day of Absence*, **Gilbert Moses**'s *Roots*, Amiri Baraka's (Leroi Jones) *Dutchman*, and **Marvin X**'s *Taking Care of Business*. The play that brought the company acclaim, however, was N. R. Davidson's *El Hajj Malik* (1991) based on the life of Malcolm X. One unique feature of this group was the sharing of directorial responsibilities. At the Baraka festival, graduates of the studio and present students combined to perform in productions with three different directors: McClintock did *Junkies*, Helmar Cooper did *Experimental Death Unit #1*, and Woody Carter did *Great Goodness of Life*. McClintock later moved to Richmond, VA, and formed the Ernie McClintock Jazz Actors.

ALDRIDGE, IRA (1807–67). Born in the United States, Aldridge was the first African American actor of record to achieve success on the international stage. He performed before kings and queens throughout Europe, garnering the reputation as the preeminent Shakespearean actor and tragedian of the 19th century. His father, a lay preacher, sent him to the African Free School in New York, but young Aldridge was attracted to the African Grove Theatre (*see* AFRICAN COMPANY [AC]/AFRICAN GROVE THEATRE [AGT]), the first black theater founded by William Alexander Brown in 1821. He apprenticed under **James Hewlett**, the first African American Shakespearean actor. Realizing he could not achieve success in the United States, young Aldridge worked his passage to Liverpool, England, as a ship's steward.

From the mid-1820s to 1860, Aldridge slowly forged a remarkable career. He performed in London, Liverpool, Edinburgh, Bath, and Bristol in *King Lear*, *Othello*, *Macbeth*, and *The Merchant of Venice*. He also freely adapted classical plays, changing characters, eliminating scenes, and installing new ones, even from other plays. In 1852, he embarked on a series of continental tours that intermittently would last until the end of his life. He performed his full repertoire in Prussia, Germany, Austria, Switzerland, Hungary, and Poland. Some of the honors he received include the Prussian Gold Medal for Arts and Sciences from King Frederick, the Golden Cross of Leopold from the czar of Russia, and the Maltese Cross from Berne, Switzerland. Aldridge died while on tour in Lodz, Poland.

ALDRIDGE PLAYERS. Active in 1926, playwright **Frank Wilson** formed this short-lived **Harlem** theater group. The company was named after **Ira Aldridge**, an actor and playwright at the African Grove Theatre (*see* AFRICAN COMPANY [AC]/AFRICAN GROVE

THEATRE [AGT]) in New York City (1821–23). The ensemble presented three of Wilson's one-act plays, *Sugar Cane*, *Flies*, and *Color Worship*, at the Harlem Library Little Theatre (July 1926) as guests of the **Krigwa Players**, who then occupied the facility. The company included William Jackson, Agnes Marsh, Charlie Taylor, Charles Randolph, Virginia Randolph, and Wilson, who both performed and directed. Another thriving group of Aldridge Players out of Saint Louis, MO, toured circa 1927 to 1935 as part of the African American Little Theatre Movement. **Frederick O'Neal** organized the ensemble with the help of the Saint Louis Urban League. The players acquired a theater, where it produced plays of black life, and its members received instruction in speech and drama for some eight years. O'Neal left the group to pursue a professional career with the **Federal Theatre Project**.

ALEXANDER, LEWIS M. (1900–45). Born in Washington, DC, Alexander was an actor, director, poet, essayist, and pioneer playwright of the 1920s. He attended Dunbar High School and Howard University and also studied at the University of Pennsylvania. As a professional actor, he made his Broadway debut in 1923 in the **Ethiopian Art Players'** production of *Salome* and the *Comedy of Errors*. He was a member of the Playwrights' Circle and the **Ira Aldridge** Players (*see* ALDRIDGE PLAYERS) and directed several black theater groups in Washington, including the St. Vincent de Paul Players, the Ira Aldridge Players of Grover Cleveland School, and the Randall Community Center Players

ALEXANDER, ROBERT. Playwright/Author. Robert Alexander may not have the name recognition of an August Wilson or a Suzan-Lori Parks, but he is one of the most significant literary lions in black theater today. Alexander has written some 30 plays, been a playwright in residence at three separate professional theaters, and cowritten four anthologies of African American plays. Alexander was born and raised in the Washington, DC, area where his parents exposed him to the world of theater. His early influence was toward the more militant fare of LeRoi Jones and Ed Bullins. After earning a bachelors degree in 1975 from Oberlin College, he headed west and settled in the San Francisco bay area. It was there that he was exposed to the works of

R. G. Davis's San Francisco Mime Troupe, where he found out humorous satire trumps hateful rhetoric every time. It was in San Francisco that he earned an M.F.A. from San Francisco State in 1980. He also served a residency with the Mime Troupe, with which he wrote six plays, including *Secrets of the Sand* (1982), *Fact Wino vs. Armageddon* (1982), and *I Ain't Yo Uncle: The New Jack Revisionist Uncle Tom's Cabin* (1993). He then married and began raising a family of his own. He returned to the world of academia in 1996, earning a second M.F.A. at the University of Iowa.

Alexander was playwright in Residence at both the Lorraine Hansberry Theatre in San Francisco, and the Wooly Mammoth Theatre in Washington, DC. His works have been performed nationwide including Actors Theatre of Louisville, Trinity Repertory Company, Jomandi Productions, Mark Taper Forum, Kennedy Center, Karamu House, the Hartford Stage Company, and Horizon Theatre. Some of the plays he has written are *Air Guitar: (A Rock Opera)*, *Alien Motel 29*, *The Last Orbit of Billy Mars*, *Will He Bop Will He Drop?*, *On a Street With No Name*, *Freak of Nature*, and *Forty Acres: The Reparations Play*. He has written or cowritten a total of four play anthologies including *Colored Contradictions* (1996), *Plays From Wooly Mammoth* (1999), *The Fire This Time* (2004), and *Plays From the Boom Box Galaxy: Anthology for the Hip Hop Generation* (2008). Alexander is the recipient of grants from the National Endowment for the Arts, and the Pew Charitable trust.

ALEXANDER, ZAKIYAH. Alexander is an emerging playwright of the 21st century. She earned a B.A. from Binghamton University and an M.F.A. from the Yale School of Drama. She has had readings at Actors Express, New Dramatists, Vineyard Theatre, and New Professional Theatre. In addition, her works have been developed and performed at **La MaMa Experimental Theatre Club**, Greenwich Street Theatre, Pace Theatre, Ensemble Studio Theatre, and the Producer's Club. Of the plays she has written, the most successful has been *The Etymology of Bird*, which won her the coveted **Theodore Ward** Prize in 2005. She was rewarded with a full production of the play at Columbia College under the direction of **Charles "Chuck" Smith**. A partial list of Alexander's plays include *Blurring Shine*, *Prayala*, *After the Show: A Play in Mask*, *Present Company*, *Sick*,

Elected, One Smart Trick, Sweet Maladies, and *Momentary Delay.* Alexander is a resident member of New Dramatists, EST Youngbloods, and Women's Work Project Playwrights Lab. She is the recipient of the James Duvall Phelan Award, New Dramatists fellowship, New Professional Award, and Theatre Playwriting Award.

ALICE, MARY SMITH. Alice is a respected character actor in theater, a profession she has worked in for over 35 years. She transitioned adeptly between working onstage, in television, and in movies. Born in Indianola, MS, Alice studied at the teachers college at Chicago State University (B.A.). She began her professional life as a teacher in the Chicago school system, but her passion was for acting. She made her stage debut in the early 1960s in **Ossie Davis**'s hilarious satire *Purlie Victorious*. In the mid 1960s, Alice moved to New York City and began studying acting with **Lloyd Richards**. She made her professional acting debut in 1967. Alice has performed in such prestigious theaters as the Long Wharf Theatre, McCarter Theatre, Goodman Theatre, **La MaMa Experimental Theatre Club**, New York Shakespeare Festival/Public Theatre, American Place Theatre, and St. Mark's Playhouse. She has appeared in a variety of plays, including *A Rat's Mass* by **Adrienne Kennedy**, *Julius Caesar* by William Shakespeare, *Zooman and the Sign* by **Charles Fuller**, *Spell #7* by **Ntozake Shange**, and *Fences* by **August Wilson**.

Since 1974, Alice has appeared in over 50 different television and movie ventures, such as *Kojak, Police Woman, All My Children, The Women of Brewster Place, Serpico, Good Times, L.A. Law, Bonfire of the Vanities, Enter, The Matrix, Law and Order, I'll Fly Away, Soul Food, Cosby, Touched by an Angel, Down in the Delta,* and *The Matrix Online.* Over the years, Alice has been fortunate to appear on Broadway four separate times, including in *Fences* in 1987 opposite **James Earl Jones**, for which she won a **Tony Award** for best actress and a **Drama Desk Award**. Alice also won an Emmy Award for her 1993 performance on television in *I'll Fly Away.*

ALLISON, HUGHES (1908–74). Born in Greenville, SC, Allison, a playwright, moved with his family to Newark, NJ, in 1919. A graduate of Upsala College, he wrote in several mediums and is reputed to have written some 2,000 radio scripts during his lifetime. During the Depression, the Works Progress Administration (WPA) hired Allison as part of the **Federal Theatre Project** group in New Jersey, providing him with his first opportunity to gain exposure in the performing arts.

Recognition for Allison as a writer came with *The Trial of Dr. Beck* (1937), a play about eugenics. A mulatto doctor is accused of killing his dark-skinned wife, who sells hair straightners for black women. The trial becomes a referendum on skin color, not evidence, and the murderer's identity comes as a shock to all. Owing to the success of the play, it was moved to Broadway, where the late William Bendix played the light-skinned doctor. Two other plays Allison penned are *Panyared* (1938), the story of a kidnapped African prince sold into **slavery**, and *It's Midnight over Newark* (1941), a *Living Newspaper* dramatization of black physicians not being allowed to practice their profession. Production plans for both shows were halted after Congress closed down the WPA in 1939. Allison continued to write for the *Newark Evening News* and other publications. In 1940, he, along with **Abram Hill**, **Langston Hughes**, **Theodore Ward**, Powell Lindsay, and George Norford, organized the nonprofit Negro Playwrights Group.

ALONZO PLAYERS. Cecil Alonzo founded the group in Brooklyn in 1966 as the Players Eight. As the administrator, director, producer, actor, and principal playwright, Alonzo changed the original name to the Alonzo Players. Growing up in Williamsburg, VA, he made his stage debut in a church pageant at age five. He received a B.A. in theater arts and English education from Norfolk State College, VA (1965), and studied acting and speech with the American Academy of Dramatic Arts (1968). He became interested in film and television production and public relations with Third World Cinema Productions in 1972. Since 1981, he has taught communication skills and public speaking for Empire State College, the School Arts League, and the New York City Board of Education.

The players are best known for their rendition of *Black Voices* and *Somewhere between Us Two*. *Voices*, a poetic review in two acts, was produced in 1969. Alonzo interlaced his own material with excerpts from African American poets to retell black history from the time blacks were brought to America to the 1960s. Alonzo opened the show at the Courtyard Playhouse in New York City (March 1971), aired it on the Public Broadcasting System (1973), telecast it in the New York City area around 1973, and produced it at the **Billie Holiday Theatre** in Brooklyn (1973). Alonzo's second work, *Somewhere between Us Two* (1972), was written in collaboration with Rob Taylor. It is a poetic love story in one act about two pen pals who are disappointed in each other when they finally meet.

AMBUSH, BENNY SATO. Ambush, a veteran of the American stage, is a native of Worcester, MA. He earned a B.A. in theater arts from Brown University and then headed West, where he earned an M.F.A. in theater from the University of California at San Diego. His first break came when the indomitable Zelda Fichlander hired him as an apprentice at Arena Stage in Washington, DC. He is the producing-director-in-residence at Emerson College in Boston, MA. He is perhaps best known as the producing director of the Oakland Ensemble Theatre, a theater that he rescued from obscurity, where he produced and directed plays from 1982 to 1990. Ambush was also an associate artistic director at the American Conservatory of Theatre and served as an interim artistic director at **Rites and Reason Theatre**.

Ambush is very much a humanist. He believes in cultural diversity, and his work reflects just that. He has directed a variety of plays, such as Ferenc Molnar's *The Play's the Thing*, Molière's *Tartuffe*, *A Bicycle Country* by Nilo Cruz, and *Gem of the Ocean* by **August Wilson**. He has directed at some of the leading theaters and educational institutions across the country, including GeVa Theatre, the Alabama Shakespeare Festival, Playwrights Horizons, Actors Guild of Lexington, California State University, Lincoln Center, North Carolina School of the Arts, Arizona Theatre Company, the National Black Theatre Festival, and Florida Stage.

AMERICAN NEGRO THEATRE (ANT). Formed by **Abram Hill**, **Frederick O'Neal**, and others in **Harlem**, ANT was an outgrowth of the illustrious Negro Unit of the **Federal Theatre Project** in Harlem. Active between 1940 and the mid-1950s, it was governed by four goals: to develop a permanent acting company trained in the arts and crafts of the theater that also reflected the special gifts, talents, and attributes of the black people; to produce plays that honestly and with integrity interpreted, illuminated, and criticized contemporary black life and the concerns of the black people (and particularly the Harlem community); to maintain an affiliation with and provide leadership for other black theater groups throughout the nation; and to utilize its resources to develop racial pride in the theater rather than racial apathy. The earliest elected officers included Hill (chairman, artistic director, and resident playwright), O'Neal (assistant chairman, company manager), and John O'Shaughnessy. The major technicians were Perry Watkins, Charles Sebree, and **Roger Furman**, set designers, and George Lewis, lighting technician.

For five years (1940–45), the theater was housed in the basement of the Harlem Branch of the New York Public Library, known as the Harlem Library Little Theatre and specially renovated for the group. In 1945, ANT was forced to move to the Elks Lodge at 15 West 126th Street, then known as the American Negro Theatre Playhouse. It later became the home of the Elks Community Theatre. ANT moved again in 1950 to a loft on West 125th Street, its last residence before the theater closed.

ANT's program was divided into three categories: stage production, a training program, and a radio program. Stage productions included *On Striver's Row* by Hill (September 1940); *Natural Man* by **Theodore Browne** (May 1941); *On Striver's Row*, the musical version by Hill (March 1941); *Three Is a Family* by Phoebe and Henry Ephron (November 1943), which transferred to Broadway (April 1944); *Anna Lucasta* by Philip Yordan, adapted by Hill (June 1945); *Garden of Time* by **Owen Dodson** (March 1945); *Henri Christophe* by Dan Hammersmith (June 1945); *Home Is the Hunter* by Samuel Kootz (January 1946); *On Striver's Row* by Hill (revived February 1946); *Angel Street* by Patrick Hamilton (July 1946); *Juno and the Paycock* by Sean O'Casey (July 1946); **You Can't Take It with You** by Moss Hart and George Kaufman (August 1946); *The Peacemaker* by Kurt Unkelbach (November 1946); *Tin Top Valley* by Walter Carroll (March 1947); *The Later Christopher Bean* by Sidney Howard (July 1947); *Rope* by Eugene O'Neill (July 1947); *The Show Off* by George Kelly (August 1947); *Rain* by John Colton and Clemence Randolph (December 1947); *The Washington Years* by Nat Sherman (March 1948); *Sojourner Truth* by Katherine G. Chaplin (April 1949); *Almost Faithful* by Harry Wagstaff Gribble (June 1948); *Riders to the Sea* by John Millington Synge; and *Freight* by Kenneth White (February 1949). The play that brought ANT the most recognition, however, was *Anna Lucasta*. It opened at the Harlem Library Theatre, but Broadway producers were anxious to move it downtown because of its commercial appeal. The show ran on Broadway for 957 performances before it toured throughout the country and later abroad in London. The success of *Anna* on Broadway had a twofold effect on the company. It caused the demise of ANT because it departed from the company's community roots, and this resulted in the loss of its founder Hill, who resigned due to the shift in goals and ideology. The second category was an aggressive training program that launched the careers of some of the more recognizable African American artists in the field, such as **Sidney Poitier**, Harry Belafonte, **Ruby Dee**, **Ossie Davis**, Frederick O'Neal, **Alice Childress**, Maxwell Glanville, Hilda Simms, **Earle Hyman**, **Clarice Taylor**, **Gordon Heath**, Isabel Sanford, Roger Furman, and **Rosetta LeNoire**. The last category was a weekly series of radio programs presented from 1945 to 1946 entitled "New World A-Coming." The format was a weekly half-hour dramatic program that ranged from William Shakespeare's *Romeo and Juliet* and Charles Dickens's *Christmas Carol* to Arthur Laurent's *The Face* and Paul Lipschutz's *The Last Page*. Operatic productions included *Pagliacci*, *H.M.S. Pinafore*, *Rigoletto*, and *The Barber of Seville*. The company also presented operatic productions on Sunday afternoons on Station WNEW.

AMERICAN THEATRE OF HARLEM (ATH). Located in New York City, the ATH was founded in 1989 by the late Hal DeWindt, who passed away in 1997. DeWindt had done it all. A former actor, director, producer, and model, he worked for **Joseph Papp** at the New York Shakespeare Festival, was a former film executive in Hollywood, and held a position as an acting professor at Loyola Marymount University at the time of his death. DeWindt started the ATH with a mission to ground the student in the fundamentals of acting in preparation for a professional career. He set up ongoing acting workshops, readings, showcases, and occasional productions. Keith Johnston, an early student of DeWindt who has put his own imprint on the program, has guided the ATH. He instituted a one-act play festival and annual film festival and created the Shine Program, an educational theater component that provides workshops for youth, community, and corporate groups.

Aside from regularly scheduled play readings, the ATH also produced plays geared to the experience level of the actors being trained. Plays are considered from one to three acts and from plays in the

African American canon to established plays in the European/American tradition. The ATH has mounted plays ranging from Tennessee Williams's *A Streetcar Named Desire* to **George C. Wolfe**'s *The Colored Museum*. The plays are performed at the South Oxford Space in the arts community of Fort Greene in Brooklyn. The ATH is a 501(c)3 nonprofit organization and is a member of the Alliance of Resident Theatres. *See also* HARLEM.

ANDERSON, CHRISTINA. Playwright and Kansas City native, Anderson graduated from Brown University. Her first play was *Sacagawea: Breath of an American Spirit*, which she developed using the research to performance method taught at the **Rite and Reason Theatre** at Brown University. It received a staged reading at the Eugene O'Neill Theatre in 2000. Other plays she wrote include *Construction of a Black Diva*, a one-woman show; *The Indian Wants the Bronx*; *Confessions Written on Brown Paper Bags*; *Revelations: The Outtakes* (2003); and *Going Home* (2006). Anderson's plays have been produced at the Provincetown Playhouse, Coterie Theatre, Mark Taper Forum, and other venues. She is the winner of a Kennedy Center Award (2003) and a **Lorraine Hansberry** Playwriting Award (2004).

ANDERSON, DIANA (1937–83). This playwright was a native of Buffalo, NY. Upon earning her A.B. from the University of Southern California (1963), she moved to New York City, where she studied at Gene Frankel's Theatre Workshop. She worked as a resident playwright/instructor at the Back Alley Theatre and a visiting artist/lecturer at the University of South Florida. Anderson is credited with writing over 15 plays. They include *A Long Way from Here*, *Let Me Count the Ways*, *Charlie Still Can't Win No Wars on the Ground*, *The Black People's Party*, *Nightcap*, *If I Were a Chameleon*, *(Mis) Judgement*, *The Unicorn Died at Dawn*, *Closing Time*, and *Black Sparrow*. Anderson's plays have been produced at the Back Alley Theatre, the West End Repertory Theatre, and other venues.

ANDERSON, GARLAND (1886–1939). A pioneer playwright and moralistic philosopher of constructive thinking, Anderson was the first African American known to have a serious full-length drama produced on Broadway. Active in the theatre for over 10 years (1920s–30s), he achieved national prominence as the "San Francisco Bellhop Playwright." Born in Wichita, KS, Anderson completed only four years of formal schooling before the family moved to California. Working as a bellhop in a San Francisco hotel, he often shared his optimistic philosophy of life with guests, who encouraged him to write about his ideas. Anderson believed an individual might achieve anything in life through faith. He got the idea of writing a play after seeing a production of Channing Pollock's moralistic drama *The Fool*. He wrote his first play, *Appearances* (1924), in only three weeks with no training in playwriting style or technique. Failing to find a producer, he personally raised $15,000 toward the production. Despite numerous obstacles, his play opened on Broadway in 1925 with the help of Al Jolson and U.S. president Calvin Coolidge. The courtroom drama is about a bellboy (played by Lionel Monagas in the first production) on trial when he is falsely accused of raping a white woman. Owing to the central character's strong moral convictions, he is eventually exonerated. Anderson spent the last period of his life lecturing on his beliefs about constructive thinking, on which he wrote a book entitled *Uncommon Sense* (1933). His achievements in the face of overwhelming racial, financial, and educational limitations were widely publicized.

ANDERSON, VALETTA. Playwright and administrator, Anderson has been involved in theater on multiple levels, including as dramaturge, director, facilitator, and professor on the collegiate level. A native of Chicago, Anderson received her education in Atlanta, GA, including instruction at the Academy Theatre School of Performing Arts. She has developed her works through workshops and staged readings at such venues as Seattle's ACT Theatre, Women Playwrights Festival, Horizon Theatre, and Theatre Emory and the Southeast Playwright's Project. Her plays have been produced by **Kuntu Repertory Theatre**, **Jomandi Productions**, **National Black Theatre Festival**, and Essential Theatre.

A partial list of Anderson's plays include *Leaving Limbo* (2006), which is about a young hip-hopper who travels back to Africa in search of identity and is puzzled at what he finds. *She'll Find the Way Home* (2003) is set in Mississippi in 1870. It is a story of a young woman's rite of passage in discovering her history. Other plays Anderson wrote are *Dorothy D.* (1994), *Dr. Love and the Fabulous Di-*

amond Jubilee, *No Virgins in Paradise* (1992), *Where Peachtree Meets Sweet Auburn* (2001), and *Traveling Thomas* (2002). Among the honors and awards Anderson received are the Georgia Council for the Arts, AT&T Award, Rockefeller Foundation Award, and Theatre Emory Commission. She is a member of Dramatists Guild, Literary Managers and Dramaturges of America, and the Southeast Playwrights Project.

ANDREWS, REGINA ANDERSON (1901–93). Andrews, a playwright and librarian, was from Chicago. She attended Wilberforce College and the University of Chicago before graduating from Columbia University (M.L.S.). She began work as assistant librarian at the 115th Street branch of the New York Public Library during the 1920s in the middle of the **Harlem** Renaissance. Bright and articulate, her influence turned a rather drab, nondescript library into a thriving oasis of culture that presented art exhibitions, a drama series, and a "Family Night at the Library" that attracted such luminaries as Marcus Garvey, Eleanor Roosevelt, and **Langston Hughes**. Her home in the Sugar Hill section of Harlem became one of the famed "salons" of the Harlem Renaissance where members of the Writers Guild and intellectuals would meet, like Gwendolyn Bennett, **Countee Cullen**, Jesse Fausett, and **W. E. B. DuBois**.

Caught in the New Negro Movement of the time in 1927, Andrews helped DuBois found the **Krigwa Players**, which later evolved into the Negro Experimental Theatre. It was an extension of DuBois's axiom of a theater "by us, for us, about us, and near us" and served as an inspiration in the development of black theater across the country. They performed all their plays at the library for a nominal fee. Anderson was also a fledgling playwright who wrote three plays under the pseudonym of Ursula Trelling. They are *Climbing Jacob's Ladder* (1931), a story of a black person being lynched while the congregation prayed in church. *Underground* (1932) is about the Underground Railroad. *The Man Who Passed* is a one-act play of eight pages. In 1947, Andrews stepped forward again and helped playwright **Loften Mitchell** found the **People's Theatre**, using the library as a base of operation. Several of Mitchell's plays were produced there, including *The Cellar* (1947), *The Bancroft Dynasty* (1947), and *The Shames of the Nation* (1952).

Andrews believed professional librarians could play a significant role in providing access and opportunity to a wide variety of people through the medium she worked in, the library. Over a period of 44 years, she did just that, as well as worked diligently to preserve African American history and culture. Some of her papers are stored at the Schomburg Center for Research in Black Culture at the 135th Street branch of the New York Public Library. Andrews is the recipient of the Asia Foundation Award.

ANITA BUSH PLAYERS (ABP)/THE ANITA BUSH ALL-COLORED DRAMATIC STOCK COMPANY. An actor, dancer, and producer, Anita Bush turned to drama after a back injury ended her dancing career in musical theater and vaudeville. She organized the ABP, a highly significant pioneer dramatic stock company. She presented her idea of launching a dramatic stock company to Eugene "Frenchy" Elmore, assistant manager of the newly renovated Lincoln Theatre in **Harlem**, a vaudeville house. Bush convinced Elmore that she could assemble a production within two weeks (even though she did not have a company). Elmore was sold on the idea and signed Bush to a contract. She secured Billie Burke, an active white director/playwright in the Harlem community, to direct the group in his play *The Girl at the Fort*, a light comedy with five characters. She assembled a promising group of actors that included Carlotta Freeman for the dramatic and emotional roles, Dooley Wilson for the comedic and light character roles, and Andrew Bishop for the juvenile lead roles.

The company opened with *Fort* at the Lincoln Theatre (November 1915). During the next six weeks, they presented a different play every two weeks with great success. Maria C. Downs, a wealthy entrepreneur of Cuban descent and proprietor of the Lincoln Theatre, ordered Bush to change the name of the group to the Lincoln Players. Bush refused and took her company to the **Lafayette Theatre**, where they opened with *Across the Footlights* (December 1915). Thereafter, ABP mounted a play each week—mainly adaptations of off-Broadway melodramas and the classics. They included *The Gambler's Sweetheart* (adapted from *The Girl of the Golden West*) and an abridged version of Dion Boucicault's *The Octoroon*. In March 1916, the Lafayette Theatre management purchased the company from

Bush and changed the name (with her consent) to the Lafayette Players, which eventually became one of the best-known black dramatic stock companies in America. Within a year, Bush organized four new groups of Lafayette Players in other cities for her circuit tour. In 1920, Bush left the Lafayette Theatre to pursue a film career in all-black films.

APOLLO THEATRE. This historic landmark **Harlem** theater located on 125th Street between 7th and 8th Avenue in New York City is the best-known black-oriented vaudeville variety house in the United States. A place where stars are born and legends are made, the Apollo has been the springboard that launched the careers of celebrated artists from the past to the present. Its luminaries span from Ella Fitzgerald, Lena Horne, Eartha Kitt, Sara Vaughn, and Pearl Bailey to James Brown, Michael Jackson, and Luther Vandross. Frank Shiffman and Leo Brecher (previous owner of the **Lafayette Theatre**) purchased the establishment and named it the Apollo. From its opening day in 1934 to the present, the amateur night has been an audience favorite. During the early years, the comedy was low and bawdy, and the artists sometimes performed in blackface. Among the more popular comedians were "Tim" Moore, Jackie "Moms" Mabley, Dewey "Pigmeat" Markham, Eddie Green, and Mantan Moreland.

The Apollo gained a reputation as the premier variety vaudeville house, but it also offered theatrical productions on occasion. In 1950, the management mounted two plays by white playwrights: One was *Rain*, with Nina Mae McKinney in the role of a prostitute. The other was *Detective Story*, with **Sidney Poitier** and Hilda Haynes in the lead roles. Both were staged with all-black casts, but neither attracted large audiences. Thereafter, management reverted to its variety vaudeville policy that appeared to meet audience expectation. For almost three decades, the Apollo survived several financial crises while accruing a million-dollar debt. Despite the deficit, Percy Sutton and the Inner-City Broadcasting Coral purchased the Apollo in 1981 to preserve it as a landmark Harlem theater. Management revived the amateur night in 1985 and celebrated the Apollo's 50th-anniversary grand reopening with a special, nationally televised Motown salute climaxed by Michael Jackson's "moon walk." Two years later, *Show*

Time at the Apollo began airing on national television. By 1991, the state of New York had acquired the theater as a nonprofit organization to ensure the theater's ongoing success. Because of this change in status, the Apollo team was able to book more high-profile shows. They mounted *Harlem Song*, a new Broadway-style musical directed by award-winning playwright and director **George C. Wolfe**, and hosted benefits in addition to headlining shows with such artists as Stevie Wonder, Vanessa Williams, and Wynton Marsalis.

ARANHA, RAY. Playwright and actor, Aranha was born in Miami, FL. He attended Florida A&M University (B.S.) and studied acting at the American Academy of Dramatic Arts. He has taught drama, conducted acting and writing workshops, and acted at leading regional theaters throughout the country. Aranha also garnered a measure of success as a playwright. His most noted play, *My Sister, My Sister* (1973), is a full-length drama set in the 1950s. A young girl attempts to cope with her family, the world, and her feelings. The Hartford Stage Company in Connecticut (September 1973) produced it for 44 performances. Ashton Springer, an African American producer, sponsored it off-off-Broadway at the Little Theatre in Greenwich Village in New York City (April–January 1975) for 119 performances.

Other Aranha plays of merit include *The Estate* (1976), a full-length historical drama. It focuses on Thomas Jefferson's' relationship with his slave mistress Sally Hemmings and a confrontation between Jefferson and Benjamin Banneker, the black scientist who surveyed and designed Washington, DC. The Hartford Stage Company produced it under the direction of Duane Jones (January 1976) for 44 performances. The Afro-American Total Theatre produced it off Broadway (January 1978). *Sons and Fathers of Sons* (1983) is a full-length drama set within three decades of the 1940s, 1950s, and 1960s. The action contrasts the development of three young men: a student, a sharecropper's son, and a college professor. Two are distraught over a lynching of a young black man in another county and is similar to one in their town, while the third works out his relationship with the past and future at a black college in Tallahassee, FL. **Walter Dallas** directed a cast of **Graham Brown**, Robert Gossett, Phylicia Allen-Rashad, Ethel Ayer, and

Eugene Lee. Aranha is the recipient of a Rockefeller playwright-in-residence grant (1975) and a **Drama Desk Award** (1974) for *My Sister, My Sister* (1973) as best playwright (**Seret Scott** won for leading actress). **Barbara Montgomery** won both the **Audience Development Committee Award** and the **Obie Award** for the role of the mother.

ARENA PLAYERS (THE COMPANY). Conceived by Samuel H. Wilson and friends after they first met in Wilson's living room, this little theater company was housed at the **Arena Playhouse** in Baltimore, MD. Comprised mostly of former members of the **Krigwa Players** from Baltimore, the playhouse has operated continuously since 1953. It is unknown when it was built. The first production was *Hello Out There*, a one-act play by white playwright William Saroyan, presented on the campus of Coppin State College. Mainly relatives and friends attended. An impressive number of players went on to work on Broadway and in movies and television.

ARENA PLAYHOUSE (THE THEATER). One of the oldest continually operating black theaters in the country, Arena Playhouse is located in Baltimore, MD. It was founded by a group of nine black actors and actresses led by Samuel H. Wilson. They called themselves the **Arena Players**, a community theater, and their first production was a double bill of William Saroyan's *Hello Out There* and Thornton Wilder's *Happy Journey*. Over the years, they have performed in a church, a gymnasium, and a recreational hall. In 1969, they acquired the old St. Mary's Church building for $10,000. Along with that came the name Arena Playhouse.

The space was renovated several times until it housed a 314-seat arena theater, classrooms, rehearsal spaces, children's theater, youth theater (13 to 18), and art gallery. By 1992, the Arena Players, the resident company, had adopted an all-black repertoire, and the audiences were primarily black. Their daily activities were augmented with poetry jams, stand-up comedians, and guest celebrity appearances, but by 1996, a sluggish economy, Samuel Wilson's death, competition by white theaters that began producing black plays, and the advent of Urban Circuit plays being produced in Baltimore caused the playhouse to plummet into serious debt.

Managing director Rodney Orange Jr., however, cut back on expenses; organized a fund-raising drive led by some of their alumni, like **Charles S. Dutton**, Trazana Beverley, and **Andre DeShields**. He also broadened the base of support by attracting private-sector companies and foundations to become involved. By 1997, Orange had erased the debt, and the theater and the land it owned were valued at over $1 million. All this was made possible at a community theater, where no one is paid, save the managing director, Orange, and any musicians jobbed in for a particular play or musical.

The playhouse grew into one of Baltimore's most celebrated institutions, with a six-play season, a thriving youth program, and a modern 314-seat theater in the heart of the Mount Vernon arts district.

ASSIMILATIONISM. During the latter part of the 1960s, along with greater opportunities for upward mobility, blacks sought access to every segment of society. They wanted to integrate financially and socially into the hegemonic culture. Assimilationism, however, came at a cost, as many blacks had to cast aside their notion of blackness and deny or lose their cultural identity and sense of self. This created a crisis in the black aesthetic movement as well as the black nationalist movement in their quest for a united black front. In **Ed Bullins**'s satire *Electronic Nigger* (1964), an "Uncle Tom" black teacher parrots the majority culture to gain access to the American dream at the expense of his own people. A post office employee in *Great Goodness of Life* (1964) by **Amiri Baraka (LeRoi Jones)** is willing to "figuratively" kill black revolutionaries to live happily in his world of bowling and whiteness. In both *Take a Giant Step* (1954) by **Louis Peterson** and *A Raisin in the Sun* by **Lorraine Hansberry**, a black family decides to leave the inner city to move into an all-white suburb to escape crime and to provide a better education for their children—the former family is from **Harlem**, the latter from Chicago. Gabe, a playwright in the play he is writing in *No Place to Be Somebody* (1969), kills his central character, Johnny Williams, because he has the "Charlie Fever," as well as his alter ego, Machine Gun, a revolutionary, so that his soul may be "White and Snow."

AUDIENCE DEVELOPMENT COMMITTEE (AUDELCO) AWARD. In 1973, Vivian Robinson (1924–96), a social reporter and theater critic for the *Amsterdam News*, formed the Audelco as a voluntary nonprofit organization. As president elect, she wanted to applaud what others ignored—recognition of African American theater—and to increase attendance by stimulating an interest and appreciation of black theater. To this end, Audelco issued an affordable theater voucher to theater patrons for $5, financed by the Theatre Development Fund. It enabled audiences to attend productions by lesser-known theater companies in the black community as well as plays off and on Broadway for as little as $1 per show. To supports its activities, Audelco conducted membership drives and fund-raising affairs, solicited contributions, organized theater parties at reduced prices, and disseminated information about black theater through a bimonthly newsletter. The organization also generated income from the New York City Department of Cultural Affairs.

In addition, Robinson initiated an annual recognition award to honor excellence in black theater and to illuminate black theater companies and artists. New York theater critics and members of the theater academy seldom recognized contributions of African American performing artists at the annual **Tony**, **Obie**, or **Drama Desk Awards**—each considered the paragon of artistic achievement. Audelco set up a nominating committee to select artists in various categories, including best actor, director, playwright, designers (lighting and set), special honorees, and pioneer and rising star awards. For a $25 fee, theater practitioners may become a member and participate actively in the voting process. The winners of the various categories are announced at Audelco's annual recognition awards held in November at Aaron Davis Hall in **Harlem**.

In 2002, Audelco celebrated its 30th anniversary. Among the Audelco award winners were actors Phylicia Allen Rashad (*Gem of the Ocean*) and **Rome Neal** (*Monk*). After 35 years of operation, it is still acknowledged as the most significant award for black artists. The awards brought prestige to Audelco, provided visibility to black theaters relatively unknown, increased theater attendance, and raised the stature and marketability of black artists. Upon Robinson's death in 1996, Audelco had awarded more than 400 theatrical practitioners for their contribution to the advancements in African American theater, a tribute in large part due to her great vision, leadership, and generosity of spirit.

– B –

BAILEY, SHERI. A playwright and educator, Bailey is from Portsmouth, VA, and her social activism manifests itself in the plays she writes, which typically reflect the history of African Americans and an attempt to give voice to the poor and disenfranchised. She weaves these elements and more into her most successful play to date, *Summers in Suffolk*. It is a tale that traces six generations of an African American family after **slavery** to the present time. The play uses music and humor in telling the story of former slave Amos Clark and his family beginning in 1870.

Bailey earned a B.A. from the University of Pennsylvania and then enrolled at UCLA, where she earned an M.F.A. in theater. She was an associate professor at the University of Southern California while also working in TV on such projects as *L.A. Law* and *Cagney and Lacey*. It was there that she began writing for the stage, and most of her earlier works were produced at the Beverly Hills Playhouse and the **Towne Street Theatre**. Bailey has since returned to her southern roots and teaches at Old Dominion University.

A partial list of her plays is *A Great and Dismal Swamp*, set in the Virginia and North Carolina swamp wilderness, where the inhabitants deal with issues of race, gender, and power; *Ben and Jefferson*, centering on the debate between African American scientist Benjamin Banneker and Thomas Jefferson; *All Kinds of Blue*, about a woman who returns from 5 years in prison and attempts to reestablish a relationship with her daughter; *Passing*, an adaptation of Nella Larson's novel set during the **Harlem** Renaissance; *Walking with a Panther*, about a stormy reunion of a former Black Panther with his family after serving 23 years in prison; and *Harriett and Harriett*, set in heaven, where the title characters meet. Bailey is recipient of the NAACP Image Award and a National Endowment for the Arts theater fellowship.

BALDWIN, JAMES ARTHUR (1924–87). A major American playwright, novelist, essayist, and short-story writer, Baldwin is the author of more than 15 books. He was born in New York City to a single mother, Emma Birdis Jones, and a father who was a Pentecostal minister. Although Baldwin's relationship with his father was somewhat contentious, religion is a recurring theme in his works. He encountered a "spiritual revelation" that called him to preach in the pulpit at age 14, only to renounce his faith five years later. In both Baldwin's semiautobiographical novel *Go Tell It on the Mountain* and his play *The Amen Corner*, his central characters are grappling with the Christian doctrine. Baldwin began to write in elementary school at P.S. 139 in **Harlem** and became coeditor of *Magpie*, a school newspaper at DeWitt Clinton High School in the Bronx.

While living in Greenwich Village in New York City, Baldwin met novelist **Richard Wright**, who encouraged him to seek writing fellowships and get work published. Disillusioned with the social attitudes in America toward black and gays, he moved to Paris in 1948, where fellow writers William Styron, Norman Mailer, and Chester Himes welcomed him. He returned to America during the late 1950s and became actively involved in the **civil rights** struggle as a literary spokesman and lecturer for the next 10 years while dividing his time between Paris and the United States. He wrote a collection of essays, *The Fire Next Time* (1963), about the role of blacks during the movement. In the 1970s, he resided in Istanbul, where he was involved in writing, directing, and making films. For many years, he lived in the south of France in St. Paul de Vence, where he died of cancer.

Baldwin wrote three plays of prominence, *Blues for Mr. Charlie* (1964), *The Amen Corner* (1954), and *One Day, When I Was Lost*. *Blues* is a protest drama that premiered at the American National Theatre and Academy Theatre (ANTA). Loosely based on the Emmett Till murder case in Mississippi, the opening of the play is dedicated to his memory and to the four black children killed in Birmingham, AL. Both whites and blacks in a small southern community react to the brutal slaying by a bigoted white storekeeper of a rebellious black youth on his return home from the North. The show was one of the first known portrayals of a black militant on Broadway. Burgess Meredith directed the show for Actors Studio on Broadway at ANTA (April 1964) for 148 performances. The star-laden cast included **Al Freeman Jr.**, Rip Torn, Percy Rodriguez, **Rosetta Lenoire**, and **Diana Sands**. It was also produced in London (1965).

With the success of *Blues*, Baldwin gained recognition as a dramatic playwright and attracted interest in his next play, *The Amen Corner*, a drama in three acts. Elders of a Harlem church question

Sister Margaret's ability to lead the congregation after her absent husband, a man of the world, comes back into her life. She has to decide between her spiritual commitment to God and the love for her dying husband and son. **Owen Dodson** first produced the show at Howard University (May 1955). Over 10 years later (March 1968), **Frank Silvera** directed and produced it at the Robertson Playhouse in Los Angeles, where it ran for about a year. He was also retained as director when it opened on Broadway (produced by Mrs. Nat King Cole) at the Barrymore Theatre (April 1965) for 24 performances. **Beah Richards** won both the Theatre World Award and *Variety*'s annual New York Drama Critic's Poll for her performance in the title role. **Lloyd Richards** directed a second version of the show in 1965, with **Claudia McNeil** in the lead role. It toured cities in Western Europe and the Near East, including Edinburgh, Tel Aviv, Vienna, and London. A musical version was also mounted in 1983. *One Day* is a biography of Malcolm X. In addition to these plays, four other works helped to establish Baldwin's literary reputation as an important writer in several genres. *Go Tell It on the Mountain* is a personal reflection on his life. *Notes of a Native Son* (1955) is a collection of essays. *Giovanni's Room* (1956) is a personal reflection on homosexuality. *The Fire Next Time* is another collection of essays exploring racial relationships and the inevitability of violence between the races if social inequities continued.

Baldwin was a member of Actors Studio of New York, the National Advisory Board of Congress of Racial Equality, the National Committee for a Sane Nuclear Policy, and the National Board of Arts and Letters. He received major fellowships and grants that included the Guggenheim fellowship (1954), as well as the Saxton fellowship, the Rosenwald fellowship, and the National Institute of Arts and Letters grant (all in 1956). He also received the National Conference of Christians and Jews Brotherhood Award (1962), the George Polk Award (1963), and the Foreign Drama Critics' Award (1964). *See also* FAITH AND RELIGION.

BARAKA, AMIRI (LEROI JONES). Playwright, poet, and social activist, Jones was a cultural and spiritual leader of the revolutionary black arts and black theater movements of the 1960s. Born in Newark, NJ, he pursued his education at Rutgers University

(1951–52) and received a B.A. in English from Howard University (1954), an M.A. in philosophy from Columbia University, and another M.A. in German literature from the New School for Social Research. He married Sylvia Robinson, the mother of five of his eight children. He founded and directed two theater companies. The first was the short-lived **Black Arts Repertory Theatre** School **(BARTS)** in **Harlem** for one year (1964–65). The Harlem Youth Opportunity Unlimited (HARYOU)/ACT funded BARTS but closed it down reportedly because of Jones's revolutionary manifesto. The second was at the Spirit House, a Newark community arts center and the home of Baraka's Spirit House Movers (also known as African Revolutionary Movers).

Baraka has lectured and taught American drama, poetry, and literature at illustrious institutions of higher learning. They include Yale University, New School, Columbia University, University of Buffalo, George Washington University, and College of New Rochelle. He was a professor of African studies at SUNY–Stony Brook. Baraka was also founder, editor, and coeditor of such journals as *Totem Pews*, *Yegen Magazine*, *Floating Bear*, *Cricket*, and *Jihad Press* (now *People's War Publications*) in Newark. He wrote and edited more than two dozen books, not including plays. With the publication of his manifesto on the "revolutionary theater" in the early 1960s, Baraka became the chief proponent of a genre that advocated direct confrontation between blacks and whites. This militancy was evidenced in plays with such titles as *Dutchman* (1964), *The Baptism* (1964), *The Slave*, *The Toilet*, *A Recent Killing*, *Jello*, *A Black Mass*, *The Death of Malcolm X*, *Experimental Death Unit #1*, *Slave Ship*, *Madheart*, *Great Goodness of Life (A Coon Show)*, *Junkies Are Full of (Shhh . . .)*, *The Sidnee Poet Heroical*, and *The Motion of History*.

Baraka's signature play that catapulted him to national prominence, however, was *Dutchman*, an absurdist allegorical one-act drama with symbolic relationships to both the Garden of Eden myth and the legend of the flying Dutchman. A young black male college student is approached, enticed, provoked, and eventually murdered by an attractive white blond on a New York subway. Theatre 1964 first produced *Dutchman* for two nights; then moved it off Broadway to the Cherry Lane Theatre (March 1964) for 232 performances, with **Robert Hooks** and Jennifer West as the leads under Edward Parone's directions. The show was also presented in Berlin, Paris, and Spoleto, Italy. Gene Persson Enterprises, Ltd. produced a film version in 1967 with **Al Freeman Jr.** and Shirley Knight.

Among Baraka's awards were an **Obie Award** for *Dutchman* as the best American off-Broadway play, a Whitney fellowship (1964), a Guggenheim fellowship (1965), a doctor of humane letters from Malcolm X College in Chicago (1972), a Rockefeller Foundation Award for drama (1981), New Jersey State Council of Arts poetry grant (1982), and National Endowment for the Arts poetry grant (1981).

BARDEN, JIMMY. A playwright and journalist, Barden is a retired editor of the *New York Times*. He is a longtime member of the Blueberry Pond Theatre Ensemble, a collective of actors, writers, and directors who meet weekly and produce plays written by members of the group. Writers bring their works to be read, critiqued, and rewritten if necessary. The process is repeated until a final script is developed. It is then produced by the group or sometimes by another theater. Born and raised in Little Rock, AR, Barden resides in Pleasantville, NY. Most of his life was consumed in making a living as a journalist until he turned to playwriting during the latter part of his life. His plays have been produced at the Philadelphia Fringe Festival, the Turnip/Globe Theatre One Act Festival, the Samuel French Off-Off-Broadway Original Short Play Festival, the Blueberry Pond Theatre, and the **Negro Ensemble Company**. Barden has written several plays. *Offspring* (2006) is a story of race, power, and obsession in which a wealthy white heiress is consumed with a desire to be inseminated by a black militant. *Menage a Femmes* (2004) portrays three generations of feminists who meet over the Thanksgiving Day holiday and debate over who fathered the third generation. His other play was *The Good Life* (1996). Barden won a Critics Choice Award for *Menage a Femmes* in 2004. He is a member of the Dramatists Guild.

BARFIELD, TANYA. In 2006, Barfield, heretofore one of hundreds of struggling playwrights, emerged as a force in theater. Her play *Blue Door*, commissioned by Playwrights Horizons, received its world premiere in 2006 by the South Coast Repertory Theatre and received productions at the Seattle Repertory Theatre and Berkeley Repertory during the 2007 season. It is a haunting look at a black professor who assimilates into the white world and loses his blackness. When his white wife leaves him, he is jolted into reality through a dream in which various ancestors visit him and question his rejection of his own culture. The title of the play comes from a belief in several third-world countries that a door painted blue will ward off evil spirits.

Barfield, a native of Portland, OR, and a New York University's Tisch School of the Arts graduate, had dreams of becoming an actor. She also earned a degree in playwriting from Julliard. Discouraged by the parts she was offered, she turned to playwriting and has steadily climbed up through the theater industry to the point of name recognition. Her plays have been workshopped at the New York Stage and Film, the Sundance Theatre Laboratory, and the Seattle Repertory Theatre's Women's Playwright Festival. Her plays have been presented at the New York Theatre Workshop, **Arena Playhouse**, and the Royal Court Theatre in London. Among the plays Barfield authored are *Dent* (2000), about two young men who commit a brutal hate crime. The women in their families embark on journeys of self-questioning, guilt, and blame. *The Quick* (2002) examines the psychological problems of teenage daughters after they learn that the United States is preparing to go to war with Afghanistan. *121o WEST* (2004) is about an eccentric family at odds in rural Oregon.

Barfields's honors and awards include the Sundance Theatre Lab Playwright-in-Residence (2006); Lark Play Development Award/ New York State Council on the Arts (2006), honorable mention; Joseph Kesselring Prize (2005); Helen Merrill Emerging Playwright Award (2003); New York Foundation for the Arts fellowship (1997); Franklin Fund Performance Art fellowship (1995); and resident artist at Mabou Mines (1995).

BARNETT, DOUGLAS Q. A producer, actor, director, and writer, Barnett has been involved actively in American theater since the moment he set foot onstage in 1961 at the Cirque Theatre in *A Raisin in the Sun*. By 1969, he had founded **Black Arts/West (BA/W)** in Seattle— the city's first professional black company. A product of the **civil**

rights movement, BA/W functioned as a three-component program: theater, dance, and an art gallery displaying the work of local and national artists. BA/W was a division of the Central Area Motivation Program, an antipoverty agency charged with providing young people with the necessary tools to survive and flourish in society. The program was able to attract a host of talented folk who thrived on the discipline and skills imparted by a top-notch professional staff, including Lorna Richards, Eve Green, Professor Abraham "Dumi" Mariare, and others. During his five-year tenure as founding director of BA/W (1969–73), Barnett produced close to 50 plays, including *Dream on Monkey Mountain*, *Wine in the Wilderness*, *A Son Come Home*, *The Great MacDaddy*, *Electronic Nigger*, *Ain't Supposed to Die a Natural Death*, and *Evolution of a Sister*. Reputable directors came out of New York City to direct plays at the theater: **Allie Woods Jr.**, **Gilbert Moses**, **Beatrice Winde**, **Jason Bernard**, Francine Major, **Buddy Butler**, and Damon Kenyatta.

A significant number of students at BA/W became professionals and performed on Broadway and in regional theaters, TV, and dance companies. Because of its success, BA/W became a nationally acclaimed entity across the United States. BA/W had three artistic directors during its duration. Barnett hired Butler to run a Technical Training Program and to direct **J. E. Franklin**'s *Black Girl*. When Barnett resigned, Butler applied for and got the position. The team of Tee Dennard and Doug Johnson succeeded Butler. After 11 years, BA/W closed its doors in the spring of 1980.

After Barnett left BA/W, a highlight of his career was serving as company manager for the National Tour (1973–74) of **Joseph A. Walker**'s **Tony Award**–winning play *The River Niger* produced by the **Negro Ensemble Company** (**NEC**). This was the first NEC production to play on Broadway, where it ran for nine months. It won the Tony Award for best play and embarked on an extensive national tour. The success of *Niger* helped ensure the continued work of the NEC and its many members over the next 10 years. Barnett has also worked for the Seattle Arts Commission and GeVa Theatre in Rochester, NY.

During a lengthy career, Barnett has acted in over 30 productions with five different companies, including BA/W, ACT Theatre, the Ensemble Theatre, and the Seattle Repertory Theatre. His directing credits include *Big Time Buck White* and *Ebony Wood*. He wrote two plays, *Da Minstrel Show* and *Days of Thunder, Nights of Violence*; he also arranged, edited, and directed two productions of African American poetry—a particular passion. In addition, he has authored articles for the *Seattle Times*, the *Seattle Post Intelligencer*, *Negro Digest*, *Black World*, and *Historylink.org*, an online repository of Pacific Northwest history. Barnett worked on this volume with Professor Anthony D. Hill of the Ohio State University. Among his other interests are dance, jazz, and African American art and poetry.

BARR, DAVID, III. Based in Chicago, Barr, a playwright and actor, evolved from the world of acting to emerge as a dynamic playwright of the 21st century. His first play, *The Death of Black Jesus* (1991), won three prestigious theater awards and established him as one of the stellar playwrights of his time. He received his B.A. in mass media arts and communications from Hampton Institute in 1985. Barr won several awards, including a Joseph Jefferson Citation for Actor for his performance in a 1992 production of *Victims*. But he tired of the way many African American roles were being written, so he embarked on a mission to improve the situation. He wanted his art to reflect the images of "real people," of blacks whom he knew and with whom he lived and associated in his daily life. He wanted to depict in his writings folks who were living, breathing, and hard-working human beings with depth of character, flaws, tragedies, and triumphs. Attracted to events rooted in history, Barr has written a series of provocative plays encompassing significant moments in the history of African Americans in this country. *My Soul Is a Witness* explores events and personalities of the **civil rights** era, such as Rosa Parks, Malcolm X, John F. Kennedy, and Dr. Martin Luther King Jr. *The State of Mississippi vs. Emmett Till* replicates events of that tragedy, and *Every Time I Feel the Spirit* explores the tragic life of contralto Marian Anderson. Barr also adapted two novels for the stage, Walter Mosely's *A Red Death* and *Billy*, a work by Albert French. Barr's other works include *Black Caesar, The Journal of Ordinary Thought, The Union Station Pullman Porter Blues Mississippi . . . And the Face of Emmett Till, Down and Out in Chicago, By the Music of the Spheres, The House That Rocked*, and *The Upper Room*.

At this juncture of his career, Barr's work has already been recognized through such prestigious awards as the National Playwriting Award (1994), Illinois Arts Council Award (1995), **Theodore Ward Best Play Award** (1997), Edgar Allan Poe Award (1998), Unicorn Theatre National Best Play Award (1999), Illinois Arts Council Award (1999), David Offner Prize (2000), and Joseph Jefferson citation for best new play (2004).

BARRETT, NATHAN. Barrett, a playwright, was born in New York City. He earned a B.A. from Brooklyn College and then studied playwriting at the **Frank Silvera Writers' Workshop.** He wrote several plays that were produced by the **Negro Ensemble Company**, the Greenwich Mews Theatre, and the **National Black Theatre**, among others. A representative listing of his plays includes *A Room of Roses, Square Root of Mother, The Aunts of Antioch City, Why Lily Won't Spin, S-C-R-E-W-E-D, Engagement in San Dominique, For Love of Mike, Itchy Bitches, Losers Weepers,* and *Cut Ups and Cut Outs.* Barrett wrote a novel titled *Bars of Adamant.* He is the recipient of the Huntington Hartford Award (1961) and a John Hay Whitney fellowship (1965–66).

BARRINGTON, ABRAHAM. *See* HILL, ABRAM "ABE" (ABRAHAM BARRINGTON).

BASS, GEORGE HOUSTON (1938–90). Bass, a director, educator, and playwright, emerged as an important figure from the black arts movement of the 1960s and 1970s, not so much for his plays but for founding and maintaining a theater on a university campus. After attending Fisk and New York Universities, he attained a Ph.D. in theater from the Yale School of Drama. Soon thereafter, he was hired to teach drama at Brown University. He worked with his friend and colleague, Professor Rhett S. Jones, in developing a unique research-to-performance method (RPM) to develop new works for the American theater. In 1970, using his own money and funds donated from students, he founded **Rites and Reason Theatre (RRT)**. Over the years, they have developed and produced over 75 plays. RRT still exists today, sustained by grants and private donations.

All the while, Professor Bass's writing continued apace, and over the years, he wrote over 20 plays. Some of the plays he authored are *Malacoff Blue*, *De Day of No Mo*, *Mama Etta's Chitlin' Circuit*, *Dreamdust*, *Function at the Junction*, *Black Masque*, *Once I Heard Buddy Bolden Play Black Blues*, *One into Another*, *Knee High Man*, and *Brer Rabbit Whole*. Bass also wrote the prologue and epilogue for **Zora Neale Hurston** and **Langston Hughes**'s *Mule Bone* that was produced at Lincoln Center in 1991. Bass died prematurely but not before being recognized for his trail-blazing work in the theater. His awards include the John Hay Whitney fellowship, Howard Foundation fellowship, Fulbright Research Grant, John Golden fellowship/Yale, and Rosenthal Award from the American Society of Cinematologists.

BATSON, SUSAN. Born in Roxbury, MA, Batson, a playwright, actress, and poet, has appeared in stage productions in Baltimore and California and worked in television. She is the author of *Hoodoo Talkin'* (1971), a one-act play about four black women who discuss aspects of the black experience. Batson received an Obie Award for her work in the ACIDC in 1971. On TV in 1985, she appeared in *Stone Pillow*, a made-for-TV film starring Lucille Ball as a bag woman.

BAYEZA, IFA. Playwright, dramaturge, and producer Bayeza, the sibling of **Ntozake Shange**, is fast becoming a playwright of note in the 21st century, as well as a producer of new plays. Her writing for the stage chronicles the bittersweet story of African American history but seeks a common ground to heal the wounds of a fractured society. Bayeza's involvement in theater includes being associate director at the **Lorraine Hansberry Theatre** and director for arts and education at the Court Theatre. Bayeza was born in Chicago and received her B.A. in English (cum laude) from Harvard University. She is also a graduate of the Tuck Business School Minority Executive Program, from which she graduated at the highest level.

As a playwright, Bayeza is perhaps best known for her 1993 play *Homer G and the Rhapsodies in the Fall of Detroit*. Based on Homer's *Iliad*, it is set in car-happy Detroit, where Afro pop, hip hop, and Motown hip mix with myth and Greek fable in a story of urban graft and drugs. The play has been produced at the **Crossroads Theatre**, Lorraine Hansberry Theatre, **National Black Theatre Festival**, and Court Theatre, among others. Bayeza has also written *Amistad Voices* (2003), a dramatization of the 1839 slave ship mutiny and trial of Cinque, leader of the revolt, with John Quincy Adams as Cinque's chief defender. It was produced at the Chernin Center, **Plowshares Theatre**, and Chicago Shakespeare Theatre, among others. *Till: The Life and Death of Emmett Till* (2006) is an exploration of the life of Emmitt Till, a boy on the threshold of manhood one month after his 14th birthday. It was produced at **Rites and Reason**, **New Federal Theatre**, Goodman Theatre, and **Providence Black Repertory Theatre**. *The Adventure of Kid Zero* (2005), a slapstick adventure comedy, is set in Mathropolis, with parents Pencilla and Rulius. *Everything There Is to Know in the World* is an adaptation of Ken Kesey's *The Sea Lion*. Among Beyeza's honors and awards are the Kennedy Center Fund for New American Plays (1994), National Endowment for the Arts Award (1999), Tuck Business School fellowship (1999 and 2000), **Arna Bontemps** residence fellowship (2003), and the Rites and Reason/Providence Black Repertory new play fellowship (2005).

BEATY, DANIEL. A multitalented actor, poet, musician, and performance artist, Beaty emerged as a bright young light of the black theater movement in the 21st century. His play *Emergence-See!*, a stunning one-man tour de force, has taken the theatrical world by storm. The play emanated from readings at **La MaMa Experimental Theatre Club** and the New York Theatre Workshop and has since toured the country at such locations as the **Shadow Theatre** in Denver and the New Freedom Theatre in Philadelphia. Beaty, a native of Dayton, OH, graduated with honors from Yale University, where he majored in English and music. Next up was the American Conservatory Theatre in San Francisco, where he earned an M.F.A. in acting in 2001. As an actor, poet, and singer, he toured the United States, Europe, and Africa, performing in operas, solo concerts, and theatrical productions. Most notably, he has performed at the White House and the Kennedy Center.

The idea for *Emergence-See!* came some five years ago, when he was exploring what it means to be free, how one can be freer, and what obstacles one has to overcome to be free. It is a 90-minute one-man show revolving around a sunken slave ship that suddenly emerges in the Hudson River opposite the Statue of Liberty on the same day as a poetry slam. Of the over 40 characters presented are a 400-year-old African chieftain, a deranged Shakespearean scholar, a scientist, a homeless man, and a Republican businessman. The play is a commentary on how a disparate group of characters all respond to the same event. It is told with humanity and humor that all humanity possesses. Beaty's other play, *Colored Contradictions*, is another one-man play in which he performs multiple characters. His latest play *Resurrection* was developed both as a one-man show and a piece for six actors. It premiered at the Arena Stage Theatre in 2008, while Beaty toured the nation in the one-man format. At a young age, he has received honors and awards, such as the Nuyorican Poets Grand Slam Champion (2004) and Denver Post Special Achievement Award for *Emergence-See!* (2005).

BELLAMY, LOU. Director and producer Bellamy founded **Penumbra Theatre** in 1976 in St. Paul, MN, by parlaying a Comprehensive Employment Training Act grant to hire 17 actors, who became the core of the company. It is one of the oldest black theaters in the country. Along with **Claude Purdy**, he was instrumental in providing a theatrical home for then fledgling playwright **August Wilson**, who premiered his early works at Penumbra. A Minnesota native, Bellamy attended Minnesota State University (B.A.) and the University of Minnesota (M.A.). He has been a member of the University of Minnesota's faculty for 30 years, serving as an associate professor in the Department of Theatre Arts and Dance. Most of his directing credits lie with Penumbra, but he occasionally directs at other regional theaters, such as the Kansas City Repertory, Trinity Repertory Company, Arizona Theatre Company, and the Tyrone Guthrie Theatre. Among the plays he directed are *Two Trains Running*, **Fences**, *Zooman and the Sign*, *Black Nativity*, *Black Eagles*, *The Mighty Gents*, *Little Tommy Parker's Celebrated Colored Minstrel Show*, *Someplace Soft to Fall*, *The African Company Presents Richard III*, *A Lovesong for Miss Lydia*, *Blues for an Alabama Sky*, *Short Eyes*, and *Seven Guitars*. His acting credits include *Joe Turner's Come and Gone*, **The Piano Lesson**, and *Talking Bones*.

Over a lengthy career, Bellamy has accrued many honors, which include the W. Harry Davis Foundation Award, the Links Excellence Award, the McKnight Distinguished Artist Award, and an honorary doctorate from Hamline University.

BENSON, FRANCE-LUC. Benson, a playwright, is of Haitian extraction, and her plays in many respects mirror that reality. She is a graduate of Florida International University, where she received a B.F.A. in theater. Benson has also studied playwriting at the Circle Repertory School in New York. Her first play was *Silence of the Mambo*, a family's tale of survival under the Haitian dictator Francois "Papa Doc" Duvalier. *Mambo* received its first professional production by the Adunde Theatre Company in Miami in 1997. It also toured schools, churches, and a women's prison. Upon moving to New York in 1999, Benson was hired as playwright in residence at the **Negro Ensemble Company** and in time supervised the playwright's workshop. The other plays Benson wrote are *Da Beat Trap*, a one-woman play exploring the lives of five women; *Ascension*; and *Mr. Sunshine and the Radio Dame*.

BERNARD, JASON (1938–96). A native of Chicago, Bernard was an actor and director. Born Ronald Johnson, he changed his name to Jason Bernard, considered a better stage name for an actor. Though Bernard became very successful in Hollywood, appearing in some 85 movies and television shows, his first love was the stage. His big break came when he was hired by Allen Fletcher of the Seattle Repertory Theatre in 1965 to become part of their 15-member acting ensemble. He appeared in several productions and directed Jean Genet's *The Blacks*. In addition, he staged several productions at **Black Arts/West** Theatre for **Douglas Q. Barnett**, notably **Derek Walcott**'s magnificent play *Dream on Monkey Mountain*. Bernard moved to Hollywood around 1970 and began building a career in the industry. His work onstage continued in such productions as *The Meeting* by **Jeff Stetson**—a dramatized version of a meeting between Malcolm X and Martin Luther King, played by Bernard.

A demanding perfectionist, Bernard combined elements of Strassberg and Growtowski in his acting. He initially found Hollywood to be somewhat insular, but in the 1980s, his fortune began to change.

He landed roles in *Cagney and Lacey*, *Days of Our Lives*, and the miniseries *V*. He reprised his role from *V* in *V: The Final Battle* and began to soar artistically. In quick succession, he appeared in a recurring role in *Herman's Head*, followed by *War Games*, *Blue Thunder*, and *The Star Chamber*. Other movies and television appearances include *No Way Out*; *Bird*; *While You Were Sleeping*; *Sophie and the Moonhanger*; *The Rockford Files*; *Wing Commander*; *Liar, Liar*; *Murder, She Wrote*; *Where on Earth Is Carmen Sandiego?*; *Designing Women*; *Perry Mason*; *The Cosby Show*; *The Rape of Richard Beck*; *Knots Landing*; *Night Court*; and a host of others. By the time of his death, Bernard had established himself as one of Hollywood's finest character actors.

BIG WHITE FOG (1938). **Ted Ward**'s historical drama *Big White Fog* is set in Chicago during the height of the Negro Renaissance of the 1920s and the Great Depression of the 1930s. It intertwines issues of Garveyism, capitalism, communism, color stratification, and intraracism to depict an African American family coming to grips with the big white fog of oppression. *Fog* was produced by the Negro Unit of the Chicago **Federal Theatre** at the Great Northern Theatre (April–May 1938) and by the Negro Playwrights Company at the Lincoln Theatre in **Harlem** (October–December 1940) for 64 performances under the direction of Powell Lindsay. **Canada Lee** was featured in the cast.

BILLIE HOLIDAY THEATRE (BHT). Named after the legendary blues singer of the same name, the BHT is one of the oldest black theaters in the country, having been founded in 1972. It came about because of a grant from the Ford Foundation to revitalize a severely depressed neighborhood. Franklin A. Thomas, the first black president of the Ford Foundation, engineered the grant that developed a supermarket, an ice skating rink, and the 218-seat BHT in one square city block. Marjorie Moon became the first artistic director and guided the company through difficult times before becoming the executive director, a position she now holds.

From the beginning, the BHT has involved the community in every phase of its operations, which has been key to its longevity. Local people were placed on the board, and local plays were written and produced. *Young, Gifted and Broke* by Weldon Irvine was so well received it sold out for 77 consecutive performances. The BHT also developed a children's theater of sorts called Theatre for Little Folks and has developed a Theatre Training Program in acting, directing, and technical aspects. It provides opportunities for aspiring artists, and the list of alumni who have trod the boards at the BHT include **Samuel L. Jackson**, Debbie Allen, **Samm-Art Williams**, and Tichina Arnold. Among the many plays the BHT has produced during their 35-year existence include *The Past Is the Past* by **Richard Wesley**, *Indigo Blue* by **Judi Ann Mason**, *Inacent Black and the Five Brothers* by **A. Marcus Hemphill**, and *Lament for Rastafari* by **Edgar White**. The theater serves over 30,000 people annually during a 40-week season and is occasionally rented out for special events.

BLACK ARTS REPERTORY THEATRE SCHOOL (BARTS). Located in **Harlem**, BARTS was founded by **Amiri Baraka (LeRoi Jones)**, **Larry Neal**, and several others in 1965 and remains an anomaly of the black arts movement. It was created in the wake of the huge success enjoyed by playwright Baraka with his play *Dutchman*, which enjoyed an off-Broadway run and received an **Obie Award** for best play. The play itself seemed a call to arms in which Baraka railed against the "system" and called for killing or overthrowing those who allowed racism to become a systematic part of the American economy and way of life. He wrote two other plays in the same vein, *The Slave* and *The Toilet*. The collective cachet of the three plays, Jones's incendiary poetry readings, and his lectures catapulted him into a leadership role in the black arts movement. Neal, an accomplished writer and essayist, seemed to be the voice of civil rights and black arts. When the formation of BARTS was announced in 1965 and that it would be located in black Harlem, the expectations were enormous. This would be the group to take blacks to the promised land and would articulate and show exactly what black art is supposed to be, what it can do, and how it should be done.

BARTS had obtained funding through the Harlem Youth Opportunity Unlimited (HARYOU)/ACT, a department of the Office of Economic Opportunity, a program set up by President Lyndon Baines Johnson to fight poverty. The first play BARTS produced was Baraka's *Experimental Death Unit #1*, a one-act play in which two black militants murder two white homosexuals and a black friend of theirs who is a prostitute. The play was laced with antigay terms, and white people were denied entrance to the theater. Additionally, lectures were held that called for armed revolution against the system, or government. BARTS was biting the hand that fed them. Accordingly, the powers at (HARYOU)/ACT cancelled BARTS's funding. Baraka moved to New Jersey, changed his name to Imamu (LeRoi Jones), and founded Spirit House. BARTS, which held such promise, closed in 1966, less than a year after it opened.

BLACK ARTS/WEST (BA/W). Founded by **Douglas Q. Barnett** in 1969, BA/W was the first known professional theater in Seattle. It evolved out of the **civil rights movement** of that decade, functioning as a three-component program—theater, dance, and an art gallery displaying the work of local and national artists. A division of the Central Area Motivation Program, an antipoverty agency, it was charged with getting young people involved and learning the necessary skills to survive and flourish in society. The program attracted a host of young people who thrived on the discipline and skills imparted by a top-notch professional staff, including Lorna Richards, Eve Green, Professor Abraham "Dumi" Mariare, and others. Over the years, the theater mounted over 75 plays, including *Dream on Monkey Mountain*, *A Son Come Home*, *The Great MacDaddy*, *Five on the Black Hand Side*, and *What the Wine-Sellers Buy*. Reputable directors out of New York, such as **Allie Woods Jr.**, **Gilbert Moses**, **Jason Bernard**, and **Beatrice Winde**, came to direct plays at the theater. A significant number of students became professionals and have performed on Broadway, in regional theaters, on TV, and in dance companies. Because of its success, BA/W became a nationally known entity across the Unites States. It had three artistic directors during its lifetime: Barnett, **Buddy Butler**, and a team of Tee Dennard and Doug Johnson. After 11 years, BA/W closed its doors in the spring of 1980.

BLACK ENSEMBLE THEATRE (BET). Based in Chicago, the BET is one of the longest running and most successful black theaters in the country, owing to the creative vision of Jackie Taylor, a 1973 graduate of Loyola University. Taylor found the roles available to an actress were demeaning and stereotypical, so she took out a loan of $12,000 in 1976 to start a theater. Initially, the BET did traditional works like *A Raisin in the Sun*, *The Glass Menagerie*, *A Streetcar Named Desire*, and Shakespearean fare like *Julius Caesar*. While somewhat successful, the theater became wildly successful when, in 1984, it began producing musical biographies, which became the signature genre of the BET. The format was simple: Tell highlighted stories from the artist's life sprinkled with songs from his or her career. Almost immediately, the theater began a string of sell-out performances, with Taylor such writing pieces as *The Other Cinderella, Muddie Waters: The Hoochie Coochie Man, The Jackie Wilson Story, Great Women in Gospel*, and *Ella: The Ella Fitzgerald Story*. In over 30 years, she has written more than 100 plays and musicals that have delighted and enthralled Chicago audiences to no end.

More important, the sold-out houses brought with them a change in demographics. The all-black audiences changed over time to 35 percent white. Taylor's goal has long been to bring the races together and to depict blacks in a realistic light. She succeeded. The success of the musical biography format was not lost on the BET. If a show becomes a sell-out hit, Taylor develops a touring unit to play the university circuit and large urban cities of the North, like New York; Washington, DC; and Philadelphia. The BET has long operated out of Hull House, a 170-seat theater in uptown Chicago, but it has outgrown that venue, and current plans call for a move into a larger space in 2008. The $12,000 that Wilson borrowed in 1976 has been parlayed into an institution that has produced over 100 productions, served over 20,000 audience members and 100,000 school students annually, and had a yearly budget exceeding $1.5 million.

BLACK EXPERIENCE. Certain black playwrights wanted to capture the essence of the black experience by depicting the interests, aspirations, customs, folkways, heroes, and experiences within their own environment without being judged by those outside their community. **Ted Ward** sets his historical drama *Big White Fog* (1938) in Chicago during the height of the Negro Renaissance of the 1920s and the Great Depression of the 1930s. It shows how Marcus Garvey's black nationalist, back-to-Africa movement was a viable option for African American liberation before the Great Depression of the 1930s. *The*

River Niger (1972) by **Joseph Walker**, set in **Harlem**, is an African American drama in two acts advocating revolution. A frustrated father, a painter and poet who is psychologically devastated because of social inequity, sacrifices his dreams for his son's aspirations. **Melvin Van Peebles**'s poetry play with music *Ain't Supposed to Die a Natural Death* opened on Broadway in 1971. It captured and exemplified the rhythms of the inner-city street types—pimps, dope addicts, crooked cops, lesbian and gay lovers, jealous lovers, and hustlers. In **Daniel Beaty**'s performance piece *Emergence SEE!*, he explores what it means for blacks to be free, how they can be freer, and what obstacles they have to overcome to be free. It is a 90-minute one-man show depicting a sunken slave ship that suddenly emerges in the Hudson River opposite the Statue of Liberty on the same day as a poetry slam. Among the more than 40 characters presented are a 400-year-old African chieftain, a deranged Shakespearean scholar, a scientist, a homeless man, and a Republican businessman. The play is a commentary on how a disparate group of characters all respond to the same event. It is told with ethnic humor from an astute African American consciousness.

BLACK MASKS. This is a bimonthly online publication that chronicles African American theater and black performing arts. The inimitable **Mary Elizabeth Turner**, a former actress, playwright, and educator, established it in 1984. Turner operates both as publisher/editor. The publication enjoys a large following, both in the United States and abroad. It was launched originally as a hard-copy newsletter but expanded to the current magazine format when it went online.

BLACK NATIVITY (1961). By **Langston Hughes**, this play is a black musical adaptation of the Christmas story. It opened at the 41st Street Theatre (11 December 1961) in New York City and ran for 57 performances. It was produced by Michael R. Santangelo, Barbara Griner, and Eric Franck and directed by **Vinnette Carroll**. Hughes infused gospel music by Alex Bradford, Marion Williams, and Princess Stewart to tell the story of the birth of Jesus. The show is in two acts: Act 1, "The Child Is Born," and Act II, "The World Is Spread." Among the cast were Marion Williams and the Stars of Faith, Alex Bradford, Clive Thompson, Cleo Quietman, Carl Ford, and Howard Sanders. After a run of 57 performances in New York City, *Black Nativity* went on tour to Spoleto, Italy; London; and New Zealand to triumphant acclaim. Hughes's plays became a Christmas classic.

BLACK SPECTRUM THEATRE COMPANY, INC. (BSTC; THE BLACK SPECTRUM FILM AND THEATRE COMPANY). Located in St. Albans, Queens, NY, the BSTC was founded in the early 1970s by CEO and executive director **Carl Clay**, a playwright, filmmaker, lyricist, teacher, and theatrical director. Among the production highlights at the BSTC were *Deadwood Dick Legend of the West; or, Them Niggers Went That Away* (c. 1972); *2000 Black* (1975); *The Pit* (1985), a full-length dramatization of the Bernard Goetz Broadway shooting incident; and Clay's film *Babies Making Babies*. In 2005, the BSTC produced *Willie and Esther* by James Graham Bronson at the **National Black Theatre Festival** in Winston-Salem, NC. After an absence of several years from the stage, Clay performed the role of Smitty. Two years earlier, the BSTC had also mounted **August Wilson**'s *The Piano Lesson* at the same festival.

BLACK THEATRE ALLIANCE (BTA). In 1965, Delano Stewart founded the BTA, a community-based theater as an embodiment of a viable theatrical organization. Initially, seven companies comprised the BTA: Brownsville Laboratory Theatre, Afro-American Singing Theatre, Afro-American Total Theatre, Bedford-Stuyvesant Theatre, Theatre Black, **Afro-American Studio for Acting and Speech**, and **New Heritage Repertory Theatre Company**. Incorporated officially in 1971, the BTA stated its goals and objectives in the first issue of its newsletter. The declared merger filled a practical need to increase box office revenue by combining publicity, fund raising, and advertising and to develop a wider audience base. Other lofty goals were to provide technical and administrative services, write grants, enhance artistic development, create a clearinghouse for information on black theater, promote members of the companies, offer low-cost graphics and technical equipment, and provide touring assistance and information. By the time the newsletter was published, the BTA's membership had expanded to 16 companies to include the **New Lafayette Theatre**; Black Vibrations; the **New**

Federal Theatre; the Cornbread Players; the Demi-Gods; the Urban Arts Corps; the Weusi KuunbaTroupe; Voices, Inc.; and the East River Players. Though the mandate came four years later, it did not deter the BTA from publicly proclaiming the formation of these African American theaters when they produced four one-act plays under the title *A Black Quartet*.

Offices were set up in **Harlem** at 415 West 127th Street where the Afro-American Studio for Acting and Speech was formerly housed. Shortly thereafter, the BTA moved to a new location farther downtown at 1564 Broadway. This move created a chasm among some alliance members, who insisted that the BTA should stay in the black neighborhood. The move, however, turned out to be more political and advantageous for the organization. Stewart, the brains of the BTA, was their first elected president (1971). Other officers included **Hazel Bryant** of the Afro-American Total Theatre as secretary, Ernie McClintock of the Afro-American Studio for Acting and Speech as vice president, **Roger Furman** of New Heritage Repertory Theatre Company as executive secretary, and Cecil Cummings of the Brownsville Laboratory Theatre as treasurer.

When Stewart assumed the presidency, revolutionary black playwrights were experimenting with the absurdist style of theater. These plays were not well received by African American audiences. Some middle-class blacks did not identify with its confrontational style, while many whites saw it as antiestablishment. Stewart expressed concern that this type of theater created a financial crisis for BTA members but conversely did not affect such white theatrical organizations as **Joseph Papp**'s NYSF/Public Theatre. The BTA received funds from local, state, and federal agencies because it included black theater productions.

The BTA's financial crisis, however, was somewhat alleviated in 1972 by a grant from the New York City Parks, Recreation, and Cultural Affairs Administration to sponsor a promotional theater festival. Also, a partnership with Theatre Communications Group (TCG) helped significantly. TCG provided information on casting and touring, announcements of student auditions, visitation and personnel programs, subscription consultation, files on directors and theater resources, publications, a theater reference book, and access to a black theater panel. This joint venture resulted in the compilation and issuance of the *Black Theatre Resources Directory*. National in scope, the directory lists black theater directors, black community theater groups, works by black playwrights, and the names of technicians and administrators.

BLACK THEATRE NETWORK (BTN). The BTN is an independent organization comprised of prominent individuals and organizations within all areas of theater, from community and professional organizations to academia, across the United States and throughout the diaspora. Its stated purpose is to celebrate the beauty and complexity of black life onstage and to preserve black theater's unique art form. Formed in 1986, the BTN celebrated its 20th anniversary in Louisville, KY in 2006. Seven of the 10 past presidents were there to celebrate this landmark occasion—Ethel Pitts-Walker (1986–88), Rhonnie Washington (1988–90), Addell Austin Anderson (1990–92), Kathryn M. Ervin (1992–94), Lundeana Thomas (1994–96), **Eileen J. Morris** (2000–2), and Gregory Horton (2005–6)—as well as incoming president Sandra G. Shannon. The other three past presidents (not present) are Mikell Pinkney (1996–98), **Lorna Littleway** (1998–2000), and Marvin L. Simms (2002–3, deceased). Every other year BTN hosts an annual theater conference in a designated city. Every odd year it convenes in Winston-Salem, NC, where the **National Black Theatre Festival** is based.

BLACK THEATRE TROUPE (BTT). Based in Phoenix, AZ, the BTT is one of the longest-running black theater operations in the country, having been conceived in the long, hot, turbulent summer of 1969 by community leader and activist Helen K. Mason. By 1970, it was up and running, and it has occupied three separate facilities during its lifetime, buoyed by strong support from the community. Indeed, in 2008, the BTT will move into a brand new $2.5 million facility as part of a revitalization project of the Helen K. Mason Center for the Performing Arts. There, the BTT hopes to accomplish three objectives: reestablish and expand programs for at-risk youth, provide performing space for youth and children's programs, and provide affordable rent space for emerging performance arts groups.

The BTT's season runs from October through June, during which they produce five to six productions. For the past 11 years, the BTT has been under the veteran artistic guidance of David Hemphill. In the past 37 years, the BTT has produced over 100 plays. What follows is a sampling of plays produced by the BTT over that period: *On Striver's Row* by **Abram Hill**; *American Menu* by Don Wilson Glenn; *Fabulation; or, the Re-Education of Undine* by **Lynn Nottage**; *The Wild Party* by **George C. Wolfe**; *A Raisin in the Sun* by **Lorraine Hansberry**; *The Piano Lesson* by **August Wilson**; *Sty of the Blind Pig* by **Phillip Hayes Dean**; *Bubbling Brown Sugar* by **Loften Mitchell** and **Rosetta LeNoire**; *Sweet Thunder* by Ben Tyler; and *The Amen Corner* by **James Baldwin**. Plans are being made for next year, its 38th season, with a gala reopening in a pristine new theater.

BLACK WOMEN PLAYWRIGHT'S GROUP (BWPG). Based in Washington, DC, the BWPG began at a 1989 seminar at **Arena Playhouse** that focused on the black female playwright. Remarks by panel member Karen L. B. Evans at the conclusion of her speech lit a fire. After a meeting at her home a month later, the BWPG was born, with Evans at the helm. Evans, who holds a B.A. in drama from Dartmouth and an M.F.A. in playwriting from Catholic University of America, has had her work produced by MetroStage, the Savannah Players, and PBS. She has guided the company in recruiting new members, hosting monthly meetings, and communicating/establishing relationships with theaters around the country. The BWPG's main goal is to support, promote, and refine the work of its members. All playwrights are afforded the benefit of working with a dramaturge to enhance the quality and integrity of the plays they write, and all playwrights pay monthly dues to underwrite ongoing costs.

Each year, the BWPG holds at selected theaters with professional actors a staged reading of selected works by playwrights in the group. Playwrights represented in the past have included Donise Stevens, Joy Jones, Betty Miller Buttram, Louise V. Gray, Joy Hunter Carroll, E. Christie Cunningham, Pat Crews, Lois A. Wiley, Pamela Armstrong, Debbie Minter Jackson, Debra Rose, Stanice Anderson, **Caleen Sinnette Jennings**, and the late **Oni Faida Lampley**. Both Jennings and Lampley have enjoyed success by having professional productions of their plays, with Lampley's *Dark Kalamazoo* and *Tough Titty* taking their place in the African American canon of must-see plays. The

BWPG is a 501(c)3 nonprofit organization. The BWPG, with the assistance of a grant from the National Endowment for the Arts, is planning a national conference in 2008. Talks are being held with Loyola University to serve as the host site.

BOND, TIM. A theater director for 25 years, Bond made his mark as an apprentice in the American Theatre with the Oregon Shakespeare Festival, Seattle's Group Theatre, the Ethnic Cultural Theatre, and other regional entities. After playing musical chairs between ethnic theater and traditional Western theater, the stars finally aligned. Bond was hired as producing artistic director of Syracuse Stage and the Syracuse University Department of Drama in October 2007. He inherits a four-theater complex with a $4 million budget that attracts over 100,000 people annually. Bond is one of several African American artistic directors of a white regional theater.

Bond is a native of Toledo, OH. He earned his B.F.A. from Howard University and an M.F.A. (magna cum laude) in theater from the University of Washington. He began his career with the University of Washington's Ethnic Cultural Theatre, a theater that was formed after student unrest in the early 1970s. Out of that experience, a group of students, including Bond, spun off and created their own theater, which they named the Group Theatre after the old group theater of the 1930s led by Lee Strasberg, Cheryl Crawford, and Harold Clurman. Bond was the artistic director, directing over 20 plays, establishing the Multi-Cultural Playwrights Festival, and leading a capital campaign resulting in the company's first artistic home at the Seattle Center over a 13-year period. He left the company to become associate director to Director Libby Appel at the Oregon Shakespeare Festival. There he directed some 11 plays over a 12-year period. More important, he worked assiduously to increase diversity in the acting and design teams. He also became a leading advocate for multicultural casting in Shakespeare and other classical offerings. Bond has mounted plays at some of the leading theaters across the land, including the Cleveland Playhouse, the Mark Guthrie Theatre, Milwaukee Repertory, Actors Theatre of Louisville, and the Indiana Repertory Theatre. He has directed the works of **Lynn Nottage**, Shakespeare, **August Wilson**, **Suzan-Lori Parks**, Octavio Soliz, **Carlyle Brown**, **Lorraine Hansberry**, and Edward Albee. Among other achievements, he served as assistant director to Peter Sellers for the world premiere of the opera *Elephant Memories* at New York's **La MaMa Experimental Theatre Club**. Bond served for four years as a board member of the Theatre Communication Group (TCG). Honors for Bond include a TCG/National Endowment for the Arts directing fellowship Award and two Garland Awards for outstanding direction from Backstage West.

BONNER, MARITA ODETTE (MRS. MARITA BONNER OC-COMY, 1899–1971). A *Crisis* and *Opportunity* magazine award winner, Bonner was a pioneer playwright of the 1920s. Born in Brookline, MA, she attended Radcliffe College (1922), where she majored in English, studied writing under Charles Townsend Copeland, and received her B.A. Bonner taught English at Bluefield Colored Institute in Bluefield, VA (1922–24), and Armstrong High School, in Washington, DC (1925–30). In 1930, Bonner married William Occomy, an accountant. She resigned from her teaching position to raise her three children. It was not long before she renewed her interest in playwriting and theater. In 1927, she submitted two one-act plays, *The Purple Flower* and *Exit, an Illusion* to the *Crisis* Contest Award, and they won first place jointly. *The Purple Flower*, Bonner's best-known play, is an allegory on black–white relations in America. Whites are depicted as "sundry devils" that live on the side of the hill, and blacks as "worms" that live below them in the valley. The "devils" find various ways to prevent the "worms" from climbing up the Hill of Somewhere to reach life at its finest, the purple flower.

Bonner also experimented with expressionist stage techniques and the psychological impact color stratification had on blacks in *Exit, an Illusion*, a one-act fantasy dream play. It involves a love triangle between Buddy, a dark-complexioned black man; his mulatto girlfriend Dot; and Exit, an admirer. In a jealous rage, Buddy shoots Exit only to discover that he has inadvertently killed Dot. To further complicate matters, Buddy discovers that Exit is actually a Death figure. This theme of a jealous lover is reprised in Bonner's *The Pot Maker* (1927). In this one-act melodrama the husband drowns his wife's lover "accidentally." *The Purple Flower* and *Exit* were published in *Crisis* and in Bonner's *Frye Street and Environs*. Between 1927 and

1935, Bonner became involved with the Washington, DC, branch of the **Krigwa Players**, where she met **Willis Richardson**. She was active as a member of a literary salon, the Saturday Nighters, that met at the home of playwright **Georgia Douglas Johnson**. She resumed her teaching career at Phillips High School (1944–49) and the Doolittle School (1950–63). She died in 1971 from the effects of a fire in her Chicago apartment.

BONTEMPS, ARNA WENDELL (1902–73). A playwright, biographer, historian, novelist, teacher, poet, editor, librarian, and author of short stories and children's fiction, Bontemps was a prolific writer and leading literary figure during the **Harlem** Renaissance. He contributed more than 30 self-written and coauthored works of American literature and has been widely published in periodicals and anthologies. Born in Alexandria, VA, his parents, Paul Bismarck Bontemps, a Roman Catholic bricklayer, and Maria Carolina Bontemps, a Methodist schoolteacher, moved the family to Los Angeles when he was three. He married Alberta Johnson in 1926 and fathered five children. He received his education at San Fernando Academy; Pacific Union College (now University of California at Los Angeles) in Angwin (A.B., 1923), California; and the University of Chicago (M.L.S., 1943). For 14 years (1924–38), he taught at several private schools. He was head librarian and later public relations director at Fisk University in Nashville, TN (1943–65). There he established the **Langston Hughes** Renaissance Collection that included books on black history, poetry, folklore, and essays. He taught briefly as a professor at the University of Illinois for three years (1965–68) and was curator of the James Weldon Johnson Memorial Collection at Yale University (1969–71). After retirement, he returned to Fisk as a librarian emeritus and writer-in-residence. He died in 1973 of a heart attack.

Bontemps's best-known play, *St Louis Woman* (1933), is a three-act musical play with book by Bontemps and **Countee Cullen**. Set in the 1890s, it is adapted from Bontemps's novel *God Sends Sunday* (1931). Lil Augie, an internationally known horse jockey involved in a lover's tryst, begins losing races after the woman's boyfriend is found dead. The Gilpin Players first produced it at the **Karamu Repertory Theatre** in Kentucky and in Cleveland, OH, in 1933 for five performances. In 1946, the show made its Broadway debut at the Martin Theatre, where it ran for 115 performances. Harold Arlen and Johnny Mercer provided the music and lyrics, respectively. Among the all-star cast were the Nicholas Brothers, Rex Ingram, and Pearl Bailey in her debut. Bontemps also authored and coauthored several literary works of various genres, such as *God Sends Sundays*, *You Can't Pet a Possum* (1934), and *The Story of the Negro* (1948). He partnered with Cullen and Hughes to write such children's books as *Popo and Fifina* (1932). His poetry was published in *Crisis* magazine. Among Bontemps's awards were the prestigious Rosenwald fellowship (1938, 1942) and a Guggenheim fellowship (1949, 1954).

BRANCH, WILLIAM BLACKWELL. An award-winning playwright and television and film producer, Branch was the sixth of a family of seven sons of the late A.M.E. Zion minister Reverend James Matthew Branch and Iola Douglas Branch of Washington, DC. Born in New Haven, CT, he began his writing career with prize-winning efforts in high school and college essays and oratorical contests. His theatrical interest took professional form when he joined the national cast of the Broadway hit play *Anna Lucasta* while still a freshman at Northwestern University in Evanston, IL. Upon graduating from Northwestern, which he attended on a four-year scholarship won in a nationwide competition, Branch went to New York to resume his acting career. Parts for black actors were few and far between, however, and he became convinced that African Americans must write and produce their own parts.

Brown's first playwriting effort was *A Medal for Willie*, which was produced on a shoestring budget at a **Harlem** cabaret to enthusiastic critical and audience response. *Medal* dramatically underscored the ironies of a black American soldier fighting and dying to secure freedoms for others abroad that he was unable himself to enjoy at home. Also, ironically, the morning after the play opened, Branch himself was promptly inducted into the U.S. Army. Since then, Branch turned out a succession of plays for theater and television. Among them is *In Splendid Error*, a historical drama about Frederick Douglass and John Brown, which the Greenwich Mews Theatre turned into an off-Broadway hit, *A Wreath for Odomo*, presented on the London stage and based upon Peter Abrahams's prophetic novel about the rise and fall of an African prime minister, *Baccalaureate*, a chilling family drama that had its world premiere in Bermuda. He also wrote *Light in the Southern Sky*, an NBC television drama about the life of beloved educator and humanitarian Mary McLeod Bethune, which won for its author the coveted Robert E. Sherwood Television Award.

As a television professional, Branch has been a staff producer at both NBC News and New York City's public broadcasting station, WNET-13. As an independent producer, he originated, wrote, and co-produced the highly acclaimed 90-minute National Educational Television (now PBS) in 1968. *Still a Brother* won the Blue Ribbon Award of the 1969 American Film Festival and was nominated for a national Emmy by the National Academy of Television Arts and Sciences—the first black-produced film to receive either honor.

Other Branch projects include *A Letter from Booker T.*, a drama on Public Broadcast Station (1987) especially commissioned by its stars **Ossie Davis** and **Ruby Dee**; *Together for Days*, a feature film starring Clifton Davis and Lois Chiles; the entire package of scripts for *Afro-American Perspectives*, a 30-program television series on black history and culture produced by the Maryland Center for Public Broadcasting in cooperation with the University of Maryland; and the story outline for *Benefit Performance*, a two-hour NBC World Premiere television feature film. In another career highlight, he once wrote a three-times-weekly newspaper column of critical comment for the *New York Post* and for syndication along with Hall of Fame baseball great, businessman, and civil rights activist Jackie Robinson.

Other articles by Branch have appeared in the *New York Times*, the *New York Amsterdam News*, *Television Quarterly*, the *Black Scholar*, and other publications. Several of his plays are published in *Black Theatre: A 20th Century Collection of the Work of Its Best Playwrights*; *Black Drama Anthology*; *New American Library*, 1972, 1986; *Black Scenes*; *Black Theatre USA: 45 Plays by Black Americans, 1847–1974*; *Standing Room Only*; *Meeting Challenges*; *Black Heroes: Seven Plays*; *Black Thunder: An Anthology of Contemporary African American Drama*; and *Crosswinds: An Anthology of Black Dramatists in the Diaspora*.

In January 1985, Branch was appointed professor of theater and dramatic literature at the African Studies and Research Center at Cornell University, where he reestablished the study and performance of materials from black drama and instituted a course on African American creative writing. Previously, he served as visiting professor of African American studies at the University of Maryland–Baltimore County (1979–82) and fulfilled a variety of other academic engagements, including visiting Luce fellow at Williams College (1983), University of California regents lecturer (1985), and visiting scholar and lecturer at numerous colleges and universities.

In 1992, Branch edited and wrote the introduction to *Black Thunder: An Anthology of Contemporary African American Drama*, which was honored with an American Book Award. In 1993, *Crosswinds: An Anthology of Black Dramatists in the Diaspora* appeared, also edited and with an introduction by Branch. When not at Cornell, Branch continues working on new projects for theater, films, and television as president of William Branch Associates, a media consulting and production firm in New Rochelle, NY, which he founded in 1973.

Branch holds an M.F.A. from Columbia University, which presented him the Hannah Del Vecchio Award for achievement in playwriting. In 1959, he received a J. S. Guggenheim fellowship for creative writing in drama. The National Conference of Christians and Jews awarded Yale University School of Drama on a Yale–American Broadcasting Company fellowship for creative writing in television and film.

BRAUGHER, ANDRE. Braugher has achieved artistic success as both a stage and screen actor. One year after graduating with an M.F.A. in theater from the Juilliard School, Braugher was cast in a small supporting role in the Civil War movie *Glory*. His intense and ambiguous performance in the movie caught the eye of the producers of a new television series, *Homicide: Life on the Street*. His portrayal of Detective Frank Pembleton led to accolades from the critics and an Emmy. The series ran for six successful seasons, establishing Braugher as one of the premier actors of his generation. Since then, Braugher has acted in over 40 film and television projects, such as *The Tuskegee Airmen, City of Angels, Gideon's Crossing, Hack, Poseidon, The Court Martial of Jackie Robinson, Primal Fear, A Better Way to Die, Salem's Lot, Law and Order, The Practice, Kojak*, and *Homicide: The Movie*.

Braugher was born in Chicago, the son of a heavy equipment operator and a postal worker. He earned a B.A. from Stanford University before attending Juilliard. He was originally a premed student but changed his major to acting after performing in a production of *Hamlet*. He returned to the stage in 1996 at the New York Shakespeare Festival in the Park, where he played the title role in *Henry V*. He received an **Obie Award** for that performance and an Emmy for his role in *Thief* for FX Network in 2006. He returned to the NYSF/Public Theatre in 2008, when he performed Claudius in *Hamlet*.

BREWSTER, TOWNSEND. A playwright, Brewster was born in Glen Cove, NY. He holds a B.A. from City College of New York (CCNY) and earned his M.A. from Columbia University in 1962. From 1967 to 1973, he functioned as playwright-in-residence at CCNY. A prolific writer, Brewster has written over 30 plays. His development was nurtured by stints at the **Frank Silvera Writers' Workshop** and the New Dramatists. During the late 1960s and 1970s, when black theater was at its peak, Brewster was hired to review black plays for several white newspapers. A linguist, he translated several operas into English for the NBC opera series. They include *Pagliacci*, *Carmen*, *Gianni Schicchi*, and *Hansel und Gretel*. His plays have been produced at such venues as the Weathervane Theatre, **American Negro Theatre**, the Riverside Church, and Circle in the Square. Among his plays are *Singapore Sling* (1955), a comedy wherein a girl from Dusty Gulch tries to break into the international set in the big city; *Please Don't Cry and Say No* (1972), about an executives wife who has an affair with a teenager; *Chief Rathebe* (1968), about Tarzan and Jane being invited by an African tribal chief to dinner; and *The Jade Funerary Suit* (1975), a comedy about a poor black family that steals an ancient Chinese burial suit for her father's internment. Other plays include *How the West Was Fun*; *Idomeneus*; *The Palm Leaf Boogie*; *Praise Song*; *The Bougival Vampire*; *Oh, What a Beautiful City*; and *Arrangements in Rose and Silver*.

BRING IN 'DA NOISE, BRING IN 'DA FUNK (1995). This dance musical was conceived and directed by **George C. Wolfe** and choreographed by Savion Glover. It traces African American history from **slavery** to the present hip-hop movement through tap, music, and song intertwined with "'da funk" (the grassroots culture) and "'da noise" (the outlet, release, and expression of self). It premiered at **Joseph Papp**'s NYSF/Public Theatre, New York Shakespeare Festival (9 April 1996) and ran for 1,135 performances before closing (10 January 1999). Wolfe was the producer, Rosemarie Tichler the artistic producer, Laurie Beckelman the executive director, Joey Pames the executive producer, and Wiley Hausam the associate producer. The book was by Reg E. Gaines; music by Daryl Waters, Zane Mark, and Ann Duquesnay; and lyrics by Reg E. Gaines, George C. Wolfe, and Ann Duquesnay, with music orchestrated by Daryl Waters with musical director Zane Mark. Ann Duquesnay did the vocal arrangements; Riccardo Hernandez the scenic design; Paul Tazewall the costume design; Jules Fisher and Peggy Eisenhauer the lighting design; Dan Moses Schreier the sound design; Batwin and Robin Productions, Inc., the projection design; and additional sound design by Jon Weston. Savion Glover received the **Tony Award** in the category of best choreographer (1997).

BROWN, CARLYLE. Born in Charleston, SC, Brown is an award-winning playwright with a penchant for writing plays that examine African American history and question people's motives. He is also an actor, director, and founder of Carlyle Brown and Company based in Minneapolis and founding artistic director of the Laughing Mirror Theatre, an experimental ensemble company devoted to the research and development of black American theatrical forms.

Brown's best-known historical play is *The African Company Presents Richard III*. This play within a play begins as the African Company ensemble assembles at the African Grove Theatre (*see* AFRICAN GROVE INSTITUTE FOR THE ARTS [AGIA]) in 1821 to rehearse *Richard III*, the first Shakespearean tragedy to be performed by an all-black theatrical troupe. The plot centers on the company's discussion of racial intolerance intertwined with an enchanting love story. *Richard III* premiered in Minneapolis before moving to **Arena Playhouse** in Washington, DC. The Philadelphia production by Venture Theatre was under the direction of H. German Wilson. Productions that followed were at the **Shadow Theatre Company** (February 2000), the North Coast Repertory Theatre, Oberlin College (October 2000), Solana Beach (October 2000), and the **St. Louis Black Repertory Theatre** (May 2005).

Other plays Brown wrote are *The Little Tommy Parker Celebrated Colored Minstrel Show*. Set in February 1895 outside of the rural town of Hannibal, MO, six black minstrel players in a Pullman porter railroad car on a cold winter's afternoon entertain each other as they wait to perform onstage. The one absent performer, Percy, returns just in time for the show and escapes a white mob. He and the troupe blacken their faces with burned cork to shield Percy's identity. During the show as the mob peruses the audience looking for Percy, he has to decide whether to conceal his identity or to give himself up to save the others. *Minstrel Show* was a Cornerstone Prize winner at a PlayLabs conference and opened at **Penumbra**. An off-Broadway production by the **Negro Ensemble Company** was nominated for six **Audience Development Committee Awards**. *Buffalo Hair* was also developed at the Minneapolis Playwrights' Center's 1992 PlayLabs conference and premiered at Penumbra Theatre in fall 1993. *A Big Blue Nail* was performed as a staged reading 18 October as one of three selected plays in San Jose Repertory Theatre's 1998 New American Playwrights Festival. The play poses the question who actually "discovered" the North Pole—Admiral Robert Perry or his African American valet, Matthew Henson. *The Negro of Peter the Great*, based on the unfinished novella by Alexander Pushkin, premiered at the Alabama Shakespeare Festival during the 2000–1 season. It was nominated for an American Theatre Critics Award. *The Beggars' Strike* (2005) is the first play Brown wrote for young people and families.

For two years, Brown was the Children's Theatre Company's (Minneapolis) playwright-in-residence through the Theatre Residency Program for Playwrights. Set in West Africa, *Strike* challenges traditional and contemporary spiritual and secular values. *Yellow Moon Rising* is a play about **slavery** and escape in 19th-century America. Brown developed the show with graduate students from New York University's Tisch School for the Arts' Acting Program. The Ohio State University produced it in February 1996. Brown's entry, *The Human Voice*, in the *Ten-Minute Plays from the Guthrie Theatre* (2001 edition) was selected along with plays by seven other outstanding playwrights to expand the possibilities of the 10-minute form. *The Fula from America: Monologue*, a semiautobiographical monologue, is a 95-minute one-man show. An African American traveling through Senegal, Gambia, Guinea-Bissau, and Sierra Leone in search of his roots discovers what it means to be an African American. Directed by Louise Smith, it was produced at the Marsh in San Francisco (March 2004). The Ohio State University Department of Theatre produced it in February 2006, with the playwright assuming the lead role. *The Pool Room*, Brown's new play, premiered at the **Freedom Theatre** under the playwright's direction as part of an exchange with the Minneapolis Playwrights' Center. Two characters talk incessantly about love, a subject about which neither knows much. *Pure Confidence* premiered at the Pamela Brown Auditorium as part of the Actors Theatre of Louisville's 29th annual Humana Festival of New American Plays (February–April 2005). **Arna Bontemps** first wrote about the little-known world of a black horse jockey in *St. Louis Blues* in the 1920s. It dealt with a three-way love relationship. Brown's *Confidence* begins in the antebellum period and continues into the post–Civil War era. It explores an ambiguous relationship between a black jockey and his white master/horse owner and the racer's pursuit of freedom. Brown made his acting debut in this production directed by **Clinton Turner Davis**. Also as an actor, Brown performed his original one-man show *Sea Never Dry* at the Arizona Theatre Company.

Brown is the recipient of major awards, including playwriting fellowships from the Minnesota State Arts Board, Jerome Foundation, National Endowment for the Arts, Theatre Communications Group, the New York Foundation for the Arts, the Creative Artist Public Service Award, the McKnight Foundation, the Rockefeller Foundation, and the Pew Charitable Trusts. He received commissions from Arena Playhouse, Alabama Shakespeare Festival, Minneapolis Children's Theatre Company, the Houston Grand Opera, and the Thurber House in Columbus, OH. He is an alumnus of New Dramatists.

BROWN, CHARLES (1957–2004). Brown was one of the most gifted actors of the past generation. He was more than competent in dramatic parts, but he also showed an expansive flair for comedy, as shown especially in his signature role of Cephus Miles in **Samm-Art Williams**'s hilarious play *Home* (1979). The next year, the play opened on Broadway to great acclaim at the Cort Theatre. *Home* had a run of 278 performances through 1981, and Brown was nominated for a **Tony Award**. It was the high point of a career that spanned some 30 years, which found him performing primarily with the **Negro Ensemble Company** in New York but also regionally with the DC Black Repertory, **Karamu Repertory Theatre**, Seattle Repertory Theatre, the Goodman Theatre, the Mark Taper Forum, and many others.

Brown was born in Talledega, AL. He served in the navy during the Vietnam conflict and then attended Howard University, where he began studying theater. His lengthy career was noted for the variety of roles he played and a smoldering intensity that marked all of his characters. Some of the plays he performed in were *Showdown* by **Don Evans**, *Rumors* by Neil Simon, *A Soldier's Play* by **Charles Fuller**, *The First Breeze of Summer* by **Leslie Lee**, *Poison Tree* by Ronald Ribman, and **Steve Carter**'s *Nevis Mountain Dew*. He also performed in several of **August Wilson**'s plays on Broadway, notably the long-running *Fences* in 1987 and *King Hedley II* in 2001, in which he received a second Tony Award nomination. At age 57, the height of his theatrical prowess, Brown died after a bout with cancer—a life cut short at the pinnacle of success.

BROWN, GRAHAM. Brown is a classically trained actor. Over a 40-year period, he became known for his eloquent diction and stately portrayal of the many roles he performed. Born in New York City, Brown went to Howard University, graduating with a B.A. in theater. He continued to hone his craft at the Actor's Studio, where he immersed himself in the Stanislavski technique of acting, commonly referred to as "the method."

Brown's first big boost came in 1962, when he was chosen by Sir Tyrone Guthrie to be a resident actor for the 1963 premiere of one of America's first regional theaters—the Tyrone Guthrie Theatre of Minneapolis. Although the regional theater movement had started years earlier, Minneapolis was the first large-scale city to build a theater where none had existed and secure a big-name director. It worked phenomenally well, and for many years, the Guthrie was the flagship theater of the regional theater movement. Brown performed in the inaugural production of *Hamlet*, followed by *The Three Sisters*, *Henry V*, *Volpone*, *Richard III*, *The Caucasian Chalk Circle*, *St. Joan*, *The Miser*, and *The Way of the World*.

Brown went on to enjoy a successful career performing in venues like Lincoln Center, Center Stage Repertory Theatre, Los Angeles

Actors Theatre, Inner-City Repertory Theatre, Theatre De Lys, New York Shakespeare Festival/Public Theatre, and the **Negro Ensemble Company**, with which he had an extended relationship. While there, he played in some of the classics of the African American canon, such as *Daddy Goodness, God Is a (Guess What?)*, *Man Better Man*, **The Great MacDaddy**, *Nevis Mountain Dew*, **The River Niger**, and *Abercrombie Apocalypse*. Brown has also performed in television and movies in such vehicles as *Clockers, Law and Order, Malcolm X, Lou Grant, Cagney and Lacey, Sanford and Sons*, and *Days of Our Lives*. He has made four appearances on Broadway, including in *The Man in the Glass Booth* and *The Black Picture Show*.

BROWN, LENNOX JOHN. An international prize-winning playwright, journalist, and poet, Brown was born in Trinidad but lived for many years in Toronto. His education consists of a senior Cambridge certificate from St. Mary's College in Trinidad, a B.A. from the University of Western Ontario (1961), and an M.A. from the University of Toronto (1969). He worked as a civil servant and freelance journalist in Trinidad, as a journalist and reporter for a number of Canadian newspapers and magazines (1956–63), and as editor/producer for the Canadian Broadcasting Corporation (CBC) and the National Network Radio News (1963–67). In the late 1970s, he resided in the United States and taught at the University of Hartford, in Connecticut, and at Queens College in Flushing, NY.

Brown set out to write more that 20 plays in two cycles. The first, *Behind the Bridge*, concerns the black mythological consciousness in the Caribbean. The second, *West Indian Winter*, deals with the consciousness in North America and Europe. His plays were produced in Trinidad, Canada, and the United States (1965–81). Four of his plays won the Birks Medal of the Canadian national one-act play competition in Ottawa. A substantial number of his plays were produced onstage in Canada, the United States, the Netherlands, and the Caribbean. He has numerous television acting credits and has published his poetry in several periodicals in Canada and London. He has membership in various organization that include the Ebo Society for Black Art, Black Arts of Canada, National Black Coalition of Canada, Canadian Newspaper and Wireless Guild, Canadian Association of Radio, and Television Actors' and Writers' Association. Since 1959,

Brown has been the recipient or winner of numerous fellowships, grants, and playwriting competitions.

BROWN, MICHAEL HENRY. Born in the Bronx, Brown, a playwright and screenwriter, writes both for the stage and film media. He graduated from Lehman College and earned an M.F.A. from Columbia University in 1987. He has also studied at the Hammerstein Center for Theatre Studies. His work includes over 20 plays and numerous film scripts. His most successful productions have been *The Day the Bronx Died*, an examination of homophobia and black and Jewish relations, and *Ascension Day*, a story of the Nat Turner slave rebellion of 1831.

Brown's plays have been produced at theaters across the country, including Playwrights Horizons, the Mark Taper Forum, Long Wharf Theatre, and **Penumbra Theatre**. Some of Brown's plays are *Blood Is Thicker*, *In Love and Anger*, *Deadly Aim of the Straight and True*, *King of Coons*, *Borders of Loyalty*, *Outlaws*, *Push*, and *Generations of the Dead, or Into the Abyss of Coney Island Madness*. In film, Brown has written three screenplays, *Dead Presidents*, *In Too Deep*, and *Freedomland*, and two teleplays, *Under One Roof* and *Laurel Avenue*. Brown has received grants from the New York Foundation for the Arts, the National Endowment for the Arts, and the Charles Revson Foundation.

BROWN, WESLEY. A playwright and educator, Brown is interested in cultural changes and transformations in art forms. He attended Oswego State University and the City College of New York (M.A.) and studied at the **John O. Killens** and **Sonia Sanchez** writers workshops. Brown taught at Livingston College (1979) in Salisbury, NC. When the New Brunswick College and Rutgers University unified, Brown was asked to expand his curriculum to include literature courses. After 26 years, Brown retired following a sterling career, where he taught creative writing, American literature, and drama. He has written three novels, edited two anthologies, and written four plays that have won an accumulated eight **Audience Development Committee Awards**. His plays have been produced at the **New Federal Theatre**, Blue Heron Arts Center, Nuyorican Café, and the Black Arts Festival in Atlanta, GA. His play *And Now Will the Real*

Bud Jones Stand Up (1971) is about an attempt by a black man to deal with the question, What is truth? *Boogie Woogie and Booker T.* (1986) is an imaginary 1904 meeting between "separate but equal" advocate Booker T. Washington and the more militant minds of the **civil rights movement**. *Life during Wartime* (1992) is an examination of police brutality in the death of a young graffiti artist. *A Prophet among Us* (2001) is an examination of the life of writer **James Baldwin** from the perspectives of both the past and the present. *The Murderess* (2004) is a commissioned play adapted from the novel of the same name by Alexandros Papadiamantis. Brown's two novels are *Tragic Magic* and *Darktown Strutters*. Brown was recipient of a Pew fellowship.

BROWN, WILLIAM WELLS (1815–84). Brown was a playwright, historian, novelist, lecturer, abolitionist, and medical practitioner. He was the first known African American to write a full-length drama on the problems of American **slavery**, *The Escape; or, A Leap for Freedom* (1856) and to have a play published in the United States. Moreover, he was a pioneer black American novelist, historian, and writer of travel books. The offspring of a black mother (Elizabeth) and a white plantation owner (George Higgins), Brown was born into slavery on a plantation near Lexington, KY. He grew up under three different masters in and around St. Louis, MO. He made several attempts to escape from bondage (once with his mother) but was unsuccessful until his master took him on a trip to Cincinnati in 1834, where he fled to freedom. Traveling through Ohio, he became ill and was taken in by a Quaker family that nursed him back to good health.

In 1834, Brown married Elizabeth Schooner, who bore him three daughters. Brown settled in Cleveland, OH, but three years later, he moved his family to Buffalo. He found employment throughout the New York area, first in Buffalo, then in Farmington, and then in a small town near Rochester. While in Buffalo, he worked for a Lake Erie steamship line transporting passengers by ferry between the United States and Canada, where he assisted the Underground Railroad in transporting escaped slaves to Canada. This was the site of fierce confrontations between escaped slaves and the local sheriff. With the passage of the Fugitive Slave Act of 1850, a slave was still considered the property of his master even if he escaped from the South to a free state.

In 1847, Brown published *Narrative of William Wells Brown, a Fugitive Slave, Written by Himself* in both the United States and Great Britain. Brown took his crusade to Paris in 1849 as a representative of the American Peace Society at the International Peace Congress and later to England, where he sought to win British support for his cause. Owing to the constraints of the Fugitive Slave Act of 1850, Brown was forced to remain in England for several years because he had not been freed legally. While there, he wrote a novel about his travels in Europe, *Three Years in Europe; or, Places I Have Seen and People I Have Met* (1852). It was published in America as *The American Fugitive in Europe: Sketches of Places and People Abroad* (1855). Brown also wrote a novel and a history of the African American male. His novel *Clotel; or, The President's Daughter* (1853) is in reference to "Clotel," the biracial daughter of President Thomas Jefferson by his slave mistress. It was published later in 1969. He wrote his first history, *The Black Man: His Antecedents, His Genius and His Achievements*, in 1863. Other histories he authored would follow much later, such as *The Negro in the American Rebellion: His Heroism and His Fidelity* (1867) and *The Rising Son; or, The Antecedents and Achievements of the Colored Race* (1874).

Brown returned to the United States as a free man in 1854 after friends in England helped to purchase his freedom. He continued to write and pursue his interest as a practical physician. In 1856, he tried his hand at drama, another medium to convey his antislavery message. He completed his first full-length play, *Experience; or, How to Give a Northern Man a Backbone*, in 1856. A Northern white minister who defended the institution of slavery in his sermons (a type referred to as a doughface) is himself kidnapped and sold into slavery. He is subjected to cruel and unbearable punishment. When the minister is released and returned to the North, he has now gained a backbone and begins to work actively for the cause of abolition. The play was read publicly for the first time under the original title of *Doughface* in Brinley Hall, Worcester, MA (April 1856). From spring 1856 to spring 1857, Brown presented dramatic readings at numerous antislavery meetings and lyceum programs in Massachusetts, Vermont, Ohio, New York, Philadelphia, Connecticut, and Rhode Island.

The following year, Brown wrote *The Escape*. It is important historically as the first recorded play by a black American playwright to treat American slavery as a theme. It is also historically significant as the first black American play to be published in the United States and the first known extant play by a black playwright to dramatize the problems of American slavery. The work is a five-act melodrama mixed with minstrel elements satirizing the institution of slavery on a Mississippi plantation during the antebellum period of the South. It comments on the inhumane treatment of slaves by their plantation owners and the slave's indomitable will to escape. Although the two plays were never staged during the author's lifetime, Brown gave numerous readings of these dramas at antislavery meetings and lyceum programs. The first recorded reading of *The Escape* was held in the town hall of Salem, MA (February 1857).

While Brown was in forced exile in Europe, his first wife died (1851). In 1860, he married Annie Elizabeth Gray. They had two children, both of whom died in early childhood. Until the end of his life, Brown actively participated in the temperance society and attended antislavery society meetings in New York, where he became a dynamic public speaker. Brown later moved to Boston, where he became a lecturer for both the Massachusetts and the American Anti-Slavery Societies. Brown died in his home in Chelsea, MA, near Boston at the age of 69 from a tumor of the bladder. His second wife and two children of his first marriage survived him.

BROWN-GUILLORY, ELIZABETH. A playwright, author, scholar, and critic, Brown-Guillory was born in Church Point, LA. She received a B.A. in English and psychology (1975) and an M.A. in English (1977) at the University of Southwestern Louisiana and a Ph.D. in British and American drama and American literature at Florida State University (1980).

Like **Zora Neale Hurston**, Brown-Guillory distinguished herself as a playwright of repute by writing about the folk culture of her native habitat, Louisiana. Two of her award-winning plays, *Bayou Relics* (1981) and *Snapshots of Broken Dolls* (1981), were produced at Lincoln Center in New York City in 1986. *Bayou* is a long one-act comedy about senior citizens in a nursing home in southwest Louisiana who envy the youth of young people. It was first produced at the Spartanburg Arts

Center, Spartanburg, SC (March 1981); at Dillard University in New Orleans (March 1983); and at colleges and universities throughout the United States. *Snapshots* is a one-act comedy set in a labor room of a hospital in Bayou town. Since 1986, many of Brown-Guillory's plays have been produced at Lincoln Center in New York City. Chautauqua artist Brown-Guillory occasionally travels the country presenting one-woman shows about historical black women figures, such as Josephine Baker, Sisserietta Jones, and Madam C. J. Walker.

Other plays by Brown-Guillory include *Mam Phyllis* (1981), a full-length comedy set in southwest Louisiana during the Depression that focuses on the influence that a nanny, midwife, friend, and grandmother have on a community. A revised version was produced at Dillard University and throughout Louisiana (March 1985). *Marry Me Again* (1984) is a one-act comedy about a newlywed couple making adjustments in their relationship. Dillard University produced it (March 1984) and toured it to select institutions in Louisiana. It won a first-place statewide playwriting competition in 1984 and received a commendation from the mayor of New Orleans.

Brown-Guillory is associate professor of English at the University of Houston and has taught English at Dillard University in New Orleans. She is the recipient of a United Negro College Foundation grant (1986–87). Among her literary work, she edited *Their Place on the Stage: Black Women Playwrights in America* (1988) and has contributed scholarly articles to *The Dictionary of Literary Biography*, *Phylon*, *Sage*, *Helicon Nine: The Journal of Women's Arts and Letters*, *Xavier Review*, and *Salem Press*.

BROWNE, ROSCOE LEE (1925–2007). Browne was a classically trained actor of distinction. Blessed with a sonorous baritone voice and impeccable diction, he brought a sense of elegance to each role he played, whether the African Babu in Robert Lowell's *The Old Glory: Beneto Cereno* or the camp cook in the western movie *The Cowboys* with John Wayne. He was no stranger to the classics, cutting his teeth at **Joseph Papp**'s New York Shakespeare Festival with a small role in *Julius Caesar* in 1956. Over the years, he landed major parts in *King Lear*, *Troilus and Cressida*, *Volpone*, and *Tartuffe*.

Browne was born in Woodbury, NJ, the son of a Baptist preacher. After serving in the army in World War II, he earned a degree from

Lincoln University, where he excelled in athletics. He held the U.S. indoor track record for the 800 meters in 1951. He also attended graduate school at Middlebury College and Columbia University, as well as the University of Florence in Italy. He returned to teach English literature and French at Lincoln University before turning to acting as a profession. Some highlights of Browne's career include his appearance in the 1961 production of Jean Genet's *The Blacks*, with an all-star cast that included **James Earl Jones**, Cicely Tyson, Godfrey Cambridge, Lou Gossett, and Maya Angelou. In that same year, he created *A Hand Is on the Gate*, a collage of black poetry read and sung by Josephine Premice and **Moses Gunn**. On television in a segment of *All in the Family*, he played a character trapped in a stalled elevator with Archie Bunker, the all-American bigot.

During his 40-year career, Browne made over 100 appearances on TV, in movies, and on radio. He appeared on such shows as *Falcon Crest*, *Will and Grace*, *Uptown Saturday Night*, *Topaz*, *ER*, *The Cosby Show*, *Maude*, *Law and Order*, and *The Liberation of L. B. Jones*. In the 1990s, he returned to his stage roots, tackling August Wilson's plays *Two Trains Running* and *Joe Turner's Come and Gone*. Browne and actor Anthony Zerbe spent decades together reading poetry in a show titled *Behind the Broken Words*. Browne was the recipient of an **Obie Award**, two Los Angeles Drama Critics' Circle Awards, and an Emmy Award and was inducted into the Black Filmmakers Hall of Fame. He was a member of Actors Equity Association, Screen Actors Guild, and the American Federation of Television and Radio Artists.

BROWNE, THEODORE R. (c. 1910–79). A pioneer playwright, actor, author, and teacher, Browne was best known for his association with the Negro Unit of the **Federal Theatre** in Seattle. He was also an original member of the **American Negro Theatre** (**ANT**) and one of the founders of the Negro Playwrights Company, both in New York. He was born in Suffolk, VA, and educated in the public schools of New York City. He received advanced degrees at the City College of New York (A.B., 1941) and at Northeastern University (M.E.D.) in Boston.

He gained theatrical experience with the Civic Repertory Theatre in Seattle during the early 1930s, a community group that later became the Seattle Negro Unit of the Works Progress Administration Federal Theatre in 1936. When the Federal Theatre began its operation in

Seattle in 1936, he became assistant director of the Negro Unit, where he also acted and directed and was its resident playwright. Between 1936 and 1937, the unit produced four plays by Browne: an adaptation of *Lysistrata*, *Natural Man*, *A Black Woman Called Moses*, and *Swing, Gates, Swing*. *Lysistrata*, an African American adaptation of Aristophanes' comedy, was first produced at the Orpheum Theatre in Seattle in 1936. Browne changed the locale from ancient Greece to Ethiopia. The subject matter had to do with women of ancient Greece who withheld sex from the returning soldiers until they stopped waging war. The production was halted after only one performance. It was deemed too risqué for Seattle audiences. Reportedly, the production was shut down because the change in locale to an Ethiopian setting troubled the Franklin Delano Roosevelt administration.

Natural Man (originally titled *This Ole Hammer*) is an eight-episode folk drama with music (produced in 1936). The play is loosely based on the legendary folktale of John Henry, who tests his prodigious skills against a steam engine, the symbol of the encroaching machine age, that makes a social commentary about injustice and oppression. John Henry epitomized the African Americans' indomitable spirit and will to survive against almost impossible odds. ANT produced it (May 1941) at the 135th Street Library Theatre in **Harlem** under the direction of Benjamin Zemach. Stanley Greene played John Henry, with a noteworthy cast that included Alvin Childress, Ruby Wallace (**Ruby Dee**), Kenneth Mannigault, **Frederick O'Neal**, and **Alice Childress**. *A Black Woman Called Moses*, a two-act drama produced in 1937, centers on Harriet Tubman and the Underground Railroad. *Swing, Gates, Swing*, a musical revue, was produced the same year.

Browne also wrote four other plays, but no record has been found of their production. *The Gravy Train* (1940), a three-act drama, is about a sensitive young man trying to work, go to school, and keep his philandering wife happy. The *Seven Cities of Gold* (written before 1974), a two-act historical fantasy with an epilogue, dramatized the legend of Esteban (Stephen) Dorantes, a Moor who escorted the Spanish conquistadors in their exploration of the Southwest. *Steppin' High*, also called *Minstrel* (written before 1974), is a musical extravaganza in five acts, loosely based on the life of Bert Williams. It dramatized the life of a black performer from his early days as a tent show performer on the minstrel circuit in the South to his rise on the Broadway stage. *The Day of the Midnight Ride of Paul Revere* (1975) is a historical play in two acts.

Browne, along with **Langston Hughes** and **Theodore Ward**, helped to found the Negro Playwrights Company in New York City, which produced Ward's *Big White Fog* in 1940. After World War II, Browne lived in Roxbury, MA, where he taught theater, lectured, and maintained ties with the New England Repertory Theatre. He received the Rockefeller/Dramatists Guild fellowship in playwriting, the first African American to be honored with this award. Browne died in Boston, reportedly at age 68.

BRYANT, HAZEL (1939–83). Bryant, a director, actress-singer, producer, theatrical administrator, teacher, and playwright, was founder and artistic director of the Afro-American Total Theatre (AATT) in New York (1968–73) and the Richard Allen Center for Culture and Arts. She was also one of the organizers and first presidents of the **Black Theatre Alliance** (1969–73) and was credited with producing over 200 musicals and plays. Born in Zanesville, OH, the daughter of an AME bishop, Bryant grew up in Baltimore, MD, where she studied singing at the Peabody Preparatory School of Music. She received a B.A. from Oberlin Conservatory of Music in Ohio (1962). An interest in opera took her to Europe, where she was trained at the Mozarteum School of Music in Salzburg, Austria. During the 1960s, Bryant sang operatic roles in most of the major opera houses in Italy, the Soviet Union, Germany, Austria, and France. Later that decade, she returned to American soil to pursue a career in theater. In New York City, she studied theater administration at Columbia University and acting with Harold Clurman and Stella Adler. By1968, she had landed roles in the Equity Library Theatre production of *Lost in the Stars* and the next year in the Milwaukee Repertory Theatre's *That's the Game, Jack.* In 1971, Gregory Peterson produced a biography of Bryant entitled *Hazel Hazel Hazel Hazel Hazel* (also known as *Hazel Five Times*), a 30-minute documentary film.

As founder and director of the AATT, Bryant produced musical productions at her theater and around New York City. She frequently revised shows from her repertory. AATT performed *Black Circles 'round Angela* (1970), a one-act musical, at the Halsey Street Block

Association in Brooklyn (August 1971) and the Afro-American Studio Theatre in **Harlem** (February 1973) and *Black Circles, Black Spirits* at the Martinique Theatre (March 1974). Set in a beauty salon, the plot examines the lifestyles of four African American women—Aunt Sarah, Peaches, Saffronia, and Sweet Thing. Interspersed throughout the show is Nina Simone's song "Four Women," while vignettes and speeches by Angela Davis initiate a spiritual interaction among the women, causing each to speak and reflect. *Makin' It* was a full-length musical produced in 1970. **Gertrude Greenidge** and Walter Miles cowrote the book with music by Jimmy Justice and Holly Hamilton. It deals with a young man from a small town who wants to break into show business. AATT produced the show at the International House (January 1972), Riverside Church (March 1972), Finch College (March 1972), street locations in the five boroughs of New York City (July–August 1972), and the Lincoln Center (November 1972). It remained in repertory until 10 June 1973.

Sheba is a one-act musical by Jimmy Justice that was performed in 1972. It premiered at the Riverside Church Theatre (December). Frederick Talbot, Guyana's ambassador to the United States, and his wife sponsored the opening, which was attended by distinguished African, Asian, and Latin American dignitaries and African American artists and celebrities. AATT also produced the show at the third annual Black Theatre Festival at the Brooklyn Academy of Music. It remained in repertory until April 1974. *Mae's Amees* is a one-act musical written in collaboration with Hope Clarke and Hank Johnson. It was mounted at the Riverside Church Theatre (August 1969) and thereafter remained in repertory until October 1969. *An Evening of Black Poetry* is a black music and letters event tracing 200 years of black poetry from Phyllis Wheatley and Paul Laurence Dunbar to **Amiri Baraka (LeRoi Jones)** and Maya Angelou. It was also performed at the Riverside Church Theatre (July 1969). Other musicals that round out AATT's repertoire were *Origins*, a one-act musical coauthored by Beverly Todd and Hank Johnson and produced at the Riverside Church Theatre (October 1969); *On Being Black in White America*, performed at International House (January–March 1970); *Soul Politiken*, with music by Jimmy Justice and shown as a street theater production at Lincoln Center (July 1973); *Carnival Song* (1973); and *Star* (1970).

In 1983, Bryant died in her home of heart disease in New York City after she had spoken at the United Nations earlier in the day. She was a member of the theater panel of the New York State Council on the Arts and the New York City Board of Cultural Affairs as well as a panelist and councilman to the National Endowment for the Arts and the National Opera Institute. She received the Harold Jackman Memorial Award for outstanding contribution to the arts in New York (1976) and a special citation from the governor of New York for producing the Black Theatre Festival at Lincoln Center (1970).

***BUBBLING BROWN SUGAR* (1976).** This musical by **Loften Mitchell** opened at the American National Theatre and Academy (2 March 1976) in New York City for 766 productions. It was produced by J. Lloyd Grant, Richard Bell, Robert M. Cooper, Ashton Springer, and Moe Septee, with songs by Danny Holgate, Emme Kemp, and Lillian Lopez under the direction of Robert M. Cooper. The history of black music on Broadway and in **Harlem** is explored—the first musical to do so. Critics praised veteran actors Avon Long, Joseph Attles, and Josephine Premice for their nostalgic walk down memory lane through songs, as well as Vivian Reed and Chip Garnett, who both won the Theatre World Award. After the show closed on Broadway, it was moved to London for a successful run.

BULLINS, ED. A playwright, editor, essayist, poet, novelist, filmmaker, and teacher, Bullins was one of America's leading and most prolific black playwrights. Born in Philadelphia, he attended public schools and William Penn Institute before moving to California, where he lived for a number of years, writing and producing his early plays. He furthered his education at Los Angeles City College and San Francisco State College. Bullins was a leader of the black arts movement on the West Coast during the 1950s and a founder of **Black Arts/West** Repertory Theatre (BA/W). It was an experimental theater group in the Fillmore District of San Francisco patterned after **Amiri Baraka**'s **(LeRoi Jones)** Black Arts Repertory Theatre School in **Harlem**. In 1967 Bullins returned to the East Coast, and the next year, he was hired as playwright-in-residence and associate director of the **New Lafayette Theatre (NLT)** in Harlem, where he served until 1972. He founded and edited *Black Theatre* magazine, which remained in existence from 1969 to 1972. He also formed the Surviving Theatre in the Bronx, beginning around 1974 until 1980. After the demise of NLT, Bullins worked for **Joseph Papp** at the New York Shakespeare Festival/Public Theatre, where he coordinated a playwrights' workshop and oversaw the Publicity and Press Department. He returned to California to write in the San Francisco Bay area and teach drama at the City College of San Francisco.

Black theater audiences began to take notice of Bullins with the staging of his three one-act plays. *The Electronic Nigger* is a tragicomedy. It is a biting satire epitomizing a certain kind of pompous, pretentious, and predictable "Negro" who parrots whiteness. *Clara's Ole Man: A Play of Lost Innocence*, is about an Ivy League college student who learns a lesson about the complexities and realities of the black urban lifestyle and about Clara's "ole' man." Robert Hartman directed a San Francisco Drama Circle production at the Firehouse Repertory Theatre (August 1965). The Theatre for New York City mounted it (January 1977) as part of Festival '77. The NLT first produced *Lifestyles* off Broadway (March–May 1986) for 86 performances, with Roscoe Orman in the cast. *A Son, Come Home* is a one-act drama produced in 1968. After being away for 10 years, a son returns home to discover his relationship with his mother had deteriorated. The American Place Theatre (APT) produced the three plays off Broadway (March 1968) with cast members from the NLT. The show reopened off Broadway at the Martinique Theatre, where it ran for a total of 86 performances. **Robert MacBeth** directed all three plays.

For six years beginning in 1968, Bullins set out to write a projected cycle of 20th-century plays. *In the Wine Time* (1968), a three-act drama, is the first play in the cycle. A young black man growing up in the ghetto feels his dreams are being thwarted. MacBeth directed it (December 1968, January 1969). *In New England Winter* (1968), a seven-scene drama, is the second play in the cycle. This story about a black family picks up where *Wine Time* left off. The two plays were produced by the NLT under the direction of MacBeth. *The Duplex: A Black Fable in Four Movements* is the third play in the cycle. It is described as a slice-of-life play about an all-night party in a black California neighborhood. It deals with the fragmented allegiances within the black community and the difficulty of a black girl to find love.

When Bullins attended the opening of the play off Broadway at the Repertory Theatre of Lincoln Center at the Forum Theatre (March 1972), he denounced **Gilbert Moses**'s directing concept of the play. Nevertheless, it ran for 34 performances until it closed on 1 April. *The Fabulous Miss Marie* (1971), a full-length drama about black life, is the fourth play in the cycle, where the author revives the role of a minor character from *The Duplex*. The show won two **Obie Awards**, one for the playwright and the other for actor **Sonny Jim Gaines**. *Home Boy* (1972), a full-length drama with music by Aaron Bell, is the fifth play in the cycle and has been described as a play about two southern black men who plan to emigrate to the North. One does, while the other stays behind, however the social environment of the 1950s and 1960s in America victimizes them both. *Daddy* (1974), a full-length drama, is the sixth play in the cycle. An absent father returns home and tries to reconcile with the family he abandoned.

Aside from his six-play cycle, Bullins wrote the prize-winning *The Taking of Miss Janie* (1975), a full-length satirical drama. A parable of race relations in the 1960s, it centers on an encounter between a black would-be poet and a Caucasian classmate and close friend whom he rapes after a prolonged friendship. It won the **New York Drama Critics' Circle Award** as the best American play of 1974–75, the successor to **Lorraine Hansberry**'s *A Raisin in the Sun* as the second black play to win this award. Gilbert Moses won an Obie Award for distinguished direction. Bullins also authored over 60 scripts, a testament to his proclivity for writing plays about the African American landscape. He rightly deserves the label of America's most prolific black playwright. His other works also reveal a plethora of rich subject matter that deserves merit. Among them are *The Gentleman Caller* (1969); *We Righteous Bombers* (1969), written under Bullins's pseudonym Kingsley B. Bass; *Goin' a Buffalo* (1968); *The Corner* (1968); *Dialect Determinism: The Rally* (1965); *How Do You Do? A Nonsense Drama* (1965); *It Has No Choice* (1966); and *The Theme Is Blackness: A One-Act Play to Be Given before Predominantly White Audiences* (1966); *The Helper* (1966), a one-act satire; *Black Commercial #2* (1967), a short television commercial; *The Man Who Dug Fish* (1967), a one-act absurdist play; *The American Flag Ritual: A Short Play or Scenario* (1969); *State*

Office Building Curse: A Scenario to Ultimate Action (1969); *One Minute Commercial* (1969); *A Ritual to Raise the Dead and Foretell the Future* (1970); and *You Gonna' Let Me Take You Out Tonight, Baby?* (1969).

Rounding out Bullins's collection of plays are *The Pig Pen* (1969); *A Street Play* (1970); *Street Sounds: Dialogues with Black Existence* (1970); *The Devil Catchers* (1970); *The Box Office: A Scenario for a Short Film* (1970); *Play of the Play: A Short Play for a Small Theatre* (1971); *The Psychic Pretenders: A Black Magic Show* (also titled *A Pageant of the Black Passion in Three Motions*, 1971); *The Night of the Beast*, a one-act screenplay (1972); *House Party: A Soulful Happening* (1973); *Malcolm '71; or, Publishing Blackness* (1975); *The Mystery of Phyllis Wheatley* (1976); *I Am Lucy Terry* (February 1976); *Jo Anne* (1976); *Sepia Star* (1977); *Storyville* (1977); *C'mon Back to Heavenly House* (1978); *Do-Wah*, a musical (1970s); *Leavings* (1980); *Steve and Velma* (1980); and *High John Da Conqueror—The Musical* (1985). Bullins also authored novels, articles, and reviews and published his works in various periodicals. In addition to the Obie and **New York Drama Critics' Circle** awards, Bullins is the recipient of three Rockefeller Foundation playwriting grants and a grant from the Guggenheim Foundation. Moreover, Columbia College in Chicago awarded him an honorary doctor of letters.

BURGHARDT, ARTHUR. Burghardt is a veteran actor. He began acting at an early age and has worked in all mediums, including the stage, film, TV, and voiceovers. He is uniquely gifted with a deep sonorous voice that gives an air of authenticity to everything he does. Much of his work is in voiceovers, where he is heard but never seen. After many years of research, he wrote a one-man play about Frederick Douglass, the escaped slave who became the leader of the abolitionist movement. He performed *Frederick Douglass in His Own Words* for the **Negro Ensemble Company** in 1972 to sell-out houses. In 1976, Burghardt received an Emmy for a television version of the play. He has continued his work onstage and in film and radio, performing the play with slightly varying titles on college campuses across the country. Burghardt received an honorary degree from the African American Studies Department at Seton Hall University.

BURRILL, MARY P. (c. 1882–1946). Burrill was an outstanding early black female playwright and influential drama teacher in the Washington, DC, educational system during the first half of the 20th century. Born and raised in Washington, DC, to John H. and Clara E. Burrill, she graduated from the M Street School (1901), later called Dunbar High. Burrill's family moved to Boston, where she earned a B.A. in three years from Emerson College (1904, then Emerson College of Oratory). While at Emerson, Burrill wrote her first play, *Unto the Third and Fourth Generations: A One-Act Play of Negro Life*. The college yearbook (1930) published it as "Best Junior Play of the Year." She returned to her alma mater, Dunbar High School, and Armstrong Manual High School, to teach English, speech, and dramatics (1905–44). She read her second drama, a monologue, *The Other Wise Man*, to high school students and also in the community every Christmas. Three of her students distinguished themselves as playwrights: **May Miller** (*Graven Images*), **Willis Richardson** (*The Deacon's Awakening*), and **James W. Butcher Jr.** (*The Seer*).

In 1919, Burrill gained fame in literary circles with the publication of two one-act plays in periodicals. *Aftermath*, a tragedy that is a period piece set in rural South Carolina and is laden with Negro dialect, is about the lynching of a World War I black soldier after he returns home. During the infamous "Red Summer" of 1919, major race riots spread throughout the country because of lynching and disillusionment. Black soldiers who fought for American values and freedom abroad were denied basic rights when they returned to the United Stated. Burrill posed the question whether blacks should serve during World War I, an issue of great debate during this period. The **Krigwa Players** staged it (May 1928) and socialist editor Max Eastman published it in *Liberator*. A propaganda play, *They That Sit in Darkness* (1919), like *Aftermath*, also caused considerable controversy. Burrill challenged the issue of women's reproductive rights (an issue that was not settled until 1965). An impoverished black woman is denied information about birth control as a means of escaping poverty. Margaret Sanger published Burrill's play in a special issue in *Birth Control Review* (September 1919) under the heading "The Negro's Need for Birth Control as Seen by themselves." Burrill retired from Dunbar in 1944. She died in New York City two years later.

BURROWS, VINIE. An actor and playwright, Vinie (pronounced vine-ee) Burrows is a treasured icon of American theater and of the world, using her theatrical skills to entertain and educate thousands of people across the planet. Critic Clive Barnes once referred to her as the "reigning diva of Black Theatre." She made her Broadway debut in 1950 in *Wisteria* with Helen Hayes. Since then, she has appeared on and off Broadway and on radio, television, and film in everything from the classical works of Shakespeare to the modern repertoire. In addition, she has toured her own works on college campuses in the United States and other parts of the world, including Germany, Denmark, Nigeria, Great Britain, and Russia. Her performance pieces have been sponsored on more than 500 college campuses. She is also a social activist involved in any number of causes, including racial discrimination, women's issues, social justice, peace and disarmament, and equal opportunity.

Burrows was born in **Harlem** and after her youthful theatrical debut went on to earn a B.A. in prelaw from New York University. She continued acting, however, and in time discovered two truths: that acting could be a part-time profession and that quality roles for black actresses were almost nonexistent. To circumvent that problem, she wrote a series of one-woman shows that she books and produces at colleges, universities, churches, and other institutions both here and abroad. Among the plays she has written are *Sister! Sister!*, *Song of Lawino*, *From Swords to Plowshares*, *Dark Fire*, *Rose McLendon: Harlem's Gift to Broadway*, *Walk Together Children*, *Daughters of the Sun*, *Africa Fire*, and *Shout Freedom*.

Burrows has taught at many institutions of higher learning across the land, including Sarah Lawrence College, Franklin and Marshall College, and the New School for Social Research. In her 60s, Burrows returned to New York University and in 2002 graduated summa cum laude with a master's degree in performance studies from NYU's Tisch School of the Arts. She has been honored many times for her theatrical and social activism work. Among her many awards and honors are the June Jordan Award, Eugene McDermott Award, Actors Equity **Paul Robeson** Award, **National Black Theatre** Living Legend Award, **Audience Development Committee** Best Actor Award, American Bar Association Silver Gavel Award, and the National Organization for Women Susan B. Anthony Award. Burrows is a permanent representative to the United Nations for the Women's International Democratic Federation.

BUTCHER, JAMES W., JR., "BEANIE" (1909–94). Born in Washington, DC, Butcher, an actor, pioneer playwright, director, and drama professor, was deeply involved in theater. He attended Howard University for three years and studied at New York's Columbia University. Butcher pursued an acting career in New York. While performing with the Morningside Players, he decided to focus on academic theater after he found it difficult to land roles as a light-complexioned "black" actor. Butcher earned his A.B. from the University of Illinois (1932) and his M.A. from the University of Iowa (1941) and attended the Central School of Speech and Dramatic Arts in London as a Fulbright Scholar. Butcher returned to his alma mater, Howard University, to help establish the Department of Drama, chaired by Anne Cooke, and to teach English and advise the Howard Players. He wrote two one-act plays that were performed at Howard, *Mand Honey* (extant), a farce set in the 1930s, and *The Seer*, his best-known work. He was a resident guest actor and director with the Atlanta University Summer Theatre (1930–mid-1950s), where he performed and directed for the Negro Repertory Theatre. During World War II, Butcher coached amateur productions at Fort Huachuca, AZ, before he was assigned overseas to Liberia. James retired from Howard University in 1976 and died eight years later.

BUTLER, CHARLES "BUDDY." Director, actor and educator, is a native of Cleveland, OH, where he directed and acted in various productions at the acclaimed **Karamu Repertory Theatre**. Butler attended Howard University (B.A.) and the University of Washington (M.F.A.). He is currently a professor in the Department of Television, Radio, Film, and Theatre at San José State University, where he teaches and directs plays.

Butler's extensive professional credits span numerous affiliations coast to coast as well as internationally. He was an original member of the **Negro Ensemble Company** of New York City, founding member of the **Black Theatre Alliance** of New York City, and the **Black Theatre Network**. He has directed at theaters throughout the country that include **Black Arts/West** in Seattle (artistic director,

1973–77); Seattle Repertory's Second Stage; Phoenix Black Theatre Troupe (artistic director); Stage 1 Theatre and New Arts Theatre (both in Dallas); the Wortham Theatre in Houston; the Houston Fine Arts Center; the Asolo Theatre in Sarasota, FL; the JFK Center for the Performing Arts in Washington, DC; and the **New Jomandi Productions** in Atlanta, GA. For 10 years, Butler was associate artistic director of the Bonfils Theatre at the Denver Center for the Performing Arts, where he directed over 35 productions. In California, he directed at the **Lorraine Hansberry Theatre** in San Francisco, the Oakland Ensemble Theatre, the Inner-City Cultural Center (*see* JACKSON, CLARENCE BERNARD [1927–96]) and the Foxx Follies in Los Angeles, the San Jose Stage Company, City Lights Theatre, San Jose Repertory Theatre, and the Tabia Theatre Ensemble. Butler directed a production of the San Jose State Theatre Arts Department play *Play On* at the Rondo Theatre in Bath, England. It was the first international production by the department. At the **St. Louis Black Repertory Theatre**, he mounted the world premiere of *Conversations on a Dirt Road* by **Samm-Art Williams** and *Othello* by David Charles. Butler was named the outstanding postsecondary theater professor in the state of California (1999), received the Multicultural Award from the California Educational Theatre Association (2001), and nominated as 1 of the 10 most influential African Americans in the San Francisco Bay Area (2001). He is also the recipient of two **Audience Development Committee Awards**.

– C –

CAESAR, ADOLPH (1938–86). An actor and playwright, Caesar was one of the outstanding actors of the 20th century. During his career, he worked with some of the leading theaters in the country, including the New York Shakespeare Festival, Center Theatre Group, Lincoln Center Repertory Company, American Shakespeare Company, and **Negro Ensemble Company (NEC)**. Caesar was born in **Harlem**, and upon graduating from high school, he enlisted in the U.S. Navy, from which he retired after 20 years, having achieved the rank of chief petty officer. After studying theater at New York University, he embarked on an acting career, relying on the discipline of his military career; an innate intelligence; and a deep, gravelly voice that conveyed authority. He joined the prestigious NEC in 1970 and played leading roles in *Sty of the Blind Pig*, *The Brownsville Raid*, and *A Soldier's Play*, among others. It was his role as the crusty sergeant in the latter play for which he became known, a role he repeated in the 1982 film version of the play. He was nominated for an **Academy Award** for his performance. In 1977, he wrote his one-man show, *The Square Root of Soul*, which was performed at the NEC. Caesar then moved on to films, making over 20, including *Che*, *Fist of Fear*, *Touch of Death*, *Club Paradise*, and *The Color Purple*, to name a few. His television appearances include *The Wild, Wild, West*; *General Hospital*; *The Twilight Zone*; *Guiding Light*; and *Tales from the Darkside*. With his rich voice, Caesar also made a living doing radio and television voiceovers. Awards for Caesar include an **Obie Award** and a **Drama Desk Award** as best actor for *A Soldier's Play*.

CALDWELL, BEN. A playwright and essayist, Caldwell was born in **Harlem**, one of nine children. He dropped out of school after his father died in 1954, abandoning his interest in graphic art. A protégé of **Amiri Baraka (LeRoi Jones)**, Caldwell was inspired to write more than 20 revolutionary one-act plays for the Spirit House Movers in Newark, NJ. His plays were mounted off Broadway and throughout the country. Caldwell's best-known play, *Prayer Meeting; or, The First Militant Preacher* (1967), is a humorous look at misguided religiosity. A thief hiding in a closet of a "sellout" black minister speaks to the clergyman as the voice of God and convinces him to become a militant preacher. The Spirit House Movers first produced the show in 1967. **Woodie King Jr.** Associates followed with a production at Tambellini's Gate Theatre (July–November 1969) for 111 performances on a program of 4 one-act plays entitled *A Black Quartet*. Dennis Tate played the burglar and L. Errol Jaye the minister under the direction of Irving Vincent. *The Job* (1966), Caldwell's most widely publicized play, criticized social programs that offer only dead-end job opportunities for blacks.

Over the course of two decades, Caldwell authored more than two dozen one-act plays that were produced off Broadway at the **New Federal Theatre (NFT)**. They include *The World of Ben Caldwell* (1982), a series of skits and monologues (April 1982), for 12 performances.

Director Richard Gant assembled a noteworthy cast of Kirk Kirksey, Reginald Vel Johnson, **Morgan Freeman**, and Garrett Morris. *The Great New York City Crisis* (1974) was first produced by the Black Vibrations at the annual **Black Theatre Alliance** Festival in New York City (1974) and later by NFT. Another play of note was *The King of Soul; or, The Devil and Otis Redding* (1969), a musical tragedy about the fate of the "soul" singer who becomes successful after making a pact with a "white devil."

During the volatile **civil rights** era of the 1960s and 1970s, the revolutionary tenor of the times influenced the subject matter in Caldwell's writings as it did with other African American playwrights. The NFT produced an evening of Caldwell's one-act revolutionary plays under the production title *What Is Going On* (November 1973). It included *All White Caste: After the Separation* (1971), about a white liberal who reinvents himself as a "Nigger of the future." *Top Secret; or, A Few Million after B.C.* (1969) addresses the use of birth control (B.C.) by women as a device to limit reproduction. The Performing Arts Society of Los Angeles first produced *Top Secret* before it was included in the *What Is Going On* program. *Family Portrait; or, My Son the Black Nationalist* (1969) deals with tensions between a black upward-bound father and his militant son.

Other productions of Caldwell's works include *Yesterday, Today and Tomorrow* (1974). *The Seven Principles*, a full-length historical pageant coauthored by Ben Caldwell and Yusef Iman, dramatizes the seven principles of the black value system called the Nguso Saba. The Weusi Kuumba Troupe produced *Principles* at the Black Theatre Alliance annual festival in New York City (summer 1974). *Rape* (1971) was produced by the Bedford-Stuyvesant Theatre, Brooklyn (October 1971). *An Obscene Play* (1971) was advertised as a play for adults only. *Recognition* (1968) is a ritualistic play whereby God gives advice to a confused African American male. *Riot Sale; or, Dollar Psyche Fake Out* opened in 1968. White policemen offer money to black freedom fighters to buy them off. *Unprecedented: What Needs to Be Done* (1968) depicts a standoff between a revolutionary spokesperson and an American president. *The Fanatic: Testifyin'* (1968) concerns a white man who has a spiritual encounter and testifies before a black church congregation about his former transgressions. *The Wall* (1967) is set before a graffiti-ridden wall that connotes different messages for blacks than it does for whites. *Mission Accomplished* (1967) is a condemnation of the role of white missionaries stationed in an African country. *Hypnotism* (1966) underscores the philosophy of nonviolence as a device to control blacks.

CALDWELL, LAVERNE SCOTT. An actress, Caldwell is a Chicago native. After studying at Northwestern University for a year, she took time off to get married and to bear a son. She renewed her education at Loyola University of Chicago, where she earned a B.A. in theater arts and communication. A few years later, she moved to New York City, where she studied with Uta Hagen and **Douglas Turner Ward**. Her first career break came in *Home* by **Samm-Art Williams**, a play workshopped at the **Negro Ensemble Company**. *Home* was moved to the Cort Theatre for a Broadway run in 1980. It was a measurable success, but more important, the world was exposed to the talents of Caldwell. In 1984, she was injured in an automobile accident that kept her out of show business for two years. Upon her return, she landed a role in the Broadway production of **August Wilson**'s *Joe Turner's Come and Gone*, for which she won the coveted **Tony Award** as Bertha Holly in 1988. Since then, Caldwell has not looked back, appearing in movies and television but also the stage, her first love, where she has performed in *A Raisin in the Sun*, *Daughters of the Mock*, *Colored People's Time*, *Macbeth*, *The Dreams of Sarah Breedlove*, *American Medea*, *Boesman and Lena*, *About Heaven and Earth*, and *From the Mississippi Delta*. Caldwell has appeared in two other Broadway shows, *Proposals* and *A Month of Sundays*.

As in life, things blow hot and cold in the theatrical world, and for now at least, it is awfully hot in the Caldwell household. She is riding a career high at the moment in playing a recurring role in the hot television series *Lost*, and her role as Rose Henderson seems to expand in every appearance. The opportunity to play the role was honed with 25 years of experience in show business, which she excelled at onstage and in television and movies. Although Caldwell started out as a stage actor, she has made over 75 appearances in television and movies. Her appearances in movies and television include *Waiting to Exhale*, *The Fugitive*, *Nip/Tuck*, *Judging Amy*, *Cold Case*, *Devil in a Blue Dress*, *The Practice*, *Without a Trace*, *Ghost Whisperer*, *Murder One*, *Chicago Hope*, *Weapons of Mass Destruction*, *Doogie Howser*,

All My Children, *JAG*, and *Up against the Wall*. Caldwell has been awarded an **Obie Award** and a Helen Hayes Award.

CALEB, JOHN RUFUS. A versatile writer, Caleb has divided his career between writing for film and stage and teaching. He was born in South Carolina but grew up in Pennsylvania, where he earned his A.B. at Dickinson College. He later attended Johns Hopkins University in Baltimore, where he attained his master's in creative writing in 1973. He has taught at various institutions since and is currently an associate professor of English at the Community College of Philadelphia.

His most successful effort has been the 1980 play *Benny's Place*, which depicts an aging black tool repairman in a steel mill who is asked to train a younger man to replace him. The result is both heartrending and tragic. *Benny's Place* earned a Best Play Award from the Eugene O'Neill Playwrights Conference in 1981 and was made into a movie with Cicely Tyson and Lou Gossett that was aired nationwide by ABC in 1982. Caleb also wrote *City Lights: An Urban Sprawl* (1984), a surrealistic examination of the progress African Americans have made. *Houston: The Day of, and the Night After* (1985) shows a day in the life of an African American college student when it is turned upside down after Martin Luther King is assassinated. *Jean Toomer's Cane* (1985) is an adaptation of Toomer's novel examining the theme of "passing" for white. *Men of Bronze* (1985) addresses the problems faced by the 369th Colored Infantry in World War I. Other plays Caleb wrote are *Slave Coffle/With Observer*, *My Dungeon Shook*, *Fathers and Sons*, *The Rehearsal: A Fantasy*, and *The Ballad of Mistuh Jack*. Awards and honors Caleb received include those from the Eugene O'Neill Playwrights Conference and the Pennsylvania Council on the Arts fellowship.

CAMPBELL, DICK (CORNELIOUS C. CAMPBELL, 1903–94). A native of Beaumont, TX, Campbell was a multitalented actor and singer, theater organizer, director, producer, playwright, and social activist. He attended Paul Quinn College (A.B. in sociology) and Catholic University (M.A.). Campbell and his wife Muriel Rahn, a singing and acting team, were featured in such early musicals as Lew Leslie's *Blackbirds* (1928), *Hot Chocolates* (1929), *Brain*

Sweat (1934), and *Cabin in the Sky* (1941). In 1935, he organized the Negro People's Theatre in **Harlem** with actress **Rose McClendon**. Three years later, he founded the Rose McClendon Players after her death in 1936.

Among Campbell's other theatrical activities, he mounted over 65 all-black United Service Organization shows that he toured during World War II; directed *On Striver's Row* (1945); served as company manager for *Tambourines to Glory* (1963); produced and acted in *A Ballad for Bimshire* (1963); appeared in the film *Come Back Charleston Blue* (1972); and wrote *The Watchword Is Forward* (1942), *Jim Crow Must Go* (1952), and *Toll the Liberty Bell* (1953). The New York City branch of the Nation Association for the Advancement of Colored People produced the latter two plays. Campbell served as chair of the board of directors of the Coordinating Council for Negro Performers, Inc. (1950s), and director of the Sickle Cell Anemia Foundation of Greater New York. He was also director of information for Operation Crossroads–Africa and chaired the Committee for the Desegregation of the Arts (1960s).

CARIBBEAN AMERICAN REPERTORY THEATRE, INC. (CART). In the mid-1970s, CART was formed in Rego Park, NY, to promote aspiring and talented actors and playwrights from the Caribbean on the New York stage. Trinidad-born Neville Richen was named artistic director and Olivier Stephenson, Jamaica-born, executive director. Located initially in the heart of West Indian culture on Eastern Parkway, Brooklyn, the group was handsomely funded by the New York State Council for the Arts. Despite good reviews, CART-sponsored shows had difficulty building a strong, supportive audience. By the fourth season (1979), CART had succeeded with such plays as *A Trinity of Four* and *Fog Drifts in the Spring*, two one-act plays by **Lennox Brown** from Trinidad; *Sweet Talk* and *Alterations* by Michael Abbensetts from Guyana; and *Journey through Babylon*, a ritual fantasy based on the poems of Olivier Stephenson dealing with the experiences of a Caribbean man in New York. Arlene Quiyou of Trinidad conceived and directed the show.

For the 1979–80 season, CART offered a pair of plays entitled *The Roomer* and *The Visitor* by Amirh Bahati (Patricia Roberts), followed by *Shango de Imam: A Yoruba Mystery Play*, where the gods (male and female) determine the fate of humankind. Cuban playwright Pepe Carril wrote the script, and Susan Sherman adapted it to English. **La MaMa Experimental Theatre Club** Dance Drama Workshop hosted the Richen-directed production. No record exists of CART's activities between 1980 and 1985 after Stephenson left the organization.

For the next few years, Jeffrey Anderson-Gunter from Jamaica, an actor and director, took the helm of CART before moving to Los Angeles. His successor, Rudolph Shaw from Guyana, presented a minifestival of one-act plays in May 1986 at the New Theatre on East Fourth Street, Manhattan. That same year, CART offered **Derek Walcott**'s *Beef in My Chicken* (October 1986). It is a slight and static comedy set in 1960 Trinidad showing a family's resistance to "industrial development."

In 1987, Stephenson came back briefly to direct Stafford (Ashani) Harrison's *Indian Play*, a "cantankerous comedy." It played for eight performances at the **Paul Robeson Performing Arts Company** in Brooklyn. Stephenson then returned to Jamaica. Shaw became CART's executive director in 1988, and he held a fund raiser at the Lincoln Center Neighborhood Theatre, at which excerpts from several Caribbean plays were enacted.

In February of the next year, CART presented *Masquerade* by Ian Valz at the United Nation Library as part of the celebration marking Guyana's 19th anniversary as a cooperative republic. Fred Tyson directed it. In May, the company revived two short plays from the "Rest of America" festival, presenting them at a regional high school in Aberdeen, NJ. The 1990s brought a resurgence of CART strengthened by the addition of Jemma Redman, a Trinidadian, as new artistic director. The company became more innovative with its season of original presentations, musical comedies, monologues, and programs featuring mainstream plays. By the beginning of the new millennium, CART had expanded its offerings to non-Caribbean plays, such as *My Children, My Africa* by South African Athol Fugard (white). The play raises a moral question about the liberation of oppressed people.

CARLOS, LAURIE. An actor, playwright, and director, Carlos is an iconic figure in the world of black theater. Known primarily as a performance artist, Carlos has worked for years in stretching the boundaries of traditional Western theater where actors are there to perform a play. Carlos is recognized as a leader in the performance art field in which she has worked for the past 20 years. She develops character studies that incorporate issues of race, class, gender, and sexuality while defying the unities of time and space, past and present, beginning and ending, to create images of wholeness.

Carlos was raised on the Lower East Side of New York and worked a variety of jobs until she met **Ntozake Shange** and began working with her on Shange's choreopoem *For Colored Girls Who Have Considered Suicide When the Rainbow is Enuf*. Carlos created the role of the "Lady in Blue" when it played at **Joseph Papp**'s NYSF/ Public Theatre and reprised the role on Broadway. After a lengthy run on Broadway, Carlos worked with the theater/dance group Urban Bush Women, but she returned to the world of theater and in time became a pioneer and trendsetter working with **Robbie McCauley**, **Keith Antar Mason**, and Sharon Bridgeforth in the evolving world of black performance art. A list of the works Carlos developed includes *Teenytown, Heat, Nonsectarian Dances with the Dead, Organdy Falsetto, Zion Science, White Chocolate for My Father*, and *The Cookin' Show*. Carlos was an artistic fellow at **Penumbra Theatre** and was also on the board of the Jerome Foundation. She was the recipient of awards from the New York Foundation for the Arts, Theatre Communications Group, National Endowment for the Arts, and the McKnight Foundation.

CARPETBAG THEATRE (CT). Based in Knoxville, TN, the CT developed out of an idea whose time had come and was fueled in part by the fervor and energy that came out of the **civil rights movement**. It was time to tell the story of racism, sexism, discrimination, and access to basic rights and services that had been denied for so long. It was founded in 1969, chartered in 1970, and began searching for and developing scripts that dealt with the death penalty, domestic violence, black feminism, environmental racism, red lining, and other issues endemic to the black community. For over 35 years, the CT has been producing work that is issue driven, historically based, and rooted in the culture of the African American diaspora.

Wilmer Lucas, a writer in residence at Knoxville College, was the original force behind the theater. Linda Parris-Bailey came in 1974 and over time guided the company to become more of a multigenerational entity. The company itself mostly generates CT plays during long improvisational sessions where everyone contributes with an emphasis on divergent viewpoints. Everything is taped, a writer is chosen—sometimes commissioned—and a hard-copy script is developed. Examples of some of the scripts developed and performed include *Red Summer*, a story of Knoxville's 1919 race riot told in documentary form. *Nitram Sacul* is a praise work for women who mentor women. *Dark Cowgirls and Prairie Queens* is a story of seven of the most colorful black women in the history of the American West. *Swopera* is a consortium of actors and poets performing in a spoken word opera. *Nothin' Nice* is a contemporary piece focusing on black family and environmental justice issues.

The CT also offers a series of workshops, residency projects, and other services focusing on empowerment, skill development, and information gathering. This includes role playing, collaborative writing, story circles and swaps, creative drama, and movement. The CT's support has come from the community and such other sources as the Rockefeller Foundation, East Tennessee Foundation, Knoxville Cornerstone Foundation, National Endowment for the Arts, and W. K. Kellogg Foundation.

CARR, GREGORY S. An actor and playwright from St. Louis, MO, Carr is a graduate of Southern Illinois University and a member of the Chicago Alliance for Playwrights. He has written *Revolution/Revelation* (1991), *A Colored Funeral* (2005), *Sandtown* (2004), *Ain't Got No Time to Die* (2004), *Jacob's Well* (1991), *No Place to Go* (1995), *Losing Mogadishu* (2003), and *Johnnie Taylor Is Gone* (2005). Carr's plays have been produced at **Karamu Repertory Theatre**, First Run Theatre, the **St. Louis Black Repertory Theatre**, and the **National Black Theatre Festival**.

CARROLL, VINNETTE (1922–2002). Carroll was a director, black theater organizer, actress, playwright, and adaptor and conceiver of original shows. She has been acknowledged as an outstanding black female director in America, receiving numerous awards for playwriting, acting, directing, and contributions to the theater.

Born in **Harlem**, Carroll lived from age three to eight in Jamaica. She was educated at Long Island University (B.A. in psychology, 1944), New York University (M.A. in psychology, 1946), and Columbia University (Ph.D., completed studies but not dissertation). She studied with Erwin Piscator at the Dramatic Workshop, Lee Strasberg at the Actors Studio (1948–50), and Stella Adler (1954–65). She also taught for several years at the High School for the Performing Arts in New York, headed the Ghetto Arts Program of the New York State Council on the Arts, and was a member of the Directors Unit of the Actors Studio.

It was at the Urban Arts Corps during the 1960s in Greenwich Village where Carroll, as organizer and artistic director, conceived and staged most of her dramatic works. Carroll coauthored with Micki Grant two of her most success musicals, *Don't Bother Me, I Can't Cope* (1970) and *Your Arms Too Short to Box with God* (1975). Carroll directed both productions. Grant, an actress, also provided the book, music, and lyrics. These two shows initiated a lasting professional partnership between Carroll and Grant. *Cope*, conceived by Carroll, utilizes song and dance based on blues, gospel, jazz, rock, calypso, and traditional ballad rhythms to celebrate coping mechanisms of African Americans. *Your Arms* is a full-length gospel musical conceived by Carroll, with music and lyrics by Alex Bradford and additional music by Grant. The Gospel of Matthew is told in the black vernacular. It was commissioned by the Spoleto Festival in Italy (summer 1975) and opened in New York City (1976) the next year for an extended run.

Other successful Carroll–Grant projects include *Through the Looking Glass* (1969); *Croesus and the Witch* (1971); *Step Lively, Boy* (1972); *The Ups and Downs of Theophilus Maitland* (1974); *I'm Laughin' but I Ain't Tickled* (1976); and *Love Power* (1974). Carroll also conceived, adapted, produced, or directed several other musicals. Among them are *Trumpets of the Lord* (1963), an adaptation from James Weldon Johnson's *God's Trombones* (1927); *But Never Jam Today* (also produced as *Alice*, 1969); *When Hell Freezes Over, I'll Skate* (1979); *The Great Gettin' Up Morning* (1963), based on *God's Trombones*; *All the King's Men* (May 1974); and *What You Gonna' Name That Pretty Little Baby* (1979).

Carroll also distinguished herself as an actress. She won the **Obie Award** (1961) for her work in *Moon on a Rainbow Shawl* and was highly praised for her role as Sojourner Truth in a segment of the CBS program *We, the Women*. She received numerous honors and awards, such as the Ford Foundation grant for directors (1960–61); Emmy Award for conceiving, adapting, and supervising *Beyond the Blues*, presented on CBS (1964); Outer Critics' Circle Award for directing (1971–72); National Association for the Advancement of Colored People Image Award (Los Angeles, 1972); Harold Jackman Memorial Award (1973); three Tony nominations, two for directing (1973 and 1977) and one for the best book for a musical (1976); **Audience Development Committee** Board of Directors Award for contributions to the theater (1973); **Frank Silvera Writers' Workshop** Foundation Award (1977); and the Dramatists Guild Committee for Women's first annual award (1972) given to an outstanding female dramatist for her contributions to the theater (shared with playwright **Alice Childress**). In 1985, Carroll started a production company in Fort Lauderdale, FL. She died on 5 November 2002 after a prolonged illness.

CARSON, GERALD. A playwright, screenwriter, and poet, Carson is an alumnus of the **Sonia Sanchez** Writers' Workshop held at the Countee Cullen Library in **Harlem** (1970–71). His most produced play is *Infirmity Is Running* (1976), a domestic drama in two acts about relationships within a black family. The Theatre of Renewal at the Stagelight Theatre in New York City produced it (September 1976). Carson's other two plays are *Friends* (1976) and *Jenny* (1976). His screenplay *The Unforgettable Experience of Billy Joe McAlester* (1977) is an adaptation of *The Ballad of Billy Joe McAlester*, about a love affair between a white woman and a black man who is killed by a jealous white rival.

CARTER, STEVE HORACE. Carter is an award-winning playwright, director, scene designer, and production coordinator. Born in the Caribbean Islands, his family migrated to the United States. Upon graduation from high school, he joined the U.S. Air Force, where he served from 1949 to 1953. Working with Maxwell Glanville at the American Community Theatre, Carter gained practical theatrical experience as a costume and set designer, lighting and sound technician, and playwright.

In 1967, Carter joined the staff of the newly founded **Negro Ensemble Company** (NEC), where he functioned as head of the playwright's workshop and in a variety of positions, including playwright in residence. The NEC selected his first play, *One Last Look* (1967), as part of the 1967–68 season. It is a satirical comedy about a dead man whose mistress, wife, and children speak about him at his funeral. During Carter's 12 years with the NEC (1969–81), he coordinated the Playwright's Workshop, and the NEC produced three of his other plays. In *Eden* (1976), tensions erupt between two family members when a West Indian follower of Marcus Garvey falls in love with a southern African American woman. *Terraced Apartment* (1968), a satirical comedy, is about a lower-income couple that feels displaced when they move into a middle-income neighborhood. *Nevis Mountain Dew* (1978) is set in a West Indian household in Queens. Family and friends gather to celebrate the 50th birthday of the patriarch, who is confined to an iron lung. After they become inebriated with "mountain dew" (whiskey), he begs the family to unplug the machine to relieve his agony.

Carter received an **Audience Development Committee (Audelco) Award** for *Eden* as best play of the year and the Outer Critics Circle Award (1976) as the season's most promising playwright. *Nevis* garnered the *Burns Mantle Theatre Yearbook*'s Best Play Award (1978–79). Carter also directed *Raisin' Hell in the Son* (1962) for the NEC and was costume designer for *The Sty of the Blind Pig* (1971).

Carter moved to Chicago in 1981 and joined the staff of the Victory Gardens Theatre (VGT) as playwright-in-residence. This was a fertile period for Carter, as he wrote some 11 plays over the next 16 years as well as established the Playwrights Ensemble for the VGT. Some of the plays were somewhat successful, such as *Dame Lorraine*, *House of Shadows*, and *Pecong*. Other plays he authored during that period include *Tea on Inauguration Day*; *Speile 36; or, The Fourth Medal*; *Mirage*; *Shadows*; and *Rampart Street*. Carter's plays have been produced throughout the world, including in Hong Kong, London, Canada, and the Netherlands.

Carter earned a Guggenheim fellowship in 1982 and in 2001 was honored by the **National Black Theatre Festival** with a Living Legend

Award for outstanding contributions to black theater. Other fellowships have come from the Rockefeller Foundation; the National Endowment for the Arts; and the McDowell, Ragdale, and O'Shaunessy Foundations. He also received an Audelco Award.

CASH, ROSALIND (1938–95). Cash was an actor of extraordinary elegance and versatility known primarily for her work as a charter member of the prestigious **Negro Ensemble Company (NEC)** in the late 1960s. A vocalist as well as an actor, Cash performed for over three years in such diverse works as *Song of the Lusitanian Bogey*, *Ceremonies in Dark Old Men*, *Kongi's Harvest*, and ***Dream on Monkey Mountain***. When the resident company was disbanded several years later, Cash found herself scrambling for work along with thousands of other New York actors. She prevailed and enjoyed a brief but distinguished career onstage, TV, and the big screen.

Cash was born in Atlantic City but moved to New York City while still a teenager. After attending City College of New York, she began her career in the acting profession. She attracted critical attention when she appeared with **James Earl Jones** and **Ellen Holly** in *King Lear* at the New York Shakespeare Festival in 1962. Her Broadway debut was in *The Wayward Stork* in 1966. Cash was known for her determination not to accept roles she felt were demeaning or stereotypical. She would work as a secretary, a keypunch operator, or a jazz vocalist until the right part surfaced. Among the many television shows and movies she made were *Uptown Saturday Night*; *Klute*; *Cornbread, Earl, and Me*; *Cagney and Lacey*; *Kojak*; *The Mary Tyler Moore Show*; *Hill Street Blues*; *Thirty Something*; *The Guyana Tragedy: The Story of Jim Jones*, and *Barney Miller*. Cash was also widely known for her recurring role as the matriarchal nurse Mary Mae Ward on the soap opera *General Hospital*. She died relatively early but was most proud of her work with the NEC and with never having wavered in being true to herself and her standards.

CASTILLO THEATRE (FORMERLY CASTILLO CULTURAL CENTER). Castillo is located at the All Stars Projects Performing Arts and Learning Center on West 42nd Street. It is an off-off-Broadway theater in New York City, bringing challenging, thought-provoking entertainment to the heart of the theater district. Since it was launched in 1983, Castillo has produced over 100 main stage productions by 20 authors from seven different nations. Fred Newman, the artistic director and playwright, is a major source for new plays and musicals produced at Castillo. The company is noted for its experimental productions and politically engaged plays. Among Castillo's signature works are *Sally and Tom (The American Way)*, a musical that explores the 30-year-relationship between Thomas Jefferson and his slave Sally Hemings. *Crown Heights*, a play performed by six African American and six young Jewish actors, examines the violence between blacks and Jews in Crown Heights, Brooklyn, in 1991. *Satchel: A Requiem for Racism* is about the incomparable black pitcher Satchel Paige. *Stealin' Home* deals with the relationship between the great African American baseball player Jackie Robinson and his southern white teammate Pee Wee Reese, and *Sessions with Jesus* presents the son of God seeking therapy.

CHAKULA CHA JUA THEATRE COMPANY (CCJTC). The CCJTC was formed in 1985 to provide an outlet for local actors, playwrights, and directors in the black arts community. Its goal was to present the works of African American playwrights as they reflect the experiences of black people in America and throughout the world. **Chakula Cha Jua** (also known as Cayette McNeill) is the company's founder and artistic director. He has been an active participant in the black arts movement for more than 25 years. Under his direction, the company has presented a variety of new and exciting works for both adults and children. The company has performed for public libraries, community centers, churches, lounges, prisons, and more than 100 schools in New Orleans and throughout the southern region. The CCJTC has been a regular fixture in the Alliance for Community Theatres' annual New Orleans Black Theatre Festival. Jua was recipient of the Alliance's Best Director Award in 1990, and the company was bestowed the award for best production in 1993. In 1991, the CCJTC was one of the few theater groups from the South represented at the **National Black Theatre Festival** in Winston-Salem, NC. The CCJTC is a member of the Alliance for Community Theatres, Inc.; the Southern Black Cultural Alliance; and the **Black Theatre Network.**

CHARLES, MARTIE. *See* EVANS-CHARLES, MARTIE (MARTHA EVANS CHARLES, MARTIE CHARLES).

CHICAGO DRAMATISTS (CD; THE PLAYWRIGHT'S THEATRE). Founded in 1979 in the old Organic Theatre, CD relocated to 1105 West Chicago Avenue in 1988. Artistic director Russ Tutterow maintains that CD's mission has not changed since its founding: to discover, nurture, and promote the plays and playwrights that will contribute to the national theater repertory and a greater goal—to touch the lives of audience members. CD's policy is to commission an artist-in-residence for a three-year renewable term. It prefers to work with the development of writers for a long period of time. CD may retain up to 24 resident playwrights and hires over 600 actors and directors each year, making it one of the largest employers of artists in Illinois. It is possibly the only program of its kind in the United States.

CHICAGO THEATRE COMPANY (CTC). Douglas Alan-Mann co-founded the CTC in 1984, along with two men from Experimental Black Actors Guild (X-BAG). Mann had begun his tenure in Chicago theater with the legendary X-BAG in the early 1970s. Located on Chicago's South Side, the CTC is an Equity-affiliated organization. Mann, the artistic and production director, defined its mission as to enhance the cultural environment of the city's South Side by presenting compelling and universal themes from an African American perspective and to provide a collaborative environment where local African American artists and craftsmen can develop and hone their talent and skills. Mann directed several major award-winning CTC productions. Among them are the critically and publicly acclaimed productions *Ritual* by Stanley-Bennett Clay, *Mr. Rickey Calls a Meeting* (world premiere) by Ed Schmidt, *Hannah Davis* by **Leslie Lee**, *Roseleaf Tea* by **Judi Ann Mason**, and *Pill Hill* by **Samuel E. Kelly**. Mann also performed in 16 productions for the company, which garnered him a Joseph Jefferson nomination for acting.

The CTC has mounted 50 professional productions (most showcasing new work). Noteworthy shows include *Sizwe Banzi Is Dead*, *Po Have You Seen Zandile*, *The Sovereign State of Boogedy Boogedy*, *The Little Tommy Parker Colored Celebrated Minstrel Show*, and

Mens. Another play, *Train Is Comin'*, a new musical by local playwright McKinley Johnson, made history by being the longest-running play in the CTC's 17-year history. It was nominated for 11 **Black Theatre Alliance (BTA)** Awards and received four excellent reviews. Standing-room-only audiences and more award nominations followed with outstanding productions of *Do Lord Remember Me* by **James de Jongh** and the critically acclaimed *Shaking the Mess Outta' Misery* by **Shay Youngblood**. The CTC has helped nurture and provide artistic and economic opportunities to more than 1,500 Chicago-based minority artists. Some of those artists have gone on to highly successful careers, such as director/actor Robert Townsend and actress Irma P. Hall. The CTC has received 20 Joseph Jefferson Award nominations and over 30 BTA nominations. The Joseph Jefferson Award was received in different categories for *Pill Hill, Po Have You Seen Zandile*, and *Do Lord Remember Me*. To date, the CTC has received 16 BTA awards, again in different categories.

CHILDRESS, ALICE (1916–94). Born Alice Herndon in Charleston, SC, Childress was a distinguished contemporary playwright, author, actress, director, and lecturer. She received her education in the **Harlem** community of New York City at P.S. 81, Julia Ward Howe Jr. High School, Wadleigh High School, and Radcliffe Institute (1966–68) as a scholar-writer. After her marriage to Alvin Childress, a veteran actor of stage, films, and television, dissolved, she married Nathan Woodard, a musician and film director. For 10 years, Childress acted, directed, and served on the board of directors at the renowned **American Negro Theatre (ANT)** in Harlem during the 1940s. In 1944, she made her Broadway debut as an actress in ANT's *Anna Lucasta*. This role led to spots on television and several off-Broadway stage plays, such as **Theodore Browne**'s *Natural Man* and **Abram Hill**'s *On Striver's Row*.

Childress has written more than a dozen stage plays; four, however, distinguish her as a playwright of prominence: *Florence* (1949), *Trouble in Mind* (1955), *Wedding Band* (1966), and *Wine in the Wilderness* (1969). *Florence* is a one-act drama that centers on a black mother sitting in a segregated waiting room at a southern bus station. She plans to visit her daughter Florence, who aspires to be an actress, in New York City. The mother decides to forgo her trip after talking with a southern white actress who is also on her way to New York. Instead, the mother sends her daughter money to pursue her dream of becoming an actress. ANT first produced *Florence* in Harlem (1949). Subsequent productions were by the Committee for the Negro in the Arts at **Club Baron** in Harlem (September 1950), the Negro Arts Players also in Harlem (August 1952), and the Southside Center of the Performing Arts in Chicago (1966).

Trouble in Mind is a two-act dramedy. Actors assemble in a rehearsal hall for a play about race relations in the antebellum South that is bound for Broadway. A veteran black stage actress comes into conflict with her white director's depiction of a black mother's relationship with a rebellious young son. The play received the **Obie Award** (1956) for best off-Broadway play. The Greenwich Mews Theatre first produced it off Broadway (November 1955) for 91 performances. Featured in this fine cast were **Clarice Taylor** and Hilda Haynes. *Trouble* was scheduled to open on Broadway (April 1957) as *So Early Monday Morning*, but ironically the same issue in *Trouble* of whites co-opting the work of African Americans erupted between Childress and the director of *Trouble*. Childress withdrew the show; however, the British Broadcasting Corporation did telecast it (twice in October and November 1964).

Wedding Band: A Love/Hate Story in Black and White is a three-act drama that addresses **miscegenation** in a South Carolina town during World War I. After a 10-year relationship, a white man and black woman plan to go North to get married because of social restrictions prohibiting such a union in the South. The University of Michigan first produced it in 1966, with **Ruby Dee** as the central character Julia, a role she reprised in several other productions. Abbey Lincoln and Jack Harkins rounded out the cast. Other productions of *Band* ran at the Virginian Theatre in Chicago (1971) and the New York Shakespeare Festival/NYSF/Public Theatre off Broadway (September 1972–February 1973) for 175 performances, directed by the author and **Joseph Papp**. It was televised as a two-hour ABC theater special (April 1975).

Wine in the Wilderness is a dramedy in one act. Set in Harlem amid the social upheaval of the 1960s, a middle-class artist learns a lesson in blackness from a woman he mistakenly believes is a street person. The National Entertainment Television (1969) first produced the show in Boston as part of an experimental series of plays; thereafter, productions were staged at the Kuumba Workshop in Chicago (1971); by the Howard University Players in Washington, DC (1972); and at the **National Black Theatre** in New York (1977).

Among the other plays Childress authored are *The African Garden* (1970) and *Just a Little Simple* (1950), a full-length musical revue. The latter is an adaptation of **Langston Hughes**'s *Simple Speaks His Mind*, about an ordinary Harlem dweller, Jesse B. Simple, who has extraordinary insight about life. The Committee for the Negro in the Arts opened the show at Club Baron in Harlem (September 1950) for a two-month run. *Gold through the Trees* (1952) is a historical dramatic revue in eight scenes chronicling the black protest movement against civil disobedience from South Africa to America and back to South Africa. *Man Bearing a Pitcher* (1955) is a full-length drama set in biblical times. A fictional family holds Christ's last supper in his home to save Christ from being crucified.

The World on a Hill (1968) is a one-act drama set on a Caribbean island about a white woman and her son, who reassess their lives after an encounter with a young black man. *The Freedom Drum* (original title, *Young Martin Luther King at Montgomery, Alabama*, 1969) is a tribute to the chief architect of nonviolence during the **civil rights movement**. Childress's husband, Nathan Woodard, wrote the musical score. The Performing Arts Repertory Theatre opened it at Symphony Hall, Newark, NJ (May 1969), and followed with a bus and truck tour for two years (1969, 1972). *String* (1969) is a one-act drama about a Rastafarian-type black character accused of stealing. A production by the **Negro Ensemble Company** was produced off Broadway at the St. Marks Playhouse (March–April 1969) for 32 performances. The cast included **Arthur French**, **Esther Rolle**, and **Clarice Taylor**. *Mojo: A Black Love Story* (1970) centers on a rekindled relationship between a divorced Harlem couple. The **New Heritage Repertory Theatre Company** premiered it in Harlem (spring 1970). *The African Garden* is a drama with music that centers on a black man's search for his African birthright. It was written while Childress was in residence at the Radcliff Institute for Independent Study, a Harvard University appointment. *When the Rattlesnake Sounds* (1975) is a one-act play depicting Harriet Tubman working in a New Jersey hotel to help the cause of abolition. *Let's Hear It for the*

Queen (1976) is a one-act drama with a theme borrowed from a Mother Goose story. *Sea Island Song* (1977) is a full-length drama commissioned by the South Carolina Arts Commission about the Gullah-speaking people of the Georgia Sea Islands off the coast of South Carolina. Stage South produced it during Alice Childress Week (1977) in Charleston, SC. *Gullah* (1984) is another full-length musical based on Childress's research of the subject title. The music was by Nathan Woodard, and the University of Massachusetts at Amherst produced it (spring 1984). *Moms* (1984) is a collaboration between Childress and Clarice Taylor. It is a three-character full-length show centering on the life and career of comedian extraordinaire Jackie "Moms" Mabley. The Hudson Guild Theatre produced it in New York (February–March 1987). **Walter Dallas** directed the show with Taylor as Moms, **S. Epatha Merkerson** as her confidante, and Grenaldo Frazier as her pianist and lover. Childress coauthored a drama, *Hell's Alley* (1938), with her first husband, Alvin.

Childress was a member of the Dramatists Guild, Actors Equity Association, New Dramatists, and the Harlem Writers Guild. Her numerous awards and honors include an Obie Award for *Trouble in Mind* (1956), a grant from the John Golden Fund for Playwrights (1957), the Sojourner Truth Award presented by the National Negro Business and Professional Women's Clubs, the Black Filmmakers first **Paul Robeson** Medal of Distinction (1977), and the **Audience Development Committee** Pioneer Award (1985).

CHILDS, KIRSTEN. Actor, composer, and playwright, Childs is a rarity in the world of theater. All her life, she has seen herself as a chameleon and "rather bubbly." A native of Los Angeles, she developed her craft at New York University's Tisch School of the Arts. Childs is a black woman who can act, dance, sing, compose, and write. She has written songs for Dianne Reeves; costarred with Chita Rivera in a touring production of the musical *Chicago*; and performed on Broadway in *Dancin'*, *Jerry's Girls*, and *Sweet Charity*. She is also the author of three musicals, one of which was the recipient of multiple industry awards.

Childs's most successful play is the musical *The Bubbly Black Girl Sheds Her Chameleon Skin* produced by Playwrights Horizons in an off-Broadway production in 2000. The production earned her an

Obie Award and three Drama Desk nominations. In addition, she has written the musicals *Wasted* and *Northstar*. She was a cowriter on the musical *Sundiata: Lion King of Mali*. Her musical *Miracle Brothers* premiered at the Vineyard Theatre in 2005 to mixed reviews. Childs has been commissioned by the McCarter Theatre to adapt the 19th-century poem "The Highwayman" for the stage and is working with novelist Walter Mosely on a musical project. She has been honored with such awards as the Edward Kleban Award, Gilman and Gonzalez-Falla Musical Theatre Award, Jonathan Larson Grant, Rockefeller Foundation grant, Multi-Arts Production Fund grant, and **Audience Development Committee Award**.

CHISHOLM, ANTHONY. A journeyman actor, Chisholm has received public acclaim for portraying the "wise fool" in the plays of **August Wilson**. He has appeared in over 45 productions of Wilson's works since his inaugural stint in *Two Trains Running* in 1992, the 5th play in the 10-play Wilson cycle. Chisholm, **Stephen McKinley Henderson**, and **Eugene Lee** remain as the key interpreters of August Wilson plays. A native of Cleveland, OH, Chisholm was raised by a single mother who wrote poetry and novels. He joined the U.S. Army and fought in the Vietnam War. While in the service, he was offered a scholarship to attend Yale University after winning a dramatic reading contest, but the scars of the Vietnam conflict had left their mark—he never used the scholarship. Chisholm joined **Karamu Repertory Theatre** and received his first formal theatrical training there. Upon moving to New York, he found work in the theater, including the plays *Ice Bridge* and *Tracers*, produced at **Joseph Papp**'s NYSF/Public Theatre. Around 1990, Chisholm crossed paths with director **Lloyd Richards**, who accepted him as a student at the Yale School of Drama. Though the Wilson canon of plays flourished at that time, Richards felt Chisholm was "not ready" and held off casting him for two years. However, Wilson felt otherwise and importuned Richards to give Chisholm a chance. Chisholm was cast. Chisholm has parlayed that opportunity into acknowledgment as one of America's best character actors. He has appeared in movies and television, but his first love is the stage. Honors for Chisholm include an **Obie Award**, a **Drama Desk Award**, and a Laurence Olivier Award.

CINCINNATI BLACK THEATRE COMPANY (CBTC). Founded by Don Sherman in 2001, the CBTC mission is to keep alive the spirit of black theater by offering top-notch theatrical productions through powerful performances, exhibits, educational programs, and a nationally renowned talent competition for the *Showtime at the Apollo* tour. The CBTC has become a model institution for the preservation of African American art, history, and culture. The company offers a full season of dance, drama, poetry, visual art, and children's programs, reaching an estimated 20,000 people annually. The workshops (all styles, including rap) are free, such as theater arts classes, history of dance workshops, "Wonderful World of Writing" workshop, "Namibian Cultural Awareness," Children's Theatre Company, and special performances and events. For the 2005–6 season, the CBTC selected an appealing cross-section of plays, such as *Amen Corner*; *Black Nativity*; *Once on This Island*; *Before It Hits Home*; and *Purlie Victorious*, a tribute to its writer, **Ossie Davis**.

CIVIC THEATRE GUILD. This short-lived theater located at the Spring Street YMCA in Columbus, OH, was active between 1935 and 1937 under the auspices of African American playwright Ronald T. Hamilton. The guild's production season included Hamilton's social problem play *Crack of the Whip* (c. 1930), about a group of black vacuum-cleaner salesmen who were all fired from a white firm. The black head salesman forms his own company and lures customers away from his previous employer. The Columbus Drama Festival produced it (April 1935). *Sharecroppers* by **Randolph Edmonds** is a social protest play set in the Deep South. Black and white sharecroppers unite to fight against inequity. The Ogden Theatre produced it (May 1938).

CIVIL RIGHTS MOVEMENT. From the time blacks were first brought to America, they have always fought for civil rights. The most notable civil rights movement in the United States was a journey that lasted roughly 14 years (1954–68). Thousands of people were killed as the nation teetered on the brink of anarchy. That effort was instrumental in getting changes to laws governing interstate commerce, voting, employment, and housing and had the net effect of leveling the playing field for people of color. The civil rights movement also had a seismic effect on the artistic endeavors of black America—particularly black theater—which transformed from a previously marginalized entity into a robust, artistic arm of the civil rights movement, but more important, it became a viable entity within the American theatrical movement.

Instead of being an unwanted stepchild begging for acceptance from an American theatrical community from which it was excluded on racial grounds, African American theater became an entity unto itself. It gained momentum by coloring itself in terms of a black cultural aesthetic, with its own plays that reflected the culture of past and present black Americans and Africans. Black theater incorporated current and ongoing issues of the movement into plays and musicals that generated a sense of excitement and approbation from a newly developing audience. The civil rights movement offered a rallying cry for black America but especially theater artists, who used their skills to create, illuminate, and comment on the movement as it lurched from one crisis to another.

Lorraine Hansberry's groundbreaking Broadway production of *A Raisin in the Sun* is a prime example of how a playwright brought to the forefront one of the seminal concerns of the civil rights movement—the issue of equal opportunities in housing for blacks in search for the American dream. A mother buys a home for her family in an all-white suburb of Chicago, while her son objects. His aspirations are to buy a liquor store and become an entrepreneur. The subject matter for this theme is drawn from the author's own life experience. Hansberry's father was a litigant in a lawsuit against restrictive housing covenants in Chicago. The suit was decided in the affirmative for the elder Hansberry by the U.S. Supreme Court ruling that the restrictive housing covenants in Chicago were illegal.

In 1961, actor and playwright **Ossie Davis**, an icon of his time, used humor in addressing a civil rights issue in his biting satire *Purlie Victorious*. A stereotypical southern plantation owner who refuses to adjust to the changes brought about by the civil rights movement is frozen in time, while his more progressive son acquiesces and works with blacks toward a more equitable solution. The play enjoyed a successful Broadway run at both the Cort and Longacre Theatres. Ten years later, it was transformed into a successful musical.

Long before the civil rights movement began to take hold in the early 1950s, the legendary poet, author, and playwright **Langston Hughes** addressed civil rights issues of injustice in much of his writing. His 1938 song-play *Don't You Want to Be Free?* unfortunately met with indifference. In 1963, however, with the civil rights movement in full swing, Hughes used the resources of his own **Harlem Suitcase Theatre**, backed by endorsements from the National Association for the Advancement of Colored People, Congress of Racial Equality, and Student Nonviolent Coordinating Committee, to write and produce *Jericho: Jim Crow*, a song-play. It was a pastiche of poetry, speeches, gospel songs, and Negro spirituals telling the story of discrimination and segregation from a historical standpoint. The play opened on 12 January 1964 and was an instant success, running until the end of April. It subsequently became a staple of the movement, and excerpts from the play were performed frequently at civil rights fund raisers.

Other plays and musicals that focused on aspects of the civil rights movement include *Fly Blackbird* (1960), written by **James V. Hatch** (white) and **Clarence Bernard Jackson**. It was a musical inspired by the sit-ins in Greensboro, NC. *Blackbird* opened in Los Angeles before playing off Broadway, where it won an **Obie Award** for best musical of 1962. *Ballad of the Winter Soldiers* (1964) by **John Oliver Killens** and **Loften Mitchell** celebrates black freedom fighters throughout history. *Don't Bother Me, I Can't Cope* (1972) is a musical by Micki Grant and **Vinnette Carroll** about a group of African Americans struggling to exercise their civil rights. It opened in 1972 and played over 1,000 performances before closing in 1974. *Cope* won **Tony Awards** for best musical, best book, and best score. *Blues for Mr. Charlie* (1964) was dedicated by its author, **James Baldwin**, to the "dead children of Birmingham" after the 16th Street Baptist Church bombing that killed four girls in 1963. It is based loosely on the killing of Emmit Till, the young teenager who was slaughtered for allegedly whistling at a white woman. *Days of Thunder, Nights of Violence* (1971) by **Douglas Q. Barnett** explores many aspects of the civil rights movement. The highlight of the play centers on the 1969 trial of the "Chicago Seven," where Bobby Seale, chairman of the Black Panther Party, was ordered bound and gagged in the courtroom by Judge Julius Hoffman. The actual transcript was used as the basis for the scene that stopped the show every night. In 1963, Ann Flagg, director of the children's theater component at the famed **Karamu Repertory Theatre** in Cleveland, OH, wrote *Great Gittin' Up Mornin'* (taken from the old Negro spiritual) about a family preparing for their daughter's first day at a previously all-white school.

The initial thrust of the civil rights movement had always attempted to redress issues that treated black people as second-class citizens. As the movement evolved, however, it incorporated themes of black pride, black power, and the black aesthetic. In addition, the paperback revolution and the development of television led to a widespread dissemination of the history of blacks in America and Africa. The black theater that evolved from the civil rights movement was unique. It wanted and achieved a theater that was independent, expressed a black cultural aesthetic, and explored the deep African-centered history of black people in America. It was not interested in replicating Western theater traditions of such masters as Arthur Miller or Eugene O'Neill. In large part, the civil rights movement defined what black theater is today—a nationwide network of independent theaters that develop and present plays from the bottomless reservoir of the black experience.

CLARK, CHINA PENDARVIS. Playwright China Clark has functioned as screenwriter, director, filmmaker, professor, and installation artist during her career and is recognized as being one of the leading writers of this era. Clark was born in Pennsylvania. She holds two M.A. degrees, one in liberal arts and the other in English literature, and a Ph.D. in philosophy. She was a staff writer on *The Cosby Show* and taught playwriting at the **New Federal Theatre** and the **Frank Silvera Writer's Workshop**. She has taught playwriting, screenwriting, and philosophy at various institutions, both here and abroad, and currently teaches at the College of New Rochelle in New York.

Clark has written well over 30 plays, and they have been produced at **La MaMa Experimental Theatre Club**, African American Total Arts Theatre, New Federal Theatre, and Urban Arts Theatre and overseas in England, Germany, and Italy. She is a member of the Writer's Guild of America. A partial listing of her plays includes *Black and Blue Visions* (2000), about three men who meet in a bar during a snowstorm in New York City. One is Irish, one is English, and the other is African American. They form an emotional bond as they wait for the storm to end so they can contact the special women in their lives, but it turns out they are all waiting for the same woman. *Sugar Brown—Divine and May* (1997) is about Sugar and May, two diametrically opposite women who meet in a metaphorical prison find they have several things in common. *Bessie Smith Speaks* (1994) is a drama with music. *Neffie* (1975) is a mythical fantasy of the undying love of a woman for a man. *In Sorrow's Room* (1975) is a story of a young black woman in search of her identity as she is pulled between a domineering mother and men who see her only as a sexual object. *Perfection in Black* (1971) shows a conflict between a black woman and a black man. Other plays Clark wrote are *The Madwoman's Room, Why God Hates Reverend Chandler, The Chinese Screen,* and *The Sabian.* Clark has received such honors and awards as the Woolrich Foundation Award, Hannah del Vecchio Award, Goldberg Award, New York Council on the Arts fellowship, Puffin Award, and Martin Award.

CLASSICAL THEATRE OF HARLEM (CTH). A not-for-profit professional theater company in residence at the **Harlem** School of the Arts (HSA), the CTH is the only year-round theater company in the Harlem community that is performing a classic repertory. In 1998, Alfred Preisser and Christopher McElroen (both white) combined their life savings of less than $9,000 to set the groundwork for the HSA. Preisser became the director of the theater program and Christopher McElroen the marketing director. The impetus for the company grew out of the success of a Shakespeare workshop Preisser and McElroen taught at the HSA in fall 1998. They were successful in persuading the HSA to use the small, underutilized HSA theater building that was next door to the school. Back then, the school used the theater solely for eight student performances a year. With more than a dozen years of combined performing and producing experience behind them, they were thrilled about starting a professional theater company that would incubate in residence in the HSA, as had the Dance Theatre of Harlem and the **National Black Theatre** many years before. To date, the HSA has created over 700 temporary jobs, and nearly 40,000 people have come to see their productions.

Since being incorporated in February 1999, the CTH has been steadily breaking new theatrical ground in New York and has attracted large and unusually diverse audiences. Its plays have varied greatly in style and subject matter, from the ancient *Lysistrata* (October 1999) to the contemporary classic *Ain't Supposed to Die a Natural Death* (June 2006) to the avant-garde *Funnyhouse of a Negro* (February 2006). Not since the heyday of the 1970s has such interest, enthusiasm, and acclaim been accorded the theatrical productions in Harlem. Each season has brought larger audiences and wider acclaim. In just six years, the CTH has established a highly productive and accomplished theater company, winning five **Obie Awards**, generating more than 100 reviews, and receiving 543 **Audience Development Committee** nominations. In May 2004, the CTH received a special **Drama Desk Award** for artistic excellence for "creative and bracing staging of the world's great playwrights."

CLAY, BURIAL (1943–78). A playwright, Clay was born in Abilene, TX. He lived a short but productive life, leaving behind a vast body of work. He earned a B.A. and an M.A. from San Francisco State University. The author of over 35 plays, his writings appeared in several major publications, and he was also the publisher/editor for the *San Francisco Black Writers Literary Magazine*. The **Negro Ensemble Company** produced two of his plays, *Buy a Little Tenderness* in 1972 and *Liberty Call* in 1974. Some of Clay's other plays are *A Dance for Demons*, *The Gentle Rose Decays*, *No Left Turn*, *Jesebelle*, *The Creation of the World*, *Greasy Spoons*, *X's*, and *Rawhead and Bloody Bones*. Clay was a member of the California Writer's Workshop. In 1975, he received a Playwright's Award from the Eugene O'Neill Theatre Center and a playwright fellowship from the American Conservatory Theatre in San Francisco.

CLAY, CARL. Clay, a director, playwright, screenwriter, and actor, was born in **Harlem**. From the age of six, he was raised in southeast Queens. He attended Newtown High School, Pace University (B.A. in theater and education), and Brooklyn College Graduate School (theater directing). He also studied under the noted Broadway director Alan Schneider. Clay received his screenwriting and directing training at the International TV/Film Institute with Emmy

Award–winning director John Kotty (director of the *Autobiography of Miss Jane Pittman*) and **Academy Award**–winning screenwriter William Kelly (*Witness*, 1988). In addition, Clay studied at the Third World Training Institute and Columbia University's Institute for Not-for-Profit Management.

Clay has worked at CBS News as a TV desk assistant to newscaster Dan Rather, an intern for **Melvin Van Peebles**'s Whiz Group, and a participant in a World Cinema Training Program initiated by **Ossie Davis**. Clay also worked as an actor and producer assistant in such featured films as *Greased Lighting*, starring Richard Pryor and Pam Grier. His work on TV shows include *The Driver*, featuring **Ron O'Neal**; *Love Boat*; *Charlie's Angels*; *The Marilyn Monroe Story*, and *The Joe Louis Story*.

As CEO at the **Black Spectrum Theatre Company, Inc.** (BSTC), Clay wrote over 15 plays and directed 20 films about African American youths, trained over 1,000 actors, and produced over 150 plays and 20 jazz concerts with such artists as Roy Ayers, Roberta Flack, Stanley Turrentine, Freddie Hubbard, and Angela Bofil. The BSTC provided a training ground to help launch the careers of such actors as Lisa Carson (*Ally McBeal*) in her first feature film, Desiree Coleman (*Mamma I Want to Sing*), David Baptist (WB Network), and Byron Mims (***Fences*** on Broadway).

Among Clay's numerous awards and honors are an **Audience Development Committee Award** as producer of the year for *Deadwood Dick Legend of the West; or, Them Niggers Went That Away*, a satire by Warren B. Burdine. He won an American Society of Composers, Authors, and Publishers Music Lyricist Award for his songs in the film *Coffey* and first place at the annual Wornen's Media Award Competition as lyrist for the ABC TV special *Turkey Treasure*. Clay also received a National Library Association Award for his breakout film *Babies Making Babies*, as well as an International Film and TV Festival bronze medal for *The Follower and Clear Vision*, a film about male responsibility in teen pregnancy. In 2000 and 200l, his films *Urban Encounters: What to Do If You Get Stopped by the Police* and *Justice Done* were recipients of the National Black Programming PBS Awards for outstanding youth programs. He was inducted into the Los Angeles film union International Alliance of Theatrical Stage

Employees and Screen Actors Guild. Clay also received acknowledgment for outstanding professional achievement at Spectrum by local and national organizations.

CLEAGE, PEARL MICHELLE. Born in Springfield, MA, Cleage grew up in Detroit. She gained a reputation as a multitalented playwright, essayist, poet, and writer of fiction and essays. Cleage is the daughter of an elementary school teacher, Doris, and prominent author, clergyman, and founder of the Pan African Orthodox Christian Church Reverend Albert B. Cleage Jr. After an unsuccessful bid for the governorship in 1962 on the Freedom Ticket, he became a black nationalist, changing his name to Jaramogi Abebe Agyemen.

Cleage enrolled at Howard University in 1966, where she studied playwriting under **Owen Dodson, Ted Shine,** and **Paul Carter Harrison.** The institution produced two of her one-act plays. Within three years, she left Howard and married Michael Lomax, a politician. Relocating with her husband to Atlanta, she earned an A.B. in drama and playwriting from Spelman College in 1971 and pursued an M.A. in Afro-American studies at Atlanta University. Meanwhile, after 10 years of marriage, Cleage and Lomax divorced in 1979.

Cleage gained notice as a playwright in the 1980s with *Puppetplay* (1981), *Hospice* (1983), *Good News* (1984), and *Essentials* (1984). In 1992, however, it was *Flyin' West* that brought Cleage national recognition with her presentation of African Americans migrating at the turn of the century to an all-black town out West. It premiered at the Alliance Theatre Company in Atlanta under the direction of **Kenny Leon.** During the season of 1992–93, *Flyin'* was the most produced African American play at regional theaters throughout the country. Other plays that added to her renown as a playwright are *Blues for an Alabama Sky* and *Bourbon at the Border.* Cleage was playwright-in-residence at Spelman College, the editor of *Catalyst*, and artistic director of Just Us Theatre Company. Most recently, she wrote a bestselling novel entitled *What Looks Like Crazy on an Ordinary Day*, an Oprah Book Club selection. She also received grants from the National Endowment for the Arts, the City of Atlanta Bureau of Cultural Affairs, and the Georgia Council for the Arts. In addition to her playwriting, Cleage has contributed essays to such national magazines as

Essence, *New York Times Book Review*, *Ms.*, and *Black World*. In 1990 and 1991, she published collections of her essays entitled, respectively, *Mad at Miles* and *Deals with the Devil*.

Cleage was the winner of the Norman Felton Playwriting Award (1976), playwright-in-residence at the University of Michigan in its Guest Artist Program (1982), recipient of first prize for poetry from *Prornethean Literary Magazine* (1968), winner of the Atlanta mayor's fellowship in the arts (mid-1970s), and recipient of National Endowment for the Arts residency grants through Just Us Theatre Company (1980s) and Georgia Council for the Arts residence grants from the city of Atlanta (1980 and 1983).

CLORINDY, THE ORIGIN OF THE CAKEWALK (1898). Called a "Negro opera," *Clorindy, the Origin of the Cakewalk* was the first musical by Will Marion Cook (1869–1944) and Paul Laurence Dunbar. Cook wrote the original sketch, composed the music, and coauthored the lyrics with Dunbar. It is a love story set on a plantation in Louisiana during the 1840s that traces the origin of the cakewalk dance. It introduced ragtime music and the cakewalk to New York audiences. The Casino Roof Garden first produced *Clorindy* on Broadway during the summer of 1898. The cakewalk became a dance craze both in the United States and abroad. *Clorindy* is the first known black musical to depart from the negative minstrel tradition of the early 1900s and to depict a more positive portrayal of African American performers.

CLUB BARON. Located at 132nd Street and Lenox Avenue in **Harlem**, Club Baron housed theater productions during the early 1950s to showcase several important productions. The Committee for the Negro in the Arts (CNA) produced three plays of record: **Alice Childress**'s *Just a Little Simple* (September 1950) and *Gold through the Trees* (April 1952) and **William Branch**'s first play, *A Medal for Willie* (October 1951). *Simple* was an adaptation of **Langston Hughes**'s "Simple" stories; *Gold through the Trees* commented on the black struggle against apartheid in South Africa. *Medal* dramatically underscored the ironies of a black American soldier fighting and dying to secure freedoms for others abroad that he was unable himself to enjoy at home. The stellar cast for *Medal* included **Clarice Taylor** (as the mother), **Julian Mayfield**, Kenneth Mannigault, Helen Martin, and Eli Wallach. The club also hosted a Burlap Summer Theatre production of an evening of one-act plays in 1953, codirected by **Maxwell Glanville** and Ruth Jett.

CLUNIE, GLORIA BOND. A playwright and educator, Clunie is from Henderson, NC. She holds a B.S. in speech and an M.F.A. in theater from Northwestern University. She worked in the Evanston, IL, school district as a drama specialist. She was the founder/director of the Fleetwood Jourdain Theatre for eight years and helped to found the Playwrights Ensemble at the Victory Gardens Theatre in Chicago. Clunie was also an accomplished director, having directed shows at Chicago Theatre Company, Fleetwood Jourdain, and Northwestern University. In addition, she assumed the mantle of playwright. Her plays have been produced in Chicago and many other black theaters across the country.

Two of Clunie's most recognized dramatic works are *North Star* (1995), a play about a character's decision in 1960 to join the historic lunch counter sit-in movement in Greensboro, NC, and a black child's bond with her father, and *Shoes*, a story of events surrounding the 1965 **civil rights**–era bombing of an Alabama church that killed four black children. Other plays by Clunie include *Sweet Water Taste*; *Secrets*; *Sing, Malindy, Sing!*; *Dreams*; *Some Enchanted Evening*; *Basket of Wishes, Bucket of Dreams, A Children's Play*; and *Mirandy and Brother Wind*, adapted from a book of the same name by Patricia McKissac. Clunie is the recipient of several awards and honors, including an Illinois Arts Council fellowship, Ann Flagg Multicultural Award, National Endowment for the Arts education fellowship, Scott McPherson Award, and **Ted Ward** Playwriting Award.

COLE, BOB (ROBERT ALLEN COLE JR., 1868–1911). An Athens, GA, native who grew up in Atlanta, Cole was a multitalented director, actor, entertainer, playwright, songwriter, and producer of vaudevilles. Active at the turn of the 20th century, Cole broke new ground in the development of African American musical theater. His professional career began as a cabaret singer in Chicago, where he joined the cast of Sam T. Jack's *The Creole Show* in 1890, for which he was stage manager. There he met his future wife, dancer Stella Wiley, with whom he performed in several early shows until their divorce two years later. By the mid-1890s, Cole was in New York City, where he established the All-Star Stock Company. He assembled a residence company of a group of aspiring young black performers at Worth's Museum at 6th Avenue and 13th Street, the first professional stock company and training school for black performers (c. 1896).

A year later, Cole starred in and cowrote with Billy Johnson *A Trip to Coontown* (1897), a musical farce with additional music by Willis Accooe. It is the first known full-length musical comedy written, performed, directed, and produced by African Americans and one of the first to depart from the negative portrayal of blacks in minstrelsy. The plot centers on a naïve old black man who is saved at the last minute from being cheated out of his pension by a con man. In the cast was Cole, who introduced the character with whom he was to become identified—Willie Wayside—a tramp whom he played in whiteface. This landmark production showed producers and theater owners that there was an audience for all-black shows. *Coontown* opened on Broadway at the Third Avenue Theatre (4 April 1898) for eight performances. The show toured for two seasons before closing in 1891. During this time, Cole and Johnson also produced the Black Patti Troubadours, starring Sissieretta Jones, dubbed the "Black Patti," who was Cole's protégée. Cole wrote many of the skits, sketches, and full-length musical comedies for the troubadours. *Coontown* was one of the few African American shows to play successfully in the South.

At the turn of the century, Cole teamed with the Johnson brothers, James and J. Rosamond, from Jacksonville, FL, both writers and composers of musical comedies. The trio's most successful show was *The Shoo-Fly Regiment* (1906), for which they assembled a cast of 50. That same year, Cole and James Weldon Johnson opened another musical comedy, *The Red Moon* (1906), about Minnehaha, the daughter of an Indian chief who leaves her father to return to a government school for Indians and blacks to claim her child. The show starred Abbie Mitchell as Minnehaha and featured Aida Walker (Mrs. George Walker) who sang and performed "Wildfire." Cole did the book and lyrics, and Johnson provided the music. The show played in Philadelphia before moving into New York's Majestic Theatre for a short run. On 2 August 1911, Cole had a mental breakdown and died.

COLEMAN, RALF "MESHACK" (1898–1976). Coleman was born in Newark, NJ. He was an actor, stage manager, theatrical director, playwright, and a pioneer of the little theater movement in New England during the 1920s and 1930s. He studied theater at Harvard University under H. W. L. Dana; at Provincetown Wharf Theatre, MA; and at Boston Experimental Theatre. Coleman acted with and directed the Allied Arts Players, Boston (1927); the Boston Players (1930–33); and the Beacon Hill Little Theatre (1930s). He made his professional debut with the New York production of Paul Green's *Roll, Sweet Chariot* (1933–34), playing the romantic lead. In addition, he directed the Negro Unit of the Works Progress Administration **Federal Theatre** of Massachusetts (1935–39) and produced and directed plays for the United Service Organization circuit during World War II and for the National Association for the Advancement of Colored People and Negro College Fund in Boston. He was also the stage manager for *Anna Lucasta* on Broadway, in Chicago, and on tour, from 1945 to 1949. He was a member of Actors Equity Association, Negro Actors Guild, and the Saturday Evening Quill Club (a Boston writers' group). Among his more representative plays is *The Girl from Back Home* (known as *The Girl from Bam*, 1929), a one-act drama about a mistress of a **Harlem** racketeer who escapes from that lifestyle. *Paradox* (1930) is a one-act play produced at the Barn in Boston. *Swing Song* (1937) is a one-act protest melodrama set in the Deep South and centering on the pregnancy of a white woman by a black man who is being threatened by a lynch mob. The Federal Theatre of Boston produced it (c. 1938).

COLLIE, KELSEY E. Collie is a director, playwright, and teacher. He was educated at Hampton Institute (A.B. in English, speech, and drama, 1967), George Washington University (M.F.A. in dramatic arts, 1970), and Howard University (doctoral studies in communication arts, 1975). He taught English and drama at various colleges in Washington, DC, prior to joining the Department of Drama at Howard in 1975 as assistant professor and director of the Children's Theatre. He developed touring programs, conducted seminars and workshops, and served as resource person for numerous groups.

His theatrical experiences include TV appearances and presentations, as well as extensive acting, directing, and producing at Howard and in the DC area. Collie made his mark, however, as a playwright of children's musicals, including *Fiesta* (1969), a musical in one act. A young man's search for truth and happiness leads him to a South American village, where he saves the fiesta from becoming a fiasco when it is discovered that the ceremonial donkey has been stolen. It was written and presumably produced at George Washington University in Washington, DC, as his M.F.A. thesis (1970). *Celebration* (1973) is a children's play with songs. People of a West Indian nation vote out of office a selfish, egotistical prime minister for stealing money. The Howard University Drama Department produced it (1973). *Randy's Dandy Circus* (1974) is a musical about a young boy who inherits a circus. His envious aunt and uncle sabotage the opening by stealing all the animals, but the boy triumphs after all with the help of his friends. It was produced by Howard University Children's Theatre in Washington, DC (summer 1974), and presented on the "Young News" segment of WRC NBC-TV, Channel 4 (November 1974).

Other plays Collie wrote include *Black Images/Black Reflections* (1975), which is a historical-ritual theater piece that is a chronicle narrative of Afro-American experiences and contributions to the United States' development, depicted through song, movement, and dramatization. Howard University's Children's Theatre produced it and presented it on *Howard University Presents* over WRC NBC-TV, Channel 4 (May 1975). *Good Friday; or, The End and the Beginning* (1962) is a morality drama in one act. Ten people seeking shelter in a cave from an atomic holocaust attempt to come to grips with themselves and each other. *It Happens Every Summer* (1963) is a musical comedy in two acts. It deals with experiences shared by a group of young people who are working as summer camp counselors for a church youth program. *Where Is Love* (1963) is a children's drama in one act and a little girl who runs away from an orphanage in search of love. *The Gift: Sermon in Three Dramatic Sketches, Including a Litany* (1964) is a one-act play depicting how humans are often unmindful of the gift of love God has given each. *How to Succeed with a Little Bit of Luck* (1964) is a musical comedy in two acts about a young woman who visits her cousin in New York City and gets a big theatrical break, but she has some minor problems in the romance department. *Hell's Belles* (1965) is a musical comedy in two acts about an angel who is sent from heaven as an emissary and promptly falls in love with an attractive hellion. *Kids!* (1966) is a musical comedy in one act about girls who want to know what the boys are doing in their clubhouse, so they send in a spy. The parents want to know what both are up to. *Ash Wednesday* (1967), a one-act play, is a morality play based on Ash Wednesday scriptures. Several persons at a cocktail party are revealed to be jealous, petty, and lustful, as they share the bread and wine served by the host, who is a priest. *It's a Mad, Mad, Mad, Mad World We Live In* (1967) is a musical revue in one act. Topical issues, including politics, religion, and minority problems, are satirized in song and dance. *Maybe Some Day* (1968) is a domestic **black experience** drama with music in one act. It centers on a young woman's conflict with her mother's teachings and her desire to have a good time with her friend and neighbor, who is very hip and popular.

***THE COLOR PURPLE* (2005).** Based on Alice Walker's **Pulitzer Prize**-winning novel, Oprah Winfrey brought the musical version of *The Color Purple* to the Broadway Theatre (1 December 2005) in New York City, where it played for 910 performances. Gary Griffin directs it, with music by Brenda Russell, scenic design by John Lee Beatty, lighting design by Brian MacDevitt, sound design by Jon Weston, orchestrations by Jonathan Tunick, musical supervision by Kevin Stites, and musical direction by Linda Twine. Told through gospel, jazz, ragtime, and blues music, the show is about a black woman overcoming adversity through forgiveness and love while finding her place in the world.

The show was nominated for nine awards. Among them, La Chanze won the **Tony Award** for best actress in a musical for the role of Celie. Also nominated for Tony Awards were *The Color Purple* (best musical); Marsha Norman (book of a musical); Brenda Russell, Allee Willis, and Stephen Bray (score, music, and/or lyrics); Felicia P. Fields, (actress, featured role, musical); Victor Dixon (actor, featured role, musical); John Lee Beatty (scenic design, musical); Paul Tazwell (costume design, musical); and Donald Byrd (choreography). *Purple* also won a Grammy Award for music and lyrics. On 10

April 2007, the four-time Grammy Award nominee Fantasia Barrino joined *Purple*, replacing Jeannette Bayardelle as Celie and becoming the first *American Idol* winner to play a role on Broadway. A touring version of *Purple* opened at the Cadillac Palace Theatre in Chicago (17 April 2007).

COLOR STRATIFICATION. During the antebellum and postslavery (*see* SLAVERY THEME) era in the South, color stratification divided the African American community and disrupted family unity. Once white men began mixing with and impregnating black women against their will during slavery, they produced biracial offspring for whom, in most instances, they relinquished all responsibility for their care and upbringing. These children were considered black by the hegemonic culture and therefore were not only shunned by white society but were also forced to live within the black community, and even there, they were sometimes treated as outsiders. Occasionally, when a white father took some responsibility for the care of his children, they were afforded greater opportunities for upward mobility. Some passed as white; others integrated into the black community; and some became leaders in the black community. Among them, some set themselves apart as being of "superior blood." In both *Rachel* (1916) by **Angelina Weld Grimké** and *Big White Fog* (1935) by **Ted Ward**, a dark-skinned young black boy is castigated because of his color. The former is by a white schoolteacher and the latter by a biracial grandmother whose intraracism is based on self-hate. These two plays show how many black children are made to feel inferior and worthless and explain why some lack motivation and do not excel in the classroom.

Lorraine Hansberry's *Les Blancs* (1970) is set in a fictitious colonized African country and has to do with three brothers, Eric, Abiose, and Tshembe. Eric, whose black mother was raped by an army general, is the most visible because of his light complexion. He is not only emblematic of the rape of Africa that sets him apart from his darker-skinned brothers, but he also represents a new warrior spirit of the "modernized" African. In Dael Orlandersmith's full-length drama *Yellowman* (2002), she portrays the psychological effect social attitudes rooted in slavery have on a biracial light-complexioned young black man. *See also* ASSIMILATIONISM.

COLORED ACTORS' LEGION (CAL)/COLORED ACTORS' UNION (CAU). In 1920, the Actors Equity Association, a white union, listed only two black actors among its members, Leigh Whipper and Leon Williams. Two African American theatrical unions, the CAL and the CAU, were formed to protect the interest of black artists. The CAL, initiated in January 1921 in Cincinnati, OH, was short lived. Elected officers were Henry Drake (president), R. C. Pugsley (secretary), Lew Henry (recording secretary), T. S. Finley (treasurer), and Salem Tutt Whitney (arbitrator of disputes between management and actors).

In July of that year, the CAL merged with the CAU based in Washington, DC. Organized by S. H. Dudley, the CAU expanded upon the goals set by the CAL: to protect members against irresponsible persons and conditions in the industry and the undesirable practices on the Theatre Owners' Booking Association circuit; to give guidance to black performers; to see that acts were sufficiently varied; to guarantee timely contracts that could not be easily broken by managers and performers; to classify and improve the quality of acts; to help provide acts with new materials, new writers, and new songs; and to protect female performers against the unwanted sexual advances of unscrupulous managers. Original CAU officers in 1921 were President Henry Wooden (trick cyclist and tab manager), Secretary Boots Hope (monologist and comedian), and Treasurer S. H. Dudley. By September 1921, membership had topped 800, and the CAU had 27 stock companies and 500 vaudeville acts enrolled from which to draw talent. Three years later, membership fees were raised from $2 to $5 under the newly elected officials: Secretary Talfair Washington, Recording Secretary Joe Watts, Chief Deputy Bart Kennett, General Manager and Treasurer Dudley. In 1926, Kennett published the *Colored Actors' Union Theatrical Guide*, an official handbook that listed the officers and membership at that time. It contained addresses of agents in the United States and abroad, provided biographies of Dudley and other noted black performers, outlined a brief history of black theatricals in America, and presented endorsements and advertisements from many leading performers, as well as other information concerning the progress of blacks in America. Negro Actors Guild of America superseded the CAU in 1937.

THE COLORED MUSEUM **(1986)**. This comedy by **George C. Wolfe** is in 11 playlets. Since winning the **Crossroads Theatre** playwriting contest and staging its debut there on 26 March 1986 under Lee Richardson's direction, *Colored Museum* has become a staple in black theaters across the nation. Set in an African American museum, the play is a scathing satire on the likes, desires, traditions, and mores of the black community. The show begins with a slave crossing from Africa to America that takes place on an airplane over the Atlantic Ocean. Thereafter, the playwright lampoons various aspects of black culture, Afro wigs, black musicals, Josephine Baker, black matriarchy, colored people's time, food, and *Ebony* magazine, as well as other icons. That same year, a New York Shakespeare Festival/Public Theatre production won the 1986 Dramatists Guild Award.

COMMUNITY ACTORS THEATRE (CAT). A nonprofit organization, CAT was founded in 1986, in San Diego by Jennie Hamilton, owner, producer, director, writer, and actor. Housed in the former ironworkers union office on the corner of 54th and College Grove Drive, CAT may have been the only black-owned theater in the San Diego Oak Hill neighborhood. Most of the plays are written, produced, directed, and performed by local black actors. CAT is the recipient of many Aubrey Awards over the years (the San Diego community theater equivalent of the **Tony Award**), and the Top Judges Award for Hamilton in 2000. Local playwright Calvin Manson received a Best Direction of a Drama Award for *Passion and Honey*, a story about a poet and her childhood friends.

CONCEPT EAST THEATRE (CET). The CET was another black arts institution that emerged from the **civil rights movement** and thrived between 1961 and 1978. **Woodie King Jr.** and David Rambeau, who raised $100 each from 10 friends to renovate an old bar into a theater space, fathered it. Their friends included the playwright **Ron Milner** and Cliff Frazier, who would play instrumental roles in the life of King and of black theater in general. The bar, located at 401 East Adams Street, was renovated into a theater space with 75 seats and an art gallery in the lobby. The 10 investors did all the work, including building sets, lighting, box office, and administration.

Nine plays were produced in their first season, including the first play ever by Milner, titled *Life Agony* (1961). It would eventually turn into *Who's Got His Own*. During the first five years of operation, the theater produced over 35 plays and also published three issues of *Black Theatre Arts Magazine*. More important, it was surviving on earned income and not falling into the grant trap. In 1971, the theater moved into an abandoned high school at 60 East Harper Street and in 1972 merged with the Spirit of Shango Theatre that Milner had started. They enjoyed one of their greatest successes with a production of **Amiri Baraka**'s **(LeRoi Jones)** *Slave Ship* in 1973. It had a cast of 150 and enjoyed sell-out houses for four months. King, who had functioned as the managing director, left the company in 1964, touring in a production of Malcolm Boyd's play *A Study in Color*. The play was a big success in New York, and King decided to stay. He found a job in his profession and has not looked back since. He rose to a preeminent position in black theater through his work at the Mobilization for Youth, the Henry Street Playhouse, the **New Federal Theatre**, and his many Broadway productions. David Rambeau took over managing the theater after King left. The CET was destroyed by fire in 1974, but attempts to revive the theater under Von Washington along with an infusion of CETA money failed, and the company formally disbanded in 1978.

CONGO SQUARE THEATRE COMPANY (CSTC). Derrick Saunders and Reginald Nelson, cofounders of the CSTC, met while pursing their B.F.A. degrees in theater at Howard University in Washington, DC. Sanders went on to receive his M.F.A. from the University of Pittsburgh, and Nelson earned his M.F.A. from the University of Illinois at Urbana–Champaign. The CSTC, based in Union Park on the Near West Side of Chicago, is a non-Equity theater with a culturally diverse ensemble of actors. The title is a reference to the New Orleans marketplace where slaves of African descent congregated from the early 1800s to the Civil War to sell various products and to celebrate their existence through drumming and dancing. The city was also considered the birthplace of jazz and became known for jazz and blues.

The company debuted with a three-show inaugural season, the first two at **Chicago Dramatists**. **August Wilson**'s *The Piano Lesson* opened in the fall of 2000. Wilson attended and spoke to the audience after the show. **Cheryl L. West**'s AIDS-themed drama *Before It Hits Home* followed. *The Island* by Athol Fugard, John Kani, and Winston Ntshona concluded the season at the Chicago Cultural Center's Studio Theatre (CCCST). The CSTC also reprised *The Piano Lesson* at Theatre on the Lake. It opened the 2001–3 season at Chicago Dramatists with the premier of *All* by Geoffrey Ewing and Graydon Royce, a play about the life of a popular prizefighter. **Endesha Ida Holland's** *From the Mississippi Delta* followed. *Playboy of the West Indies*, set in Trinidad, was the last offering. The CSTC also showcased the troupe's women artists. By the sixth season (2006–7), CSTC audiences were applauding the three-show offering of *African Company Presents Richard III* by **Carlyle Brown** (directed by Aaron Todd Douglas, founding ensemble member), *Black Nativity* by **Langston Hughes**, and *Joe Turner's Come and Gone* by August Wilson (directed by Derrick Sanders, founding artistic director).

COOKE, ANNE M. (1907–87). Cooke was a theatrical troupe organizer and actress of the academic stage. A significant female director of African American academic theater, she founded and headed a successful drama program at several black universities. Known by her students as "Queen Anne," Cooke was an active theater practitioner from the **Harlem** Renaissance (1920s) through the volatile 1960s and 1970s. Born in Washington, DC, Cooke grew up in Gary, IN. She received her advanced education from Oberlin College (B.A., 1928), Yale University School of Drama (Ph.D. in theater, 1972), and the American Academy of Dramatic Arts, where she studied for one year. She taught at North Carolina A&T College and at Spelman College in Atlanta, GA, in 1927.

Cooke cowrote *Our Old Kentucky Home*, a drama of slave heroism during the Civil War. She also played the role of a Creole slave in the show. Other acting roles included the title character in *Clarisse* (1893) at Spelman College. The show was taken to Chicago. That same year, she traveled to the West Indies, Panama, and Costa Rica, giving a series of dramatic performances on a dual program with the contralto soloist Nonie Bailey Hardy. On her return to the United States, she became interested in Marcus Garvey's Universal Negro Improvement Association (UNIA), particularly his back-to-Africa movement, and joined the UNIA in 1917. By 1919, she was one of the top officers of the movement and began traveling on behalf of the organization to Jamaica and Liberia. In 1927–28, she staged the pageant *Ethiopia at the Bar of Justice* for the UNIA in Kingston, Jamaica, and other locations. She remained with Garvey's organization until about 1930. Cooke died in Washington, DC, at age 80.

CORTHRON, KARA LEE. Corthron is a 2006 graduate of the Lila Acheson Wallace Playwriting Program. Her most recent play, *Wild Black-Eyed Susans*, was produced at **Elizabeth Van Dyke**'s "Going to the River 2006," a celebration of African American female playwrights. The play was developed at Juilliard and received another major reading in July at the Circle East Repertory Theatre at the University of New York in New Paltz. Corthron is also a winner of the New Professional Theatre Writer's Award (2006) for her play *End Zone Zepher* and a finalist for the 2006 **Theodore Ward** Prize for African American playwrights.

CORTHRON, KIA. A playwright, Corthron was born in the small town of Cumberland, MD. She received a B.A. in communications from the University of Maryland and an M.F.A. in theater arts from Columbia University in 1992. Considered an attractive woman who speaks rapidly in a high-pitched voice, Corthron is admittedly a political writer who wants people to think. Her writings have explored such themes as cloning, police brutality, abandoned land mines, gang violence, and homelessness. She is prominent among the tidal wave of African American female writers who emerged as a dominant force in the 1990s and into the 21st century. Corthron's plays have been produced in the United States and around the world, and professional theaters have commissioned 9 of the 15 plays she wrote. The commissions have come from the Long Wharf Theatre, the Mark Taper Forum, Goodman Theatre, Second Stage, and the Royal Court Theatre in London, among others.

Among Corthron's plays are *Wake Up Lou Riser* (1992); *Cage Rhythm* (1993); *Come Down Burning* (1993); *Life by Asphyxiation* (1995); *Seeking the Genesis* (1996); *Splash Hatch on the E Going Down* (1997); *Digging Eleven* (1999); *Force Continuum* (2001); *Breath, Boom* (2001); *The Venus De Milo Is Armed* (2003); *Slide Glide the Slippery Slope* (2003); *Snapshot Silhouette* (2004); and *Light Raise the Roof* (2004). In a relatively short career, Corthron has earned significant honors, including the Kennedy Center Fund for New American Plays, Joe A. Callaway Playwriting Award, New Professional Theatre Playwriting Award, Manhattan Theatre Club Van Lier playwriting fellowship, National Endowment for the Arts/Theatre Communications Group residency, Daryl Roth Creative Spirit Award, and Mark Taper Forum's Fadiman Award.

COTTER, JOSEPH SEAMON, JR. (1895–1919). Cotter, a playwright, journalist, and poet, was born and reared in Louisville, KY. He was the son of Joseph Seamon Cotter Sr., a talented journalist, playwright, poet, teacher, and community developer. Carter Jr.'s education began with his older sister Florence Olivia, who taught him to read. He graduated from Central High School in 1911, where his father was the school principal and his teacher. His mother, Maria F. Cox, was also a teacher. Cotter attended Fisk University in Nashville, TN, for two years before being stricken with tuberculosis, a disease that claimed the lives of both his sister in 1914 and himself seven years later. During the last seven years of his life, Cotter completed a collection of one-act plays and poetry before his untimely death at age 24. *On the Fields of France* (1920) is a protest play in one short act. It is a story about two American army officers, one black, one white, both mortally wounded. As they lie dying hand in hand on a battlefield in northern France, they wonder why they could not have lived in peace and friendship in America. Cotter's plays *The White Folks' Nigger* and *Caroling Dusk* were never published.

COTTER, JOSEPH SEAMON, SR. (1861–1949). Cotter, the father of poet-playwright **Joseph Seamon Cotter Jr.**, distinguished himself as a playwright, poet, author, and educator. He was historically significant as an early African American playwright of record to be published. He was a Kentuckian born in Bardstown and reared in Louisville. His father, Michael J. Cotter, was of Scotch–Irish ancestry, and his mother, Martha Vaughn Cotteran, was an African American. Cotter married Maria F. Cox, a teacher, on 22 July 1891. They had three children: Leonidas died in 1900 before his adolescence, and tuberculosis claimed the lives of Florence Olivia (died 1914) and Joseph Seamon Cotter Jr. (died 1919).

Cotter was essentially a self-educated man who learned to read at age three. He worked as a manual laborer until he was 24 to help his poverty-stricken family, attended night school for 10 months, and emerged a teacher at Western Colored School (1893–1911). He also taught in several private and public schools in Kentucky (1885–93) and distinguished himself as founder and principal of Samuel Coleridge Taylor School (1911–42) in Louisville, KY. He was elected to the Louisville Board of Education in 1938 and instituted storytelling contests at the town's public libraries.

Cotter's most significant play, *Caleb, the Degenerate: A Study of the Types, Customs, and Needs of the American Negro* (1901), is a four-act thesis play. It gained him the distinction of being the second black American ever to have a play published, the first being **William Alexander Brown**, proprietor of the African Grove. *Caleb* dramatizes Booker T. Washington's educational philosophy of the "accommodations," as in industrial education over liberal arts education, as a means of achieving race progress. Caleb, the central character, is emblematic of the rebellious "bad" black man pitted against the "good" black man at an industrial school administered by the Bishop and Pious Olivia. The show was read publicly but never staged. Two other representative plays by Cotter were published around the turn of the century, *Caesar Driftwood* and *The Chastisement*. The former is a one-act comedy set the night before a wedding. There is a rumor that Caesar will disrupt the proceedings, however it is only a joke initiated by the bride. *Chastisement* is a one-act moralistic thesis play written in short staccato dialogue. In it, a miserly, stern, and hypocritical father's family teaches him a lesson. Cotter also wrote six volumes of poetry and a poem, "The Tragedy of Pete," a folk ballad. In addition, he utilized Italian sonnets and dialect verse as written by Paul Laurence Dunbar. Cotter died on 14 March 1949.

COUNTS, ANGELA M. A playwright, Counts was born and raised in Detroit. She earned her M.F.A. in theater from the University of Southern California. She is a working playwright in the theater world whose work has been rewarded by several awards of note. These include a **Lorraine Hansberry** Award for her 1994 play *Hedy Understands*

Anxiety, focusing on a woman searching for her grandmother as a key to the past. *Edge of Blue Light* is the story of a woman of color living with HIV/AIDS. Other plays she has written include *Sari Yams, Flower Child, Saxophone Me Baby, Seein' Eyed Dogs, To Thine Self*, and *Ocean Waves*. Counts has also been bestowed with a Van Lier playwriting fellowship.

COURTNEY, WARD. A Hartford, CT, playwright, Courtney was associated with the local **Charles Gilpin** Players (CGP) and later the Negro Unit of the **Federal Theatre Project** in Hartford. The CGP (not associated with the Gilpin Players of Cleveland, OH) had been an important part of Hartford cultural life for more than 15 years and was reorganized as a Negro Unit of the Works Progress Administration Federal Theatre Project. Ward is the author of two plays produced and published by the Hartford Negro Unit of the circa 1939. *Stars and Bars*, a full-length drama, appeared in the *Living Newspaper* and addresses abuses in housing, medicine, employment, and inequities of public facilities in Ward's home town of Hartford. *Trilogy in Black*, a full-length modern drama, incorporates themes from Greek tragedies to examine issues by African Americans after World War I.

CRESCENT THEATRE (CT)/CRESCENT PLAYERS (CP). Built in 1909, the Crescent Theatre located on West 135th Street may be **Harlem**'s first theater. Martinson and Nibur, two white liquor dealers, initiated the idea of catering to the new black trade coming into the Harlem community. Under these two owners, the CT became a Mecca of entertainment for the affluent class of African Americans who were gradually replacing the whites then moving to other communities in New York City. Comedian Eddie Hunter became the moving force behind the CT. The owners had approached him during the CT's first year of operation to present his comedy act *Goin' to the Races*. This was the first known black show to use the stage and screen simultaneously to create the effect of talking pictures. Hunter subsequently wrote and produced several shows at the CT, including *The Battle of Who Run*, *Why Husbands Leave Home*, and *Broadway Sal*. During the next few years prior to World War I, a variety of other programs were presented. Among the members of the company were

Edmona Addison (a singer) and the team of Hodges and Lauchmere (former vaudeville artists). The CT premiered H. Lawrence Freeman's grand opera *The Tryst* and began attracting talent from other competitors. Because of the popularity of shows at the CT, the nearby Lincoln Theatre was forced to emphasize a vaudeville and motion picture policy to lure customers back to the Lincoln.

The CP also got its start at the CT. The Muse and Pugh Stock Company founded by Clarence and Ophelia Muse and Willard Pugh moved their group from the Franklin Theatre in Harlem to the CT. They changed their name to the CP, presented a repertoire of plays, and resided there for one year (1914–15). The group moved to the Lincoln Theatre to form the Lincoln Players (after the **Anita Bush Players**). Unable to compete, the CT was soon forced to close its doors shortly thereafter. The CP apparently produced several plays, including *Another Man's Wife*, featuring Clarence Muse as a comic philanderer and his wife as stereotypical "poor little orphan girl." After one season, the group moved to the Lincoln Theatre, where it was absorbed into the Lincoln Players.

CROSSROADS THEATRE COMPANY. In 1978, two Rutgers graduates, Ricardo Khan and L. Kenneth Richardson, shared a dream of establishing a professional black theater in New Brunswick, NJ. They succeeded beyond their wildest dreams with the founding of Crossroads Theatre Company. Their mission was to provide opportunities for black theater artists and to present positive images of black life and culture. They converted the second floor of an old sewing factory into a 132-seat theater and with the aid of the Comprehensive Employment Training Act and Ford Foundation money mounted their first production, **Leslie Lee**'s *First Breeze of Summer*. Initially, the audiences were small, but they grew over time. They specialized in new works, developing a program called "New Play Writes" and attracting such new names as Dominic Martin, Emily Mann, and others. Crossroads was in the forefront in regard to gender equity. They hired Sydne Mahone as director of play development, resulting in over 20 productions by women playwrights. Taking advantage of $20,000 from CBS and Dramatists Guild, a nationwide contest led to their pick of **George C. Wolfe**'s *The Colored Museum* for production. It became a huge hit and was picked up by **Joseph Papp**, who produced it at the NYSF/Public Theatre. Within 10 years, Crossroads had a budget of $1.25 million. Along the way in 1988, the board for "personal issues and health" dismissed cofounder L. Kenneth Richardson.

In 1990, with a budget of $2.8 million, the company moved into a new 264-seat theater located in the New Brunswick Cultural Center. Essentially, they were tenants, and it cost them from $80,000 to $90,000 per year in rental costs. Also in 1990, Crossroads became a member of the League of Resident Theatres, thus joining 265 other theaters with regional equity status. Again, costs went up exponentially. The move coincided with a 50 percent cut in State Arts Council funding. They embarked upon a massive fund-raising effort that was not entirely successful. It did, however, enjoy a tremendous success that year with its production of *It Ain't Nothing but the Blues*, which became a national staple. Nonetheless, the company plunged on and in 1991 gained national attention by mounting Leslie Lee's *Black Eagles*, a play about the Tuskegee airmen of World War II. President George H. W. Bush, Chairman of the Joint Chiefs of Staff General Colin Powell, and **civil rights** icon Rosa Parks all hailed the production.

Between 1992 and 1999, the company went through four managing directors. The company struggled on, and on its 20th anniversary in 1998, it mounted a world-class production of **August Wilson**'s *Jitney*. In the spring of 1999, Crossroads was awarded the **Tony Award** for a continuous level of artistic achievement contributing to the theater nationally. It was a tremendous recognition of all that Crossroads had achieved. Then, inexplicably, Artistic Director Ricardo Khan left the theater for his native Trinidad, stating he needed "rest and renewal." The dam broke, however, in September 2000. It was announced that Crossroads was some $1.7 million in debt. The New Brunswick Cultural Center canceled their lease, and Crossroads cancelled the season. The theater was dark during the 2000 and 2001 seasons. Efforts continued behind the scenes to revive the theater, led by new board chairman Rheinhold Ponder, but an agreement with debtors and financial agencies fell apart, and Ponder resigned.

Since then, Khan returned and resumed his former post, albeit with a revised mission for Crossroads as follows: to explore beyond traditional black theater and to connect the dots between all people—European,

Hispanic, and Asian peoples—who identify with the African American diaspora. His goal was to make the **black experience** more exciting onstage without being viewed as a victim because he says it gets stale artistically. The theater worked out a debt-reduction plan, reducing its deficit down to four figures. The board was revitalized, and many of its former subscribers returned. It opened the 2005–6 season with New Jersey native Savion Glover's *Tap Legends* and followed with *Cookin' at the Cookery*, a new play about blues legend Alberta Hunter by Marion J. Caffey. With a new board, a financial restructuring, and a new mission, Crossroads intends to regain the swagger and verve it once had. But to do that, critics feel the company must avoid the temptation of submerging itself in "soft money."

CULLEN, COUNTEE PORTER (1903–46). A playwright, novelist, and author of children's books, Cullen was also a leading African American poet and one of the outstanding figures of the **Harlem** Renaissance. Cullen's birthplace has been listed variously as Louisville, KY; Baltimore, MD; and New York City. Records, however, show he was adopted by the Reverend Frederick Cullen, pastor of Salem Methodist Church in New York City. He was educated at DeWitt Clinton High School in New York, New York University (A.B., 1925, Phi Beta Kappa), and Harvard University (A.M., 1926). In 1928, he married Yolande DuBois, daughter of **W. E. B. DuBois**, but the marriage dissolved a year later. He remarried 14 years later to Ida Mae Robinson. That same year, he went to Paris on a two-year Guggenheim fellowship for study and creative writing. There he wrote *The Black* (1929). When he returned, he began teaching in the public schools of Harlem, where he remained until his death in 1946. The next year, Harold Jackman established the Countee Cullen Memorial Collection at Atlanta University (now Clark Atlanta University).

Cullen's literary efforts took various forms. Among his dramas and adaptations, his best-known play is *St. Louis Woman* (1933), a three-act musical with book by Cullen and **Arna Bontemps**. Set in the 1890s, it is adapted from Bontemps's novel *God Sends Sunday* (1931). Lil Augie, an internationally known horse jockey, involved in a lover's tryst, begins losing races after the woman's boyfriend is found dead. The Gilpin Players produced it first at the **Karamu Repertory Theatre** in Kentucky (1933) and then in Cleveland, OH, for five performances (November 1933). It premiered on Broadway at the Martin Beck Theatre (March–July 1946) for 115 performances. Harold Arlen did the music and Johnny Mercer the lyrics. The cast featured Ruby Hill in the lead role with Pearl Bailey—her Broadway debut.

Among Cullen's other dramatic renderings are *The Medea* (original title: *By-Word for Evil*, 1935), a two-act play with a prologue and epilogue. It is a modern adaptation of the tragedy of Euripides, written originally for the popular Broadway veteran actress **Rose Mc-Clendon**. It was scheduled to open at Hedgerow Theatre in Moylan–Rose Valley, PA, but was canceled after McClendon's untimely death. Under its original title, the show, directed by **Owen Dodson**, premiered at Atlanta University (March 1940). *Medea in Africa*, an adaptation by Dodson, was produced by the Fisk University Stagecrafters in Nashville, TN (1944–45). The Howard Players mounted it at the Howard University Drama Department in Washington, DC (April–May 1963). From there, it was taken on tour to a number of colleges in New England, including Dartmouth, the University of New Hampshire, Bowdoin, Middlebury, and Williams. Dodson also directed these versions of the show. *One Way to Heaven* (1936) is a full-length dramatic adaptation based on Cullen's novel by the same title. The importance of a black church in Harlem is exemplified through the relationship of a devout woman and her atheist husband. Directed by Jasper Deeter, it was produced by the Hedgerow Theatre in Moylan–Rose Valley, PA (September 1936) and subsequently by the American Negro Theatre at the 135th Street Library Theatre in Harlem (November 1943) for 37 performances, at the Harlem YMCA, and at the Hempstead, NY, United Service Organization.

The Conjur Man Dies (1936), a three-act farcical mystery adapted by Cullen and Bontemps, was considered the most popular **Federal Theatre** play among Harlem audiences. More than 20,000 theatergoers saw the dramatization of Rudolph Fisher's novel *The Conjur Man Dies: A Mystery Tale of Dark Harlem*. Superstition, voodoo, sorcery, and Harlem come into play when a conjure man is murdered. **Arena Playhouse** first produced it two years after Fisher's death as part of the Negro Unit of the Federal Theatre Project at the **Lafayette Theatre**, New York (March–April 1936), for 24 performances. J. Augustus Smith and Joe Losey directed it, with music performed by the

Works Progress Association (WPA) Orchestra under Joe Jordan's direction. It went on tour with a traveling unit of the WPA players as part of the New York City Recreation Department's Outdoor Recreation Program. The Cleveland Federal Theatre opened it first (1936), and later, the Gilpin Players presented it at the **Karamu Repertory Theatre** (February 1938). *The Third Fourth of July* (1946) is a one-act symbolic drama Cullen coauthored with Owen Dodson. Black and white families are brought together during World War II after the death of a son. It is intertwined with movement, poetry, and music. The Drama Division of the New School for Social Research, New York, commissioned the show.

Cullen might be best known for his poetry. While a student at New York University, he began writing poetry. As a sophomore, he placed second in the national Witter Banner Poetry Contest for "The Ballad of the Brown Girl" (1922). In 1925, he won the Witter Banner Award and also published his first volume of poetry, *Color*, which established his reputation as a poet. He also won the Harmon Foundation's gold medal for literature in 1927, and in the same year, he published his second and third poetry volumes, *Copper Sun* and *The Ballad of the Brown Girl*, and edited an anthology of black American poetry, *Caroling Dusk*.

CULTURAL ODYSSEY. Idris Ackamoor founded Cultural Odyssey in 1997 in San Francisco and assumed the position of executive director. Rhodessa Jones joined the company four years later as coartistic director. Together they developed over a dozen original productions that demonstrate their vision of arts and social activism. Since its inception, artists of all cultures have committed the two to the creation of original work. They have undertaken a series of innovative collaborations with nationally renowned artists, such as dancer/choreographer Bill T. Jones, jazz percussionist Don Moye of the Art Ensemble of Chicago, and pianist Cecil Taylor. Odyssey is one of the bay area's leading touring ensembles that regularly travels throughout the United States, as well as Japan, the Caribbean, and Europe. The company has developed deep artistic roots and community support in San Francisco by showcasing productions, presenting local and national acts for bay area audiences, and creating innovative arts training programs for the community. Odyssey is dedicated to interacting with its community to develop performances and services that have transforming effects. In 1989, Jones set up a residence at the San Francisco County Jail that resulted in the Medea Project: Theatre for Incarcerated Women, a visionary model for using art to transform a population in need. This is one example of an art-based project that helped to reduce the numbers of women returning to jail.

CUNEY-HARE, MAUD (1874–1936). Born in Galveston, TX, Cuney-Hare was married to William P. Hare. She was a pioneer playwright of the 1920s and leading figure in the Negro little theater movement in Boston. Cuney-Hare was associated prominently with the Allied Arts Theatre Group as an author, pianist, lecturer, musicologist, and composer. She received her education from Howard University and the New England Conservatory of Music. After graduation, she established the Musical Art Studio in Boston and gave concert piano recitals in the New England area. Later, she became the director of music at the Deaf, Dumb and Blind Institute of Texas, a position she also held at Prairie View State College.

The work that distinguished Cuney-Hare as a playwright is *Antar of Araby* (1926). It is a historical romance in poetic prose, with an overture and incidental music and a prologue in four short acts. The overture is by Clarence Cameron White and the incidental music by Montague Ring, a pseudonym for Amanda Ira Aldridge, daughter of **Ira Aldridge**. *Antar* is adapted from Cuney-Hare's article "Antar, Negro Poet of Arabia." It follows the legendary exploits of Antar Bin Shaddad, a celebrated black Arabian poet and storyteller. The story centers on this warrior of humble origins who has to find a way to win the hand of his beloved Abla, an Arabian maiden of noble heritage. Allied Arts Center produced it in Boston first in 1926 and again in 1928.

Cuney-Hare was also recognized as an author of poetry, nonfiction, and scholarly books on black music history. Among her books are *Norris Wright Cuney: A Tribune of the Black People* (biography, 1913), *The Message of the Trees: An Anthology of Leaves and Branches* (poetry, 1918), *Six Creole Folk Songs: With Original Creole and Translated English Text* (1921), and *Negro Musicians and Their Music* (1936), a classic in its field. In addition, she edited a music column in *Crisis* for many years.

– D –

DALLAS, WALTER. A director, producer, and playwright, Dallas is a veteran theater practitioner who has worked at most major theaters in the country, including the Lincoln Center Theatre, NYSF/Public Theatre, **New Federal Theatre**, **Negro Ensemble Company**, **Plowshares Theatre Company**, and Long Wharf Theatre, to name a few. He has directed over 25 world premieres and been an integral figure in developing emerging playwrights with his work at the Eugene O'Neill Playwrights Center, New Dramatists, Sundance, and Philadelphia Young Playwrights Festival and overseas in Africa, France, Russia, and England. Dallas was born in Atlanta, GA, in 1946. He earned a B.A. at Morehouse College and an M.F.A. from the Yale School of Drama and also studied music and theology at Harvard. He has taught theater at Antioch College and the University of California at Berkeley and created the School of Theatre for Philadelphia's University for the Arts in 1982, an institution he ran for over 10 years. He resigned from that position in 1993 to become the artistic director of the Philadelphia **Freedom Theatre**. Dallas resigned as artistic director in June of 2008. During a busy career, Dallas also found time to write plays. His most representative play is *Lazarus, Unstoned* (2002), a religious pageant play depicting the death and resurrection of Lazarus, the close friend of Jesus. He also wrote *Manchild* (1973) and *Willie Lobo* (1973). Among the awards and honors Dallas has received are the National Endowment for the Arts director fellowship (Center Stage), Bronze Jubilee Award, and **Audience Development Committee Award**.

DASHIKI PROJECT THEATRE (DPT). **Ted Gilliam**, an assistant professor in the Theatre Department at Dillard University in New Orleans, was the driving force behind the DPT. Gilliam arrived at Dillard in 1962 with a degree from the Yale School of Drama. The **civil rights movement** was at its zenith and had spawned the black arts movement. As black theater companies spread throughout the country, the only known black theater in the South was the innovative **Free Southern Theatre** in Jackson, MS, started by **Gilbert Moses**, Doris Derby, and **John O'Neal**.

Gilliam soon found himself in charge of an on-campus theater group, the Players Guild. At a cast party, one of Gilliam's students lamented he would not have a career in acting when he graduated. That was all the encouragement Gilliam needed. In 1968, he founded the DPT to establish a high-quality black aesthetic and to provide an outlet for young black people in the theater. They were an inclusive theater, not subscribing to the more militant ethos of **Amiri Baraka (LeRoi Jones)** and **Larry Neal**, who espoused a separate but equal theater for black folks only. The name of the company, *Dashiki*, represents freedom, and *Project* was a reference to the company's first location, Saint Francis de Sales Church, an old Catholic church in a rundown black section of New Orleans surrounded by projects. The DPT had a small proscenium stage with 150 folding chairs. Gilliam assumed the position of artistic director, while **N. R. Davidson** wrote most of the early shows, and Guy West Jr. became managing director. Their earliest success was Davidson's *El Hajj Malik*, a mélange of poetry, slides, dancing, and music that told the story of the mercurial Malcolm X. Touring throughout the country, *El Hajj* became the DPT's signature piece. Gilliam was also a playwright, and the DPT produced several of his plays, including *Mahalia, Praise Song!, The Pride of Lions*, and *What You Say? Or How Christopher Columbus Discovered Ray Charles*.

Over the years, the DPT produced an eclectic mix of theater and black plays, with such hits as *Inacent Black* by **A. Marcus Hemphill**, *Dream on Monkey Mountain* by **Derek Walcott**, *Eden* by **Steve Carter**, *Phaedra* by Racine, *The Blacks* by Jean Genet, and an all-black production of *A Streetcar Named Desire* by Tennessee Williams. Although their actors and personnel were all black originally, the company eventually changed its policy so people of all races were able to work freely in the theater at every level of participation.

A significant development occurred in 1973, when the DPT developed the Ethiopian Youth Workshop, a training academy where young people gained experience in all aspects of the theater. Another highlight was when the DPT was invited to perform for the Black Playwright Project at the John F. Kennedy Center for the Performing Arts in 1979. That same year, they also mounted a production at the Black Theatre Festival at Lincoln Center, *The Amen Corner* by **James Baldwin**, and *The Duplex* by **Ed Bullins**.

Box office receipts sustained the DPT financially in the early years, and over time, they built audience support and received grants from various sources. Nevertheless, they were never able to build or sustain an endowment and very seldom ran in the black. Over the 20-plus years of their existence, the DPT moved five times. Finally, their luck ran out. In 1990, the DPT filed for chapter 7 bankruptcy. In a last ditch effort to save the theater, Gilliam mounted a production of **August Wilson**'s *Joe Turner's Come and Gone* in 1991. However, Gilliam became ill, and the assistant director, Carol Sutton, took over his directing duties. The money raised was not enough, and Gilliam died shortly thereafter.

DAVID, JAMAL. *See* POLE, CHARLES (JAMAL DAVID).

DAVIDSON, NORBERT R., JR. A playwright and magazine editor, Davidson was born in New Orleans. He received degrees from Dillard University (A.B.) and Stanford University (M.F.A.). During the 1960s, he was playwright-in-residence with the **Dashiki Project Theatre (DPT)** in New Orleans and one of the editors of *The Black Collegian* magazine. Among his representative plays are *El Hajj Malik: The Dramatic Life and Death of Malcolm X* (1967), a ritual drama in two acts that evolved from improvisations by M.F.A. students at Stanford based on Malcolm X's biography. It was first produced for 40 performances by the **Afro-American Studio** off Broadway under the direction of Ernie McClintock at the Martinique Theatre (November 1971). *The Further Emasculation Of* (1970) is a comedy in one act about a mental patient who comes to grips with the cause of his mental breakdown—his family. The DPT produced it in July 1970. *Window* (1970) is a psychological drama in three acts about two gay black college professors who are on the verge of a mental breakdown. *Jammer* (1970), a comedy in one act, is a stud metaphor of American racism.

DAVIDSON, WILLIAM F. Davidson, a playwright, has one play of note, *Learn, Baby, Learn* (1969), a full-length comedy. Set in a large high school, it concerns two couples with divergent ambitions who find consolation in each other. Among Davidson's honors and awards are the Emmy Award for his role in *Teacher, Teacher* (1969, Hallmark

Hall of Fame), Frederick Douglass Award by the Urban League of New York (1970), Actor's Equity Association **Paul Robeson** Citation (1975), and induction into the Black Filmmakers Hall of Fame (1974). He also received honorary doctorates from Howard University, the University of Massachusetts, Wilberforce University, and Virginia State University.

DAVIS, A. I. Playwright and short-story writer, Davis was born in **Harlem**. He wrote short stories and a radio script at the University of Wisconsin and amassed a number of plays, including *Better Make Do* (1971), a domestic drama in one act about less fortunate individuals who rebel against those of privilege. *Sometimes a Switchblade Helps* (1969) is a drama in one act about a black man who works for a large corporation and must decide whether to play the game with the establishment or to report his white manager for sexual harassment of a black woman. *Gallivantin' Husband* (1973) is a drama in two acts about a Harlem husband who abandons his wife and child for another woman. *Sporting Times* (1973) is a comedy in one act about a black Harlem pimp who recites rhymes for his prostitute. *Nightmare* (1970) is a fantasy in one act; in a dream, a black man learns a lesson about the **black experience**. *Love Songs* (1972) is a short skit for street theater about a man singing a love song to a woman who has been disheartened by love and challenges the lyrics in the love song. *More Power to the Grape* (1974) is a domestic comedy in one act that depicts a black New Yorker who changes his "slave" name to an African one as a source of identity and creates tension in his relationship with his wife. *Black Rage in Suburbia* (1974) is a drama in three acts about a black maid who talks two Harlem hoodlums out of robbing the home of a white family where she works. *Precious* (1975) is a drama in one act dealing with a black father trying to raise two daughters in a ghetto. Davis was the recipient of a grant from the New York Council on the Arts in 1972.

DAVIS, CHERYL L. Davis is an aspiring playwright by night and a practicing attorney in New York City by day. After receiving an A.B. from Princeton, she enrolled at Columbia University, graduating with a journalism degree in 1986 and a law degree in 1987. She also took classes in musical theater and playwriting. As a playwright, nine of her plays and musicals have been produced. She has also been commissioned by three separate theaters to write plays for them. Among theaters performing her works are Manhattan Theatre, Circle in the Square Lab, Cleveland Playhouse, Actors Theatre of Louisville, Playful Repertory Theatre, and the Kennedy Center. Among the plays she has written are *Carefully Taught*; *The Bones of Giants*; *Equal Justice*; *The Real Ma Rainey*; *Dementia Americana Phyllis: A Slave to Poetry*; *In Review*; *The Virgin*; *Oscar Michaeux*; *Barnstormer, A Musical*; and *Sugar Dumplings* (a musical). Her *Oscar Michaeux* played at the prestigious Edinburgh Festival in 2004, and in 2005, she shared the distinguished Edward L. Kleban Award as most promising librettist with fellow writer Ken Stone for *Barnstormer*. The musical also won a Jonathan Larson Award.

DAVIS, CLINTON TURNER. Davis is a director, actor, dramaturge, and educator. For over 30 years, he has been involved in every aspect of the theater, from acting to managing and producing. Today he stands at the apex of his career as one of the finest directors of his generation. He is perhaps best known as the founder of the Non-Traditional Casting Project, an organization devoted to the eradication of racism in American theater. Davis graduated magna cum laude with a B.F.A. in theater from Howard University and attended graduate school at City College of New York before finding work with the **Negro Ensemble Company** (**NEC**) in the late 1960s. He was hired as an assistant stage manager, but over the next decade, his rise was meteoric as he successfully assumed the mantle of stage manager, casting director, literary manager, and director of plays during his tenure with the NEC.

In 1982, Davis made his directorial debut at the NEC with **Paul Carter Harrison**'s *Abercrombie Apocalypse*. He left the NEC after 14 years and embarked on a three-pronged career as an arts advocate, educator, and director that now finds him at the peak of his profession. He has directed plays at the GeVa Theatre, **Arena Playhouse**, Oregon Shakespeare Festival, Cincinnati Playhouse, Trinity Repertory, American Place Theatre, and other regional theaters and over 10 **August Wilson** productions. Davis has guest-lectured at such institutions of higher learning as Yale University, Dartmouth College, Columbia University, University of California at Berkeley, the Ohio

State University, Colorado College, and Howard University and has directed productions at Juilliard, Brandeis, and Colorado College, among others. While working at Actors Equity, he cofounded the Non-Traditional Casting Project, an ongoing entity. He is the associate artistic director and producer at the **New Federal Theatre** and an adjunct associate professor in the Drama and Dance Department at Colorado College. Honors for Davis include the Pew/Theatre Communications Group national theater artist residency grant, Howard University Distinguished Alumni Award, Dallas Theatre Critics Award, Bay Area Critics Award, Dramalogue Critics Award, and **Audience Development Committee Award**.

DAVIS, EISA. Davis, a playwright, actor, and vocalist, tries to incorporate in her work the concept of Sankofa, a return to the past to understand what happened there and move on in the future. She was named after her aunt, the famed revolutionary of the 1960s Angela Davis, but she prefers the name Eisa. She was born in Berkeley, CA, and earned a B.A. from Harvard University and an M.F.A. degree from the Actors Studio Drama School in New York. Davis is a multitalented artist who has acted in regional theater, film, and television. She is also an aspiring playwright who has received development support from such institutions as Cherry Lane, Seattle Repertory, Soho Repertory, Yale University, and the Schomburg Center for Black Research. She has performed as a vocalist at Joe's Pub, the Jazz Gallery, and the Showtime series *Soul Food*. Of the six plays she has written thus far, only one, *Bulrusher*, has received a professional production. It premiered at Urban Stages Theatre in March 2006. The other plays she has written are *Angela's Mix Tape*, *Paper Amor*, *Umkovu*, *Six Minutes*, and *Hip Hop Anansi* (a musical). Davis has accrued honors and awards that include the Cave Canem fellowship, Van Lier fellowship, McDowell Colony fellowship, Helen Merrill Award for Emerging Playwright, Mellon Foundation Award, and John Lipman New Frontier Award.

DAVIS, OSSIE (1917–2005). A veteran actor, playwright, and film director, Davis grew up in Waycross, GA. He attended Howard University for three years before leaving to pursue an acting career in New York City with the **Rose McClendon** Players (1941–42).

Within a year, he was inducted into the military (1942). While stationed in Liberia in the medical corps and special services, he wrote several musicals. Upon his return to civil service, he landed a role on Broadway in *Jeb*, which launched his professional career, and it was in this play that he met **Ruby Dee**, his future wife and lifetime mate of over 50 years. They became legendary for their involvement in theater and **civil rights** and for their contribution to the American stage, television, and film industry. In black theater circles, they are known affectionately as the "first couple of black theater." They worked together as actors onstage, screen, and television (often appearing in the same shows); hosted television shows; starred in Broadway plays; and had fulfilling film careers. For five years, they had their own radio series, *Ossie Davis and Ruby Dee Hour*.

Davis was also playwright and director. His best-known play was *Purlie Victorious* (1961), a satire on black and white stereotypes in the South. Among the other plays Davis wrote are *Alice in Wonder* (1952), a drama in one act. Set in the 1950s during McCarthyism, an African American television actor is asked to testify before a congressional committee. A year later, *Alice* was expanded into a three-act version entitled *The Big Deal. Curtain Call, Mr. Aldridge Sir* (1963) is a dramatic reading in one act highlighting the life and career of **Ira Aldridge**, the eminent black Shakespearean actor of the early 19th century. The University of California at Santa Barbara produced it with Davis and Dee in the cast (summer 1968). *Escape to Freedom* (1978) is a full-length historical play for children about Frederick Douglass, the famous abolitionist and orator. It opened at Town Hall in New York City (March 1976). *Langston: A Play* (1982) is a full-length biographical drama about playwright/poet/short-story writer **Langston Hughes**. *Bingo* (1985) is a full-length musical based on William Brashler's book *Bingo Long's Traveling All Stars and Motor Kings* (made into a film in 1976), about the rise and fall of a black baseball team of the 1930s. Davis directed an AMAS (Latin for "You Love." Repertory Theatre production in New York City (October 1985) that was also presented at the **Audience Development Committee** Black Theatre Festival (October 1986). *Montgomery Footprints* (1956) is a one-act drama about the Rosa Parks incident that spearheaded the bus boycott in Montgomery, AL, led by Dr. Martin Luther King.

DAVIS, THULANI. A writer and playwright, Davis is an accomplished writer in many genres. She has written novels, essays, opera librettos, screenplays, documentaries, poetry, and newspaper articles. That she has found time to write for the stage is a blessing unto itself. She was born in Virginia, attended Putney School, and graduated with a B.A. from Barnard College. She attended graduate school at the University of Pennsylvania and Columbia University.

Upon graduation, she found herself working with other poets in the frenetic New York scene, such as **Gylan Kain** and Felipe Alou of the Last Poets, Jessica Hagedorn, and Janice Mirikitani. But the work was unsteady, so she took a job with a San Francisco newspaper. She returned to New York in the late 1970s and resumed working with people like **Ntozake Shange**, Oliver Lake, and **Laurie Carlos**. Her brother, filmmaker Collis Davis, introduced her to other young blacks in the field, exposing her to yet another form of writing. Thereafter, she took a job at the *Village Voice*, where over the next 13 years she rose to the position of senior editor. This was a period of fruition for Davis. She began working in longer forms, producing novels, documentaries, recordings, musical works, opera librettos, screenplays, books, and plays.

Plays Davis wrote include *The Souls of Black Folk* (2003), *Everybody's Ruby: Story of a Murder in Florida* (1999), an adaptation of Bertolt Brecht's *The Caucasian Chalk Circle* (1990), *Paint* (1982), *Sweet Talk and Stray Desires* (a one-woman show, 1979), and *Where the Mississippi Meets the Amazon* (1977) with Shange and Hagedorn.

Davis is the recipient of numerous honors and awards that include the Charles H. Revson Fellows Award (2003–4); Black Writers Hall of Fame Award (1998); **Paul Robeson** Cultural Democracy Award (1998); Ralph Metcalfe Chair, Marquette University (1999); and the Lila Wallace *Reader's Digest* Award (1996–99); in addition, she received the Pew National Theatre Artist Residency grant (1993–95); Chicago Humanities Festival Award (1992); New York Foundation for the Arts Award (1988); Gregory Millard Fellowship Award, fiction (1988); New York State Council on the Arts Writer in Residency Award (1987); Fannie Lou Hamer Award (1987); and Medger Evers College Women's Center Award (1987).

DE JONGH, JAMES. Born in St. Thomas, Virgin Islands, de Jongh is a playwright, college professor, novelist, and actor. He was educated at Williams College (B.A. 1964) and assumed a position as associate professor of English at City College of New York. He began his career as an actor in **Woodie King Jr.**'s *Death of a Prophet*. His passion, however, was playwriting. He often collaborated with Charles Cleveland in such plays as *Hail Hail the Gangs!* (1976), a full-length experimental theater piece about a black teenager who joins a **Harlem** street gang. The New York Theatre Ensemble produced it off-off-Broadway (April 1976). It was also featured at the **Black Theatre Alliance** Festival and the Lincoln Center Outdoor Festival.

De Jongh's most produced play is *Do Lord Remember Me* (1978), a full-length memory play with music. It is a tribute to the triumphs of African Americans over **slavery** from emancipation through the **Federal Theatre Project**. The **New Federal Theatre** opened it in New York (March 1978) under the direction of Reggie Life. He also directed a later production off-off-Broadway at the American Place Theatre (October 1982) with **Glynn Turman** and **Frances Foster** in the cast. Among the awards and honors de Jongh received were a Fulbright fellowship from the University of Madrid (1964), CAPS fellowship in fiction (1977), National Endowment for the Humanities summer fellowship at Yale University (1980), Center for Black Studies fellowship at the University of California at Santa Barbara (1981–82), and **Audience Development Committee** Recognition Award as musical creator (1984).

DEAN, PHILLIP HAYES. A playwright and actor, Dean was born in Chicago and educated in the public schools of Pontiac, MI. He moved to New York City in the late 1950s to pursue an acting career. He appeared on Broadway in *Waiting for Godot* and *The Wisteria Trees*. His plays have attracted interest in such venues as the American Place Theatre (APT), the Chelsea Theatre Center, the **Negro Ensemble Company (NEC)**, and the **Afro-American Studio**, all in New York City. Dean has been praised by different critics as a young black writer of major potential.

His representative plays include *This Bird of Dawning Singeth All Night Long* (1968), a two-character play. In it, a black woman claiming to be her twin sister confronts a white prostitute. The APT first produced it at St. Clements's Church (December 1968) on a program of three one-act plays with Billie Allen and Josephine Premice in the cast. *Every Night When the Sun Goes Down* (1968) is a drama in two acts. It concerns an ex-convict and his relationships with his old friends in a black ghetto. The APT first produced it in 1969. The Eugene O'Neill Theatre Center mounted it for the National Playwrights Conference in Waterford, CT, at the Amphitheatre (August 1974) under the direction of **Harold Scott**. The APT revived it (January 1976) for 46 performances under the direction of **Gilbert Moses**. Frank Adu played the central character. *Thunder in the Index* (1969) is a drama in one act about a Jewish psychiatrist and a street-wise black youth who have a racial dialogue. It was produced by the Chelsea Theatre Center in Brooklyn (January 1969) and the New Media Studio (August 1975). *The Owl Killer* (1971) is a drama in one act. In it, a black laborer frustrated with his life takes out his bitterness and sense of worthlessness on his family. The Afro-American Total Theatre in New York City produced it (December 1973). *The Sty of the Blind Pig* (1971) is a drama in three acts. Set in an apartment house in Chicago's inner city, it deals with a blind street singer's influence on an aging unmarried woman and her dominating mother. *Time* magazine honored *Sty* as one of the year's best plays, and it won for Dean a **Drama Desk Award** (1971–72) as the year's most promising playwright. The NEC first produced it at St. Marks Playhouse for 64 performances (November 1971). Featured in this exceptional cast were **Frances Foster**, **Clarice Taylor**, and **Moses Gunn** under the direction of **Shauneille Perry**. Other productions that followed were at the **Karamu Repertory Theatre**; in the Proscenium Theatre in Cleveland for one month (January 1973); by the Howard University Players in Washington, DC (1972–73); and at the Afro-American Studio Theatre in **Harlem** (1973–74). It was also aired on *Hollywood Television Theatre* (May 1954). *Minstrel Boy* (1972) is a tragedy in one act that deals with an aging black vaudeville performer. *Freeman* (1973) is a drama in two parts about a radical son of middle-income parents who wages an unsuccessful insurrection. The APT first produced it (January 1973) for 37 performances starring Bill Cobbs (Drama Desk Award recipient) under the direction of **Lloyd Richards**. The NEC offered it during the 1976–77 season, with **Dick**

Anthony Williams in the title role and Richard Ward. Ernie Mc-Clintock also directed *Freeman* at the Afro-American Studio (March 1977).

Paul Robeson (1978) is perhaps Dean's most contentious play. It is a full-length one-man show portraying the controversial life and career of **Paul Robeson**, the dynamic actor, singer, and political activist. Lloyd Richards directed the piece on Broadway at the Lunt-Fontanne Theatre (January 1978) for a total of 77 performances. **James Earl Jones** was featured in the title role. The play caused just as much controversy offstage among the black intelligentsia about Dean's depiction of Robeson as did Robeson's life. Akin Babatunde and Thelma Carter codirected a production at **Rites and Reason** at Brown University in Providence, RI (May 1983). Dean was awarded a Drama Desk Award (1971–72) as the year's most promising playwright and a Dramatists Guild Award—both awards for *The Sty of the Blind Pig*, which was also selected by *Time* magazine as one of the year's 10 best plays.

DEANDA, PETER. A playwright and actor, DeAnda was born in Pittsburgh, PA. He attended acting classes for teenagers at the Pittsburgh Playhouse before dropping out of high school to join the U.S. Air Force (1955–59). His interest in theater was perked when he was assigned to special services, where he appeared in several theatrical productions. While in the service, he completed high school, got married, and fathered three children. He renewed his passion for theater at the Pittsburgh Playhouse School of Drama, where he performed with the Irene Kaufman Players. He also studied with the Actors' Workshop in New York City and appeared in several New York stage productions and on television and in films.

He made his mark as a playwright in such shows as *Sweetbread* (1964), a drama in three acts about a black Muslim who tries to put his young brother on the right track. *Ladies in Waiting* (1968) is a drama in two acts about a pretty, young, liberal-minded white girl who is arrested for marching in a picket line to protest prison conditions for women and is incarcerated in the same cell with three black women: a lesbian, a prostitute, and a mentally unstable woman. The **Negro Ensemble Company** produced an off-Broadway workshop production at St. Marks Playhouse (June 1968), and other productions followed.

Vinnette Carroll directed it for the Urban Arts Corps in Greenwich Village (1970–71). The **New Federal Theatre** mounted it in New York (1973), as did the **Alonzo Players** at the **Billie Holiday Theatre** in Brooklyn (1974) under Cecil Alonzo's direction.

DEE, RUBY. Active since the 1940s, Dee is a celebrated dramatic actress of stage, film, and television as well as a playwright. Born in Cleveland, OH, she received a B.A. from Hunter College (1945). This accomplished actress honed her skills working with Morris Carnovsky (1958–60) and at the Actors' Workshop. She performed in several minor parts at the **American Negro Theatre** before landing a role as Libby in the Broadway play *Jeb*. It not only launched her professional acting career, but it was in this show that she met **Ossie Davis**, her future husband and lifetime partner. The role, however, that brought Dee national acclaim was that of Ruth Younger opposite **Sidney Poitier** in **Lorraine Hansberry**'s *A Raisin in the Sun* (1959). For the next 40 years, she has distinguished herself as an actress in plays, films, and television shows. Dee is also the author of two plays, *Glow Child and Other Poems* (1972) and her own one-woman show, *My One Good Nerve* (1998), an autobiographical account of her life, marriage, and career. Among her awards, Dee is the recipient of both the **Obie Award** and **Drama Desk** awards for her portrayal of Lena in *Boesman and Lena* (1961). She was elected to the Black Filmmakers Hall of Fame (1975) and to the Theatre Hall of Fame (1988).

DENT, TOM. Dent, a director, poet, and playwright, was a significant figure in the black arts movement of the 1960s. Dent was associated with the **Free Southern Theatre (FST)** founded by **Gilbert Moses**, Doris Derby, and **John O'Neal**, who realized their goal of establishing a legitimate theater in the Deep South. Later, Dent took over as associate director after Richard Schechner's departure in 1965, generally overseeing the administrative end of the theater. He was also a poet and a playwright of considerable depth who regularly contributed plays to the repertoire of the FST. Dent was born in New Orleans. He earned a B.A. from Morehouse College in 1952 and organized the Umbra Writing Workshop the same year. Dent also cofounded BlkArtSouth, a community writing workshop of the theater. He returned to college and earned his M.A. from Goddard in 1974.

Dent was a prolific writer. His articles and essays were published in leading African American journals. He also helped found the Congo Square Writers' Union and *Callaloo*, a literary magazine. Dent has written two books of poetry, *Magnolia Street* (1976) and *Blue Lights and River Songs* (1982). His plays, mostly produced by the FST, include *Feathers and Stuff* (1960), *Ritual Murder* (1966), *Negro Study #34A* (1969), *Riot Duty* (1969), *Snapshot* (1969), *Song of Survival* (1969, coauthored with **Kalamu Ya Salaam**), and *Inner Black Blues* (1972). Dent is the recipient of the Whitney Young fellowship (1973–74).

DESHIELDS, ANDRE. DeShields, an actor, singer, director, choreographer, and college professor, has been hailed as a phenomenal Broadway song-and-dance man for his role as the amazing Wizard of Oz in *The Wiz* (1975) and more recently for his spell-binding portrayals at the **Classical Theatre of Harlem** (**CTH**). Born in Baltimore, MD, DeShields received his education at Baltimore City College High School, the University of Wisconsin at Madison (B.A.), and the New York University Gallatin School of Individualized Study (M.A.), where he is currently a faculty member.

DeShield's Broadway debut was in *Warp* (1973), which closed after eight performances. His next scheduled Broadway show, *Rachael Lily Rosenbloom (And Don't You Ever Forget It)*, never opened. Shortly thereafter, however, he had greater success as the choreographer of a Bette Midler concert. His breakout performance, however, came in 1975, when he dazzled audiences in the title role of the hit musical *The Wiz*. He went on to star in *Ain't Misbehavin'*; *Play On!*, the Duke Ellington revue; *The Full Monty*; *Prymate*; and *André DeShield's Haarlem Nocturne*. On the regional theater stage, DeShields has performed in *Death of a Salesman* (as Willy Loman), *The Full Monty*, *The Man Who Came to Dinner*, *Waiting for Godot*, *Play On!*, and *Dusyanta: A Tale of Kalidasa*. At the CTH, he has become a mainstay performer, playing many of the central characters in *Caligula*, **Dream on Monkey Mountain**, *Black Nativity*, and *King Lear*.

DeShields's television appearances include *Another World, Cosby, Sex and the City, Great Performances*, and *Law and Order*. He won an Emmy Award for outstanding special achievement for his performance in the 1982 NBC broadcast of *Ain't Misbehavin'*. Among his other honors, DeShields is the recipient of an **Obie Award** for sustained excellence of performance (2007) and an Outer Critics Circle Award nominee for best featured actor in a musical (*The Full Monty*, 2001). He is a three-time nominee for the **Drama Desk Award** for outstanding featured actor in a musical (*Play On!*, 1997; *Ain't Misbehavin'*, 1978; and *André DeShield's Haarlem Nocturne*, originated at **La MaMa Experimental Theatre Club**—which he conceived, wrote, directed, and performed in); and a Drama Desk Award for outstanding featured actor in a play (*Prymate*, 2004). He also received the Jeff Award and **Black Theatre Alliance** Award for *Play On!* at the Goodman Theatre in Chicago. In 2007, DeShields gave the commencement address at his alma mater—the University of Wisconsin at Madison.

DETROIT RENAISSANCE THEATRE (DRT; AFRICAN RENAISSANCE THEATRE). The DRT started out as the African Renaissance Theatre in 2003 with its founder, Oliver Pookram. After only two short years, Pookram renamed the theater in honor of his native city Detroit. Pookram is a graduate of Cass Technical High School in Detroit and holds a B.F.A. from Wayne State University. He has acted in 4 films, 10 television productions, and 14 live-stage productions. The fledgling theater has produced only four plays thus far, and Pookram has either acted in or directed all of them. The plays, divergent in nature, range from **Anna Deveare Smith**'s polemic on race relations *Twilight: Los Angeles, 1992–1993* to Stephen Adly Guirgis's contradictory psychological study of religion in *Jesus Hopped the A Train*. Other plays the DRT has produced are *The Trip*, a madcap comedy by Crystal Rhodes and the **Pulitzer Prize**–winning play *Topdog/Underdog* by **Suzan-Lori Parks**. The theater has no venue of its own, so their plays are presented in various locales, like the Hasting Street Ballroom or the YMCA Theatre in Detroit.

DEVEAUX, ALEXIS. Playwright, poet, fiction writer, teacher, self-taught artist, and political activist, DeVeaux was born in New York

City, where she grew up. She received a B.A. from Empire State College of State University of New York (1976). She has published books on children, a novel, short stories, poems, and other writings. DeVeaux's best-known plays include *Circles*, a drama in one act (1973) about a young black woman who attempts to break away from the influence of her domineering grandmother to realize her dreams of becoming a dancer. *The Tapestry* (1976) is a drama in two acts about a young black female law student who questions her relationship with her boyfriend as well as her best friend. *A Season to Unravel* (1979) is a drama in one extended act about a psychologist who explores aspects of herself through other characters while hallucinating. The **Negro Ensemble Company** mounted a production at the St. Marks Playhouse in New York City (January 1979) that ran for 15 performances. **Glenda Dickerson** directed a notable cast of **Barbara Montgomery**, **Michele Shay**, **L. Scott Caldwell**, **Graham Brown**, and **Adolph Caesar**. *A Little Play* (1972) is a dream fantasy in one act about a young girl who has a discussion with her lover. *Whip Cream* (1973) is a drama in one act about a young woman who is caught jumping the turnstile of a New York subway. *The Fox Street War* (c. 1979) is a full-length drama about a group of black women who use voodoo to persuade their landlord to make improvements. DeVeaux is the recipient of *Black Creation*'s national fiction contest (first prize, 1972), Best Production Award from Westchester Community College Drama Festival (1973), and two Art Books for Children Awards from Brooklyn Museum (1974, 1975).

DEWINDT, HAROLD "HAL." DeWindt is a director, playwright, actor, teacher, and former model. He has appeared in such New York productions as *Entertain a Ghost* (1962), *Day of Absence* (1965), *Happy Ending* (1965), and *Volpone* (1967). DeWindt served as stage manager for the New York Shakespeare Festival Mobile Theatre (summer 1965) and directed the Summer Lab for the Working Actor at the Stanleigh School of Theatre in New York (1960s). In the late 1960s, he worked with the Inner-City Repertory Company of Los Angeles as producing director and later with the **Negro Ensemble Company** in New York as a workshop director (1972). He also formed the Hal DeWindt Theatre in San Francisco (1977). As a playwright, he is primarily known for *Raisin' Hell in the Son* (1962), a full-length play satirizing *A Raisin in* *the Sun* and its characters. DeWindt also directed *Raisin'* off Broadway at the Provincetown Playhouse (July 1962) for a three-week run that starred **Barbara Ann Teer**.

DIAMOND, LYDIA R. A playwright and educator, Diamond earned a B.S. in theater and performance studies at Northwestern University. She is among the black female playwrights who almost dominated the black theater scene during the 1990s and into the 21st century. Upon graduation, Diamond formed her own production company named Another Small Black Theatre Company with Good Things to Say and a Lot of Nerve Productions. Diamond produced most of her own works, including *Solitaire*, *The Inside*, and *Here I Am See Can You Handle It*, a show that comprises the writings and poetry of Nikki Giovanni. Since then, despite marrying, having a son, and teaching part time, she has emerged as a playwright, writing plays that have gathered widespread recognition. Some of her plays are *Gift Horse* (2001); *Stage Black* (2003); *Stick Fly* (2006); *The Bluest Eye* (2006), adapted from the Toni Morrison novel; and *Voyeurs de Venus* (2006). The Steppenwolf Theatre Company commissioned two of her plays, *Voyeurs de Venus* and *The Bluest Eye*. Diamond is a contributing editor at *TriQuarterly*. She has taught at Loyola, Columbia College, and **Chicago Dramatists**, where she is a resident playwright. Diamond is a recipient of the **Theodore Ward** Prize for best play for *The Gift Horse*, and in 2003, she received a fellowship from the Illinois Arts Council.

DICKERSON, GLENDA J. Born in Houston, TX, Dickerson is a director, folklorist, adaptor, writer, choreographer, actress, black theater organizer, and teacher. She received a B.F.A. from Howard University (1966) and an M.F.A. from Adelphi University (1968) and studied with British director Peter Brook. Dickerson gave up acting for directing in 1968 because of the paucity of roles for black actresses in New York City. Undaunted, while in New York, she founded Tough on Black Actors Players and became its director (1967–68). She began experimenting with various theatrical forms, integrating the use of drama, poetry, and black heritage with an emphasis on the adaptation of myth and classical plays. This became her trademark.

Dickerson taught at Spelman College in Atlanta, GA, and presently is professor of theater (directing, theater studies) and head of the African American theater minor at the University of Michigan School of Music. She has directed professionally for over 20 years throughout the country at institutions of higher learning and regional theaters as well as on Broadway. She conceived and implemented the Ford Foundation–supported Project for Transforming through Performing that produced *Kitchen Prayers*, a series of performance dialogues on 9/11 and global warming. Since 2001, Dickerson has been director of the International Institute's Center for World Performance Studies.

Her representative plays include *Unfinished Song: Reflections in Black Voices* (1969), a full-length theatrical collage with drums, finger instruments, and choreography that celebrates African oral poetry and drama by African Americans from Jupiter Hammond to **Larry Neal**. Howard University in Washington, DC, produced it (1969), and it received a citation from the mayor of Washington. *Jesus Christ-Lawd Today* (1971) is a full-length biblical musical with music by Clyde Barrett. The Savior lands in present-day urban black America. The Black American Theatre produced it (summer 1971) under the direction of the author, with choreography by Debbie Allen (of television's *Fame* series). It was also presented at Howard University (1970s). *Trojan Women* (1971) is a full-length adaptation of Euripides' play set in present-day West Africa depicting the devastation of war and oppression. The **Ira Aldridge** Theatre at Howard University produced it (1971). *Jump at the Sun* (1972) is a full-length adaptation of **Zora Neale Hurston**'s novel *Their Eyes Were Watching God* (1937), about a young black woman in the rural South who meets and falls in love with a man but has difficulty trying to overcome obstacles that threaten to keep them apart. The Theatre Lobby in Washington, DC, produced it (1972). *The Torture of Mothers* (1973) is a full-length adaptation of Truman Nelson's novel by the same title, about six mothers who tell a story about the role their sons played in igniting the **Harlem** riots in 1964. The Back Alley Theatre produced it (1973). *Owen's Song: A Tribute to Owen Dodson* (1974) is a two-act theatrical collage conceived, directed, and choreographed by Dickerson and Mike Malone, with music by Clyde Barrett and Dennis Wiley. Coauthored by Dickerson and Malone, it incorporates the plays and poetry of **Owen Dodson**. *Magic and Lion*

(1978) is a full-length theatrical collage of Egyptian mythology utilizing the prose and poetry of Ernestine Walker. The Women's Interart Theatre of New York City produced it (1978). *Rashomon* (1982) is a full-length adaptation of the Japanese classic set in Ethiopia in the 13th century, weaving the African trickster and queen of Sheba tales. It was produced in Ethiopia (1982). *Saffron Persephone Brown* (1983) is a full-length one-woman show conceived and performed by Dickerson about the liberation of a black woman. *Haitian Medea* (1983) is a full-length adaptation of Euripides' tragedy set in Dahomey, Africa, in the early 19th century. Medea is a Haitian "voodoo" queen and folk heroine of New Orleans who flies across the Atlantic Ocean. Dickerson was awarded a Ford Foundation Grant (2003); the Peabody Award (*For My People* on WTOP Television, 1972); the Lilly Endowment teaching fellowship (1987–88); two **Audience Development Committee Awards** (*Magic and Lions*, 1978); a special award for *Owen's Song* at the Lyric Theatre (1982); a citation by the mayor of Washington, DC, for *Unfinished Song*; and an Emmy nomination for her production of *Wine in the Wilderness* for WRC-TV (1971).

DINWIDDIE, MICHAEL. Dinwiddie is a playwright whose works have been produced in New York City and regional and educational theater. A cofounder (along with Kathryn Ervin) of Detroit's Satori Theatre Company, he won a Best Play Award at the Furay Theatre Festival (Detroit Institute of Arts) for the Satori production of *The First Day*. Other produced works include *The Beautiful LaSalles* at **Crossroads Theatre** and Westbeth Theatre Center (**Audience Development Committee [Audelco])** nomination, best play], *The Carelessness of Love* at the Juneteenth Festival (Actors Theatre of Louisville), *Hannibal of the Alps* at Detroit Repertory Theatre and Masque (Richard Allen Center for Culture and Art's Seaport Salon), *Dacha* (Audelco nomination, best play) at the Wonderhorse Theatre and Westbeth Theatre Center, *Original Rags* (Genesis Festival) at Crossroads (New Brunswick, NJ) and Florida A&M University, and *A Guest of Honor* (commission) at St. Louis University. His musical tableaux *Mood Ellington* featured Broadway star **Andre DeShields** and ran at Bobby Militello's Traf Club in Buffalo, NY, while *Cotton Club Rhapsody* was produced at **La MaMa Experimental Theatre**

Club under the direction of Mercedes Ellington. As inaugural Disney Fellow at Touchstone Pictures, he worked as a staff writer on the ABC Television series *Hangin' with Mr. Cooper* and was awarded a playwriting fellowship from the National Endowment for the Arts.

Dinwiddie has been playwright-in-residence at Florida A&M University and St. Louis University. Currently, he is an associate professor at the Gallatin School of Individualized Study at New York University. He has taught writing courses and workshops at California State University at San Bernardino, Michigan State University, State University of New York at Stony Brook, College of New Rochelle (School of New Resources), Wayne State University (Black Theatre Program), and La Universidad de Palermo in Buenos Aires, Argentina. He has served as a peer panelist for the National Black Film Consortium, the Los Angeles Arts Council, and on the boards of the **Black Theatre Network**, the **Classical Theatre of Harlem**, and the **New Federal Theatre**. Dinwiddie is a member of the Writers Guild of America and the Dramatists Guild.

DIXON, IVAN (1931–2008). An actor and director, Dixon is a man with multiple talents who has functioned as an actor and a director onstage, in movies, and on television. He is perhaps best known as the lead character Duff Anderson in the 1964 film *Nothing but a Man* and his 1964 movie of Sam Greenlee's *The Spook Who Sat by the Door*. A New Yorker by birth, Dixon began his career on the stage appearing as Jamie in the 1957 production of *The Cave Dwellers* and later Joseph Assagai in the record-breaking 1959 production of *A Raisin in the Sun*, with **Sidney Poitier**, **Diana Sands**, and **Claudia McNeil**. He branched off into the emerging television medium, where he made numerous appearances in such shows as *The Twilight Zone*; *Dr. Kildare*; *Ironside*; *The Mod Squad*; *Magnum, P.I.*; *The Name of the Game*; *Have Gun, Will Travel*; *Tenspeed and Brownshoe*; *The Fugitive*; and *The Bob Hope Chrysler Theatre*.

Over a 5-year period, he appeared in more than 140 episodes of *Hogan's Heroes* as Sgt. James Kinchlow. Dixon resigned from that series to apprentice under veteran TV director James Goldstone. His big break came when Bill Cosby tapped him to direct an episode of *The Bill Cosby Show*. Afterword, he became one of the most sought-after directors in the industry, directing such shows as *Magnum, P.I.*;

The Price Is Right; *Palmerstown, U.S.A.*; *The Rockford Files*; *The Waltons*; *Starsky and Hutch*; *The Nancy Drew Mysteries*; *Wonder Woman*; and *The A Team*. At the time of is death, he was one of Hollywood's most respected directors.

DODSON, OWEN VINCENT (1914–83). A director, teacher, poet, novelist, and playwright, Dodson for many years was a professor of drama and the chairman of the Department of Drama at Howard University, Washington, DC. He was revered as one of the most influential academicians in African American theater from the 1940s to the 1970s. Born in Brooklyn, he was educated in the public schools of New York City and Bates College (B.A., 1936), where he was elected to Phi Beta Kappa and received an honorary doctorate of letters (1967). At Yale University, he received his B.F.A. in playwriting and directing (1939) under a General Education Board fellowship. He served in the U.S. Navy (1942–43), where he wrote, produced, and directed a number of short, morale-building plays while stationed at Camp Robert Smalls at the Great Lakes Naval Training Station in Illinois.

Dodson is one of the founders of the Negro Playwrights Company (1940). He has been a mentor and inspiration to a number of well-known, successful theatrical talents, including **Gordon Heath**, **Earle Hyman**, **Ossie Davis**, **Ted Shine**, **James Hatch**, Charles Sebree, Hilda Simms, **Richard Wesley**, **Frank Silvera**, and many others. He taught and directed plays at Atlanta University (1939–42), Hampton Institute (1943–44), and Howard University (1949–70). Professionally, he directed the premier production of **James Baldwin**'s *The Amen Corner* in 1935, nine years before it opened on Broadway. He is also the author of several books of poetry, two novels, short stories, articles, poems in periodicals and anthologies, and over 30 plays, operas, and theatrical works. Among his plays of note include *Divine Comedy* (1938), a verse drama with music in two acts about the charismatic religious leader, Father Divine. *Bayou Legend* (1948) is in two acts. It is a poetic black American version of Henrik Ibsen's *Peer Gynt*, set in Louisiana's bayou country, and has been directed by **Shauneille Perry**. *Medea in Africa* (1959) is a full-length black adaptation of Euripides' classic set in Africa. Dodson was the recipient of numerous honors and awards, including an **Audience Devel-**

opment Committee Outstanding Pioneer Award (1975) for his contribution to the growth and development of black theater, the Maxwell Anderson Verse Play Contest (1940) for his *Garden of Time* (1939), the Tuskegee Institute playwriting contest (first prize of $100, 1941) for the *Gargoyles in Florida* (1936), the Rosenwald fellowship (1944–45), a Guggenheim fellowship (1953–54), and a Rockefeller grant (1969–70).

DONOGHUE, DENNIS. Donoghue was one of the few black playwrights to have a show produced on Broadway, *Legal Murder* (1934). It is a melodrama in three-acts based on the infamous Scottsboro case, where nine black youths were falsely accused of raping two white girls. This version, however, depicts the youths as a neighborhood singing group that flees to Chicago to sing on the radio. *Beale Street* (1934) is a full-length play focusing on the seamier side of black life in Memphis, where the blues are said to have originated. It was produced at the Mecca Temple in New York (December 1934). *The Black Messiah* (also called *The Demi-God*, 1939) is a full-length comedy coauthored with James H. Dunmore. It is another version of the popular prophet, Father Divine. The Cooperative Players at the Transport Theatre produced it in New York (June 1939). Donoghue wrote five plays in New York City between 1929 and 1939, but no records of these have been found.

***DON'T BOTHER ME, I CAN'T COPE* (1972).** *Cope*, directed and conceived by **Vinnette Carroll**, with music by Micki Grant, was the first Broadway show to be directed by an African American woman. It utilizes song and dance based on blues, gospel, jazz, rock, calypso, and traditional ballad rhythms to celebrate coping mechanisms of African Americans. It was produced by Edward Padula, Arch Lustberg, and Vinnette Carroll's Urban Arts Corps (UAC). The show evolved out of Carroll's UAC's Theatre Workshop. A year before it made its journey to Broadway, Grant assembled a talented cast of herself, Alex Bradford, Hope Clark, Bobby Hill, and Arnold Wilkerson and infused traditional black folk music, such as the blues, calypsos, and spirituals, to develop the plot. The world premiere was held at Ford's Theatre in Washington, DC (September 1971), where it ran for 32 performances. From there,

Carroll moved a revised version to the Playhouse Theatre on Broadway (April 1972) that ran for 1,065 performances. *Cope* became the UAC's first major successful hit. Carroll then transferred it to another Broadway house, the Edison Theatre (June 1972), where it continued to run with most of the same cast until it closed (October 1973). The Center Theatre Group at the Mark Taper Forum in Los Angeles opened it for 54 performances (August 1972) before it settled at the Huntington-Hartford Theatre in Los Angeles for a long run. Paula Kelly was featured in the cast. That same year, it was produced at the Happy Medium in Chicago (1972). It returned to the Ford Theatre (April 1973) for another run of 44 performances. The American Conservatory Theatre in San Francisco also mounted it as a guest production (July 1973) for 55 performances. *Cope* won the Outer Critics' Circle Award, two **Obie Awards**, two **Drama Desk Awards**, and a National Association for the Advancement of Colored People Image Award.

DRAMA DESK AWARDS. Founded in 1955, the award was originally known as the Vernon Rice Award, named after the theater critic of the *New York Post*. The name was changed to the Drama Desk Award during the 1963–64 season. Its purpose was to celebrate and honor creative excellence in theater on Broadway, off Broadway, and in other nonprofit community theaters. A panel of theater critics, reporters, editors, and even the incumbent mayor of New York City select representatives in respective theater categories. Past winners, presenters, and current nominees along with stage and television luminaries attend the annual award presentation. Its prestige has helped launch the careers of many black artists, such as Cicely Tyson, the first African American recipient of the award for best performer in *Moon on a Rainbow Shawl* (1961–62).

The winners from the 1960s include **Gloria Foster**, best performance (*In White America*, 1964–65); *In White America*, best overall production; **James Earl Jones**, best performance (*Othello*, 1964–65); **Barbara Ann Teer**, best performance (*Home Movies*, 1964–65); **Douglas Turner Ward**, best playwright (*Day of Absence/Happy Ending*, 1965–66); **Ed Bullins**, best playwright (*The Ed Bullins Plays*, 1967–68); the **Negro Ensemble Company**, one of the best theaters (1967–68); James Earl Jones, outstanding performer (*The Great*

White Hope, 1968–69); **Ron O'Neal**, outstanding performer (*No Place to Be Somebody*, 1968–69); Nathan George, outstanding performer (*No Place to Be Somebody*, 1968–69); Douglas Turner Ward, outstanding performer (*Ceremonies in Dark Old Men*, 1968–69); **Michael A. Schultz**, outstanding director (*Does a Tiger Wear a Necktie?*, 1968–69); **Charles Gordone**, most promising playwright (*No Place to Be Somebody*, 1968–69); **Lonnie Elder III**, most promising playwright (*Ceremonies in Dark Old Men*, 1968–69); Cleavon Little, outstanding performer in a musical (*Purlie*, 1969–70); and Melba Moore, outstanding performer in a musical (*Purlie*, 1969–70).

The winners from the 1970s include James Earl Jones, outstanding performer (*Les Blancs*, 1970–71); **Adolph Caesar**, outstanding performer (*A Soldier's Play* (1981); Gylan Kain, outstanding performer (*The Black Terror*, 1971–72); **J. E. Franklin**, most promising playwright (*Black Girl*, 1971–72); **Richard Wesley**, most promising playwright (*The Black Terror*, 1971–72); **Gilbert Moses**, most promising directing (*Ain't Supposed to Die a Natural Death*, 1971–72); Micki Grant, most promising lyricist (*Don't Bother Me, I Can't Cope*, 1971–72); **Melvin Van Peebles**, most promising book (*Ain't Supposed to Die a Natural Death*, 1971–72); **Ruby Dee**, outstanding performer (*Boesman and Lena*, 1971–72); **Sonny Jim Gaines** (*Don't Let It Go to Your Head*, 1972–73); Ben Vereen, outstanding performer (*Pippin*, 1972–73); Bill Cobbs, most promising performer (*Freeman, What the Wine Cellars Buy*, 1972–73); **Joseph A. Walker**, most promising playwright (*The River Niger*, 1972–73); Ruby Dee, outstanding performance (*Wedding Band*, 1972–73); **Ray Aranha**, outstanding playwright (*My Sister, My Sister*, 1973–74); **Seret Scott**, outstanding performance (*My Sister, My Sister*, 1973–74); Ralph Carter, outstanding performer (*Dude*, 1973–74); Stephanie Mills, outstanding actress in a musical (*The Wiz*, 1974–75); George Faison, outstanding choreography (*The Wiz*, 1974–75); Geoffrey Holder, outstanding costume design and outstanding director (*The Wiz*, 1974–75); Hinton Battle, outstanding featured actor in a musical (*The Wiz*, 1974–75); Ted Ross, outstanding featured actor in a play (*The Wiz*, 1974–75); Richard Williams, outstanding featured actor in a musical (*Black Picture Show*, 1974–75); Mabel King, outstanding featured actress in a musical (*The Wiz*, 1974–75); Charlie Smalls, outstanding music and lyrics (*The Wiz*, 1974–75); and *The Wiz*, outstanding musical (1974–75). Other awardees include Billy Wilson, outstanding choreography (***Bubbling Brown Sugar***, 1975–76); Vivian Reed, outstanding featured actress in a musical (*Bubbling Brown Sugar*, 1975–76); **Oz Scott**, outstanding director in a play (***For Colored Girls Who Have Considered Suicide When the Rainbow Is Enuf***, 1976–77); *For Colored Girls Who Have Considered Suicide*, unique theatrical experience (1976–77); Trazana Beverley, outstanding actress in a play (*For Colored Girls Who Have Considered Suicide*, 1976–77); Ken Page, outstanding actor in a musical (*Ain't Misbehavin'*, 1977–78); Nell Carter, outstanding actor in a musical (*Ain't Misbehavin'*, 1977–78); James Earl Jones, outstanding actor in a play (*Paul Robeson*, 1977–78); **Charlayne Woodard**, outstanding actress in a musical (*Ain't Misbehavin'*, 1977–78); **Morgan Freeman**, outstanding featured actor (*The Mighty Gents*, 1977–78); *Ain't Misbehavin'*, outstanding musical (1977–78); Debbie Allen, outstanding featured actress in a musical (*West Side Story*, 1979–80) (*Tintypes*, 1979–80); **Samm-Art Williams**, outstanding new play (*Home*, 1979–80); and **La MaMa Experimental Theatre Club**, special award (1979–80).

The winners from the 1980s include Lena Horne, outstanding actress in a musical (*Lena Horne: The Lady and Her Music*, 1980–81); *Lena Horne: The Lady and Her Music*, outstanding musical (1980–81); Gregg Burge, outstanding featured actor in a musical (*Sophisticated Ladies*, 1980–81); Jennifer Yvette Holliday, outstanding featured actress in a musical (***Your Arms Too Short to Box with God***, 1980–81); Jennifer Yvette Holliday, outstanding actress in a musical (*Dreamgirls*, 1981–82); Sheryl Lee Ralph, outstanding actress in a musical (*Dreamgirls*, 1981–82); Douglas Turner Ward, outstanding director in a play (*A Soldier's Play*, 1981–82); Cleavant Derricks, outstanding featured actor in a musical (*Dreamgirls*, 1981–82); Ben Harney, outstanding featured actor in a musical (*Dreamgirls*, 1981–82); Adolph Caesar, outstanding featured actor in a play (*A Soldier's Play*, 1981–82); *A Soldier's Play*, outstanding new play (1981–82), **Charles S. Dutton**, outstanding featured actor (*Ma Rainey's Black Bottom*, 1984–85); Charlayne Woodard, outstanding featured actress in a musical (*Hang on to the Good Times*, 1984–85); *Ma Rainey's Black Bottom*, outstanding new play (1984–85); Whoopi Goldberg, outstanding one-woman show (1984–85); Morgan Freeman, outstanding actor in a play (*Driving Miss Daisy*, 1986–87); James Earl Jones, outstanding actor in a play (*Fences*, 1986–87); **Lloyd Richards**, outstanding director (*Fences*, 1986–87); **Mary Alice**, outstanding featured actress in a play (*Fences*, 1986–87); Vickilyn Reynolds, outstanding featured actress in a play (*The Colored Museum*, 1986–87); *Fences*, outstanding new play (1986–87); Delroy Lindo, outstanding actor in a play (*Joe Turner's Come and Gone*, 1987–88); Lloyd Richards, outstanding director in a play (*Joe Turner's Come and Gone*, 1987–88); Ed Hall, outstanding featured actor in a play (*Joe Turner's Come and Gone*, 1987–88); Kimberly Scott, outstanding featured actress in a play (*Joe Turner's Come and Gone*, 1987–88); *Joe Turner's Come and Gone*, outstanding new play (1987–88); and *Black and Blue*, outstanding musical (1988–89).

The winners from the 1990s include Gregory Hines, outstanding actor in a musical (*Jelly's Last Jam*, 1991–92); **George C. Wolfe**, outstanding book of a musical (*Jelly's Last Jam*, 1991–92); Hope Clarke, Gregory Hines, and Ted L. Levy, outstanding choreography (*Jelly's Last Jam*, 1991–92); Toni-Leslie James, outstanding costume design (*Jelly's Last Jam*, 1991–92); George C. Wolfe, outstanding director of a musical (*Jelly's Last Jam*, 1991–92); outstanding director of a play (*From the Mississippi Delta*, 1991–92); Savion Glover, outstanding featured actor in a musical (*Jelly's Last Jam*, 1991–92); Tonya Pinkins, outstanding featured actress in a musical (*Jelly's Last Jam*, 1991–92); *Jelly's Last Jam*, outstanding musical (1991–92); Luther Henderson, outstanding orchestration (*Jelly's Last Jam*, 1991–92); **Anna Deveare Smith**, outstanding one-person show (*Twilight: Los Angeles, 1992*, 1993–94); Brian Stokes Mitchell, outstanding actor in a musical (*Ragtime*, 1997–98); *Jitney*, outstanding play (**August Wilson**, 1999–2000); and **Marion McClinton**, outstanding director in a play (*Jitney*, 1999–2000).

The winners from the 2000s include *The Bubbly Black Girl Sheds Her Chameleon Skin*, outstanding musical (2000–1); La Chanze, outstanding actress in a musical (*The Bubbly Black Girl Sheds Her Chameleon Skin*, 2000–1); **Ruben Santiago-Hudson**, outstanding performance, *Lackawanna Blues* (2000–1); **Charles Brown**, outstanding featured actor in a play (*King Hedley II*, 2000–1); Viola Davis, outstanding featured actress in a play (*King Hedley II*, 2000–1); **Kirsten Childs**, outstanding book, outstanding lyrics, and outstanding music for a musical (*The Bubbly Black Girl Sheds Her Chameleon Skin*, 2000–1); *Topdog/Underdog*, outstanding play (2001–2); **Jeffrey Wright**, outstanding actor in a play (*Topdog/ Underdog*, 2001–2); **Dael Orlandersmith**, outstanding actress in a play (*Yellowman*, 2002–3); Brian Stokes Mitchell, outstanding actor in a musical (*Man of La Mancha*, 2002–3); Keb' Mo', Anderson Edwards, and **Keith Glover**, outstanding music (*Thunder Knocking on the Door*, 2002–3); **Charlayne Woodard**, outstanding solo performance (*In Real Life*, 2002–3); Russell Simmons, unique theatrical experience (*Def Poetry Jam on Broadway*, 2002–3); *A Raisin in the Sun*, outstanding revival (2003–4); **Phylicia Allen-Rashad**, outstanding actress in a play (*A Raisin in the Sun*, 2003–4); **Audra Mc-Donald**, outstanding featured actress in a play (*A Raisin in the Sun*, 2003–4); George C. Wolfe, outstanding director in a musical (*Caroline; or, Change*, 2003–4); the **Classical Theatre of Harlem**, special award (2003–4); and Audra McDonald, outstanding actress in a play (*110 in the Shade*, 2006–7).

DREAM ON MONKEY MOUNTAIN **(1967).** This play by West Indian playwright **Derek Walcott** won the Nobel Prize in drama (1967). First performed at the Central Library Theatre in Toronto, Canada (12 August 1967), *Dream on Monkey Mountain* premiered in the United States at the Mark Taper Forum in Los Angeles in 1970. The cast featured **Roscoe Lee Browne**, **Ron O'Neal**, and **Jason Bernard** under the direction of **Michael Schultz**. Subsequent productions were at **Black Arts/West** of Seattle (directed by Bernard in 1971) and the **Negro Ensemble Company (NEC)** in New York (1971). *Dream* is illogical and contradictory, as it exists in the mind of Makak, an old charcoal burner. It takes place somewhere in the West Indies on an unspecified island and either in the past or the present, where Makak, after seeing his face for the first time, embarks on a journey to search for his identity. His exploration confronts notions of Christianity, English law, colonialism, the teachings of Gandhi, and the demise of Haile Selassie. Much like a dream, the play is left unresolved. It is augmented with the music of the West Indies, warrior dances, and voodoo. The 1971 production by the NEC won an **Obie Award** for best play.

***DREAMGIRLS* (1981).** Tom Eyen's (white) musical opened at the Imperial Theatre (20 December 1981) in New York City and ran for 1,522 performances. It was produced by Michael Bennett, Bob Avian, Geffen Records, and the Shubert Organization, with composition by Henry Krieger under the direction of Michael Bennett. Set in the early 1960s, *Dreamgirls* is a story of friendship, romance, and greed. A trio of Supremes-like singers dream of rising to the top in the rhythm and blues industry. They land a job as backup singers for a James Brown–type singer, James "Thunder" Early—but not for long. They get their wish after their manager replaces the lead singer, Effie, to give them a smoother sound and crossover look and appeal as a pop group.

The Broadway cast featured Obba Babatunde (C. C. White), Cleavant Derricks (James "Thunder" Early), Loretta Devine (Lorrell Robinson), Ben Harney (Curtis Taylor Jr.), Jennifer Holliday (Effie Melody White), Sheryl Lee Ralph (Deena Jones), and Vondie Curtis Hall (Marty). Jennifer Holliday won a **Tony Award** (1982) in the best performer in a musical category as Effie. Her performance of the act one finale, "And I Am Telling You I'm Not Going," brought the curtain down nightly to rousing ovation. Ben Harney as the manager and Cleavant Derricks as the James Brown–type singer won Tony Awards as well. The show also received Tony Awards for best book of a musical, best actor in a musical (Ben Harney), best featured actor in a musical (Cleavant Derricks), best lighting design, and best choreography. The show was revived on 28 June 1987, playing for 177 performances.

Dreamgirls was made into a film in 2006 with great success, starring Jamie Foxx (Curtis), Beyoncé Knowles (Deena), Eddie Murphy (Early), and Jennifer Hudson (Effie). As did her predecessor, Hudson dazzled audiences with her rendition of "And I Am Telling You I'm Not Going." Additionally, she won an **Academy Award** for best performance by an actress in a supporting role. Eddie Murphy was also nominated for an Oscar for best performance by an actor in a supporting role.

DUBOIS, SHIRLEY GRAHAM (MRS. W. E. B. DUBOIS, 1906–77).
A playwright, biographical historian, and composer, DuBois was born

in Indianapolis. She received her education at the Sorbonne in Paris (advanced musical composition, 1926–29), Oberlin College (B.A., 1934; M.A., 1935), and Yale University School of Drama (Julius Rosenwald Fellow, 1936–40). Most of her plays were written and produced between 1932 and 1942, while she was a student at Oberlin and Yale. She was a music teacher at Morgan State College (now a university), Baltimore (1929–31), and head of the Fine Arts Department, Tennessee State College (now a university, 1935–36). For two years (1936–38), she was director of the Negro Unit, Chicago Federal Theatre. She was also actively involved in producing, directing, designing, and writing music for such shows as *Little Black Sambo* (1937) and *The Swing Mikado* (1939).

DuBois was the author of a number of biographies of famous persons of color. Among them are George Washington Carver, **Paul Robeson**, Phyllis Wheatley, Jean Baptiste Point de Sable, Pocahontas, Booker T. Washington, and Gamel Abdel Nasser. She also wrote other plays, such as *Dust to Earth* (original title *Coal Dust*, 1938), a three-act tragedy about a black owner of a coal mine in West Virginia who dies trying to rescue his son. *It's Morning* (1940) is a one-act tragedy about a black mother who kills her daughter rather than have her be sold into **slavery**. The Yale University School of Drama produced it in New Haven (1940). Otto Preminger, a faculty member at the time, directed it. *Elijah's Ravens* (1941) is a comedy in three acts about a preacher whose sister dies and leaves an inheritance, and he wants God to favor him as the benefactor. The Gilpin Players produced it in Cleveland, OH (1941).

DUBOIS, WILLIAM EDWARD BURGHARDT (1868–1963). DuBois was a distinguished American scholar and educator. He graduated from Harvard University in 1895 with a Ph.D., the first African American to do so. He was a founding member of the National Association for the Advancement of Colored People (NAACP) in 1910 and editor for *Crisis* magazine, the NAACP journal. He wrote some 17 books and was a leading and controversial advocate for full civil rights for blacks. To that end, he utilized theater as a tool depicting blacks as living, breathing human beings with the same attributes and failings as their white counterparts. He also wrote several plays, notably *The Star of Ethiopia* in 1911. DuBois taught at Atlanta University and several other institutions.

His most famous works were two essays, both written in 1903. One is titled "Souls of Black Folk," the other "The Talented Tenth." DuBois is known as a staunch advocate of **civil rights**, and the NAACP, through his leadership, expanded to over 30 branches nationwide and became known as the face of civil rights in America, if not the world. Moreover, he used his position as president as a pulpit to push theater as one more tool to erase negative depictions of blacks and replace them with positive ones. As editor of *Crisis*, he regularly printed plays and poetry and sponsored paid play competitions through the magazine. His insistence that theater should be political brought him into conflict with Alain Locke, a Rhodes Scholar and professor of philosophy at Howard University. Locke argued for a more humanistic depiction of blacks, warts and all. These two proud, brilliant men would spend over 30 years in a philosophical argument about the direction of black theater. DuBois's mandate for black theater, however, still holds true today. He advocated a black theater that would be by, about, for, and near the black community. He also developed the first "little theater," the **Krigwa Players** at the Krigwa Theatre in 1926, which served as inspiration for that movement. It was centered in Harlem, where plays by **Eulalie Spence** and **Willis Richardson** were presented. DuBois is known today for his work as a scholar, editor, and activist for civil rights under the banner of the NAACP. Additionally, he made lasting and meaningful contributions to black theater in this country that should not be forgotten.

DUMAS, CHARLES. A Chicago native, Dumas is an actor, director, and educator. He became entranced with theater in a high school class project when he memorized a speech from Shakespeare's *Macbeth*, for which he received praise from the teacher and classmates. His foray into theater as an actor, however, in the 1960s was unsuccessful. Unable to find consistent work, he turned to academia, earning a B.A. from the State University of New York at New Paltz, and a master's in urban studies at the New School. He enrolled in graduate theater studies at Hunter College and later received a juris doctorate from the Yale Law School. He entered private practice in 1979, seemingly set for life in his new profession, however he still had a passion for acting, so he decided to scratch that itch. This time he was successful, and today Dumas is recognized as one of America's fine character actors onstage, in television, and on the big screen. He has carved out acting roles in such varied plays as *Titus Andronicus*, *Joe Turner's Come and Gone*, *Death of a Salesman*, *The Meeting*, *A Christmas Carol*, *Fences*, *You Can't Take It with You*, and *Much Ado about Nothing*. His film and television credits include *Asbury Park*, *The Peacemaker*, *Deep Impact*, *Die Hard with a Vengeance*, *Where God Left His Shoes*, *100 Centre Street*, *A Man Called Hawk*, and a recurring role in *Law and Order* as the husband of Lt. Anita Van Buren (**S. Epatha Merkerson**). Dumas has also trod the boards as an actor and director at the McCarter Center, **Kuntu Repertory Theatre**, Circle in the Square, **New Federal Theatre**, **Arena Playhouse**, Pennsylvania Shakespeare Company, Pennsylvania Center Stage, the Milwaukee Repertory Theatre, and Theatre by the Sea.

The instability of the acting profession is a reminder to Dumas not to give up his day job. For 12 years, he was an associate professor in theater at Penn State University. Today, he occupies the same position at Temple University.

DUNBAR-NELSON, ALICE MOORE (FORMERLY MRS. PAUL LAURENCE DUNBAR, 1875–1935). A playwright, poet, teacher, and editor, Dunbar-Nelson, was credited with being a precursor to the **Harlem** Renaissance as well as a participant in it. Although she was a playwright and poet in her own right, Dunbar-Nelson was often identified through her husband, famous African American poet, Paul Laurence Dunbar. Born in New Orleans, she was educated at Dillard University in New Orleans (1892), the University of Pennsylvania, Cornell University, and the School of Industrial Arts in Philadelphia.

Dunbar-Nelson taught school in New Orleans and Brooklyn and later chaired the English Department at Howard High School in Wilmington, DE (1902–20). Her most important play, *Mine Eyes Have Seen* (1918), was performed there. It begs the question whether black soldiers who fought in the war should be loyal to a nation that denies them equal opportunity at home.

DUNBAR REPERTORY THEATRE (DRT). Darryl Willis Sr. and Ramon James Morris founded this important theater in 1987, located in the southern part of New Jersey. Willis studied theater under **Harold Scott** and holds a degree in theater from Montclair State University. He has functioned as the producing artistic director of the DRT since its inception. The road has not been smooth for the DRT over the years, sometimes suspending production when the money was not there. Having no home of its own, they performed in small venues and churches during their first 11 years of operation. They presented such fare as **Langston Hughes**'s joyous gospel song play *Black Nativity* and made it almost an annual event. Other efforts have been dramatized versions of James Weldon Johnson's epic book of poetry *God's Trombones* and **James Baldwin**'s church corner drama *The Amen Corner.* Other plays they produced were *Hambone* by Javon Johnson, *Shakin' the Mess Outta Misery* by **Shay Youngblood**, and *Jitney* by **August Wilson**. Twenty years after its foundation, Willis is optimistic about a bright future ahead.

DUNCAN, THELMA MYRTLE (1902–c. 1937). Duncan was a pioneer playwright of the 1920s and 1930s. She studied playwriting at Howard University under professors Alain Locke and Montgomery Gregory. While there, she developed two of her plays, *The Death Dance* and *Sacrifice*. They were among the first plays to be produced at Howard and to be included in Locke and Gregory's anthology. *Death* (1923), an African play, is a one-act drama with African music, drumming, and dancing. A "trial by ordeal" is set in an African village for a powerful conjure man who tries to influence the outcome of the trial. The Howard Players opened the show in Washington, DC (April 1923). *Sacrifice* (1930) is a drama in one act. It concerns the sacrifices a widowed mother and a good friend have to make that will affect whether her daughter can graduate from college. *Black Magic* (1931) is a comedy in one act satirizing African American folk traditions. A husband who believes his wife has left him enlists a fake spiritualist to win her back. It met great success when it opened in White Plains, NY, moved to St. Albans, Queens, and then to the **Harlem** Showcase. The stage manager was **Loften Mitchell**, and Harold Cruise was the associate producer and director.

***DUTCHMAN* (1964).** **Amiri Baraka**'s **(LeRoi Jones)** signature play catapulted him to national prominence and was credited with launching the revolutionary black theater movement of the 1960s. It is an absurdist allegorical one-act drama with symbolic relationships to both the Garden of Eden myth and the legend of the flying Dutchman. On a New York subway, an attractive white blond approaches a young black male college student and entices, provokes, and eventually murders him.

Producers Clinton Wilder, Richard Barr, and Edward Albee opened *Dutchman* at the Playwright's Unit Workshop in New York City (1964) for two nights under Edward Parone's direction. They moved it off Broadway to the Cherry Lane Theatre (23 March 1964) for 232 performances with the cast of **Robert Hooks** (Clay) and Jennifer West (Lula). It was also presented in Berlin, Paris, and Spoleto, Italy. Gene Persson Enterprises, Ltd., produced a film version in 1967 with **Al Freeman Jr.** and Shirley Knight. *Dutchman* shared the **Obie Award** with **Adrienne Kennedy**'s *Funnyhouse of a Negro* as best off-Broadway play of the season (1964). The play became one of the most produced African American plays.

Forty-three years after its initial production, the Cherry Lane Theatre again hosted *Dutchman* (16 January–24 February 2007). This time, director Bill Duke's production team conceptualized an innovative interactive multimedia environment that set the audience inside the subway. They entered a wooden turnstile as the conductor opened the "subway" to let "passengers" on the "train." Once seated, they witnessed the interaction between Lula and Clay and the image of subway trains moving left and right upstage through the subway window (with the use of videotapes). The show featured Dulé Hill (of the TV series *West Wing*) and Jennifer Mudge, with set by Troy Hourie, costumes by Rebecca Bernstein, and lights by Jeff Croiter.

DUTTON, CHARLES S. A Baltimore, MD, native, Dutton is a character actor extraordinaire and a testament to an enduring will to overcome adversity and to turn one's life around. The son of a truck driver, he was a seventh-grade dropout who spent time in and out of reform school. At age 17, he was convicted of manslaughter and spent over eight years in prison. While there, he earned a high school equivalency diploma, completed two years of college, and found his

EASTON, WILLIAM EDGAR • 159

passion in life—acting. He studied acting technique and practiced his craft on inmates, whom he captivated with his portrayals. After his release in 1978, the Yale School of Drama, a prestigious institution of higher education, accepted him into its program. There he met and came under the tutelage of director **Lloyd Richards** and later playwright **August Wilson**. Richards cast Dutton as Levee, the central character in the Yale Repertory Theatre production of Wilson's *Ma Rainey's Black Bottom* (6 April 1984), along with Joe Seneca as Cutler, Robert Judd as Toledo, Leonard Jackson as Slow Drag, and Theresa Merritt as Ma Rainey. Dutton reprised the role of Levee for his Broadway debut in *Rainey*, for which he received a **Tony Award** nomination. The production established Dutton as one of the preeminent actors of his time. So moved was Wilson by Dutton's raw energy, charisma, and creativity in *Rainey* that he was inspired to develop the character of Boy Willie Charles with Dutton in mind for *The Piano Lesson* (1990)—Wilson's second **Pulitzer Prize**–winning play. Dutton might have become a staple in Wilson's plays if he had not been contacted by Fox television to star in his own show, *Roc* (1991–94), with fellow actors from *The Piano Lesson* **Carl Gordon** and Rocky Carroll. In 1989, a few years before the show premiered, Dutton married actress Debbi Morgan, but that marriage dissolved simultaneously with the end of his television show.

Dutton went on to perform in over 100 plays, movies, and television episodes. They include *Without a Trace*; *Cookie's Fortune*; *Get on the Bus*; *A Time to Kill*; *Gothika*; *The Sopranos*; *Homicide: Life on the Street*; *The Practice*; *Cry, the Beloved Country*; *Crocodile Dundee*; and *Menace to Society*. Dutton began directing in 1997, and he also formed his own production company. He received critical acclaim as the director of *The Corner*, an HBO miniseries about the streets of East Baltimore, an area with which he was most familiar. Awards thus far for Dutton include three Emmy Awards, two National Association for the Advancement of Colored People Image Awards, a **Drama Desk Award**, and a Theatre World Award.

– E –

EASTON, WILLIAM EDGAR (1861–?). A pioneer playwright and newspaperman, Easton was born in New Bedford, MA, to Charles F.

Easton and Marie Antoinette Leggett-Easton. His paternal ancestors fought in the Revolutionary War, and his mother was from Haiti. His great-grandfather was a captain of Indian Scouts. His great-uncle James Easton designed the fortification for Bunker Hill, then known as Breed's Hill. Easton received his formal education in Canada and the United States. In the early 1920s, Easton moved to Texas, where he was active in the Republican Party and became editor of the Texas Blade Publishing Company.

Dissatisfied with the comic portrayals of blacks on the stage during his time, Easton wanted to write serious plays about heroic blacks with a noble history. Drawing from his family's historical past, Easton wrote two plays on Haitian history that were similar in construction, *Dessalines: A Dramatic Tale: A Single Chapter from Haiti's History* (1893) and *Christophe: A Tragedy in Prose of Imperial Haiti* (1911). *Dessalines* is a four-act historical melodrama in verse on the life of Jean-Jacques Dessalines (1758–1806), the revolutionary general who became the emperor of Haiti, reigning for two years from 1804 until his assassination in 1806. Henrietta Vinton Davis produced *Dessalines* with a company of black actors at the Haitian Pavilion of the Chicago World's Fair (January 1893). *Christophe* is a melodramatic tragedy in prose also set in imperial Haiti. Easton dramatizes the overthrow and death of Henri Christophe (1767–1820), the Haitian revolutionary general who became king of Haiti (1811–20) after the assassination of Dessalines. It was produced at the Gamut Auditorium, Los Angeles (1912). Easton was also a newspaperman who held posts in various municipal and federal agencies during his lifetime, including an appointment to the National Bureau of Speakers for the War Department during the World War I, for which he traveled around the country speaking in favor of the United States' involvement in the war.

EDEN THEATRICAL WORKSHOP. Lucy M. Walker founded Eden Theatrical Workshop (Eden is an abbreviation of East Denver, CO, where Eden is located) in 1963. Eden is Denver's first multicultural theater and specializes in social dramas on such topics as depression, sexuality, and chemical dependency. Eden takes pride in being the oldest continuously active theater organization guided by an African American woman. At the time of their 30th anniversary celebration in 1993, the company had produced/was responsible for 150 major productions and over 200 experimental productions.

EDMONDS, RANDOLPH "SHEPP" (1900–83). A pioneer director, playwright, drama teacher, and organizer of drama associations and festivals, Randolph "Shepp" Edmonds was affectionately known as the "Dean of Black Academic Theatre." He was born in Lawrenceville, VA, the son of sharecroppers and the grandson of ex-slaves. He attended St. Paul's Normal and Industrial School (now St. Paul's College) in Lawrenceville, graduating from high school as valedictorian in 1921 and winning both the English and history prizes. His passion for playwriting was realized as a student at Oberlin College in Ohio (B.A. in English, 1926). There he organized the Dunbar Forum, a cultural organization for black students that produced several of his early plays. Edmonds took a position as instructor of English and drama (moving up to professor and chairman of the department) at Morgan College (now Morgan State University) in Baltimore, MD. He also organized and directed another theatrical group—the Morgan State College Players from 1926 to 1934. In 1931, he married Irene Colbert, a pioneer playwright and director in the children's theater at Dillard University (DU) in New Orleans and Florida A&M University (FAMU) in Tallahassee. After Irene died in 1968, Edmonds married Ara Manson Turner, a Lawrenceville widow and businesswoman.

Edmonds continued his education at other prestigious institutions, such as Columbia University (A.M. in English and drama, 1934) and Yale University School of Drama (on a General Education Board fellowship, 1934–35). He also received a Rosenwald fellowship (1937–38) to study abroad at Dublin University and the London School of Speech Training and Dramatic Arts. There he observed how amateur drama groups were organized in England, Ireland, Scotland, and Wales. Upon his return to the United States, Edmonds joined the faculty of DU, where he directed the Dillard Players' Guild from 1935 to 1947. Edmonds's tenure at DU was interrupted when he was drafted in the U.S. Army (1943–44). Stationed at Fort Huachuca, AZ, as a captain in the Special Services Division, he was assigned to develop theatrical shows with black troops. Three years after his return to civilian life, Edmonds left DU and moved to FAMU. There he served as chairman of the Department of Speech and Drama for more than 20 years and directed the FAMU Playmakers Guild (1947–69). When Edmonds retired, he returned to his hometown of Lawrenceville. Edmonds gained a reputation as an organizer of drama associations and festivals at predominantly black colleges in the Southeast.

Edmonds was also a prolific writer. He published 3 collections of plays, more than 50 individual plays, and numerous articles on drama and theater. Beginning in 1922, for over four decades, he gained distinction as a writer of merit and a director of his own plays. Representative plays Edmonds wrote and directed during the 1920s include *Job Hunting* (1922), *Christmas Gift* (1922), *A Merchant in Dixie* (1923), *The (Black) Highwayman* (1925), *Illicit Love* (1926), *Peter Stith* (1926), *Old Man Pete* (1934), *Rocky Roads* (1926), *A Virginia Politician* (1927), *Bleeding Hearts* (1927), *Silas Brown* (1927), *Takazee: A Pageant of Ethiopia* (1928), *One Side of Harlem* (1928), *Sirlock Bones* (1928), *Stock Exchange* (1928), and *Denmark Vesey* (1929). Representative plays Edmonds wrote and directed during the 1930s include *Everyman's Land* (1930), *Hewers of Wood* (1930), *Shades and Shadows* (1930), *The Devil's Price* (1930), *Drama Enters the Curriculum* (1930), *The Man of God* (1931), *Bad Man* (1932), *For Fatherland* (1934), *The High Court of Historia* (1934), *Old Man Pete* (1934), , *Breeders* (1934), *Nat Turner* (1934), *The New Window* (1934), *Yellow Death* (1935), *The Land of Cotton* (original title, *Sharecroppers*, 1938), *Wives and Blues* (1938), *Simon in Cyrene* (1939), *G. I. Rhapsody* (1943), and *Gangsters over Harlem* (1939). Representative plays Edmonds wrote and directed during the 1940s include *The Shape of Wars to Come* (1943), *The Trial and Banishment of Uncle Tom* (1945), *Earth and Stars* (1946, revised in 1961), *Whatever the Battle Be: A Symphonic Drama* (1947), and *Prometheus and the Atom* (1948). Representative plays Edmonds wrote and directed during the 1950s and 1960s include *Career or College* (1956), *FAMU's Objective IV* (1964), *Down in the Everglades* (1964), and *Climbing Jacob's Ladder* (1967).

Honors and awards for Edmonds were numerous. They include a Carnegie Foundation grant-in-aid (1948) to write a "history of the Negro in the Western world theater," an honorary doctorate of letters from Bethune-Cookman College (1959), appointment as a fellow by the American Educational Theatre Association (1968), election to the board of trustees of St. Paul's College (1972), and a special citation from the American Theatre Association (1972) for his contributions to that association and the theater. The National Conference on Black American Drama and Theatre at Morgan State University in Baltimore (1985) presented posthumously along with the Mister Brown Award (named after the playwright Mister Brown, manager of the **African Company/African Grove Theatre Institute for the Arts**) for excellence in theater.

EDWARDS, CARLOS (1969–2004). A playwright and educator, Edwards lived a short but fruitful life. A native of Cincinnati, OH, he was a founding member and artistic director of the Cincinnati Black Theatre before his untimely death at the age of 35. He earned a B.A. and an M.A. in public relations, journalism, and advertising from Morehead State University. He was an assistant director of academic services at the University of Cincinnati. His best-known play is *Kitchen Committee* (2003), about women who discuss racism and politics in the church kitchen. His other plays include *Transition Patterns in Black Manhood*, in which four men in a support group tell the story of their lives; *Hue of Blues Cause Your Blues Ain't Like Mine*; and *Smokin' It Over*.

EDWARDS, GUS. A playwright, actor, and director, Edwards was born in Antigua and grew up in St. Thomas, U.S. Virgin Islands. **Sidney Poitier** encouraged him to come to the United States in 1959 to pursue a career in the theater. He studied acting and theater in New York City at Uta Hagen and Herbert Berghoff's studio. Edwards is generally acknowledged as one of the finest African American playwrights of the 20th century. He worked at a number of jobs and appeared in minor roles in two films, *The Pawnbroker* (1965) and *Stilleto* (1969), while developing his skills as a playwright. In 1977, he became resident playwright with the **Negro Ensemble Company (NEC)**, which produced his first two scripts in a single season and later produced three more of his plays. In 1983, he moved to Arizona State University at Tempe to become the playwright-in-residence.

Edwards's most noted plays include *The Offering* (1977), a drama in two acts about a young black hit man who offers to give financial help to his former mentor, who is down and out and receiving public assistance. When the mentor refuses the offer, he and the young man engage in a psychological struggle for dominance. The NEC produced it at the St. Marks Playhouse (November 1977). It reopened (February 1978) for a total run of 59 performances under the direction of **Douglas Turner Ward** (who also played the older man). *Black Body Blues* (1977) is a melodrama in two acts about a black ex-boxer who works for a kindly white man. He is at odds with his dope-peddling brother who wants to take drastic actions to liberate the fighter from what he sees as a master–slave relationship. The NEC produced it at St. Marks Playhouse (January 1978) for 40 performances under the direction of Ward. **Samm-Art Williams** played the role of the former boxer. *Old Phantoms* (1979) is a drama in two acts about three children who reminisce about the destructive effects their deceased father had on them. The NEC produced it at St. Marks Playhouse (February 1978) under the direction of Horacena Taylor.

Fallen Angels (original title, *Scenes from the City*, 1979) is a drama in one act about a young college-bred drifter who becomes involved in a triangular relationship with a factory coworker and his attractive wife, with whom the drifter falls in love and seduces. He leaves town, leaving the wife pregnant and the unsuspecting husband happy because he thinks he is going to be a father. It was commissioned and produced by the North Carolina School of the Arts under its original title (October 1979) and at the American Premiere Stage in Boston (November 1981). *Weep Not for Me* (1981) is a domestic drama in two acts about the psychological impact that living in the South Bronx ghetto has on a downtrodden African American family. The NEC produced it (January 1981) for 48 performances under the direction of Ward, featuring Ethel Ayer and Bill Cobbs. *Manhattan Made Me* (1983) is a drama in two acts about four unemployed actors, two blacks and two whites, living together in a Manhattan apartment while trying to find work as actors. The NEC produced it at Theatre Four in New York City for 32 performances under the direction of Ward. *Go Tell It on the Mountain* (1985) is a full-length adaptation of **James Baldwin**'s autobiographical novel by the same title about a young boy growing up in Harlem under an overbearing preacher-father. PBS telecast it on the American Playhouse series (1985) with a cast that included Paul Winfield, **Rosalind Cash**,

Olivia Cole, Douglas Turner Ward, **Ruby Dee**, and Alfre Woodard. *Ramona* (1986) is a full-length drama set in the Caribbean in the 1950s about an uninhibited woman who lives her life for love or the illusion of it. The NEC produced it during its 1986–87 season. *Ages of Douglass* (pre-1985) is a full-length dramatic collage of the life of Frederick Douglass. Other plays authored by Edwards include *Frederick Douglass, Lifetimes on the Street, Dear Martin, Dear Coretta, Love and Ophelia, Voices in the Wind, Snapshots and Duets,* and *Black Resurrection.*

Edwards has written several books for the black student actor. They include *Monologues on Black Life* (1976), *The Black Actors Book of Original Scenes,* coauthored with Tanya Kersey (1995), *50 African American Audition Monologues* (2002), *Advice to a Young Black Actor* with Douglas Turner Ward (2004), and *Black Heroes in Monologues* (2006).

In addition to writing plays, Edwards has conducted theater workshops for Lehman College in the Bronx and the North Carolina School of the Arts (where he was also judge of a playwriting contest). He has served on literary advisory committees for the Theatre Communications Group and the New Dramatists. He was a judge for the **Obie Awards** (1981–82), a script panelist for the Artists Foundation (1982), and a member of the TV Panel on Playwriting for the American Theatre Wing. He was also a recipient of a Rockefeller Foundation Playwrights Award (1979–80) and received a fellowship from the National Endowment for the Arts, a Drama League Award, an Arizona Commission on the Arts grant, and the Arizona State University Fine Arts Research Award.

EL-SHAIR, JAMIL F. A playwright, editor, and publisher, El-Shair was born in Tallahassee, FL. He received his education at Hempstead High School in Hempstead, NY; at Clark University in Worcester, MA; and at Georgia State University in Atlanta. Among El-Shair's most recognized plays are *A View through the Blinds* (1981), a one-act drama. It deals with African American family members placing their elders in nursing homes. The Mass Communications Department at Clark College in Atlanta produced it under the direction of Joan Lewis. *Blood Knot: Blood Ties* (1982) is in one act. It centers on a couple's inability to communicate. *Praying for Lynn* (1982) is a three-act drama. An older man leaves his wife for a younger woman only to discover he had made a serious error in judgment. *Street Corner Symphony* (1984) is in three acts. Five high school buddies who sang together as a group in the 1960s reconnect and reminisce by singing songs from the past. *The Sandman* (pre-1985) is in two acts and is a diabolical play that deals with humans who are preoccupied with satanic possession. *Crik Crak* (pre-1985), a children's play based on African folklore, explains why adult frogs do not have tails. *Joshua and David* (pre-1985) is a children's play about the importance of telling the truth.

ELDER, LONNIE, III (1931–96). A playwright, actor, and screenwriter for film and television, Elder was best known for his play *Ceremonies in Dark Old Men* (1965) and as scriptwriter for the film *Sounder* (1972), which was nominated for an **Academy Award**. Born in Americus, GA, Elder grew up in Jersey City, NJ. He received his education from Jersey City State Teachers College (now Trenton State Teachers College, c. 1959–60), the Jefferson School, the New School for Social Research (c. 1950–52), and the Yale University School of Drama (1965–67). He also studied acting under Mary Welch. At age 19, he moved to **Harlem** to pursue a career in the theater, but he was drafted into the army (1952). After his discharge, he returned to Harlem, where he joined the Harlem Writers Guild. There his contact with **John Oliver Killens** and Dr. Robert Hayden stimulated his interest in writing fiction and poetry. While sharing an apartment with **Douglas Turner Ward** (1953–56), the cofounder of the **Negro Ensemble Company (NEC)**, Ward urged him to hone his playwriting skills.

Elder married Judy Ann Elder, an actress he met at the NEC. They had one son. Elder worked as an actor and scriptwriter during the earlier part of his career. He played Bobo in the Broadway and road productions of *A Raisin in the Sun* (1958) and the role of Clem in the New York production of Ward's *Day of Absence* (1965). He was a scriptwriter for the *Camera Three* TV series (1963), coordinator for the Directors and Playwrights Unit for the NEC (1967–69), staff writer and writer-producer for Talent Associates in New York, scriptwriter for the *NYPD* TV series (1968), writer-producer for Cinema Center Films in Hollywood (1969–70), staff writer at Universal Pictures in Hollywood, scriptwriter for the *McCloud* TV series (1970–71), and staff writer for Radnitz-Mattel Productions at 20th Century-Fox Studios in Hollywood (1971).

Elder's most successful play was *Ceremonies*, a two-act drama set in a Harlem barbershop. A disheartened, recently widowed, ex-vaudevillian resorts to selling bootleg whiskey in the back room of his barbershop rather than doing honest work to provide for his daughter and two sons. The NEC produced it off Broadway at the St. Marks Playhouse (February 1969) for 40 performances. Director Edmund Cambridge assembled a cast of Douglas Turner Ward, **Arthur French**, William Jay, David Downing, **Rosalind Cash**, Samuel Blue Jr., and Judyann Johnson. Later that year, Cambridge also directed *Ceremonies* at another off-Broadway house, the Pocket Theatre (April), for 320 performances. He recast this production with Richard Ward, Arnold Johnson, Billy Dee Williams, Richard Mason, Bette Howard, Carl Lee, and Denise Nicholas. It was telecast on ABC (1975), where it won the Christopher's Television Award. The NEC also revived it at Theatre 4 in New York City (May 1985).

Other representative plays by Elder include *Charades on East Fourth Street* (1967), a thesis drama in one act that posits a nonviolent approach through legal channels when dealing with corrupt policemen. It was commissioned by Mobilization for Youth, Inc., in New York City and performed at Expo 67 in Montreal (1967). *A Hysterical Turtle in a Rabbit Race* (1961) is a drama in three acts. A social-climbing black matriarch meets resistance when she tries to cajole her husband and children into becoming part of the upper social class. *Kissin' Rattlesnakes Can Be Fun* (1966) is a tragicomedy in one act. It deals with black–white relationships in Greenwich Village. *Seven Comes Up, Seven Comes Down* (1966) is a comedy in one act about a double con game. The National Black Theatre in New York City produced it (1977).

Among Elder's numerous honors and awards, *Ceremonies* garnered the most recognition. It was nominated for a **Pulitzer Prize** (1969) and won the Vernon Rice/**Drama Desk Award**, the Outer Critics' Circle Award, the Stella Holt Memorial Playwrights Award, and Christopher's TV Award, and the Los Angeles Drama Critics' Circle Award, and Elder received $500 for the Stanley Drama Award. He was also the recipient of the ABC Television fellowship

(1965–66), John Hay Whitney fellowship for playwriting (1965–66), John Golden fellowship (1966–67), and Joseph E. Levine fellowship in filmmaking at the Yale School of Drama (1966–67). As scriptwriter for *Sounder*, he received the Writers Guild of America Award at the Atlanta Film Festival Silvera Award, Christopher's Award, National Association for the Advancement for Colored People Image Award, Stanley Award, and the Los Angeles Drama Critics' Circle Award. As a scriptwriter for *Part 2, Sounder* (1976), Elder received a second Christopher's Award.

ELLA B. MOORE THEATRE (THE CHINTZ AND ELLA B. MOORE THEATRE). This Dallas, TX, black-controlled theater, active in the 1920s, was owned and operated by vaudevillians Ella B. Moore and Chintz Moore (her husband), who also owned the Park Theatre in Dallas. It was on the Managers and Performers circuit in 1922, which merged with the reorganized Theatre Owners Booking Association (TOBA) circuit the following year. Reportedly, the theater was remodeled when it reopened (October 1924). It was considered the most fashionable theater on the TOBA circuit in the Southwest, with a ground floor that could accommodate more than 600 persons and a balcony (seated 500) as well as a loge (seated 100) and 4 box seats. The structure was topped with a roof garden with seven dressing rooms and included an orchestra pit. Backstage, artists were afforded the luxury of a shower and bath. Among the groups that played at the Ella B. were the famed Lafayette Players and the Dusty Murray Company.

ELLIS, KIMBERLY "KIM" C. Ellis is a rising young actress (performance artist), choreographer, dancer, teacher, and scholar of African American literature and history. Her goal is to become one of the most important voices of the 21st century, for which she is making giant strides. Ellis grew up in the Hill District of Pittsburgh, PA, the setting made famous by playwright **August Wilson**—her uncle. She received a Ph.D. in American studies from Purdue University (2002). Ellis is known in the industry as "Dr. Goddess" for her one-woman show *Homegirl's Homecoming* that premiered at the Pittsburgh Playwrights Theatre (April 2006) to critical acclaim. Ellis describes her performance piece as a multimedia, coming-of-age variety show about a young woman in urban America, whose neuroses in academia meets the social commentary of the comedic stage. Ellis assumed the role of 15 characters. She aptly dramatizes the life of this woman through spellbinding monologues, poetry, and African, jazz and hip-hop music and dance.

Since 2004, under the direction of **Eileen J. Morris**, *Homegirl* has appeared at the Women's Theatre and Performance Conference in Toronto, ON (July 2004); Kent State University (August 2004); De-Paul University (October 2004); University of Houston (March 2005); Vanderbilt University (April 2005); National Black Theatre Festival and International Colloquium, Winston-Salem, NC (4 August 2005); Inglewood City Playhouse (September 2005); Lehman College in the Bronx (October 2005); Slippery Rock University of Pennsylvania (November 2005); Kansas State University (February 2006); Williams College (March 2006); Boston Center for the Arts (March 2006); Emory University (March 2006); Miami University of Ohio (April 2006); and the Black Theatre Network's 20th-anniversary conference in Louisville, KYy (July 2006). Her latest production, *Dr. Goddess Goes to Jail in Church*, opened at the Kelly-Strayhorn Theatre in Pittsburgh, PA (August 2007). She is also working on *Tulsa Race Riot, War and Massacre of 1921*, and *June*, a piece based on the Tulsa incident. Ellis, an award-winning, spoken word poet and new playwright, was appointed literary and historical expert consultant to the Reparations Coalition Committee legal team that includes Harvard law professor Charles Ogletree.

ENSEMBLE THEATRE. Founded in Houston, TX, by the late George Hawkins in 1976, Ensemble Theatre has introduced several generations of African Americans to performance art. Ensemble's mission is to preserve African American artistic expression and to enlighten and enrich a diverse community. It has 501(c)(3) status and serves as the nation's largest African American theater. It owns, operates, and produces a main-stage season of five to six contemporary and classic works. The Ensemble also provides a Tour Education Program portraying the African American experience for young audiences at schools and through community outreach and trains young artists through the Young Performers Program.

Ensemble's recent main-stage production was a slapstick comedy, *The Complete Works of William Shakespeare (Abridged)*, generously underwritten by BP America. Under the direction of Ed Muth, it was described as zany yet smart, linguistically funny, and brazenly incorrect. Three of Houston's finest actors play all the male and female roles in all 37 plays in 97 minutes. The production showcases the talents of a multiethnic cast of Keith Caldwell, Alvaro Saar Rios, and Henry Edwards. Veteran director Ed Muth is a resident faculty member at the Houston Community College Central Campus. He enjoyed a close professional relationship with the late George Hawkins and with former artistic director and producing artistic director Marsha Jackson-Randolph.

Ensemble's $4.5 million facility includes the George Hawkins main stage with seating for 200 patrons; the Audrey Lawson Arena, seating up to 125; and a performance center accommodating up to 500 people. The theater's most recent accomplishment occurred when it celebrated two major milestones: the retirement of its $360,000 deficit that remained from its $4.5 million capital campaign and the dedication of METRO, the commuter stop named in the theater's honor. In 2006, Eileen Morris returned to assume the helm of artistic director of Ensemble.

EPPS, SHELDON. Epps is a producer, director, conceptualizer, and the artistic director of the Pasadena Playhouse, a once storied theater that had given birth to such actors as Gene Hackman, Robert Young, Charles Bronson, Eve Arden, and Sally Struthers. This theater, established in 1917, had fallen on hard times, and Sheldon Epps was brought onboard in 1997. Epps is among a handful of African Americans who have assumed the mantle of artistic leadership of a white regional theater. During Epps's 10-year tenure, the playhouse has grown from a marginal entity teetering on the brink of extinction to a cultural center with a diverse, young, multiethnic audience that now come from over 350 zip codes who witness a broad cross-section of theater, everything from Shakespeare to **August Wilson**.

Epps is a native Californian whose family moved east when he was 11 years old in 1963. He graduated from Carnegie Mellon University in 1973 and was a cofounder of the Production Company, where he began his theatrical career. Epps is known for his vivid imagination in the creation of new plays and musicals from old material. He conceived and directed the musical *Play On!*, inspired by Shakespeare's

Twelfth Night. The title is taken from the first line in the show, "If music be the food of love, play on." Set in the magic kingdom of **Harlem** in the swinging 1940s, it features the music of Duke Ellington. The show premiered at the Goodman Theatre in Chicago and received three **Tony Award** nominations. A Pasadena Playhouse production of the musical was broadcast nationally on the PBS Great Performance series. Epps did something similar in 1982 with the musical *Blues in the Night*, featuring the music of Bessie Smith, Johnny Mercer, Fats Waller, and others. Patrons at the Pasadena Playhouse have enjoyed a diversified palette of plays directed by Epps that include the aforementioned *Play On!*, *A Midsummer Nights Dream*, *A Musical Portrait of Edith Piaf*, *Mr. Rickey Calls a Meeting*, *The Importance of Being Earnest*, *And I Ain't Finished Yet*, *The Old Settler*, *Les Liaisons Dangereuses*, and *Purlie*. Epps has not only diversified the play selection but has also changed the culture of the playhouse by implementing youth programs, workshops, and seminars to develop emerging playwrights and directors.

Epps has also directed at Playwrights Horizons, **Crossroads Theatre Company**, Seattle Repertory Theatre, Manhattan Theatre Club, Old Globe, **Arena Playhouse**, and Cleveland Playhouse among others. When he is not active stagewise, Epps retreats to the small screen, where he is the director of record for *Frazier*; *Everybody Loves Raymond*; *Evening Shade*; *Sister, Sister*; *Girlfriends*; and *My Wife and Kids*. Epps is the recipient of two Theatre Communication Group/Pew Charitable Trust grants to underwrite his four-year tenure as associate artistic director at the Old Globe Theatre. In 2007, Epps was awarded the $125,000 James Levine Irvine Foundation Leadership Award.

THE ESCAPE; OR, A LEAP FOR FREEDOM: LIFE IN THE SOUTH (1856). **William Wells Brown**'s semiautobiographical play is important historically as the first recorded play by a black playwright. It is also the first extant play by an African American playwright to dramatize the problems of American **slavery** and the first to be published in the United States by a black dramatist. The work is a five-act melodrama mixed with minstrel elements satirizing the institution of slavery on a Mississippi plantation during the antebellum period in the South. It comments on the inhumane treatment of slaves by their plantation owners and the slaves' indomitable will to escape. Although the play was never staged during the author's life-time, Brown gave numerous readings of the *Escape; or a Leap for Freedom* at antislavery meetings and lyceum programs. The first recorded reading of the play was held in the town hall of Salem, MA (February 1857).

ESTELLE, MARSHA. A Chicago-based writer, Estelle is both a play-wright and actress. She received an Illinois Arts Council fellowship in 2000 and is a member of the **Chicago Dramatists** Playwrights Net-work. She has written three plays: *Big Butt Girls and Other Fantasies*, a one-woman play; *Heat*, about three generations of women who con-verge on a small Midwestern town for a birthday during a heat wave; and *Mama Said There'll Be Days Like This*, a history of the Shirelles, Martha and the Vandellas, the Chiffons, and the Supremes, women's singing groups of the 1970s and 1980s.

ETHIOPIAN ART PLAYERS (EAP; ORIGINALLY THE CHICAGO FOLK THEATRE, 1923–25). The EAP was a well-in-tentioned but short-lived enterprise that thrived between 1923 and 1925. Raymond O'Neil, a well-regarded white director with an ex-tensive European theater background, formed the EAP in Chicago. He was one of a few Caucasians who moved easily between the white and black worlds. Sensing opportunity, he resigned from the Cleve-land Playhouse, moved to Chicago, and began to form a cadre of ex-perienced black actors. He promised them another world of theater, leaving behind the stilted stereotypes, underwritten plays, and shabby theaters they had been used to playing. He believed that blacks pos-sessed a primitive talent, which if harnessed with classical training would elevate their art to a new level. They would be performing plays in the classic continuum of Molière, Shakespeare, Sheridan, and other giant figures. It worked, and he attracted some of the finest black actors of the day, including Evelyn Preer, Solomon Bruce, Laura Bowman, and Arthur Ray.

After a year of extensive rehearsals, workshops, and occasional performances, the EAP took off on a lengthy tour of the Eastern Seaboard. The repertoire included **Willis Richardson**'s folk play *The Chip Woman's Fortune*, sandwiched between *A Comedy of Errors* and *Salome*. *Chip Woman* received the most praise from critics and made history by being the first serious play by a black playwright to be presented on Broadway. It centered on the unsuccessful attempt of a young black man who is deeply in debt to rob an old chip woman of her savings who earns a meager living by picking up chips of wood and bits of coal in the street. He believed she has money stashed away in a secluded spot. The cast included Evelyn Preer (Liza), Sidney Kirkpatrick (Silas), Marion Taylor (Emma), and Laura Bow. They were met with tepid reviews by the primarily white audiences, who were used to seeing black actors cavort in minstrel shows, not the staples of a European Anglo–Saxon society. There was also some evidence that not all of the company had mastered the nuances of speech, pauses, manner, and movement needed to perform a classical repertory. Whatever the reason, the EAP did not survive the tour and closed in 1925.

EUELL, KIM. A playwright, Euell is one of the most experienced dramaturges in the country, but that changed once she has stepped out of the shadows, put pen to paper, and began writing her own plays. Euell holds degrees from American University in Washington, DC, and Stanford University and is a graduate of Playwrights Workshop. She has served as the director of new play development at Hartford Stage and the New American Playwrights Festival for the San Jose Repertory Theatre, director of the Mark Taper Forum's Blacksmyths Play Development and Playwrights Lab, and staffer for the Sundance Theatre Lab. She has also taught playwriting and dramaturgy at Trinity College, Wesleyan University, and the University of Hartford. In 2002, Euell's first play, *Diva Daughters Dupree*, premiered at the **Plowshares Theatre Company** in Detroit and was a rousing success. It has since played at **Penumbra Theatre**, Actors Theatre of Louisville, **Robey Theatre**, and other theaters across the country. The play also won the prestigious **Theodore Ward** Prize for best play. Euell is currently at work on her second play, *Otto Bingo*, set during the **Harlem** Renaissance. She is also the coeditor with **Robert Alexander** of the book *Playz from the Boom Box Galaxy: An Anthology from the Hip Hop Generation*. Fellowships include a Dove, MacArthur, and **August Wilson**, as well as one from the University of Minnesota.

EVANS, DONALD "DON" THOMAS (1938–2003). A playwright and professor, Evans was born in Philadelphia. An only child, he was raised by his mother, Mary Evans, and he never knew his father. After serving in the U.S. Marine Corp and the reserves, Evans attended Cheyney State College in Westown, Pennsylvania (the name was changed to Cheyney University in 1983), majoring in secondary English education. Upon graduating in 1962, he took a job teaching at a public school. The same year, Evans married Frances Gooding, and they eventually had three children, Todd, Rachel, and Orrin. He attended graduate school at Temple University (M.A., 1968; and M.F.A., 1974, in theater arts). Even more important to his training as a playwright, Evans studied acting, directing, and playwriting at the Hagen-Berghof Studios in New York City (1969–70). In 1971, he was hired by Trenton State College (now the College of New Jersey) to chair the Afro-American Studies Department, serving in that capacity from 1971 to 1983. Since 1983, he has directed such plays as **Ed Bullins**'s *The Taking of Miss Janie* and **August Wilson**'s *Ma Rainey's Black Bottom* at the suburban residential college and taught African American literature and drama and jazz as well as courses at Rutgers and Princeton Universities as a visiting professor. His other academic activities include publishing scholarly articles, such as a study of black playwrights of the 1950s in *Black World*; editing *Black Theatre News*, a quarterly magazine; and helping the University of San Diego and other schools develop a theater program. Along with August Wilson, he helped organize the Black Theatre Summit at Dartmouth University (1997–98), out of which was formed the **African Grove Institute for the Arts**. As a playwright, Evans was part of the black arts movement of the 1970s. A contemporary of Ed Bullins, his creative energies came out of the **New Lafayette Theatre** and the **Negro Ensemble Company (NEC)**, both in New York City. James Oliver, a professor at Cheyney State University, as well as **Alice Childress** and Ron Milner, encouraged Evans to try his hand at writing for the stage after Evans wrote reviews of their plays.

Evans's first play was *Sugar Mouth Sam Don't Dance No More* (1972), a drama in one act. Sammy, a sweet-talking but irresponsible drifter, returns to Verda Mae's life after a three-year absence hoping that they can resume their former love affair. She tells him, however, that she can no longer share him with his wife, and he leaves her once again. *Sugar Mouth* was produced at several theaters, including the HB Playhouse (HBP) off Broadway in New York City (Fall 1972), the **Concept East Theatre (CET)** in Detroit (1973), the **Freedom Theatre (FT)** in Philadelphia (spring/summer 1974), and the NEC off Broadway (May 1975) for eight performances.

Other plays Evans authored include *Orrin* (1972), a domestic drama in one act. A young man with a history of dope and thievery comes home to "check things out." He hopes to be invited back without having to change his life. His father, solid as a rock, holds fast to his responsibility to the family and refuses his son's reentry on those terms. It was produced off Broadway by the HBP (1972). Subsequent productions were at the De Lys (January 1972), the CET (1973–74), and the NEC (May 1975) for eight performances. *Change of Mind* (1972) is a comedy in two acts. Possibly a retelling of Evans's *It's Show Down Time* (pre-1976), it concerns a black man from the South who initiates his own black revolution in the North by using the sexual myths about black men to his own advantage in his romantic conversation. The Hansberry Arts Workshop produced it (May 1972), as did the Morehouse-Spelman Players in Atlanta (1974). *Matters of Choice* (1974) is a serious comedy in two acts. The Washingtons, a middle-class black couple, return home from a night out to find their home broken into. The police show no interest, and Oscar has to investigate on his own. He finds, when he goes back to the black ghetto, that he does not know the dynamics of his own people. *Matters* was produced at the HBP in New York City (fall 1974); **Karamu Repertory Theatre** in Cleveland, OH (February 1975); and Players Company in Trenton, NJ (spring 1975). *Showdown* (1976) is a comedy in two acts with seven scenes. It was an adaptation of Shakespeare's *The Taming of the Shrew* for a black cast in a Philadelphia setting. The first two productions were at the FT in Philadelphia (prior to 1976) and the **New Federal Theatre (NFT)** in New York City (February 1976). Both shows, produced under the title of *Showdown* under **Shauneille Perry**'s direction, were taken on a national tour after the initial run at these two theaters.

In 1978, Evans wrote *Mahalia*, his first musical. It is in two acts and is based on the life of Mahalia Jackson. Esther Marrow played the title character in productions by the NFT at the Henry Street Playhouse in New York City (May 1978) for 14 performances under the direction of **Oz Scott** and at the Hartman Theatre, Stamford, CT, for the 1981–82 season. His second full-length musical, *Louis* (original title *Satchmo*, 1981), is about the legendary performer, Louis Armstrong. The NFT produced it at the Henry Street Playhouse in New York City (September 1981) for 12 performances under the direction of **Gilbert Moses**. Norther J. Calloway played Louis.

Other plays Evans wrote include *A Lovesong for Miss Lydia* (1981), a full-length drama. A romantic relationship develops between a respectable widow and her gentleman boarder to the dissatisfaction of her friends. The **Crossroads Theatre** first produced it. The Arts Playhouse on the Arts and Entertainment Network televised it (May 1981) with **Earle Hyman** and Pauline Myers. *One Big Happy Family* (1983) is a full-length comedy. It is an exploration of black and white sexual fantasies and attitudes through the eyes of an accomplished white businesswoman whose college-aged daughter was raised in a black environment. The American Folk Theatre's Ensemble Acting Company produced it at the Richard Allen Center for Culture and Art in New York (May 1983). *One Monkey Don't Stop No Show* (1984) is a full-length domestic comedy about the life of a snobby middle-class black family. The **National Black Theatre** produced it in New York (March 1984).

Sweet Daddy of Love (1985) is a full-length farce about an overweight lover who has a passion for food and poetry. Crossroads Theatre Company produced it in New Brunswick, NJ (April 1985). *The Trials and Tribulations of Stagerlee Booker T. Brown* (1985) centers on the infamous player Stagerlee of African American folklore. Now older, he wonders whether he has the right stuff to uphold his reputation with the ladies. The National Black Theatre produced it in New York City (November–December 1985). His more recent play, *When Miss Mollie Hit the Triple Bars* (1999), was based on the life of Evans's mother. Evans has had 18 plays produced and 6 published. His plays have been produced in virtually every major city of the United States, as well as in England, Germany, and Hong Kong.

Evans has won fellowships in playwriting from the National Endowment for the Arts, the New Jersey Council of the Arts, and the New Jersey Historical Society. In 1974, the **Arena Playhouse** named Evans outstanding playwright. Evans was the artistic director of Karamu Repertory Theatre in Cleveland (1983–88). Until his death,

Evans wrote, directed plays, taught college students, and enjoyed his seven grandchildren.

EVANS-CHARLES, MARTIE (MARTHA EVANS CHARLES, MARTIE CHARLES). An actress-playwright, Evans-Charles is hailed as a powerful new female playwright on the scene. She is the daughter of actress Estelle Evans and the niece of actress **Esther Rolle**. She received her education at Fisk University and Hunter College (A.B., M.A.). She was an assistant professor of speech and drama at Medgar Evers College in Brooklyn.

Evans-Charles honed her playwriting skills as an alumna of the **Harlem** Black Theatre Workshop and the **New Lafayette Theatre (NLT)** in New York City. She received a Rockefeller grant to develop her talents as a writer. Among the more recognizable plays she wrote is *Job Security* (1970), a drama in one act. A bright student who feels alienated takes revenge on a teacher who is more interested in job security than responding to the needs of the student. Among the companies that produced *Job* are the Black Magicians at Third World House in New York City (June 1970) and the University Players in Elizabeth City State University in Elizabeth City, NC (spring 1975), directed by Bernard L. Peterson Jr.

Black Cycle (1971) is a dramatic invocation in two acts. It is set in a beauty shop where operators and customers tell tall tales about the "hood." One story has to do with a young black girl's repulsion of her mother and authority figures. Productions were mounted at the Black Theatre Workshop at NLT (1971), **Afro-American Studio for Acting and Speech** in New York City (1973), and Kuumba Workshop in Chicago (1973–74). *Jamimma* (1971) is a drama in three acts. A black woman is trying to hold on to the man she loves in spite of numerous obstacles. Professionally, it was produced off-off-Broadway by the **New Federal Theatre (NFT)** at the Henry Street Playhouse (March 1972) for 8 performances; it reopened (May 1972) at the NFT for 41 additional performances under the direction of **Shauneille Perry**. *Where We At?* (1971) is a one-act play. A selfish black woman refuses to help her unfortunate sister. The Playwrights Workshop of the **Negro Ensemble Company** first produced it as a work-in-progress at St. Marks Playhouse (1972). *The Guest House* (c. 1981) is a one-act play depicting the seedy side of urban life. The 18th Street Playhouse produced it in New York City (1982). *Daisy's Dilemma* (c. 1984), a children's play in one act, is a lighthearted story about how a daisy finds a home of her own.

– F –

FAITH AND RELIGION. Over 400 years ago, Africans, displaced from their homeland and stripped of their religious practices, were forced to accept Christianity in America. Nevertheless, they found ways to retain their traditions through ancestor worship and rituals they brought across the "big pond." Their religious faith provided a conduit to connect with ancestors spiritually and gave them a sense of hope, identity, and wholeness. Contemporary playwright **August Wilson** says that Africans were becoming too far removed from their cultural roots by identifying with a God that had failed them. In **James Baldwin**'s semiautobiographical play *The Amen Corner*, his central character is grappling with the Christian doctrine. Baldwin was raised in **Harlem**, where his father was a Pentecostal minister and with whom he had a contentious relationship, yet religion is a recurring theme in Baldwin's work. Baldwin encountered a "spiritual revelation" that called him to preach in the pulpit at age 14 only to renounce his faith five years later. The play is set in Sister Margaret's church in Harlem, where she is an overly devout pastor. Elders of the church question her ability to lead the congregation after her absent husband, a man of the world, comes back into her life. She has to decide between her spiritual commitment to God and her love for her dying husband. She chooses to be with her husband in his final hours but has to relinquish her position as pastor. At this revelatory moment, she realizes her love for her husband is more important than the Word. Ironically, she is now better equipped spiritually to lead the congregation. James Weldon Johnson's *God's Trombones* (1927), a collection of seven vignettes taken from the Old Testament, illuminates and celebrates Christianity by setting the "sermons" to gospel music, song, and dance, starting with the Creation and ending with Judgment Day. This play is one of the most produced shows throughout time. *Trombones* puts an exclamation point on how entrenched the Christian faith is within the black community.

In August Wilson's *Joe Turner's Come and Gone*, Bertha, the proprietor of a rooming house in Pittsburgh, PA, acknowledges both the African and Christian traditions in her establishment. Although a practicing Christian, she sprinkles salt over the threshold and allows Bynum, the conjure man, to perform rituals in the backyard with his pigeon blood, bless the table, and perform the juba dance clockwise around the dinner table with the boarders. Wilson contends Africans should not lose their ancestral ties or spirituality.

FEDERAL THEATRE PROJECT (FTP; NEGRO UNITS). In the middle of the Great Depression, in 1935, President Franklin Delano Roosevelt implemented the Works Progress Administration FTP as part of the New Deal, an economic recovery program. Negro units, also called the Negro Theatre Project (NTP), were set up in 23 cities throughout the United States. This short-lived (1935–39) project provided much-needed employment and apprenticeships to hundreds of black actors, directors, theater technicians, and playwrights. It was a major boost for African American theater during the Depression era. These units were situated throughout the country in four geographical sectors. In the East, the most productive units were located in New York City; Boston; Hartford, CT; Philadelphia; and Newark, NJ. In the South, units were placed in Raleigh, NC; Durham, NC; and Birmingham, AL. In the Midwest, they were situated in Chicago; Peoria, IL; and Cleveland, OH. In the West, units were in Seattle and Los Angeles.

The best-known and most active FTP was the New York Negro Unit (1935–39). Located at the **Lafayette Theatre** in **Harlem**, it staged some 30 productions. Two white directors, John Houseman and Orson Welles, headed it for one year (1935). Three black directors, Edward Perry, **Carlton Moss**, and H. F. V. Edward, eventually replaced them (1936). The unit's most popular production was the Haitian, or "voodoo," *Macbeth* (1935), an adaptation of Shakespeare's play set in the Caribbean under the direction of Welles. Other productions included **Frank Wilson**'s folk drama *Walk Together, Children* (1936), which deals with the deportation of 100 African Americans from the South to the North to work for menial wages. **Arna Bontemps** and **Countee Cullen**'s *The Conjur Man Dies* (1936), a farcical mystery in three acts, is a dramatization of Rudolph Fisher's mystery-melodrama. J. Augustus Smith and Peter

Morrell coauthored *Turpentine* (1936), a social drama in 3 acts and 10 scenes. It is about the evils of the Southern labor camp system. George MacEntee's *The Case of Philip Lawrence* (1937) is a courtroom melodrama. *Haiti* (1938) by William DuBois (not to be confused with **W. E. B. DuBois**), is a historical drama about the overthrow of Haiti. A subdivision of the New York Negro Unit was the Negro Youth Theatre, which produced Conrad Seiler's social drama *Sweet Land* (January 1937) and toured the streets of New York with the production during the following summer.

The Newark Negro Unit, in combination with the white New Jersey unit, produced one of the most successful FTP productions by a black author, *The Trial of Dr. Beck*. **Hughes Allison**'s play is a courtroom melodrama about color stratification among upward mobile blacks. It was produced at Union City and Newark, NJ (1937), and then transferred to the Maxine Elliott Theatre on Broadway, where it ran for four weeks.

The Philadelphia Negro Unit produced *Prelude in Swing* (1939), a musical documentary by Carlton Moss. The Boston Negro Unit was directed and run by Ralf Coleman, also a playwright and one of the leading performers. His brother Warren Coleman and H. Jack Bates, the main resident playwright, assisted him. Broadway and film actor **Frank Silvera** was also a member and leading actor with this unit. Among the plays this unit produced (c. 1937–38) were Bates's *Cinda*, a black version of Cinderella; *Dear Morpheus*, a fantasy of love and marriage; *Streets of Gold*; *Black Acres*; *The Legend of Jo Emma*; *The Lost Disciple*; and Coleman's *Swing Song*. The Hartford Negro Unit produced *Trilogy in Black* by Ward Courtney (c. 1937). Down South, the Raleigh Negro Unit produced *Heaven Bound* (1936), a black morality play adapted by Laura Ward.

In the Midwest, Shirley Graham (later Mrs. W. E. B. DuBois) headed the Chicago Negro Unit (1936–39). It rivaled the New York unit in the originality, popularity, and variety of its offerings. The unit's most acclaimed production was ***The Swing Mikado*** (1939), a jazzed-up version of the Gilbert and Sullivan operetta, which was a hit both in Chicago and New York City (1939). Other productions by this unit included Lew Payton's *Did Adam Sin?* (1936); *Little Black Sambo* (1937), a children's operetta; and **Theodore Ward**'s drama of the Depression ***Big White Fog*** (1938).

In the Far West, the Seattle Negro Unit's (1936–39) play production season was boosted greatly by the presence of playwright-in-resident **Theodore Browne**. The unit staged four of his plays, including *Lysistrata*, an African American adaptation of Aristophanes' comedy, and *Natural Man*, a dramatization of the John Henry legend. *Go Down Moses* is a play about Harriet Tubman and her involvement in the Underground Railroad. *Swing, Gates, Swing* is a musical revue. The Los Angeles Negro Unit produced two plays by black playwrights. *John Henry* (1936) by Frank B. Wells is about the legendary railroad worker. *Run Little Chillun'!* (1938–39) is a revival of Hall Johnson's folk drama that was produced on Broadway (1933).

FENCES **(1983).** This **Pulitzer Prize**–winning drama catapulted **August Wilson** to national and international acclaim in 1987. *Fences* was first read at the National Playwrights Conference in 1983, and then it opened at the Yale Repertory Theatre in 1985 before it made its Broadway debut on 26 March 1987. The play centers on a father–son conflict, a dream deferred, betrayal and denial, and the impact these issues have on the family. It featured a stellar cast that included **James Earl Jones**, **Mary Alice**, **Charles Brown**, and Courtney Vance. The production was a smash success, running for 525 performances. It won four **Tony Awards**—best play, director (**Lloyd Richards**), actor (Jones), and actress (Alice)—the Theatre World Award, and **Drama Desk Award**. *Fences* ran until 26 June 1988 and grossed over $11 million, a record for a nonmusical play at that time.

FERDINAND, VAL. *See* SALAAM, KALAMU YA (VAL FERDINAND).

FIRES IN THE MIRROR: CROWN HEIGHTS, BROOKLYN AND OTHER IDENTITIES **(1992).** A performance piece conceived, written, and performed by **Anna Deveare Smith**, *Fires in the Mirror: Crown Heights, Brooklyn and Other Identities* was first mounted at the NYSF/Public Theatre in New York City in 1992. Smith dramatizes the tension and rioting between Jews and blacks that occurred in the Crown Heights section of Brooklyn the previous year. She recorded numerous interviews within both communities with those who had intimate knowledge of the incident; put the story line together, with verbatim excerpts from the interviews about the incident; and portrayed each character, shaping the monologues into a riveting performance piece. She played over 30 characters, black, white, old, young, without pause and with no costumes and very few props. *Fires* was the recipient of an **Obie Award**, **Drama Desk Award**, Drama League Award, and a **Pulitzer Prize** nomination. The play also stands as a landmark performance piece of the research-to-performance method developed by the late **George Houston Bass** of Brown University.

***FLY BLACKBIRD* (1960)**. This musical by **C. Bernard Jackson** and **James V. Hatch** opened at the Mayfair Theatre (5 February 1962) and ran for 127 performances. It was produced by Helen Jacobson, with composition, lyrics, and libretto by Jackson and Hatch. It is about integration and the struggle for **civil rights** in the United States. Director Jerome Eskow assembled a talented cast that featured Avon Long (William Piper), Robert Guillaume (Carl), Mary Louise (Josie), Thelma Oliver (Susie), Chele Abel (Gladys), and Micki Grant (Camille).

***FOR COLORED GIRLS WHO HAVE CONSIDERED SUICIDE WHEN THE RAINBOW IS ENUF* (1976)**. **Ntozake Shange**'s (Paulette Williams) play touched upon new ground—exploring the relationship among black men and women from a feminist perspective. During the early 1970s, Shange joined Halifu Osamare's dance company at Mills College in Oakland, CA, where she worked with poets, writers, and performers. There she also met Paula Moss. The two began working on *For Colored Girls Who Have Considered Suicide When the Rainbow is Enuf*, a mixture of poetry, music, and dance that would become known as a "choreopoem." Shange and Moss moved to New York City in 1975, where Shange contacted **Oz Scott** to help shape and focus the piece. They gave a series of performances in the jazz lofts of Soho and in selected bars on the Lower East Side. Producer **Woodie King Jr.** saw them perform, contracted the show, and expanded the production for an open-ended run at his **New Federal Theatre**. It ran for six months. In a special arrangement with **Joseph Papp**, artistic director of the NYSF/Public Theatre,

King and Papp produced the play jointly at the Booth Theatre on Broadway. It opened there on 15 September 1976 and closed on 16 July 1978, running for 742 performances. After the Broadway run, the show was taken on tour.

Colored Girls was an instant success—and highly controversial. The theme of black men–black women relationships told from a feminist perspective, about black women living and surviving, sparked wails of protest from both sides of the gender divide, but the richness of its prose could not be denied. The ramifications of the issues raised in the play still reverberate today. Nevertheless, it is a drama of self-celebration, utilizing poetry, dance, color symbolism, and intimate personal experiences to explore the many facets of a black woman's psyche. It is performed by seven black women. Each character is distinguished by the colors of a rainbow—Lady in Brown, Lady in Yellow, Lady in Red, Lady in Green, Lady in Purple, Lady in Blue, and Lady in Orange. *Colored Girls* was made into a television movie in 1982, with the author and Trazana Beverly reprising their roles. Beginning in the late 1970s, it became one of the most produced African American plays. It was the recipient of numerous awards, an **Obie Award** and Outer Circle Award, as well as several **Tony**, Grammy, **Drama Desk**, and Emmy Award nominations. Shange has written other "choreopoems" since then, but none have garnered the acclaim, honors, and success of *Colored Girls*.

FORD, MARGARET. *See* SNIPES, MARGARET FORD-TAYLOR.

FOREMAN, FARRELL J. A poet, writer, playwright, and drama and English teacher, Forman is a native of Philadelphia. He attended Antioch University in Philadelphia (B.A. in elementary education, 1977) and the University of California at San Diego (UCSD; M.F.A. in theater and playwriting, 1982). He was on the faculty of the Drama Department of UCSD in 1980. He was a playwright-in-residence at Northern Illinois University at Dekalb (1978 and 1982), a faculty assistant at the Center for Minority Studies, and an administrator in the Office of the Dean at the Ohio State University (1994–97).

Among Farrell's best-known plays are *The Ballad of Charley Sweetlegs Vine* (1978), which won the **Lorraine Hansberry** Award for playwriting at the American College Theatre Festival (ACTF), was produced by Northern Illinois University at Dekalb, and entered in the ACTF (1978). *Daddy's Seashore Blues: A Play in Three Tides* (1979) is a full-length drama about love, happiness, and hatred but, most of all, about survival. Other plays include *The Teachers' Lounge* (1977), a one-act produced by Texas Southern University in Houston (1977); *Lone Eagle* (1985), dealing with black flyers in World War II that was produced by UCSD (summer 1985); and *Black Gravy* (1982), produced at Northern Illinois University at Dekalb (1982). *Gym Rats* (1982) was produced at the Olde Globe Theatre in San Diego (1982), the New Dramatists in New York (1983), and the Ohio State University (1995). One of Foreman's poems published in *Atlantic Monthly* won a student writing award in 1971. Other awards include the National Association of Dramatic and Speech Art Award for playwriting (1978), the Samuel Goldwyn Award for creative writing (1980), the National Endowment for the Arts Award for playwriting (1980s), and the McDonald's Gold Award (1983).

FOSTER, FRANCES HELEN. Active since the 1950s, Foster, a veteran of the Broadway and off-Broadway stage, is a dramatic actress of stage, screen, and television. She is best known as an original member of the **Negro Ensemble Company (NEC)**. A native of Yonkers, Foster gained theatrical experience with Levicus Lyon and Ed Cambridge at the **Harlem** YMCA as a company member of the Harlem "Y" Drama Group in the late 1940s and early 1950s. She also studied theater at the American Theatre Wing (1949–51). This led to a role as a television extra in *Lamp unto My Feet*, *Playhouse 90*, and *Studio One* and later to a regular role in *All My Children*, a television soap opera. Foster made her Broadway debut in Helen Hayes's *Wisteria Trees* (1955) as Dolly May. She returned to Broadway the next year in the Equity Library production of *Take a Giant Step* (1956). Off Broadway, she appeared in *The Crucible* (1958) as Tituba. She left the show to eventually replace **Ruby Dee** as Ruth Younger in *A Raisin in the Sun* (1959) on Broadway, with which she also toured. Foster appeared in several films, such as *Edge of the City* (1957) and *Take a Giant Step* (1961), before joining the NEC during the late 1960s and 1970s, where she played most of the elderly character roles and directed several plays. On Broadway, she played in the

NEC production of *The River Niger* (1973). Foster won the Sara Siddons Award (1960) and the **Obie Award** (c. 1984) for sustained excellence in performance.

FOSTER, GLORIA (1933–2001). Foster was among the finest actresses of the 20th century, a pioneer in playing roles previously denied to actors of color. During a distinctive career, she played roles in *Mother Courage*, *A Midsummer Night's Dream*, *The Cherry Orchard*, *Coriolanus*, *Long Day's Journey into Night*, *Medea*, and *A Raisin in the Sun*, among others. Foster performed for the Seattle Repertory Theatre, the New York Shakespeare Festival, Theatre De Lys, Sheridan Square Playhouse, Vivian Beaumont Theatre, Longacre Theatre, and Goodman Theatre, among others. Foster was born in Chicago, where she studied drama at the Goodman Theatre School of Drama. She moved to New York City and attended an open audition, where she landed a part in *In White America*. The play was a huge success, catapulting Foster into the upper echelon of actors on the New York scene. A demanding performer, Foster refused to play demeaning or stereotypical parts and because of this was often unemployed. While filming the movie *The Cool World* in 1963, she met and married Clarence Williams III. During a lengthy career, Foster appeared in over 10 films, including *Nothing but a Man* (1964) with **Ivan Dixon**, *The Matrix* (1999), and *The Matrix Reloaded* (2003). Foster was one of the prime actors in **Joseph Papp**'s black and Hispanic Shakespearean company in 1977. She was frequently sought after by world-class directors, like Andre Serban and Joseph Chaiken, to play choice roles. During her career, she appeared on Broadway four times. Awards for Foster included three **Obie Awards**, two **Drama Desk Awards**, and a Theatre World Award.

FRANK SILVERA WRITERS' WORKSHOP (FSWW). The FSWW has been associated with more than 75 off-off-Broadway productions that have been mounted as a result of their play readings, workshops, and professional feedback. In 1973, Garland Thompson, a director and playwright from the West Coast, and **Morgan Freeman**, an actor, founded the FSWW in **Harlem**. Thompson named it after **Frank Silvera**, a distinguished actor, producer, and director. Its mission was to provide a workshop for African American playwrights and a place to hear their works read by professional actors and to get feedback from a professional and nonprofessional audience. The readings and discussion of new plays were held on Monday and Saturday afternoon. By 1977, the number of plays being read had reached 90 a year. Initially, Thompson rented space for the readings in and around the Harlem vicinity at such venues as the Harlem Performance Center, City College of New York, Pace College, St. Mark's Playhouse, and the Martinique Hotel. Within a year, the FSWW found a permanent home for the next 29 years at 125th Street and St. Nicholas Avenue in Harlem with the funding received primarily from the New York State Council of the Arts and the National Endowment for the Arts.

FRANKLIN, J. E. (JENNY E.). A playwright, author, and teacher, Franklin was born in Houston, TX. She received a B.A. from the University of Texas and took graduate courses at Union Theological Seminary in New York City. She was formerly a lecturer in the Education Department of Herbert H. Lehman College, a branch of City University of New York. She was also the director of the Theatre for Artcentric Living, Church of Crucifixion, in New York City, where she applied her skills as an artist-therapist. Franklin has written a number of short stories. She has also completed a series of articles on education through art. Franklin's book *Black Girl from Genesis to Revelations* (1976) contains an introduction to her best-known play, *Black Girl* (1969).

Franklin has an attractive track record of plays produced that include *The In-Crowd* (1967), which is a thesis play in one act that is also a full-length rock musical (1977). Young gang members hang an effigy of their parents as punishment for the way the parents have been treating them. All is well after they realize the role of parents and the importance of family. The Mobilization for Youth (New York) produced it at the Montreal Expo, Canada (1967). The **New Federal Theatre (NFT)** in New York City produced it as a rock musical for the young (1977). *Black Girl* (also a feature film and full-length screenplay, 1972) is a domestic drama in two acts and an autobiographical play about a teenager who wants to be a dancer but cannot negotiate how to separate herself from the family without losing their love. It won a **Drama Desk Award** (1971–72) for her as most promising playwright. The NFT first produced it as a videotape on WGBH/Boston (1969). The NFT also produced it off-off-Broadway at St. Augustine's Chapel in New York City and then transferred it to the Theatre De Lys on Broadway (June 1971), where it played one year for 247 performances under the direction of **Shauneille Perry**. The College Little Theatre also produced it (October 1973) for three performances. **Ossie Davis** directed a film version produced by Lee Savin and released by Cinema Releasing (1972) with Leslie Uggams, Brock Peters, Claudia McNeil, and Ruby Dee.

Cut Out the Lights and Call the Law (1972) is a full-length drama. A group of black students at a white college arm themselves in anticipation of an attack by white students. *The Prodigal Sister* (1976) is a musical in two acts. It follows the basic plot and theme of the *Prodigal Daughter* (1962). A young girl becomes pregnant, leaves her home and family for the big city, and sinks into a sordid life, finally returning home to the love and protection of her parents. It was produced off Broadway at the Theatre De Lys in New York City (November 1974) for 40 performances under the direction of Shauneille Perry. In *Throw Thunder at This House* (1970s), a group of undergraduate students desegregate a Southern university but learn that the fight for equity is an ongoing battle. The Theatre for Artcentric Living produced it (1970s) at Skidmore College in Saratoga Springs, NY (1970s). *Where Dewdrops of Mercy Shine Bright* (1983) is a sequel to *Christchild* about a mother's loss of her second child. **Rites and Reason** produced it at Brown University in Providence, RI (February 1983). *Under Heaven's Eye til Cockcrow* (1983) centers on a young girl who searches for her roots but is apprehensive about embracing them. Theatre of the Open Eye produced it in New York City (1984).

FREE SOUTHERN THEATRE (FST; 1964–68). During the early 1960s, scores of Northern-reared and Northern-educated young idealists went south to participate actively in the black liberation movement. Among them were the organizers of the FST. In the winter of 1963, Doris Derby, **Gilbert Moses**, and **John O'Neal** met at a college drama workshop at Tougaloo College in Jackson, MS, to identify possible play scripts to start a theater company in the Deep South. They came to the conviction that a theater in Jackson was not only needed but also feasible. As artists, they perceived the rural areas of Mississippi as a veritable cultural wasteland. A prospectus was drawn up outlining the general plan for the FST. The objectives were to establish a legitimate theater in the Deep South located in Jackson, MS; to produce political, social, and economic changes in the lives of Southern blacks; to create an atmosphere where people could come together for intellectual and social involvement; and to celebrate black culture.

The theater's nucleus was composed of Derby, who served as scenic designer, and O'Neal, a recent graduate of Southern Illinois University who was in charge of production and organization. Derby and O'Neal were also field directors for the Student Nonviolent Coordinating Committee (SNCC) in Jackson. They were the theater arm of SNCC's **civil rights** campaign to register voters. Moses, who had some experience in off-Broadway theater, was responsible for actor training. In addition, Moses was a writer for the *Mississippi Free Press*.

The FST began as a completely integrated theater that aspired to artistic and political relevance. At first, white involvement did not appear to threaten the theater's objectives. However, in need of experience and organizational expertise, the founders contacted Richard Schechner, a white professor at Tulane University and editor of *Tulane Drama Review*. The first white actor to join the FST was Murray Levy. The FST opened the season in New Orleans with a company of five blacks and five whites with Martin Duberman's (white) black history documentary *In White America* (August 1964). Following this premiere production, the play was presented in 15 rural Mississippi communities. A second one that lasted from November 1964 through January 1965 and covered over 20 small towns in Mississippi and Tennessee followed this initial tour. The repertoire included Beckett's *Waiting for Godot* and *In White America*.

The FST did not have a criterion for dealing with the dichotomy between a black-styled theater and an integrated company and audience. Having to begin somewhere, they fell back on the theater of social consciousness and the theater of revolt by doing works by such playwrights as Bertolt Brecht, Sean O'Casey, Eugene Ionesco, and Samuel Beckett. However, they may have shown a lack of courage in their selection of a black play by a black playwright and selected **Ossie Davis**'s mild *Purlie Victorious* over **James Baldwin**'s fiery *Blues for Mister Charlie*.

To motivate the audience to reflection and discussion, the FST held open forums at the end of the performances. Since the majority of these rural inhabitants had never seen a live performance, these discussions helped audiences to form a better understanding of and an appreciation for theater. The occasion gave them the opportunity to articulate their own views on issues that affected their lives. There were even times when these discussions broke through social barriers and brought whites and blacks together in an exchange of opinions. Despite this success, the FST was still faced with the difficult task of finding suitable plays to produce and solve the problem of grossly inadequate finances. Neither of these problems, it turned out, were easily overcome. Not quite a month after the second tour, in February 1965, the troupe traveled to New York to raise funds by staging benefit performances. A New York committee had been set up and assisted in the fund-raising efforts. Although scarcely enough money was raised to pay the troupe members, who now consisted of the four original members who remained after Levy left, others defected. With 19 new recruits, the company outlined plans that included another extended tour, a repertory company that would travel continually, a permanent community theater, and workshops for playwrights and actors.

For its third tour, the FST's repertoire consisted of *In White America*, Brecht's *The Rifles of Senora Carrar* as adapted by George Tabori, Sean O'Casey's *Shadow of a Gunman*, and James Baldwin's *Blues for Mister Charlie*. The company's weekly overhead of $1,000 was offset slightly by the willingness of private individuals in the towns they toured to supply the troupe with free room and board. But the FST's determination to live up to its name by offering free admission merely added to its financial woes. At the same time that the FST was metamorphosing into an all-black theater, Schechner, with some reservation, became chairman of the racially mixed, middle-class board of directors.

More in the spirit of altruism than authoritativeness, the New Orleans–based board of directors aided the company by providing it with food and lodging, ratifying decisions, making suggestions for fund raising, and in desperate times personally donating lump sums of $500 or more. As it was, the FST's magnanimity worked against it in that foundations required theaters to be self-supporting as a condition for funding. Even as early as 1965, the theater projected an annual operating budget of $98,000 to $100,000. Obviously, some perspicacious thinking was needed to make the theater attractive to funding institutions while it was reestablishing itself as a completely ethnic theater.

The FST is important to the black theater movement because it was one of the very first theater companies established during the early stages of the civil rights era of the 1960s. It set an example when it switched from the ideology of the civil rights movement to that of black nationalism. This move came in the middle of 1965 and is attributed to the upheaval sparked by the publication of *The Autobiography of Malcolm X*. The impact of Malcolm X's life and ideas shifted the sphere of influence in the liberation movement from the South to the urban North. As an overt response to this shift, many activities within the civil rights struggle became radicalized and repudiated the doctrine of nonviolence and integration for that of separation and resistance. Consequently, black intellectuals and rebels looked to the Northern ghettos instead of the Southern towns and plantations for inspiration and guidance.

A second phase of the liberation movement, one might say, began at that point. Since the more radical elements of the FST found in black nationalism the theoretical base that had eluded them, they argued a strong case for reshaping the company around nationalist principles. Moses, Denise Nicholas, and Orman waged the strongest challenge for an all-black theater. O'Neal believed that the FST was already an ontological entity and therefore should not fall victim to racial doctrine. Instead of being influenced by popular ideas, they believed, the FST should impress the audiences by displaying its own liberation. On the other hand, the arguments of Moses were broader and more complex. He argued first in favor of tapping and putting onstage that element of black society that ignores and is ignored by the American cultural mainstream. Excluded from TV, film, and theater, this neglected subculture deserved to have its values, images, and experiences portrayed through some theatrical medium. Moreover, in light of the notion that the American theater industry remained discriminatory, Moses declared that black people needed to face the problem by creating theaters in their own communities and proposed that the FST reflect the concept of a theater for black people established and run by blacks rather than following the white-oriented liberal idea of uplifting the culturally deprived. He further suggested that the FST find its direction in black consciousness and encouraged the creation of new plays that dealt seriously with the **black experience**. Moses also believed that renaming of the FST to Third World Theatre would help the company project a more appropriate image. After the ideological upheaval that led the theater to more fully embrace the concept of ethnic purity, Levy left the group, the last white to abandon the fold. Curiously, the metamorphosis of the FST from an integrated theater to a black theater was more the result of evolution than revolution. The defection and circumstantial departure of certain key members from the company caused dissolution within the administrative ranks. It was the height of the Vietnam War, and after receiving his draft notice, O'Neal filed for conscientious objector status. Following several hearings, he was ordered to do alternative service by working in a children's home in New York. Naturally, this meant that he had to uproot himself from New Orleans. He left in January 1966 to fulfill his military obligation. Moses left the FST in the spring of that same year. Eventually, Nicholas defected to the **Negro Ensemble Company** and Orman joined the **New Lafayette Theatre**. Schechner resigned as board chairman around the same time that Moses quit as artistic director to pursue his interest in "happenings" and "environmental theater" as a professor at New York University. The disintegration of the FST highlights a major difference between the two prominent theater movements during the era, the black theater movement and the radical theater movement.

The reason the FST seemed so much like bourgeois university theater was because the college-trained and college-influenced architects viewed theater academically. What the company may have needed at this juncture was leadership from someone who perceived theater not with awe and reverence but as a vehicle to further the goal of total liberation. Thus, the addition of Tom Dent to the board of directors was a move in the right direction. On a trip to New York in 1964, Moses and O'Neal met Dent, a New Orleans–born poet and writer who wanted to return home. The FST directors invited Dent to join the company. With the departure of Moses and O'Neal and the resignation of Schechner as board chairman, Dent became chairman of the board. Almost immediately, he began the task of straightening things out administratively and artistically.

FREEDOM THEATRE (FT). Located at 1346 North Broad Street in a mansion built in 1855 by the actor Edwin Forrest, the FT in Philadelphia is perhaps the nation's largest and Pennsylvania's oldest African American theater. John Allen Jr. and Robert E. Leslie founded it in 1966. For over 25 years, the FT was a training ground for artists and presented over 150 performances a year. In 1992, **Walter Dallas** assumed the directorship after founder Allen died the same year. Dallas attended Morehouse College in Atlanta and the Yale Drama School in New Haven, CT. He directed the inaugural production of **August Wilson**'s *Seven Guitars* (1995) at the Goodman Theatre in Chicago, which was nominated for a **Pulitzer Prize**. Dallas also adapted the film *Cooley High* (1996) into a stage production that became the FT's most successful production in its 33-year history. Owing to a hefty grant of $425,000 from a Ford subsidiary in 1966 and to the philanthropists' policy of teaching theater administrators how to manage their money, the FT by 1998 had a surplus of $11,000. The FT also became the second black theater to join the League of Resident Theatre (the other being **Crossroads Theatre**), a move that gave it status and prestige. In June of 2008, Dallas resigned as artistic director of FT. *See* WALTER DALLAS.

FREEMAN, ALBERT "AL" CORNELIUS, JR. Freeman has been an actor, director, producer, screenwriter, and drama instructor for over 50 years. Born in San Antonio, TX, he and his family were deserted by his father, who moved to Columbus, OH, when he was nine. His interest in theater as a young man brought him to Los Angeles, where he enrolled at Los Angeles City College (LACC) in 1951 to study acting. His schooling was interrupted by a three-year stint in the U.S. Air Force. Upon his return to civilian life, he reenrolled at LACC, where he took courses in speech, broadcasting, and drama. While still a student, he made his stage debut in an Ebony Showcase Theatre production of *Detective Story* in 1954. Freeman relocated to New York City in 1959, where he landed a part in the 1960 Broadway play *The Long Dream*, adapted from a novel by **Richard Wright**.

Thereafter, during the volatile decade of the **civil rights movement**, he was cast mostly as an angry young militant. This depiction onstage was for Freeman his way of contributing to the struggle. Off Broadway, he played the lead role in **Amiri Baraka**'s **(LeRoi Jones)** *Dutchman* and *The Slave* and **James Baldwin**'s *Blues for Mister Charlie*.

By the early 1970s, Freeman was active onstage, on television, and in films. He played **Sidney Poitier**'s Oscar-winning role in the musical *Lilies of the Field* (1963), titled *Look to the Lilies*. Freeman made his film debut in 1960 in *The Rebel Breed*. His film credits include *The Detective, The Lost Man, My Sweet Charlie* (a series in which he costarred with Patty Duke for three years), *A Fable, Finian's Rainbow, Once Upon a Time . . . When We Were Colored*, and *Assault at West Point* (a movie made for television). He also wrote the screenplay for **Ivan Dixon**'s *Countdown at Kusini* (directed by Dixon, 1976), and Freeman directed *A Fable* (a 1971 feature film). Beginning in 1972, for the next 17 years, Freeman played stoic police detective Hall on the daytime drama *One Life to Live*. Also in that year, he played Malcolm X in the miniseries *Roots: The Next Generations*. He left *One Life* in 1988 to teach at Howard University, a position he holds today. In 1993, he made a dramatic comeback on the silver screen as Elijah Muhammad in Spike Lee's *Malcolm X*, for which he won an Image Award. Other awards he received were an Emmy Award in 1979 for outstanding actor on *One Life to Live* and an Emmy nomination for his performance in the miniseries *Roots: The Next Generations*.

FREEMAN, BRIAN. A playwright, actor, director, and theater producer, Freeman was born in Boston. He spent the years from 1973 to 1975 at the University of Pennsylvania. Migrating west, he caught on as an actor with the San Francisco Mime Troupe, where he worked from 1977 to 1985. His work as an actor fed into a yearning for directing, and he soon began doing both. He served as a director-in-residence at **Joseph Papp**'s NYSF/Public Theatre (1988–89) and later helped found Pomo Afro Homo, a performance group he stayed with until they disbanded in 1995. Later he served as director of the Blacksmyths Theatre Lab at the Mark Taper Forum. He began writing in the 1980s and has produced several works that have received great acclaim. Some of the plays he has written are *A Night at the Apollo*, *I Think It's Gonna Work Out Fine*, *Dark Fruit*, *A Slight Variance*, and *Civil Sex*. Freeman's plays have been produced throughout the country at such venues as the **La MaMa Experimental Theatre Club**, **Ensemble Theatre**, **Cultural Odyssey**, and Public Theatre. He has taught theater, playwriting, and performance at the Art Institute of Chicago, California Institute of Arts, the San Francisco Arts Institute, and Colorado College. Freeman has been awarded the following honors: the Gerbode Foundation Playwriting Award, Will Glickman Best Play Award, California Arts Council playwriting fellowship, Rockefeller Foundation Multi-Arts Production grant, National Endowment for the Arts research grant/Mark Taper Forum, and CalArts Alpert Award in theater.

FREEMAN, MORGAN. Freeman is one of the leading character actors of this generation, using his distinct voice and eloquent diction to bring dignity and gravitas to a variety of characters. He came into his own in the late 1980s with memorable performances in *Driving Miss Daisy* and *Glory*. The ante was upped in the 1990s when he appeared in the films *Amistad*, *Kiss the Girls*, *Seven*, and *The Shawshank Redemption*. The 21st century found him reprising his role as detective Alex Cross in *Along Came a Spider*, then *Bruce Almighty*, and finally *Million Dollar Baby*, for which he won an **Academy Award** as best supporting actor. But all of this did not happen overnight, for Freeman spent over 20 years onstage as a working actor honing his craft before the opportunity to perform on the silver screen presented itself.

Freeman was born in Tennessee, but a family breakup resulted in being brought up with grandparents in Mississippi. He served a five-year stint in the U.S. Air Force before attending Los Angeles Community College and acting at the Pasadena Playhouse. Upon migrating to New York, Freeman found himself competing for roles with the cream of the crop. He worked at many venues in New York and also helped found the **Frank Silvera Writers' Workshop** with **Garland Lee Thompson**. His first Broadway performance was the all-black version of *Hello Dolly* with Pearl Bailey. Other notable productions he appeared in were *The Three Penny Opera*, *The Mighty Gents*, *The Gospel at Colonus*, *The Taming of the Shrew*, and the title role in *Coriolanus* with **Gloria Foster**. Freeman and Foster were two of the prime actors in **Joseph Papp**'s black and Hispanic Shakespeare company in 1977. Freeman's work on the stage resulted in his winning the esteemed Clarence Derwent Award, four **Obie Awards**, and a **Tony Award** nomination. When Hollywood knocked, Freeman was ready.

FREEMAN, NATHAN ROSS. A dramaturge, playwright, filmmaker, and educator, Freeman is a native of Philadelphia, where he graduated from St. Joseph's University in 1972. He began his career as a playwright and wrote eight plays before transitioning into a life of academia and filmmaking. He is perhaps best known for his musical play *The Contract* (1982). A prominent pastor of a large church begins to doubt his faith until he is thrown into the greatest challenge of his career. In December 1985, Freeman became the first playwright-in-residence at the **North Carolina Black Repertory Theatre (NCBRT)**. He coordinated the Residency Program and had a profound influence on its operations. He established a program whereby guest playwrights had the opportunity to have their unproduced works read before an audience. During his stay at the theater, he eventually filled the positions of assistant director and literary manager. Since leaving the theater in 1995, Freeman has held a variety of positions both in the private sector and in academia, teaching and lecturing at Duke University, **Freedom Theatre**, University of North Carolina, **National Black Theatre Festival**, Montage Showcase Ensemble, and others. His plays have been produced at the American Theatre Project, NCBRT, Bushfire Theatre Company, SoHo Repertory Company, and other notable venues. Freeman currently teaches playwriting and screenwriting at the University of North Carolina at Charlotte. He is the founder of Montage Showcase Ensemble and the Assegai Film Group.

Among the plays Freeman wrote are *Hannah Elias* (1989). It is a story of Hannah Elias, one of many post–Civil War philanthropists who used her resources to help less fortunate African Americans. *Ancestors* (1997), a one-woman play, asks the question, Have the ancestors stopped talking to us? Nine characters explore the question through a series of scenes set in Haiti, Africa, and America during the time of **slavery**. Other plays Freeman wrote are *Zero* (1974), *Joshua* *and Hazel* (1974), *Evening Sunrise* (1976), *Getting Further* (1982), *Virgins* (1992), *Winter Isn't Over Yet* (1996), and *Your Side Mine* (1997). Freeman received the North Carolina Arts Council playwright fellowship (1997).

FRENCH, ARTHUR W. French has been a working actor for over 40 years, quietly going about his work in an unassuming manner but always doing a first-rate job. He has acted onstage, in movies, and on television, where he prevails in episodic television, soap operas, and especially commercials and voiceovers. Though not well known to the general public, in the industry he is a household name. French is a native New Yorker who graduated from Brooklyn College and was a social worker when he became interested in acting. His early studies were with Maxwell Glanville and Peggy Fleury, with whom he became a disciple of the Lee Strasberg technique. He worked his way up the ladder quickly, appearing in Circle in the Square productions with Jason Robards in *The Iceman Cometh* and George C. Scott in *Death of a Salesman*. His work in **Douglas Turner Ward**'s play *Day of Absence* led to his selection as a charter member of the **Negro Ensemble Company** in 1968. Three years later, French made his Broadway debut in **Melvin Van Peebles**'s collage of poetry and music *Ain't Supposed to Die a Natural Death*. Since then, he has appeared in 10 other Broadway productions. French's list of movie and television credits number over 100, including *Law and Order*, *Crooklyn*, *Malcolm X*, *Three Days of the Condor*, *The Stone Killer*, *Third Watch*, *A Hero Ain't Nothing but a Sandwich*, *Sanctuary*, *Entrapment*, and *The Wiz*. French's recent stage work was in **August Wilson**'s *Two Trains Running* at the Signature Theatre in New York City in 2007. French is the recipient of an **Audience Development Committee Award**, a Lucille Lortel Award, and an **Obie Award** for sustained excellence of performance.

FULLER, CHARLES. One of the most accomplished playwrights of his time, Fuller was awarded the **Pulitzer Prize** in drama for *A Soldier's Play* (1981). He is a graduate of LaSalle College in his native Philadelphia. In 1967, he cofounded the Afro American Arts Theatre and assumed the mantle of playwright-in-residence. He began writing plays with a particular emphasis on refuting stereotypes of

African Americans as "slow, stupid, and lazy." Fuller tried to demystify stereotypes by basing his writings on historical events because he says you can't argue with history. Against the backdrop of the halcyon black arts movement, Fuller wrote a series of plays that captured the mood and tenor of the times, the first being *The Perfect Party* (1969), a two-act drama that deals with the problems of interracial marriage. Over the next decade, he authored a series of highly successful plays. Three of Fuller's plays gained national acclaim because of his attention to crucial issues facing the black community and to African American history. *Zooman and the Sign* (1980), an **Obie Award** winner, is a melodrama in two acts. A black teenage "gang banger" terrorizes a Philadelphia neighborhood after he accidentally kills a 12-year-old in full view of witnesses who are afraid to identify him to the police. *The Brownsville Raid* (1975) is a historical drama in three acts. It is based on an actual incident in 1906 in Brownsville, TX, where an entire black regiment was accused of raiding a town. *A Soldier's Play* is a historical drama in two acts. A black captain investigates the murder of a black sergeant during World War II. In 1984, it was made into a movie, retitled *A Soldier's Story*, and received **Academy Award** nominations for best movie and best screenplay, which Fuller wrote. Fuller's interest changed over time. He turned to screenwriting in an effort to reach more people. He is one of four African American playwrights to have won a Pulitzer Prize. His other honors include fellowships from the Guggenheim Foundation, the Rockefeller Foundation, and the National Endowment for the Arts. He is a member of the Writers Guild of America and serves on the Board of the Dramatists Guild Fund.

FUNNYHOUSE OF A NEGRO **(1963).** This signature work by **Adrienne Kennedy** influenced the growth of the off-Broadway black avant-garde movement in the 1960s that challenged traditional theatrical forms. It centers on a mulatto girl's unsuccessful attempts to resolve the psychological conflicts of her black/white heritage. In a surrealistic rooming house, Sarah is visited by various historical figures that represent facets of her divided self. The play won the author a Stanley Award from Wagner College in Staten Island (1963) and an **Obie Award** (1964). It was first mounted as a workshop production for one night at the Circle in the Square in New York City

(1963) under the direction of Michael Kahn. Featured in the cast were **Diana Sands**, Yaphet Kotto, **Lynn Hamilton**, and Andre Gregory. Edward Albee and others opened it off Broadway at the East End Theatre (January–February 1964) for 46 performances, also under the direction of Kahn. The cast consisted of Billie Allen as the young girl, Ruth Volner, Leonard Frey, Leslie Rivers, Cynthia Belgrave, **Ellen Holly**, Gus Williams, and Norman Bush. It was produced in many theaters, including in London (1968), at the University of Houston (October 1984) as a student production under the direction of **Ntozake Shange**, and at New York University (November–December 1984) by the Undergraduate Department of Drama, directed by Billie Allen, with music by Carman Moore.

FURMAN, ROGER (1924–83). Furman was a playwright, theatrical designer, community theater organizer, director, and actor. He studied at the Drama Workshop of the New School for Social Research under Edwin Piscator and was an apprentice under Rafael Rijospray at the National Theatre of Puerto Rico. He began his acting career in the 1940s with the **American Negro Theatre (ANT)** in **Harlem**. In addition to his stage credits, Furman also acted in such films as *The Fight Never Ends* (1949) and *Georgia, Georgia* (1972).

Furman is best known for founding and directing the **New Heritage Repertory Theatre Company (NHRTC)**, Harlem's oldest black nonprofit theater group. Furman first became involved in theater at the old ANT as a scene designer in the 1940s. When ANT folded, Furman faded into obscurity, except for an ill-fated adventure in 1954, when he founded the Harlem Experimental Theatre Group, which failed after one production. In 1964, Furman was appointed field director for the Harlem Youth Opportunity Unlimited (HARYOU), a New York City–based antipoverty agency. Furman formed a summer program at the local YMCA, which he named the NHRTC. Columbia University came forward and gave him a grant to teach young blacks and Puerto Ricans the technical aspects of theater. The program grew exponentially, and by the time federal funding ran out, they had renovated a loft on 125th Street and installed a 110-seat theater.

The theater grew into a yearround training and producing center, usually presenting two to six plays a year. Some of their most successful plays that Furman wrote include *Hip, Black, and Angry* (1967) and *The Long Black Block* (1971). *Hip* is a full-length variety program conceived and directed by Furman with input from Jim Williams, Nathaniel Juni, Warren Cuney, Ted Joans, Carl Boissiere, and Frances Ernest Kobina Parks from South Africa. It was produced at the NHRTC in Boston and schools throughout Harlem, Brooklyn, and Mount Vernon, NY. *Black Block* is a two-act drama with music. It deals with the aspects of black people's struggles against apathy, exploitation, dissension, and the destructive moral crises brought on by the drug plague. It had it inaugural production at the NHRTC (January 1972), after which it was produced in repertory (1972–73), and at the Brooklyn Academy of Music (September and November 1972).

Furman was a multitalented man. He not only administered the program but also functioned as fund raiser, lighting designer, and set builder, all with students by his side. Among the other plays he wrote are *Fat Tuesday; or, Drawers Down, Bottoms Up*; *The Gimmick*; *Renegade Theatre*; *Another Shade of Harlem*; *To Kill a Devil*; *Fool's Paradise*; *The Quiet Laughter*; and *Three Shades of Harlem*. Furman died in New York City (November 1983) of heart and kidney disease. After Furman's death, Jamal Joseph, an ex–Black Panther, became artistic director. Joseph was a jack-of-all-trades and one of the seminal figures in the black arts movement of the 1960s and 1970s. He parlayed funds from Lyndon Johnson's war on poverty into training young people in the arts, into what eventually became the NHT (New Horizon Theatre). It was a producing entity that brought some of the finest work of that period to the stage.

– G –

GAINES, JAMES. E. "SONNY JIM". An actor and playwright, Gaines has had a long career in the arts, first as a playwright and then as an actor in theater, TV, and films. He has appeared onstage in the Public Theatre production of *Julius Caesar*, a 1974 production of *What the Wine Sellers Buy*, and the 1991 production of *Mule Bone* at Lincoln Center. He started out as a playwright and wrote the following plays: *It's Cullid, It's Negro, It's Black Man* (1971); *Kuumba,*

Don't Let It Go to Your Head (1972); *Sometimes a Hard Head Makes a Soft Behind* (1972); *What Lilt Had Turned Up Heads* (1972); and *Folks Remember a Missing Page (The Rise and Fall Harlem)*(1991). Gaines has appeared in over 18 movies and TV episodes, including *Law and Order, Good Times, Freedom Road, Malcolm X,* and *The Pelican Brief.*

GARDLEY, MARCUS. A playwright and poet, Gardley was born in Oakland, CA. He earned his B.F.A. from San Francisco State University (SFSU), where he received the Eugene O'Neill Memorial Scholarship and the SFSU African American Student of Outstanding Achievement Award for 2000–1. He continued his education at the Yale School of Drama (M.F.A., 2004). Upon graduation, he began teaching creative writing at Columbia University.

Gardley's first play, *Living Tired,* premiered at SFSU under the direction of Amy Mueller. It centered on a well-liked man who lived in a cemetery. Owing to the success of this show, Gardley has been showered with praise by critics with terms like "a unique new talent" and "destined for greatness." Needless to say, he has made an early impact on the theatrical scene in America. His second play was *Shadow Men,* about homeless people in San Francisco. Gardley's most recent play, *Like Sun Fallin' in the Mouth* (2002), is set in a toxic heap that breeds defeat and hopelessness among the people society often discards, the West Oakland community. He received the Playwrights Foundation fellowship (PFF) of San Francisco, which gave him an opportunity to complete his play with the assistance of a dramaturge and to have a staged reading with a cadre of seasoned actors.

Gardley is best known for his play *And Jesus Moonwalks on the Mississippi* (2004), a poetical allegory where the protagonist is propelled back in time to events surrounding the Civil War. It was a launching pad for a career that is still rocketing, as he seemingly has an unending reservoir of material from which to draw. Other plays Gardley wrote between 2002 and 2007 include *(L)imitations of Life*; *Moon Bitch*; *Sweet Dream Grandpa*; *Moth on the Mother Tongue*; *Jonah Bell, A Musical*; *Lorin District Project*; and *Dance of the Holy Ghosts: A Play on Memory.* Gardley has also written for the San Francisco Mime Troupe. At age 30, he has already been awarded a

Sundance residency (2003). He has earned prestigious awards and honors, such as the PFF, Eugene O'Neil Memorial Scholarship, American Society of Composers Award, Artists and Publishers Cole Porter Prize, and Sundance/UCross playwright fellowship. He is a member of New Dramatists.

GARRETT, JIMMY. Born in Dallas, TX, in 1947, Garrett, a playwright, was raised in Los Angeles. Like many others of that era, he became actively involved in the burgeoning **civil rights movement**. He worked with the Student Nonviolent Coordinating Committee in both California and Mississippi. It was while attending San Francisco State University that he became involved with **Sonia Sanchez**, Nathan Hare, and other leaders in the movement for social justice. That is also where he wrote *We Own the Night* (1967), a searing commentary on the differences between generations. A young black revolutionary kills his mother because she will not accept his brand of militancy. The play was successful at the time, playing at the Spirit House in New Jersey and other hard-core black theaters. Garrett, along with contemporary **Amiri Baraka (LeRoi Jones)**, was labeled as one of the most militant playwrights of the time because of *We Own the Night* (and his philosophy). He believed that a black writer had the responsibility of collecting, distilling, clarifying, and directing the energies of black people toward purposeful, meaningful action. For many years, Garrett's name was mentioned in the top tier of black playwrights, with the promise of better things to come. The anger and furor that accompanied the civil rights movement has long since dissipated. So, too, has Garrett; records indicate no further plays or writings of any kind by him.

GARRETT, TRE. A native of Houston, TX, Garrett is a fledgling playwright and director of the 21st century. He attended the High School of the Performing Arts in Houston and holds an M.F.A. from the North Carolina School of the Arts. Garrett has studied under Broadway director Gerald Freedman and was assistant director for Dan Sullivan in the 2005 Broadway production of *Julius Caesar* starring **Denzel Washington**. He was also a directing fellow at the 2003 Eugene O'Neill Playwrights Conference. His directing efforts include works for the African Continuum Theatre, the Young Playwrights Theatre

Tour, and the **New Horizons Theatre**. Garrett's playwriting credits since 2003 include *Loving Langston* and *A Month of Sundays*. They were both produced at the Horizon Theatre's Young Playwrights Festival. Other plays by Garrett are *Rain and Rivers, Color and Light, That's Got His Own*, and *Creole Fire*. Garrett is a member of the **Black Theatre Network** and the Society of American Stage Directors and Choreographers. He has received the John Gielgud directing fellowship and the Thomas S. Kenan fellowship and has been honored as director-in-residence at the John F. Kennedy Center for the Performing Arts.

GIBSON, EDWIN-LEE. Gibson is a journeyman actor and burgeoning playwright from Houston, TX. He was born there in 1941 and almost from the beginning was attracted to the stage. After graduating from Paul Quinn, a small African American college in Waco, TX, he spent several years working for the **Ensemble Theatre** in Houston. He left for New York to pursue his career and has been a working actor since. Gibson wrote his first play in 1989, *Anatomy of a Knucklehead*, which ran for eight months in Brooklyn and four months in New York. Broadening his genre, Gibson began teaching theater at the Harbor Conservatory for Performing Arts in 1989. He juggles a career of teaching, acting, and writing. In 2006, he won a prestigious *Village Voice* **Obie Award** for his over-the-top performance in Will Power's off-Broadway production of *The Seven*. Gibson's other plays are *Morning*; *The Morning of 9/11/2001*; *Five Till*, about the five minutes before an inmate is scheduled for electrocution; and *Placebo*.

GIBSON, P. J. (PATRICIA JOANN). Gibson is an award-winning playwright, teacher, scriptwriter, director, administrator, and consultant. She is among the burgeoning group of African American female playwrights who came to the fore in the 1990s. Gibson has worked at various institutions of higher learning and theater organizations as well as in the public sector. From her first lauded play, *Shameful in Your Eyes* (1971), to her latest work, *The M. Odyssy* (2006), she continues to contribute powerfully to the black theatrical diaspora.

A native of Pittsburgh, PA, she holds a B.A. in drama, religion, and English from Keuka College (1973). She earned an M.F.A. (under a Schubert fellowship) in theater arts from Brandeis University, Waltham, MA (1975), and she studied under J. P. Miller (*Days of Wine and Roses*). Although Gibson began writing poems and short stories while in college, she did not find her voice until she did additional study under **George Houston Bass** at **Rites and Reason Theatre** at Brown University in Providence, RI. Gibson's voice has resonated loud and clear on the theatrical scene with dramatic works like *Void Passage* (1973), *Konvergence* (1973), *Miss Ann Don't Cry No More* (1980), *Brown Silk and Magenta Sunsets* (1981), and *Long Time since Yesterday* (1985).

Void is a realistic/surrealistic drama in one act. The setting is a vast pyramidal structure considered the "void passage." It addresses the conflict between two women who have both had to live with the title "strong black woman" and must now learn to find strength from each other. *Void* is a companion piece to the author's *Konvergence*, a drama in one act set in a mountain lodge about a couple who wants to reevaluate their relationship after a year's separation. The two plays were produced on a double bill by several theater-producing organizations, such as Players Company in Trenton, NJ (March 1973); Rites and Reason as part of its "Image and Reality" Project (April 1977); and Kuumba Workshop in Chicago (1978). *Konvergence* was also produced alone at the Oakland Ensemble Theatre (December 1982).

A National Endowment for the Arts grant (NEA) enabled Gibson to develop *Miss Ann*, a two-act drama. It explores the lives of four tenants who live in separate households in the inner city. The Frederick Douglass Creative Arts Center in New York City produced it (March 1980). *Brown Silk* is a stylized drama in two acts set in the luxurious apartment of Lena Larden Salvinoni, a wealthy recluse. She is traumatized by three life-size paintings of people from her past who come to life in her subconscious. *Long Time* is a drama in two acts. A group of ex-college women gather after attending the funeral of a friend who committed suicide. While reflecting on the past, they discover that one in the group is gay and learn secrets about each other that will change their lives forever. The **New Federal Theatre** produced it twice (February and October 1985), both under the direction of Bette Howard. *Long Time* won five **Audience Development Committee Awards**, including best dramatic production of the year and awards for direction, costuming, and scenic design. It also garnered Gibson a Playwright of the Year Award (1985). In addition, Gibson received several grants and commissions during her career. Among them are the NEA fellowship; the Schubert fellowship; a commission from Rhode Island Committee for the Humanities to write her historical drama *My Mark, My Name* (1977–78); artist-in-residence award at the Music and Drama Institute, Khartoum, Sudan (1978); and key to the city from the mayor of Indianapolis.

GIBSON THEATRE (PHILADELPHIA). *See* DUNBAR REPERTORY THEATRE (DRT).

GILLIAM, THEODORE "TED" E. (c. 1937–1991). A playwright director, and educator, Gilliam founded the now defunct **Dashiki Project Theatre** in 1962 located in New Orleans. Arriving with degrees in hand, one from the Yale School of Drama, Gilliam assumed the position of associate professor in the School of Drama at Dillard University (1968). Dashiki had a long and proud history before expiring in 1991. Gilliam was the artistic director of the company, directing many of the shows, including several of his own, such as *What You Say? or, How Christopher Columbus Discovered Ray Charles* (1970). It is a children's play in one act based on a story about Columbus by Flip Wilson. It calls for black children to play roles of Africans, Native Americans, and Europeans. Dashiki produced it during the summer of 1973. *The Pride of Lions* (1973) is a family drama in three acts based on two short stories from *Lover Man* by Aston Anderson. Gilliam also wrote *Mahalia: My Name Is Naomi* (1982), a one-act musical narrative with songs on the life of gospel singer extraordinaire Mahalia Jackson. Dashiki in collaboration with the Desire Community Housing Corporation produced it at two churches and at the New Orleans Jazz and Heritage Festival (1983). *Praise Song!* (1983) is an adaptation from the novel *Praise Song for the Widow* by Paule Marshall. During his tenure at the Dashiki Project Theatre, Gilliam returned to school and obtained his Ph.D. from Tulane University. Gilliam also provided opportunities for women in all phases of the theater. He produced *For Colored Girls Who Have Considered Suicide When the Rainbow Is Enuf* as a vehicle for his growing cadre of female actors. Carol Sutton, Barbara Taker, Patricia Hall, Francesca Roberts, Claudia Miller, and Adele Gautier were up to the task, and the show was a smash success. In time they were called the Dashiki Divas. At the time of his death, Gilliam was chairman of the Theatre Department at Dillard University.

GILPIN, CHARLES SIDNEY (1878–1930). An actor, singer, and vaudevillian dancer, Gilpin is best known for his portrayal of Brutus Jones in Eugene O'Neil's *The Emperor Jones* (1919). A Richmond, VA, native, Gilpin attended St. Francis School, a Catholic institution for colored children, until age 12 and served as a printer's assistant at the *Richmond Planet* (c. 1890–93). Gilpin married three times. His first wife was Florence Howard (married c. 1897); his second Lillian Wood, whom he was with at the Lafayette Players; and his third Alma Benjamin Gilpin.

Gilpin showed great promise early on as a singer appearing in amateur theatricals in Richmond. He went to Philadelphia in the early 1890s, where he worked briefly for the *Philadelphia Standard* but was let go after some employees complained about working with a black man. Thereafter, he toured as a performer with several traveling minstrel and vaudeville shows (1896–1904) and the Gus Hill's Smart Set for one season. He played Remus Boreland, the mayoral candidate in *The Black Politician* (1905). Gilpin also sang with the male chorus in Bert Williams and George Walker's *Abyssinia* (1906) on Broadway and on tour. After the tour, Gilpin founded the Pekin Stock Company (PSC) at Robert T. Motts's famed **Pekin Theatre** in Chicago. Gilpin acted in a variety of roles in such plays as *Captain Rufus* (1907), *Tie Husband* (1907), *The Merry Widower* (1908), *The Man Upstairs* (1909), and *The Chambermaid* 1908). Gilpin also starred in several productions for Jesse A. Shipp's stock company (1910–11) that absorbed the PSC. From Chicago, Gilpin moved to New York City, where he performed at the **Lafayette Theatre** in *The Old Man's Boy* (as Tom Bolden and the vocal director, 1913–14). The following year, Gilpin joined the **Anita Bush Players** at the Lincoln Theatre in **Harlem** as one of the featured players. Bush changed the name of the players to the Lafayette Theatre Players after it was relocated to the Lafayette Theatre, also in Harlem. As the star performer, he played in *For His Daughter's Honor*, *The Octoroon*, and *Within the Law*. In 1916, Gilpin left the show during the rehearsal of *Paid in Full* over a salary dispute. In between shows, Gilpin worked as a barber, Pullman porter, and elevator operator before landing a small part as Reverend Custis, a former slave, in John Drinkwater's *Abraham Lincoln* on Broadway in 1919. A year later, he landed the title role in *The Emperor Jones* at the Neighborhood Playhouse in New York City for a short run. The Provincetown Players mounted the show in Greenwich Village, where it ran for 399 performances, after which it toured throughout the United States and later in London, establishing Gilpin as the most recognized black actor on the American stage to play the lead in a serious drama. Due to his failing health and a nervous breakdown, **Paul Robeson** replaced Gilpin in the role. Gilpin died at age 52 in Eldridge Park, NJ. In 1921, Gilpin was named by the Drama League as one of the 10 best artists who had made valuable contributions to American theater.

GLANVILLE, MAXWELL (1918–92). A veteran actor, director, playwright, and producer, Glanville was born in Antigua. He attended the New School of Social Research in New York before embarking upon an acting career with the **American Negro Theatre (ANT)**, founded by **Abram Hill** and **Frederick O'Neal** in 1940. Its mission was to provide training and acting opportunities for black actors by producing plays that attract black audiences. Glanville became an important figure onstage and offstage, serving on the Committee for the Negro in the Arts at a time when discrimination was rampant.

Glanville's talent as a playwright surfaced upon the demise of ANT in 1951. That same year, Glanville founded a theater company, the American Community Theatre (ACT). Though he produced other plays, Glanville used the ACT as a vehicle to mount his plays, which included *Swing Wedding* (1945), a short skit of a wedding in swing time. It was produced at the Champaign, IL, United Service Organization (1945) and the **Harlem** YMCA (1947). *Broadway Sadie* (1955) is a comedy in one act about a lady who lives in a Broadway subway station. It was performed at the Greenwich Mews Theatre in New York City (1955). *Long Stretch—Short Haul* (1960) is a full-length romantic drama that centers on a love triangle among a woman and two men, all unemployed actors. The ACT produced it in theaters throughout New York City (1969).

The Bonus (1961), produced under several titles, is a comedy in one act. A newlywed couple are about to take a vacation when the wife's offbeat mother shows up for a visit. They must decide whether to leave or to stay. It was produced at the ACT; Clark Center YWCA; Westchester Community Theatre; Bedford-Stuyvesant Civic Theatre, Brooklyn; and Yonkers Community Theatre and for other New York community groups. *Cindy* (1970), a children's play in one act, is a black adaptation of the Cinderella story. It was produced in New York City at the ACT (1962), the Adam Clayton Powell Jr. Theatre (1976), and the Drew Hamilton Community Center (1976). *Dance to the Nosepicker's Drum* (1970) is a domestic drama in two acts coauthored with Rudy Gray. It involves three generations of a black family, with a focus on a young son who steals to get attention. The ACT produced it (1970), and subsequent productions were given at the Clark Center YWCA and the Concourse Village Community Center in the Bronx.

The Wire (1973) is a screenplay coauthored with **Gertrude Greenidge**. It is based on an actual case about a black policeman who goes undercover to solve his father's murder. *Twit* (original titles: *Twit for Twa'* and *Twit for 'Wat*, 1974) is a full-length musical farce coauthored with Greenidge. It is a black adaptation of Shakespeare's comedy *Measure for Measure* set in the country of Blackolovia, where blacks rule and sex without marriage is a hanging offense. *The Injectors* (c. 1960) is a playlet about representatives of the devil wanting to change their fate.

In 1970, Glanville decided to curtail producing plays and stressed instead actor training in all phases of the theater. During this time, he produced plays sporadically at community theaters in New York City, especially in Harlem, such as *China Gold* (1983), a short playlet about two methadone patients discussing their addiction. *The Commutables* (1985) is a one-act drama. Two people, commuting between Harlem and Westchester, become engaged emotionally in dialogue. In his later years, Glanville turned to directing, using his vast experience in such plays as *Light in the Cellar*, *God's Trombones*, *Branches from the Same Tree*, and *Outside Daughters*.

Glanville was the recipient of numerous awards, including three poetry awards, an award from the Junior Page of *Amsterdam News* (1932–35), Rosenwald scholarship (1943, declined because of induction into the U.S. Air Corps), YMCA Community Service Award for contributions in the theater (1954), Bedford-Stuyvesant Civic Club (Brooklyn) Award for community work in theater (1972), the American Community Theatre Award from members of the ACT for dedication and direction (1958–80), and the WLIB (radio station) Community Civic Award for contribution to the arts.

GLENN, ROBERT. An adaptor of plays and a director, Glenn resides in New York City. He adapted and directed two works of significance, including **Langston Hughes**'s *Montage of a Dream Deferred* (1951), which was adapted into a full-length poetic collage entitled *Shakespeare in Harlem* (1959). It was produced during the 1959–60 season at various locations in New York City; off Broadway at the Theatre De Lys (American National Theatre and Academy Matinee Series); the White Barn Theatre in Westport, CT; and the **Karamu Repertory Theatre** in Cleveland, OH (April 1961). The second adaptation was of James Weldon Johnson's book of poems *God's Trombones* (1960) into a full-length poetic collage. It was produced in New York (February 1960). Glen's directing credits include New York productions of *Soul Gone Home* (1959), *Victims of Duty* (1960), *Time to Go* (1960), and *The Coggerers* (1960).

GLOVER, KEITH. An actor, director, and playwright, Glover is a protégé of **August Wilson**. Born in Bessemer, AL, he moved to New York in 1980. At age 15, he studied with Lee Strassberg, eventually finding work as a teenager on television in *As the World Turns*. Later he worked in films and regional theater as well as television. He has appeared onstage at the GeVa Theatre, the **Arena Playhouse**, Mark Guthrie, and Center Stage, among others. His TV and film work included *Law and Order* and *New York, Undercover*.

While not acting, Glover turned his attention to playwriting. He made his New York debut at the NYSF/Public Theatre (April 1995) with *Dancing on Moonlight* (April 1995), his first play. It is set backstage of the famous **Apollo Theatre** in 1935. Black folks are playing the numbers and gambling as a woman dies in the act of giving birth to her child. The father abandons the scene after being accused of cheating. Twenty-five years later, the now grown child who inherited the illegal gambling operation finds himself torn between the pull of the family business that has expanded into drug dealing and his earnest desire to be legitimate. Directed by **Marion McClinton**, *Dancing* was one of three plays at the NYSF/Public Theatre presented under the American identity rubric. Another well-received play was *Coming of the Hurricane* (1996). Set in 1880s during the post–Civil War period after the Reconstruction, it presents Crixus, a middle-aged black man who is a survivor of the numerous bare-knuckle boxing matches held during the Civil War. The contestants had to fight until one kills the other. A newly freed slave, Crixus is not prepared for the life of freedom. After his house is burned down mysteriously, he is forced to resume boxing for a lucrative payday and challenge "The Hurricane," a white symbol of the South, to one final bout. Produced at the Arena Playhouse in Washington, DC (February 1996), *Hurricane* was a finalist for the American Theatre Critic's Award for best play.

Glover's fourth play, *In Walks Ed* (1997), was a huge success. Set in a **Harlem** bar, the play features Ed, a hit man who returns to his old barroom hangout after being away for 15 years working for the mob. He is back to close an unsettled account. There is an outpouring of stories in the bar that are accompanied by rock and roll, jazz, and the blues. *Walks* premiered at the Long Theatre in New Haven, CT, under the direction of the author. It earned Glover a **Pulitzer Prize** nomination (1997). Another play, *Thunder Knocking at the Door*, was given an off-Broadway production (2002). It was set in 1966 in Glover's hometown. It is an African American fable that combines drama, mystery, comedy, magic, and music to tell the story of the Dupree family, leading to a guitar duel between brothers Jaguar and Marvel "The Conqueror" Thunder. *Thunder* was the winner of the Osborn Award given by the American Critics. Other representative plays by Glover include *The Rose of Corazon: A Texas Songplay* (2004), a tale of Rosa, a rescued World War I war bride who starts her new life with a husband with mystical powers. Glover also wrote *Coming of the Hurricane, Swerling with Merlin, The Curious Walk of the Salamander, Heaven and Hell (On Earth), Dark Paradise: The Legend of the Five-Pointed Star*, and *Jazzland*. An alumnus of the New Dramatists, Glover is also the writer of the *134th Edition of Ringling Brothers and*

Barnum and Bailey Circus: The Greatest Show on Earth. Glover has received several awards during his career, which include the Lois and Richard Rosenthal New Play Award, the Helen Hayes Award, and the American Theatre Critics Association Award.

GORDON, CARL. Born in Richmond, VA, Gordon is a veteran character actor with over 40 years of experience. He made his Broadway debut in 1969 in *The Great White North*—his first of four Broadway appearances. Gordon formed a close alliance with the **Negro Ensemble Company**. He performed in nearly 30 productions, including the national tour of **Joseph Walker**'s *The River Niger*; **James de Jongh**'s *Do Lord, Remember Me*; and **Charles Fuller**'s *Zooman and the Sign*. He has appeared in over 50 television episodes and movies, including *ER*, *Law and Order*, *The Practice*, *The Brother from Another Planet*, *The Bingo Long Traveling All-Stars and Motor Kings*, *Sesame Street*, *Nash Bridges*, *Gordon's War*, *JAG*, and *The Wedding*. His most cherished memories, however, lie in the television sitcom *Roc* with **Charles Dutton**, which relished portraying positive images of black people rather than negative stereotypes. The series aired for three years between 1991 and 1994. Previously, Gordon had worked with Dutton in **August Wilson**'s *The Piano Lesson* (1990) onstage and in the film in 1995.

When Gordon retired to his home state of Virginia in 2004, returning to the stage was the last thing on his mind. When he found out, however, that a new black theater, the African American Repertory Theatre, was forming in his hometown of Richmond, he offered his help. In the best tradition of "giving back to the community," he even performed the title role in their production of Wilson's *Joe Turner's Come and Gone* in 2007. He had acted in the original Broadway cast of the same show in 1990. Although he had not planned it, he had come full circle. Gordon is now in the phalanx of veteran black actors who are providing input to the burgeoning crop of young people who see black theater as a viable, vital part of the future.

GORDON, CHARLES. *See* OYAMO (CHARLES GORDON).

GORDONE, CHARLES (1925–95). A playwright, actor, and director, Gordone was the first African American writer to win the esteemed **Pulitzer Prize** in drama for *No Place to Be Somebody: A Black-Black Comedy* (1967). Born in Cleveland, OH, he was the son of carnival dancer Camille Fleming and the stepson of an auto mechanic. After his birth, the family, including his six siblings, moved to Elkhart, IN, his mother's hometown. Although he enrolled in University of California at Los Angeles in 1942, Gordone left after only a semester to join the U.S. Army Air Corps Special Services, where he helped organize entertainment services. Gordone returned to Indiana the day after his army discharge. There he married Juanita Burton, and they had two children. After the marriage failed, Gordone fell into a period of promiscuity and alcoholism. He moved to Los Angeles in 1945, where he worked as a police officer before deciding to use the G.I. Bill of Rights to complete his education. In 1952, he completed his B.A. at California State University in Los Angeles. He gave up plans to be a singer and moved to New York City. As a waiter in Greenwich Village, he gravitated toward the stage. He went on to win an **Obie Award** in 1953 for his performance as George in an all-black off-Broadway production of *Of Mice and Men*.

Through the early 1960s, Gordone directed several plays. In 1964, he made his playwriting debut with *Little More Light around the Place*, cowritten with Sidney Easton. Social issues also found their way into Gordone's life. He cofounded the Committee for the Employment of Negro Performers and chaired the Congress of Racial Equality's committee for employment of black performers. Gordone reached the pinnacle of success in theater, however, with his Pulitzer Prize–winning play *No Place* in 1969. While working in the Greenwich Village bar, Gordone was inspired to write about the fantastic stories he heard from an array of character types who provided rich subject matter for the play. First staged off Broadway, *No Place* soon drew critical and popular attention. A drama in three acts, it deals with the question of identity. Set in a New York City bar, it focuses on characters whose lives intersect with barkeeper Johnny Williams, a gangster; black and white prostitutes; an ex-convict; politicians; and idealists. Johnny, inflicted with the "Charlie fever," is trying to gain control of the local rackets from the area syndicate by enlisting a number of his associates in his scheme.

For over 15 years, *No Place* was the most produced African American play both professionally and at institutions of higher education. Productions were mounted at the Sheridan Square Playhouse in New York City, where it was first presented (November 1967); the Richard Barr's Playwrights Unit in New York City (December 1967); off Broadway by **Joseph Papp** at the Other Stage (April 1969); and at the New York Shakespeare Festival at the NYSF/Public Theatre (May 1969–October 1970), for a total run of 312 performances. This run was interrupted for a special engagement presented on Broadway by American National Theatre and Academy (ANTA) at the ANTA Theatre for 16 performances (1970). In 1971, Gordone received a grant from the National Institute of Arts and Letters (1972) that allowed him time and funding to develop his craft as a playwright. Under the direction of the author, the show was produced again on Broadway at the Promenade Theatre (1970–72) and at theaters throughout the country with the National Black Touring Company (1970–74) with a cast headed by Philip Thomas and Terry Alexander. Following the national tour, the production returned to the Morosco Theatre on Broadway for a limited run (1974).

Gordone continued to write plays throughout the 1970s. As successful as *No Place* was, his later plays failed to attract critical or popular attention. This had a momentarily debilitating effect on his writings until he became reenergized after hearing a reading of *Anthem* by legendary cowboy-poet Buck Ramsey. Around this time he began working with inmates, using theater as a rehabilitative tool, at the Cell Block Theatre in Yardville and Bordentown Youth Correctional Institutions in New Jersey in 1975.

Some 10 years after winning the Pulitzer Prize, Gordone moved to Los Angeles, where he met Susan Kouyomjian, whom he would later marry. They founded a multicultural theater that performed the works of John Steinbeck, Arthur Miller, and Tennessee Williams. Gordone also found time to direct and lecture in community theaters throughout the country. In 1986, he began a nine-year teaching career at Texas A&M University until his death (November 1995) in College Station, TX, of cancer. In addition to the aforementioned honors, Gordone also won a **New York Drama Critics' Circle Award**, a **Drama Desk Award**, and the Vernon Rice Award, all for *No Place*.

In 1987, he won the prized fellowship at the D. H. Lawrence ranch just outside of Taos, NM.

GOSS, CLAY E. A playwright, Goss was born in Philadelphia. He was a playwright-in-residence at Howard University (1970–73), where he received a B.F.A. He came into prominence during his senior year at Howard when his play *The Corner* (1973) was produced off Broadway by the New York NYSF/Public Theatre. *Homecookin* (1970) centers on two childhood friends who meet by chance in a subway. One is a college student and aspiring writer, and the other is a sergeant in the Marines home from Vietnam. The **New Federal Theatre** (**NFT**, 1972), Howard University, Washington, DC, produced it (1974), as well as the La Mont-Zeno Community Theatre in Chicago (1975). *Andrew* (1970) is a tragedy in one act. A murder victim symbolically confronts his killers. It was produced by Johns Hopkins University in Baltimore, MD; St. Marks Playhouse, off Broadway, for two performances (January 1971); off Broadway by the New York Shakespeare Festival; and at the NYSF/Public Theatre (June–July 1972) for 46 performances. *Oursides* (1974) is a drama about a black man and a black woman who reach a common bond of mutual understanding about life.

Goss has been a prolific writer of 15 plays and a book. Theatres nationwide, such as Theatre Black, DC Black Repertory, **Billie Holiday Theatre**, and **Plowshares Theatre**, have produced his plays. Other plays by Goss include *A Walking Disorder* (1970), a full-length screenplay. A 16-year-old boy and five children must find their way amid unusual circumstances. *Mars: Monument to the Last Black Eunuch* (1972) is a drama with music. A black man disenchanted with life is reenergized after he reads an article about blacks on the planet Mars. Howard University produced it in Washington, DC (1972).

China Gold (1983) is a playlet that centers on two methadone addicts. *The Commutables* (pre-1985) is in one act. Set in a 125th Street/Park Avenue subway station, two commuters are linked while connecting between **Harlem** and Westchester. *A Hip Rumplestiltskin* (1969) is a black rock musical version of the well-known fairytale. The Department of Recreation in Washington, DC, produced it (1969), along with the Ebony Impromptu in Washington, DC (1971); Theatre Black at the Third Annual Black Theatre Alliance Festival held at the Brooklyn Academy of Music (1973); and Summer in the Parks of New York City (1974). *Keys to the Kingdom* (1975) is a domestic drama in three acts. After the death of a young person's grandmother, he inherits her property, causing a problem among the family. *Ornette* (1970) is a ritualistic drama in three acts about avant-garde innovator of jazz music Ornette Coleman set during the 1940s. It was produced by the Drama Department at Howard University (winter 1970) on a program of one-act plays by Goss entitled *Changes: Three Plays for Elgba.* It was also presented at New York University (1973) and the University of Massachusetts (1975).

GRAHAM, ARTHUR J. Born in Kingston, Jamaica, Graham, a playwright, educator, and accountant, became a U.S. citizen in 1963. He received a B.A. in accounting at San Diego State University (1967) and a Ph.D. in English and American literature at the University of California at San Diego (1980). He wrote his doctoral dissertation on the Manichean leitmotif. It dealt with the ideology and psychology of racism in American fiction. By 1983, he had settled in San Diego.

Graham is the author of four plays of note. *The Captain and His Crew* (1972) is a children's story. *The Nationals: A Black Happening in Three Acts* (1968) is about the inclusion of an improbable segment of the African American community that played a part in the **civil rights** struggle of the 1960s—the prostitutes, pimps, and winos. *The Last Shine* (1969) is a drama in one act about an old shoe-shine boy who questions his attitude about racial identity during the civil rights era of the 1960s. Productions were mounted at the Inner-City Reader's Theatre in Los Angeles (February 1976) and the West Coast Black Repertory Theatre, Inc. (June 1976), in San Francisco. *Daddy Was a Welfare Check* is a drama in three acts about a family's determination to get off welfare and break the cycle of dependency. Stage 7 presented it (August and November 1975) in San Diego, and the Performing Arts Society of Los Angeles mounted it for a special showing in December 1975.

GRAHAM, BILLY (1935–1996). Born in New York City, Graham was a playwright, actor, writer, set designer, and poster designer. He has the distinction of being the first black commercial artist and cartoonist/

illustrator hired by the Marvel Comics Group, producers of Super-man, Spider Man, and the Hulk, among others. The **Frank Silvera Writers' Workshop (FSWW)** showcased Graham's work along with the **Negro Ensemble Company** and the **New Federal The-atre (NFT)**, all in New York City. Graham earned his diploma from the High School of Music and Art and the School of Visual Arts, made possible by his G.I. Bill after serving a four-year enlistment in the U.S. Navy. He studied playwriting with **Steve Carter** and acting with Jim Moody, Bill Duke, **Gilbert Moses**, and **Dick An-thony Williams** at the NFT (at the Henry Street Settlement). He also studied theater with **Maxwell Glanville** at the American Com-munity Theatre/Pro/Workshop.

Graham began his career as a commercial artist. He became art di-rector of Warren Publishing, the world-famous horror magazine com-pany and publishers of *Creepy, Eerie, Vampirella,* and *Famous Mon-sters* magazines. Then he turned to freelance artwork for Marvel Comics Group and became illustrator for many of their comic books. Since 1974, Graham has turned his talents to the theater as play-wright, actor, set and poster designer, and publicist. He has also writ-ten "spec" scripts for television and films.

He was twice nominated for **Audience Development Committee (Audelco)** Recognition Awards for set design and was winner of this coveted award in 1982–83 for his designs for **Garland Lee Thomp-son**'s play *Tut-Ankh-Amen* (1982). He was also nominated by Au-delco as most outstanding playwright (1983–84) for *The Trial of Adam Clayton Powell, Jr.* (1981), a drama in two acts chronicling the life of Congressman Adam Clayton Powell Jr., the powerful black chairman of the Education and Labor Committee for 14 years, a post that earned him seniority in the House of Representatives. Powell was later forced to relinquish his position. The FSWW mounted the show for a long, successful run (c. 1982–83). Its presentations in-clude the three performances at the Second Annual Audelco Black Theatre Festival, produced by Vivian Robinson at City College of New York (1983); off Broadway by the NFT (October–20 Novem-ber1983); and 24 performances with Timothy Simonson in the title role for which he won an Audelco Award as best actor of the year.

The Dreams of Dr. King and the Memphis Mission (1985) is a two-part play about Dr. Martin Luther King Jr. Both parts deal with the next to last day in King's life. *Dreams* incorporates selected speeches and sermons of the great **civil rights** leader and shows some of his fears and frustrations as well as his premonition of his death from an assassin's bullet. *Mission* dramatically reveals how King defied warnings and journeyed to Tennessee to give his support to the striking sanitation workers. The Theatre in Progress produced the work in New York City (December 1984–January 1985).

Ghost Stories of the Blacksmith's Curse (1995) is a favorite around Halloween time or during Black History Month in February. It chronicles African American history through an experience in terror, drama, mystery, and ghostly humor, with touches of spooky sound effects, eerie music, howling winds, lighting, thunder, and a graveyard-walking ghost in white. All these elements make this a fun play for the entire family, young and old. **Woodie King Jr.** produced it at the **National Black Theatre Festival** in Winston-Salem, NC (1995). The Ohio State University (OSU) Department of Theatre produced it at the Riffe Center in downtown Columbus (2005) under the direction of Anthony D. Hill. It also played at the Ohio Union at OSU and was taken on tour to the local schools.

GRAY, ALFRED RUDOLPH. A playwright and educator, Gray is a native New Yorker. He earned an M.A. from Hunter College in 1945 and taught English and drama in the New York public school system. After earning his doctorate at the Graduate Center of the City of New York, he became an instructor at the John Jay College of Criminal Justice. Gray is the author of a number of plays that have been produced at the **New Lafayette Theatre**, Company in Black, AMAS (it means "'you love" in Latin) Repertory Theatre, the Hunter College Playwrights Unit, the 13th Street Repertory Theatre, and other venues. Representative plays Gray wrote are *Tryst* (1959), in which a former star athlete tries to live life through his son; *Lucy, My Rose Petal* (1964), a bittersweet comedy about a couple that tries to put their lives back together after being robbed; and *Conversation with a Kleagle* (2005), a story inspired by events in the life of **civil rights** leader Walter White. His other plays are *Dance to a Nosepicker's Drum* (1970), cowritten with **Maxwell Glanville**; *Dreams from a Far Region of the Soul* (1972); and *Eye for an Eye* (1972). Gray is a member of the **Frank Silvera Writer's Work-**

shop, the Frederick Douglass Creative Arts Center, the Writers Guild of America, and the Dramatists Guild. Honors and awards he has received are the John Golden Playwriting Award (1972, 1973, and 1974), Creative Artists Public Service Award (1980), Writers Guild of America screenwriting fellowship (1980), and American Award for filmmaking.

GRAY, LAYON. An actor, director, playwright, and choreographer, Gray is among a new breed of African American playwrights who write for the stage and the silver screen. He was born in Louisiana and earned his B.A. in theater arts at the University of Louisiana. He moved to Los Angeles in the 21st century and established his own theater, now called the Mighty Gents of Hollywood. He has appeared onstage in such plays as *Miss Ever's Boys*, *The Crucible*, and *A Raisin in the Sun* and directed such plays as **Ntozake Shange**'s *For Colored Girls Who Have Considered Suicide When the Rainbow Is Enuf*, **August Wilson**'s *Fences*, and **Charles Fuller**'s *A Soldier's Play*. Gray has written several plays that have gained prominence among theatergoers. *Meet Me at the Oak* is a family play. *Soldiers Don't Cry* is a military drama. Among his other plays are *Diary of a Catholic School Dropout*, *The Girls of Summer*, *American South*, *When April Snow Falls in June*, *Black Man*, *Get Ready*, *8 Shades of Layon Gray*, and *Brick*. Gray's latest play is WEBEIME, the story of the last day of a man sentenced to die in the electric chair. The man is seated upstage center while a seven-man ensemble portray scenes from the man's life from birth to death. The play was shown at the National Black Theatre Festival in 2007, and in 2008 at the Negro Ensemble Company in Harlem. Gray has appeared in 10 films, including *The Gates-trix*, *Hood Angels*, *Like a Woman Should*, and *Demon Slayer*. He has also directed two films, *Soldiers Don't Cry* and *The Lost Girl Society*.

THE GREAT MACDADDY (1973). **Paul Carter Harrison**'s **Obie Award**–winning play *The Great MacDaddy* is a ritualized, episodic, imagistic African American event in two acts. It is based on African storyteller Amos Tutuola's mythic novel *The Palm Wine Drinkard*. It is an episodic journey through time in which MacDaddy searches for the Spirit of Wine who holds the secret of the race. The play is set at the wake of the elder MacDaddy in Los Angeles. The son now becomes heir to his father's lucrative bootlegging operation, however Wine, the protector of the race, is the only one who knows the formula for the home brew, and he disappears into the spirit world. The son, with his African juju stick as protection, begins a journey eastward toward the motherland, Africa, in pursuit of Wine. As the journey unfolds, Mac-Daddy encounters an array of emblematic folk characters—an Uncle Tom, a preacher, a pimp, a drug addict—all of whom contribute to his search, but some do their best to lead him astray. Most are in various disguises, such as Scag, Spirit of Woe, Shine, and Signifying Baby. When the son finally finds Wine, whom he was unaware had guided him throughout his journey, the son is rewarded with something much greater than what he had set out to find—the essence of life. The play becomes a spiritual odyssey through African American folk traditions in which the son gains force by encountering manifestations of the oppression and spiritual resistance of blacks throughout American history before he can become the Great MacDaddy—the savior of his people. The ending is ambiguous, leaving it to the audience to decide the fate of the black race. The play is augmented by music, everything from reggae to "Amazing Grace." *MacDaddy* premiered at **Black Arts/West** in 1973 before the **Negro Ensemble Company** produced it in 1974, where it won an Obie Award for best play.

GREEN, DAVID. A playwright, Green was born in New York City, where he attended the New School for Social Research. He began writing in the early 1960s when the black arts movement was becoming a force. His plays include *Gonna Make That Scene*, about two black men who aspire to become part of the American middle-class community but continually fail. *Do Your Thing* tells the story of a man visiting a paranoid friend in **Harlem** who refuses to let him enter his home. *Georgia Man and Jamaican Woman* (1970) is a comedy about cultural differences. His other plays include *My Cherie Amour* (1970); *Mr. B* (1971); *One Hundred Is a Long Number* (1972); *Those Wonderful Folks* (1972); *Bubba, Connie, and Hindy* (1973); *Sporty* (1974); and *Wally Dear* (1974).

GREEN, JOHNNY L. A playwright, Green was based in New York City, where he participated in the New York Black Writers Conference in 1971. His plays of note include *Black on Black*, a mystery-drama in one act. The action occurs in the interior of an old cabin in the woods, where a traitor is discovered among the group. *The Night of Judgment* is a drama of ethics in one act. Four black men are brought to trial by a hooded figure who determines whether they live or die by their actions in the community. *The Trials and Tribulations of Ma and Pa Williams* is a domestic drama in three acts. A young wife puts status and image before the human interests of her husband's mother and father.

***THE GREEN PASTURES* (1930).** Marc Connelly's (white) religious fantasy with music opened on Broadway at the Mansfield Theatre (26 February 1930). Laurence Rivers produced it under the direction of the author, with numerous spirituals provided by choir director Hall Johnson. It is a black preacher's version of the Old Testament set in the black side of heaven. The principal character, De Lawd, was played by a black man, Richard B. Harrison, who received special praise from critics; he comes down to earth in the form of a human to get a closer look at corruption and decay in society. *Pastures* has been praised for providing opportunities onstage on and off Broadway for literally hundreds of black actors and was awarded the **Pulitzer Prize**. Connelly's play has also been criticized by black writers and audiences for its use of Negro dialect and portrayal of black stereotypes from the minstrel tradition. Aside from that controversy, *Pastures* provided black actors, singers, and songwriters work onstage in New York and in theaters throughout the United States during the difficult times of the Great Depression; furthermore, it swayed investors to support black musicals and dramas.

GREENIDGE, GERTRUDE. A native New Yorker, Greenidge has been a playwright, librettist, and screen writer since 1962. Four representative plays by Greenidge have been produced frequently. *Shadow of the Birth Tree* (1963, revised in 1977 to a three-act form) is a domestic drama in two acts set on a Midwestern farm. The arrival of the youngest brother in a family with his new bride is the catalyst that disrupts the family tranquility when a deep dark secret is revealed. It was produced in New York City at the **Harlem** YMCA Theatre Group (1967) for three performances, and the Franklin

Thomas Theatre Group (July 1977). *Shadowplay* (1966) is a fantasy in one act. A young couple enters a theater that is due for demolition, and they find two men seated on the bare stage. Their meeting changes the course of the young couple's lives. Productions in New York City opened at the "Riverdale Showcase" at Christ Church Parish House in the Bronx (January 1968) for six performances and by the Adam Clayton Powell Repertory Company (June–July 1977). *Ma Lou's Daughters* (original title, *Daughters*, 1979) is a domestic drama in one act. A woman raped by two white men as a teenager returns to the South for her mother's funeral. She finds that she must now deal with her mulatto daughter, whom she has left behind since infancy. New York City productions include those by the Afro-American Total Theatre (March–May 1975), American Community Theatre (ACT)/Pro/ Workshop, the Harlem YMCA (January 1980), the Redfield Theatre of the No Smoking Playhouse (an Equity minishowcase directed by **Glenda Dickerson**, September 1983), and the **Hadley Players Theatre** (December 1985 and February–March 1986) directed by **Maxwell Glanville**. *Outside: A Psychological Evaluation* (1983) is in one act. A young woman, the victim of amnesia, tries desperately to convince the director of the mental institution where she is confined that she is not insane. New York City productions include the ACT/ Pro/Workshop (January 1983) for three performances and the Hadley Players Theatre (December 1985 and February–March 1986) directed by Maxwell Glanville. Greenidge was a member of the **Negro Ensemble Company** Playwrights Workshop under the direction of **Steve Carter**. She has been associated with the **Frank Silvera Writers' Workshop**, the Harlem YMCA Little Theatre, the Adam Clayton Powell Repertory Company, the Afro-American Total Theatre, and the Franklin Thomas Little Theatre—all in New York City—as well as the TAPS Community Theatre and the **Paul Robeson** Players in Brooklyn. She was a playwright-in-residence at the ACT Professional Workshop in New York City.

Greenidge has been honored with the **Lorraine Hansberry** Best Play Award, National Endowment for the Arts/Theatre Communication Group Residency Award, National Endowment for the Arts Award, and Richard Maibaum Award, among others. In 1983, she received an award for literary excellence from the Paul Robeson Players in Brooklyn.

GREENIDGE, KIRSTEN. Born in Arlington, MA, Greenidge, a playwright, earned a B.A. from Wesleyan University (1996) and an M.F.A. from the Playwrights Workshop at the University of Iowa (2001), where she was a Barry Kemp Fellow. In addition to writing plays over the years, she has continued to hone her skills at such venues as the New Dramatists Writers Retreat, the Sundance/UCross Theatre Lab, the Humana Festival, and the Eugene O'Neill Playwrights Festival. She is among an increasing number of emerging young black female writers who have thrust themselves into the forefront of the African American theatrical world. Her works tend to be nonlinear, surreal comedies that explore race through the prism of comedy intermixed with history.

Her plays have been either workshopped, read, given staged readings, or performed at some of the leading theaters in the country, including the Mark Taper Forum, the Oregon Shakespeare Festival, the Eugene O'Neill Theatre Center, and Actors Theatre in Louisville, among others. One of her more produced play is *The Gibson Girl* (August 1995), about two rebellious young girls reared as fraternal twins. The tension between them has to do with color stratification. One is dark, and the other is light-complexioned. The mother tries to lure the absentee father back home to straighten them out. Other plays Greenidge wrote are *Sans Culottes in the Promised Land*; *A More Perfect Union*; *Yes Please, and Thank You*; *Familiar*; *Rust: An Illustrative Limbo*; *Hinges Keep a City: Neighborhood Stories*; *Bossa Nova*; *103 within the Veil: A Theatrical Collage*; *What If They're Wrong*; *The Joys of Childhood*; *Feeding Beatrice: A Gothic Tale*; and *Josephine 65*. Greenidge has been honored with the **Lorraine Hansberry** Best Play Award, National Endowment for the Arts/Theatre Communication Group Residency Award, National Endowment for the Arts Award, and Richard Maibaum Award.

GREENLEE, SAM. A playwright, poet, and novelist, Greenlee is a writer whose life has been circumscribed by one event: the writing of his best-selling novel *The Spook Who Sat by the Door* (1969). Until then, he was a nondescript federal employee for the U.S. Information Agency (USIA). Born in Chicago, Greenlee received a B.S. in political science from the University of Wisconsin (1952). After a two-year stint in the U.S. Army, he continued his graduate studies at the

University of Chicago and the University of Thessalonski in Greece. He joined the USIA (1957) with the intent of becoming a career employee, but disenchantment with U.S. policies prompted him to resign in 1965. This was at the height of the **civil rights movement** in the United States, and Greenlee decided to make his contribution to the cause.

For the next two years, he worked on *Spook*, a fictional novel. In reality, it was a handbook for urban warfare, showing the tactics, techniques, strategies, and planning to gain the upper hand in inner-city fighting. Greenlee received 40 letters of rejection before Allison and Bigsby, Ltd., a small London press, decided to publish it. *Spook* became an instant cult classic. It sold over 1 million copies and was printed in six languages. It gained a reputation from the radical sector of the African American community as the first black nationalist novel. United Artists made it into a film in 1973, with **Ivan Dixon** directing. Greenlee cowrote the screenplay with Melvin Clay. The release came during the period of the blaxploitation movies and was filling movie-houses across the land until United Artists abruptly withdrew the film. The FBI had warned the distributor of the "film's dangerous and radical revolutionary content." The novel was made into a play in the 1980s, but it had a short run. Greenlee wrote one other play of record, *Blues for Little Prez*, a musical about the life and drug-related death of Chicago bluesman Lil Prez. It was work-shopped at the **Frank Silvera Writers' Workshop** and produced at the Martinique Theatre in New York City (1976). Greenlee is the recipient of numerous awards.

GREENWOOD, FRANK. A playwright, Greenwood has resided in Los Angeles and New York City. His most known plays include *Brother Malcolm X: Reminiscences of a Black Revolutionary* (1986), a full-length biographical drama about the life of the dynamic leader of the **civil rights movement**. **Roger Furman**'s **New Heritage Repertory Theatre Company** in New York City first presented it (May–June 1986). It was then taken on the **National Black Touring Circuit** (April 1987) under the direction of **Ron Milner**. Greenwood's other play, *Cry in the Night* (1963), is a one-act drama that explores the subject of black militancy.

GRIMKÉ, ANGELINA EMILY WELD (1880–1958). Grimké, a playwright, poet, and educator, was born in Boston. She gained wide recognition from the National Association for the Advancement of Colored People (NAACP) for her play *Rachel* (1916), a scathing indictment on lynching and its aftermath. She is the first black female playwright of record to use the stage as a propaganda tool against racial violence and prejudice. Grimké is the offspring of a biracial marriage between her half-black father and a wealthy white woman of a prominent Boston family. She was named after her great-aunt, Angelina Grimké (Weld), a noted white abolitionist. Owing to her family's good name, she was afforded an education (not available to nonwhites at the time) at Boston Normal School of Gymnastics and Harvard University. Grimké moved to Washington, DC, to teach English, first at the Armstrong Manual Training School, then at Dunbar High School.

Grimké began writing poetry at an early age and continued writing most of her life. *Rachel*, a full-length play, is her most important work as a playwright. A sensitive young black teacher whose greatest love is for children is traumatized by the discovery of a lynching 10 years earlier and by the hostile racial attitudes against young black children, especially the darker ones. She is faced with a dilemma as to whether she should marry and bring children into this environment. The Drama Committee of the NAACP first produced *Rachel* in Washington, DC (March 1916), and a year later in Boston and New York City. Grimké died in 1958 in New York City, where she had retired.

GUILLORY, LETITIA. An actor and director, Guillory is one of the new breed of performance artists who utilize space, mixed media, current events, and spontaneity in creating works that evolve with each performance. No one work ever remains the same. Her performance pieces have been mounted in Ohio, Connecticut, Maryland, North Carolina, and New York City. In 2002, she was the first black performance artist to be invited to the Eugene O'Neill Playwrights Conference, where she gave her piece *The Further Adventures of Gussie Mae in America*, a one-woman show exploring three generations of black women in America. Other performance pieces Guillory is known for include *Crossing the Holy Waters*, a journey through history; *Free at Last*; *A Look at the Harlem Renaissance*; *Red*; *The Beginning of the End, Shelter: A Photograph of Hope*; and *Dancing in Her Head: The Life and Times of Katherine Dunham*. Guillory served as the artistic director of the AIDS Theatre Project. She also works in educational theater, presenting workshops to homeless shelters in the community and college campuses.

GUNN, MOSES (1929–93). Gunn was an unassuming, powerful actor who excelled not only in playing Shakespearean parts but also in nuanced, textured roles of authoritarian figures. During his lifetime, Gunn appeared onstage with the Yale Repertory Theatre and the New York Shakespeare Festival and was a charter member of the **Negro Ensemble Company**. He made over 60 television and movie appearances in his career in such vehicles as *Hill Street Blues*, *A Man Called Hawk*, *The Killing Floor*, *Little House on the Prairie*, *Good Times*, *Roots*, *The Iceman Cometh*, *Hawaii Five-O*, *Shaft*, *Gabriel's Fire*, *The Cosby Show*, and *Homicide: Life on the Street*. Gunn was born in St. Louis, MO, the oldest of seven children. When he came of age, Gunn enrolled in and served in the U.S. Army for three years. Taking advantage of his service benefits, he earned a B.A. from Tennessee State University in 1959. Subsequent studies were in the Graduate Program for Speech and Drama at the University of Kansas. Gunn made his stage debut in the remarkable 1962 production of Jean Genet's *The Blacks* that featured **James Earl Jones**, Cicely Tyson, **Roscoe Lee Browne**, Godfrey Cambridge, and **Esther Rolle**. He was equally comfortable with Shakespearean roles, which he performed with the Yale Repertory and **Joseph Papp**'s New York Shakespeare Festival (NYSF). At the NYSF he appeared in *Measure for Measure*, *Romeo and Juliet*, and *Titus Andronicus* and played the lead role in *Othello*. Gunn was honored with a Lifetime Achievement Award from the **National Black Theatre Festival** in 1991. He is also the winner of two **Obie Awards** for his work onstage, one in performance for *The First Breeze of Summer* (1974–75) and the other for distinguished performance (1967–68).

GUNN, WILLIAM "BILL" HARRISON (1934–89). A playwright, actor, filmmaker, screenwriter, and novelist, Gunn was one of the most respected, admired, and versatile artists. He broke new ground in the area of black independent film in the 20th century. Born in Philadelphia, Gunn grew up in a middle-class environment and attended an integrated high school. Early on, his parents nurtured his creative ability. His mother, Louise Alexander Gunn, an actress, founded her own theater. His father, William Harrison, was a poet, songwriter, and musician. After serving a short stint in the U.S. Navy, he settled in the East Village in New York City in the 1950s to pursue a career in the performing arts, playing roles on and off Broadway. By the early 1960s, Gunn had minor or secondary roles regularly in many of the popular television series and films. Gunn saved enough money as a performer on and off Broadway to be able to write, study art, and buy a historic house in New York State.

The inaugural production of Gunn's first stage play, *Marcus in the High Grass*, opened at the Theatre Guild at the Westport Theatre in Connecticut in 1958. It is a melodrama about a young black man's search for his biological father only to discover his father is someone he already knows. The Theatre Guild produced it off Broadway at the Greenwich Mews Theatre (1960) starring David Wayne and Elizabeth Ashley. *Marcus* was followed by four of his more commercially successful plays, *Johnnas* (1968), *Black Picture Show* (1975), *Rhinestone* (1982), and *Family Employment* (1985). *Johnnas* is a tragedy in one act. It centers on a self-destructive, talented young black poet whose parents had sacrificed their careers in show business for him to have a better life. It won an Emmy as best teleplay (1972). The Chelsea Theatre Center first produced it in Brooklyn (1966). The **Dashiki Project Theatre** in New Orleans mounted it as a premiere production (summer 1971) directed by **Theodore Gilliam**. It was telecast over WRC-TV (NBC) in Washington, DC (1972). In addition, the Afro-American Studio in New York City produced it the next year (1973–74). *Black Picture Show* is a musical play adapted from Gunn's novel by the same title. It is set in a psychiatric unit in a Bronx hospital. A successful poet-playwright seduced by ambition and the movie industry is reflecting on his life, trying to ascertain what went wrong. The New York NYSF/Public Theatre/Public and **Joseph Papp** produced it at the Vivian Beaumont Theatre at Lincoln Center in New York City (January–February 1975) for 41 performances. Under the direction of Gunn, **Dick Anthony Williams** received a **Tony Award** nomination for acting in the role of the title character. *Rhinestone* (adapted by Gunn from his novel *Rhinestone Sharecropping*) is a drama with music and dance in three acts. It explores the relationship between a sensitive black director-writer and a white producer uninformed of how a famous black football hero should be depicted. *Family Employment* is a full-length domestic drama. A black family of privilege has earned its wealth by exploiting African Americans through gambling.

From the late 1960s until his death, Gunn also wrote for movies and television and acted in several of his screenplays. The film that garnered Gunn recognition nationally and internationally was *Ganja and Hess* (original title, *The Vampires of Harlem*, reedited as *Blood Couple*, 1973), a full-length feature film. A vampire doctor is obsessed with blood. Gunn wrote the screenplay; played the role of George Meda, the assistant to Green (played by Duane Jones); and directed it. It was shown at the Mexican Film Festival, the Philadelphia Art Museum, and the Museum of Modern Art. In the 1970s, Gunn's contributions to the stage and screen were recognized. *Johnnas* won the 1972 Emmy Award for the best television play. *Ganja* was selected as one of the 10 best American films of the decade at the Cannes Film Festival in France (1973) and became part of a collection at the Museum of Modern Art. In 1975, Gunn received two **Audience Development Committee Awards** for best playwright and best play of the year for *Black Picture Show* and a 1980 John Simon Guggenheim Memorial Foundation fellowship award in filmmaking. In 1991, Phillis Klotman codedicated *Screenplays of the African American Experience* to Gunn and to his friend **Kathleen Collins Prettyman**. On 5 April 1989, one day before his play *The Forbidden City* opened at the NYSF/Public Theatre, Gunn died of encephalitis in Nyack Hospital in New York City.

– H –

HADLEY PLAYERS THEATRE. Hadley is a community theater located in the basement of 207 West 133rd Street in **Harlem**. **Gertrude Jeannette**, veteran actress, producer, and playwright, founded this community theater in 1979. Her goal was to enrich the cultural life in

Harlem by affording artists a chance to develop their talents and skills in the theater. Hadley recently celebrated 25 years of excellence in Harlem with a production of *American Menu* by Don Glenn. Under Ajene Washington's astute direction, *Menu* garnered the Dramatic Production of the Year Award at the **Black Theatre Festival** in Winston-Salem, NC (2003). The theater's latest offering was *The Diva and the Rapper* (2005). A diva, representing the older generation, teaches a young rapper about the importance of respecting his elders. Jeannette is now retired and resides in New York City.

HAIRSTON, ANDREA. Professor Hairston is a playwright and educator from Pittsburgh, PA. She holds a B.A. (cum laude) from Smith College and an M.A. in creative writing from Brown University. She was associate director of Brown University's **Rites and Reason Theatre** from 1988 to 1992, working with the late **George Houston Bass**. She taught at Trinity College, Holyoke Community College, Brown University, and the University of Hamburg in Germany and was a professor of theater at Smith College.

She is an award-winning playwright and founder and artistic director of Chrysalis, a cross-cultural, multidisciplinary performance ensemble that develops new music theater productions, often using the medium of performance to explore social issues of the day. Chrysalis has produced some 50 productions over the years, with Hairston being the motivating force. Hairston's early plays are written in a more traditional format and reflect themes of the day. Her later work has reflected her strong interest in science fiction and fantasy. Among the plays she wrote are *Lonely Stardust*, *Soul Repairs*, *Hummingbird Flying Backwards*, *Archangels of Funk*, and *SF Theatre Jam*. Hairston was awarded a National Endowment for the Arts (NEA) fellowship, a Rockefeller/NEA grant, a Ford Foundation fellowship, and a Schubert fellowship.

HAIRSTON, JEROME. Most young playwrights never enjoy the luxury of having one of their plays professionally produced. Hairston, however, at age 19 had two plays produced off Broadway. He is from a biracial background: his father is African American, and his mother is Korean. He received his B.A. from James Madison University (1998), followed by an M.F.A. in theater arts from Columbia University

(2001). His plays have been polished and burnished at the Humana Festival; the Eugene O'Neill Theatre Center; Young Playwrights, Inc.; and the Manhattan Theatre Club. Prior to graduation from high school at age 18, Hairston's play *Live from the Edge of Oblivion* was produced off Broadway by Playwrights Horizon. The play is a look at the corrosion of the American dream. A year later in 1994, the New York NYSF/Public Theatre produced his play *The Love of Bullets*, a love story between a drug dealer and an addict trying to escape the drug life. Other plays Hairston wrote include *Carriage*, a family drama set in a trailer park. *A.M. Sunday* (2002) is about a turning point in an interracial couple's relationship. *A Trip down the Caramel Road* is an autobiographical look at biracial families. *Three Dimensions* (2003) is a 10-minute play about a love triangle. Hairston was also the recipient of a one-year fellowship at the Manhattan Theatre Club.

HALL, KATORI. An actor and award-winning playwright, Hall received her B.A. from Columbia University in African American studies and an M.F.A. in theater from Harvard University. Additional training has come from the American Repertory Theatre, the Moscow Art Theatre School Institute, and the **Harlem** School of the Arts. In her fledgling career, she has worked in the film, television, radio, and print mediums. As an actor, Hall performed with the **Classical Theatre of Harlem** and the American Repertory Theatre as well as at the Kennedy Performing Arts Center. Hall's plays have been well received in the United States and abroad. They have been presented at the Eugene O'Neill Playwright's Center, the John F. Kennedy Center, and the Minor Latham Playhouse. Her one-woman show *Diaspora*, a blending of music and poetry, was taken to Cape Town, South Africa. Among the other plays she penned are *Awake*, *Freedom Train*, *Miss Emma Brown*, *Oreogirl: The Miscegenation Of*, *Hoodoo Love*, and *On the Chitlin Circuit*. Hall has received prestigious honors, such as being named a Cherry Lane Theatre Mentor Project finalist (mentor, **Lynn Nottage**, 2005), Eugene O'Neill/Kennedy Center Playwriting Fellow (2005), and New York Foundation of the Arts Playwriting Fellow (2006) and receiving a **Lorraine Hansberry** Playwriting Award (2005), and Vogel Award (2005).

HAMILTON, LYNN. Hamilton is a veteran actor who has had a long, steady career on both stage and television. She is perhaps best known for her recurring role as Redd Foxx's girlfriend in the sitcom *Sanford and Son*, which played from 1972 to 1977. She considers the highlight of her career, however, to be her selection to President John F. Kennedy's Cultural Exchange Program that toured Europe, the Near East, and South America. With the program, she played major roles in Thornton Wilder's *The Skin of Our Teeth* and William Gibson's *The Miracle Worker*.

Hamilton was born in Yazoo City, MS. After moving north, she earned a B.A. from the Goodman Theatre of Chicago's Art Institute. One of her earliest appearances was in the groundbreaking 1961 off-Broadway production of Genet's *The Blacks* at St. Mark's Playhouse. The show was directed by Gene Frankel and featured an all-star cast of **Roscoe Lee Browne**, **James Earl Jones**, Maya Angelou, Lou Gossett, Cicely Tyson, Godfrey Cambridge, Cynthia Belgrave, and Raymond St. Jacques. For five years, she was a resident member of **Joseph Papp**'s New York Shakespeare Festival Theatre, where she played feature roles in *Romeo and Juliet*, *Macbeth*, *Henry V*, and *The Taming of the Shrew*. Hamilton also appeared on Broadway in four separate productions over a four-year period, including **Langston Hughes**'s *Tambourines to Glory*. After a stint with the then fledgling Seattle Repertory Theatre in the mid 1960s, Hamilton moved south to Los Angeles, appearing in over 70 television episodes and movies. They include *Judging Amy*; *The Practice*; *Port Charles*; *Moesha*; *The Young and the Restless*; *Murphy Brown*; *Sister, Sister*; *The Golden Girls*; *Quincy, M.E.*; *The Waltons*; *Roots: The Next Generations*; *The Rockford Files*; *Starsky and Hutch*; *Buck and the Preacher*; *Ironside*; *Gunsmoke*; *Mannix*; and *The Bill Cosby Show*. She has returned to the stage occasionally and performed in *A Raisin in the Sun*, *Reunion in Bartlesville*, *The Amen Corner*, *A Change Is Going to Come*, and *The Divorce*. Hamilton is the recipient of a 1989 Image Award and a Living Legend Award from the **National Black Theatre Festival** in 2003.

HANSBERRY, LORRAINE (1930–65). Hansberry will be forever known in the annals of American theater as the first black female playwright to have a play, *A Raisin in the Sun* (1959), produced on

Broadway. Even though she was able to complete only two plays during her short lifetime, she was a significant and influential playwright of the 20th century. She was born in Chicago to a prominent and affluent family. She received her education at the University of Wisconsin, Roosevelt University, and the New School for Social Research. She also studied African history and culture under **W. E. B. DuBois** at the Jefferson School for Social Research. She became involved in political causes and wrote articles for **Paul Robeson**'s *Freedom Magazine*.

Hansberry wrote what became an American classic, *A Raisin in the Sun*, based on a childhood incident when her family moved into an all-white neighborhood in Chicago. It played New Haven, CT; Chicago; and Philadelphia prior to opening in New York at the Ethel Barrymore Theatre. Overnight it became a raging success, propelled by dynamic performances from **Sydney Poitier**, **Diana Sands**, and **Claudia McNeil**. It ran some 530 performances, winning a **New York Drama Critics' Circle Award** and four **Tony Awards** for best play, director, actor, and actress. In 1961, it was made into a movie, with Poitier, Sands, Ruby Dee, and McNeil reprising their stage roles. Her second play, *The Sign in Sydney Brustein's Window* (1964), was not as successful. It opened in 1964 and closed after 101 performances. Ironically, Hansberry died the same day it closed. She left behind a significant body of unfinished work, which her divorced husband, Robert Nemiroff, fell heir to when he was named executor of her estate.

Nemiroff has edited and published her unfinished manuscripts and produced them in several forms. One was her play *To Be Young, Gifted, and Black (A Portrait of Lorraine Hansberry in Her Own Words)*. This is a collage of her most personal writings, telling the story of her life and work. The Cherry Lane Theatre produced it in 1969, and it ran for a record 380 performances. It was published in 1970. That same year, *Les Blancs: The Unfinished Plays of Lorraine Hansberry* was published. It encompassed the title production as well as *The Drinking Gourd* and *What Use Are Flowers? Gourd* was commissioned by NBC years earlier to commemorate the centennial of the Civil War, but the network considered the script too controversial and never aired it. In 1973, Nemiroff and Charlotte Zaltzberg adapted *Raisin* into a musical that ran on Broadway for three years. Hansberry lived a short but remarkable life. Over 40 years after her death, the love of audiences around the world for her work has elevated her to an almost iconic status in the world of theater. Her place is assured in the canon of great African American playwrights. *See also*, MANHOOD.

HANSBERRY PROJECT (HP). One cannot help but think of the late Greg Falls, founder of A Contemporary Theatre (ACT) in Seattle, smiling with approbation as his theater lends a helping hand to a new venture called the HP, for it was the ACT that hired the first black actors in the early days of the regional theater movement in 1950, and it was the ACT that broke with past custom by hiring an all-local black cast for **Pearl Cleage**'s *Blues for an Alabama Sky* in 1997. Now they have lent their theater and resources to a new African American venture called the HP under the leadership of two veterans of the theater, **Valerie Curtis Newton** and Vivian Philips. In partnership with the ACT, the HP will produce a main-stage show, workshops, and other community-related activities during the ACT's regular season. Their avowed mission is to make significant and long-lasting contributions to Seattle's performing arts community by producing work that is stimulating, relevant, emotionally satisfying, culturally specific, multifaceted, entertaining, and artistically excellent. They have also committed themselves to producing the best plays that black theater has to offer, classics and new works alike. Newton, who holds an M.F.A. from the University of Washington and is head of the University's School of Drama Directing Program, is the artistic director of the HP. Philips, the executive director of Sankofa Theatre, functions as managing producer. The HP is named after the late playwright **Lorraine Hansberry**, whose landmark 1959 play *A Raisin in the Sun* was the first play written by an African American woman to be produced on Broadway.

Their inaugural production was in June 2006, when they presented *Wine in the Wilderness* by **Alice Childress**, an improbable love story set in **Harlem** during the middle of a race riot. Since then, they have presented the following as evidence of building community involvement and support: a black-tie fund-raising event titled Juneteenth Gala; a reading of short stories by Childress in the Town Hall Series; the Black Salon, a small group of select artists who meet monthly to network, share, and support one another; the BlackStage Theatre Group, whose goal is to bring a group to every black theater presentation in the city, regardless of who is the producing entity; and the Louise Jones McKinney Playwright Scholarship for aspiring black playwrights.

The HP produced its second main-stage production in September 2007, *The Mojo and the Sayso* by **Aishah Rahman**. Newton and Philips also presented a reading of a new play by **Dan Owens**. The third main-stage production in 2008 was Michael Bradford's *Fathers and Sons*. While the HP's avowed goal is to attract and preserve a black audience, it is an uphill battle in a city where the black population is in decline. Thus far, they have reached a broad and discerning audience. The challenges continue with optimism.

HARLEM. From the time Harlem evolved into the cultural capital of black America during the Harlem Renaissance (1915–29) to the present, it also became a popular setting for black playwrights. Harlem symbolized the dreams, aspirations, and disenchantment of the big-city urban-dwelling blacks. **Langston Hughes's** *Little Ham* and *Simply Heavenly* present Harlem as a humorous, lighthearted, bustling, and energetic environment. **Ted Ward's** *Big White Fog* shows why millions of Harlem residents both hailed and resisted Marcus Garvey and his back to Africa movement. **Abram Hill's** *On Striver's Row* is set on a block made famous by wealthy Harlem illuminati and pokes fun at bourgeoisie black middle-class snobbery. **James Baldwin's** *The Amen Corner* is set in a black Harlem church. A black female pastor must choose between the love of God and her husband, a worldly musician. **Lonnie Elder III's** *Ceremonies in Dark Old Men* depicts a desperate ex-vaudevillian who resorts to selling illegal bootleg whiskey from his Harlem barbershop as a last-ditch effort to change his mundane lifestyle. **Jeff Stetson's** *The Meeting* portrays a secret meeting of two **civil rights** giants, Malcolm X and Dr. Martin Luther King, in Harlem at the legendary Lorraine Hotel to talk about survival strategies for the black race. *See also* HARLEM ENSEMBLE COMPANY; HARLEM REPERTORY THEATRE; HARLEM SHOWCASE THEATRE (HST); HARLEM SUITCASE THEATRE (HST); HARLEM THEATRE COMPANY (HTC).

HARLEM ENSEMBLE COMPANY. Artistic director Evelyn Collins founded the **Harlem** Ensemble Company in 2000. A Detroit native, Collins has directed over 35 plays in New York; Ann Arbor, MI; and Detroit. This 501(c)3 tax-exempt organization solicits donations from patrons and encourages directors and designers to submit resumes. The company accepts scripts from playwrights yearround that focus on the **black experience**. The ensemble's inaugural production was **Leslie Lee**'s *The First Breeze of Summer* (May 2002) at the Little Theatre in St. Martin's Episcopal Church in Harlem. The 2004–5 season boasted an ambitious offering that included *In Celebration: A Tribute to Musical Theatre* (honoring Micki Grant); *Dreamgirls* by Tom Eyen and Henry Krieger; and *A Soldier's Play*, the **Pulitzer Prize** winner by **Charles Fuller**.

HARLEM REPERTORY THEATRE. This is an arm of the City College of New York's (CCNY) Theatre Department and is supported by the DuBose Heyward Foundation and CCNY's College Now Program. The theater is under the direction of Associate Professor Keith Lee Grant, who also is chair of the Theatre Department at CCNY. Grant holds an M.A. from Pennsylvania State University and an M.F.A. from the Yale School of Drama. He has directed or choreographed over 70 productions on both the university and professional level. The theater produces from two to six productions each year with visiting professionals, Equity actors, faculty members, and the theater's most advanced actors. A listing of typical productions includes *Cabaret* (book by Joe Masteroff, music and lyrics by John Kander and Fred Ebb), *For Colored Girls Who Have Considered Suicide When the Rainbow Is Enuf* by **Ntozake Shange**, *The Wiz* (book by William F. Brown, music by Charlie Smalls), *Bye Bye Birdie* (book by Michael Stewart, music and lyrics by Lee Adams and Charles Strouse), *Dreamgirls* (book by Tom Eyen, music by Henry Krieger), *Hair* (book by James Rado and Gerome Ragni, music by Galt McDermott), and *Tambourines to Glory* by **Langston Hughes**.

HARLEM SHOWCASE THEATRE (HST). Founded by **Loften Mitchell**, the HST, a playwright's workshop and theater, reportedly evolved out of Mitchell's People's Theatre (1946–48). The names were often used interchangeably. The HST's first production was Mitchell's *The Shame of the Nation* (c. 1952), which had to do with the Trenton Six rape case. It was produced at a location in **Harlem**. After the success of this production, the company relocated to its permanent home at 290 Lenox Avenue in Harlem, where motion-picture cameraman Don Tatum and Harlem businessman Raphael Lowman had converted a house into a loft. The newly acquired theater produced Mitchell's *The Cellar*. Set in Harlem, a black blues singer hides a fugitive from the South in her cellar who is being pursued by the woman's fiancée, a ruthless detective. The play had a long run at the HST (November 1952–April 1953). Mitchell's *City Called Norfolk* (1953) was the next production. The New Playwright's Company produced the fourth play at the HST, Sidney Easton's *Miss Trudie Fair*. It is set in a Harlem boarding house occupied mostly by vaudevillians. A charitable landlord marries one of the boarders, who almost ruins the proprietor's life. Mitchell was the associate producer, and Harold Cruise was the stage manager.

HARLEM SUITCASE THEATRE (HST). Based in **Harlem**, this distinguished little theater group was active between 1937 and 1939. The HST was founded as a proletarian theater to give a voice to the black masses by **Langston Hughes**; Hilary Phillips, the director; and Thomas Richardson, the executive director. It was influenced greatly by agitprop theater of the time, which came into popularity during the 1930s, and the *Living Newspapers* of the Works Progress Association **Federal Theatre Project**. Hughes and his cofounders hoped to develop a permanent repertory theater with its base in the Harlem community for black people.

Located in a loft in the International Workers Order Community Center, a fraternity hall at 317 West 125th Street in Harlem, the HST produced five plays by Hughes between 1937 and 1938. They were *Angelo Herndon Jones, Em-Fuehrer Jones, Little Eva's End, Limitations of Life, De Organizer*, and *Angelo Herndon Jones*. This last play is about the celebrated Herndon case in which a black man was sentenced to 20 years on a chain gang for protesting being unemployed in the United States. It received the best play award in the New Theatre League contest of 1936.

One of Hughes's more popular productions was *Don't You Want to Be Free?* It is an agitprop musical that tells in dramatic form the history of black oppression in America through the use of spirituals, work songs, poetry, sketches, and the rhythms of jazz and swing. It was one of the longest-running plays in Harlem. Playing mostly on weekends, *Free* amassed a record run of 135 performances. Under the direction of the author, the cast included Robert Earl Jones (father of **James Earl Jones**). The other plays the HST produced were Elizabeth Yates's *The Slave*, Paul Green's *The Man Who Died at Twelve O'Clock*, Powell Lindsay's *Young Man of Harlem*, and Hughes and Dorothy Peterson's translation of Lope de Vega's *Fuente Ovejuna*. In 1939, the HST closed due to economic instability.

HARLEM THEATRE COMPANY (HTC). Located at 432 West 150th Street (between Convent and Amsterdam Avenues), the HTC was founded by director James Pringle c. 1996. It was inspired by Sammy Davis Jr., Miles Davis, and Elijah Muhammad. The mission of the HTC was to help young people develop their acting skills through a rigorous program of voice and speech, stage makeup, script and character analysis, stage movement, dance, music, song, pantomime, and study of various periods and styles. Pringle was a native of Chicago but fine-tuned his acting skills at Los Angeles City College and in Pittsburgh, PA. Among the plays Pringle directed were *Inacent Black* (1978), a full-length mystery-comedy by **A. Marcus Hemphill**, and *Steal Away* (1971), a folktale by Ramona King. For over 10 years, the HTC garnered a reputation as one of New York's finest actor training programs that specialized in speech, dance, and advanced acting. Many HTC graduates have appeared in such sitcoms and movies as *Malcolm X*, *Boomerang*, *Above the Rim*, *New York Undercover*, and *America's Most Wanted*.

HARRIS, BILL. A playwright, poet, and novelist, Harris is a writer out of Detroit who earned his M.A. from Wayne State University. He worked briefly with **Concept East Theatre** in Detroit and the **New Federal Theatre (NFT)** before beginning his life's work as a professor of creative writing at Wayne State. Harris has written well over 30 plays and has enjoyed over 70 productions of his plays both locally and nationally. A sampling of Harris's plays includes *Every Goodbye Ain't Gone* (1983), about a show business marriage gone sour. It opened at the NFT with **Denzel Washington** and **S. Epatha Merkerson** and won an **Audience Development Committee Award**. *Stories about the Old Days* (1986) has to do with a church being demolished, triggering a confrontation between a gospel and a blues singer. It premiered at the NFT and starred jazz singer Abby Lincoln. *Holy Smoke, Society of Men* (1983) is a comedy about dueling preachers. One is a man, the other a woman. *Warn the Wicked* (1974) presents a clash of political beliefs within a close-knit family. *Queen of Sheba Boo!* is a musical fantasy. *Langston* is the life story of poet and playwright **Langston Hughes**. Among the honors and awards Harris received were the Guggenheim Foundation fellowship, Rockefeller Foundation fellowship, Naomi Long Madgett Poetry Award, Tomkins Writing Award, and **Paul Robeson** Cultural Arts Award.

HARRIS, NEIL SHAW. A playwright, Harris was born in Valhalla, NY. After attending Shaw University for two years, he left to make his own way in the world. He formed the Neil Harris Experimental Theatre in Mount Vernon, NY, which served as an incubator for many of his plays; and he studied at the **Frank Silvera Writers' Workshop**. The **New Lafayette Theatre** and the New York Shakespeare Festival produced several of his plays in the 1970s. *Passion without Reason* (1977) is Harris's most produced play. It portrays the complexities within relationships through two male and female characters. Other plays he authored include *The Vampire* (1971), a melodrama in three acts about a junkie vampire who strings his victims out on drugs; *Cop and Blow* (1972), which exposes police corruption and payoff in a **Harlem** barroom; *Players Inn* (1972), showing dope pushers pimping off the black community; *So Nice They Named It Twice* (1976), depicting a middle-class romance in the big city that clashes with life on the street; and *Straight from the Ghetto* (1976), a musical revue of Harlem street life. Harris's honors and awards include the Westchester Council for the Arts Award (1972) and the American Film Institute Award (1973).

HARRIS, TED. A playwright, Harris is a product of the Playwrights' Workshop of the **Negro Ensemble Company (NEC)** in New York

City. Two of his plays of note are *Playstreet* (1973), a drama in one act in which a married couple relives the experiences of their unfulfilled life together while staying in an abandoned building. The NEC produced it as a workshop production (February 1973). *Sandcastles and Dreams* (pre-1976) is a drama in one act in which two lonely, middle-aged women on vacation at a beach resort fantasize and dream of sexual gratification.

HARRIS, THOMAS W. A playwright, Harris, a career librarian since 1961, has written many plays that have been produced locally and around the country. He was born in New York City and served in the U.S. Army from 1951 to 1953. His educational credentials include a B.A. from Howard University (1957), an M.A. from the University of California at Los Angeles (1959), and an M.L.S. from the University of Southern California (1961). Harris wrote a number of plays, including *Always with Love*, a comedy about a black maid who murders a white family in humorous ways, and *A Number One Family*, showing the struggles of a black immigrant family in the school system. Harris also wrote *Suds*; *Fall of an Iron Horse*; *Pray for Daniel Adams*; *Daddy Hugs and Kisses*; *All the Tigers Are Tame*; *Beverly Hills Olympics*; *The Relic*; and *Divorce, Negro Style*. Harris's plays have been produced at Actors Studio and the Pasadena Playhouse. Harris has also written two novels, *Always with Love* (1973) and *No Time to Play* (1977).

HARRIS, VALERIE. A playwright, film consultant, scriptwriter, and essayist, Harris was born in Philadelphia. She attended Cheyney State College (B.A.) in Pennsylvania and American University (M.A. in performing arts and theatre) in Washington, DC. Harris's essays have been published in several periodicals, and her plays were produced at major cities and institutions of higher education. Her plays include *Nights Alone in the Naked City* (original title, *Nights Alone*, 1970s), a drama in one act in which an old white woman sharing an apartment with a young drifter reminisces about and reenacts incidents from the past with him. It was produced in Washington, DC, at American University and in Cleveland, OH. *Ice Game* (1970s) is a one-act drama in which an actor in a performing troupe trying to get out of his contract refuses to go onstage.

HARRISON, PAUL CARTER. Harrison, a playwright of world renown, is also known as an educator, author, and director. He holds both a B.A. and M.A. He has taught at Howard University, the State University of California, and the University of Massachusetts (where he is now professor emeritus). In 1980, Harrison was hired for a one-year contract as playwright-in-residence at Columbia College in Chicago. That stint turned into a 26-year sojourn, where he redeveloped the Theatre Department into one of the finest in the nation. He recently retired in 2006.

During his illustrious teaching career, Harrison taught **Phylicia Allen-Rashad**, **Clinton T. Davis**, **Pearl Cleage**, and many other artists of acclaim. He has written numerous works, but his signature play is *The Great MacDaddy* (1973), which won an **Obie Award**. It is a ritualized African American event in two acts based on Amos Tutuola's novel *The Palm Wine Drinkard*. Other plays Harrison wrote include *Abercrombie Apocalypse*, *Tabernacle*, *Pavane for a Deadpan Minstrel*, *The Experimental Leader*, *Dialogue from the Opposition* (essays based on his play *The Experimental Leader*, 1965), *Americain Gothic*, *Tophat*, and *The Death of Boogie Woogie*.

Harrison is known as the spiritual and philosophical father of black theater for his many books and articles on the subject. Perhaps the most prominent are his groundbreaking books, wherein he examines the relationship between black theater and the rituals of the motherland, Africa. They are *The Drama of Nommo: Black Theatre in the African Continuum* (1972), *Kuntu Drama: Plays of the African Continuum* (1974), and *Black Theatre: Ritual Performance in the African Diaspora* (2002). Harrison currently resides in New York City.

HATCH, JAMES VERNON. A playwright, archivist, filmmaker, and professor emeritus of English and theater at City University of New York, Hatch, Ph.D., has authored and coauthored 11 books. The most recent is *A History of African American Theatre* (2003) with **Errol G. Hill**, for which they received the Theatre Library Association's George Freedley Award for the best book published in theater that year, as well as the Bernard Hewitt Award from the American Society of Theatre Research. Other volumes by Hatch include *Lost Plays of the Harlem Renaissance*, *Inside the Minstrel Mask*, *Black Theatre USA*, and *Sorrow Is the Only Faithful One*, for which he received a second Bernard Hewitt Award (1993). In 1975, Hatch, together with his wife Camille Billops, founded the Hatch–Billops Collection, an archive of African American cultural materials. This library, open to all scholars, has published interviews of the lives and works of over 300 minority artists in a series of annual programs titled *Artist and Influence.* This year's journal (2008) will be volume 26 of the annual publication.

Hatch's awards include two National Endowment for the Humanities fellowships. He has lectured and directed plays for the U.S. Information Agency in the Philippines, India, Sri Lanka, and Pakistan and also held Fulbright fellowships in Egypt, Germany, and Taiwan. In the creative arts, he has been recognized with two **Obie Awards** for off-Broadway productions, as well as with membership in the College of Fellows in American Theatre. In 1992, he shared with his wife the Grand Jury Prize at the Sundance Film Festival for *Finding Christa.*

HAY, SAMUEL A. Hay, a playwright, critic, educator, and theater historian, was born in Barnwell, SC. He attended Bethune-Cookman College (B.A. in speech and theater, 1955), Johns Hopkins University (M.A. in playwriting, 1967), and Cornell University (Ph.D. in theater history and criticism, 1971). Hay held positions at several institutions of higher learning, such as chairperson of the Department of Communication and Theatre Arts and professor of theater at Morgan State University, Baltimore, MD (1979–84); assistant professor of English and African American studies at the University of Maryland at Baltimore (1974–78); director of the Africana Studies and Research Center and associate professor of theater at Purdue University (1974–78); and director of the Black Studies Program and professor of theater at Washington University in St. Louis, MO (1978–79). He was also chair of the Department of Speech Communication, Mass Communication, and Theatre Arts at North Carolina A&T State University in Greensboro.

Hay is also a playwright of note. His plays include *Yes in a Pleasant Country* (1970), a two-act fantasy; *Parting Shocks*, involving a couple who finds it too painful to stop their extramarital affair; and *Getting Some*, about a 14-year-old seducing the 28-year-old friend of his mother. *The Robeson Place Singers* (1976) is a full-length drama that was produced at Purdue University (1976) and portrays drunks in an alley who are inspired by the life of **Paul Robeson**. *An American Passport* (1981) is a full-length drama about Robeson's appearance before the House Un-American Activities Committee. *Sistah Rachel* (1982) is a full-length musical drama adapted from **Owen Dodson**'s *Divine Comedy* that plots Father Divine's rise to fame and his downfall. *A Woman against Apartheid* (1985) is a full-length drama about a South African woman who is tortured for standing up against apartheid. It won the National Playwriting Contest sponsored by the Detroit Center for the Performing Arts. Hay is the author of *African American Theatre: A Historical and Critical Analysis* (1994), a seminal study of theater and drama, and *Black Theatre of the Sixties* (1986). In addition, he is coeditor of a six-volume series, *Focus on Literature* (1978). He was also founder of the now defunct National Conference on African American Theatre held annually in Baltimore, MD.

Hay has been funded by the Maryland Council for the Humanities and received a fellowship from the Ford Foundation for doctoral studies at Cornell University (1968–71), a grant from the University of Maryland for study of West African theater (1972), a grant from the American Bicentennial Commission for the study of oral history of blacks in Indiana (1976), and a grant from the U.S. Department of Education to improve reading via black studies (1979).

HAYES, LOREY. Born in Wallace, NC, Hayes is a veteran performer and playwright. After graduating from North Carolina A&T, she journeyed to New York and began a successful theatrical career. Hayes was a replacement actor in **Ntozake Shange**'s breakout production *For Colored Girls Who Have Considered Suicide When the Rainbow Is Enuf* (1976). To pursue her writing career, she worked at **Frank Silvera Writers' Workshop**, the **Negro Ensemble Company**'s playwrights' workshop, the **New Heritage Theatre**, and Mark Taper's Blacksmith's Laboratory Theatre. While juggling an acting career in television, film, and stage work, she wrote over 10 plays. Her latest offering is *Lipstick, Chilli, Grits and Grace*, which was presented at the **National Black Theatre Festival** in Winston-Salem, NC, in 2007. Her other plays include *Sex, Sin, and Salvation*; *Dragonfly Tale*; *An Almost Perfect Marriage*; *Legend of Sylvia's Son*;

Left to right: Theatre patron and former director/choreographer Bambi Lynn Nickelberry, M.D., hosting at her home in Los Angeles, playwright August Wilson, director Lloyd Richards, and actor Charles Dutton after the "Fireside Chat with August Wilson," sponsored by the Center Theatre Group, c. 1992. Wilson won two Pulitzer Prizes in drama—Fences in 1987 and The Piano Lesson in 1990. He also wrote an epic 10-play cycle chronicling the African American experience for each decade of the 20th century. Wilson's mentor, Richards, was the dean of the Yale School of Drama and directed Wilson's first five plays on Broadway. Richards won the Tony Award as best director for Fences. Dutton made his Broadway debut in Wilson's Ma Rainey's Black Bottom (1985).

James Hewlett as Richard III at the African Grove Theatre in New York City, 1821, where he gained the reputation as the first professional African American actor in the United States.

Ira Aldridge performing Othello *in Frankfurt, Germany (From a lithograph by S. Buhler, 1852.). Expatriate Aldridge was internationally acclaimed throughout Europe for over 40 years.*

George and Aida Walker with Bert Williams and Stella Wiley doing the Cake Walk, c. early 1900s. The duo of Williams and Walker became one of the most successful and celebrated vaudeville teams around the turn of the century.

Krigwa Theatre Company makes a curtain call after a performance in Harlem, 1926. At this theatre, Krigwa founder W. E. B. DuBois mandated that theatre should be by, about, for, and near the black community.

A rehearsal in Seattle of Langston Hughes's Simply Heavenly by the Contemporary Players, directed by Keve Bray. Anthony D. Hill is downstage center as Boyd, c. late 1960s.

Joe Staton as Petrarch (center to right), Sarah Oliver as Kate, and Robert A. St. Clear as the preacher in the wedding scene from the Seattle Negro Repertory Company's production of The Taming of the Shrew, 1939. This was one of the many Negro units established throughout the country by President Franklin Delano Roosevelt's Works Progress Administration Federal Theatre Project during the Great Depression.

Uta Hagen as Desdemona and Paul Robeson in the title role of Othello at the Shubert Theatre on Broadway in 1943. Othello played for 296 performances, breaking the record of 157 of any Shakespeare play in America at that time. The show also broke down the racial barrier of an integrated production on Broadway.

The production staff of Summer Theatre Lincoln at Lincoln University in Jefferson City, MO. Left to right: Bertram Martin, Owen Dodson, Whitney LeBlanc, and Winona Fletcher; Tom Pawley is standing, 1960.

Ellen Holly as Regan, James Earl Jones as King Lear, and, Rosalyn Cash as Goneril in King Lear by the New York Shakespeare Festival/Public Theatre, Joseph Papp, producer, at the Delacorte Theatre, 1973.

Obie Award–winning playwright Amiri Baraka (Leroi Jones), author of Dutchman *and* The Slave Ship, *is a cultural and spiritual leader of the revolutionary black arts and black theatre movements of the 1960s.*

Jane White as Goneril in a scene from the American Shakespeare Festival Theatre/Public Theatre production of King Lear, 1975.

A production of Coriolanus *featuring Roscoe Orman and Frankie Faison as Senators, Robert Christian as Tullus Aufidius, and Morgan Freeman as Coriolanus at the New York Shakespeare Public Theatre Festival/ Public Theatre , Joseph Papp, producer, 1979.*

Left to right: Alexander Conley III, Jason Bernard, and Charles Canada rehearsing Dream on Monkey Mountain *at Douglas Q. Barnett's Black Arts/West, c. 1971.*

A production of Fortunes of the Moor *by Barbara and Carlton Molette, directed by Anthony D. Hill at the Ohio State University, February 1998.*

Ifa Bayeza is a playwright, dramaturge, and theatre producer who works out of San Francisco and Chicago.

The plenary session of American theatre and the African diaspora at the 27th Comparative Drama Conference in Columbus, OH, April 2003. Right to left: Professor Samuel A. Hay, dean, North Carolina A&T; Professor David Krasner, Yale University; Professor Anthony D. Hill, the Ohio State University; Professor Sandra L. Richards, Northwestern University; Professor Harry J. Elam Jr., Stanford University; Professor James V. Hatch, City University of New York; Eileen Morris, artistic director, Kuntu Theatre/The Ensemble Theatre; and Professor Tisch Jones, University of Iowa.

Woodie King Jr. is producer, director, author, educator, founder, and artistic director of the New Federal Theatre in New York City. A producer and director of more than 200 plays, King is the most prolific African American dramatist.

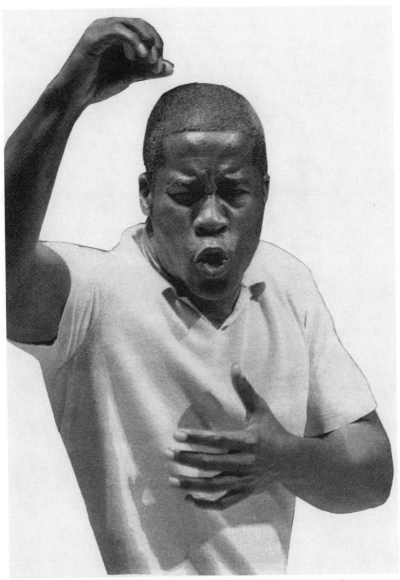

Daniel Beaty in a scene from his highly acclaimed performance piece Emergence-SEE! *at the National Black Theatre Festival in Winston-Salem, NC, 2007.*

George C. Wolfe is playwright, producer, and artistic director of the New York Shakespeare Theatre Festival/Public Theatre. His best-known play, The Colored Museum, is a satirical look at black culture.

Lynn Hamilton is a veteran stage, television, and film actress. For five years, she was a resident member of Joseph Papp's New York Shakespeare Festival Theatre/Public Theatre, where she played feature roles in Romeo and Juliet, MacBeth, Henry V, *and* The Taming of the Shrew.

Derek Walcott is a Caribbean playwright, poet, educator, and Nobel Prize winner for literature, 1992. His most-produced play is Dream on Monkey Mountain.

Valerie Curtis-Newton, artistic director at A Contemporary Theatre in Seattle, where she oversees the Hansberry Project, discusses with William Hall, Jr., a scene from Michael Bradford's Fathers and Sons.

Suzan-Lori Parks, the first African American woman playwright to win the Pulitzer Prize in drama for her linear play Topdog/Underdog (2002)—a departure from her abstract, expressionist avant-garde form.

Haiti's Children of God (a musical); *Massinassa and the Tragedy of the House of Thunder*; *Power Play*; and a one-woman play, *Little Lorey's Song*. Hayes is a member of Actors Equity and the Dramatists Guild. She is also the recipient of an **Audience Development Committee Award**.

HEATH, GORDON (1918–91). Heath was an actor, director, and folk singer with exceptional talent who chose not to fight the inherent racism he found in the United States and eventually moved to Paris, France, where he spent most of his life. He was born in New York City, the son of Haitian parents. As a youngster, he was musically inclined, slowly mastering the guitar and singing wherever he could. After high school, he attended Hampton Institute, where he studied drama under **Owen Dodson**, an old friend. Among the plays he took on in college was *Hamlet*, in which he played the title character. His Broadway debut was a small role in *South Pacific* in 1943. Two years later, he played a substantial role in a Broadway production of *Deep Are the Roots* by Arnaud D'usseau and James Gow under the direction of Elia Kazan. The play ran for 477 performances and established Heath as an actor of substance. He reprised his role in a London West End production, but when the run was over, he once again could not find work.

He moved to Paris, where he believed the racial atmosphere would be more hospitable for African American actors. He opened a night club, L'Abbaye, with his partner Lee Payant. The club became enormously popular with fellow expatriates, other artists, and the locals. Heath and Payant both sang and performed there for over 25 years. Heath acted in several films shot in France over the years, including *Mr. Arkadin* with Orson Welles, *The Madwoman of Chaillot* with Katherine Hepburn and Charles Boyer, and *The Lost Command* with Anthony Quinn and George Segal. He also found occasional roles, as in 1950, when he played the title role in *Hamlet* in a production directed by Tony Richardson, a production reprised in 1955 on the BBC. In 1960, Heath in concert with the American Church of Paris founded a new English-speaking theater and named it Studio Theatre of Paris. There they performed many American plays, including *The Skin of Our Teeth*, *The Slave*, *In White America*, *After the Fall*, and *The Glass Menagerie*. Heath either directed or acted in many of the plays. In

1970, he returned to the United States in the midst of the **civil rights** and black arts movements and was astonished at the progress made for black actors. As an expatriate, Heath was among American artists like Josephine Baker, Eartha Kitt, and **James Baldwin** who found acceptance and appreciation for their artistic talents abroad.

HEMPHILL, A. MARCUS (1930–86). A versatile playwright, director, musician, and comedy writer, Hemphill was a native of Fort Worth, TX. He earned a B.A. from Houston-Tillotson College and migrated to New York City, where he studied at the **Frank Silvera Writers' Workshop** and worked with the jazz group the Pair Extraordinaire, with whom he recorded five albums. Hemphill also toured with Bill Cosby as his principal writer in 1985 before becoming artistic director of the drama component at Riverside Church in New York City. Hemphill's most successful play was *Inacent Black* (also known as *Inacent Black and the Brothers*), first presented at the **Billie Holiday Theatre** in 1979. After playing to sellout houses for a year, it was moved off Broadway for a run at the Biltmore Theatre, where it failed to catch on. Other plays by Hemphill are *Breakin' Light: The Life and Times of John Henry*, *Seven Days before the Flood*, *The Eternal Question* (first play in the trilogy), *And I Killed Him* (second play in trilogy), and *The Big Game* (third play in trilogy).

HENDERSON, STEPHEN MCKINLEY. An actor, Henderson overcame a poverty-stricken environment during his childhood in Kansas City, MO, to become one of theater's finest character actors and a tenured professor at the University of Buffalo. He has made four appearances on Broadway and has performed at leading regional theaters across the country as well as in Ireland and England. He has made several television appearances as well, with a recurring role as a judge on *Law and Order*. Henderson could have ended up as another inner-city statistic if he had not discovered an outlet for his pent-up emotions—acting. His acting ability and disciplined learning landed him a scholarship at the North Carolina School of the Arts and Juilliard in New York City. He continued his education at Purdue University, where he earned his M.A. in theater (1977).

Henderson has played a variety of parts onstage, including Creon in *Antigone*; Sitting Bull in *Indians*; Azdak in *Caucasian Chalk Cir-*

cle; Falstaff in *The Merry Wives of Windsor*; and Abraham Van Helsing in *Dracula, the Musical*. He is also widely known as one of the strongest actors in the works of **August Wilson**. He appeared in *King Hedley II, Jitney, Ma Rainey's Black Bottom*, and *Joe Turner's Come and Gone*. Henderson also directed the successful production of *Ali* in 1992, which won an **Obie Award**. Other plays he has directed include *The Meeting, Benito Cereno, Great Goodness of Life*, and *Oleanna*. Henderson was a contributing director to the first International Women's Playwrights Conference in 1988, and in 2004, he worked at the Sundance Theatre Lab. Henderson is a member of Actors Equity Association, American Federation of Radio and Television Arts, and the Screen Actors Guild. Honors for Henderson include an Obie Award, a **Drama Desk Award**, an **Audience Development Committee Award**, and a Los Angeles National Association for the Advancement of Colored People Theatre Award.

HEWLETT, JAMES (1778–1836). An actor and singer from the West Indies with keen features and dark black eyes, Hewlett was active between 1810 and the late 1830s. He was the first recognized black professional actor in the United States. As a free black man, he earned his living as a tailor, but on weekends, he created quite a stir doing his impressions of professional actors at William Alexander Brown's tea garden (1816–21) in lower Manhattan. When Brown moved farther uptown and formed the first black theater company at the **African Grove Institute for the Arts** (AGIA; 1821–23), he hired Hewlett as his principal actor. The theater mounted over 10 productions. Hewlett, playing the title role in such productions as *Richard III* and *Othello*, became known as the "celebrated tragedian." His portrayal of Shakespearean characters was a novelty that generated excitement among black audiences and curiosity among the white patrons across the street at the famous Park Theatre, who began frequenting the AGIA. Concerned with losing his clientele and revenue, Park Theatre owner Steven Price had his friend the constable close the AGIA and arrest Hewlett along with the cast. In order to be released, the actors had to agree never to perform Shakespeare again; nonetheless, when they were released, the actors returned to the AGIA and continued to perform. Hewlett also played the role of the black Caribbean tribal chief Joseph Chatoyer in Brown's *King Shotaway*

244 • HICKS, HILLY, JR.

(June 1823), an original drama and the first **slavery** sketch in America. Soon thereafter, the police succeeded in closing the theater for good for "disturbing the peace."

Hewlett reverted to doing performances of his one-man imitations in hotels and halls in New York City to favorable reviews by critics. In 1924, he took his show to London and performed excerpts from Shakespeare at the acclaimed Coburn Theatre that were well received. Upon his return to the United States, Hewlett was armed with fresh material for his one-man imitations. His show was now comprised of burlesques of popular English and American actors, such as Charles Mathews, Edwin Booth, Edmund Kean, William Charles McReady, and J. W. Wallack. Records indicate that Hewlett last performed in 1836.

HICKS, HILLY, JR. An emerging young playwright of the 21st century, Hicks is the son of the legendary character actor Hilly Hicks, who performed in over 30 Hollywood films. Hicks, a Los Angeles native, is a graduate of New York University's School of the Arts and the Columbia University Graduate School of the Arts. He is a former staff writer for the Fox TV series *Pasadena* and also cowriter for the Discovery Channel. Hicks has had three of his works commissioned by theaters, including his highly acclaimed children's plays *The Breeze, the Gust, the Gale and the Wind*, which premiered at the La Jolla Playhouse in 2003. Other plays he wrote are *A Hole in the Dark*, *Home Life of Polar Bears*, *How to Unload a Dishwasher*, *Artists and Criminals*, *Note to Self*, *Kick Me*, and *The Trophy Room*. In his brief career, Hicks has won a Van Lier playwriting fellowship and a Berrila Kerr Foundation Award. He has also been received two Sundance Theatre Lab Awards (2000, 2006). Hicks is a member of the Dramatists Guild and the Writers Guild of America.

HICKS, ISRAEL. A director and teacher, Hicks is one of the few African Americans to make a living teaching and directing both traditional and black plays. A native of South Carolina, Hicks grew up in Brooklyn. He attended Boston University on a football scholarship but became interested in theater inadvertently—he fell in love with a student actress who spurred his interest in theater. Hicks went to graduate school at New York University, where he studied directing under **Lloyd Richards**, the mentor and director of **August Wilson**'s first six shows on Broadway. Hicks had met Richards previously at Boston University. On Broadway, Hicks worked as an assistant director on *Does a Tiger Wear a Necktie?* in 1969 with a cast that included Al Pacino. Thereafter, Hicks was asked to direct a production at the prestigious Tyrone Guthrie Theatre in St. Paul, MN. From there, his career was launched as a director. Early in his career, colleague Earle Gister and Wilson gave Hicks some advice that would set his professional career on course. Gister told him that if he could do the classics, the rest would come easily. He thought this was being dismissive of his own culture but realized that directing black plays would be only 10 percent of his work. This changed, however, with the arrival of Wilson and his 10-play cycle of black plays, 1 for every decade of the 20th century. Hicks took Gister's advice and became one of the most sought-after black directors of theater in the country. Also, Richards had advised Hicks to find a balance between directing and teaching. That he did. For one year, he directed plays at the Duke Ellington School of the Arts (high school) in Washington, DC, and between 1970 and 1975, Hicks taught acting at Carnegie Mellon. For 16 years, he was the dean of theater and film at the State University of New York at Purchase before he became head of the Theatre Program at Rutgers, where he still resides. Hicks has combined both his academic and directing career ever since.

Among the plays Hicks has directed are *The Piano Lesson* at the NYSF/Public Theatre in Pittsburgh, PA; *Like Other People* at Actors Theatre of Louisville Humana Festival; *Day of Absence* and *Happy Ending* at A Contemporary Theatre in Seattle; *Cat on a Hot Roof* at American Conservatory Theatre in San Francisco; and the Ibsen-inspired world premiere of **OyamO**'s *Selfish Sacrifice* along with *The Mad Woman* at the Denver Center Theatre. Hicks was nominated for the Bay Area Critics Award in theater for *Cat on a Hot Roof*. In 1990, he received the Boston University College of the Fine Arts Distinguished Alumni Award.

HILL, ABRAM "ABE" (ABRAHAM BARRINGTON, 1911–86). A playwright, black theater organizer, director, and drama critic, Hill was a leader of the **Harlem** theater movement in the 1940s. He was founder and director of the historic **American Negro Theatre (ANT)** of the 1940s and was also a pioneering black playwright and professor at Lincoln University. Born in Atlanta, GA, he and his family moved to New York in 1925. Hill received his education at Roosevelt and DeWitt Clinton High Schools at City College of New York, where he pursued premedical courses (1930–32). At Lincoln University in Pennsylvania (A.B., 1937), he majored in English, studied drama, and wrote and directed plays. After graduating from Lincoln, he joined the faculty for one semester as an assistant in drama. He studied playwriting on a Theresa Helburn Scholarship at Columbia University, at the Dramatic Workshop of the New School for Social Research in New York City, and at the Atlanta University Summer Theatre.

In 1938, he joined the Works Progress Association **Federal Theatre Project (FTP)**. One of his special projects was to read and evaluate scripts by black authors and to write a case history of black people entitled *Liberty Deferred* for the *Living Newspaper*. The FTP dissolved before the work could be produced. Two years later, Hill organized the Negro Playwrights Company (NPC) in Harlem but left after a few months because of creative differences. That same year, he and **Frederick O'Neal** cofounded ANT. As artistic director and playwright-in-residence, Hill directed and codirected his own plays there as well as plays by others. ANT thrived for the next seven years (1941–48), presenting successful productions in the Harlem community. Famous luminaries in drama who got their start at ANT include **Sidney Poitier**, Harry Belafonte, **Ruby Dee**, **Earle Hyman**, and such budding young playwrights as **Alice Childress** and **Ossie Davis**.

The zenith of Hill's career was his adaptation of *Anna Lucasta* (1944) from the work of the same name by white playwright Philip Yordan. An immense hit in Harlem, it went on to play on Broadway. *Anna* is a three-act drama about a prostitute who wants to become a respectable citizen. A father sends his naïve young son to Brooklyn to find a wife. The young man houses with an unscrupulous family who schemes to get the money his father gave him to financially secure a marriage. The parents talk him into marrying their daughter, Anna, a courtesan who upon meeting the country bumpkin, falls in love with him. A crisis occurs when Anna's former boyfriend, a sailor, returns home on leave. *Anna* became the longest-running play with an all-black cast at that time and launched the careers of many of the stars in film and the emerging television industry, such as Sammy Davis Jr., **Frank Silvera**, Ossie Davis, Ruby Dee, **Rosetta LeNoire**, **Frank Wilson**, Ralf Coleman, **Maxwell Glanville**, **Harold Scott**, and Eartha Kitt. In 1948, United Artists produced it as a film featuring Sammy Davis Jr. and Eartha Kitt.

Hill's most successful play is *On Striver's Row: A Comedy about Sophisticated Harlem* (1939), a three-act play. It satirizes middle-class social snobbery and pretentiousness among the black "Sugar Hill" residents of the Harlem community. Other plays Hill authored include *Stealing Lightning* (1937); *So Shall You Reap* (1937); *Hell's Half Acre* (1938), a drama in three acts; *Liberty Deferred: Living Newspaper* (1938), a full-length drama coauthored with John Silvera; *Booker T. Washington* (1939, revised 1983), a biographical drama about the illustrious founder of Tuskegee Institute; *Walk Hard* (1944), a drama in three acts; *The Power of Darkness* (1948), a full-length drama; *Miss Mabel* (1951), a drama in two acts; and *Beyond the Bush* (1970), a drama in one act. After the demise of ANT in 1948, Hill retired from the theater. Hill was the recipient of a Schomburg Award and a Riverdale Children's Association Award for promoting interracial understanding and for his contributions to the theater. Hill died in New York in October 1986.

HILL, ERROL GASTON (1921–2002). Born in Trinidad, West Indies, Hill was a playwright, author, editor, critic, director, and educator. He received his education at the Royal Academy of Dramatic Art in London (1951), Yale University (B.A., summa cum laude, 1962; M.F.A. in playwriting, 1962; and D.F.A. in theater history, 1966). He was author-director of the Dimanche Gras carnival shows for the government of Trinidad and Tobago (1963–64). He performed as an actor in amateur and professional productions and produced and directed numerous pageants in the Caribbean, United States, Nigeria, England, and Wales. He was a tutor of drama and radio and a guest lecturer in creative writing, and he received teaching fellowships in theater history, dramatic literature, and playwriting.

He was an associate professor of drama at Richmond College and City University of New York (1967–68), a guest lecturer/director at the Graduate Theatre Workshop at Leeds University in England (Fall 1978), and professor of drama at Dartmouth College from 1961 until his retirement in 1989. He was also a visiting professor at the University of California at San Diego (winter 1982) and the Chancellor's Distinguished Professor at the University of California at Berkeley (spring 1983).

Hill has edited numerous articles and books on theater. His publications include *The Trinidad Carnival* (1972), *Theatre of Black Americans* (1980), *Shakespeare in Sable* (1984), *The Jamaican Stage: 1655–1900* (1992), and *The Cambridge Guide to African and Caribbean Theatre* (with Martin Banham and George Woodyard, 1994). He was also contributing editor to numerous Caribbean plays. His last book before his untimely death, *A History of African American Theatre* coauthored with **James V. Hatch**, is a seminal study of theater and drama.

He was also an accomplished playwright, whose plays includes *Square Peg* (1949) a domestic drama in one act is about a young man who runs away from home; *The Ping Pong: A Backyard Comedy-Drama in One Act* (1950), about a West Indian steel band; *Dilemma* (1953), a drama in one act about industrial pollution produced by the University of West Indies in 1966; *Man Better Man: Trinidad Folk Musical* (1954), a play in three acts in which a man uses Trinidadian folklore to win the love of the woman he wants to marry; *Wey-Wey* (1957), a comedy in one act concerning an illegal lottery that holds the hopes and dreams of the West Indian people and which University of West Indies produced (1957); and *Strictly Matrimony* (1959), a domestic comedy about a West Indian couple who is living together happily but faces difficulties after they are tricked into marriage.

Other plays are *Away from Home* (1979), a two-act comedy about a black man who, after relocating to a big city, loses his family because he finds he does not like intellectuals or whites; *Heartshift* (1982), a drama in two acts showing the incestuous relationship between a daughter and her father who wants to keep her home to exploit her sexually; *The Courtship* (1983), a romantic comedy in two acts about interracial love; *Never Enough* (1984), a dramedy in two acts about a misogynous male who keeps his feelings unknown; and *Equal Time* (1964), a comedy in one act in which two wives have to compete with the television to get noticed.

Hill was the recipient of several honors and awards. Among them were the British Council Scholarship (1949–51); Rockefeller Foundation fellowship (1958–60 and 1965); Theatre Guild of America fellowship (1961–62); gold medal for drama, government of Trinidad and Tobago (1973); visiting scholar, Bellagio Study and Conference Center, Italy (fall 1978); and a regional citation for teaching and scholarship.

HILL, LESLIE PINCKNEY (1880–1960). An educator, poet, and pioneer playwright, Hill was for many years president of Cheyney State College in Pennsylvania. Born in Lynchburg, VA, Hill was educated in the public schools of Orange, NJ, his hometown. He was elected to Phi Beta Kappa and was a member of the debating team at Harvard University (A.B. cum laude, 1903; A.M., 1904), ironically where he worked as a waiter at a fraternity house. He taught at Tuskegee Institute (1904–7), where he was department head; Manassas (VA) Institute (1907–13); and the Institute for Colored Youth in Cheyney, PA, where he became principal and retired as president emeritus (1913–51).

Hill is the author of *The Wings of Oppression* (1921), a volume of poetry, and *What the Negro Wants*, which outlines six things that black people insist are necessary for achieving equality. His plays include *Toussaint L'Ouverture* (1928), written in blank verse about the title character, and *Jethro* (1931), a full-length historical musical pageant about the Ethiopian contemporary of Moses. Among the awards and honors Hill garnered were honorary degrees from Lincoln University in Pennsylvania (Litt.D., 1929), Morgan State College (L.L.D., 1939), Haverford College, and Cheyney State Teachers College. He was the recipient of the Seltzer Award for distinguished service to the Mercy-Douglass Hospital in Philadelphia.

HILL, MARS. A playwright and engineer, Hill was born in Pine Bluff, AR, and raised in Chicago. He received a B.A. in architecture from the University of Illinois (1954), a degree in business law at the University of Washington (1971–72), and an M.A. in black studies from the State University of New York (SUNY) at Albany (1974). While working for the Boeing Company in Seattle, he was asked to perform in Eugene O'Neill's play *The Emperor Jones*. Thus began his love for theater, and upon moving back to Albany and continuing his work as a civil engineer, he began to take playwriting courses. Eventually he founded a theater, the **Black Experience** Theatre, and began writing plays and teaching black theater courses at SUNY. He was a prolific writer and over the years wrote dozens of plays, including *Eclipse*, *Cavorting with the Whartons*, *Huzzy*, *Malice in Wonderland*, *The Buzzards*, *House and Field*, *To Have and Have Not*, *Monkey Motions*, *Man in the Family Tree*, and *The Very Special Occasion*. Hill retired in 1983 and went back to school, achieving a Ph.D. in humanistic studies at the University of Albany in 1997. Also, his novel *The Moaner's Bench* (1998) was nominated for a **Pulitzer Prize**.

HINES, KIM. An actor, director, and playwright, Hines has made the stage her home since childhood, when she was a member of the Children's Theatre of Minneapolis. After earning a B.A. in speech and drama at Macalester College, she carved out a life in the theater, acting, directing, teaching, and playwriting. She has either acted, directed, or had her plays performed at such venues as Illusion Theatre, the Great History Theatre, **Penumbra Theatre**, Blood Theatre, Cornell University, Kansas University, and the Guthrie Theatre. Among the plays Hines wrote are *Home on the Mornin' Train*, a children's play; *From Slavery to Freedom*; *Hip Hop Shakespeare*; *My Lord, What a Morning*; *The Story of Marian Anderson*; *Magical Adventures of Pretty Pear*, a children's play; *Cut on the Bias*; *Do Not Pass Go*; *If You Don't Really Want to Know, Then Don't Ask Me*, a one-woman show; and *Ain't I a Woman*. Hines's honors and awards include the Bush playwright fellowship (1997) and Artist of the Year (1992).

HITTITE EMPIRE. A predominantly male performance art group, the Hittite Empire is based in Santa Monica, CA. **Keith Antar Mason**, Ellis Rice, and Michael Keith Woods founded it in 1977 to fill a cultural void. Mason, a poet and performance artist, serves as the company's artistic director. It is comprised of 10 men but may be expanded to an ensemble of 35. Their mission was to articulate the new black aesthetic and to deal with current social problems in the black community. The ensemble blends history, audience participation, and the arts into thought-provoking, harsh, and confrontational scenarios. They also have a youth program for urban young men aged 16 to 25 to build trust, teamwork, and self-esteem and to think about their lives. They have toured throughout the country from Los Angeles and Columbus, OH, to Pittsburgh, PA, and New York City. Mason's most popular performance piece is *49 Blues Songs for a Jealous Vampire*, a two-hour show performed with five other members of Hittite.

HOLDER, LAURENCE. A playwright and educator, Holder has been a bedrock of strength in the black theater movement. He has focused on creating, writing, and directing plays and novels illuminating the lives of trailblazing African Americans. They include Ethel Waters, Duke Ellington, Valaida Snow, and Malcolm X. His plays were performed at Theatre for the New City; Castillo Theatre; **North Carolina Black Repertory Theatre**; Cairo, Egypt; and the Edinburgh Festival, among others. Holder is a native New Yorker born to Goldie and Wilson Holder. He married Andrea Jackson, an actress, on the island of Barbados in 1994 and is the father of three children. Laurence has had affiliations with the New York Theatre Ensemble, **La MaMa Experimental Theatre Club**, and the **Frank Silvera Writers' Workshop**. He attended the City College of New York, completing studies in the areas of geology and creative writing.

Holder has written seven novels and over 20 plays. His most acclaimed play was the **New Federal Theatre** production of *When the Chickens Come Home to Roost* (1981), featuring a then unknown **Denzel Washington** as Malcolm X and Kirk Kirksey as Elijah Muhammad. The production, directed by **Allie Woods Jr.**, was a huge success, vaulting Holder into the top rank of American playwrights. Another widely produced play by Holder is *Zora Neale Hurston* (1998), an American Place Theatre production and winner of an **Audience Development Committee (Audelco) Award** for best playwright. It was a portrait of the well-known author and folklorist of the **Harlem** Renaissance. **Elizabeth Van Dyke** played the title role under the direction of Wynn Handman. The Ohio State University Department of Theatre produced *Zora* directed by Anthony

D. Hill (1994). Two other plays Holder wrote that received acclaim are *M: The Mandela Saga* (1995), a drama about the South African husband-and-wife activist team of Nelson and Winnie Mandela, and *Monk*, a one-act play about the life of the legendary jazz pianist Thelonius Monk, which was named for two Audelco Awards, with actor **Rome Neal** receiving the Audelco for best solo performance and Laurence being nominated for best writing. In addition, Laurence won the Otto Rene Castillo Award for political theater and the **Garland Anderson** Award from the National Black Arts Festival for overall body of work. Both awards honored the body of his work. Other representative plays Holder wrote are *Juba* (a musical), *Bussa*, *MonknBud*, *Urban Decalogue*, *They Were All Gardenias* (a musical), *Red Channels*, *Hot Snow*, and *The Gospel According to Max Roach*. Holder has also received a New York Foundation grant. He continues to teach English and write at John Jay College, where he has been a professor for the last 30 years.

HOLLAND, ENDESHA IDA MAE (1944–2006). An educator and playwright, Holland was born in poverty-stricken Greenwood, MS. Her mother raised her making a living as a midwife and taking in boarders to make ends meet. She was a strong-willed woman who continually urged Holland to control her own destiny. In her late teens, it seemed as if Holland was out of control after being kicked out of high school and getting arrested for prostitution. In the early 1950s, she took a step in the right direction when she became involved in the burgeoning **civil rights movement** in Mississippi. Tragically, because of her involvement in the movement, the Ku Klux Klan burned her mother's house down, killing her mother. This incident affected Holland immensely but also strengthened her resolve. She left Mississippi to go to Minnesota with a newfound determination to fulfill her mother's wishes by earning a high school equivalency diploma. Enthralled with the knowledge that she could succeed, she enrolled at the University of Minnesota. Within 13 years, she had received a B.A. in African American studies (1979), an M.A. (1984), and a Ph.D. (1985).

Holland's signature play is *From the Mississippi Delta* (1986). It is an autobiographical account of her life from obscurity in Greenwood, MS, to her involvement in the civil rights movement to the completion of her doctorate in American studies (1985). It premiered at Buffalo's **Ujima Theatre Company** and subsequently moved to the Henry Street Settlement and the **Negro Ensemble Company** in New York City. Oprah Winfrey partly financed the production at the Circle in the Square (1991) that was nominated for a **Pulitzer Prize**.

Earlier plays that Holland wrote include *Second Doctor Lady* (1980), a drama in one act based on Holland's mother when she worked as a midwife, portraying the black midwife assisting a white woman with a difficult birth in a hospital and then delivering a baby in a poor black home. *Mrs. Ida B. Wells* (1982) is a full-length one-woman show highlighting the renowned activist-journalist whose contributions to the black press were extensive. *The Reconstruction of Dossie Ree Hemphill* (1980) is a drama in one act based on the author's mother's experiences as "madam" and midwife. Other plays she wrote include *Fanny Lou*, *Requiem for a Snake*, and *Prairie Woman*. In 1981, Holland was the recipient of the **Lorraine Hansberry** Playwriting Award. Holland taught in the Women's Studies Department at the University of Buffalo (1985–93) and at the University of Southern California (1993–2000) until she was forced to take early retirement because of ataxia, a degenerative disease that took her life in 2006.

HOLLY, ELLEN. Holly is a gifted actor and author of the 20th century whose light skin complexion was both a boon and an impediment. She was considered too dark for white roles and too light for black roles. She overcame this obstacle to carve out an outstanding career primarily onstage and later in film and television. Born in New York City, Holly's early education was at Hunter College, where she received a fine arts degree with a minor in theater. Shortly thereafter, she was accepted into the Actor's Studio headed by Elia Kazan and Lee Strasberg. Holly was of the select few chosen to participate in this august group. She made her professional debut in Anton Chekhov's *The Anniversary* in 1955 and her Broadway debut in Alan Paton's *Too Late the Phalarope* in 1956. It was around this time that she began to encounter casting difficulties because she "looked too white." Nevertheless, **Joseph Papp**, a strong proponent of nontraditional casting, hired her for his New York Shakespeare Festival production of William Shakespeare's *Antony and Cleopatra*. Papp had seen Holly in her debut role a few years earlier.

Holly became a regular with the company and over the years cemented her reputation as a classical actress with roles in *A Midsummer Nights Dream, King Henry V, Macbeth, King Lear, The Taming of the Shrew*, and *Othello*. She has also appeared in plays like *Moon on a Rainbow Shawl*, **Funnyhouse of a Negro**, *The Cherry Orchard, John Brown's Body, A Hand Is on the Gate, Camino Real, The Comedy of Errors*, and many others. Her movie credits include *Take a Giant Step, Cops and Robbers, 10,000 Black Men Named George*, and *School Daze*. Holly was also one of the first black actors to achieve success in daytime soap operas, where she parlayed a one-time appearance in ABC's *One Life to Live* into a permanent role that lasted 17 years. This opened the door for other African American actors, who are now an integral part of daytime television. In addition, Holly is a published author for her critically acclaimed book *Autobiography of an African American Actress* (1994).

HOLMAN, M. CARL. A poet and **civil rights** leader, Holman was 1 of the 100 most influential black Americans as listed by *Ebony* magazine in 1968. Born in Minter City, MS, Holman lived in Washington, DC. His poetry has been published in numerous periodicals and anthologies. Holman's representative play is *The Baptizin'* (1971), which premiered at the Little Theatre of Tulsa, OK (summer 1971). It received first prize at the National Community Theatre Festival of the American Community Theatre Association (1971). Holman was the recipient of a Rosenwald and a John Hay Whitney fellowship and winner of the John Fisk Poetry Prize from the University of Chicago and a Blevins Davis Playwriting Prize from Yale University.

HOLMES, WILLIE. A playwright and educator, Holmes is a native of Birmingham, AL. He is an educator in the Dallas Public School System, where he is striving to make a difference both as an educator and as the founder and executive director of Blacken Blues Theatre, located in Dallas, TX. His avowed goals are to save the children "by any means necessary" and to share the beauty of African American life through his theatrical efforts.

Holmes received his bachelor's degree from Bethune-Cookman College and his M.A. from Ohio State University. In Dallas, he founded Blacken Blues Theatre in 1998, which has slowly developed into a reliable producing entity. Holmes's own plays produced there were well received. They include *Suspects in America*, a political satire on Homeland Security efforts to put black men on trial for using hip-hop to destroy the American dream; *Eve's Garden*, depicting a young girl coming of age and fighting the age-old dilemma of what is love and what is desire; *Acts of Love*, four vignettes of love, lust, and seduction; and *Daddy's Girl: The Corporate Plantation*, which centers on a successful African American executive who fights the battle of greed, ambition, and family. He has also written *The Wounded*, *A Fool's Redemption*, *E-Love*, *The Family Debt*, and *Heaven for a Gee*.

HOOKS, ROBERT. Hooks, an actor and theater administrator, was born in Washington, DC. He cofounded the **Negro Ensemble Company** and organized the New York's Group Theatre Workshop and DC Black Repertory Company. In his debut as a professional actor on Broadway in the original production of **Lorraine Hansberry**'s *A Raisin in the Sun*, he won a **New York Drama Critics' Circle Award**. He also originated three roles on Broadway in *Dutchman*, *A Taste of Honey*, and *Where's Daddy?* On television, he was the first African American to have a leading role on the original *N.Y.P.D.* series. In 1980, he was a regular on *Dynasty* as Dr. Walcott. On the silver screen, Hooks played Reeve Scott in *Hurry Sundown*, Mr. T. in the 1972 film *Trouble Man*, and Fleet Admiral Morrow in *Star Trek III: The Search for Spock*. Among Hooks's awards and honors are a nomination for a **Tony Award** for his lead role in the musical *Hallelujah, Baby!*; both the Pioneer Award and the National Association for the Advancement of Colored People Image Award for lifetime achievement; and induction into the Black Filmmakers Hall of Fame. Also, he won an Emmy for his PBS special *Voices of Our People* and a Theatre World Award for *Where's Daddy?*, a Broadway production.

HOPKINS, LINDA. Mahalia Jackson discovered this actress-singer, who sang for more than 10 years with the Southern Harp Spiritual Singers. Her first appearance on Broadway was in a supporting role as church soloist in *Purlie* (1970). She won both a **Tony Award** and a **Drama Desk Award** for her performance in *Inner City* (1971). Her play of note is *Me and Bessie* (1974), a full-length musical about the life and legend of Bessie Smith portrayed through reminiscences, anecdotes, and songs.

HOPKINS, PAULINE ELIZABETH (1859–1930). A playwright, actress, novelist, short story writer, essayist, editor, and stenographer, Hopkins was born in Portland, ME, raised in Boston (some accounts say she was born in Cambridge, MA), and educated at the Girls High School in Boston. At a young age, Hopkins won $10 in an essay competition sponsored by **William Wells Brown** and the Congressional Publishing Society of Boston. *The Escape; or, A Leap for Freedom* (1858), written by Brown, was possibly the first full-length drama published by a black author. Inspired by Brown's play and the dramatic form, Hopkins at age 20 wrote *Slaves' Escape; or, The Underground Railroad* (1880; original title, *Peculiar Sam; or, The Underground Railroad*, 1879). It was a historical musical drama in three acts about how the railroad helped blacks escape from the South in their search for freedom in the North. The show ran briefly in Boston in 1880, receiving acclaim. Hopkins died in a fire on 13 August 1930.

HORNE, J. W. ROBINSON. Born in Richmond, VA, Horne is a playwright, theater critic, actor, designer, choreographer, and impresario. He received his education at Virginia Union University (B.S.), the Fashion Academy of New York City, and Virginia Commonwealth University. He was founder, playwright, and producing director of the Christian Arts Company (1951–present), a resident performing arts company of the Second Baptist Church in Richmond.

Horne's plays have focused primarily on religious subjects, such as *Garden of Easter* (1952), *The Acts of Four Men* (1959), *That Man John* (1961), *Great Day* (1964), *The People vs. the Nazarene* (1965), *Soul at Sunrise* (1970), *Miracle Morning: A Celebration in Christ for Singers* (1974), *Entrances and Exits* (1976), *Easter: A Jesus Jubilee:*

A Musical Jubilation in Jesus Christ (1981), *Rejoice in the Re-deemer: A Pageant of Rejoicement in Jesus Christ with Music and Drama* (a three-act work, 1983), and *Morningstar: A Musical of the Messiah* (1985). Horne wrote a few dramas that diverged from his religious theme. *Lena Mitchell Walker: Vanguard Virginian* (1980), a semidocumentary play with music and projections in two-acts, is based on Maggie L. Walker, Richmond's most famous black woman. Ten black high school students in Walker's senior class of 1883, taught by an all-white faculty, launch a protest because they are refused commencement exercises in the same theater as whites. *Sisters: The African-American Experience of the Black Woman* (1980) is a drama with music about the "Soul Sister" from the great black queens of Africa.

THE HOT MIKADO. *See THE SWING MIKADO* (1939) AND *THE HOT MIKADO* (1939).

HOUSTON, DIANE. An actress, director, and playwright, Houston has a special interest in children's theater. Born in Washington, DC, she received training in the theater at DC's Workshops for Careers in the Arts and at Howard University, where as a drama student she was named best director for two consecutive years for **Peter De-Anda**'s *Ladies in Waiting*, **Kelsey Collie**'s *Black Images/ Black Rejections*, and Saundra Sharp's *The Sistuhs*. She has worked with several theater groups, including the Ebony Impromptu Theatre in Washington, DC, and the City Street Theatre in New York. Two representative plays Houston wrote are *AsaGa Kimashita: Morning Has Broken* (1982), a full-length drama that won two national first prize awards in the American College Theatre Festival (1982)—the **Lorraine Hansberry** Award for the best play about the **black experience** and the David Lib Playwriting Award for the best new play about American freedom—and *American Dreams* (1984), a full-length drama that depicts the realities of life in America when a black soldier returns home after World War II with a Japanese bride.

HUDSON, RUBEN SANTIAGO. *See* SANTIAGO-HUDSON, RUBEN.

HUGHES, LANGSTON JAMES (1902–67). The poet laureate of **Harlem** and dean of black American professional writers, Hughes was a prolific playwright who wrote in all genres for six decades beginning in the 1920s. He was a poet; radio and television scriptwriter; essayist; editor; novelist; and writer of autobiographies, histories of drama and entertainment, librettos, lyrics for operas and musicals, books for children, articles for newspapers and magazines, and short stories. His literary output encompassed more than 35 books.

Born in Joplin, MO, Hughes and his family were deserted by his father when he was a youth. Hughes's mother and maternal grandmother raised him in Lawrence and Topeka, KS, and Cleveland, OH. At age 18, he visited his father in Mexico during the summer, and there he wrote some of his early poems and short stories. In 1921, Hughes enrolled at Columbia University but dropped out within a year to travel to the motherland, Africa, and then to Europe. Upon returning to the United States, he continued his pursuit of education at Lincoln University in Pennsylvania (B.A., 1929). He received commissions to write during the 1930s and 1940s for several theater groups as playwright-in-residence at the **Karamu Repertory Theatre** in Cleveland, OH (1936, 1939), and as resident poet at the University of Chicago Laboratory School (1949). This experience helped prepare Hughes to develop theater companies at the **Harlem Suitcase Theatre** (1938); the New Negro Theatre, Los Angeles (1939); and the company known as the Skyloft Players, Chicago (1941).

Hughes was among a few early black playwrights to have a play produced on the "Great White Way." In 1935, *Mulatto* became the longest-running drama (373 performances) on Broadway at that time. It is a tragedy in two acts influenced by Hughes's relationship with his father. **Rose McClendon** played the mother. Martin Jones adapted the play for its opening on Broadway at the Vanderbilt Theatre (October 1935). It toured for eight months, appearing at the Studebaker Theatre in Chicago for three weeks (December 1935); at Karamu Repertory Theatre by the Gilpin Players in Cleveland, OH (March 1938); and at Compagnia del Teatro Italiano in Rome and Milan (1950s) for two weeks. It was later adapted into an opera, *The Barrier* (1950).

Hughes's outpouring of plays was astronomical. *The Gold Piece* (1921) is a children's play in one act. *Cock o' de World* (1931) is a musical comedy in three acts adapted by Hughes from a play by Kaj Gynt with lyrics by Duke Ellington. A black sailor traveling from New Orleans through the Caribbean to Paris encounters discrimination. *Scottsboro Limited* (1931) is a one-act play in verse about the celebrated Scottsboro case of nine black youths accused of raping two white women in Alabama. *The Emperor of Haiti* (original titles, *Troubled Island* and *Drums of Haiti*, 1935) is a three-act tragedy about the heroics of Haitian emperor Dessalines during the Napoleonic era. *Blood on the Fields* (1935) is a social drama in three acts. Migrant cotton workers attempt to organize a union to improve their working conditions. *Little Ham* (1935) is a comedy in three acts about the antics of the lovable Hamlet Jones, a popular ladies' man. *St. Louis Woman* (1936) is a full-length adaptation revision of **Arna Bontemps** and **Countee Cullen**'s original play of the same name. *Angelo Herndon Jones* (1936) is a drama in one act. A black man is sentenced to a chain gang for 20 years for protesting against the U.S. government for not paying him his unemployment check. The play won the New Theatre League's contest (1936) as the best play about the Herndon case. *No Left Turn* (1936) is a comedy in one act that deals with a black man's social life. The Community Laboratory Theatre, a unit of the Works Progress Administration **Federal Theatre Project**, produced it at the Karamu Repertory Theatre in Cleveland, OH (1936). *When the Jack Hollers; or, Careless Love* (1936) is a folk comedy in three acts about superstitious poor black and white sharecroppers on a plantation in the Mississippi Delta region. *Joy to My Soul* (1937) is a farce in three acts about a wealthy bachelor who corresponds through a "lonely Hearts" racket. *Soul Gone Home* (1937) is a fantasy in one act. The spirit of a dead son accuses his mother of causing his untimely death through her misconduct and neglect. *Don't You Want to Be Free* (1937, revised 1963) is a musical pageant in one long act narrating the history of blacks in America from **slavery** through the blues to the 1930s, incorporating spirituals, blues, poetry, dramatic sketches, jazz, and work songs. *De Organizer* (1938) is a blues opera in one act, with music by James P. Johnson, supporting the organization of a union of sharecroppers. *Like a Flame* (1938) is work in one act dramatizing Alice Holdship Ware of Hughes's poem "Tomorrow." An American tourist tries to persuade a French nightclub owner to segregate the black and white audience members. *Em-Fuehrer Jones* (1938) is a satirical skit in one act parodying Eugene O'Neill's *The Emperor Jones*. The Harlem Suitcase Theatre produced it along with two other plays. *Little Eva's End* (1938), a satirical skit in one act of Harriet Beecher Stowe's character in *Uncle Tom's Cabin* who became a symbol of white purity and innocence, was Hughes's version of Little Eva's ascension into heaven. *Limitations of Life* (1938), a satirical skit in one act, is a parody of Fanny Hurst's film *Imitation of Life* (1934). Hughes reverses the role of the black faithful mammy and the benevolent young white mistress.

Other plays Hughes authored are *Front Porch* (1938); *Way Down South* (1939), a screenplay for a full-length feature film; *Mule Bone* (1930s), coauthored with **Zora Neale Hurston**; *Trouble with the Angels* (1930s), a drama in two acts; *Tropics after Dark* (1940), a musical theater work in two acts; *Cavalcade of the Negro Theatre* (1940), a black pageant; *The Sun Do Move* (original title, *Sold Away*, 1941), a musical drama with a prologue and three acts; *That Eagle* (1942), a patriotic play with music; *Hotel Black Majesty* (c. 1943), a drama set in a hotel lobby; *Popo and Fifina* (1943), a children's play; *Street Scene* (1947), a folk opera in two acts; *Troubled Island* (1949), an opera in four acts based on Hughes's play *The Emperor of Haiti* (1935); *Simple Takes a Wife* (1955), a full-length folk comedy; *Shakespeare in Harlem* (1959), a full-length theater work; **Black Nativity** (1961), a gospel pageant in two acts; and *Tambourines to Glory* (1963), a gospel play in two acts with 12 scenes.

Hughes was the recipient of the *Opportunity* Poetry Prize (1925), the Harmon Gold Medal for literature (1931), the Guggenheim fellowship for creative writing (1935), the Rosenwald fellowship (1942), the American Academy of Arts and Letters grant (1947), the Anisfeld-Wolf Award (1953), and the **Spingarn Medal Award** (1960).

HUGHES, VIRGINIA. *See* RAHMAN, AISHAH (VIRGINIA HUGHES.

HUNTER, LARRY. A playwright and editor from Houston, TX, Hunter graduated from Wiley College and then spent many years abroad in Africa and Paris before returning home to the United

States. After studying creative writing in Carmel, CA, and writing his first book, he returned to his native Houston and began writing plays. His interest in youth manifested itself when he joined Writers in the Schools (WITS), an organization that places authors in local schools and other facilities. Hunter was largely successful in teaching creative writing, poetry, and playwriting to a growing number of students, all the while writing his own plays, which were produced by the University of Houston and other entities.

Hunter eventually established Colourwhirl, Inc., Youth, a nonprofit yearround organization that introduces inner-city kids to the world of the arts. He has written over 20 plays. Among them are *The Elder Comes to Town*, about a faith healer who wanders into town frightening the townspeople; *The Rawley Street Whistler*, a thinly based autobiography about Wilton Felder, saxophonist for the Jazz Crusaders; *Passing Times*, a comedy about three elderly women who move to the country to escape crime in the inner city; *Wildcat Inn*, telling the story of black colleges during the era of segregation; and *The Juke Box*, a comedy. Hunter also wrote two books, a novel titled *The Whispering Call* (1987), and a book of poetry titled *My Reflections* (1987).

HURSTON, ZORA NEALE (c. 1891–1960). Hurston was a prolific and famous novelist, folklorist, anthropologist, playwright, and critic whose fictional and actual accounts of African American cultural traditions are unprecedented. She was born in Notasulga, Macon Country, AL. In 1894, the family moved to the all-black small town of Eatonville, FL, the first incorporated black municipality in the United States. Hurston's father, a Baptist preacher and carpenter, was elected mayor of Eatonville in 1897 for three terms.

Hurston attended Hungerford School in Eatonville. After the death of her mother in 1904, which forms a crucial episode in her autobiography *Dust Tracks on a Road*, she continued her studies in Jacksonville. During her childhood and adolescence, she held diverse jobs throughout the South until she moved to Washington, DC, in 1918. There she entered the preparatory school at Howard University and started her degree in 1920. She became involved in the literary club formed by philosophy professor Alain Locke, which enabled her to publish her first short stories.

In 1925, Hurston moved to New York, where she studied anthropology with Franz Boas at Barnard University. In New York, she met such influential intellectuals as **Langston Hughes, Countee Cullen,** and Carl Van Vetchen and was encouraged to enter several literary works in the *Opportunity* contest. One short story, "Spunk," was later included in *The New Negro*, a landmark anthology of the **Harlem** Renaissance edited by Alain Locke.

Married twice and engaged once, all of Hurston's relationships were short lived. Her marriage to Herbert Sheen in 1927, her longtime fiancée, lasted four years (they divorced in 1931). Her marriage eight years later to Albert Price III, a 23-year-old Works Progress Administration playground worker, was also short lived, and her engagement later to James Howell Pitts did not materialize. Thanks to a $1,400 research fellowship, Hurston left New York in 1927 to collect folklore in the South. That was the first of the many field trips during her career that would take her throughout the South as well as to the Bahamas (1930), Haiti (1935), the West Indies (1936), and Honduras (1947). This research formed the basis of her collections of folklore for *Mules and Men* (1935), *Tell My Horse* (1938), and many of her articles and essays.

Hurston found a conduit for her one-act dramas through the annual *Opportunity* Contest Awards of 1925 and on Broadway. *Spears* (1925) received honorable mention. She won second prize for *Color Struck* (1925), a melodrama about color discrimination among blacks. The next year, she was awarded honorable mention for *The First One* (1925), a satire of the biblical story of Noah's curse on his son Ham, portrayed as the ancestor of the black race. *Fast and Furious* was produced on Broadway in 1931. It is a musical credited to several black writers and includes three of her comedy sketches. The next year, *Great-Day* (1931) was produced in New York City (1932). When the show moved to Florida in 1933, it was retitled as *From Sun to Sun* (1932).

Nearly 60 years later, Hurston's third play was produced on Broadway, *Mule Bone* (1930s). Coauthored with Langston Hughes, it was based on folk material from Eatonville. The Lincoln Center produced it (January 1991) with an all-star cast that included Akosua Busia, Marilyn Coleman, Paul S. Eckstein, Clebert Ford, **Frances Foster,**

Arthur French, Sonny Jim Gaines, Leonard Jackson, Ebony Jo-Ann, Robert Earl Jones, Reggie Montgomery, Mansoor Najeeullah, Vanessa Williams, and **Allie Woods Jr.** *Mules and Men* is but one example of Hurston's research and interests in black folk traditions resulting in the immortalization of her hometown of Eatonville.

Other plays, such as *Jonah's Gourd Vine* (1934), are based on the story of Hurston's parents. *Their Eyes Were Watching God* (1937) is about a young black woman's quest for self-identity and is intertwined with rich folktales. It was panned by a young **Richard Wright** and Alain Locke. *Dust Tracks on a Road* (1942), her autobiography, won the *Saturday Review*'s Anisfield Award (1943) for the best book on race relations.

In the twilight of her years in Florida, Hurston found herself impoverished and in ill health. In addition, the accusation of sexually molesting a 10-year-old child took its toll on her, a case that was eventually dismissed. Hurston died on 28 January 1960 in the Saint Lucie County Welfare Home. With no funds for her funeral, she was buried in an unmarked grave with the help of a few friends. Some 20 years later, **Pulitzer Prize**–winning novelist Alice Walker placed a headstone on Hurston's unmarked grave and paid tribute to her place in the American literary canon as a folklorist. Walker and members of her literary society make an annual trek to Hurston's gravesite to commemorate her death and pay homage to her work.

HYMAN, EARLE. Hyman is a veteran actor whose career encompasses some 60 years, during which he has played some of the great characters in dramatic literature, including title roles in Shakespeare's *Richard III, Julius Caesar, Antony and Cleopatra, Coriolanus,* and *Hamlet.* He also played Vladimir in Samuel Beckett's *Waiting for Godot,* James Tyrone in Eugene O' Neill's *Long Day's Journey into Night,* and Firs in Anton Chekhov's *The Cherry Orchard.* In recent years he has been best known as Bill Cosby's father in the long-running TV series *The Cosby Show.*

Hyman was born in 1924 in Rocky Mount, NC, but grew up in Brooklyn. He attended Howard University, where he majored in theater and played Hamlet, his first Shakespearean role. In 1944, Hyman was cast as the romantic lead in the **American Negro Theatre**'s

Broadway production of *Anna Lucasta* that played for over a year. He became a charter member of the American Shakespeare Festival in Stratford, CT, in 1955. For five years, he shared equal billing with the likes of Fritz Weaver, Morris Carnovsky, Katherine Hepburn, and Alfred Drake in *The Tempest*, *Othello*, *The Winter's Tale*, and *A Midnight Summers Night's Dream*, establishing himself in the top rank of American actors. Hyman performed many years in Norway, where he worked and lived and still has a home. He speaks fluent Norwegian and was honored with the St. Olaf Medal in 1988 for his work on the Norwegian stage.

During his extensive career as an actor, Hyman has performed the works of the leading playwrights of the day, including Edward Albee, Alfred Uhry, Henrik Ibsen, and **Lorraine Hansberry**. He was the first black actor to play four giants of the Shakespeare canon in *Othello*, *King Lear*, *Macbeth*, and *Hamlet*, moreover playing over 29 roles in Shakespearean plays. Among the awards of which he is most proud are the Theatre World Award (1956) and the **Tony Award** (1980).

– I –

IMAN, YUSEF. A playwright, poet, and actor, Iman was born in Savannah, GA. He grew up in the South, where he became actively involved in both the **civil rights movement** and the arts. After moving to Newark, NJ, he joined a radical theater group, Spirit House Theatre, headed by **Amiri Baraka (LeRoi Jones)**. There he was inspired to put the pen to the page in response to the social upheaval of the times. One of his more popular early plays is *Praise the Lord, but Pass the Ammunition* (1967), a one-act that deals with ideological differences between the forces of self-defense and nonviolence. *Praise* was first produced by Spirit House in Newark (1967). After Spirit House closed, Iman continued to write and perform at **Roger Furman**'s **New Heritage Repertory Theatre Company** in New York City. Later Iman founded the Weusi Kuumba Theatre Troupe in Brooklyn, where he directed most of the plays. Among his other acting credits, Iman portrayed Malcolm X opposite **Morgan Free-**

man in the 1981 film *The Death of the Prophet*. For over two decades, he wrote more than 20 plays. Among them are *Dope: The Cause and the Cure* (1967); *Jihad* (1968); *Resurrection* (1969); *Confusion* (1970); *The Verdict Is Yours* (1971); *The Price of Revolution* (1971); *We Wear the Mask* (1973); and *Yesterday, Today, and Tomorrow* (1971), coauthored with **Ben Caldwell**. Iman is also a published poet.

IMPACT REPERTORY THEATRE. Based in New York City, Impact Repertory Theatre was founded in 1964 by the late **Roger Furman**. It is a branch of the **New Heritage Repertory Theatre Company**, one of the oldest black theaters in the country. In 1997, Voza Rivers and Jamal Joseph, artistic director and executive producer, respectively, of New Heritage, committed to establishing an arts training component for young people. Thus was born Impact, an intensive training laboratory open to young people between the ages of 12 and 18. New members undergo six weeks of studying the rudiments of history, leadership and teamwork, communication skills, hygiene, and current youth issues. They are also exposed to the basic vocabulary of drama, music, dance, and self-assessment in order to track their progress on the next level, which includes dance (modern jazz, traditional African, hip hop, and ballet); movement (martial arts, stage combat, pantomime, stepping); music; voice; composition; keyboards; musical theater; drama (scene study, improvisation, monologues, audition and performance techniques); writing (poetry, short stories, plays, movie scripts); and leadership (public speaking, career planning, time management, community organizing). New Impact members are required to attend a 12-week boot camp of intensive arts and leadership training before they can perform with the theater company. Members receive training in all areas, which enables the group to create pieces for performance. The group also initiated a community service aspect. Each year, members visit nursing homes, help in block cleanups, and organize food drives in their neighborhoods. Impact also travels throughout the New York area to churches, the **Harlem** Health Fair, the United Nations, hospitals, the **Apollo Theatre**, and prisons and has appeared on CBS and HBO.

IN DAHOMEY (**1903**). This is the first hit musical for the comic team of Bert Williams and George Walker. It opened in New York City (18 February 1903). Hertig and Seamon produced it, J. A. Shipp wrote the book and directed it, Will Marion Cook composed for it, and Alex Rogers wrote the lyrics. In the first two acts, Williams and Walker search for a missing silver box. Pursued by the law, they escape to Africa, where they decide to remain because they like the way they are treated—like kings.

Williams played Shylock Homestead, and Walker played Razerback Pinkerton. The cast also included Alex Rogers (George Reeder), J. A. Shipp (Hustling Charley), J. Leubrie Hill (Officer Still), Abbie Mitchell (Pansy), Aida Overton Walker (Sosetta Lightfoot), Chares Moore (JeJe, a caboceer), William Elking (Menuki, messenger of the king), William Barker (Mose Lightfoot), Pete Hampton (Hamilton Lightfoot), Fred Douglas (Dr. Straight), Walter Richardson (Henry Stampfield), George Catlin (Me Sing, a Chinese cook), Richard Conners (Leather, a bootblack), Green Tapley (White Wash Man), Theodore Pankey (Messenger Rush), Hattie McIntosh (Cecilia Lightfoot), and Lottie Williams (Mrs. Stringer). After the Broadway run, Williams and Walker took the show to London, where it played before Edward VII. They returned the show to America and took it on a successful tour between 1904 and 1905.

INNERACT PRODUCTIONS. This is a member of the Alliance of Resident Theatres in New York City, a consortium of Quality Theatres by artists of color. Operating for six years as a not-for-profit production company, InnerAct Productions provides a venue for actors to develop their craft freely, to produce works of quality within the heart of the New York theater district, and to provide ongoing training. Since 1999, InnerAct has produced at least one vital stage performance that depicted and represented cultural norms and experiences of both historical and current African American life. In the spring of 2000, the company began offering the actors workshops, a free two-hour lecture and demonstration series run by the artistic director to all career-seeking performing artists. In the fall of 2001, InnerAct implemented a mentoring program of 45 students to provide exposure to high school and college students. It gave the students an opportunity to work with professional artists in a theater and to gain hands-on experience in the areas of marketing, directing, lighting, costume design, stage design, sound, stage management, producing, and the box office.

INNER-CITY CULTURAL CENTER. *See* JACKSON, CLARENCE BERNARD.

– J –

JACKMON, MARVIN E. *See* X, MARVIN (MARVIN E. JACKMON).

JACKSON, CLARENCE BERNARD (1927–96). Born in Brooklyn, Jackson was a composer, playwright, and community activist. He graduated from the High School of Music and Arts (arts major), earned a B.A. and M.A. from Brooklyn College, and was musical director at the Dance Center in Los Angeles (1954–56). Approximately 10 years later, in the midst of the 1965 Watts riot, he set the groundwork for the Inner-City Cultural Center. For the next 30 years, he ran the center with the notion of bringing art that was multicultural to Southern California. Jackson theorized art was the only tool left to save the world from self-destruction.

As a playwright, Jackson was known primarily for *Fly Blackbird* (1960), a musical in two acts he coauthored with **James V. Hatch**. A satire set during the sit-in movement of the 1960s, it was about a group of blacks in the Deep South who were trying to decide the most effective methods of securing their **civil rights**. Producers expanded *Blackbird* to a full-length play for its production at the Shoebox Theatre in Los Angeles (fall 1960) with student performers, many of whom went on to professional stage and film careers, such as Micki Grant and Thelma Oliver. The show was produced off Broadway in a revised and expanded version, with additional material by the director, Jerome Eskow, at the Mayfair Theatre for 127 performances (February 1962). Avon Long assumed the leading role. *Blackbird* earned the authors an **Obie Award** (1961–62). It was produced at the Institute in Black Repertory Theatre, housed at the University of California at Santa Barbara (summer 1968). Jackson also wrote his own musicals, *Earthquake* (1973) and an adaptation of Shakespeare's *Othello* called *Iago* (1996). Other musicals followed.

Jackson was the recipient of numerous honors and awards. Among them were the Obie Award for best musical (1961–62); Unity Award, Los Angeles (1960); John Hay Whitney fellowship (1963–64); special commendation from the Los Angeles City Council (1969, 1978); three Dramalogue Awards (one each for writing, production, and direction) for *Iago* (1979) *Los Angeles Weekly* Award for best play, *Iago* (1980); Drama Logue Award for directing *Piano Bar* (1980); City of Los Angeles Certificate of Appreciation (1982); and Los Angeles Human Relations Commission Certificate of Merit (1982).

JACKSON, ELAINE. A playwright, Jackson graduated from Wayne State University. A recurring theme in her plays is a loss of innocence in the world of young black girls and women. Jackson's first published play, *Toe Jam* (1971), explores the realities of black girlhood. It is unique, given the abundance of plays at the time dealing with black manhood and social crises. The play received wide recognition. Jackson produced three other plays of note. *Paper Dolls* (1979) is an attack on the hegemonic construct of American beauty that inundated the entertainment business. The late **Hazel Bryant** at the Richard Allen Center for Culture and Art in New York City (January 1983) produced it under the direction of Duane Jones. *Cockfight* (19787) is set on a chicken farm outside San Francisco and centers on relationships among black men and women in American society, with one set of partners filled with demands and ambitions, while the other only dreams of being a writer or a country-and-western singer. **Woodie King Jr.** directed a production at the American Place Theatre (1978), with a cast of **Morgan Freeman, Charles Brown, Gylan Kain,** and Cynthia McPherson. *Birth Rights* (1987) is a comedy. It is a portrait of nine anxious expectant mothers in a delivery room of an overburdened metropolitan hospital in New York City and of the lack of communication among the overworked doctors and the authoritarian nurses. Among the awards Jackson received were the Rockefeller Award for playwriting (1978–79), **Langston Hughes** Playwriting Award (1979), and National Endowment for the Arts Award for playwriting (1983).

JACKSON, SAMUEL L. Over the past 20 years, Jackson, an actor and producer, has emerged as a highly respected and sought-after actor in Hollywood. He is among the top three African American actors financially, as his films have grossed over $4 billion worldwide. Jackson's portrayal of the bible-quoting hit man Marcellus Wallace in Quentin Tarantino's film *Pulp Fiction* drew the attention of both audiences and critics. Since then, he has worked steadily in films and costarred with such A-list actors as Bruce Willis, John Travolta, Sharon Stone, and Kevin Spacey. Jackson has appeared in over 100 films, including the *Star Wars* trilogy and films like *Shaft, The Red Violin, Jurassic Park, Die Hard with a Vengeance, The Long Kiss Goodnight, S.W.A.T., Do the Right Thing, Mo' Better Blues, Patriot Games, Rules of Engagement,* and *The Negotiator.*

Born in Washington, DC, Jackson was raised in Chattanooga, TN. He attended the historically black college of Morehouse in Atlanta, GA, as a student of architecture. After participating in a school production of Bertolt Brecht's *Three Penny Opera*, he changed his major to drama. Morehouse was also where Jackson met filmmaker Spike Lee, who later cast him in *Do the Right Thing* and *Jungle Fever*. At Morehouse, he was schooled in the basics of drama, including voice production, elocution, script and character analysis, movement, and choreography and appeared in such plays as *King Heroin* by Al Fann, *Getting It Together* by **Ed Bullins**, and *Dr. B. S. Black* by **Barbara and Carleton Molette**.

Jackson moved to New York after graduation and eventually found work with the Yale Repertory Theatre, **Joseph Papp**'s New York Shakespeare Festival, and the **Negro Ensemble Company**. During a decade of work, he appeared in Brecht's *Mother Courage and Her Children*; **Ntozake Shange**'s *Spell #7*; **Richard Wesley**'s *The Mighty Gents*; and three of the 10-play **August Wilson** canon, *The Piano Lesson, Fences,* and *Two Trains Running*. By this time, he was also working in films but not consistently. In the late 1980s, Jackson developed a severe addiction to drugs and alcohol. After an overdose in 1991, Jackson was committed to a rehabilitation facility in New York, where he finally conquered his habit. He returned to the screen in Spike Lee's *Jungle Fever*. Jackson played secondary roles until his breakout role in *Pulp Fiction* (1994). Jackson's many awards include a National Association for the Advancement of Colored People Image Award as well as awards from the Berlin Film Festival, Acapulco Black Film Festival, the British Academy of Film and Television Arts, and a star on the Hollywood Walk of Fame.

JAHANNES, J. ARTHUR. Jahannes is a playwright, poet, and scientist. He received his education at Lincoln University (cum laude, 1964), Hampton University (M.A., 1966), and the University of Delaware (Ph.D., 1972). Among the plays he wrote is *One More Sunday* (1985), an operatic folk story that shows how a church congregation maneuvers politically in preparation for receiving Dr. Martin Luther King. *Ain't I Something!* (1985) is a musical set in the 1950s and 1960s about life growing up black. *And Yet We Sing* (1986) focuses on black family life in America from 1600 to the 1980s. *La Dolorosa* (1986), in oration and music, depicts the life, death, and rebirth of Jesus Christ. *Go Down Death* (1985) is an adaptation of James Weldon Johnson's vignettes from the Bible.

JEANNETTE, GERTRUDE. An actress, playwright, director, and teacher, Jeannette was one of the great ladies of the American theater. She spent over 50 years as a performer on and off Broadway, at regional theaters, in films, and on radio and television. In 1942, aside from taking bookkeeping classes, Jeannette became the first female licensed cab driver in New York due to the paucity of males during the war. Three years later, she took speech classes at the **American Negro Theatre**, where she launched her theatrical career with a part in *Our Town*. During her lengthy career, Jeannette appeared in such plays as *God's Trombones* and *The Great White Hope* and in such films as *Cotton Comes to Harlem*, *Shaft*, *Nothing but a Man*, *Vieux Carre*, and *Lost in the Stars*.

In 1979, at age 65, Jeannette founded the **Hadley Players Theatre**, a community theater headquartered in **Harlem**, where she lives, as her way of giving back to the community. Her goal was to hone theatrical abilities and to enhance the artistic and cultural life of Harlem. To that end, Jeanette wrote and directed many of the productions and cultivated and trained hundreds of young people who wanted to pursue a career in the theater. Jeanette has been recognized with numerous awards and honors across the span of her career. They include the **Audience Development Committee** Outstanding Pioneer Award (1984), **National Black Theatre Festival** Living Legend Award (1991), Lionel Hampton Legacy Award (1998), Arkansas Black Hall of Fame (1999), and Actors Equity **Paul Robeson** Award (2002).

JELLY'S LAST JAM **(1992). George C. Wolfe** wrote and directed this 2-act, 12-scene musical drama retrospective of Jelly Roll Morton. The music was arranged by Luther Henderson, who composed additional music with lyrics by Susan Birkenhead. *Jelly's Last Jam* was developed at **Crossroads Theatre Company** in New Brunswick, NJ (1991), before it moved to the Mark Taper Forum in Los Angeles (winter 1991–92). It opened on Broadway at the Virginia Theatre (April 1992), with Wolfe as director, Hope Clarke as choreographer, and Gregory Hines and Ted L. Levy doing the tap choreography. The life and death of Morton, a New Orleans jazz musician of mixed heritage, is celebrated on the eve of his death by an African spiritualist, Chimney Man, and characters from his past life as Morton wrestles with his repulsion against being neither black nor white. Among the original cast were Gregory Hines (Jelly Roll Morton), Savion Glover (Young Jelly), Keith David (Chimney Man), and **Ruben Santiago-Hudson** (Buddy Bolden, a musician). Among the awards *Jelly* received were **Tony Awards** for Hines for best leading actor; Tonya Pinkins for best featured actress; Wolfe for best book and best director; Luther Henderson for best original score; Hines, Levy, and Clarke for best choreography; and Toni-Leslie James for best costume design.

JENKINS, FRANK SHOCKLEY. Born in Seattle, Jenkins, a playwright and poet, is a veteran writer who lives in Los Angeles. He traveled throughout the world as a merchant marine seaman, lived in France and New York City, and worked a variety of jobs, including at the U.S. Post Office. He has written several books of poetry, including *My World*, which was presented by him and his actress wife, **Lynn Hamilton**, at Purdue University, Northwestern University, Massachusetts Institute of Technology, and University of Southern California. His plays have been produced at such venues as the Matrix Theatre, Amistad Cultural Center, and the Back Lot Theatre. As a playwright, he has written *Driving While Black in Beverly Hills* (1969), which centers on a middle-class black family's drives through Beverly Hills; *Nobody: The Checkered Life of Bert Williams*; *My World* (1978); and *The Boy and the Bird* (2006). Jenkins's books of poetry include *I Didn't Start Out to Be a Poet* (1977), *Black Mac Say* (1981), *What It Is?* (1981), *Curious about Myself* (1987), and *From behind My Eyes* (2002).

JENNINGS, CALEEN SINNETTE. Jennings, a playwright, is professor of theater at American University in Washington, DC. She is the author of over 80 plays and is a two-time Helen Hayes Award nominee for outstanding new play. In 2002, she received the Heidman Award from Actor's Theatre of Louisville for her play *Classyass*, which has been published in five anthologies. In 2000, her play *Free Like Br'er Rabbit* was performed at the Kennedy Center New Visions/ New Voices Children's Play Festival. In 1999, she received a $10,000 grant from the Kennedy Center's fund for new American plays for her play *Inns and Outs*. Her *Playing Juliet/Casting Othello* was produced at the Folger Elizabethan Theatre in 1998. Jennings received her B.A. in drama from Bennington College and her M.F.A. in acting from the New York University Tisch School of the Arts. She has been a faculty member of the Folger Shakespeare Library's Teaching Shakespeare Institute since 1994. In 2003, Jennings won the award for outstanding teaching of playwriting from the Play Writing Forum of the Association of Theatre in Higher Education. She received the university's 2003 Scholar/Teacher of the Year Award.

JOHNSON, GEORGIA DOUGLAS (1886–1966). A playwright and poet, Johnson was one of the leading members of the Washington, DC, literati during the **Harlem** Renaissance of the 1920s. Born in Atlanta, GA, she received her education at Atlanta University, Howard University, and Oberlin Conservatory of Music. She taught school for a brief period in Atlanta before moving to Washington, DC, with her husband, Henry Lincoln Johnson, a lawyer who was appointed recorder of deeds by President Howard Taft.

For some 40 years, her home in Washington, DC, located on S Street in the northwest section, earned the distinction of being a literary haven for black artists and intellectuals of the area. Because they met on Saturday nights, they were called the "Saturday Nighters." Among the well-known figures who frequented her home were **Langston Hughes**, Alain Locke, **Jean Toomer**, **Countee Cullen**, **May Miller**, Sterling Brown, **Owen Dodson**, **Angelina Grimké**, **Marita Bonner**, and Richard Bruce Nugent.

Johnson wrote and published four volumes of poetry, her husband's biography, a novel, numerous short stories, and about 30 one-act plays. Among the plays she penned is *Sunday Morning in the South* (1925), a tragedy in one act set in a small southern town. A frail grandmother learns her innocent grandson has been arrested and accused of assaulting a white woman the night before. While she is seeking help from a prominent white woman, she is told her grandson has been lynched by a white mob, a fatal blow to the grandmother, who collapses and dies. There are two versions of the play, one in which singing is heard from a black church in the background throughout the play and the other in which the singing is heard from a white church. *Blue Blood* (1926), a drama in one act, explores black social snobbery, **miscegenation**, and incest. On their wedding night, a black couple and their respective mothers learn that the bride and groom have the same father, a wealthy white southern aristocrat. *Blood* received honorable mention in the *Opportunity* Contest Awards (May 1926). In its first production by the **Krigwa Players** in New York City, there were three performances (April 1927). *Plumes* (1927) is a folk tragedy in one act. It explores the superstitions and funeral practices of lower-class blacks during the 1920s. A desperately ill daughter's indigent mother struggles with a decision whether to spend the $50 savings on an emergency operation not guaranteed to save her mother's life or on a lavish funeral "with plumed horses." The mother makes her decision based on the coffee-ground readings of a superstitious friend who declared the operation would do no good. The play won first prize in the *Opportunity* Contest Awards of 1927. It was followed by productions at the Harlem Experimental Theatre, New York (1928), and the Cube Theatre in Chicago (1928). Other plays Johnson wrote are *Safe* (c. 1929), a one-act drama; *Blue-Eyed Black Boy* (c. 1930), a drama in one act; and *William and Ellen Craft* (1935), a black history play in one act. Johnson gained a modicum of attention for writing plays dealing with lynching, such as

And Still They Paused, Midnight and Dawn, A Bill to Be Passed (about the need for an antilynching law), *Camel-Leg, Heritage, Miss Bliss,* and *Money Wagon.* Johnson remained in Washington, DC, still writing and publishing her work until her death at 80.

JOHNSON, JAVON. An actor and playwright, Johnson is a multitalented young man from Pittsburgh, PA. He is widely regarded as a protégé of the late **August Wilson,** who befriended him at the Edward Albee Theatre Conference held in Valdez, AK, in 1998. As an actor, Johnson has also performed in several of Wilson's plays. A native of Anderson, SC, Johnson holds a B.A. from South Carolina State University and an M.F.A. in Theatre Arts from the University of Pittsburgh (1999).

Johnson had already begun writing plays in college, winning the **Lorraine Hansberry** Award for the first play he wrote, *Papa's Blues* (1998). The next year (1999), he won the coveted **Theodore Ward** Award for best play for *Hambone.* Johnson's plays include *The Spanish Jade, Breathe, Runaway Home, The House That Jack Built, A Noose for Bettyanne, Cryin' Shame, Eighty Six, Things That Lovers Do*—with George Faison, *The Pawn, Sanctified, Hobo King,* and *Homebound.* As an actor, he has appeared in *Fences, Measure for Measure, Pericles,* and *Macbeth,* as well as in several films. He is a founding member of the Chicago-based Congo Square Theatre Company and functions as its literary manager. In a relatively short period, Johnson has earned several prestigious awards. They include best one-act play at the American College Theatre Festival competition (1996), Kennedy Center fellowship for the Eugene O'Neill Playwright Conference (1998), Yukon/Pacific New Play Award (1998), Pittsburgh Playwright Award (1999), and the Sundance Theatre Lab (2000).

JOHNSON, OKORO HAROLD. Johnson, a veteran director, actor, and administrator, has worked in the Chicago area for years to help improve the cultural life of the citizenry. He was born in Chicago in 1925, eventually earning a B.A. in theater from Roosevelt University and an M.A. from Governors State University. Johnson holds the distinct honor of cofounding the eta Creative Arts Foundation with **Jackie Taylor** in 1969. He functioned as the artistic director of eta for the next 17 years. Johnson also served as director of the South Shore Cultural Center in Chicago and has taught at the collegiate level. Johnson has directed such shows as *A Candle in the Wind, A Change Is Gon' Come,* **Purlie Victorious,** *Fats Waller: His Life and Times,* and *Jazz Set.* The plays he has written include *The Regal Theatre, SCLC: Second Coming, Last Chance, Strange Fruit,* and *Kintu and the Law of Love.* He has also appeared in the film versions of *A Raisin in the Sun, The Wedding,* and *The Spook Who Sat by the Door.* Johnson is a recipient of the **Paul Robeson** Award.

JOMANDI PRODUCTIONS. Based in Atlanta, GA, Jomandi is one of the oldest black theaters in the country. It was cofounded in 1978 by **Thomas W. Jones II** and Marsha Jackson Randolph. The production company evolved from a play Jones wrote as a tribute to his father that became its initial production. Jomandi eventually incorporated as a nonprofit 501(c)3, producing theater for the eclectic city of Atlanta. It has developed into one of the leading theaters in the country in producing cutting-edge new work and providing a forum for a new generation of black writers. Jones, an actor and playwright of increasing renown, led the company for 22 years in producing over 100 productions, including the premiering of over 50 new plays. Jomandi has toured in over 40 states and five countries. Among the plays they have presented are *If God Was a Blues Singer; Josephine Live; Zooman and the Sign; Buddy Bolden's Blues; Do Lord Remember Me; That Serious He-Man Ball; Boesman and Lena; The Black Play; Every Now and Then I Get the Feeling; The Wizard of Hip; House of Cold Funk; Harlem Nutcracker; Trick the Devil; And the Men Shall Also Gather; Black Nativity; Hip 2: Birth of the Boom;* and *Welcome Home, Marian Anderson.*

The theater has garnered much acclaim and many awards over the years, including the 1990 Governor's Award for the arts, the Bronze Jubilee Award, the Back Stage Dramalogue Award, an **Audience Development Committee Award**, and eight Helen Hayes Awards. The theater, however, went through a transitional phase. Jones left the company in 2000 in pursuance of other interests. Jackson Randolph also left soon thereafter. In 2002, though, it moved into their first permanent space, a 99-seat black box theater located at City Hall East. Since then, the theater has initiated a theatrical training program called JADA, the Jomandi Academy of the Dramatic Arts. The program is being run under the direction of Carol Mitchell-Leon, head of the Theatre Arts Program at Clark Atlanta University.

JONES, DANIEL ALEXANDER. Jones is an interdisciplinary performance artist. This form of theater took root in the late 1980s, flourished in the 1990s, and is now recognized as a theatrical art form, albeit not without detractors. Jones works from a large canvas, incorporating visual art, poetry, live music, tape recordings, slideshows, and other elements designed to clarify the message of the event, though the message can be interpreted several ways.

A native of Springfield, MA, Jones received a B.A. in African studies from Vassar College (1991) and earned an M.A. in theater from Brown University (1993). His works have been performed in Seattle; New York City; Boston; Atlanta, GA; Dublin, Ireland; London; and a host of other cities. He has worked in collaboration with many of the leading performance artists in the world, including **Robbie McCauley**, Erik Hen, **Carl Hancock Rux**, and Helga Davis, among others. Two of his more popular performances were *Bel Canto*, a drama set in New England in which opera and jazz intermix. It is a story of a shy, young man abandoned by his father. The other piece, *Blood: Shock: Boogie*, is the story of a young man discovering his homosexuality and the fantasy world he inhabits to counteract societal pressures. Other "plays" Jones wrote are *Earthbirths: The Blackbird Cipher*, a jazz play; *Ambient Love Rights*; *Black Barbie in the Hotel de Dream*; *Whale*; *Phoenix Fabrik*; *Clayangels*; and *La Chanteuse Nubienne*.

Jones taught at the University of Texas at Austin as a professor in playwriting. In 2006, he won a prestigious Alpert Award of $50,000 given to "early midcareer" artists in the fields of dance, film, video, music, theater, and the visual arts. Jones was also awarded a 2000 National Endowment for the Arts/Theatre Communications Group playwright-in-residence fellowship at Boston's Theatre Offensive. In addition, he has received other grants and awards from such organizations as the Jerome Foundation, Playwrights Center, Creative Capital Foundation, and Rockefeller Foundation. Jones received the 2008 Screen Actors Guild Lifetime Achievement Award.

JONES, JAKE ANN. An actor, composer, and playwright, Jones is one of a growing cadre of young artist who are re-inventing the art of the theater. She was born in Harlem, New York, where she earned a degree from CCNY in 1988. Jones then enrolled at Brown University, where she studied in the Rites and Reason program, obtaining an M.F.A. in 1996. Thereafter followed a life of modeling, acting, and eventually writing after she enrolled in the Frank Silvera Writers Workshop. She has also worked with the New York Theatre Workshop, the Public Theatre, and the Trinity Repertory Theatre.

Her most prominent work to date has been *Death of a Ho*, which she later developed into a musical *Magic Kingdom: A Ho's Tale*. The musical has quickly become a staple at performance venues around the country. Other performance pieces written by Jones include *Pedisyon* (1996) in which a Catholic woman ponders what to do after her fourth pregnancy. The play is an exploration of guilt, race, and class interlaced with Haitian voodoo. *Black Bitches Brew* (1995) a solo performance piece with the kitchen as a metaphor for the power and empowerment of women. *Sojourner Truth Meets Napoleon* (1993) is an imaginary meeting between two opposites from different centuries who attempt to find common ground. Jones is the recipient of a Jonathan Larson Award for her musical, *The Magic Kingdom: A Ho's Tale*.

JONES, JAMES EARL. An actor, Jones has one of the most recognizable and distinctive basso voices of the past half century that is the very symbol of authority. People throughout the world recognize him both as the iconic voice of Darth Vader in the *Star Wars* trilogy and the voiceover for a world news network when he tones, "This is CNN." Born in Arkabutla, MS, Jones was raised by his grandparents on a farm in Michigan. He overcame a severe stuttering problem with the aid of a teacher, using acting as a tool to correct it. He quit medical school at the University of Michigan to pursue acting but wound up in the army. After military service, he moved to New York City, where he made his theatrical debut in 1957. He has performed in over 200 stage, movie, and television projects, including *The Lion King, Clear and Present Danger, The Great White Hope, Field of Dreams, The Hunt for Red October, **Fences**, Othello, Light, Dr. Strangelove, Homicide: Life on* *the Street, King Lear, As the World Turns, Cry, The Beloved Country, Patriot Games, Baal, Moon on a Rainbow Shawl, The Defenders,* and *Gabriel's Fire,* to name but a few. Jones has been recognized for his acting with many awards and honors during his lifetime, including two **Tony Awards**, five **Drama Desk Awards**, two **Obie Awards**, two Cable Ace Awards, four Emmy Awards, and a National Association for the Advancement of Colored People Image Award. President Bill Clinton awarded him a National Medal of Arts Award in 1992 for his distinguished career in theater.

JONES, LEROI. *See* BARAKA, AMIRI (LEROI JONES).

JONES, SARAH. Jones, a performance artist and playwright, was born in Baltimore, MD. She attended Bryn Mawr College on a Mellon minority scholarship intending to be a lawyer but put her education on hold when her sister died. She also attended the United Nations International School, where she was introduced to people of various nationalities and learned many different speech patterns, nuances, and inflections. Her interest turned to writing, and she became involved in the renowned Nuyorican Poets Café (NPC) in New York, eventually winning the Grand Slam Championship in 1997. She began developing monologues from her poetry based on experiences with relatives of her parents after they divorced while she was growing up in Washington, DC; Boston; and New York City. Jones performed her first solo show, *Surface Transit,* at the NPC in 1998. Owing to its success, it attracted the attention of several feminist organizations as well as Equality Now, which commissioned Jones to write a play addressing discriminatory laws against women, *Women Can't Wait.* It premiered in 2000 at the United Nations International Conference on Women's Rights.

Jones wrote three more plays, each one adding to her reputation as one of the fine wordsmiths of her generation. Each play features multiple characters, all deftly handled by Jones, who has no formal training in acting. She has appeared in off-Broadway productions of *The Vagina Monologues* and on the PBS series *City Life.* She also performed on CBS, ABC, and NBC. In 2000, *Variety* magazine named her among the "Top Ten Comedic Talents of the Year." Abroad, Jones has performed in India, Nepal, Europe, and South Africa and locally at such diverse locations as the American Place Theatre, the **Apollo Theatre**, Riker's Island, and the 92nd Street YMCA in New York City. Other plays Jones wrote are *Waking the American Dream*, *A Right to Care*, and *Bridge and Tunnel*. The latter was produced off Broadway (2005) at the Circle in the Square Theatre. In 2006, it premiered on Broadway at the Helen Hayes Theatre. Of the awards and honors bestowed on Jones, the most significant are the W. K. Kellogg Foundation Commission Award, Helen Hayes Award, Theatre World Award, Drama League Award, and the Ford Foundation Award.

JONES, SILAS. A University of Los Angeles City College playwright, Jones was born in Paris, KY. He studied literature and creative writing at Washington State of America Open Door Program. His plays were produced by the **Negro Ensemble Company** and at the Mark Taper Forum, **Penumbra Theatre**, and other venues across the country. His most successful plays are *American Medea* and *The Afrindi Aspect*. Other plays Jones wrote include *Canned Goods*, *The Eight Planet*, *God in Little Pieces*, *The John Doe Variations*, *Night Commander*, *Romancing Stereotypes*, *Vagaries*, and *Waiting for Mongo*. Jones has also written several short stories and a TV documentary. He is a member of Dramatists Guild of America and is the recipient of a Gwendolyn Brooks Literary Award.

JONES, SYL. Jones, a playwright and journalist, graduated from Augsberg College in 1970 with a journalism degree. He has worked in that profession while juggling a career that includes both film- and playwriting. As a playwright, he has written over 50 plays, mostly in conjunction with the Mixed Blood Theatre Company in Minneapolis. His plays have also been produced at the Kennedy Center, **Penumbra Theatre**, Indiana Repertory Theatre, **Arena Playhouse**, Mark Guthrie Theatre, and Great American History Theatre, among others. One of his plays, *Black No More*, won the prestigious Roger Stevens/Kennedy Center Award for best play in 1998. A representative sampling of his plays is *Mother of the Movement*, *Lazarus*, *Gunplay*, *Cincinnati Man*, *The Brotherhood*, *Burnt*, *Gunplay*, *Shine*,

Sacrament, and *Fire in the Bones*. During a lengthy career, Jones has been duly recognized for his work, accumulating such awards as the Cornerstone Award, a Jerome fellowship, a National Endowment for the Arts fellowship, the McKnight Foundation Award, and the Mixed Blood American National Playwrights Award.

JONES, THOMAS W., II. Jones, a longtime actor, director, and producer, has mounted over 200 productions worldwide. He is perhaps best known as the founder/director of **Jomandi Productions** in Atlanta, GA, a company he started in 1978, which still exists today. Jones was born and raised in Queens, where he began writing as a child. He earned a B.A. with honors from Amherst College. Jones started Jomandi Productions as a vehicle to produce a play he had written as his senior thesis, *Every Father's Child*. It was quickly expanded to become a broad-based community theater dedicated to providing a forum for new work and expanding visions.

As a playwright, Jones has written several plays of note. They include *Hip II*; *Birth of a Boom*; and his critically acclaimed one-man show, *The Wizard of Hip*. Probably one of his most acclaimed works is *Bessie's Blues*, a tribute musical to the great blues singer Bessie Smith. Jones's main interest is in music, and his efforts have resulted in the following musicals of note: *Three Sistuhs*; *Point of Revue*; *Two Queens, One Castle*; *Cool Papa's Party*; *Harlem Rose: A Love Song to Langston Hughes*; and *Bricktop*, written with Calvin A. Ramsey. Jones has been the recipient of many awards during his career, including a National Association for the Advancement of Colored People Award and 12 Helen Hayes Awards. After 22 years with Jomandi, having built the theater into the third largest African American theater in the country, Jones resigned in 2000 and created his own new company, VIA Theatrical. Jones continues to write, direct, and perform in venues around the country and the world.

JONES, WALTER. An actor, director, and playwright, Jones is a native of Fayetteville, NC. He has been involved in theater for over 25 years, either as an actor or director. His plays have been produced at venues throughout the United States, including the New York Shakespeare Festival/Public Theatre, **New Federal Theatre**, **La MaMa**

Experimental Theatre Club, Museum of Modern Art, **Penumbra Theatre**, and regional theaters and colleges across the country. Jones adapted **Langston Hughes**'s musical *Black Nativity* and produces it each year with great success. Other plays are *Jazznite, Nigger Nightmare, Fish and Chips, Reverend Brown's Daughter, Dudder Lover, The Boston Party at Annie Mae's House, Mom's Long Leash, The Withering Rose*, and *Underground*. He also collaborated with Edgar White and Norma Jean Darden in writing a musical, *The Lady from Philadelphia*, a tribute to the operatic diva Marian Anderson. Jones was also a staff writer for the Norman Lear–Bud Yorkin sitcom *What's Happening?* Jones is the recipient of a Rockefeller fellowship grant for playwriting.

JORDAN, JUNE (1936–2002). A playwright, poet, and educator, Jordan was one of the most acclaimed and prolific writers of the 20th century, producing over 50 volumes of poetry, plays, children's books, and political essays. She was also an educator, a professor who taught English, women's studies, and African American studies at City University of New York, Yale, Sarah Lawrence, and the University of California at Berkeley during her lifetime. Her birthplace was **Harlem**, and she was educated at Barnard College, where she excelled. She is known primarily as a poet but had some success with the three plays, enjoying productions at Lincoln Center, American Place Theatre, Seven Stages Theatre, Eureka Theatre, John Jay Theatre, and several theaters in Europe. Jordan also served as playwright-in-residence at the New Dramatists Theatre in 1987–88. The plays Jordan wrote include *All My Blessings*, a semiautobiographical play about a young woman growing up with a tyrannical father in Bedford-Stuyvesant during the **civil rights movement**. *Bang Bang, Uber Alles!* is a musical in which activists hold a benefit concert in Ku Klux Klan territory to protest racism. *I Was Looking at the Ceiling and Then I Saw the Sky* is about a diverse group of people who are trapped together during the Los Angeles earthquake and have to overcome their differences. Among the numerous awards and honors Jordan received were the Lila Wallace Readers Digest Award, a McDowell fellowship, a Yado fellowship, Ground Breakers Dream Award, and Chancellors Distinguished Lectureship at the University of California at Berkeley and from such organizations as the New York Foundation for the Arts, Prix de Rome, National Endowment for the Arts, Rockefeller Foundation, and Massachusetts Council on the Arts.

JOYCE, ELLA. Joyce is an up and coming actor of the 21st century who has made a name for herself both onstage and in television. She is best known for her role as Eleanor in the 1990s sitcom *Roc* with **Charles Dutton**. Born as Cherron Hoye in Chicago, Joyce was raised in Detroit, where she studied acting at the Performing Arts Curriculum at Cass Technical High. She also attended Eastern Michigan University to hone her dramatic talents. Joyce has performed in regional theaters throughout the country, including the Pittsburgh Public Theatre, the Seattle Repertory Theatre, the Goodman Theatre, South Coast Repertory Theatre, Boston Huntington, Yale Repertory Theatre, and the **Juneteenth Legacy Theatre**. She has the unique distinction of creating two roles from the **August Wilson** canon—Risa in *Two Trains Running* (1992) and Tonya in *King Hedley II* (1999). Other plays she performed in include *Crumbs from the Table of Joy* by **Lynn Nottage**, *The Mighty Gents* by **Richard Wesley**, *Split Second*, *Medea*, and *Anna Lucasta*.

Joyce has also made over 30 television and movie appearances in shows like *PBS Hollywood Presents*; *Bubba Ho-tep*; *Selma, Lord, Selma*; *The Jamie Foxx Show*; *Sabrina, the Teenage Witch*; *Seinfeld*; *Clockin' Green*; *The Client*; *Bid Whist Party Throwdown*; and *Who Made the Potato Salad?* Her most recent project, *A Rose among Thorns*, is a one-woman biopic of the life of **civil rights** icon Rosa Parks. It met with great success at the 2007 **National Black Theatre Festival**, her eighth consecutive appearance at the festival as a performer. The carefully researched play debuted at New York's Richard Allen Center in 2006 and has been constantly touring since. Joyce has been the recipient of an **Audience Development Committee Award**, a Jeff Award, and a **Black Theatre Alliance** Award.

JUA, CHAKULA CHA (CAYETTE MCNEIL). Jua, born Cayette McNeill, is known as an actor, director, writer, producer, and enabler of all things theatrical. He is a living legend in his hometown of New Orleans, where he has been involved in theater since 1968. As a youngster, he was enthralled while witnessing a performance by the **Free Southern Theatre (FST)**. Following his stint in the U.S. Air Force, he returned and worked as a staffer for the FST not knowing this was the beginning of a long theatrical career. After the demise of the FST in 1972, he began working for the Ethiopian Theatre as an actor and later directing plays for them. Eventually he founded the **Chakula Cha Jua Theatre Company** in 1985, and they have performed continuously. Jua has been an active presence in New Orleans theater for many years, at one time teaching theater at Xavier University and serving as president for the Alliance of Community Theatres. He regularly tours the schools and libraries of New Orleans, either involving students in storytelling or performing one of his one-man shows, such as *Has Anyone Here Heard of Langston Hughes?*

JUBILEE THEATRE. Based in Fort Worth, for over 25 years, Jubilee Theatre has been providing black theater of high quality to the people of Texas. Rudy and Harriett Eastman founded Jubilee (1981), with Rudy serving as its artistic director. The first five years, it was a gypsy operation, performing in churches, lobbies, and schools. By 1986, it had made great strides in obtaining 501(c)3 nonprofit status and obtaining an Actors Equity contract. This enabled Jubilee to bring in professional actors, to merge with its resident company, and to elevate the quality of productions. Most of the productions were traditional plays, such as *God's Trombones*, **Langston Hughes's** Christmas spectacle *Black Nativity*, and original musical *The Blues Ain't Nothin'*.

In 1993 and 1995, Jubilee held two successful fund-raising campaigns, which the administration used to enlarge office space and increase staffing. They also began to produce more challenging work by staging *Crumbs from the Table of Joy* by **Lynn Nottage**, *Cookin' at the Cookery* by Marion J. Caffey, and *Home* by **Samm-Art Williams**. The 2003–4 season marked another turning point. They increased the seating capacity to 150 seats, renovated the lobby, and increased dressing room and lobby space without going into debt. Jubilee also launched an educational outreach program in the school system that involved over 38,000 students. The theater has seen its audience rise each year and serves an average of 12,000 patrons yearly. Unexpectedly, artistic director Rudy Eastman passed away. A year later, a nationwide search produced his successor—Professor Edward Smith, a theater veteran with an impeccable record. The transition has been seamless, with Smith introducing a program of staged readings in the 2006–7, along with *A Lovesong for Miss Lydia* by **Donald T. Evans** and **August Wilson**'s epic journey *Joe Turner's Come and Gone*.

JUNEBUG PRODUCTIONS, INC. (JP). In the late 1960s, **John O'Neal**, a playwright, actor, and director, founded JP, an African American theater company based in New Orleans. It was one of the many multicultural artistic collaborations O'Neal organized. Earlier in the decade, he had cofounded the historic **Free Southern Theatre** (FST) and later the Color Line Project, a social-justice group. O'Neal began his theatrical journey at the height of the **civil rights movement**. Growing up in Mound City, IL, O'Neal had been subjected to racial tensions and social upheaval in what he described as a rigidly segregated community of 2,200 people divided along racial lines.

After the demise of the FST (late 1960s), O'Neal embarked upon a one-man show utilizing dance, music, and storytelling. Although O'Neal came from a family of privilege, that did not protect him from being subjected to oppression and exploitation. To combat social injustice, O'Neal put together a performance piece akin to the storytelling traditions of the Deep South called *Don't Start Me to Talking or I'll Tell You Everything I Know*. He embodied onstage the character of Junebug Jabbo Jones, a modern-day African American storyteller who enlightened audiences with humorous introspection. After the success of this show, he added three other works that comprise the Junebug Cycle—*You Can't Judge a Book by Looking at the Cover*, *Till the Midnight Hour*, and *Trying to Find My Way Back Home*, for which O'Neal's son made his stage debut. Each piece was interactive. JP engaged audiences through six humorous tales using down-home charm to tell the truth about coming of age in the cotton fields of Pike County, MS; leaving home, and getting old. For more than 30 years, O'Neal traveled to numerous community and educational institutions and regional theaters with versions of the Junebug Cycle, captivating audiences throughout the country from east to west.

JUNETEENTH LEGACY THEATRE (JLT). The JLT is Kentucky's only professional African American theater company. It is a testament to the day blacks gained their freedom. On 19 June 1866, slaves of Ashton Villa in Galveston, TX, first learned they were free owing to the executive order of President Abraham Lincoln (he had signed the Emancipation Proclamation on 1 January 1863, three and a half years earlier). It became a day of celebration and family reunions for blacks akin to the Fourth of July in the United States.

In 1993, producer, director, playwright, actress, and educator **Lorna Littleway** founded the JLT in Louisville and assumed the mantle of artistic director of the Minority Theatre Workshop. She also served as codirector of the African American Theatre Program at the University of Louisville (1994–99). As an assistant professor there, she designed courses in African American theater history, dramatic literature, and performance. Littleway also initiated the Juneteenth Festival of New Works: A Cultural Celebration of Emancipation, which she produced from 1997 to 1999. Littleway has directed extensively on the regional theater circuit and at colleges and universities.

– K –

KAIN, GYLAN. A playwright, poet, actor, and musician, Kain was one of the founding members of the Last Poets. David Nelson and Felipe Luciano were the other two members of this popular group that made waves during the black arts movement. New York born and raised, Kain was a forerunner in a style of poetry that eventually evolved into what is now called rap. Kain was also director of the East Wind Cultural Center, a writer's workshop. The zenith of their popularity came with the release of the 1971 film *Right On*, which was produced by **Woodie King Jr.** and Herb Danska. Kain wrote two plays. One is a 1968 effort titled *Epitaph to a Coagulated Trinity*, in which a black wino points out the absurdities of Christianity to a group of white priests and nuns waiting for a train on a subway platform. The other is a 1973 vehicle with a self-explanatory title, *The Urination of Gylan Kain*. As an actor, he was selected for **Joseph Papp**'s black and

Hispanic Shakespeare company in 1977. Kain left the United States and now lives abroad.

KARAMU REPERTORY THEATRE (KRT)/COMPANY. Karamu was preceded by the Gilpin Players and the Dumas Dramatic Club (DDC) and KRT/Company of Cleveland, OH. Founded by two white Oberlin College (1915) graduates, Rowena Jelliffe and her husband Russell, the KRT gained the reputation as America's longest-running African American integrated little theater group.

The Jelliffes had gained practical experience in theater management at the Hull House in Chicago. From, there they organized the KRT with six players. They called themselves the DDC, named after Alexandre Dumas père (1802–70), a biracial French writer. The KRT's mission was to develop a multicultural arts center within the black community in Cleveland. It started out as a children's theater, but as the area changed racially, so did their focus. In 1923, **Charles Gilpin** appeared in Cleveland as the title character in *The Emperor Jones*. So moved by Gilpin's performance were the Jelliffes that they co-opted his name for their company, the Gilpin Players (1927–c. 1945). By the mid-1940s, the players began producing plays that better represented this racially diverse community. They thrived until the outbreak of World War II and then ceased to exist. While living in Cleveland, **Langston Hughes**, one of America's more prolific playwrights, frequented the KRT. The Jelliffes produced several of his plays between 1915 and 1960, including *Little Ham*, *Joy to My Soul*, *Front Porch*, *Drums of Haiti*, *Mulatto*, *Simply Heavenly*, and *Shakespeare in Harlem*, adapted by **Robert Glenn**.

Other nationally acclaimed playwrights also mounted their plays at the KRT. Among them were **Willis Richardson**'s *Compromise*, Andrew Burris's *You Mus' Be Bo'n Again*, **Zora Neale Hurston**'s *Sermon in the Valley*, **Countee Cullen** and **Arna Bontemps**'s *St. Louis Woman*, Shirley Graham DuBois's *Coal Dust*, **Louis Peterson**'s *Take a Giant Step*, and **Lorraine Hansberry**'s *A Raisin in the Sun*. Also, the KRT offered plays by white playwrights that intertwined themes and subject matter relating to African Americans. They included Ridgely Torrence's *Granny Maumee*, *Simon the Cyrenian*, and *The Rider of*

Dreams; Paul Green's *The No 'Count Boy* and *In Abraham's Bosom*; Eugene O'Neill's *The Emperor Jones*; Dorothy and Dubose Heyward's *Porgy*; and Carson McCullers's *The Member of the Wedding*.

KEIN, SYBIL. A playwright, poet, musician, and historian, Kein was born in New Orleans. After graduating from Xavier University with a degree in instrumental music in 1958, she married and raised a family. After the marriage dissolved, she returned to school, earning an M.A. in theater arts and communication from the University of New Orleans (1972) and a Ph.D. in American ethnic literature from the University of Michigan (1975).

Kein's playwriting efforts include *Get Together* (1970), which is about a gathering of invited guests, both black and white, who are subjected to stereotypical comments at a dinner party. Her other plays are *Saints and Flowers* (1965), *Projection One* (1966), *The Black Box* (1967), *The Christmas Holly* (1967), *Deep River Rises* (1970), *The Reverend* (1970), *When I Grow Up* (1974), *Rogues althethe River Flint* (1977), and *River Rogues* (1979).

Kein spent over two decades researching the history and culture of native Louisiana Creoles, which resulted in her seminal book *The History and Legacy of Louisiana's Free People of Color*, which was published in 2000. A musician as well as a writer, Kein has written three volumes of poetry: *Visions from the Rainbow*, *Gumbo People: Poésie de La Nouvelle-Orléans*, and *Delta Dance*. She also wrote several essays and papers and over 28 plays (10 of which have been produced), made several recordings of music and poetry, and performed in various locations. She received honors and awards as the best playwright from Louisiana State University (1970), as well as the Avery Hopwood Award for poetry (1975); Creative Achievement Award, University of Michigan (1978); Michigan Association of Governing Boards Award (1982); and the Michigan Council of the Arts Artist Award (1981, 1990).

KELLEY, SAMUEL L. A playwright and educator, Kelley was born in Memphis, TN, and grew up in Marvell, AR. He holds degrees from Arkansas University (B.A., M.A.), Yale School of Drama (M.F.A.), and the University of Michigan (Ph.D.). In addition, he has studied screenwriting, playwriting, and film script development at New York University. His career as a playwright began when he was a student at Yale, where he penned his first script, *Blue Vein Society*, which eventually was produced by several theaters. He has been writing ever since, with his plays finding homes at **Jomandi Productions, Karamu Repertory Theatre, Penumbra Theatre**, Actors Theatre of Louisville, **Billie Holiday Theatre**, the **Paul Robeson Performing Arts Company**, and even in Wales. His most successful play has been *Pill Hill*, which received national acclaim by winning the Kieffer Award for best production and the Molly Kuhn Award for best play at the Yale School of Drama in 1990.

Herewith is a listing of other plays by Kelley: *Skeletons*; *Ain't Got No Time to Die*; *Driving While Black*; *White Chocolate*; *Thruway Diaries*; *A Hero for McBride*; *August Revival*; *Bicycle for Kim*; and *Faith, Hope, and Charity: The Story of Mary McLeod Bethune*. Kelley's plays are published in *Dramatic Publications, Best Monologues for Male Actors*, and *New American Plays*. His many honors and awards include the 2005 Chancellors Award for excellence in research and creativity and appointment to the Phi Kappa Phi National Honor Society. He has received a National Endowment for the Humanities grant and served as the James Thurber playwright-in-residence at Ohio State University. He is a member of the Dramatists Play Service and the **Black Theatre Network**. Kelley is currently a professor at State University of New York in Cortland.

KELLY, NAMBI E. A budding playwright and actress, Kelly was born in New York City and reared in Chicago, where she earned a B.F.A. in playwriting from the Theatre School of DePaul University. Her acting skills landed her roles on live television, in film, and onstage. As a playwright, she wrote several plays, such as *Antigone, Chris T., Girl to Be Named Later, Bus Boyz, The First Woman, The Tale of Nambi and Kintu, Milk, He She and My White Mama*, and *Hoochie Mama*. Her works have been produced at the Steppenwolf Theatre, **St. Louis Black Repertory Theatre**, and Lincoln Center. Kelly is associated professionally with the Women's Theatre Alliance, Chicago Alliance for Playwrights, Alliance for Los Angeles Playwrights, and Playwright's Center in Minneapolis. She was a playwright-in-residence with Chicago Dramatists and **Ma'at Production Association**

of **Afrikan-Centered Theatre**. Kelly was recipient of a Lila Wallace Readers Digest Fund Award and a Berkshire Theatre Festival acting scholarship.

KENNEDY, ADRIENNE. A playwright and educator, Kennedy is the "Grande Doyenne" of American theater. Born in Pittsburgh, PA, she received B.A. from Ohio State University (OSU; 1952) and an M.A. in creative writing from Columbia University (1956) as well as an honorary doctorate from OSU (2003). She also studied playwriting at the American Theatre Wing and Circle in the Square workshop with Edward Albee. She married Joseph C. Kennedy in 1953. They are the parents of two children, Adam and Joe. She has been a lecturer in playwriting at such prestigious institutions as Yale University (1972–73) on a Yale teaching fellowship.

Over a span of four decades, Kennedy has produced a variety of thought-provoking nontraditional plays that have intellectually challenged audiences from New York City to London. Her nonlinear expositions are plays that dramatize a dreamlike, surrealistic state where characters in the present, past, and historical past are juxtaposed to impart meaning. Characters are emblematic. Different personalities of characters are sometimes portrayed by a single actress. Stories are often told from different time periods by historical personages, such as Chaucer, Malcolm X, Jesus Christ, and Queen Victoria, who regularly visit contemporary settings. These plays are closely aligned with the theater of the absurd.

Kennedy has written more than 20 plays and won numerous awards, including three **Obie Awards** for *Funnyhouse of a Negro* (1963), *June and Jean in Concert* (1996), and *Sleep Deprivation Chamber* (1996). This last play was cowritten with her son Adam. Kennedy is best known for her signature work, *Funnyhouse*, an avant-garde play in one act. It has to do with a mulatto girl's unsuccessful attempts to resolve the psychological conflicts of her black/white heritage. In a surrealistic rooming house, Sarah is visited by various historical figures that represent facets of her divided self. The play won the author a Stanley Award from Wagner College in Staten Island (1963) and an Obie Award (1964). It was first mounted as a workshop production for one night at the Circle in the Square in New York City (1963) under the direction of Michael Kahn. Featured in the cast were **Diana Sands**, Yaphet Kotto, **Lynn Hamilton**, and Andre Gregory. Edward Albee and others opened it off Broadway at the East End Theatre (January–February 1964) for 46 performances, also under the direction of Kahn. The cast consisted of Billie Allen as the young girl, Ruth Volner, Leonard Frey, Leslie Rivers, Cynthia Belgrave, **Ellen Holly**, Gus Williams, and Norman Bush. Among the places it was produced were London (1968), the University of Houston (October 1984; as a student production under the direction of **Ntozake Shange**), and New York University (November–December 1984; by the Undergraduate Department of Drama, under the direction of Billie Allen, with music by Carman Moore).

Other one-act avant-garde plays Kennedy penned include *Rat's Mass* (1963), about a black brother and his sister, characterized as Brother and Sister Rat, who struggle to rid themselves of white-Christian oppression. It was first produced in Rome, Italy. Subsequent productions were by the Theatre Company of Boston (April 1966) and off Broadway by **La MaMa Experimental Theatre Club** (August 1969), with music by Lamar Alford under the direction of Cecil Taylor. *The Owl Answers* (1963) illuminates a mulatto girl's search for her identity. It received the Stanley Award (1963) and was produced at several locations, the White Barn Theatre in Westport, CT (1965); off Broadway at the New York Shakespeare Festival (NYSF); and the **New Federal Theatre** (4 January–March 1969) for 67 performances on a double bill with *A Beast's Story* (1965), under the direction of Gerald Freedman. The cast included Joan Harris, Cynthia Belgrave, **Moses Gunn**, and Henry Baker. *A Lesson in Dead Language* (1964) depicts a white dog that attempts to teach a class of adolescent girls but fails to communicate. It was produced in London (1968) and in New York City at St. Mark's Church (April 1971). *A Beast's Story* (1965) is a symbolic play about the sexual fears of a black woman. It was first produced in New York City (1965) and then off Broadway by the NYSF/Public Theatre (4 January–March 1969) for 67 performances on double bill with *The Owl Answers*, under the direction of Freedman. The cast was comprised of Amanda Ambrose, Moses Gunn, Cynthia Belgrave, and Tony Thomas.

Kennedy's representative full-length adaptations include *The Lennon Play: In His Own Write* (sometimes listed as *The Lennon*

Play, 1967), an adaptation by Kennedy and Victor Spinette from John Lennon's stories and poems dealing with the rite of passage. It was first produced in London by the National Theatre Company (1967); subsequently at the Summer Theatre Festival in Kingston, RI (August 1968); and at the Arena Summer Theatre at State University of New York at Albany (August 1969).

Kennedy also wrote avant-garde monologues in one act. *Sun: A Poem for Malcolm X Inspired by His Murder* (1969) is about the scattering of a man's atoms into the cosmos after his body has been shattered into fragments. It was produced in London's West End at the Royal Court Theatre (August 1969). *An Evening with Dead Essex* (1973) is a one-act document paying tribute to Mark Essex, a youth shot by police in New Orleans. It was produced off Broadway at the American Place Theatre (November 1973) and at the Yale Repertory Company in New Haven, CT (1974). *A Rat's Mass/Procession in Shout* (1976) is a full-length improvisational jazz opera in one act. Cecil Taylor adapted and staged it from Kennedy's *A Rat's Mass*. La MaMa produced it in New York (March 1976). *A Movie Star Has to Star in Black and White* (1976) is a full-length work produced off-off-Broadway as an experimental workshop production by the NYSF/Public Theatre (November 1976). Joseph Chaikin directed the production at the University of Houston in Texas (February 1985) under the direction of Ntozake Shange. *A Lancashire Lad* (1980) is a children's musical. It is a fictionalized version of the boyhood of Charlie Chaplin. Other plays Kennedy authored are *The Ohio State Murders*, *She Talks to Beethoven*, *The Dramatic Circle*, *Orestes and Electra*, *A Lesson in Dead Language*, and *Oedipus Rex 2001*. In 1995, **Joseph Papp** and the Signature Theatre Company acknowledged Kennedy as a major American playwright by presenting a prospective of seven of her plays at the NYSF/Public Theatre. The critics agreed and rewarded the productions with praise.

Kennedy has spent her career teaching at various educational institutions, including Yale, Harvard, the University of California, Princeton, Brown, and OSU, her alma mater. In 2003, the 50th anniversary of her graduation from that institution, OSU presented her with an honorary doctorate of literature. She also cofounded the Women's Theatre Council. In addition to her plays, Kennedy's prose offerings include a memoir, *People Who Led to My Plays*, and a novel, *Deadly Triplets*. Over a lengthy career, Kennedy has accumulated many awards and honors. They include a Guggenheim fellowship, two Rockefeller playwriting grants, a National Endowment for the Arts grant, Creative Artist Public Service grant, Stanley Award for writing, Lila Wallace Reader's Digest Award, and the Pierre Lecomte du Novy Award. She was named the chancellor's distinguished lecturer at the University of California at Berkeley (1980 and 1986). In addition, in 2003, she was the recipient of the Lifetime Achievement Award by the Anisfield-Wolf Book Awards Jury.

KENNEDY, SCOTT J. A playwright, director, composer, actor, and company manager, Kennedy was born in Knoxville, TN. He is the recipient of a B.A., M.A., and Ph.D. from New York University. He studied in Paris; London; and Heidelberg, Germany, and attended professional schools of theater and acting. He was a professor of theater arts at the School of Performing Arts in Brooklyn College, City University of New York. Kennedy married Janie Sykes Kennedy, an actress and educator. They have three children. He was a university teacher and professor for more than 25 years and founder/director of a number of university, community, and professional theater groups. As a performer, he has appeared in films and onstage, radio, and television in the United States and abroad and is also an actor-director and Africanist.

His playwriting credits include *Ham's Children* (1962), a three-act drama with music on the **civil rights** struggle set in a church and a jail in the Deep South. The African Theatre and the Related Arts (ATRA) produced it in New York City (1962). *Dramatic Voices of Protest* (1964) is a theatrical collage utilizing music, poetry, narration, and drama to present various figures of history who represent the "Voices of Freedom." ATRA produced it (1964). *Commitment to a Dream* (1965) is a historical drama with music and dance. Historical black heroes who fought for the cause of freedom are resurrected by a high priestess from Ghana in order to inspire a group of players who are rehearsing a play about freedom. Among the figures invoked are Cinque, Nat Turner, and Frederick Douglass. ATRA produced it (1965).

Kennedy's other representative plays include *Threshold of the Dawn* (1965); *Negritude: A Speak Out on Color* (1965); *Beyond the Veil* (1965); *Behind the Mask* (1965); *Cries from the Ghetto* (1966); *The Poetic Life of Langston Hughes* (1957), cowritten with his wife, Janie Kennedy; *They Sang of a Nation* (1968); *The Rivers of the Black Man* (1969), cowritten with his wife, Janie Kennedy; *The Spirit That Creates* (1970); *The King Is Dead* (1971); and *Cries! How African!* (1973).

KHAN, RICARDO. An artistic director and graduate of Rutgers University, Khan was cofounder with L. Kenneth Richardson of **Crossroads Theatre Company** in Brunswick, NJ, in 1977—a theater with a checkered history. It was the first African American theater to become a member of the League of Resident Theatres and the first to receive a **Tony Award** (1999) for outstanding regional theater. Conversely, it has been forced to close its doors twice because of financial problems but continues to function as of this writing. During his tenure, Khan initiated a New Playwrights Program, which has attracted the likes of such writers as Emily Mann, **Leslie Lee**, Denise Nicholas, and **George C. Wolfe**. He hired Sydne' Mahone as director of play development, and the result was a more balanced exposure for female playwrights. Under Khan's direction, Crossroads produced a variety of plays that brought the theater national acclaim. Among them were *The Screened-In Porch* by **Marian X**, *Jitney* by **August Wilson**, *The Darker Face of the Earth* by Rita Dove, *The Colored Museum* by George C. Wolfe, *Two Hah Hahs and a Homeboy* by **Ruby Dee**, *The Love Space Demands* by **Ntozake Shange**, and *Black Eagles* by Leslie Lee. Khan was president of the Theatre Communications Group's board of directors from 1995 to 1998. He took a leave of absence from Crossroads in 1999.

KILLENS, JOHN OLIVER (1916–87). A native of Macon, GA; playwright; novelist; and essayist, Killens was often considered one of the finest writers to grace American soil and a seminal figure in the world of black arts and letters. Over a lifetime, he has written some 10 plays, of which 1 remains unpublished; 2 screenplays; and hundreds of short stories, essays, and opinion pieces that have appeared in numerous publications. Killens aspired to be a lawyer, but education was a struggle for him financially. After attending two other colleges, he finally obtained his baccalaureate through evening classes at Howard University. After serving 41 months in the U.S. Navy in World War II, he returned to the United States and decided to become a writer, taking writing courses at Columbia University while working full time at the National Labor Relations Board.

In the early 1950s, Killens, Rosa Guy, and John Henrik Clarke founded the **Harlem** Writers Guild, a group that would eventually include Maya Angelou, **Ossie Davis**, **Lonnie Elder III**, Paule Marshall, and Audrey Lorde. That led to the writing of his first novel, *Youngblood* (1954), the story of a southern family dealing with racism and Jim Crow laws in the early 20th century. His two biggest successes were *And Then We Heard the Thunder* (1962) and *The Cotillion; or, One Good Bull Is Half the Herd* (1971). *Cotillion* was so successful that Killens adapted it into a play. **Woodie King Jr.** produced it at the **New Federal Theatre** (1975) under the direction of **Allie Woods Jr.** *Cotillion* is a hilarious, satirical look at the cultural politics of the 1960s and 1970s between militants, social climbers, and the black middle class on the occasion of a cotillion. Other plays Killens wrote include *Ballad of the Winter Soldiers*, coauthored with **Loften Mitchell**, and *Lower than the Eagles*. Killens was a writer-in-residence at Fisk University, Howard University, Bronx Community College, Medgar Evers College at City College of New York, and Columbia University. Over the years, his students included Terry McMillan, Arthur Flowers, Bebe Moore Campbell, and Nikki Giovanni. Killens received a National Endowment for the Arts fellowship in 1980 and a Lifetime Achievement Award from the Before Columbus Foundation in 1986.

KILONFE, OBA. *See* PENNY, ROBERT LEE (OBA KILONFE).

KIMBALL, KATHLEEN. A playwright Kimball, was based in New York City, where she was associated with Theatre Genesis, the **Afro-American Studio for Acting and Speech (AASAS)**, and the New York Shakespeare Festival/Public Theatre during the 1970s. One of her representative plays is *Meat Rack* (1972), a comic fantasy about the mental wanderings and dreams of a black prostitute who wants to quit her profession. Her fantasies concern what she might otherwise have become. The AASAS produced it (January 1975). *Jimtown* (1972), another representative play, was produced by Theatre Genesis (April 1972).

KING, WOODIE, JR. A theater pioneer, King is a director, actor, playwright, screenwriter, television scriptwriter, essayist, short-story writer, and consultant. Hailed as the "Renaissance Man of Black Theatre," he was the most successful and prolific black producer in the world. For over 35 years, as founding director of the seminal **New Federal Theatre (NFT)**, King produced nearly 200 theater productions; over 5,000 performances; and a showcase for over 1,000 actors, directors, and designers. A Detroit native, King received his theatrical training at Cass Technical High School in Detroit (mid-1960s); Will-O-Way School of Theatre, Bloomfield Hills, MI (1958–62); Wayne State University; and the Detroit School of Arts and Crafts. He also studied drama with **Lloyd Richards** under a John Hay Whitney fellowship (1965).

As cofounder of the **Concept East Theatre** in Detroit with **Ronald Milner** in 1960, King held the position of manager and artistic director. He directed several plays by some of the leading black writers, such as Milner and **Amiri Baraka (LeRoi Jones)**, and by white playwrights, such as Edward Albee. While touring a production of *A Study in Color* (1964) that played in New York City at the newly formed American Place Theatre, King was asked to stay and direct five plays as works-in-progress. He soon attracted the attention of the **Harlem** Youth Opportunity Unlimited/American Community Theatre (Harlem Youth Opportunities Unlimited, Inc., Associated Community Teams), which asked King to write a proposal for a cultural arts program. The group was awarded a budget of $225,000 to start a theater program. King was hired as cultural arts director of Mobilization for Youth (MFY) to teach dance, arts, and theater. From 1965 to1970, he produced and directed a number of plays and award-winning short films and was also involved in several other projects. King is also the author of two plays, *Simple Blues*, an adaptation of work by **Langston Hughes** (1957), and the *Weary Blues* (1966), also adapted from Hughes.

After the demise of the MFY in 1970, King conceived the idea of the NFT (named after the Hallie Flannigan Federal Theatre of the **Federal Theatre Project**) at the Henry Street Settlement in New York City. This location on the Lower East Side has housed a combination of black, Jewish, Asian, and Latino theaters. Since its doors opened, King's creative endeavors have produced a legacy of theatrical excellence. King is the recipient of an array of theater honors and awards. Among them are the John Hay Whitney fellowship (for directing 1965, 1966) and several **Audience Development Committee Awards** and **National Black Theatre Festival** awards. King's alma mater, Wayne State University, awarded him an honorary doctorate in humanities (2000). In 2005, King was honored along with **Douglas Turner Ward** as a theater pioneer at Town Hall on 13 February 2005.

KISSOON, FREDDIE. Kissoon is an Afro-Caribbean playwright who has often been described as a "leading light" in Caribbean theater. He was born in St. James, Trinidad, the last of seven children, but subsequently moved to the United States. Kissoon has always had a keen interest in drama. As a young man, he joined the Nelsonian Cultural Club, a community group based in the area where he lived. In 1957, he founded the legendary Strolling Players, a dramatic group that is still performing and one that enjoys the status of Trinidad's longest-operating dramatic group. To date, Kissoon has written over 70 plays and has directed almost twice as many. Most of his plays have been self-published. These include *Common Entrance*; *God and Uriah Butler*; *He Died for Us*; *Doo-Doo*; *Do Your Homelessons, Daddy*; *A Promise for Christmas*; *Fugitive from the Royal Gaol*; *King Cobo*; *Girls Wanted*; *The Miracle Man*; *Like Hog Love Mud*; *Pahyol*; and *Papa Look de Priest Passing*. *Mamaguy* and *Zingay* were published by the Extra-Mural Department of the University of the West Indies in 1966. *Calabash Alley* (1970) was written as a radio play, but because of its overwhelming popularity, it was scripted into a stageplay and self-published in 1973. It was a success on the local and regional theater circuit and became a television series, with Kisson writing new episodes for this sitcom. Kissoon was one of the first to do a book-length study on West Indian creative drama. He also wrote the script for Trinidad and Tobago's first full-length movie, *The Right* *and the Wrong*, and is involved in the production and presentation of an annual Lenten play, *We Crucify Him*.

KRIGWA PLAYERS, KRIGWA LITTLE THEATRE, KRIGWA LITTLE NEGRO THEATRE MOVEMENT. This landmark theater group, theater, and movement, was active between 1925 and the early 1930s. Krigwa Theatre was formed by the erudite Dr. **W. E. B. DuBois**, editor of *Crisis* magazine, an organ of the National Association for the Advancement of Colored People. KRIGWA was an acronym for *Crisis* Guild of Writers and Artists, CRIGWA, which changed to KRIGWA, to the Krigwa Players, and to the Krigwa Little Negro Theatre Movement, a name that was gaining popularity around the country. It was at Krigwa that DuBois first articulated his now seminal declaration for African American theater: that it should be by, about, for, and near the black community. DuBois wanted to use drama as a vehicle to support cultural uplift of his people and to encourage the writing and production of plays for racial propaganda. To this end, DuBois established the *Crisis* literary contest (1925–27) and the *Crisis* Guild of Writers and Artists, comprised of the prize-winning writers of the *Crisis* contest. It presented annual awards for the best original literary and dramatic works.

The renamed players (Krigwa Little Theatre) was housed for three years (1925–27) at the **Harlem** Library Little Theatre in the basement of the 135th Street Branch of the New York Public Library, the first drama group to make its home there. It was comprised of approximately 30 members. Other branches were established in Washington, DC; Cleveland, OH; New Haven, CT; Baltimore, MD; and other cities in the East and West. With DuBois as the driving force and Charles Burroughs the artistic director of Krigwa Players, the group's first show, Burroughs's *Black Man: A Fantasy* (1925), was given at the Harlem Library Little Theatre. It was a pageant-masque that focused on the future development of black theater—the development of drama, art, music, and literature in America. Soon thereafter, the Krigwa Little Theatre mounted several programs (1926–27), producing many of the prize-winning plays from the *Crisis* contest. These included **Willis Richardson**'s *The Broken Banjo* and *Compromise*, **Georgia Douglas Johnson**'s

Blue Blood, and **Eulalie Spence**'s *Foreign Mail Here* and *The Fool's Errand*. Spence's latter play, *Errand*, was presented in the National Little Theatre Tournament at the Frolic Theatre in New York City (May 1927). It was awarded the Samuel French prize of $200 as the best unpublished play, but Spence did not receive her prize money. In an uncharacteristic move, DuBois kept it to pay for production expenses. His action displeased Spence and other members of the ensemble, causing the demise of the Krigwa Players (September 1927) at the New York branch. However, branches in other cities continued to operate, and many remained active into the early 1930s. The second most active branch of Krigwa was in Washington, DC. It produced several plays by Richardson, such as his *Mortgaged*, *The Chasm*, *Flight of the Natives*, and *The Peacock's Feather*, as well as Spence's *The Hunch* and Lewis M. Alexander's *Pierrot at Sea*. The Baltimore branch produced **May Miller**'s *Riding the Goat*. Although the different groups of Krigwa Players throughout the country were short lived, the group helped to stimulate the formation and activity of many other little theater groups in New York City and elsewhere in the nation.

KUNTU REPERTORY THEATRE (KRT). Associate Professor **Vernell A. Lillie** founded the KRT in 1974 as an adjunct to the African Studies Department at the University of Pennsylvania. *Kuntu* is a Bantu word meaning "the way." The purpose was to provide opportunity for the presentation of plays by Associate Professor and Playwright-in-Residence **Rob Penny**, **August Wilson**, and other aspiring African American playwrights. The mission has been to examine African American life in all its nuances and to entertain, enlighten, and educate the audience to social action. To this end, the KRT has developed a three-pronged approach: to train students in all areas of the theater; to produce four main-stage productions each year; and to develop a producing touring unit that performs at schools, universities, community organizations, social service agencies, and state and federal prisons.

The KRT has been very successful in all three areas, credited with over 80 productions since its inception and producing the works of Wole Soyinka, **OyamO**, **Kathleen Collins Prettyman**, **James Baldwin**, **Lorraine Hansberry**, and Marta Effinger. Other productions include *The Meeting* by **Jeff Stetson**, *Seven Guitars* by August Wilson, *Little Willie Armstrong Jones* by Rob Penny, and *Keepers of the Dream: A Celebration of Significant Sistahs!* by Jacqueline Moscou. Lillie, also a playwright and the head of the Theatre Department, has produced and directed her own plays. Each year, 10 to 20 plays are sent on the touring circuit to practically every venue in the state and throughout the world, appearing in New York City, New Orleans, and Toronto and at the Edinburgh Fringe Festival in Scotland. The KRT has also developed special interactive programs for senior citizens that are a yearly occurrence. Over 15 residency workshops are held each year in Pittsburgh public schools, involving students, teachers, parents, and theater professionals, all coordinated by Artistic Director Lillie. The programs focus on music, dance, and theater as psychodrama, culminating in a performance. The KRT has been a true pioneer in exposing and developing new playwrights and their plays for over 30 years. Penny, who chaired the African Studies Department from 1978 to 1984, passed away in 2003. Lillie succeeded Penny as department chair. She held this position until she retired at the end of the 2006–7 academic year.

– L –

LA MAMA EXPERIMENTAL THEATRE CLUB. Based off Broadway on the Lower East Side of New York City's Greenwich Village, this world-renowned cultural theater club has a proud heritage as an international theater. Founder and director Ellen Stewart organized La MaMa in October 1961. A leader of the avant-garde movement of the 1960s, Stewart's premise was to develop new, creative, risk-taking, experimental work beyond the influence of Broadway. She also wanted to make a strong commitment to cultural pluralism—to theater that was ethnically diverse and that sustained a universal global vision. She has succeeded within the last 47 years in developing, nurturing, supporting, producing, and presenting new and original performance work by artists of all nationalities from around the world. An amazing number of film, theater, and television luminaries got their starts at La MaMa.

La MaMa is a complex of three theaters, the First Floor Theatre, the Club, and the Annex. It was one of the first theaters to house full-time directors with resident companies. Among this list were Wilford Leach's La MaMa Troupe, Lee Bruer's Mabou Mines, Wilford Leach's ETC, Joel Zwick's La MaMa Plexus, and Andrei Serban and Elizabeth Swados's Jones Repertory. Many of these troupes and others from La MaMa have performed throughout the world. The theater also presented, in collaboration, over 1,000 original musical scores to become one of the country's foremost producers of international performance. In 1967, Stewart, in collaboration with Ted Hoffman, a professor at New York University, introduced the Eastern European Theatre to America when they brought in Jersey Godowsky, Richard Islam, and Ludwig Lassen. Among its honors and awards, La MaMa has received over 30 **Obie Awards** and several **Drama Desk**, Bessie, and Villager Awards.

LAFAYETTE THEATRE/PLAYERS (STOCK COMPANY). Built in 1912, the 2,000-seat Lafayette Theatre was located at 132nd Street and 7th Avenue in **Harlem**. At the time, because of a large presence of whites in the area, the theater was segregated. When C. W. Morganstern, a Broadway booking agent, took over the lease, he desegregated the theater after he hired Lester A. Walton, a black critic for the *New York Age* to comanage the theater. The first production at the Lafayette was *Across the Footlights* (27 December 1915) by the **Anita Bush Players**. Bush had formed the ensemble at the Lincoln Theatre in Harlem before moving her company to the Lafayette because of artistic differences between Bush and management. At the Lafayette, she changed the name of her acting troupe to the Lafayette Players.

In February 1916, Robert Levy took over the management of the Lafayette Theatre; thereafter, the players presented a new show every week, all by white authors. They produced more than 250 short shows (called "tabs") for the next seven years. More than 360 actors performed in such shows as *The Octoroon*, *The Count of Monte Cristo*, *Madam X*, and *Dr. Jekyll and Mr. Hyde*. Some of the noted performers to appear at the Lafayette Theatre include Clarence Muse, **Charles Gilpin**, Evelyn Ellis, **Frank Wilson**, Edna Thomas, Evelyn Preer, and Abbie Mitchell. The lone dramatic play production by a black playwright mounted at the Lafayette was Tom Brown's *The Eternal Magdaline* (1917) a "neoromantic" drama. Owing to the success of the players at the Lafayette, Levy added a second and third troupe of players at the Howard Theatre in Washington, DC, and the Grand Theatre in Chicago.

The original Lafayette Players thrived in Harlem until 1928, when they could no longer compete with the silent film industry. Although the black actors portrayed white characters by white authors, the players succeeded in developing an appreciation within black audiences for theater, provided opportunities for black actors to shed the image of the minstrel buffoon by performing in straight dramas and melodramas, and helped to advance the fledgling African American theater industry. Thereafter, the Lafayette Theatre struggled through the early stages of the Great Depression with vaudeville shows and silent films, but it was forced to close its doors in 1932.

LAMONT, ALONZO JR. A playwright, Lamont is a native of Baltimore, MD. He graduated from Marlboro College (B.A.) and the University of Iowa (B.A., playwriting). His early work attracted the attention of Hollywood, where he worked as a staff writer on the TV series *A Different World*. His return to the theater was highlighted by a long, productive relationship with **Jomandi Productions**, where several of his plays were produced. Lamont's plays have also been seen at the Goodman Theatre, **Arena Playhouse**, **Ensemble Theatre**, Seven Stages, and off Broadway at the American Place Theatre. Some of his plays are *The Black Play* (1979); *Twenty-First Century Outs and Backs* (1985); *That Serious He-Man Ball* (1987), depicting a basketball game where three men explore life's problems; *Vivisections from the Blown Mind*; *Life Go Boom*; and *21st Century Groove*. Lamont is the recipient of the **James Baldwin** Playwriting Award and the Florida Arts Commission playwriting fellowship.

LAMPLEY, ONI FAIDA (1959–2008). An actor and playwright, Lampley is a veteran performer and writer from Massachusetts with a long career in the theater. She earned her B.A. from Oberlin College and an M.F.A. from New York University's Graduate Acting Program. She also studied at Julliard's Playwright Program, where she received the prestigious Lincoln Center Lacombe du Nouy Award.

Her first play, *Mixed Babies*, won the coveted Helen Hayes Award for outstanding new play in 1991. It was produced widely and eventually published by Dramatists Play Services. Lampley is an acclaimed performer whose acting career in theater, film, and television has dominated her writing efforts. She has appeared in *Third Watch*, *Law and Order*, *The Sopranos*, *Two Trains Running*, and *Dragonfly*. Nonetheless, she is an avid, opportunistic writer whose persistence has resulted in writing such plays as *The Dark Kalamazoo*, *Waiting for My Man*, *Put My Father in the Ground*, and *Tough Titty*. In 1998, she was invited to the prestigious Sundance Screenwriters Lab. She has been a guest lecturer at George Mason University and has also taught writing to young people in New York City and Washington, DC, public school systems. Other honors and awards for Lampley include those from such organizations as the Rockefeller Production Fund, Playwrights Center, Jerome Foundation, William and Eva Fox Foundation, New York State Foundation on the Arts, and DC Commission on Arts and Humanities.

LANGE, THEODORE "TED" WILLIAM. Lange is a well-known actor, director, and playwright who has excelled in television, film, and stage. This global recognition stems from a 10-year run on the TV sitcom *Love Boat*. An Oakland, CA, native, he graduated from San Francisco City College and attended the Royal Academy of Dramatic Arts in London, where he was steeped in all phases of theater. This prepared his foray into the theatrical world. He soon found success on *Love Boat*, where he not only acted but also wrote seven of their scripts and directed some 17 episodes.

While still an actor, Lange has also written for the stage, penning over 20 plays. His efforts include *Lemon Meringue Façade*, a comedic look at the lives of four disparate women; *Behind the Mask: An Evening with Paul Laurence Dunbar*, a one-man show about the title character; *Born a Unicorn*, a rock musical depicting the life of the African American Shakespearean actor **Ira Aldridge**; and *Four Queens—No Trump*, which depicts four black women playing bid whist (a card game) as they reveal aspects of their lives, for which Lange received the National Association for the Advancement of Colored People Best Play Award in 1997. He has also written *A Foul Movement* and *Day Zsa Voo*. His latest play is *George Washington's*

Boy, an exploration of George Washington's close relationship with his personal slave Billy Lee. Lange has appeared on Broadway in *Hair* and in numerous theaters across the country in such Shakespearean roles as Petruchio, Bottom, and Macbeth. He has taught film directing at University of Southern California's School of Cinema and Television. Lange has also written numerous screenplays and film scripts.

LAWRENCE, REGINALD (SHEPSU AAKHU). *See* AAKHU, SHEPSU (REGINALD LAWRENCE).

LEE, CANADA (LEONARE LIONEL CORNELIUS CANEGATA, 1907–52). Active between the 1930s and 1940s, Lee was a stage and screen actor. He first gained notice for his portrayal of Banquo in Orson Welles's *Voodo Macbeth* (1936) at the **Lafayette Theatre**, the home of New York Negro Unit of the **Federal Theatre Project** (FTP). He received critical acclaim as Bigger Thomas in **Richard Wright**'s *Native Son* (1941), for other Broadway roles, and for his work in such films as *Lifeboat* and *Body and Soul* (1947).

Born and raised in **Harlem**, Lee left home at age 14. After his career as a welterweight boxer was cut short by an eye injury, he made his professional debut as an actor in *Voodoo Macbeth*. Subsequent FTP roles followed with *Brown Sugar* (as Henry, 1937), *Haiti* (as Bertram, 1938), *Mamba's Daughters* (as Drayton, 1939), and *Big White Fog* (as Victor Mason at the Lincoln Theatre, 1940). Lee made his Broadway debut in *Native Son*, followed by *Anna Lucasta* (as Danny, the sailor, 1944), *The Tempest* (as Caliban, 1945), *On Whitman Avenue* (as David Vennett, 1946), *The Duchess of Malfi* (as Bosolo, in whiteface, 1946), and *Set My People Free* (as the slave leader George, 1948). During the 1930s and 1940s, Lee came under congressional scrutiny for his involvement in the Communist Party, resulting in him being blackballed in the entertainment industry. The father of one child, Carl Lee (b. 1933), the elder Lee died in 1952 from complications of pneumonia. In 1976, he was enshrined in the Black Filmmaker's Hall of Fame.

LEE, EUGENE. Lee, an actor and director, was a veteran of the theater wars. He worked for the prestigious **Negro Ensemble Company** (NEC) in New York where was in the original production of

Charles Fuller's *A Soldier's Play*; and many regional theaters across the country and abroad. Lee is well known as an interpreter of **August Wilson**, having appeared in almost every play the late writer wrote. In addition, Lee works in film and TV and is a playwright. He is best known for *East Texas Hot Links* (1994), set in the 1950s in the South, where the Ku Klux Klan still roamed at will. It centers on random killings and disappearances in a community where blacks and whites are all "good ol' boys." Lee also wrote *Fear Itself* (1996). Lee graduated from Southwest Texas State University. He was an adjunct professor of playwriting in the School of Theatre at the University of Southern California.

LEE, LESLIE. A playwright, television scriptwriter, and fiction writer, Lee was born in Bryn Mawr, PA. He was educated at the University of Pennsylvania (B.A. in biology and English) and at Villanova University (M.A. in theatre), where he began writing plays. Two of his plays were first produced while he was working at Ellen Stewart's **La MaMa Experimental Theatre Club** (1969–70). He has taught playwriting at the College of Old Westbury in New York (1975–76), was a playwright-in-residence at the University of Pennsylvania (1980), and coordinated a playwriting workshop at the **Negro Ensemble Company (NEC)** in 1985 and the Douglass Creative Arts Center in New York.

Lee's award-winning play, *The First Breeze of Summer* (1975), is a semiautobiographical drama in two acts. It reflects three generations of a black middle-class family whose quarrels cause the revered grandmother to start reminiscing about the heartaches and sacrifices it took for the family to achieve middle-class status. It won an **Obie Award** as best play (1974–75), a **Tony Award** nomination, a John Gassner Medallion for playwriting, and three distinguished acting awards. **Woodie King Jr.** produced it in association with the NEC off Broadway at St. Marks Playhouse (March–April 1975) under **Douglas Turner Ward**'s direction. **Frances Foster** played the role of the grandmother with Reyno (who won both an Obie Award and a Clarence Derwent Award) and **Moses Gunn** (who won an Obie Award). The play opened on Broadway at the Palace Theatre (June–July 1975), running for 48 performances. Thereafter, King directed it at the Center Stage in Baltimore,

MD (March 1977), for 36 performances, with **Claudia McNeil** as the grandmother. The Theatre of Universal Images mounted it in New York City (January–March 1983). It was also adapted into film by PBS on WNET-TV's "Theatre in America" series (1976), starring Moses Gunn. It won a Mississippi ETV Award for best film adaptation (1977).

Between Now and Then (1975) is a drama in two acts. A white man is paralyzed with fear that mixing of the colored and white races will cause the white race and culture to disappear. The play was produced by the New Dramatists in New York City (February 1975) and by the **Billie Holiday Theatre** in Brooklyn (1983). *The War Party* (1975) is a political drama inspired by the author's personal experiences of a political power struggle within a **civil rights** organization. The play depicts a young mulatto woman's search for her own identity. The New Dramatists produced it in New York (1975) under the direction of Douglas Turner Ward, and the NEC produced it at Theatre Four in New York (October–November 1986). *Colored People's Time* (1982) is a full-length historical play. It depicts events from the Civil War to the Montgomery bus boycotts. The NEC produced 32 performances of the play (March–April 1982) under the direction of Horacena Taylor. Among the cast were **L. Scott Caldwell**, **Charles Weldon**, and Debbie Morgan. The play received a best play nomination in 1983 for an **Audience Development Committee Award**. *Phyllis* (1986) is a full-length musical with book by Lee and music and lyrics by Micki Grant. It is based on the life and work of the eighteenth-century black American poet Phyllis Wheatley, a slave born in Senegal who learned to read and write and gained the admiration of George Washington and Thomas Jefferson. It was produced by Ralph Madero Productions in association with the United Negro College Fund. It previewed at the **Apollo Theatre** in **Harlem** (October 1986). *Hannah Davis* (1987) is a full-length domestic drama focusing on the grown children of an upper-middle–class black family coming to terms with their own lives as well as with the illness of their father. The **Crossroads Theatre Company** in New Brunswick, NJ, produced it (March–April 1987).

Lee was the recipient of a Rockefeller Foundation playwriting grant (1966–68), Shubert Foundation playwriting grants (1971–72), Obie Award, Isabelle Strickland Award for excellence in the fields of arts and human culture, a National Endowment for the Arts playwriting grant (1982), and a Eugene O'Neill Playwriting Conference (Waterford, CT) playwriting fellowship (1980).

LENOIRE, ROSETTA (1911–2002). An actor, singer, dancer, and producer, LeNoire was a renaissance figure of the 20th century. She fought back from her own personal adversity to become not just a formidable talent onstage but also a leading advocate for nontraditional casting to provide opportunities for actors of color. She also founded the Amas Repertory Theatre in 1968 to develop original musicals and provide training and opportunity for actors of color.

LeNoire was born with rickets, which doctors treated by breaking both legs so they could grow in a proper fashion. Her godfather, the great Bill "Bojangles" Robinson, taught her dancing as a learning exercise for her legs. She also studied music and voice under musician Eubie Blake. When she grew of age, she performed in several revues with Robinson. One of her first legitimate stage appearances was the groundbreaking 1936 **Federal Theatre Project** production of *Macbeth*, directed by the legendary Orson Welles. Over a lifetime, LeNoire built a fabulous career in which she made 23 Broadway appearances in such vehicles as *Anna Lucasta*; *The Royal Family*; *A Streetcar Named Desire*; *You Can't Take It with You*; *Blues for Mister Charlie*; *Finian's Rainbow*; *The Hot Mikado*; *Paul Robeson*; and her own creation, **Bubbling Brown Sugar**. LeNoire was also a frequent television performer, appearing in episodes of *The Guiding Light*, *Search for Tomorrow*, *A World Apart*, *Gimme a Break*, and *Family Matters*. Movies include *Moscow on the Hudson*, *Playing for Keeps*, and *Brewster's Millions*.

LeNoire received a Theatre World Special Award in 1993. She received the prestigious National Medal of the Arts Award by President Bill Clinton in 1999, who said, "Rosetta did more than dream of a theater with no color bar; she actually built one." Her work in this field was recognized in 1989 by Actors Equity Association, who initiated the Rosetta LeNoire Award, given annually for outstanding contributions to the universality of the human spirit in the American theater. LeNoire was the first recipient.

LEON, KENNY. A director, actor, and producer Leon represents the new generation of theater artists who have worked their way up through the trenches to assume a prominent role in the industry. He is cofounder and presently artistic director of the True Colors Theatre Company based in Atlanta, GA, and Washington, DC. Their mission is to preserve African American classics while producing a diverse group of plays from the traditional canon of Western culture. The company was founded in 2002. Prior to that, Leon was head of the Alliance Theatre in Atlanta. He is one of a few black artistic directors of a traditional white regional theater, joining **Harold Scott, Sheldon Epps, Tim Bond, Tazewell Thompson, George C. Wolfe**, and **Benny Sato Ambush.** Leon served in that capacity from 1990 to 2001, during which the company grew to over 100 employees with a $7 million budget. The Alliance Theatre produced an eclectic selection of plays, everything from Shakespeare and Molière to Arthur Miller and **August Wilson.**

Leon, a native of Florida, graduated from Clark Atlanta University. During his early career as an actor, Leon was featured in such plays as *Blood Knot, A Christmas Carol, Ma Rainey's Black Bottom,* and *The Island.* Over a lengthy career, he has directed plays at the Hartford Stage, New York Shakespeare Festival/Public Theatre, Goodman Theatre, Seattle Repertory Theatre, **Arena Playhouse**, and Huntington Hartford Theatre. On Broadway, he directed the 2004 production of *A Raisin in the Sun* with **Phylicia Allen-Rashad** and Sean Combs that garnered two **Tony Awards** and a **Drama Desk Award** nomination for Leon. As a result, before his death, Wilson chose Leon to direct the last 2 plays in Wilson's 10-play cycle, *Gem of the Ocean* and *Radio Golf. Gem* was produced on Broadway in 2004–5 and *Golf* in 2005, shortly after the author's death. That both productions were received so well is confirmation of Leon's ascendancy to the top rank of American directors. Leon's honors and awards include the Boston Theatre Award, Bronze Jubilee Award, Connecticut Critics Circle Award, Morehouse College Candle in the Dark Award, and Massachusetts Institute of Technology Eugene McDermott Award.

LEWIS, DAVID. A playwright, Lewis was born in New York City, and his upper education was at the New School for Social

Research. He has several plays. A representative sampling includes *Gonna Make That Scene* (1967), about an elevator that is a metaphor for two black men trying rise to middle-class status; *Do Your Thing* (1970), a comedy in which a man visits a paranoid friend in **Harlem**, who refuses to allow the visitor to enter his home; and *Georgia Man and Jamaican Woman* (1970), a comedy about cultural differences between American blacks and Jamaicans. Other plays include *My Cherie Amour* (a comedy, 1970); *Sonny Boy* (a comedy, 1970); *A Knight in Shining Black Armor* (1971); *Mr. B.* (1971); *One Hundred Is a Long Number* (a children's comedy, 1972); *Heaven—I've Been There; Hell—I've Been There Too* (1972); and *Bubba, Connie, and Hindy* (a satire, 1975). Lewis is a recipient of the New American Playwriting Award (1959).

LIGHTS, FREDERICK L. Brother of Ellen Stewart (founder and director of **La MaMa Experimental Theatre Club** in New York City), Lights is known for two plays, *The Underlings* (1948), about **miscegenation**, and *Mood Indigo*, about the life of Duke Ellington. Lights has written at least six other plays, *All over Nothing* (1948), *Samson and Lila Dee* (1952), and *Barbershop Boogie, Boys Like Us, Perepity*, and *Pigeons en Casserole*, all of which were pre-1976.

LILLIE, VERNELL A. A director, educator, producer, and playwright, Lillie is the former chair of the Africana Studies Department at the University of Pittsburgh and the "apple pie mother" of the black theater movement. Lillie became an associate professor at the university in 1972. In 1974, she established the **Kuntu Repertory Theatre (KRT)** as a platform for the plays of fellow associate and playwright **Rob Penny** and to examine African American life from a sociopolitical and historical perspective. The theater has produced over 100 plays and at one time served as an incubator for a novice, beginning playwright—**August Wilson**. Like her counterpart, **Woodie King Jr.**, she has done it all, from acting to directing and producing to founding a theater of long-standing merit in the KRT.

Lillie is highly credentialed, holding both a Ph.D. and an M.A. from Carnegie Mellon University, a B.A. in speech and drama from Dillard University, and a graduate studies in education and English from Texas Southern University. She has been trained in psychodrama, playback theater, and problem-solving theater. Lillie has directed plays from the classical repertory and plays from the black theater movement, like *The Miracle Church* by Sybil Berry, *Tambourines to Glory* by **Langston Hughes**, *Blues for an Alabama Sky* by **Pearl Cleage**, *Over Forty* by **Celeste Bedford Walker**, and *Seven Guitars* by August Wilson.

As a playwright, she has written several plays, including *Crawford Grill Presents Billie Holiday, Mahalia Jackson: Standing on Holy Ground, The Buffalo Soldiers Plus One*, and the stirring tribute to Martin Luther King *Lift Every Voice and Sing*. She has also been a strong supporter of the distaff side of theater and is credited with nurturing the careers of **Elizabeth Van Dyke**, **Eileen J. Morris**, Jacqueline Moscou, Marta Effinger, **P. J. Gibson**, Phylicia Allen-Rashad, and Marta Jones, among others.

In a career exceeding 50 years, Lillie has amassed many awards for her work as both an educator and a theater artist. They include an Alpha Kappa Alpha Outstanding Teacher Award, a Governor's Award for the arts, University of Pittsburgh Chancellor Distinguished Teaching Award, and a Career Achievement in Education Award. Additionally, the Vernell Lillie Endowed Scholarship Award was established at Dillard University in 1997. She retired in 2006.

LITTLEWAY, LORNA. Like most theater people, Littleway, a director, is a jack of all trades, functioning equally as an actress, playwright, producer, and educator. She is founding director of the **Juneteenth Legacy Theatre** in Louisville, KY, a position she has held since the company's inception in 1993. A New Yorker, Littleway holds not only a B.A. from the University of Southern Maine and an M.A. in playwriting from Goddard College but also an M.F.A. in directing from Southern Methodist University. She has worked in regional theaters and colleges and universities across the country, including the New Horizon Theatre **St. Louis Black Repertory Theatre**, Stamford Theatre Works, Queens College, Lehigh University, Lincoln Center Theatre's Director Lab, and Brown University.

Among the plays she has directed are *Ceremonies in Dark Old Men, The Grapes of Wrath, Ma Rainey's Black Bottom*, **Funnyhouse of a Negro**, *Miss Evers' Boys, Shakin' the Mess Outta Misery, Your*

Obituary Is a Dance, Trouble in Mind, **A Raisin in the Sun,** and *Trick the Devil.* Littleway is also a working playwright and has written the following plays: *Young Sistas*; *A Collective Piss and the Devil's Beating His Wife*; *Billy, Lena, and the Duke: A Night of Ellington Music*; *Juneteenth Cotton Club Revue*; and *Kinder, Gentler Nation.* Littleway is a member of the Lincoln Center Directors Lab and is a past president of the **Black Theatre Network.** Honors for Littleway include a Dramatist Guild fellowship, the Sallie Bingham Award from the Kentucky Foundation for Women, and a playwright fellowship from the Kentucky Arts Council. Littleway is professor of theater arts at the University of Louisville.

LIVINGSTON, MYRTLE SMITH (1902–74). A playwright and teacher, Livingston was born in Holly Grove, AR, and reared in Denver, CO, where she received her elementary and high school education. She studied pharmacy at Howard for two years (1920–22) and was a member of a medical sorority, Rho Psi Phi. In 1925, she married William McKinley Livingston, a physician. She received an A.B. from Colorado State Teachers College at Greeley (1927) and an M.A. from Columbia University (1940). Livingston taught in the public schools of Denver prior to accepting a position at Lincoln University in Jefferson, MO, where she taught health and physical education from 1928 to her retirement in 1972. She spent the remaining two years of her life sharing a condominium with her sister in Hawaii, where she died in 1974 at age of 72.

Livingston won third prize in the *Crisis* Contest Awards for her play *For Unborn Children* (October 1925). It is a plea in one act against intermarriage and was the first play published in *Crisis* (July 1926). *Frances* (1925) is a melodrama in one act centering on the relationship among a black woman, a white landowner, a teacher, and a **civil rights** worker. The Norman Players of Philadelphia produced it at St. Peter Claver's Auditorium (1925). It received first prize in the *Opportunity* Contest Awards (May 1925).

LORRAINE HANSBERRY THEATRE (LHT). Located in San Francisco, the LHT is one of a handful of black theaters that have been in existence for over 25 years, celebrating its anniversary in 2006. Over the years, the LHT has worked out of four different locations and has mounted over 100 plays from such playwrights as **Ifa Bayeza** and Shakespeare. It was founded in 1981 by Artistic Director Stanley Williams and Managing Director Quentin Easter, whose goal was threefold: to establish a quality theater able to present America's foremost black playwrights, to provide opportunities for local actors and technicians, and to foster youth development through workshops and outreach programs. The LHT has presented the works of Nobel laureates **Derek Walcott** and Toni Morrison, **Pulitzer Prize** winners **August Wilson** and Alice Walker, and award-winning plays from **Langston Hughes**, **Lorraine Hansberry**, **James Baldwin**, and others. One of its biggest successes was the 1999 production of Marcia Leslie's play *The Trial of One Short-Sighted Woman versus Mamie Louise and Safreeta Mae.*

Success did not come easy for Easter and Williams. The early years were rough, but they persevered. It was not until they moved to their present site in downtown San Francisco that things turned around. With help from then-mayor Willie Brown, the LHT moved into a downtown theater at Sutter and Mason. The theater, a 300-seat modified proscenium thrust stage with excellent sight lines, proved to be a hit with all involved. The theater continues to put on five to six productions every year and works collaboratively with other high-profile institutions, like the American Conservatory Theatre, *Cultural Odyssey*, the San Francisco Museum of Modern Art, and the San Francisco Mime Troupe, in mutually beneficial endeavors. The theater has attracted over 20,000 patrons over the years and has been honored with many awards, including six Dramalogue Awards, two **New York Drama Critics' Circle Awards**, the National Black MBA Association Award, San Francisco Chamber of Commerce Cyril Magnin Award, Charles Schwab Renditions Award, **National Black Theatre Network** Winona Fletcher Award, and California Alliance for Arts Education Award.

LOTT, KARMYN BERTRINA. A playwright, Lott is a native of Amarillo, TX. A graduate of West Texas State University, she studied playwriting at the Henry Street Settlement and at the Negro Ensemble Playwrights unit under Steve Carter. She has written over 15 plays, including *We Shall*, a celebration of Martin Luther King's activities during the civil rights movement, and *Once upon a Time*, an adaptation of Shakespeare's *Twelfth Night*. Other plays she authored are *His Dream*, a children's play; *Pepperwine*, a musical play; *Old Soldier*; *Breakfast for My Friend*; *Hot Sauce*; *Songs from My Sister*; *Stop and Think*; and *Hush Sweet Baby*. Lott's plays have been produced at the Negro Ensemble Company and the Theatre Guinevere. During her career, she has received a Ragdale Foundation writer's scholarship, a McKnight Foundation fellowship, and a College Access Program Public Service grant. She is a member of the Writer's Guild.

– M –

M ENSEMBLE. Based in Miami, FL, the M Ensemble was established in 1971 by the late T. G. Cooper. Previously, he had been chair of the Theatre Department at Howard University in Washington, DC. Into the void stepped Patricia E. Williams and Shirley Richardson, who have performed as producer/manager and executive director, respectively. Both women hold full-time positions away from the theater, Williams as director of the after-school program of Greater Miami and Richardson as a substance abuse prevention specialist with Miami-Dade Rehabilitative Services. The commonality is that both women hold bachelors degrees in theater. They have worked hard in keeping the theater lights on for over 35 years, producing well over 150 plays and musicals and serving countless thousands in the process. The M Ensemble has represented the United States at the World Festival for Black Arts in Lagos, Nigeria, in 1972 and participated in the **National Black Theatre Festival** in Winston-Salem, NC, in 1995 and 1997. They have also exposed Miami-Dade inner-city youth to the hard-core fundamentals of theater, both as entertainment and as a work opportunity. Over the years they have presented an eclectic bill of fare that includes "funky" musicals like Fats Waller's *Ain't Misbehavin'*; dramas with a comedic edge, such as **Lonnie Elder III**'s *Ceremonies in Dark Old Men*; and gospel songfests, like **Langston Hughes**'s *Tambourines to Glory* or Lanie Robertson's biographical cabaret treatment of Billie Holliday's last days in *Lady Day at Emerson's Bar and Grill*. Miami-Dade has been well served by the M Ensemble as they continue into the 21st century with plans for a new theater to serve an ever-expanding community.

MA'AT PRODUCTION ASSOCIATION OF AFRIKAN-CENTERED THEATRE (MPAACT). This is a different type of theater that emanated from a group of students at the University of Illinois who were disenchanted with the usual form and content of theater. Accordingly, they formed a multidisciplinary collective of actors, writers, vocalists, musicians, and others and called themselves the Afrikan-centered theater based on the ancient East African civilization of Kamit. Although it is a collective, Reginald Lawrence (**Shepsu Aakhu**) has emerged as the spokesperson for the group. Since 1995, MPAACT has lost a few original members, but the ones who stayed continue to perform their original works at the studio theater in the Victory Gardens Theatre and in the Chicago area. The main-stage productions are still done at MPAACT. Two shows are produced annually at Victory Gardens, and a few tour the college circuit. The company has also developed a playwrights workshop, out of which emerged such playwrights as Carla Stillwell, Shepsu Aakhu, and Nambi Kelley. Aakhu's play *Kiwi Black* won the prestigious **Theodore Ward** Prize for African American playwriting in 1999. Some of the other works produced by MPAACT are *Kosi Dasa* by Aakhu, *Relevant Hearsay: Stories from 57* adapted from the short stories of Shirley Carney written by Aakhu and Mignon McPherson Nance, and *Afrosynthesis: Hoochie Mama* by Nambi E. Kelley. MPAACT has won several awards, including the **Negro Ensemble Company** Award for best production (2004), BTAA for best sound design (2003), and Scott Joplin Award (2003).

MACBETH, ROBERT. A director, actor, playwright, filmmaker, critic, and teacher, Macbeth became widely known as the founder and artistic director of the **New Lafayette Theatre (NLT)**. Located in **Harlem** on the site of the landmark **Lafayette Theatre** of the Negro Renaissance (1920s), the NLT epitomized the black nationalistic philosophy of the 1960s. During his six-year tenure at the NLT (1967–73), MacBeth garnered a reputation as a leading African American director in New York City and as an advocate of black rituals and directed four NLT plays to unite black people in their struggle against racism.

A Charleston, SC, native, Macbeth was prepared for the position at the NLT. He received his education at Morehouse College (1950–52) and Newark College of Engineering (1952–53). His studies were interrupted by a stint in the U.S. Air Force (1953–57). Upon his return, he enrolled at City College of New York (1957–60). MacBeth has taught at such institutions as New York University School of the Arts for many years, and beginning in 1977, he was a professor at City College of New York at the Leonard Davis Center for the Performing Arts. In the early 1960s, MacBeth's acting career landed him parts both on and off Broadway. At the NLT, he directed **Ron Milner**'s *Who's Got His Own*, Athol Fugard's *Blood Knot*, and plays by **Ed Bullins**. He also mounted plays locally at the American Place Theatre and the New York Shakespeare Festival. In addition, he produced a film, *In the Streets of Harlem/The Ritual Masters* (1972). Among the plays MacBeth authored are *A Black Ritual* (1968), about the raising of black consciousness, which the NLT workshop produced (1968), and *The Fly in the Coffin* (pre-1986), a one-act comedy. The NLT burned down in 1973, under suspicious circumstances amid accusations that the theater catered to the more radical elements of the black struggle.

MACKEY, WILLIAM WELLINGTON. A playwright and actor, Mackey was born in Miami, FL. He received a B.A. in 1958 from Southern University in Baton Rouge, LA, where he was actively involved in the theatrical productions of the River Bend Players under the tutelage of Rhoda Carmichael. Mackey taught high school for one year in Miami before entering the M.A. Program at the University of Minnesota in 1960, where he began writing his first two plays. In 1975, Mackey was selected by the bicentennial committee of Miami, his hometown, to write the script for the model city's cultural contribution to the celebration. Mackey completed the script he began writing at the University of Minnesota after graduation while he worked as a recreational therapist at Colorado State Hospital in Pueblo. From Denver, he went to Chicago and from there to New York City, where his plays were produced off Broadway.

His representative plays include *Saga* (1976), a bicentennial musical in five acts commemorating Africans who helped to develop America. Third Century, the bicentennial committee, commissioned it in the author's hometown. *Love Me, Love Me, Daddy—or I Swear I'm Gonna Kill You!* (pre-1976) depicts a wealthy black man who is dying while his seven sons fight over the family dynasty. The Holy Name House in New York produced it (1980). Other plays Mackey wrote are *Behold! Cometh the Vanderkellans* (1964), a three-act drama; *Requiem for Brother X* (1965), a dramatic monologue in one act; *Family Meeting* (1968), a surrealistic drama in one act; *Billy Noname* (1970), a two-act musical in 15 scenes, with a book by Mackey and music and lyrics by Johnny Brandon; and *Living Is a Hard Way to Die* 1974), a tragicomedy in two acts. Mackey is the recipient of a Rockefeller Foundation playwriting grant.

MALIK, HAKIM SULAIMAN. An actor, playwright, and poet, Malik was born in the 1950s during the turmoil of the **civil rights movement** and the flowering of the black arts movement. He attended Queens College in Flushing, NY, and studied playwriting at the **Frank Silvera Writers' Workshop** and the Playwrights Unit at the **Negro Ensemble Company**. Malik became resident playwright at the Afro-American Repertory Theatre during the 1975–76 season. He has performed in *Ceremonies in Dark Old Men* under the direction of Anthony D. Hill at Queens College in Flushing and in *The Sign in Sidney Brustein's Window*. The plays Malik wrote are *What It Is!*, about five men asking the question of what it means to be black and working in the theater; *Get the One with the Star on the Side*, in which a black woman bemoans her husband for leaving her for a white woman; and *The Transients*, about a man and woman who meet in the afterworld and try to change who they were in life. Other plays he wrote are *In the Service of the Chairman* and *The Murder of Cyrene Vignette*. Malik is a member of Actors Equity and the Screen Actors Guild.

MANHOOD. The institution of **slavery** in America greatly disrupted the black family structure. This dilemma is tied, in part, to the notion of black manhood due to his lack of employment; inability to take care of his family; absence in the household; incarceration; drugs;

high death rate; sexual orientation; and loss of motivation, self-esteem, and identity. Manhood was and still is an important issue in the black community. Like Minister Louis Farrakhan with the Million Man March, black playwrights mandated black men to take responsibility as providers for their families and their own lives. *Take a Giant Step* (1953), **Louis Peterson**'s critically acclaimed Broadway play, depicts the effect that urban flight by a black family to an all-white New England community has on a young middle-class black male adolescent in his quest toward manhood. In **August Wilson**'s *Fences* (1983), the manhood theme is exemplified through both the father and son. The patriarch, Troy Maxon, was raised by a father who expressed his love through working hard and taking care of the family but stayed detached emotionally from Troy and the rest of the family. Troy's manhood is put to the test when he physically confronts his father, who is caught trying to rape Troy's girlfriend. His father beats him unmercifully, but Troy had taken a stance and fled his father's house at age 14. Troy's son, Cory, also takes his first step toward manhood when he threatens his father with a baseball bat during an argument. He joins the Marines to get away from his father. Cory's true test of manhood occurs at the end of the play, when he reconciles his conflicting emotions for his father at Troy's funeral, aided by his mother's words of enlightenment. The defining moment of manhood for Walter Lee Younger in **Lorraine Hansberry**'s prize-winning play *A Raisin in the Sun* (1959) comes when he refuses the money offered to the family by a member of the White Citizen's Council if they do not move into the all-white neighborhood.

MARCON ET FERRAND, JUAN VICTOR SEJOUR. *See* SEJOUR, VICTOR (JUAN VICTOR SEJOUR MARCON ET FERRAND).

MARSHALL, WILLIAM (1924–2003). Marshall was a classically trained actor with a booming bass voice, excellent diction, matinee idol looks, and a physique of Adonis-like proportions at 6'5" and 220 pounds. After studying acting at the famed Actor's Studio in New York and the Neighborhood Playhouse, he embarked on a career that at its height had him playing Othello and other classical roles before adoring audiences in the United States as well as in London and

Paris, France. It is ironic, however, that this man of immense talent is best known worldwide for his performance in a 1972 blaxploitation film *Blacula*, in which he played an African American version of Count Dracula. Marshall brought a quiet, intense dignity to the role, however, elevating the character beyond stereotype. The film instantly achieved cult status, and he reprised the role in the 1973 movie *Scream, Blacula, Scream!*

Marshall was born in Gary, IN; moved to New York City as a young man; and after studying art at New York University, changed course and decided to become an actor. He performed Shakespeare and other works, including one-man shows of both Frederick Douglass and **Paul Robeson**, whose works he studied assiduously. During a lengthy career, Marshall appeared in over 50 movie and television efforts, including *Studio One*; *Ben Casey*; *The Man from U.N.C.L.E.*; *Tarzan*; *Star Trek*; *The Boston Strangler*; *Benson*; *The Jeffersons*; *Bonanza*; *Rawhide*; *The Wild, Wild West*; and *Pee Wee's Playhouse*. Toward the end of his career, Marshall taught acting workshops at selected colleges and at the Mafundi Institute in Watts, CA. He retired from acting in the late 1990s.

MARTIN, LYNN. Martin, a playwright, was born in Washington, DC. She received an A.B. in English from Georgetown University (1987) and an M.F.A. in playwriting from Columbia University (1990). While serving an internship at the **Arena Playhouse** in Washington, DC, she began writing. Her plays have been produced at Zebra Crossing, Lincoln Center, New Georges Theatre, Arena Playhouse, and Playwrights Horizon, among other venues. A listing of Martin's plays includes *Summer Feet Hearts*, about three women from the same family who disagree about their absentee father who returns after a long hiatus, and *Babes in Boyland*, a surrealistic fantasy depicting violence in the big city. She also wrote *Waltzing de Niro*, *The Wait*, *Still Waters*, *The Bodhisattva Locksmith* (a romantic comedy), *Pinto and Bone*, *Psyche Was Here*, and *The Misanthrope* (an adaptation of Molière's play). Martin has been honored with awards and fellowships. Among them are the Mark A. Klein Playwriting Award (1990), New York Foundation for the Arts fellowship (1991), Juilliard School fellowship (1993), Van Lier fellowship (1993–95), and W. Alton Jones grant (1994).

MARTIN, RENITA. Martin is a Boston-based actor, performer, and playwright with an M.F.A. in playwriting from Brandeis University. She has been both a dancer and actor during her career and performed in venues all across the United States. In 1996, she founded Rhythm Visions Production Company, a nonprofit devoted to teaching and producing artists of color. Her plays have been published and produced widely in such venues as the Cherry Lane Theatre, Boston Theatre, and African Repertory Troupe. She was nominated for the Cherry Lane's Mentors Project for her play *Lo, She Comes*. The list of plays Martin wrote includes *The Brunch, Peace in the Midst, Frisco's Café, Shotgun Café,* and *Five Bottles in a Sixpack.* Martin was the recipient of an Annette B. Miller fellowship and a Herbert and Nancy Beigel New Play Award.

MARTIN, SHARON STOCKARD. Born in Nashville, TN, Martin is a playwright, poet, theater critic, freelance writer, and editor. She received her education from Howard University, Bennington College (A.B. in general studies, 1969), Yale School of Drama (M.F.A. in playwriting, 1976), and the University of Southern California (Ph.D. in cinema/TV, 1982). Martin honed her writing skills at **Ed Bullins**'s Black Theatre Workshop in New York City (1968–69), the **Free Southern Theatre (FST)** Writers' Workshop in New Orleans (1970–73), the **Frank Silvera Writers' Workshop** in New York City (1973–76), the Congo Square Writers Union in New Orleans (1976–77), and the Los Angeles Actor's Theatre Playwrights Workshop (1980) in California. One of Martin's more produced plays is *Proper and Fine: Fanny Lou Hamer's Entourage* (1968), a comedy in one act about two black shoppers waiting to be served by an indifferent salesperson in a department store in the segregated South. The Touring Ensemble of the FST produced it (1969). Other plays Martin authored include a comedy in two acts, *Hair Products* (1980). Most of her plays, however, are one-act comedies, such as *The 20-Minute Workout* (1983), *Further Elaborations on the Mentality of a Chore* (original title, *Edifying Further Elaborations on the Mentality of a Chore*, 1972), and *Entertaining Innumerable Reflections on the Subject at Hand* (1973). Two of her one-act plays are absurdist protests, *Canned Soul* (1974) and *Deep Heat* (1975). Martin is the recipient of a Schubert fellowship, Yale School of Drama fellowship (1974–75), a Eugene O'Neill Award (while a student at Yale), a CBS Foundation Prize in playwriting (1976), a John F. Kennedy Center Black Playwright Award (1979), a Mary Roberts Rinehart Foundation grant (1980), and a Beaumont fellowship at the University of California at Los Angeles (c. 1982).

MASON, CLIFFORD. Born in Brooklyn, Mason is a playwright, actor, director, producer, administrator, author, critic, and teacher. He earned a B.A. at Queens College (1958) and taught at institutions of higher education, such as Manhattanville College of the Sacred Heart in Purchase, NY (1969–75); the Graduate School of Education, Rutgers University at the New Brunswick campus (1971–74); and Medgar Evers College at City University of New York at Brooklyn (1981–83).

Mason is a freelance writer of books on drama, literature, and the West Indies. One of his representative plays is *Gabriel: The Story of a Slave Rebellion* (1965), a historical drama in three acts. It dramatizes the unsuccessful slave rebellion led by Gabriel Prosser in Virginia in 1800. New Dramatists produced it as a workshop (fall 1968). *Gabriel* was entered in a nationwide contest by Elmwood Playhouse, Nyack, NY, where it won first prize of $1,000 and was produced by several colleges. Other plays Mason authored are *Sister Sadie* (original title, *Sister Sadie and the Son of Sam*, 1968), a domestic drama in three acts; *Time out of Time* (1980), a full-length domestic drama; *Captain at Cricket* (1982), a full-length Caribbean comedy; and *The Trial of Denmark Vesey* (1974), a historical drama in three acts on Vesey, the ex-slave who was executed in 1822 for plotting a rebellion against **slavery** in Charleston, SC. Mason is the recipient of a National Endowment for the Humanities grant of $15,000 (1978) to research black theater of the 1930s through the 1960, a National Endowment for the Arts (NEA) writer-in-residence grant of $5,000 (1979) to develop play material and hold workshops at the Gene Frankel Theatre in New York, and an NEA grant of $10,000 (1980) for playwriting.

MASON, JUDI ANN. A playwright and freelance journalist, Mason was born in Shreveport, LA. She received her education at Grambling State University (B.A., 1977). At age 20, Mason was one of the youngest women to have an off-Broadway play produced in New York. Two years later, she was named one of the top 10 college women by *Glamour Magazine* (1976). Mason is best known for *Livin' Fat* (1974), a "soul farce" in two acts. A bank janitor who finds $15,000 left behind in a bank robbery has to wrestle with his family and his conscience over the moral implications of what happens if he keeps the money. Grambling University in Louisiana produced it (1974). It won the Norman Lear Award at the American College Theatre Festival (ACTF). The **Negro Ensemble Company (NEC)** in New York City mounted it (June–18 July 1976) for 61 performances. The **Hadley Players** produced it at St. Philip's Church in New York City (c. 1984) under the direction of **Gertrude Jeannette**. *A Star Ain't Nothin' but a Hole in Heaven* (1976) is a tragicomedy about a young black woman who resists the pursuit of conventional education. Grambling State University entered the play at the ACTF, where it received the **Lorraine Hansberry** Award (1976). *Daughters of the Mock* (1978) is a full-length drama about an elderly voodoo priestess who wants her daughter, "the Mock," to carry on the powers of voodoo, but the daughter wants to get married and does not want the responsibility. Productions of *Daughters* were mounted by the NEC at St. Mark's Playhouse in New York City (December 1978) for 23 performances and the **Billie Holiday Theatre** in Brooklyn (March 1987) for an extended engagement. Other plays Mason wrote include *Jonah and the Wonder Dog* (1986), a full-length domestic drama, and *Tea at Kat's Place* (1986), a one-act play.

MASON, KEITH ANTAR. Mason, a performance artist and playwright, is the cofounder and artistic director of the **Hittite Empire**, a performance art theater company based in Los Angeles. In 1980, he began his mission to transform bullets into words and to save the lives of young black American men who live in the projects or poor neighborhoods of major cities. Hittite has performed in the United States, the United Kingdom, and other parts of the world. Virtually all of their performance pieces are written, directed, and sometimes performed by Mason. Their scripts are shaped organically by current events as interpreted through the lens of the brothers on the street. As such, the scripts are sometimes angry, confrontational, lyrical, and ever changing but with a core theme, much like jazz. Some of their performance pieces they presented throughout the country and abroad include *The Anatomy of Deep Blue*, *I Drink Televised Gods*, *Field Holler and Other Screams from the Night*, *The Skeletons of Fish*, *In My Living Condition*, *Black Folks and Heroes*, *Sexual Illegals*, *The Punic Wars*, and *For Black Boys Who Have Considered Homicide When the Streets Were Too Much*. Mason and the Hittite Empire have received honors and awards from the Brody Arts Fund, Franklin Furnace, Art Matters, and Barbara Mandingo and have been recipients of the Kelley Peace Award.

MASSAT, SHERRY SHEPHARD. A playwright, Massat writes dialectically about common folk who are attached to a community and creates characters who are amalgams of her family members. Massat is a native New Yorker who served a stint in the U.S. military before deciding what she wanted to do with her life and career. She spent a year as an intern at the London Royal Court Theatre and earned a degree back in her homeland in theater from New York University's Tisch School of the Arts. Her first play, *Waiting to Be Invited*, was developed at the Eugene O'Neill Playwrights Conference before being premiered at the Denver Theatre Center in 2000. Set in 1961, the play focuses on four black women who decide to integrate an all-white lunch counter in downtown Atlanta that had resisted a Supreme Court decision to integrate. *Waiting* marked Massat's debut as a playwright with great potential, and she has not disappointed. Other plays followed: *Someplace Soft to Fall* (2001), *Levee James* (2002), *Deeds* (2003), and *Starving* (2005). Her plays have been produced at Victory Gardens, Berkeley Repertory Theatre, American Conservatory Theatre, **St. Louis Black Repertory Theatre**, and the Black Theatre Troupe, among others. Her awards and honors include the Roger L. Stevens, Francesca Primus, **Adrienne Kennedy**, and Elizabeth Osborn Emerging Playwrights Awards.

MATHEUS, JOHN FREDERICK. Matheus, a playwright and native of West Virginia, is best known for *Cruiter* (1926). The plot centers on the pre-Depression rush of blacks leaving the South going north to find jobs. Matheus also collaborated with Clarence Cameron White, an African American composer, in writing the opera *Wanga 193*.

MAUTI. A playwright, Mauti wrote one play of note, *Cop 'n Blow* (1972), a drama in one act, with three scenes that he wrote while an inmate at Norfolk, VA, Prison. It depicts the irony of a situation in which a destitute black prison parolee robs the company that wants to offer him a job. Mauti was vice president of the National Association of Dramatic and Speech Arts (NADSA) and a member of the Southwest Theatre Conference and the Louisiana State Arts Council (the youngest and only black member appointed by the governor). He received the **Randolph Edmonds** Award by NADSA (c. 1975) and won the Norman Lear Award (1974) and the **Lorraine Hansberry** Award (1976), both at the American College Theatre Festival (ACTF). He was the first two-time winner of the ACTF Awards.

MAYFIELD, JULIAN HUDSON (1928–84). Mayfield was a playwright, novelist, screenwriter, journalist, actor, director, producer, teacher, and political activist. A native of Greer, SC, he grew up in Washington, DC. After his tour of duty with the U.S. Army in the Pacific, Mayfield studied at Lincoln University in Pennsylvania and at Paul Mann Actors Workshop (1951–54) in New York City. An aide to President Kwame Nkrumah of Ghana (1963–66), Mayfield was also founding editor of various black journals and contributor of short stories. He received fellowships and taught at institutions of higher education, such as the Afro-American Studies Department at the University of Maryland (c. 1966), the Society for the Humanities at Cornell University (1967–68), the Schweitzer Program in the Humanities at New York University (1968–70), and Africana Studies and Research Center (as distinguished visiting fellow) at Cornell University (1970–71). He was named writer-in-residence at Howard University in 1978 and remained there until his death in 1984.

Mayfield wrote for the medium of television, theater, and film. NBC and ABC produced a series of TV scripts, *The Other Foot* and *Johnny Staccato* (1959–60). His play offerings include *Fount of the Nation* (1963), set in West Africa (possibly Ghana) about a president who wants to build a $20,000 harbor with aid from America but meets resistance from his own countrymen. Other dramas he wrote are one-acts, *417* (1954), *The Other Foot* (1950), and *A World Full of Men* (1952). Mayfield did the screenplay for the full-length film *Uptight* (1968), an adaptation by Jules Dassin of Liam O'Flaherty's novel. The star-laden cast included Mayfield, **Ruby Dee**, Raymond St. Jacques, **Frank Silvera**, **Roscoe Lee Browne**, and Janet MacLachlan. It was one of the first films to depict the black revolution.

MAYFIELD, WILLIAM FRANCIS. Mayfield was an electrician, playwright, and author specializing in computerized playwriting and publication. He earned his education from Lindbloom Technical High School in Chicago (1968), Kuntu Writers' Workshop, and the Black Studies Department at the University of Pittsburgh. He was active theatrically at the **Frank Silvera Writers' Workshop** in New York prior to 1985. He authored *Playwriting for the Black Theatre* (1985) and *Odella* (c. 1965), which was set in a video arcade and addressed the frustrations of modern black women of the 1980s. Mayfield was last known to be living in Pittsburgh, PA.

MCCAULEY, ROBBIE. Actor, performing artist, playwright, and educator, McCauley was born in Norfolk, VA. As an actress, McCauley appeared in the original cast of *For Colored Girls Who Have Considered Suicide When the Rainbow Is Enuf* (1976) by **Ntozake Shange**. In the 1990s, she received both an **Obie Award** (best play) and a New York Dance and Performance Award for *Sally's Rape*, which she wrote, directed, and performed nationally and internationally. Written in a circular, historical style, *Sugar* is the latest installment in a series of performance pieces by McCauley that refer to her family's survival since the 19th century as part of the African American working class.

MCCLENDON, ROSE (SOSALIE VIRGINIA SCOTT; MRS. HENRY P. MCCLENDON, 1884–1936). Active between the 1920s and 1930s, McClendon was hailed as the "undisputed black first lady of the American theater" for her body of work as a dramatic actor both on and off Broadway. A native of Greenville, SC, McClendon relocated with her family around 1890 to New York City, where she attended public school and Hunter Normal School (later, Hunter College). By the early 1900s, she had become involved in the theater as an actress and director, and in 1904, she met and married Dr. Henry P. McClendon, a chiropractor.

For three years beginning in 1916, she received a scholarship to study under Franklin Sargent at the American Academy of Dramatic Arts. She made her professional debut on Broadway in *Justice* (1919). Within five years, she returned to Broadway in *Roseanne* (1924) and *Taboo* (1924). McClendon got the attention of Broadway audiences in 1926 as Octavie, an elderly quadroon madam in *Deep River*, a jazz opera set in Creole New Orleans during the 1830s. Her breakout performance, however, was as Goldie opposite Jules Bledsoe as Abraham in Paul Green's **Pulitzer Prize**–winning play *In Abraham's Bosom* (1927) at the Provincetown Playhouse. Later, **Frank Wilson** played Abraham. That same year, Wilson and McClendon (as Serena) starred in *Porgy* (1927), a Theatre Guild Broadway production. The show enjoyed a long run and later toured the United States and Europe. In the 1930s, McClendon became the most active and identifiable black female actress on Broadway, appearing in such productions as *Never No More* (as Mammy, 1932), *Brain Sweat* (as Carrie Washington, 1934), *Roll Sweet Chariot* (as Sadie Wilson, 1934), and **Langston Hughes**'s *Mulatto* (as Cora Lewis, 1935), the last role for McClendon before she died. A year earlier, McClendon had coorganized with **Dick Campbell** the Negro People's Theatre (NPT), which lasted for a year until her death. In 1936, the NPT was absorbed into the New York Negro Unit of the **Federal Theatre Project**. A few years later, Campbell and Muriel Rahn (his wife) cofounded the Rose McClendon Players and Rose McClendon Workshop Theatre (1938–41) in recognition of its namesake.

MCCLINTON, MARION. McClinton is a director, actor, and playwright. A college dropout from Minneapolis, he worked in relative obscurity in the theatrical world until he took over as **August Wilson**'s favorite director in the mid 1990s. The breakup between director **Lloyd Richards** and Wilson over "artistic differences" portended trouble, but the transition to old friend McClinton turned out to be almost seamless. McClinton had been working his way up in the theatrical world since 1978, when he met Wilson at **Penumbra Theatre** in Minneapolis. Since then, McClinton has worked in regional theater and off and on Broadway and has also served as an artistic associate at Center Stage Theatre in Baltimore, MD; Mark Taper Forum; Playwrights Horizons; and Pillsbury House Theatre. His mastery of plays by Beckett, Genet, Shakespeare, and Strindberg and his work with younger playwright like **Kia Corthron** and **Suzan-Lori Parks** have made him a director in much demand. McClinton was an early advocate for Wilson. He worked on the early script of *Jitney* for productions that never happened. McClinton also spent three years as a dramaturge for the Sundance Theatre Lab.

Inspired by Wilson's *Joe Turner's Come and Gone*, McClinton began writing for the stage in 1989 with his play *Walkers*. Like many plays McClinton had written, *Walkers* explores themes of race, sex, violence, and the precarious balance between sanity and insanity. *Stones and Bones* (1994) deals with two couples struggling to bridge the language barrier between the vernaculars of the hip-hop culture and the accepted patterns of speech. *Police Boys* (1995) is about a conflict that arises in a police squad room between wildly divergent characters. McClinton's record of productions he directed on Broadway was also impressive. They were *Drowning Crow*, *The 24 Hour Play*, and three of Wilson's plays, one of which he was nominated for a **Tony Award** in 2001 (*King Hedley*). Honors and awards McClinton has received include the **Audience Development Committee Award** (twice), National Association for the Advancement of Colored People Image Award, **Obie Award** Laurence Olivier Award, Joseph Calloway Award, and **Ira Aldridge** Award, as well as the Joseph Kesselring Prize and National Endowment for the Arts/Theatre Communications Group charitable trust grant.

MCCRAY, NETTIE. *See* SALIMU (NETTIE MCCRAY).

MCCREE THEATRE (MCT). The MCT and Fine Arts Centre was named in honor of Floyd McCree, the first African American mayor of Flint, MI. Located on the north side of Flint at the Sacred Heart Catholic Church, the MCT was established by the Genesee County Model Cities Program in 1970 to provide training in the performing arts for African American youth and young adults and to promote racial harmony. The inaugural season in September 1970 was comprised of three one-act plays directed by Ron Kieft, artistic director for the University of Michigan at Flint's Theatre Program. They were *Happy Ending* by **Douglas Turner Ward** and *A Son Comes Home* and *Electronic Nigger* by **Ed Bullins**. Thereafter, the MCT mounted

The Amen Corner by **James Baldwin** and *El Hajj Malik* by **N. R. Davidson**. For the next 35 years, the MCT produced over 100 main-stage productions.

After the MCT was placed in trust by the Urban League of Flint in 1974, the theater was deluged by a large turnover of artistic directors. Charles Michael Moore, a visionary and energetic writer and director, was actively involved in all levels of production at the theater before he left for Chicago in 1976. Moore's replacement, Ben Spillman, built upon Moore's success. Spillman's administrative skills helped to raise the artistic level of productions. Ronald Parsons, a film actor in *Barbershop II*, followed Spillman. Parson's replacement was Faye Turner Johnson, a former MCT theater student. Finally, Moore returned briefly as artistic director in 1986, the last year the theater would successfully mount a full season of productions.

In 1979, the MCT relocated to the former Model Cities Activity Center at 115 East Pierson Road, but operating costs eventually absorbed funds normally set aside for programming supplied primarily by an HVAC grant. Billie Scott Lindo, an actress, singer, dancer, director, and stage manager, reconfigured the new MCT in 1981 as artistic director. She directed and wrote children's plays and founded the Youth Repertory Group. Due to poor economic conditions in Flint and the loss of local funding for the arts, Lindo resigned, but she returned in 2003 to revitalize the then-inactive MCT.

MCDONALD, AUDRA. An actress and singer, McDonald was born in Berlin, Germany, and raised in Fresno, CA. She studied classical voice and acting at the Juilliard School of Music, graduating in1993. At age 28, McDonald became a three-time **Tony Award** winner in the best supporting actress category for her performances in *Carousel*, *Master Class*, and *Ragtime*. She received a Tony Award nomination for her role in *Marie Christine* and won her fourth Tony for *A Raisin in the Sun* in 2004. Only three other actresses have achieved this feat—Angela Lansbury, Gwen Verdon, and Mary Martin.

On television, McDonald has won acclaim as outstanding supporting actress in a miniseries for *Wit*, the HBO film starring Emma Thompson and directed by Mike Nichols. She also has appeared on *Homicide: Life on the Street*, *Law and Order: Special Victims Unit*,

Having Our Say: The Delaney Sisters' First 100 Years, *Mister Sterling*, and *Kidnapped* and as Daddy Warbucks's secretary Miss Farrell in the 1999 television remake of *Annie*. McDonald's film credits include *Best Thief in the World* (2004), *It Runs in the Family* (2003), *The Cradle Will Rock* (1999), *The Object of My Affection* (1998), and *Seven Servants* (1996). In the television series *Private Practice*, a *Grey's Anatomy* spin-off, McDonald plays Naomi Bennett, the wife of Sam (Taye Diggs). In 2007, she sang with the New York Philharmonic in a concert of songs from movies televised on *Live from Lincoln Center* by PBS. The same year, McDonald received yet another award for best actress in a musical. She shared the **Drama Desk Award** with Donna Murphy for the role of Lizzy in the Roundabout Theatre Company's revival of *110 in the Shade* directed by Lonny Price at Studio 54.

MCGLOWN, JERRY EUGENE. A playwright and educator, Mc-Glown was born in Oxford, MS. He received a B.A. from the University of Mississippi and an M.F.A. from Memphis State University. He taught at Toogaloo College and was an assistant professor in the Theatre Department at Radford College. McGlown has written several plays over the years, with *King Uzziah* being his most produced play. Other plays he authored are *The Quiet in the Land* (1982), and *Every Horse and Rider* (1987), *The Lonely Christmas Tree* (1976), *Mansions in the Sky* (1976), *Lamentations* (1977), and *The Great White Sea* (1977).

MCIVER, RAY. McIver, a playwright and educator, was born in Darien, GA. He graduated from Morehouse College with a B.A. in 1935. After serving three years in the U.S. Army during World War II, McIver made a career of teaching English and drama in the Atlanta public school system. Motivated by the emergence of professional black theater during the 1960s, McIver sent his unsolicited script of *God Is a (Guess What?)* to the **Negro Ensemble Company** in New York City. To his delight and surprise, **Douglas Turner Ward** included it as part of the 1968 season. *God* is a satirical look at race relations, using minstrelsy and vaudeville as a backdrop. The plot centers on a potential lynching prevented by the intervention of a god who turns out to be neither black nor white. Another play McIver wrote is *The Fly in the Coffin*, a comedy about a man who is supposed to be dead but rises from the coffin during the funeral.

MCNEIL, CAYETTE. *See* JUA, CHAKULA CHA (CAYETTE MC-NEIL).

MCNEIL, CLAUDIA (1917–93). McNeil is one of those actors forever associated with one role, that of mother Lena Younger in **Lorraine Hansberry**'s *A Raisin in the Sun*. Though she made over 20 movie and television appearances in a late-blooming theatrical career, she was never able to escape the overarching shadow of *Raisin*. McNeil was born in Baltimore, MD, but her family moved to New York City soon thereafter. A family breakup resulted in her being raised by a Jewish couple who later adopted her. Though trained as a librarian, she began her career as a singer and was very successful at it. McNeil toured with the Katherine Dunham Dance Troupe in South America. She turned to acting in 1953, and her first role was as an understudy in a Broadway production of Arthur Miller's *The Crucible*. Later her appearance in **Langston Hughes**'s *Simply Heavenly* established her as an actor of substance. It was, however, her performance in the 1959 Broadway production of *Raisin* that opened the doors to multiple movie and television projects. McNeil reprised her role as Lena Younger in the 1961 film version of *Raisin*. She also appeared in *Roots*; *Mod Squad*; *Profiles in Courage*; *Roots: The Next Generations*; *To Be Young, Gifted, and Black*; *The Last Angry Man*; *Tiger, Tiger, Burning Bright*; *The Amen Corner*; *Contributions*; and *Roll of Thunder, Hear My Cry*. In 1983, McNeil retired from acting, 30 years after entering the profession.

MEADOWS, KAREN JONES. Meadows, an actor, playwright, and educator from North Carolina, was active in the theater for many years. Her plays are full of heroic characters in stories that reflect a universal humanity and positive resolutions. They have been produced by the **Negro Ensemble Company**, **Penumbra Theatre**, Kennedy Center, Women's Project, and many others. She is best known for *Harriet's Return*, a one-woman play about the life of Harriet Tubman that premiered at **Crossroads Theatre Company** in the late 1990s. Her play was not fully appreciated until Debbie Allen played the role at the Geffen Playhouse in Los Angeles some years later. Other plays Meadows wrote include *Henrietta* (1984), and *Tapman* (1987), an adaptation of a popular fairytale as told through the eyes of African griots. Meadows also writes for film. Her screenplays include *Laying Down Harriet's Soul, Losing Time, Crystals*, and *Laurinburg*. She is a member of the Black Filmmakers Hall of Fame and a recipient of a New York Drama League Playwright Award.

MEADOWS, LEROY. A playwright from Miami, FL, Meadows was associated with the Inner-City Cultural Center (ICCC) in Los Angeles. He attended Florida A&M University in Tallahassee as a technical theater major and Howard University in Washington, DC, as a theater major on a William Morris Agency scholarship. His professional training included positions as technical assistant at St. Marks Theatre in New York (1969); lighting designer for the U.S. Army, winning the Best Lighting Designer Award (1971); floor director for MPLG-TV in Miami, FL (1973–74); news announcer for WMBM-Radio, Miami (1974); and technical director for Ebony Showcase Theatre in Los Angeles (1975–78).

Meadow's representative plays include *Blues Song: A Soap Opera for Live Theatre* and *Serial of the Manipulations of a Narcissistic Matriarch* (1983). The ICCC in Los Angeles began producing *Blues* in 1983. *Everything's Happening Here* (1976) is a musical in two acts about a young woman in a small town who becomes disenchanted with the image of the big city. *When It Rains* (1980) is a drama in one act that centers on a conflict among a female trickster, a dying mother, a conniving lesbian, and a dishonest partner. *Ellen* (1981) is a two-act drama in which a black family has to come together because of economic hardships. *Julio* (1985) is a multimedia theatrical work in two acts about an Olympic boxer who must weigh his chances of becoming a professional fighter or staying an amateur.

MEDLEY, CASSANDRA. A playwright and educator, Medley is a veteran playwright known mostly as a contributing writer for the 1984 off-Broadway hit *A . . . My Name Is Alice.* She is also an educator of long standing, having taught at the University of Iowa Playwrights Project, New York University, Columbia University, University of Michigan, and currently Sarah Lawrence College. Medley also has a history of film work as a staff writer for *One Life to Live* on ABC and author of several screenplays, including *Esther* and *Almost Famous*. Her latest play, *Relativity*, examines the issue of stem cell research and racial superiority. Her plays have been produced at Eureka Theatre, the Women's Project, the Ensemble Studio Theatre, Indiana Repertory Company, and the **St. Louis Black Repertory Theatre**, among others. Her other plays include *3 by EST*, *Ma Rose*, *Flesh of My Flesh II*, *Mildred*, *Terrain*, *Waking Women*, *Dearborn Heights*, *Maiden Lane*, and *Noon Day Sun*. Medley is a member of the Ensemble Studio Theatre, Dramatists Guild, and the Writers Guild of America. During her career, she has been the recipient of awards from the Sloan Foundation, the National Endowment for the Arts, the New York State Foundation for the Arts, and the Walt Disney Foundation.

MELONCON, THOMAS. Meloncon is a nationally known playwright of long standing whose plays continue to be a staple of the Urban Circuit. Born in Houston, TX, he graduated from Texas Southern University with a B.A. in journalism and an M.A. in journalism. His career has been that of an educator in the Houston school system and as an adjunct professor at Texas Southern. He began writing poetry in the early 1970s but soon turned to playwriting. His plays mostly deal with the relationship between black men and black women with a positive twist. Meloncon has written well over 30 plays and 2 books of poetry. His most noted play is *The Diary of Black Men*, which had a lengthy off-Broadway run in 1982 and has since toured almost continuously in southern and some northern cities that constitute the Urban Circuit. Other representative plays by Meloncon are *The Laws of Storms* (2002), about a family who struggles to survive after storm hits; *Whatever Happened to Black Love* (1998), a family courtroom drama; and three children's plays, *The Tree That Grew Human*, *The Rainbow Celebration*, and *Young Mandela*.

MERKERSON, SHARON EPATHA. An actress, Merkerson is best known as Lt. Anita Van Buren on the long-running television series *Law and Order*. Entering its 20th season in 2008, Merkerson has played the stern, no-nonsense lieutenant for 14 consecutive years, setting a record for the longest-running African American character on television. Merkerson has continued to work in films, television, and her first love, the stage. She has appeared in films like *Random Hearts, Radio, Black Snake Moan,* and *Jersey Girl.* Television appearances have included *Lackawanna Blues,* for which she won an Emmy Award; *South Beach; Frazier; The Cosby Show;* and *A Place for Annie.* She returned to the stage in 1998 in **Marion McClinton**'s play *The Old Settler* and again in 2003 to perform in *Fucking A* by **Pulitzer Prize** winner **Suzan-Lori Parks**.

Born in Saginaw, MI, Merkerson grew up in Detroit. After graduating from Wayne State University with a B.F.A. in theater, she moved to New York City and began the hard, tedious work of making a mark on the New York theater scene. Merkerson played bit roles and mainly worked as an understudy in the early years. Her first break was in 1986, when she played "Reba, the mail lady" on the Pee Wee Herman children's television show *Pee Wee's Playhouse.* That led to the role of Berniece in **August Wilson**'s **Pulitzer Prize**–winning play *The Piano Lesson* (1990). Producer Dick Wolf, who had seen her on *Pee Wee's Playhouse,* hired her to play Lt. Anita Van Buren on *Law and Order,* where she was retained as a regular on the show.

Merkerson returned to the stage again in 2005, playing the lead role in **Cheryl L. West**'s *Birdie Blue* to great acclaim. Though Merkerson continues in her role on *Law and Order,* she made a triumphant return to the Broadway stage in 2008 in the William Inge play, *Come Back Little Sheba,* for which she was nominated for a Tony Award for her outstanding performance. Among the numerous awards Merkerson has received are a Golden Globe Award, Helen Hayes Award, **Obie Award** Lucille Lortel Award, **Drama Desk Award**, Screen Actors Guild Award, and six National Association for the Advancement of Colored People Image Awards.

METROPOLITAN EBONY THEATRE (MET). Located in Largo, MD, the MET is the resident professional theater on the campus of Prince George's Community College. It was started in 1999 by Cheryl Collins, a professional actor and storyteller for over 25 years. Collins holds a fine arts degree from Avila College and an M.A. from the University of Missouri. Initially, she made a living as an actor, director, writer, and dancer at regional theaters and institutions across the country. After becoming an assistant professor of theater and speech at Prince George's, she soon realized the need to raise the bar and provide a working, professional environment for aspiring students. Thus, the MET was born, a professional theater that focuses on all aspects of African American life and provides access and opportunity for students of color. Collins has cast a wide palette for her students by staging such productions as Lee Breur's musical *The Gospel at Colonus*; Shakespeare's *A Midsummer Night's Dream*, set in Jamaica with music by Bob Marley; **August Wilson**'s **Pulitzer Prize**–winning *Fences*; and *Having Our Say*, Emily Mann's adaptation of the remarkable Delaney sisters; as well as **James de Jongh**'s powerful dramatization of the enslavement of African Americans in *Do Lord, Remember Me*.

MILLER, MAY (MRS. JOHN SULLIVAN, 1899–1995). Born in Washington, DC, Miller was a poet, teacher, playwright, and anthologist. Her mother, Kelly Miller, was a well-known professor and dean at Howard University (1907–25). At an early age, Miller was introduced to the writings of Paul Laurence Dunbar and **W. E. B. DuBois**, whom her father entertained in their home. Miller became involved with the Howard Players while attending Howard University. She also joined **Georgia Douglas Johnson**'s literary salon called the Saturday Nighters. Johnson was a family friend who became one of Miller's mentors. After graduation from Howard, Miller continued her studies at American University and Columbia University.

For 20 years (1922–42), Miller taught English, speech, and dramatics at the Frederick Douglass High School of Baltimore, MD, and served as supervisor of English in the junior high schools of that city. Also during the mid-1920s, she joined the new Negro literary movement in Washington, DC. She submitted plays to the *Opportunity* literary contests of 1925 and 1926. One received third prize, and another received honorable mention. Her other scripts were produced by various drama groups in North Carolina; Baltimore, MD; and Washington, DC.

Miller coauthored two plays with **Willis Richardson**, *Pandora's Box* (1914), an adaptation of the Greek classic myth in two acts, and *Within the Shadow* (1920), which won first prize for the Howard University Drama Award (1920). Howard University students produced *Within* in 1920 at the Howard commencement upon the author's graduation. Other plays Miller wrote include *The Bog Guide* (1925), a drama in one act that weaves an intriguing web among a biracial African family that results in an unexpected consequence. *Bog* won third prize in the *Opportunity* Contest Awards (May 1925). The Intercollegiate (Drama) Association at the Imperial Elks Auditorium produced it on West 129th Street in New York City (May 1926). Additional plays Miller authored include *The Cuss'd Thing* (1926), a drama in one act; *Scratches* (1929), a drama of black ghetto life; *Riding the Goat* (1930), a folk comedy in one act; *Graven Images* (1930), a children's play in one act; and *Nails and Thorns* (1933), a biblical drama involving the Crucifixion. It won third prize in a drama contest at Southern University in Baton Rouge, LA (1933). During the 1930s, Miller coedited two drama anthologies with playwright Richardson. She married John Sullivan and retired from teaching and drama in 1943, devoting her time to a literary career as a poet in her native Washington, DC.

MILNER, RONALD "RON" (1938–2004). A playwright, author, editor, and director, Milner was born in Detroit, where he graduated from high school at Highland Park Junior College. He attended the Detroit Institute of Technology and Harvey Swados's writing workshop at Columbia University (1965). Milner and **Woodie King Jr.** were cofounders of the **Concept East Theatre (CET)** in Detroit (1962) along with David Rambeau, artistic director. In the early 1970s, Milner was also founder/director of the Spirit of Shango Theatre Company (which merged with the CET) and the **Langston Hughes** Theatre in Detroit (1975). In 1964, Milner followed King to New York City in a touring production of three plays by the Reverend Malcolm Boyd. There he remained after King joined the staff of the American Place Theatre (APT), which was being formed at that time. At the APT, King directed two of Milner's plays, *Who's Got His Own*, as a work in progress in 1965, and *The Warning: A Theme for Linda* in 1969. Milner and King also coedited *Black Drama Anthology* (1972), one of the earliest collections of plays by new African American playwrights.

Milner's most noted plays are *Life Agony* (early 1960s, an original version of the author's three-act play *Who's Got His Own*, 1965). A drama in three acts, it depicts a heated confrontation between a black youth and his mother and sister immediately following his father's funeral. The CET in Detroit produced it during the early 1960s with King in the lead role. **Robert Hooks**'s Group Workshop later produced it in New York TV's Channel 47 Experimental Negro Theatre, again starring King. The APT first presented it as a work in progress in New York (October 1965) under King's direction. *Life*'s first professional production was at the APT (October 1966) for 19 performances under **Lloyd Richard**'s direction. The cast was comprised of **Glynn Turman, Barbara Ann Teer**, Estelle Evans, L. Errol Jaye, Sam Laws, and Roger Robinson. The production toured New York state colleges under the auspices of the New York State Council of the Arts.

The Monster (1968) is a drama in one act about the dilemma faced by black students on a college campus who force an "Uncle Tom" black dean to reveal himself. The Louis Theatre in Chicago produced it (October 1969). *The Warning: A Theme for Linda* (1969) is a drama in one act with four scenes. A young woman finds love and happiness in a household of three generations of black women whose marriages have been unfulfilling. Woodie King Jr. Associates produced it at Tambellini's Gate Theatre in New York (July 1969) for 111 performances on a program of four one-act plays titled *What the Wine-Sellers Buy* (1973), a drama in three acts. A black pimp tries to persuade a young high school student to coerce his girlfriend into prostitution to get money for the student's sickly mother. The Henry Street Settlement House produced it in New York City (May 1973). Other productions included the Mark Taper Forum in Los Angeles (October 1973) and the New York Shakespeare Festival at the Vivian Beaumont Theatre at Lincoln Center (February–March 1974) for 37 performances under **Michael Schultz**'s direction. The cast included Glynn Turman, Loretta Greene, Marilyn Coleman, and **Dick A. Williams**, who won a **Drama Desk Award** in the role of Rico, the pimp. *Roads on the Mountaintop* (1986) is a full-length drama about the internal struggles of Dr. Martin Luther King Jr. and his family after he received the Nobel Peace Prize. Milner was the recipient of the John Hay Whitney Award (1962–63) and a Rockefeller Foundation grant (1965–66).

MISCEGENATION. During the 1920s and 1930s, black female playwrights expressed concern about losing their black men to atrocious acts of violence by white mobs that were often related to an alleged interaction with a white woman. They took it as a personal affront and were confronted with the additional burden of raising children alone in a hostile environment. This greatly disrupted the family structure. In addition, marriage between the races, in most cases, was unacceptable to both the black and white communities. *Mulatto* (1935) by **Langston Hughes** is a play on miscegenation set in the Deep South after the Reconstruction. It is about a relationship between a black woman and a plantation owner. While the play comments on an ill-fated social taboo, it is also about entitlement among black offspring who walk through the front door with feet planted firmly demanding their birthright.

Alice Childress's three-act drama *Wedding Band: A Love/Hate Story in Black and White* (1966) deals with the issue of miscegenation in a South Carolina town during World War I. It is about a 10-year relationship between a black woman, Julie, and a white man, Herman, who are engaged to be married. They plan to go north to get married because of his mother's objections and social conventions prohibiting such a union in the South. Julie is also being pursued by Albert, an African American soldier on leave. Julie rejects Herman's offer and the advances of Albert. The play comments on the precarious position of a black woman in an interracial relationship and the inability of the black man to provide for and protect the black woman from harm without risking the threat of being hanged. In **Myrtle Smith Livingston**'s one-act play *For Unborn Children* (1925), she does not equivocate on the subject of miscegenation; she makes a strong plea against intermarriage. This concern is with the safety of a black man and the verbal and psychological abuse the children would have to endure in a hostile racial climate if he married a white woman.

MITCHELL, LIONEL H. (1942–84). A critic, novelist, and playwright, Mitchell was born in New York City. His father, Alexander John ("Razz"), was a drummer with Louis Jordan's company Five and was also with the Savoy Sultans. Mitchell received his education at Louisiana State University (1961–63). He became a freelance writer and drama critic for the *New York Amsterdam News* (1977–84) and novelist with *Traveling Light* (1980). Two representative plays by Mitchell are *L'Ouverture* (1972), a full-length avant-garde ritualistic drama with choreography. It is about three figures of the Haitian Revolution, Toussaint L'Ouverture, Dessalines, and Henri Christophe, for which **Frank Silvera Writers' Workshop** gave a reading in New York City (1975). *Uncle Tom's Cabin* (1974) is a full-length updated adaptation of Harriet Beecher Stowe's novel, with George L. Aikin's dramatization and choral arrangements by Mitchell. Tom is a Martin Luther King Jr.–type character who is anticipating being with Jesus after his death. The Works Progress Administration Theatre Group produced it in New York City (February–March 1975). Mitchell won an American Book Award from the Before Columbus Foundation (1981) for literary excellence for *Notes from the New Underground* (1968).

MITCHELL, LOFTEN (1919–2001). A major historian of African American theater and drama, Mitchell was a playwright, essayist, and teacher, as well as an important writer for the musical stage. Born in Columbia, NC, he spent his early childhood growing up in **Harlem**. Mitchell graduated with honors from DeWitt Clinton High School (1937). It was during this time that he joined a local church group, the Salem Community Dramatizers (1936–37), which produced two of his plays. His interest in playwriting continued at institutions of higher education, such as City College of New York (1937–38), Talladega College (A.B., 1943), and Columbia University Graduate School, where he studied playwriting under John Gassner (1947–51). While Mitchell was a student at Columbia, he married Helen March in 1948. He also studied at Union and General theological seminaries.

Between 1937 and 1938, Mitchell performed as an actor at the **Rose McClendon** Workshop Theatre in *Having a Wonderful Time* (1938) and *The Black Messiah* (1939). He also acted with the Pioneer Drama Group at the 115th Street branch of the New York Public Library (1938–40), where they also produced some of his early plays, *Cocktails* (1938) and *Crossroads* (1938). Also at this library, Mitchell organized the People's Theatre Workshop (1946–48) after returning home to Harlem from his stint with the U.S. Navy during World War

II. There he wrote and produced several of his plays, including *Blood in the Night* (1946), *The Cellar* (1947), and *The Bancroft Dynasty* (1947). In the 1950s, the People's Theatre was absorbed by the **Harlem Showcase Theatre**, which Mitchell cofounded. Mitchell as associate producer also produced other plays there, such as *Shame of the Nation* (1952), *A City Called Norfolk* (1953), and Sidney Easton's *Miss Judy Fair* (1953).

Beginning in 1946, Mitchell expanded his writing talents to film, TV, radio scripts, novels, and articles, as well as periodicals and anthologies. One of the significant plays Mitchell wrote is *A Land beyond the River* (1957), a documentary drama in three acts about the historical Supreme Court school desegregation decision of 1954. The Reverend Dr. Delaine, a schoolteacher and minister from South Carolina, filed a suit against the U.S. government to desegregate the public schools and major transportation system, resulting in this landmark decision. The Greenwich Mews Theatre produced it in New York City (March–June 1957) for 99 performances. The cast featured **Graham Brown** in the lead role, with **Diana Sands**. Between 1958 and 1959, *Land* toured to Great Neck, Long Island; Brooklyn; and Newark, NJ. It was also a popular choice for productions at colleges and community groups throughout the country.

Since 1960, Mitchell has authored *Ballad for Bimshire* (coauthored with composer-singer Irving Burgie, 1963), a musical in two acts with a prologue and 11 scenes; *Ballad of the Winter Soldiers* (coauthored with **John O. Killens**, 1964), a two-act dramatic documentary/pageant at the Lincoln Center New York; *Star of the Morning* (off Broadway, 1965); **Bubbling Brown Sugar** (on Broadway, 1976, and in London, 1977); *The Phonograph* (1961), a domestic drama in two acts; *Tell Pharaoh* (1967), a concert drama in two acts infusing music from Africa into present-day America; *Sojourn to the South of the Wall: And the Walls Came Tumbling Down* (1973, revised 1983), a historical drama; *Cocktails*, a satirical comedy in one act about the notion of Father Divine being elected to the presidency of the United States; *Crossroads*, a drama in one act about the Harlem riot of 1935; and *Of Mice and Men* (1953), a full-length all-black adaptation of John Steinbeck's novel. Mitchell also gained attention for his two seminal works on

African American theater history: *Black Drama: The Story of the American Negro in the Theatre* (1967) and *Voices of the Black Theatre* (1975). The latter was comprised of interviews of **Abram Hill**, Eddie Hunter, **Regina Anderson Andrews**, **Ruby Dee**, **Dick Campbell**, and **Frederick O'Neal**.

Mitchell was a professor at State University of New York at Binghamton, Department of Theatre and Afro-American Studies. He is the recipient of the Guggenheim Award for creative writing in drama (1958), the Harlem Cultural Award for playwriting (1969), the Research Foundation grant at State University of New York (1974), **Tony Award** nomination for *Bubbling Brown Sugar* (1976), an award for best musical of the year in London (1977), an **Audience Development Committee Award**, and an Outstanding Theatrical Pioneer Award (1979). Mitchell died on 14 May 2001 in Queens.

MOLETTE, BARBARA JEAN AND CARLTON W. The Molettes, a husband-and-wife theatrical playwriting team, wrote eight plays, a book, and a newspaper column about theater, motion pictures, and television. Barbara is professor emerita at Eastern Connecticut State University. She received her education at Florida A&M University (B.A)., Florida State University (M.F.A.), and the University of Missouri (Ph.D.). She has taught at Spelman College, Texas Southern University, and Baltimore City Community College. She was an administrative fellow for the Mid-Missouri Associated Colleges and Universities, director of arts-in-education programs for the mayor's advisory committee on art and culture in Baltimore, director of writing across the curriculum at Baltimore City Community College, and chair of the English Department at Eastern Connecticut State University. Her play *Perfect Fifth* won third place in the WMAR-TV competition and was produced by **Arena Playhouse** of Baltimore.

Carlton studied at Morehouse College (B.A.), University of Iowa (M.A.), and Florida State University (Ph.D.). He is professor of dramatic arts and senior fellow of the Institute for African American Studies at the University of Connecticut. He has taught at Spelman College, Florida A&M, Howard University, and Atlanta University. He has served as chair of the Division of Fine Arts at Spelman College, dean of the School of Communications at Texas Southern University, dean of arts and sciences at Lincoln (Missouri) University, and vice president of academic affairs at Coppin State College in Baltimore, MD. He has been a guest director at the University of Michigan and a seminar leader at the University of Iowa and has served on boards of civic and arts organizations in Atlanta, Baltimore, and Houston.

Prudence (2007), coauthored by the Molettes, was inspired by Prudence Crandall's academy for "young ladies and little misses of color." In 1832, in Canterbury, CT, Sarah Harris, a young African American woman, sought to enroll in Prudence Crandall's all-white academy. Crandall's consent unleashed a firestorm of bigotry. After most students withdrew, Crandall vowed never to teach white students again and reopened for "young ladies and little misses of color." Crandall was arrested for violating a law that was enacted for the purpose of closing the school. After three trials and several violent attacks, the school was forced to close.

In addition to *Prudence*, the Molettes have collaborated on other plays, scholarly papers, workshops, articles, and a book, *Black Theatre: Premise and Presentation* (1986), now in its second edition. Their playwriting collaborations began in 1970 with *Rosalee Pritchett* (1970), a drama in one act with four scenes. A well-to-do black woman, critical of the black revolutionary movement, learns she is not exempt from the racial upheaval. It was presented by the **Negro Ensemble Company**, the **Free Southern Theatre**, and several university theaters and published by Dramatists Play Service and in *Black Writers of America*. A year later, the Molettes collaborated with Charles Mann on a musical, *Dr. B. S. Black* (1969). Just Us Theatre in Atlanta, GA, produced it with **Samuel L. Jackson** in the title role. Other black theater companies also mounted it in Washington, DC; Houston; and Memphis, TN. Their play *Noah's Ark* (1974), a drama in two acts, is set in 1983 as war rages in Africa. Daniel, a college professor and pacifist, is inducted into the army. It was produced by the Morehouse-Spelman Players and published in *Center Stage*. *Booji* (original title *Booji Wooji*, 1971) is a full-length drama. A young black lawyer questions his purpose in life as he sees the African American community being eroded by the influence of drugs. The Atlanta University Summer Theatre presented it and broadcast it on KPRC-TV in

Houston. *Fortunes of the Moor* (1995) picks up where Shakespeare's *Othello* leaves off. The male child of Desdemona and Othello is placed secretly in a Venetian convent. He is heir to the fortune of both Desdemona and Othello. Desdemona's father, Brabantio, is resurrected and claims the child as his heir. Othello's family also arrives in Venice to return the child to their homeland in Africa. The play becomes a child custody battle. *Fortunes* has been produced by the **Frank Silvera Writers' Workshop (FSWW)** in New York, the National Theatre Company of Ghana, and the eta Creative Arts Foundation in Chicago. Among the universities that produced it are **Rites and Reason Theatre** at Brown University, the Ohio State University (Anthony D. Hill directed it), University of Louisville, **Kuntu Repertory Theatre** at the University of Pittsburgh, and University of Connecticut.

More recently, their *Our Short Stay* was presented as a reading at the **National Black Theatre** Festival and New York's FSWW in 2003 and then premiered in 2005, produced by **M Ensemble** at the African Heritage Cultural Center, Miami, FL. *Presidential Timber* was presented as a reading at the University of Connecticut in 2000, the National Black Theatre Festival in 2001, and New York's **New Federal Theatre** in 2001. The Molettes are both members of the Dramatists Guild.

MONTGOMERY, BARBARA C. Montgomery is an actor and director of distinction. She is recognized as one of the great ladies of the American theater, having trod the boards for over 40 years both in the United States and abroad. She has also performed at some of the leading theaters in the country—**Arena Playhouse**, Cincinnati Playhouse in the Park, A Contemporary Theatre, the **Negro Ensemble Company (NEC)**, **La MaMa Experimental Theatre Club**, Intiman Theatre, New York Shakespeare Festival Theatre, Long Wharf Theatre, and Yale Repertory Theatre.

Born in East Orange, NJ, Montgomery came to the theater late, after being married and raising a child. Early on, she studied with the late **Vinnette Carroll** at Variety Arts, which gave her the confidence to pursue theater as a profession. Over a 30-year period, she worked at **Joseph Papp**'s NYSF/Public Theatre and Ellen Stewart's La MaMa Theatre and was a member of **Douglas Turner Ward**'s NEC. She was also an artist-in-residence with the Great Jones Repertory

Theatre. She performed there in *As You Like It*, *Caligula*, and *Macbeth* and toured overseas with La MaMa, primarily in Italy. Among the other notable plays Montgomery has appeared in are **Leslie Lee**'s *The First Breeze of Summer*, **Alice Childress**'s *Wedding Band*, Jean Genet's *The Blacks*, and **James Baldwin**'s *The Amen Corner*. She also performed on Broadway five times and made numerous television appearances, including in *Fresh Prince of Bel Air*, *Living Single*, *Married People*, and *Women of Brewster Place*. In 1983, she cofounded Black Women in Theatre, Inc., where she served as artistic director. Recently, Montgomery has turned her attention to directing, both for the stage and film. She continues to conduct acting workshops and is in the process of directing her first film, *Mitote*. She has been honored with an **Obie Award**, four **Audience Development Committee Awards**, and a New York State Council on the Arts grant.

MOORE, CHARLES MICHAEL (1949–2003). An actor, director, and playwright, Moore worked extensively at the eta Creative Arts Foundation and other theaters in Chicago, like **Congo Square Theatre Company**, **Black Ensemble Theatre**, and **Chicago Theatre Company**. His work with eta's Playwrights Discovery Program was memorable, as was his work with Urban Gateways and the Illinois Arts Council. A gifted playwright, his plays were produced at the **New Federal Theatre**, Four Star Theatre, Madam Walker Theatre Center, and other venues. His list of play includes *Love's Light in Flight*; *The Hooch*; *Tatum Family Blues*; *Say-Rah*; *One Nickel on This Wine*; *Roommates*; and *That's the Way It Was, Walter*. Moore is the recipient of the Jefferson Wing citation and American College Festival Library Award.

MORRIS, EILEEN J. Multitalented black female directors, actresses, and administrators have always been an integral part of African American theater; Morris is the latest of many. She is a graduate of Northern Illinois University, where she earned a B.A. in theater. Also, she graduated with honors from the Tuck School of Business at Dartmouth University. Morris has over 25 years of theatrical experience that includes acting and directing in over 75 productions. Presently, she is artistic director of the Ensemble Theatre in Houston,

TX, a position she was appointed to in 2006. With over 30 years of history, it has been one of the longest-running black theaters in the country. Prior to Morris's appointment, she was the managing director of the **Kuntu Repertory Theatre (KRT)** in Pittsburgh, PA, for seven years.

Among her directing credits are **Pearl Cleage**'s *Blues for an Alabama Sky*, *Flyin' West*, and **Charles Fuller**'s *A Soldiers Play*. As an actress, she has performed in **August Wilson**'s *Joe Turner's Come and Gone*, *Two Trains Running*, and *The Piano Lesson* and the **Lorraine Hansberry** classic *A Raisin in the Sun*. Also, she has either performed in or directed plays at the Alley Theatre, New Heights Theatre, the KRT, the Houston Grand Opera, and other venues. Morris was president of the **Black Theatre Network** (2000–2) and served on artistic and cultural review panels for the National Endowment for the Arts, Cultural Arts Council of Houston, the Heinz Endowment, and the Texas Commission on the Arts.

MOSES, GILBERT (1942–95). A director, actor, musician, and playwright, Moses will be remembered forever as the intellectual force behind the founding of the **Free Southern Theatre** (FST) in 1964. He established himself as one of the quintessential stage directors to emerge from the black arts movement of the 1960s and 1970s. During an all too brief career, he directed on Broadway, off Broadway, and at major regional theaters across the country. In addition, he directed three episodes of the celebrated *Roots* television series, an episode of *Law and Order*, and five major films.

Moses was born in Cleveland, OH, and caught the acting bug early, performing onstage at the **Karamu Repertory Theatre** at age nine. His early education was at Oberlin College, majoring in theater, but like many students of the time, he dropped out to work in the **civil rights movement** in Jackson, MS. It was there while working as a field secretary for the Student Nonviolent Coordinating Committee that he conceived the idea of bringing free theater to the people of the South. He enlisted **John O'Neal** and Doris Derby to assist him, and the FST was born in 1964. Moses was the artistic guru. He not only chose the plays but acted in and directed them as well. They presented an eclectic bill of fare, everything from *Waiting for Godot* to *In White America*. It was there that Moses wrote *Roots*, which was also incorporated into the repertoire. Two years later, artistic and philosophical differences disenchanted him, and he returned to finish his education at New York University. He also studied with **Lloyd Richards**, Paul Sills, and Kristin Linlater.

After a year at the Sorbonne in Paris, he returned to New York and embarked on a directing career with his monumental production of **Amiri Baraka's (LeRoi Jones)** *Slave Ship* at the Chelsea Theatre Center in 1969. From a bare-bones script of some 20 pages, Moses used improvisational techniques to flesh out the story. He changed the language to Yoruba and enlisted musician **Archie Shepp** to jointly compose a score that played from the moment of audience entrance to when the last audience member left the theater. Aided by a huge multilevel slave ship that swayed and creaked with the bow cut out so the audience stared directly into the bowels at the "slaves," it was a gut-wrenching production that left audiences stunned. Moses won an **Obie Award** for this production, which subsequently played at other venues and then toured in France, Italy, and Switzerland. He was hailed as the "wunderkind" of black theater, and the opportunities seemed endless for a career of great expectations.

Moses then began his odyssey of the regional theater circuit, directing, among other plays, Athol Fugard's *Blood Knot* for the American Conservatory Theatre (San Francisco) and **Charles Gordone's** *No Place to Be Somebody* at **Arena Playhouse**. In 1971, Moses was contracted to direct **Melvin Van Peebles's** poetry play with music *Ain't Supposed to Die a Natural Death* on Broadway, to open in October. Prior to the opening, however, he workshopped an eight-week summer program at **Douglas Q. Barnett's Black Arts/West** in Seattle, where he developed and shaped the 20 poems into a play. The play opened on Broadway at the Ethel Barrymore Theatre and was a big success, capturing seven **Tony Award** nominations, including one for Moses for best director. His next success was his production of **Ed Bullins's** *The Taking of Miss Janie* at the **New Federal Theatre** in 1975, for which he won a **New York Drama Critics' Circle Award**.

Moses also loved filmmaking, but his efforts in that area were not as successful because they came in the era of blaxploitation films. The opportunity was there, but controlling the product was not. The results were two eminently forgettable films: *Willie Dynamite* and *The Fish That Saved Pittsburgh*. He fared much better in his 1986 film *A Fight for Jenny* and the 1989 film *Wonderwork-Runaway*, featuring **Charles Dutton**. An insidious bone cancer disease, however, began to take its toll, and Moses died at the age of 53, with the glorious promise of his talent largely unfulfilled.

MOSS, CARLTON (1910–97). Moss was director of the Works Progress Administration (WPA) **Federal Theatre Project**, a film writer, producer, consultant, critic, actor, and radio scriptwriter. Born in Newark, NJ, Moss received his early education in North Carolina. In the late 1920s, he studied and participated in theater under the tutelage of **Randolph Edmonds** at Morgan (State) College in Baltimore, MD. He left to pursue a career in acting and writing in New York. In 1931, one of his scripts was produced by the **Harlem** Players. For a two-year period (1932–33), he wrote radio plays for NBC and wrote and acted in the radio series *Community Forum*, which was broadcast over Station WEVD. In addition, he acted in a number of plays and appeared in some of the early films of Oscar Micheaux.

In 1934, Moss was a Harlem YMCA drama director under a federal rehabilitation program launched by President Franklin D. Roosevelt's New Deal. When the WPA Federal Theatre was begun in New York in 1935, he was hired as a consultant and later appointed to director of the Harlem Unit when white directors Orson Welles and John Houseman were replaced by three black directors. Moss was the community man who went to black lodges and churches to try to win audiences for the unit. His goal was to create an environment where the community felt comfortable and would consider the theater its own. While with the Federal Theatre (1935–39), Moss wrote and directed an original show for the Philadelphia Negro Unit, apparently based on his own popular booklet *Negro Music Past and Present*, also written for the WPA. By 1943, he was given a place on the Schomburg Collection's Honor Roll for Race Relations because of the success of his film *The Negro Soldier*, which was considered one of the best documentaries on the black soldier produced during the war. After World War II, he wrote and produced a number of short film biographies of famous black Americans. He wrote several film scores and an outpouring of plays, such as *Prelude in Swing* (1939), a full-length theatrical collage, and *Salute to Negro Troops* (1942), a patriotic stage show.

MOTOJICHO (VANTILE EMMANUAL WHITFIELD, 1930–2005).
A designer, actor, director, and administrator, Motojicho was a man of
the theater. Trained in acting and lighting design, he will be forever
known as the founding director of the Expansion Arts Program of the
National Endowment for the Arts (NEA). Over a seven-year span, he
dispensed some $47 million in grants to the black, Appalachian, Latino,
and Native American communities. For the first time in the storied history of the NEA, taxpayer dollars were being funneled to the various art
groups on the community level along with their European American
counterparts.

He was born in Washington, DC, and attained his B.A. in theater
and design from Howard University in 1957. Ten years later, he received an M.A. in film production from the University of California
at Los Angeles. In the interim, he cofounded the Theatre of Being
with the late **Frank Silvera** in 1963. Then in 1964, using his own
money, he built a 100-seat theater that he named the Performing Arts
Society of Los Angeles (PASLA). At the urging of his friend **Robert
Hooks**, he returned to Washington, DC, where they founded the DC
Black Repertory Theatre. In 1965, Motojicho became one of the first
production designers to work a Broadway show when he did the sets,
lights, and costumes for **James Baldwin**'s play *The Amen Corner* at
the Ethel Barrymore Theatre. He was also a playwright, and some of
his plays have become classics in the black theater repertoire, such as
Changes, in which he intertwines folklore, the dozens, street chants,
and mythic heroes into a collage of black pride. Other plays he authored are *The Creeps, Don't Leave Go My Hand, East of Eden, In
Sickness and in Health,* and *Wanted.*

By 1970, he had done it all, and when Nancy Hanks, director of the
NEA, was eager to shed its elitist image, she decided on a community outreach program and hired Motojicho for the job. He named the
department Expansion Arts. Over the next seven years of his stewardship, the budget grew from $375.00 to $1 million annually, and he
was instrumental in funding some 600 groups annually. After his
NEA experience, he returned to the theater, writing, teaching, and directing shows primarily with the eta Creative Arts Foundation in
Chicago. Motojicho accrued many honors and awards over the years,
including the National Association for the Advancement of Colored
People Image Award (1969), Los Angeles Drama Critics' Circle Award

(1970), eta Creative Arts Award/epic man of the 20th century (1992), and the **Audience Development Committee** Pioneer Award (1996).

MULATTO **(1935). Langston Hughes**'s two-act tragedy about **miscegenation** set in the Deep South after the Reconstruction was among the earliest plays to be produced on the "Great White Way." *Mulatto* became the longest-running drama (373 performances) on Broadway at that time. The plot was influenced by Hughes's relationship with his father. It depicts a union between a black woman and white plantation owner. They have five children and live as common-law man and wife. When their son returns home from college up North and walks through the front door, his father confronts him because social customs dictate that blacks must use the back door. The father pulls a gun but cannot kill his own son. They struggle over the gun, and the father is killed. The son escapes from an angry mob but returns home to his mother only to take his own life rather than let them get the satisfaction of killing him as the mother goes insane. Martin Jones adapted the play for its opening on Broadway at the Vanderbilt Theatre (October 1935). It toured for eight months, appearing at the Studebaker Theatre in Chicago for three weeks (December 1935); at **Karamu Repertory Theatre** by the Gilpin Players in Cleveland, OH (March 1938); and at Compagnia del Teatro Italiano in Rome and Milan (1950s) for two weeks. It was later adapted into an opera, *The Barrier* (1950).

MYTHIC THEME. During the black power movement of the 1960s, a segment of the theater community embraced themes and rituals connecting them with their ancestors from the motherland, Africa. Many black playwrights were attracted to **Paul Carter Harrison**'s notion of black mythology and rituals. His theory of Kuntu drama incorporated song, music, and drum to seek ultimate truths about African American history and traditions. It provided African American playwrights the format and freedom to break from the linear form and juxtapose images and ideas to convey greater meaning.

    Adrienne Kennedy's **Obie Award** winning play *Funnyhouse of a Negro* (1963) is an abstract, surrealistic theater piece and a manifestation of Harrison's theory. The props in the play represent numerous ideas, and characters transform into multiple people, sometimes simultaneously, creating the effect of nightmares. However, as in a dream, behind her kaleidoscopic vision hovers a literal story. *Funnyhouse* is the madhouse of racism steeped in mythology. A biracial woman is torn between the paradoxes of black and white, past and present, flesh and spirit. The play centers on a mulatto girl's unsuccessful attempts to resolve the psychological conflicts of her black/white heritage. In a surrealistic rooming house, Sarah is visited by various historical figures that represent facets of her divided self. Another Obie Award–winning play is *The Great MacDaddy* (1973) by Paul Carter Harrison, a ritualized African American event in two acts based on Amos Tutuola's mythic novel *The Palm Wine Drinkard*. It is a spiritual odyssey through African American life in which the leading character gains force by encountering manifestations of oppression and spiritual resistance of blacks throughout American history.

Derek Walcott's Nobel Prize–winning drama *Dream on Monkey Mountain* (1967) is both illogical and contradictory. It exists in the mind of Makak, an old charcoal burner. *Dream* takes place somewhere in the West Indies on an unspecified island and either in the past or the present, where Makak, after seeing his own face for the first time, embarks on a mythical journey to search for his identity. His exploration confronts notions of Christianity, English law, colonialism, the teachings of Gandhi, and the demise of Haile Selassie. It is augmented with the music of the West Indies, warrior dances, and voodoo practices and shows the psychological devastation colonialism had on blacks.

– N –

NATIONAL BLACK THEATRE (NBT). Located in **Harlem** on 125th Street, the NBT was organized in 1968 by the late Dr. **Barbara Ann Teer**, a well-known writer, producer, director, teacher, organizer, and actress from East St. Louis, IL. Teer's journey to the NBT began in 1960 after a promising career at the **Negro Ensemble Company** and her disenchantment with portraying stereotypical images of blacks on Broadway. She redirected her creative expression to experimenting with an Afrocentric theory of performance training. Audiences and performers undertake a spiritual and cultural journey that liberates spirits, strengthens minds, and raises African American consciousness. This process is achieved through a five-cycle self-awareness technique: "the Nigger," "the Negro," "the Militant," "the Nationalist," and "the Revolutionary." Her mission was to maintain and develop cultural traditions of African descent and to counteract the negative aspects of European culture. The NBT became known as the Sun People's Theatre of Harlem because of its attention to politics, education, entertainment, social- and psychodrama, and African cultural rituals that were reportedly grand, highly energized, and functional. In 1983, Teer expanded her entrepreneurial aspirations for the NBT by purchasing a 64,000-square-foot city block of property on 125th Street and 5th Avenue. The NBT may be the first revenue-generating black theater arts complex in the country and one of the few viable theatrical ventures to survive into the third millennium. This is a testament in large part of the vision and creativity of Teer.

NATIONAL BLACK THEATRE FESTIVAL (NBTF). The NBTF began in 1989, the brainchild of Larry Leon Hamlin, artistic director of the **North Carolina Black Repertory Theatre** of Winston-Salem. The festival is held every other odd year. It was conceived with the goal of uniting black theater companies in America and ensuring the survival of the genre into the next millennium. It has succeeded beyond its wildest expectations, attracting theater companies, celebrities, and people from all over the world. The NBTF is now considered one of the most historic and culturally significant events in the history of black and American theater. The first festival attracted over 10,000 people. Seventeen theater companies were involved, such as the **Negro Ensemble Company**, **Jomandi Productions**, **Freedom Theatre**, and **Cultural Odyssey**. They gave over 30 performances in a one-week span. Since then, the NBTF has attracted more than 60,000 people during the six-day event.

The festival has proven to be a windfall for the city of Winston-Salem, bringing in revenues of over $10 million during the one-week period. It has succeeded because of Hamlin's determination. He was also ably assisted by the venerable Dr. Maya Angelou, an early supporter and professor at nearby Wake Forest University. She served as chairperson for the inaugural festival. Since then, each festival has been overseen by two cochairpersons. Each festival has an overall theme and a set of events structured around performances. Over the years, the bill of fare has changed. There are still workshops on subjects common to black theater but also a reader's theater of new works, a poetry slam, a black film festival, and offerings of hip-hop theater. Hamlin also initiated a new Performance Black Theatre Series for performance artists. An ongoing feature is the Living Legends Awards Project, where outstanding members of the theatrical profession are honored. Over the years the festival has honored **Sidney Poitier**, **Ossie Davis**, **Ruby Dee**, **August Wilson**, Cicely Tyson, **Ed Bullins**, **Amiri Baraka (LeRoi Jones)**, Diahann Carroll, **Jason Bernard**, **Lloyd Richards**, and a host of other theater artists. By 2001, the NBTF had become an international event. Performances climbed exponentially to over 100 during the week-long event. The plays presented during the festival are disparate and versatile, such as *The Dance on Widows Row* by **Samm-Art Williams**, *Dink's Blues* by **Phillip Hayes Dean**, *From the Mississippi Delta* by **Endesha Mae Holland**, *The Jackie Wilson Story* by **Jackie Taylor**, *Rhyme Deferred* by Kamilah Forbes, and *The Piano Lesson* by August Wilson. The festival has grown to the point where it is now underwritten by major corporate sponsors like Coca Cola, Sara Lee, Bank of America, American Express, R. J. Reynolds, Wachovia Bank and Trust, and the city of Winston-Salem. Over the years, the NBTF has become a focal point of cultural significance for black people involved in theater and the arts. On 8 June 2007, the founder and driving force behind the NBTF, Larry Leon Hamlin, died.

NATIONAL BLACK TOURING CIRCUIT (NBTC). The NBTC is based in New York City through the offices of the **New Federal Theatre**. For the last 32 years, the NBTC has been presenting black plays of substance and clarity to an increasing audience both in the United States and abroad. Conceived by the ubiquitous **Woodie King Jr.** with the support of the **Black Theatre Alliance (BTA)**, its purpose was twofold: to make black theater productions available to a larger audience and to create a viable mechanism for the economic development of the participating organization by sharing the net proceeds.

King was assisted in the development and nurturing of the plan by Gloria Mitchell of the BTA and by **Shauneille Perry**, veteran actor

350 • NEAL, LAWRENCE "LARRY" PAUL

and director. After years of fund raising, working out union contracts, and making key contacts, the NBTC opened its first production at the Terrace Theatre in the John F. Kennedy Center in 1975. Using small casts and working on tight budgets, the NBTC has performed in over 175 cities and numerous festivals, including the **National Black Theatre Festival** in Winston-Salem, NC, and festivals in Bermuda; England; and Osaka, Japan. Examples of productions over the years include *Love to All, Lorraine* by **Elizabeth Van Dyke**, a one-woman show based on the life of the late playwright **Lorraine Hansberry**; *Celebration* by Shauneille Perry, comprised of poetry and music from Paul Laurence Dunbar, Sojourner Truth, Stevie Wonder, and others celebrating the African American tradition; *Monk 'n Bud* by **Laurence Holder**, a play based on a true incident honoring the spirit and friendship between jazz greats Thelonious Monk and Bud Powell; *Rosa Parks* by **Von H. Washington Sr.**, a play revealing why Parks refused to move from her bus seat in Montgomery AL, and her life after moving to Detroit; and *Grandma's Quilt* by Karen Annette Brown, a one-woman show from the postslavery (*see* SLAVERY THEME) era to the present day wherein a grandmother explains to her family what the workings on a quilt represent.

NEAL, LAWRENCE "LARRY" PAUL (1937–81). A playwright, author, and scholar, Neal was an important figure of the **civil rights movement** of the 1960s. He was a prime architect in the flowering black arts movement that emerged during this tumultuous time period. A native of Atlanta, GA, Neal grew up in Philadelphia, where he earned a B.A. from Lincoln University (1961) and an M.A. from the University of Pennsylvania (1963). He set the tone for a new black aesthetic in his 1964 article "The Negro in the Theatre" and quickly followed with "The Cultural Front," asserting the need for separate and equal black cultural endeavors. In 1968, he teamed with **Amiri Baraka (LeRoi Jones)** in writing *Black Fire: An Anthology of Afro-American Writing*. It featured the works of Hoyt Fuller; **Sonia Sanchez**; Harold Cruse; Calvin C. Hernton; Ed Spriggs; and other poets, playwrights, and short story and essay writers of the **black experience**. It is the seminal work of the black arts movement.

Between 1963 and 1976, Neal taught writing at Yale University, City College of New York, and Case Western Reserve University.

Also, he spent three years as executive director of the DC Commission on the Arts and Humanities. In 1965, Neal and his wife purchased a large brownstone in the Sugar Hill section of **Harlem**, and it attracted literary figures like Ishmael Reed, Quincy Troupe, and Stanley Crouch, who met there almost weekly for discussions of the arts. During this period, Neal founded and edited several of the most influential journals of the 1960s, *Liberator*, *Soulbook*, *The Journal of Black Poetry*, and *Black*. In addition, he assisted Baraka in founding the **Black Arts Repertory Theatre School** in 1964 and served as its administrator. Neal is also the writer of two books of poetry, *Black Boogaloo* (1969) and *Hoodoo Hollerin' Bebop Ghosts* (1974).

Neal wrote two plays of note. *The Glorious Monster in the Bell of the Horn* (1976) is a full-length poetic drama. A day before U.S. forces dropped the atom bomb on Hiroshima, Japan, a group of African American artists and writers talk about what life means to them. **New Federal Theatre** produced it in New York City (July 1979) for 12 performances. **Glenda Dickerson** directed the show with music by Max Roach. *In an Upstate Motel* (1981) is a full-length crime drama. Two convicts hide out from the mafia in an upstate motel. The **Negro Ensemble Company** produced it in New York City (April–May 1981) for 45 performances. **Paul Carter Harrison** directed a fine cast featuring **Phylicia Ayers-Allen** and **Carl Gordon**. The Guggenheim Foundation awarded Neal a fellowship in 1970 for Afro-American critical studies. After Neal died in 1981, the DC Commission on the Arts and Humanities established the Larry Neal Writer's Award. The competition is open to all District of Columbia residents, 8 to 18, for artistic excellence in three genres: poetry, fiction, and essays. Cash awards are presented in each category.

NEAL, ROME. Raised in New York City, Neal is a man of many talents, a performing artist, director, producer, and jazz singer. Since the early 1980s, he has been artistic director of the world-famous Nuyorican Poets Café in Manhattan. His interest in theater began in the early 1970s after he took an acting class at Baruch College and the professor put him in a play. This was the beginning of Neal's independent self-promotion. He began creating, producing, and directing himself in his own work. Neal burst upon the theatrical scene with his breakout performance in *Shango de Ima*, which was nominated for and received 11 **Audience Development Committee (Audelco) Awards.**

Neal's best-known one-man performance piece is *Monk 'n Bud* by **Laurence Holder**, for which Neal received five Audelco Awards—two for acting, two for directing, and one for light design. *Monk* is about the legendary jazz musician, bassist Thelonious Monk, who died on 17 February 1982, and Bud Powell. The play opened at the Nuyorican in February 2000, where it ran for two months. Neal and Holder moved it to a theater space on 42nd Street and then to the Theatre for the New City and back to the Nuyorican for three weeks before it went on tour. Thereafter, they took it to the **National Black Theatre Festival (NBTF)** in Winston-Salem, NC (2001), and from there to Philadelphia to the Cleft Note Club, where they performed it twice, and then to Hartford, CT, at the Artists Collective. *Monk* received critical acclaim at the NBTF and from Jason Zinoman of the *New York Times*. Neal also collaborated with Holder on two other plays that Holder wrote and Neal directed—*Ruby and Pearl*, about women in the burlesque business, and *Red Channels*, about McCarthyism in the 1950s. Another piece Neal both acted in and directed was *Signs* by Gabrielle N. Lane, a four-character piece that was done at Theatre for the New City and for which he won an Audelco Award as lead actor. Neal and Holder's next project is *The Jazz Singer*, in which he sings. It is about a down and out jazz singer who is trying to put his life back together.

NEGRO ENSEMBLE COMPANY (NEC). The NEC was founded in the summer of 1967 under the direction of actor **Robert Hooks**; actor, playwright, and director **Douglas Turner Ward**; and producer and director Gerald Krone (white). From its beginning, the NEC was criticized for its integrated administration, its grant from the Ford Foundation, its location in Greenwich Village, and its first season's bill. Clearly, in its nascent stage, the objective of the NEC was to survive. Events that culminated in the formation of the NEC began in 1965–66 with the production of two one-act plays by Ward, *Happy Ending* and *Day of Absence*, both satires. They ran for 15 months off Broadway, and both were popular and critical successes. Hooks was the producer, Krone the producer/manager, and Philip Meister the director, who five years earlier had been unsuccessful in raising enough capital to produce the plays.

Owing to the attention his plays engendered, Ward was asked by the *New York Times* to write an article on the Afro-American in the theater titled "American Theatre: For Whites Only?" (14 August 1966). Ward stressed the need for an established black theater by African American playwrights with an unfettered, imaginative black angle of vision. He targeted blacks to be his primary audience, but he also wanted to attract a better-informed black audience that shared common experiences to readily understand, debate, and confirm or reject the truth or falsity of the playwrights' explorations. He also emphasized that he did not want whites to be excluded. Ward's *Times* article attracted the attention of W. McNeil Lowrey at the Ford Foundation, motivating them to recommend a grant for such a theater. A formal proposal was written up and submitted, which Ford accepted. Along with cofounders Hooks and Krone, Ward eventually received a Ford grant of $434,000 to establish the NEC. A nucleus already existed in the form of Hooks's three-year-old Group Theatre Workshop. There was therefore no problem in finding a talent pool. Ward and his cofounders decided to make the St. Marks' Playhouse at 133 Second Avenue the permanent home of the NEC because it had been the site of Ward's successful playwriting debut. A clearly defined policy established the company as a black-oriented, black-controlled theater of high professional standards with an extensive training program in all facets of theater from acting to backstage crafts.

The NEC's inaugural season began in January 1968 with a production of Peter Weiss's polemic on Portuguese colonialism *Song of the Lusitanian Bogey*. Generally, critics agreed that the production was skillful and intense, overshadowing the mediocrity of the script. It was this polished and poised production that impressed the critics and the public and established the NEC's credibility and gave reason to believe blacks could control their destiny in the theater. Much of the NEC's success, however, was clouded by adverse criticism. Some white critics condemned the Ford Foundation for encouraging black theater groups to remain segregated. Ward came under attack for what was perceived as his dictatorial control over the company and his sanctioning of mediocrity through the production of bland, innocuous plays. Some New York critics and black theatergoers raised a pertinent question: Is the NEC *really* black theater? Supporting this argument was Harold Cruse's definition of black theater as an institution completely controlled by blacks financially, technically, and administratively. Because the Ford Foundation, seen by many to epitomize the capitalist establishment, financed the operation of the NEC, it meant the company could not lay claim to financial independence.

Perhaps in capitulation to strong ethnocentric pressure, the NEC's 1968–69 season was highlighted by a series of black-oriented, black-authored plays. To commemorate its second season (1969–70), the NEC presented *God Is a (Guess What?)* by Ray McIver and **Lonnie Elder III**'s *Ceremonies in Dark Old Men*. Featured also was a bill of one-act plays that included *String* by **Alice Childress**, *Contribution* by **Ted Shine**, *Malcochon* by **Derek Walcott**, and *Man Better Man* by **Errol Hill**, and a European tour finished off the season.

The plays selected during the theater's early days were Peter Weiss's *Song of the Lusitanian Bogey*, Australian playwright Ray Lawler's *Summer of the Seventeenth Doll*, and Nigerian playwright Wole Soyinka's *Kongi's Harvest*. These plays reflected the **black experience**, but they were not written by African American playwrights. As the company developed, the directors produced more black-authored plays, but they continued to repudiate revolutionary plays, feeling they were simply "bad plays." Ward said he was tired of handing out leaflets on street corners and writing for the *Daily Worker*. Ward was no longer interested in what he called the leftist writing. He felt a strong desire to deal with the black experience in all its complexity. That style for Ward may have been naturalistic plays, which the NEC soon started producing. Ward believed black audiences wanted to see these kinds of plays because they could closely identify with the aspirations of the characters.

The NEC produced a line of successful plays, all more or less naturalistic evocations of black family life, most notably Lonne Elder III's *Ceremonies in Dark Old Men* (1969), **Phillip Hayes Dean**'s *The Sty of the Blind Pig* (1971), **Joseph Walker**'s *The River Niger* (1972), and **Leslie Lee**'s *The First Breeze of Summer* (1975). Although these plays did do well commercially, the NEC did not restrict itself to naturalistic family dramas. To back its promise to introduce new playwrights and actors, to develop new resources, and to explore uncharted aesthetic frontiers, the company experimented with plays that varied in style, form, content, and perspective. The range of styles extended from the symbolic realism depicted in John Scott's *Ride a Black Horse* (1970–71) to **Lennox Brown**'s use of symbolic expressionism in *A Ballet behind the Bridge* (1971–72). After **Paul Carter Harrison** mildly rebuked the NEC in his book *The Drama of Nommo* for ambivalently capitulating to white standards, the NEC mounted Harrison's "cosmic focused" ritual *The Great MacDaddy* during the 1973–74 season. Clearly, a precedent was set this second season, for the company went on to produce new plays by young and previously unknown black playwrights. In a decade, the NEC had compiled a stellar roster of playwrights that listed the names of Lonne Elder III, Joseph A. Walker, Paul Carter Harrison, Leslie Lee, Phillip Hayes Dean, Derek Walcott, Wole Soyinka, Lennox Brown, John Scott, **Silas Jones**, **Judi Ann Mason**, **Steve Carter**, **Charles Fuller**, **Gus Edwards**, and **Samm-Art Williams**.

Besides promoting playwrights, the NEC has boosted the careers of many actors and actresses, some of whom went on to achieve greater exposure in film and television. At one time or another, the NEC boasted a roster that included **Moses Gunn**, **Frances Foster**, **Adolph Caesar**, Denise Nicholas, Roxie Roker, **Esther Rolle**, **Rosalind Cash**, David Downing, Judyann Elder, **Arthur French**, Hattie Winston, **Clarice Taylor**, **Allie Woods**, and **Ron O'Neal**. Others who performed with the NEC are Stephanie Mills, Cleavon Little, Richard Roundtree, Lauren Jones, and **Roscoe Lee Browne**. A large portion of contemporary African American dramatic literature has come from NEC productions. And most certainly, the artistic quality of many of those productions was enhanced by such designers as Edward Burbridge. Before going on to design for Broadway, the movies, and television, scene designer Burbridge worked with the NEC on such shows as *The Lusitanian Bogey* and the road company production of *The River Niger*.

Just as the **Free Southern Theatre** had done several years earlier, the NEC in 1978 faced the reality of possible extinction and decided to devise constructive plans to ensure its survival. New programs were instituted to revitalize and reinstitutionalize the organizational structure. Through developmental projects, production activity was increased and strengthened. While a complete overhaul of the administrative and artistic staffs was affected through changes in personnel, the corporate board was expanded. Professionals were hired to administer, attract outside support, and ensure the institution's stability. Classroom instruction was replaced by an apprenticeship program and on-the-job training. The company expanded its playwrights' unit and continued its commitment to the discovery of new playwrights. Certainly, the NEC demonstrated its interest in showcasing the works of young black playwrights with its "Works in Progress" Program for the 1971–72 season. Playwrights from other theater companies were also asked to participate. By presenting the plays of **Ed Bullins**, **Martie Evans-Charles**, and **Sonia Sanchez**, the NEC used the occasion to show its impartiality and nonsectarianism. The company was not indifferent toward other mediums of entertainment, especially television, which broadcast *The First Breeze of Summer* (WNET) and *Ceremonies in Dark Old Men* (ABC). A film version was made of *The River Niger*, but because the NEC was allowed only minuscule input, the company escapes blame for the movie's artistic and commercial failure.

In July 1980, the NEC moved to a larger theater farther uptown at 424 West 55th Street. Its first major production in the new Theatre Four facility was not until October 1980, when they presented Samm-Art Williams's *The Sixteenth Round*. *New York Times* critic Mel Gussow gave the play and the performance a less than enthusiastic review. Although opening night had been postponed while the script was shortened and some roles strengthened, it seems the play was still not ready for production. That aside, the NEC saw the move as a renaissance of sorts. The main goal was to make the theater company, at least, completely self-sufficient. Consensus among NEC members was that the company should try to get along on box-office receipts and subscriptions rather than foundation largesse. Nonetheless, the company expected to receive a $300,000 grant from their biggest benefactor, the Ford Foundation. By 1980, Ford had granted NEC nearly $2 million. Still, the company felt it could generate enough income to maintain its self-sufficiency by raising ticket prices, mainly producing works by established playwrights, and depending on its new location to attract a larger, mixed audience. A year before the NEC's historic move uptown, Douglas Turner Ward represented the company in Zambia, Central Africa. For two weeks during the summer of 1979, Ward directed a project jointly sponsored by the Zambian government and the International Theatre Institute of Paris. Working in a village not far from the Zambian capital of Lusaka, Ward helped young African actors prepare skits designed to entertain and educate the villagers.

After Ward, the original founder of the NEC, left the company, O. L. Duke took over as artistic director in 2002. His tenure was short lived, as he died in an auto accident in 2004. **Charles Weldon**, an NEC member since 1970 and a veteran of stage and screen, was selected as the new artistic director. Under his direction, the NEC had diversified into a more full-service theater. The company took on an aura of a school or academy by adding several components to its overall program. In addition to their long-standing curriculum of acting, playwriting, and technical theater, the NEC also offered courses in video production, commercial theater management, producing, advertising, and a public school training component. It was one of the more diversified theaters in the country.

The NEC still takes pride in its playwrights' workshop that has developed so many fine writers over the years and exposed their work to thousands of people, but it is no longer a producing entity grinding out five to six productions a year. Instead, Artistic Director Weldon has opted to produce one play each year to keep a firm hand on overall operations. In 2006, Weldon chose **Jimmy Barden**'s *Offspring*, a play that explores the insidious ways in which racial prejudice nearly always triumphs over racial solutions. In 2007, the NEC welcomed back NEC alumnus Samm-Art Williams and his new play *The Waiting Room*. The play is a dramedy set in a hospital waiting room where strange things happen when friends and relatives gather around a loved one who appears to be at death's door.

The NEC has also changed its fund-raising approach, staying away from the troubles of "soft money" that plagued them so much in the past. Aside from tuition fees and touring production money, they have been successful in attracting funding from a variety of sources on an ongoing and long-range basis. At this writing, the NEC seems to have found a formula that augurs well for the long-term success of the company. But it is a far cry from its storied, checkered past, when they reigned as the premier black play–producing entity in the land, staging such classics as *A Soldier's Play*, *The River Niger*, *Sty of the*

Blind Pig, **Dream on Monkey Mountain**, *The Great MacDaddy*, and *God Is a (Guess What?)*. Whether it will once again become a producing entity is difficult to foresee, but here in the 21st century, it has its two feet on the ground, stable funding, and a richly deserved reputation for turning out grounded, knowledgeable, and talented people in every area of the theater.

NELSON, MARCUS. A black theater director and playwright, Nelson was executive director of the New Concept Theatre (NCT) in Chicago, now defunct. His play of note was *The Essence of Pathos* (1975), a drama about **Richard Wright**, short-story writer, playwright, and author of *Native Son* (1940) who fled America to become an expatriate in France. The NCT produced it in 1975.

NELSON, NOVELLA. Functioning as an actor, administrator, director, and cabaret singer, Nelson has had a broad and diverse career in the arts. In a lengthy 30-year career, she has made numerous appearances onstage, in nightclubs, on television, and in movies. Born in Brooklyn, Nelson began her career as a vocalist but soon became interested in the theater. **Joseph Papp** of the New York Shakespeare Festival saw a production of *Nigger Nightmare* by **Walter Jones**, a play Nelson had directed, and was so impressed that he hired her as his artistic consultant. She wore many hats, serving as a conduit to the black community, as Papp's personal assistant, and as producer of the "Sundays at the Public" Program. This was during the volatile **civil rights** period of the 1970s, when she also directed several plays, including **Richard Wesley**'s *Black Terror* and **Edgar White**'s *Les Femmes Noires*.

Since then, Nelson has worked primarily as an actor and director, with an occasional cabaret performance in between. Between 1970 and 1995, she appeared on Broadway 11 times, either as a producing consultant, actor, director, or understudy. She has performed in several regional theaters across the country. They include the Mark Taper Forum in Los Angeles, the Seattle Repertory Theatre, the Goodman Theatre in Chicago, and Lincoln Center in New York City. Her list of television and movie credits includes *The Starter Wife*, *Antwone Fischer*, *Bailey's Café*, *Preaching to the Choir*, *Girl 6*, *Law and Order: Special Victims Unit*, *100 Centre Street*, *The West Wing*,

Head of State, *The Littlest Victim*, and *The Cotton Club*. Nelson remains a working professional actor, an icon of the American theater.

NEW FEDERAL THEATRE (NFT). The NFT was formed by **Woodie King Jr.** in 1971. A few years earlier, he had helped to organize **Concept East Theatre** in Detroit with **Ron Milner**. For over 35 years, the NFT accomplished an unparalleled record of excellence with over 180 theatrical productions, encompassing 5,000 performances with some of the finest performers and playwrights in the country. It was named after the Hallie Flannigan Federal Theatre that was active during the Great Depression of the 1930s. The NFT was housed at the Henry Street Settlement on New York's Lower East Side. It was not a black theater per se but rather a multicultural institution that served a diverse, low-income community in lower Manhattan. It had a number of programs and components to serve the community.

The theater was a godsend for performers and playwrights. Among the array of performers whose careers were launched at the NFT are **Denzel Washington, Morgan Freeman, Phylicia Allen-Rashad**, and Laurence Fishburne. Playwrights too were afforded opportunities to workshop their plays at the NFT, such as **J. E. Franklin**'s *Black Girl*; **Ntozake Shange**'s *For Colored Girls Who Have Considered Suicide When the Rainbow Is Enuf*; **James de Jongh**'s *Do Lord, Remember Me*; Ron Milner's *What the Winesellers Buy*; and David Henry Hwang's *The Dance and the Railroad*. Aside from productions, the NFT also offered vocational training workshops in all phases of theater, dance, and film. The emphasis was to provide the tools necessary for low-income and minority students to compete in the workplace for employment in the arts or related areas.

Almost from the beginning, the theater prospered because of the plays King selected for production. The NFT won **Audience Development Committee Awards, Obie Awards, Drama Desk Awards, Tony Awards**, and a host of others. Milner's *What the Winesellers Buy* attracted the interest of **Joseph Papp** of the New York Shakespeare Festival NYSF/Public Theatre. In collaboration with King, they moved the play to Lincoln Center. It was the first black play to be presented there. The team of King and Papp also took Shange's *Colored Girls* to Broadway, where it played for over a year. After the

Broadway run, it toured nationally and recouped its investment three times over. It was also presented on television via American Playhouse. David Henry Hwang's *The Dance and the Railroad* was moved to the NYSF/Public Theatre, where it ran for six months, winning three **Obie Awards**. In addition, Damien Leake's *Child of the Sun* won the coveted Richard Rodgers Production Award from the American Academy and Institute of Arts and Letters.

NEW HERITAGE REPERTORY THEATRE COMPANY (NHRTC). Two significant factors within the **Black Theatre Alliance** have been the NHRTC and its founding artistic director, **Roger Furman**. When Furman formulated the NHRTC in 1964, he had already established himself as a moving force in black theater. Furman's involvement in black community theater goes back to the 1940s, when as a very young artist he designed sets for the **American Negro Theatre**. Even before the dynamic 1960s, this artist, writer, set designer, producer, and director had responded to the needs of black theater by organizing the Negro Art Players in 1952. Furman's purpose was to bring summer stock to **Harlem**. This modest venture was undertaken ambitiously with little money and few convinced backers. Despite obstacles, Furman was successful in negotiating with the Elks Community Theatre to present three one-act plays in July 1952. This bill included Tennessee Williams's *Mooney's Kid Don't Cry*, Furman's *The Quiet Laughter*, and Charles Griffin's *The Oklahoma Bearcat*. Furman's contributions during this time are even more noteworthy because they were several years in advance of the events and personages credited with launching the black theater movement. Furthermore, in 1964, Furman served as field supervisor of the Harlem Youth Opportunity Unlimited, a Harlem-based arts and cultural program that funded **Amiri Baraka's** (**LeRoi Jones**) epochmaking **Black Arts Repertory Theatre School**.

Furman originally called the group the New Heritage Players but later renamed it the NHTRC. Being somewhat older than most of the theater artists he worked with during the 1960s, Furman felt no inner pressure to conform to the philosophy of the black arts movement. Denying any inspiration from that sector, he declared his own purpose to be the production of quality plays as a means of communicating with the masses of black people in the New York City area. Although the NHTRC was seriously involved in street theater as a medium serving the liberation struggle, Furman objected to overly rhetorical, didactic theater. He believed that to preach to people in deprived communities about injustice and inequality is to be redundant and that street theater should emerge out of the communities by using the language and experiences of the people who live there. Furman also believed theater of the street required a special program of actor training with emphasis on discipline and that plays should be short and fast and deal with such problems as housing, drugs, police–community relations, and welfare.

Because actors are subordinate to the community that is both the source of and the actual milieu for their action, Furman initiated a system of on-the-job training that permitted NHRTC actors to receive training through public performances. The company began in 1964 with a rigorous schedule of daily workshops and rehearsals that culminated in street theater productions. *Three Shades of Harlem*, coauthored by Furman and Don Brunson, was presented in June 1965. It was performed at the YWCA on 125th Street and was the company's formal stage debut. Though the staging of the play was more conventional, this work was said to reflect Furman's concept of street theater. It was a moving, humorous panorama of the community and told of the community's problems, hopes, and dreams. Before finally settling down in one place, the NHRTC was forced into a peripatetic existence. This journey began in the fall of 1965, when the company accepted an invitation to use space in Public School 125 on 127th Street. Two years later, another move took the company to East Harlem and a larger space at Intermediate School 201. In late 1969, the NHRTC moved to the location that became its permanent residence: 43 East 125th Street. Furman turned what was a veritable wasteland in the form of an empty, dilapidated loft into a well-designed intimate amphitheater. The company presented plays that were either written or directed by Furman, including *Three Shades of Harlem*, with Doris Brunson (1965); *Hip, Black and Angry*, an original company production directed by Furman (1967); *Renegade Theatre* (1968); *The Gimmick, To Kill a Devil* (1970); *Another Shade of Harlem* (1970); and *The Long Binck Block* (1972).

Furman's version of street theater was the Grass Roots Players, the name he gave to these performers who appeared regularly in NHRTC productions. True to his goal, Furman went directly to the community to find audiences for his company's productions. Word of new productions was spread primarily through a grassroots grapevine because limited funds prohibited commercially bought publicity. The group also got notice through organs dedicated to serving the black theater movement, such as Black 46 Black Theatre. Furman's method of interviewing the audience after each performance was an effective way of acquiring empirical, on-the-spot feedback without relying on analyses from interpretative critics. This way he could assess the success of the production from the point of view of the audience itself. Direct audience contact, moreover, allowed him to personally promote black theater and black culture and solicit community support.

NEW HORIZON THEATRE (NHT). Located in Pittsburgh, PA, the NHT was established in 1992. Its goals, according to Ernie McCarthy, the artistic director, were to bring high-quality cultural events that glorify and reflect the African American aesthetic and to provide a professional venue for their development. It has been a godsend for local writers, performers, directors, and technicians. It evolved from its humble beginnings in a church community center to its current home, the majestic Kelly Strayhorn Theatre in East Liberty. The play offerings for the 2005–6 season attest to the variety of themes: *A Soldier's Play* by **Charles Fuller** (September–October 2005), readings and excerpts from *My One Good Nerve* by **Ruby Dee** (February 2006), *Purlie Victorious* by **Ossie Davis** (February 2006), and *American Menu* by Don Wilson Glenn (May–June 2006).

NEW LAFAYETTE THEATRE (NLT). Established in 1966, the NLT reflected the aesthetic and social philosophy of its founder and director, **Robert MacBeth**. During its six-year existence (1967–73), the NLT was a prolific and resourceful black theater company in **Harlem**. MacBeth attended Morehouse College in Atlanta and served in the armed forces before studying at the Actor's Studio. There he met another young director, Adam Miller, and they decided to form a regional theater in which plays about blacks written primarily by black playwrights would be presented. This was in the late 1960s, and MacBeth was averse to the proposition of integration in the theater merely for the sake of integration. He believed that too many plays by black playwrights had been inordinately concerned with black–white social problems. What was needed, he felt, was a community of artists and a community of audience that are equal participants in the theatrical event. MacBeth also criticized the missionary syndrome prevalent in American society that takes an "outside to inside" approach to social, political, educational, and cultural matters in the black community. He sensed something distasteful and even destructive in the posture of "advantaged" outsiders bringing educational and cultural enlightenment to the "disadvantaged." Deprived minorities faced problems in the inner city, but MacBeth proposed techniques, methods, and concepts that were organic to the body politic.

Consciously reflected in the theater's name, the NLT was an attempt to bridge history and recreate conditions of the past. The old **Lafayette Theatre** of the early decade of the 1900s had served the Harlem community and in turn was served by it. MacBeth intended to bring black artists into closer contact with the black community so they could be reoriented to black life. He viewed the black community in a national rather than a local sense. There were black artists and black communities all over the United States, but there was no point at which they could converge and commune.

The NLT, according to MacBeth, would become a Mecca to be visited by artists from across the country, who would take back to their communities the inspiration and knowledge gained from their experience. This way, the NLT proposed to serve as a "national community theater." The infrastructure for this cultural nerve center was composed of 40 participating black artists who were actors, musicians, designers, and technicians. Their singular purpose was to perform at the highest possible level of excellence.

The NLT added another philosophical and creative dimension to its structure. MacBeth avowed that plays by white playwrights would be accepted as long as they depicted the playwright's experiences with blacks. Also, plays by socially conscious white writers, such as Bertolt Brecht, were acceptable if they portrayed the experiences of blacks honestly. Under no circumstances would plays by whites about blacks be welcomed. **Ed Bullins** was in complete agreement with MacBeth on the purposes and goals of a black theater, and he quickly became a spokesman for the NLT. Bullins's vision for the

NLT and black theater was for artists to learn how to come together and form their own institutions and their own vehicles and corporations, to take their talents and give them to the people, and to have something to build upon. Bullins also saw the need for black publishing, film, radio companies, and black communications so that a black person would never have an excuse to go someplace else to work.

Bullins's vision was realized, but a suspicious calamity befell the NLT before it could make its most impressive accomplishments. On 31 January 1968, a fire destroyed the first theater, which had opened in October 1967 at 132nd Street and 7th Avenue. This site had sentimental value because it was the original location of the old Lafayette Theatre of the 1920s and 1930s. But in December 1968, the company opened a new theater at 137th Street and 7th Avenue. After this, a succession of events occurred. From December 1968 through January 1969, Bullins's *In the Wine Time* was presented. This was followed in by a revival of *Who's Got His Own* by **Ron Milner** (February 1969). *We Righteous Bombers* by Bullins under his pseudonym Kingsley B. Bass Jr. was produced (April–June 1969). The first of a series of black rituals began (August 1969) with *A Ritual to Bind Together and Strengthen Black People So That They Can Survive the Long Struggle That Is to Come*. In the middle of all this production activity, in September 1969, the NLT launched the New Lafayette Theatre Agency, a nonprofit play service that handled the plays of NLT playwrights. Two plays by Bullins were also presented, *Goin' a Buffalo* (October–December 1969) and *To Raise the Dead and Foretell the Future*, a black ritual (March 1970). Bullins's *The Duplex* ran from May through July 1970. That August, the NLT presented a play without words, *A Black Time for Black Folk*. Described as a "New Lafayette creation," *The Devil Catchers* ran from November 1970 through January 1971. While awaiting the opening of their new theater, the NLT had not been idle. With members of the NFT, MacBeth directed three of Bullins's plays off Broadway at the American Place Theatre (March 1968). They were *A Son, Come Home*; *The Electronic Nigger*; and *Clara's Ole Man*.

In September 1968, the NLT issued its first publication, *Black Theatre: A Periodical of the Black Theatre Movement*. Several members of the company's playwriting corps achieved name recognition, especially **Richard Wesley**, **Sonia Sanchez**, **Sonny Jim Gaines**, **Ben**

Caldwell, **Marvin X**, Sharon Stockard (Martin), and **Martie Evans-Charles**. Whitman Mayo and Roscoe Orman were two of the company's stand-out actors. The NLT also offered free acting classes for children aged 8 to 12 and provided free theater tickets to the community and general public, graciously funded by the Ford Foundation, the Rockefeller Foundation, the New York Foundation, and individual patrons.

Although the NLT began with the promise that black theater should draw upon the community it serves for talent and material, critics have alleged that in some ways the organization, rather than living up to its promises to the community, became exclusive and sectarian. Some of the critics even charged that the addition of Bullins as playwright-in-residence made the theater a virtual showcase for his plays. Critic Ron Neal seemed convinced that the NLT's rituals could not have been done at the **Apollo Theatre**, where the tastes of the black masses prevail. In Neal's opinion, these rituals wasted creative and artistic energy. He found the rituals to be pretentious and self-consciously pedantic when compared with the **National Black Theatre**'s rituals, which were reportedly grand, highly energized, and functional. The NLT was also criticized for wasteful expenditures, for not using the best talent available, and for letting the artistic level of its productions drop considerably. For whatever reasons, the NLT in the winter of 1972 voted itself out of existence. For some people, this was the end of a glorious epoch of black theater that began in the mid-1960s.

NEW YORK DRAMA CRITICS' CIRCLE AWARDS. On 22 September 1935, a prominent group of theater critics of the New York City newspapers, magazines, and wire services (except the *New York Times*) met at the Algonquin Hotel and formalized the New York Drama Critics' Circle Awards. They established an annual award for the best new play produced in New York City by an American playwright. The winners would be awarded the Poor Plaque, named after and designed by artist Henry Varnum Poor. It became the second major drama award in that city; the Toast of New York (Tony) Awards being the first.

The founding members comprised New York's finest critics, George Jean Nathan (*Vanity Fair*, *Esquire*, *Newsweek*, *Scribner's*, and *Life*), Burns Mantle (*New York Daily News*), Percy Hammond (*New York Herald Tribune*), John Mason Brown (*New York Post*), Robert Benchley (*The New Yorker*), Walter Winchell (*New York Mirror*), Stark Young (*The New Republic*), Gilbert Gabriel (*New York American*), John Anderson (*New York Evening Journal*), Whitney Bolton (*New York Morning Telegraph*), and Joseph Wood Krutch (*The Nation*), along with New York theater critics Robert Garland, Kelcey Allen, Richard Lockridge, Rowland Field, and Arthur Pollack. As the first order of business, the group elected Atkinson as president and mandated that the award winner must receive a three-quarters simple majority vote from the organization. For the 1937–38 season, the group voted to expand the best American play category to include a best new foreign play category.

The first African American to win the Best New Play Award was **Lorraine Hansberry** during the 1958–59 season for *A Raisin in the Sun*; she was also the youngest winner at age 28. Other plays by black writers to receive citations for this award were *Ain't Misbehavin'* for best musical (1977–78), *A Soldier's Play* (1981–82), and *Ma Rainey's Black Bottom* (1984–85). *Ma Rainey* was **August Wilson**'s first award and the first of his eight plays the group honored with this award. The others were *Fences* (1986–87), *Joe Turner's Come and Gone* (1987–88), *The Piano Lesson* (1989–90), *Two Trains Running* (1991–92), *Seven Guitars* (1995–96), *Jitney* (1999–2000), and *Radio Golf* (2005–6). In between the Wilson cycle of plays, writer/actress **Anna Deavere Smith** won this award for her unique contribution to the theatrical form (1993–94).

NEWTON, VALERIE CURTIS. Newton is a working director whose home base is the University of Washington, where she is an associate professor in acting and directing and head of directing. She is also the artistic director of the **Hansberry Project**, an African American theater lab—an adjunct of A Contemporary Theatre (ACT), one of Seattle's three professional theaters. She has directed plays or been involved in new play development with the Southern Repertory Theatre, Actors Theatre of Louisville, Alabama Shakespeare Festival, New York Theatre Workshop, Children's Theatre Company of Minneapolis, Seattle Repertory Theatre, Women Playwrights Festival, and the Mark Taper Forum. Among the plays she has directed are

Stevedore; *Stop Kiss*; *Wine in the Wilderness*; *Mojo and the Sayso*; *Yellowman*; *Flight*; *Twilight: Los Angeles, 1992*; *Wedding Band*; and *To Be Young, Gifted, and Black*.

Newton's father was in the military and finally settled down long enough to guide her studies at Holy Cross University in 1981. She accepted a scholarship by the University of Washington, which included managing its Ethnic Cultural Theatre. That experience and her previous stint as artistic director for the Performing Ensemble of Hartford paved the way for her appointment to the Drama School at the University of Washington. Newton worked in the 1997–98 National Endowment for the Arts/Theatre Communications Group Career Development Program for directors, assisting Tina Landau, Gordon Edelstein, Douglas Hughes, and Sharon Ott, among others. Newton is also the recipient of the prestigious Sir John Gielgud directing fellowship, awarded by the Stage Directors and Choreographers Foundation.

NO PLACE TO BE SOMEBODY: A BLACK–BLACK COMEDY (1967). A drama in three acts by **Charles Gordone**, *No Place to Be Somebody* was the first African American play to be awarded the esteemed **Pulitzer Prize**. Set in a New York City bar, it focuses on characters whose lives intersect with barkeeper Johnny Williams, a gangster, and black and white prostitutes, an ex-convict, politicians, and idealists. Inflicted with the "Charlie fever," Johnny is trying to gain control of the local rackets from the area syndicate by enlisting a number of his associates in his scheme. For over 15 years, *No Place* was the most produced African American play both professionally and at institutions of higher education. First staged off Broadway, it soon drew critical and popular attention. Productions were mounted at the Sheridan Square Playhouse in New York City, where it was first presented (November 1967); the Richard Barr's Playwrights Unit in New York City (December 1967); off Broadway by **Joseph Papp** at the Other Stage (April 1969); and at the New York Shakespeare Festival at the Public Theatre (May 1969–October 1970) for a total run of 312 performances. This run was interrupted for a special engagement presented on Broadway by American National Theatre and Academy (ANTA) at the ANTA Theatre for 16 performances (1970). Under the direction of the author, the show was produced again on Broadway at the Promenade Theatre (1970–72) and at theaters throughout the country with the National Touring Company (1970–74) headed by a cast of Philip Thomas and Terry Alexander. Following the national tour, the production returned to the Morosco Theatre on Broadway for a limited run (1974). In addition to the aforementioned honors, Gordone also won a **New York Drama Critics' Circle Award**, and a **Drama Desk Award** (Vernon Rice Award), all for *No Place*.

NORTH CAROLINA BLACK REPERTORY THEATRE (NCBRT). The NCBRT, founded by the mercurial Larry Leon Hamlin, the dominating force behind the success of the theater, has been in existence since 1979. Though the NCBRT is one of the more successful black theaters in the country, it is perhaps known best as the home of the **National Black Theatre Festival**, an event held every other year that attracts the crème de la crème of black theater from all over the world. The event is one of the biggest tourist attractions in the state of North Carolina.

Hamlin, who has a business degree from Johnson and Wales University, also studied theater at Brown University under the late **George Houston Bass**. Hamlin started the NCBRT in an innovative way, by selling memberships ranging from $10 to $100. Over $2,000 was raised to underwrite the first production, *Sizwe Bansi Is Dead* by Athol Fugard, John Kani, and Winston Ntshona, which was held at Winston-Salem State University. Hamlin used grassroots techniques in selling theater to the community by performing excerpts and monologues in living rooms, churches, sorority and fraternity houses, libraries, and other establishments of note. Excerpts from such plays as **Joseph White**'s *Ol Judge Mose Is Dead* and **Amiri Baraka**'s **(LeRoi Jones)** *Great Goodness of Life* were then later performed in full at various venues around the city. Building his base further in 1981, Hamlin created the theater's own Theatre Guild, a kind of reverse subscription base to support the theater on a long-range basis. Support continued to grow through the years but escalated when the NCBRT attained nonprofit 501(c)3 status in 1984. They not only attracted funding from the Winston-Salem Arts Council but also from corporate sponsors like the R. J. Reynolds Tobacco Company and Sara Lee.

The NCBRT has continued producing theater at venues like the Arts Council and at four other locations in the Winston-Salem area. They have continued apace, producing such plays and musicals as *Don't Bother Me, I Can't Cope* by Micki Grant; *Who's Got His Own* by **Ron Milner**; *And Still I Rise* by Maya Angelou; *The Emperor Jones* by Eugene O'Neill, *Black Nativity* by **Langston Hughes**; and *Fences* by **August Wilson**. In 2004, the NCBRT celebrated its 21st anniversary. Unfortunately, three years later on 8 June 2007, its founder Larry Leon Hamlin died. The fate of the NCBRT remains uncertain.

NOTTAGE, LYNN. A playwright and educator, Nottage has emerged as one of the finest playwrights of the 21st century. Her play *Intimate Apparel* (2004) received unanimous praise and two prestigious awards for best play from the **New York Drama Critics' Circle** and the Outer Critics Circle. Another play, *Crumbs from the Table of Joy*, also garnered praise from critics and audiences across the nation. Nottage, a native of Brooklyn, had already written her first play at age eight. She received a B.A. from Brown University (1987) and an M.F.A. in playwriting from the Yale School of Drama (1989), where she was also a visiting lecturer in playwriting. Immediately thereafter, she spent four years working for Amnesty International. Her first play, *Poof*, was entered in the short play competition at the Actors Theatre in Louisville and won the Heideman Award. It was subsequently mounted at the Human Festival and was a rousing success. *Poof* and subsequent plays have been produced all over the country by such theaters as Playwrights Horizons, Oregon Shakespeare Festival, Center Stage, and Yale Repertory Theatre. They have also been performed in Europe, China, and Ireland. Despite taking a seven-year break from writing, Nottage has produced a representative number of plays, including *Por' Knockers*; *Mud, River, Stone*; *A Walk through Time, A Children's Musical*; *A Stone's Throw/The Antigone Project*; *Snapshot*; *Las Meninas*; and *Fabulation; or, The Re-Education of Undine*. Nottage received numerous honors and awards. They include the Laura Pels Award, New Dramatists fellowship, Manhattan Theatre Club fellowship, New York Foundation for the Arts fellowship, National Endowment for the Arts/Theatre Communications

Group grant for a year-long residency at **Freedom Theatre**, Francesca Primus Award for emerging female playwright, and Guggenheim fellowship.

NUBIAN THEATRE COMPANY (NCT). Based in Memphis, TN, the NTC is a vibrant professional musical theater company with members in Washington, DC; Texas; and New York. The talented company began in 1980 in Washington, DC, under the creative leadership of Ayubu Bakari. Two years later, Deborah Adero Ferguson brought the company to Memphis, where their animated performances have delighted audiences of all ages throughout the Mid-South. The NCT is the only folkloric musical theater company in the region that specializes in presenting folklore and dance in Africa and African American cultures. Their performances have taken them from the John F. Kennedy performing center in Washington, DC, to the Isle of Bermuda and throughout the East Coast and the Mid-South. Instrumental in the development of the "Arts in the School" Program in the Memphis City Schools, the educational and entertaining performance ensemble is one of Memphis's and the world's most delightful treasures.

– O –

OAKLAND ENSEMBLE THEATRE (OET). Benny Sato Ambush established the OET in Los Angeles in 1972. Within a few years while operating in a 99-seat playhouse, it attained nonprofit status. Sato developed a cadre of actors and on average would produce five to seven plays a year. After five years, the OET moved to the Alice Arts Center, a larger venue with some 500 seats. By 1982, with a budget that had grown to over $500,000, Ambush signed a Bay Area Actors Equity contract to employ five to seven Equity actors. They continued to produce plays, but by 1994, with dwindling audiences and a fixed overhead, the budget had shrunk to $260,000. Ambush left, and Zerita Dodson took over as producing director. The OET had a long and glorious history, not the least of which includes the world premiere of **Roger Guenveur Smith**'s 1996 one-man show *Huey Newton* that smashed box office records.

OBIE AWARDS, THE. Initiated by theater critic Jerry Tallmer, *The Village Voice*, started the annual Off-Broadway Theater Awards, or "Obies" in 1956. Initially, the awards were limited to only Off-Broadway shows. By 1964, the *Voice* began including Off-Off-Broadway shows. Each year, the winners are selected in the category of performance, best production, direction, design, special citations, sustained achievement, lifetime achievement. The *Voice* also awards annual grants to selected companies, and a Ross Wetzsteon Grant in honor of its former theater editor. The African American recipients of these awards are listed in each decade as follows:

– 1960s –

1960–61, *The Blacks* won for Best New Play, Godfrey M. Cambridge, for Distinguished Performance as an Actor (*The Black*); 1961–62, **C. Bernard Jackson, James Hatch**, and Jerome Eskow for Best Musical Award (*Fly Blackbird*), **James Earl Jones** for Best Actor (*Clandestine on the Morning Line, The Apple*, and *Moon on a Rainbow Shawl*), **Vinnette Carroll** for Distinguished Performance as an Actress (*Moon on a Rainbow Shawl*); 1963–64, *Dutchman* for Best American Play, **Adrienne Kennedy** for Distinguished Play (*Funnyhouse of a Negro*), **Gloria Foster** for Best Performance (*In White America*), **Diana Sands** for Distinguished Performer (*The Living Premise*); 1964–65, James Earl Jones for Distinguished Performer (*Beal*), **Roscoe Lee Browne** for Best Performance (*In White America*); 1965–66, Gloria Foster (*Medea*) and **Douglas Turner Ward** (*Day of Absence*) for Distinguished Performances; 1967–68, **Michael A. Schultz** for Best Director (*Song of the Lusitanian Bogey*), **Moses Gunn** for Distinguished Performance (**The Negro Ensemble Company** repertory); 1968–69, James Earl Jones for (*The Great White Hope*), **Ron O'Neal** (*No Place To Be Somebody*), Nathan George (*No Place to be Somebody*), Douglas Turner Ward (*Ceremonies in Dark Old Men*) all won for Outstanding Performers, Michael A. Schultz for Outstanding Director (*Does a Tiger Wear a Necktie*), **Charles Gordone** (*No Place to be Somebody*), and **Lonnie Elder III** (*Ceremonies in Dark Old Men*) for Most Promising Playwright; 1969–70, **Gilbert Moses** for Distinguished Direction (*Slave Ship*).

–1970s–

1970–71, Athol Fugard (white, *Boesman and Lena*), **Derek Walcott** (***Dream on Monkey Mountain***) both won for Best Foreign Play, **Ed Bullins** for Distinguished Plays (*The Fabulous Miss Maria* and *In New England Winter*), John Berry for Distinguished Direction, **Ruby Dee** for Best Performance by an actress (*Boesman and Lena*), Kirk Kirksey for Best Distinguished Performance (consistent excellence of performance); 1972–73, **Joseph A. Walker** won for Best American Play (***The River Niger***), Roxie Roker (*The River Niger*) and Douglas Turner Ward (*The River Niger*) for Distinguished Performance; 1973–74, *The Great MacDaddy* won for Distinguished Play, Loretta Greene (*The Sirens*) and **Barbara Montgomery** (*My Sister, My Sister*) for Distinguished Performance; 1974–75, *The First Breeze of Summer* won for Best New American Play, Ed Bullins for Playwriting (*The Taking of Miss Janie*), Gilbert Moses for Direction (*The Talking of Miss Janie*), Moses Gunn (*The First Breeze of Summer*), Reyno, *The First Breeze of Summer*) for Best Performance, **Joseph Papp** (white) and Ellen Stewart for Special 20-Year Obies; 1976–77, **Ntozake Shange** (poet), **Oz Scott** (director), and entire cast won for Distinguished Production (***For Colored Girls Who Have Considered Suicide When the Rainbow Is Enuf***); 1977–78, Nell Carter won for Best Performance (*Ain't Misbehavin'*); 1978–1979, **Morgan Freeman** won for Best Performance (*Mother Courage* and *Coriolanus*), **Mary Alice** for Best Performance (*Nongogo* and *Julius Caesar*); 1979–80, Morgan Freeman (*Mother Courage* and *Coriolanus*) and Hattie Winston (*Mother Courage* and *The Michigan*) won for Best Performance.

–1980s–

1980–81, **Charles Fuller** won for Best Playwriting (*Zooman and the Sign*), Giancarlo Esposito (*Zooman and the Sign*) and Michele Shay (*Meetings*) won for Best Performance, The Negro Ensemble Company for Sustained Achievement; 1981–82, **Adolph Caesar**, Larry Riley and **Denzel Washington** won for best performance (*A Soldier's Play*);

1983–84, Lee Bruer (white) and Bob Telson (white) won for Best Musical (*Gospel at Colonus*), Morgan Freeman for Best Performance (*Gospel at Colonus*); **Frances Foster** won for Best Performances for Sustained Excellence in Performance; 1986–87, Morgan Freeman won for Best Performance (*Driving Miss Daisy*); 1988–89, **The Frank Silva Writers Workshop** for Best Playwriting, Gloria Foster for Best Performance (*The Forbidden City*); 1989–90, **Suzan-Lori Parks** won for Best New American Play (*Imperceptible Mutabilities in the Third Kingdom*), Liz Diamond (white) for Best Direction (*Imperceptible Mutabilities in the Third Kingdom*) and **George C. Wolfe** for Best Direction (*Spunk*), Pamela Tyson for Best Performance (*Imperceptible Mutabilities in the Third Kingdom*), Courtney B. Vance for Best Performance (*My Children! My Africa!*), Danitra Vance for Best Performances (*Spunk*); 1990–91, **S. Epatha Merkerson**, (*I'm Not Stupid*), Lynne Thigpen, (*Boesman and Lena*), Athol Fugard (white) for Sustained Achievement.

–1990s–

1990–91, La Chanze won for Outstanding Actress in a Musical (*Once on This Island*); 1991–92, **Robbie McCauley** won for Best New American Plays (*Sally's Rape*), Lynne Thigpen for Best Performances (*Boesman and Lena*); 1993–94, **Anna Deavere Smith** won for Best Play (*Twilight: Los Angeles, 1992*); 1995–96, Adrienne Kennedy won for Best Play (*June and Jean in Concert* and *Sleep Deprivation Chamber*), Suzan-Lori Parks won for Best Playwriting (*Venus*), Adina Porter (*Venus*) and Savion Glover (***Bring in 'da Noise, Bring in 'da Funk***) for Special Citation, Lisa Gay Hamilton for Best Performance (*Valley Song*); 1996–97, Special Citations were awarded to **Arthur French** (sustained excellence of performance), **Roger Guenveur Smith** and Mark Anthony Thompson (*A Huey P. Newton Story*), and **James Hatch** and Camille Billops; 1997–98, Heather Gillespie won for Best Performance (*Mamba's Daughters*), Target Margin Theater for (*Mamba's Daughters*); 1999–2000, **Marion McClinton** won for Best Direction (*Jitney*), the entire cast of *Jitney* for Excellence of Ensemble Performance.

–2000s–

2000–01, Bill Sims, Jr. won for Best Playwriting (*Lackawanna Blues*), **Ruben Santiago-Hudson** for Special Citation (*Lackawanna Blues*), **Kirsten Childs** for Best Music and Lyrics (*The Bubbly Black Girl Sheds Her Chameleon Skin*), **Classical Theater of Harlem** received a Ross Wetzsteon Grant; 2001–02, George C. Wolfe won for Best Direction (*Topdog/Underdog*), **Jeffrey Wright** for Best Performance (***Topdog/Underdog***); 2002–03, Mos Def won for Best Performance (*Fucking A*), John Kani and Winston Ntshona for Special Citation (*The Island*); 2003–04, Ty Jones for Best Performance (*The Blacks: A Clown Show*), J. Kyle Manzay for Best Performance (*The Blacks: A Clown Show*); 2003–04, Tonya Pinkins won for Best Performance (*Caroline, or Change*), George C. Wolfe for Special Citation for his stewardship of the Public Theater; 2004–05, **Lynn Nottage** (*Fabulation*), LaChanze (*Dessa Rose*), Lynn Nottage (*Fabulation*) won for Best Performance; 2005–06, Edwin Lee Gibson won for Best Performance (*The Seven*), S. Epatha Merkerson for Best Performer (*Birdie Blue*), Peter Francis James for Best Performance (*Stuff Happens*), Robert O'Hara for Special Citation (*In the Continuum*), **Billie Holiday Theatre** received a $3,000 grant; 2006–07, Roslyn Ruff won for Best Performance (*Seven Guitars*), **Lou Bellamy** for Best Direction (*Two Trains Running*), Bill T. Jones for Best Music and Choreography Excellence (*Spring Awakening*), **Daniel Beaty** for Special Citation in Writing and Performance (*Emergence-SEE!*), Nilaja Sun for Best Performance (*No Child*), **Andre De Shields** for Sustained Excellence of Performance.

OCCOMY, MARITA BONNER. *See* BONNER, MARITA ODETTE (MRS. MARITA BONNER OCCAMY).

O'HARA, ROBERT. O'Hara has been acclaimed as a young, exciting, fresh, promising, and provocative performance artist, director, and vital playwright. He seems to be living up to his potential by writing a series of plays tackling some of the most vexing and troubling problems of humankind. O'Hara believes he is operating in the theater of choke, in that if one of his plays earns him money, he wants to be there for the ride. His plays include *Insurrection: Holding History*, which he wrote for his graduate thesis at Columbia University. A native of Cincinnati, OH, O'Hara graduated from Tufts College before enrolling in Columbia University, where he earned an M.F.A. in directing in 1996. *Insurrection* was produced by the NYSF/Public Theatre in New York City in June, the same year he graduated. He is the prolific writer of such plays as *Brave Brood, Beowulf, Antebellum, Booty Candy* (10 one-act plays), *An American Ma(u)l,* and *In the Continuum.* In such a short time, O'Hara has earned some prestigious honors and awards that include the John Golden Award, Mark Taper Forum Sherwood Award, Oppenheim Award, National Endowment for the Arts/Theatre Communications Group theater residency/American Conservatory Theatre, Tanne Award for exceptional body of work, Rockefeller fellowship, and Van Lier fellowship at New Dramatists.

OLYMPIAN PLAYERS. This little theater group located in Pittsburgh, PA, was active between 1935 and 1941. It was the main African American theater company in Pittsburgh during the years of its activity. The players exchanged plays with other dramatic organizations in the city and participated in the annual citywide play tournament. It was one of the theatrical groups supported by the Pittsburgh Playhouse, a liberal white nonsectarian organization. After the outbreak of World War II, all dramatic groups in Pittsburgh were absorbed by public and private recreational centers.

O'NEAL, FREDERICK (1905–92). A director, actor, and theater administrator of the regional and professional stage, O'Neal was one of the chief architects of the **American Negro Theatre (ANT)** in **Harlem** in the 1940s. He was involved actively in professional theater for over 40 years between the 1930s and the 1970s. He held several positions in theater associations, including president of the Negro Actors Guild (1951–52) and Actors' Equity Association (1964–73)—the first African American to do so. He also performed in numerous Broadway and off-Broadway productions. Born in Brooksville, MS, he moved with his family to St. Louis, MO, where he began putting on shows in his neighborhood. Before the age of 13, he was bitten by the acting bug. Still a teenager, he landed roles in *As You Like It* as Silvius in 1926 and *Black Majesty* in 1927, both sponsored by the St.

Louis Urban League. He then organized his own group, the **Aldridge Players**, with the support of the league. The players were active for eight years (c. 1927–35).

In 1935, the glitter of New York City beckoned this young thespian. There he studied at the New Theatre School in New York City, the American Theatre Wing, and privately with Theodore Komisarjevsky and Lem Ward. The move to New York could not have come at a better time for O'Neal. He landed a role in *Twenty Million Others* with the Civic Repertory Theatre in New York City (1935), and he was selected for the acting company of the celebrated New York Negro Unit of the **Federal Theatre Project**, the brainchild of the Works Progress Administration of President Franklin D. Roosevelt. O'Neal was involved with this unit from 1935 to its demise in 1938. A few years later, he cofounded with **Dick Campbell** the **Rose McClendon** Players (and Workshop Theatre) that thrived from 1938 to 1940. It was O'Neal's next theatrical venture, however, that had the greatest influence on the development of African American theater, the cofounding of ANT with **Abram Hill** in Harlem. O'Neal served as cochairman and company manager from 1940 to the early 1950s and played in many of the productions. Among them were *Natural Man* as Preacher (1941); *Three's a Family* (1943); *Anna Lucasta* as Frank on Broadway (1944), in Chicago (1945–46), and in London (1947); and *Henri Christophe* (1947). In addition to numerous regional and out-of-town productions, O'Neal appeared on and off Broadway in productions of *Take a Giant Step* as Lem Scott (1953), *House of Flowers* as Houngan (1954), *Shakespeare in Harlem* as Preacher, *God's Trombones* (1960), and *Ballad for Bimshire* as Neddie Boyce (1963). O'Neal also played in several films, such as *Anna Lucasta* (1959) and *Take a Giant Step* (1961). On television, he portrayed Moses in the Hallmark Hall of Fame production of *The Green Pastures* (1959).

O'Neil was the recipient of numerous awards for *Anna Lucasta*, the Clarence Derwent Award and the **New York Drama Critics' Circle Award** (1944–45), the Chicago Critics' Award (1945–46), the Motion Picture Critics' Award (1959), the **Ira Aldridge** Award (by the Association for the Study of Negro Life and History, 1963), the **Canada Lee** Foundation Award (c. 1966), and the **Audience Development Committee Award** (1976). In 1975, he was also elected to the Black Filmmakers Hall of Fame.

O'NEAL, JOHN. An actor, playwright, and theater practitioner, O'Neal may be best remembered as an icon of the **civil rights movement** and as cofounder of the **Free Southern Theatre (FST)** with **Gilbert Moses.** Born in Mound City, IL, O'Neal earned a B.A. from Southern Illinois University in 1962. His desire was to become an actor, but like many students of that era, he found himself caught in the frenzy of the movement. O'Neal believed it was the most important thing happening in his life. He reassessed his way of thinking about being in theater and became a field secretary for the Student Nonviolent Coordinating Committee in New Orleans. Meanwhile, as an outlet for his acting talent, he cofounded the FST in 1965. He wanted to use theater to stimulate critical and reflective thought among black people in the South. Following the demise of the FST in 1980, he formed his own production company, **Junebug Productions**, and toured his one-man performance piece across the country each year.

O'Neal wrote several plays but became best known for his portrayal of an African folk character named Junebug Jabbo Jones. It is a one-man performance piece he wrote utilizing dance, music, and storytelling. O'Neal has also collaborated with other writers and groups, including *The Mozambique Caper* with Joan Holder and members of the San Francisco Mime Troupe; *Black Power, Green Power, Red in the Eye* (1972), a melodrama depicting the games some black politicians use to exploit black folk; and *Where Is the Blood of Your Fathers* (1973), a stage documentary about the contribution of African Americans during the Civil War whose script the FST developed through workshops. O'Neal and Ben Spillman edited it, and it was produced by the FST for 18 performances at Memphis State University (winter 1974) and at Florida A&M University (spring 1975). *Hurricane Season* (1973) examines the impact of the unprincipled use of computer technology on the life and family of a New Orleans black dock worker. It was produced by the FST (1973) for 19 performances and in Buffalo, NY, by the Buffalo Theatre (winter 1974). *Going against the Tide* (1974) is a melodrama focusing on a conflict between a conservative housing project mother and her revolutionary daughter, which the FST produced in New Orleans (summer 1974) for 18 performances. *When the Opportunity Scratches, Itch It!* (1974–75) is a satire that is an indictment of opportunism among elements of the black bourgeoisie. The FST produced it (1974–75) for approximately 40 performances.

O'Neal also organized the Color Line Project. This group gathers and preserves personal stories of the civil rights movement. The stories are then archived, preserved, and made available to the general public with the assistance of the Clarice Smith Center. O'Neal received awards from such organizations as the National Endowment for the Arts, the Ford Foundation, and the Rockefeller Foundation.

O'NEAL, REGINA SOLOMON. A playwright, teacher, TV scriptwriter, producer, and broadcaster, O'Neal was born in Detroit. She received her formal education at Wayne State University (B.A., M.A., 1965) and was a teacher and reading coordinator in the Detroit Public Schools; a workshop director at the Edward MacDowell School in Milwaukee, WI; a coproducer-director at African Fables of WilCas Records; and a writer-producer at Wayne State University. Representative plays by O'Neal are *Walk a Tight Rope* (1974), about a young teacher who is the first black to teach in an all-white Midwestern school during the early 1960s; *And Then the Harvest* (1974), a 30-minute drama in one act that examines the cause of a race riot in the late 1960s and in which the resolve of a black family is tested after moving from the rural South to a northern ghetto; and *Night Watch* (1974), which deals with the convictions of a shallow white liberal after he is put to the test. O'Neal is the recipient of the Emmy Award from the Detroit chapter of NATAS (1979) and the NAEB Leadership Award in minority telecommunications (1979).

O'NEAL, RON (1937–2004). O'Neal, a journeyman actor, catapulted to national fame in the 1972 blaxploitation film *Superfly*. With a pulsating score by Curtis Mayfield, O'Neal utilized his classical training to advantage in playing the lead role of Priest to make the film a huge financial success. Many folks in the black community criticized the film for glorifying the life of a pimp. A sequel, *Superfly T.N.T.*, produced a year later, did not fare as well, and subsequent films by O'Neal were mediocre at best. O'Neal was born in Utica, NY, and raised in Cleveland, OH. He attended the Ohio State University but soon dropped out and pursued his interest in theater at **Karamu Repertory Theatre** in Cleveland, one of the oldest interracial theaters in the country. O'Neal appeared in a variety of plays there, including *Finian's Rainbow*, *A Streetcar Named Desire*, and *A Raisin in the Sun*. Upon moving to New York City, he found work at **Joseph Papp**'s New York Shakespeare Festival. It was there that he received his first break, being cast in a lead role in **Charles Gordone**'s play *No Place to Be Somebody*. The play was awarded a **Pulitzer Prize** for best play of the year, and O'Neal won a **Drama Desk Award** and a Theatre World Award for his performance. It was O'Neal's performance in *No Place* that cemented his selection to play the lead in *Superfly*. O'Neal subsequently appeared in more than 40 films and made TV appearances in *The Equalizer*; *Remington Steele*; *Roots*; *Hill Street Blues*; *Frank's Place*; and *Murder, She Wrote*, among others. Awards for O'Neal include an **Obie Award** and Clarence Derwent Award.

ORLANDERSMITH, DAEL. A playwright and actor, Orlandersmith was born in East **Harlem**. She is among a phalanx of bright, young African American female writers who emerged in the 1990s as a dominating force in the topsy-turvy world of black theater. She, along with **Suzan-Lori Parks**, **Cheryl L. West**, **Anna Deveare Smith**, and **Kia Corthron**, has written some of the more penetrating theater of the decade. Orlandersmith became interested in writing at a young age, writing mostly poems while attending a Catholic school one block from the barrio where her friends were black and Puerto Rican Americans. She attended Hunter College but left early to take her writing and performing talents to the Nuyorican Poets Cafe. This led to a worldwide tour with the group to Australia, Europe, and parts of the United States. Over the years, her poems developed into longer, more emphatic monologues. She also performed in such stage productions as *Romeo and Juliet* and *Macbeth* and in a film, *Amateur* by Hal Hartley. Realizing there were few parts for plus-sized women, Orlandersmith was prompted to write a one-woman performance piece, *Beauty's Daughter*. It premiered at the American Place Theatre in 1995 to great acclaim and won an **Obie Award**. Her next play, *Monster*, premiered at the New York Theatre Workshop in 1996.

Owing to the success of her literary output, Orlandersmith was invited to the esteemed Sundance Theatre Laboratory, where she worked assiduously. She assembled another one-woman show, *The*

Gimmick, which was produced in 1998–99, yet she felt the need to expand her work into a vehicle for multiple characters. This opportunity materialized when *Gimmick* was workshopped at the Sundance Theatre Lab. The revised version was better received in the McCarter Theatre, the Long Wharf Theatre, Seattle's A Contemporary Theater, and other venues across the country. *Yellowman* (2002) was another expansion to this full-length form. It deals with the tensions between light-skinned and dark-skinned black people that had their roots in **slavery**. It was a **Pulitzer Prize** finalist, for which the author is writing a screenplay. The play was originally commissioned, developed, and produced by McCarter Theatre at the Wilma Theatre and Long Wharf Theatre with the support of the Sundance Theatre. The Cincinnati Playhouse in the Park also produced it (February–March 2006). Other plays she authored include *Liar, Liar*; *My Red Hand, My Black Hand*; and *Raw Boys*. Orlandersmith was the recipient of several prestigious awards, including the AT&T onstage grant, Kennedy Center Roger Stevens Playwriting Award, **New York Drama Desk Award**, Helen Merrill Emerging Playwright Award, New York Foundation for the Arts fellowship, and Guggenheim Foundation fellowship.

OSBORNE, PEGGY ADAMS. A playwright, Osborne wrote one play of note, *The Meeting* (1968), an educational play in one act. It takes a pedagogical approach to teaching sixth-graders and beyond about their African American heritage. It contains a teaching and production guide with stage settings, costume guide, and character portraits of such well-known black historical and contemporary personages as Jean Baptiste Point Du Sable, Frederick Douglass, and **Sidney Poitier.**

OUI BE NEGROES (ORIGINAL AFRICAN AMERICAN IMPROV/SKETCH COMEDY TROUPE). Shaun Landry, a past member of Chicago's Second City, was cofounder and artistic director of the nationally acclaimed Oui Be Negroes. In 1993, Landry recruited a cast of talented improvisers from the Second City Outreach Program in Chicago. Their first show was at Café Voltaire in Chicago. The name of the group changed several times, from Oui Be Negroes to Sheffield's Improv Olympus to Turn around Theatre to the Original African American Improv/Sketch Comedy Troupe. The group has toured the country, especially during Black History Month, to festivals from New York to San Francisco and throughout the world over the past decade. Landry also organized the two-person ensemble Black and Tan Improvisation, cofounded the San Francisco Improvisation Cooperative, and produced the San Francisco Improv Festival. He also did improvisation and sketch work with the National Touring Company of the Second City, the Second City Geese Theatre Company, and Playback Theatre Midwest. He was on the board of directors of the Next Stage Theatre.

OWA. A playwright and photojournalist, Owa was born in New York City. He studied playwriting with the **Negro Ensemble Company**'s **(NEC)** Playwrights Workshop. He was the first Rockefeller writer-in-residence with the **Frank Silvera Writers' Workshop** in New York City. Owa has worked in East Africa and Europe as a photojournalist. His plays have been produced by **La MaMa Experimental Theatre Club**, Urban Arts Corps, Brooklyn College (City University of New York), Hudson Valley Freedom Theatre, Bijou Theatre, and Eugene O'Neill National Playwrights Conference.

Among the plays Owa wrote, *The Soledad Tetrad* is noteworthy. Part 1 is *A Short Piece for a Naked Tale: A Study in Chaos* (1975). The NEC produced it (spring 1975). Part 2 is *Transitions for a Mime Poem: A Study in Transcendence* (1975). It was written as a living memorial to George and Jonathan Jackson and the Soledad Brothers. The NEC Playwrights Workshop produced it in New York City (spring 1975). Part 3 is *Rejections: A Study in Development* (1973). It is a morality drama in one act about a confrontation between a black boy and a white man on a park bench that leads to tragedy. Part 4 is *The Bloodrite; or, In between the Coming or Going* (1977). It is a full-length morality drama depicting a dialogue and confrontation on a New York pier between a businessman and an ex-convict It was produced by the NEC Playwrights Workshop in New York City (spring 1975) and by the Eugene O'Neill Theatre Center's National Playwrights Conference. Other plays Owa authored are *Heaven Must Be a Very Complicated Place* (1982), about blacks in the 1940s. The **Billie Holiday Theatre** produced it (1982). *Hip Niggas* is a tragedy in one act. Two young, hip black youths mug an old black woman for $3 to buy a bottle of wine.

OWENS, DAN (DANIEL W.). A playwright, poet, teacher, and theatrical director, Owens was born in Malden, MA. He received his education at Bryant and Straton Junior College (certificate in computer programming, 1968), Boston State College (1968), the University of Massachusetts at Boston (B.A. in English, 1971), Yale University School of Drama (playwriting, 1971–72), and Harvard University School of Education (Ed.M.). He taught black theater and playwriting at Boston University and the University of Massachusetts (early 1970s). He was resident playwright at New African College of Boston (1969–71); assistant educational director at Store Front Learning Center, Boston (1969–71); director of playwrights' workshops at National Center of Afro-American Artists, Boston (1969–73); coordinator at Columbia Point in Massachusetts (1969); and associate director for the Roxbury, MA (summer, 1971). He was one of 12 playwrights selected for the Eugene O'Neill Theatre Program, National Playwrights Conference in Waterford, CT (1973). Owens produced his own plays in Boston and New Haven (1969–72).

Since 1972, plays by Owens have been produced by the People's Theatre in Cambridge, MA; the Eugene O'Neill Theatre Center; and National Playwrights Conference. In New York City, his plays were presented at the **Afro-American Studio for Acting and Speech**, the **Black Theatre Alliance**, the **Frank Silvera Writers' Workshop**, the **New Federal Theatre**, the **Negro Ensemble Company**, the Frederick Douglass Creative Arts Center, and the Richard Allen Center for Culture and Art. He is also a published poet. In 1972, Owens was writer for *Brotherlove*, Channel 7 in Boston. While at the University of Massachusetts, he was associate editor of *Viewpoint*, a student publication.

Owens's output as a playwright has been prolific. Most of his plays were presented in and around Boston and the state of Connecticut. His representative plays include *The Box* (1969), a symbolic drama in one act in which three young black people are trapped in a box and must learn to understand attitudes that are different from their own. *Nigger, Nigger, Who's the Bad Nigger* (1969) is a drama in one act about color prejudices among blacks and between two brothers, one dark and one fair. *Clean* (1969) is a tragedy in one act in which the admiration of a young man for a black pimp leads to a tragic consequence. *Joined* (1970) is a melodrama in one act portraying the conflict of a black assassin whose job it is to kill a white liberal. *Imitatin' Us, Imitatin' Us, Imitatin' Death* (1970) is an absurdist drama in one act dealing with the conflicts and contradictions within the black revolutionary movement. *Bus Play* (1972) is a drama in one act in which five black women compete for one supervisory position in a hospital. *Misunderstanding* (1972) is a drama in one act centering on a conflict between a black man and his girlfriend, who does not share his dreams. *Where Are They?* (1972) is a drama in two acts that begs the question, What happened to the young black revolutionaries of the 1960s? *Refusal* (1973) is a drama in one act that asks the question, Who writes for black aesthetic—black or white critics?

Emily T: Emily Tillington (1973) is a drama in one act. A black woman examining her life tries to find her identity. It was first produced at Emerson College, Boston (1973). *What Reason Could I Give* (1973) is a musical drama in three acts. It concerns the problems of a black writer who is unable either to give or to experience love. *Acife and Pendabis: Noirhomme* (1974) is a drama in three acts. The play deals with a young West Indian whose rejection of his people's tradition brings about his downfall. *One Shadow Behind* (1974) is a poetic drama in two acts. Three sensitive and talented people (two men and a woman) struggle among themselves for self-expression until one dies. *Debts* (1975) is a drama that deals with the problems and consequences of past due debts. The Eugene O'Neill Theatre Center presented it at the National Playwrights Conference at the amphitheater (outdoors) in Waterford, CT (July 1975), for two performances. *The Michigan* (1979) is a full-length comedy. The title is a gambling term that refers to a phony wad of money consisting of blank paper on the inside and large bills on the outside. A con man is trying to find the one big scam that will make him rich. *Lagrima Del Diablo: The Devil's Tear* (1980) is a dialogue between a guerrilla leader and an archbishop who is his prisoner. *Forever My Darlin'* (1984) is a play with music by Chapman Roberts. It is a humor-laced play with music that shows the effect that the suicide of rhythm-and-blues star Johnny Ace has on an adolescent girl singer who is obsessed with fantasies of fame.

OYAMO (CHARLES GORDON). A playwright and educator, OyamO was born in Elyria, OH. His parents, Earnest and Bennie

Gordon, moved him and his six siblings to a home on East 32nd Street in Lorain, OH, soon after his birth. After serving a period with the U.S. Naval Reserve, he received an honorable discharge in 1966. OyamO earned an M.A. in playwriting from Yale University School of Drama (1981). He changed his name to OyamO because his real name is similar to **Charles Gordone**, the **Pulitzer Prize**–winning playwright.

He has taught at several universities and conducted workshops at the College of New Rochelle, Emory University, New Dramatists, and the University of Iowa Playwrights' Workshop. Presently, OyamO is associate professor at the University of Michigan in Ann Arbor.

His greatest success as a playwright is *I Am a Man* (1995), which tells the story of T. O. Jones and other sanitation workers who went on strike in Memphis, TN, in 1968. The characters are inventions of Jones's mind and show his struggle to lead and resolve this occurrence during the days of Martin Luther King Jr. Another well-known play by Jones is *Breakout* (1969), a symbolic drama in two acts encouraging blacks to break all social confinements that imprison them. The Eugene O'Neill Theatre Center National Playwrights Conference in Waterford, CT, produced it (July 1972) for two performances. It was also produced by the Manhattan Theatre Club, New York (April 1975), under **Harold Scott**'s direction.

OyamO has authored more than 30 plays, most of which are agitprop, street theater, and satires that were produced in New York City. Among them are *Out of Site* (1969), *His First Step* (1969), *Willie Bignigga* (1970), *The Lovers* (1970), *The Thieves* (1970), *Crazy Nigger* (1971), *The Barbarians* (1972), *Erotic Love Chartune* (1975), *Blue Journey* (1977), *Mary Goldstein and the Author* (1979), *Fuck Money* (1969), *Unemployment* (1969), *Chumpanzee(s)* (1970), *The Revelation* (1970), *The Advantages of Dope* (1971), *The Ravishing Moose* (1972), *A Star Is Born Again* (1975), *The Star That Could Not Play* (1973), and *The Place of the Spirit Dance* (1980). OyamO has received many awards, including a Guggenheim fellowship, a Rockefeller Foundation playwright-in-residence grant, three National Endowment for the Arts fellowships, and numerous others.

OYEDELE, OBAMOLA. A playwright Oyedele is based in New Haven, CT, where he was actively involved in the black theater activities of his community during the 1970s. Oyedele's play of note is *The Struggle Must Advance to a Higher Level* (1972), a mock-ceremonial play. It satirizes the screaming of radical slogans and cliché-ridden phrases by the pseudorevolutionaries and calls for the advancement of the black struggle to a higher level of action.

– P –

PAPP, JOSEPH PAPIROFSKY (1921–91). An actor, director, and producer, Papp (white) was the founder of the New York Shakespeare Festival and Public Theatre. His stewardship of those dual entities made him one of America's most important and influential theatrical producers of the 20th century. He succeeded in bringing live Shakespearean theater to thousands of people who might otherwise have never experienced seeing the plays of Shakespeare. The plays were performed in New York's Central Park for free after a bruising battle with parks commissioner Robert Moses. Papp produced two of the longest-running Broadway productions— **Ntozake Shange**'s *For Colored Girls Who Have Considered Suicide When the Rainbow Is Enuf* and Michael Bennett's *A Chorus Line*. The success of *Chorus Line* underwrote the operations of the theater for many years. Papp was also a pioneer in providing opportunity to black playwrights and actors, producing an all-black production of Chekhov's *The Cherry Orchard* in 1973 and introducing an all-black/Hispanic company in 1978 to produce the plays of Shakespeare. In between, he discovered and produced **Charles Gordone**'s **Pulitzer Prize**–winning play *No Place to Be Somebody* in 1969. Papp also produced **George C. Wolfe**'s biting satire *The Colored Museum* in 1987.

PARKER, LEONARD R. An actor, producer, and director, Parker was born in Cleveland, OH. He received his education at the Cleveland Institute of Music (B.A. in music and voice, 1951) and Case Western Reserve University (M.A. in theater arts, 1956). At a young age, he was introduced to theater at the **Karamu Repertory Theatre** in Cleveland (1946–48), where he also returned eight years later (1956–58). Thereafter, he moved to New York City and assumed the position of executive director of Arts and Culture. Parker's plays of note are *Second Chance* (1979), a full-length dramatization of the song "Love Is Lovelier the Second Time Around," which Arts and Culture produced in New York City (fall 1979) under the direction of **Gertrude Jeannette**, and *Oh, My Mother Passed Away* (1982), a full-length drama set in a **Harlem** bar where patrons reveal their lives and fortune and which Parker produced with Arts and Culture at the Renny Theatre in New York City (May 1982) under the direction of Kirk Kirksey.

PARKER, WILLIAM. A playwright, Parker was born in Stockton, CA, in 1960. He attended Morehouse College briefly before transferring to California State University, where he earned a B.A. in drama in a course designed by black theater guru **Paul Carter Harrison**. He graduated in 1982 and made Sacramento, CA, his home. He toiled in obscurity, writing and producing his plays locally under the banner of his production company, Parker's Place. His major break came when **Woodie King Jr.** produced *Waitin' 2 End Hell* in New York City. It is an examination of black marital relations. It opened at the 47th Street Playhouse in Manhattan (May 2004) and was a huge success, running over 15 weeks. It soon caught the eye of other theater companies, such as **Penumbra Theatre**, **Ensemble Theatre**, and **New Federal Theatre**. It was a highlight at the **National Black Theatre Festival** in Winston-Salem, NC, in 2005. Other plays Parker wrote are *The Awakening*, *Me and My Boy*, *The Difference between Men and Women*, *AIDS . . . Killing Me Softly*, *The Ghost of Willie Lynch*, *Baby Girl*, *Buyah*, *Ganked*, *The Hustle*, and *On Parole*.

PARKS, SUZAN-LORI. A playwright, Parks, the daughter of a military officer, was born in 1964 in Fort Knox, KY. She showed an early penchant for writing, but it did not take root until her college years, when she took a class in creative writing from the renowned **James Baldwin**, who encouraged her to try playwriting. She graduated with a B.A. (cum laude) from Mount Holyoke College in

1985. Two early efforts failed, but the third play she wrote, *Imperceptible Mutabilities in the Third Kingdom*, won an **Obie Award** (1989) for best new off-Broadway play. She continued writing at a feverish pace and won another Obie in 1996 for *Venus*, based on the legend of "Hottentot Venus." In what was a portent of things to come, her play *In the Blood* was nominated for a **Pulitzer Prize** in 2000 but did not win. In 2002, however, Parks won the Pulitzer Prize for her play *Topdog/Underdog*. She became the first African American woman to win the coveted award in drama since its inception in 1917. Initially, Parks's plays were structured in a jazz-like scenario of theme introduction, improvisation off the main theme, and then return and resolution. Later efforts became more structured in a linear fashion with multiple themes introduced in wildly poetic language. She has been described as a "black Samuel Beckett."

Parks was appointed head of the CalArts Dramatic Writing Program in 2000. Like many other playwrights, she has branched out into other areas, including screenwriting. She wrote the screenplay for Spike Lee's *Girl 6* and Oprah Winfrey's TV production of **Zora Neale Hurston**'s *Their Eyes Were Watching God*. She also wrote a TV adaptation of Toni Morrison's novel *Paradise* and her own novel *Getting Mother's Body*. Some of Parks's other plays are *The Sinners Place*, *Betting on the Dust Commander*, *The America Play*, *Greeks*, *The Death of the Last Black Man in the Whole World*, *Devotees in the Garden of Love*, and *Fucking A*. Recognition for Parks's work has come from many sources. She has received an honorary degree in fine arts from Spelman University; fellowship grants from such entities as the National Endowment for the Arts, Rockefeller Foundation (twice), Ford Foundation, New York State Council for the Arts, and Simon Guggenheim Foundation; and such awards as the Lila Wallace Readers Digest Foundation Award and the MacArthur "Genius" Award.

PATTERSON, CHARLES. A playwright and poet, Patterson was born in Fayetteville, NC. At an early age, he moved to New York, where he finished high school. He was associated with **Amiri Baraka (LeRoi Jones)** and his **Black Arts Repertory Theatre School (BARTS)**, which had a short life in **Harlem** in 1965. His poetry has been published and anthologized, and he made a recording for the Umbra Poets (1967).

One of his two plays of note is *Black Ice* (1965), a drama in one act in which a group of black nationalists kidnap a congressman and hold him hostage to free one of their disciples from prison. BARTS produced it in Harlem (1965). The other notable play, *Legacy* (1970), is a drama in two acts that deals with the crisis of a well-to-do family created by the relationship between their daughter and a black nationalist.

PAUL ROBESON PERFORMING ARTS COMPANY (PRPAC).
The PRPAC is a program affiliated with the African American Studies Department at Syracuse University. It is under the directorship of William H. Rowland, an assistant professor at the university. The PRPAC was initially formed in 1982 by Rowland and Roy E. Delemos in response to the lack of opportunity for minority actors, dancers, vocalists, writers, directors, and technicians to develop the necessary skills to amplify and celebrate the diversity inherent in African American culture. The company was named after the late **Paul Robeson**, a legendary actor, singer, and activist of the 20th century. In 1989, the company began an extended residency at Syracuse University, which also provided the PRPAC with its own rehearsal hall, the Katherine Dunham Room, enabling the company to rehearse and perform in its own facility. Rowland moved up to become executive artistic director of the PRPAC. Since then, the PRPAC has worked in close collaboration with the African American Studies Department in producing a set number of plays each year, bringing in celebrities and working professionals to enhance the program and assist in fund raising. They have also joined together with the Syracuse Department of Parks and Recreation Youth Program in creating an "arts experience summer camp," where various theatrical skills are taught. They have brought in such working professionals as **Ruby Dee**, **Ossie Davis**, and **Clarice Taylor** to teach and perform. Productions include such musicals as *The Wiz*, *From Cotton Club to Motown*, and *What's Goin On: The Musical Genius of Marvin Gaye*. Plays produced from the African American canon include *White Chocolate* by **Laurie Carlos**, *Topdog/Underdog* by **Suzanne-Lori Parks**, *A Soldier's Play* by **Charles Fuller**, and *God's Trombones* by James Weldon Johnson. The PRPAC has been the recipient of many awards and honors since its inception, such as the National Associa-

tion for the Advancement of Colored People Service Award, Harriett Tubman Award by the Syracuse Urban League, Syracuse Newspapers Post Standard Achievement Award, and Martin Luther King Humanitarian Award.

PAWLEY, THOMAS D., III. Pawley, an actor, director, playwright, educator, and administrator, was a key figure in the development of theater at the collegiate level for almost 50 years. He began teaching at Lincoln University in 1940, a time when theater was almost a stepchild of the Speech Department. Over the years, Pawley instituted a Theatre Department that became the envy of the nation, particularly among black colleges. He initiated the nation's first college summer theater for black students in 1952, wrote over 10 plays, and directed at least 75 student productions.

Pawley was born in Jackson, MS. He earned an A.B. at Virginia State College in 1937 and an A.M. and Ph.D. in theater from the University of Iowa. He has taught at Prairie View College, Atlanta University, the University of California, and other institutions. At Lincoln University, he served in several administrative positions, rising to the position of dean of the College of Arts and Sciences. He retired in 1988. His *Jedgement Day* (1941) depicts a backsliding churchgoer who is reformed after having a nightmare. *The Tumult and the Shouting* (1969) is a two-act tragedy. A black teacher at an all-black college, dedicated to uplifting the race through education, is rejected by his own institution. *Freedom in My Soul* (1948) is a historical drama in eight scenes about Nat Turner, a fiery preacher who led a slave insurrection in South Hampton, VA, that killed 51 whites. *Crispus Attucks: Son of Liberty* (1948) is the story of the first known black man to die in the American Revolution. *FFV* (*First Family of Virginia*, 1963) is a full-length drama depicting the affects of a mixed marriage on a black family during the 1920s. Pawley coauthored with William Reardon the seminal book on black pedagogy, *The Black Teacher and the Dramatic Arts* (1970). He is a member of the National Association of Dramatic Speech and Arts, Actors Equity Association, and Dramatists Guild. Honors accrued by Pawley include an Outstanding Teacher Award, National Theatre Conference fellowship, and Shields-Howard Creative Writing Award.

PAYNE, LORI. A playwright and journalist, Payne was born in New Orleans in 1970. She attended the University of New Orleans, where she earned a B.A. in drama and communications. For the next 10 years, she wrote feature articles for various publications and was publisher and arts editor for *SDM* magazine. She began performing as a vocalist for a poetry fusion band and was featured in their video *Poets Sanctuary*. She moved to New York in 2004 and focused on writing plays. One play of note is *Bling*, a one-act play extracted from *Ulterior Side Dishes* and produced by Payne at three different venues in 2005, including the American Theatre of **Harlem** Season Festival. Other plays Payne wrote include *What This Is*; *Tulsa*; *Catherine Street*; and *Ulterior Side Dishes, A Trilogy*. Payne has also written a screenplay, *Death and Produce*.

PEKIN THEATRE (PT). Between 1900 and 1910, eight black-oriented and managed theaters went by the name of the PT, most of which housed a Pekin Stock Company (PSC). These theaters were scattered throughout the country. In Cincinnati, OH, on Fifth Street, it was controlled by Oscar Hawkins. In Jackson, TN, on Lane Street, it was owned by William Blakely and managed by E. D. Lee. In Lexington, KY, on West Main Street, the proprietors were Gray and Combs. In Memphis, TN, on South Fourth Street, it was administered by blacks. In Norfolk, VA, on Queen Street, it was handled by C. W. Mosely. In Savannah, GA, on West Broad Street, it was owned by W. J. Stiles and managed by Tim Owsley. This theater produced one play of record, *The Wrong Mr. Right* (c. 1910), a musical revue, before the Russell and Owens Stock Company out of Georgia bought it (c. 1911). Seven years later, its name was changed to Bob Russell Stock Company. It had been on the Southern Consolidated Circuit (1916–21) but switched to the Theatre Owners Booking Association Circuit (1920) when it was reorganized. In Chicago on 27th and State Streets, it was managed by Robert T. Motts.

Of the eight PTs located throughout the country, the best known was based in Chicago. Between 1906 and 1910, Robert T. Motts offered audiences a novel form of entertainment—dramas performed onstage by black actors. The theater also housed the first professional African American stock company in residence at a black theater PSC. The original PT, known as the "Temple of Music" at the corner of

27th and State Streets, featured vaudeville and variety shows. Motts was a former saloon and restaurant owner who had experimented with musical shows early on with *A Beautiful Spectacular Musical Comedy*. This play by the stage manager, Charles S. Sager, was about the black person of the 20th century. The new PT opened in March 1906 with a three-act musical comedy by Sager, *The Man from 'Bam*, with book by Collins Davis, lyrics by Arthur Gillespie, and music by Joseph Jordan. That same year, an itinerant actor and vaudevillian, **Charles Gilpin**, persuaded Motts to establish a stock company there on an experimental basis. For the first season, Gilpin organized the PSC with a troupe of 11 aspiring actors. They produced plays by white authors with black casts as a departure from the stereotypical images of themselves popularized by minstrel shows for over 40 years. The PSC presented sophisticated comedies, such as Bronson Howard's *Young Mrs. Winthrop*, C. Haddon Chambers's *Captain Swift*, and Paul Potter's *Trilby*. By 1910, due to dwindling attendance, Motts reverted to the staple that had sustained the theater during the early years—the song and dance troupes. Several members of the original PSC, including Gilpin, were absorbed into these acts that eventually made the PT famous. The last PT under control of black ownership was in Tulsa, OK.

PENNY, ROBERT LEE (OBA KILONFE, 1941–2003). Professor Penny, also known as Oba Kilonfe, was a playwright, educator, and unsung hero of black theater in his stewardship of **Kuntu Repertory Theatre**, an arm of the Department of African Studies at the University of Pittsburgh. Penney lobbied for an Africana Studies Department in 1969. When it was established in 1974, Professor **Vernell A. Lillie** instituted Kuntu as a showcase for Penny's plays and student playwrights. Kuntu produced over 80 plays by such authors as Marta Effinger, Javon Johnson, **Pearl Cleage**, Wole Soyinka, and **August Wilson**. Penny ran the theater while he chaired the Department of Africana Studies at the University of Pittsburgh (1978–84).

A native of Opelika, AL, Penny was raised in Pittsburgh, PA. In 1968, he and friend Wilson started the Black Horizon Theatre. That venture was short lived, but in 1974, the two men created the Kuntu Writer's Workshop, which is still extant. Penny's plays have been produced throughout the country, including at the **Billie Holiday**

Theatre, eta Creative Arts Foundation, and **New Federal Theatre (NFT)**. Penny wrote several poems and over 30 plays. Among his plays are *Deeds of Blackness and Dance of the Blues Dead* (1967), a one-act play in two parts that Black Horizon Theatre produced on a double bill at A. Leo Weil Auditorium (August 1968) under Wilson's direction and again (November 1968) on a double bill of three one-act plays, also directed by Wilson, and *Sugar and Thomas* (1970), a melodrama in one act in which Thomas leaves his black girlfriend, Sugar, for a white woman—but Sugar gets revenge. Oduduwa Productions produced it at the Black Studies Department at the University of Pittsburgh. In the 1970s, Lillie directed three plays by Penny at the University of Pittsburgh. *Little Willie Armstrong Jones* (1973) is a full-length drama about southern racial oppression. *Good Black Don't Crack* (1977) is a full-length drama encouraging black people to move toward social freedom (April 1977). The third play was *Dianne's Heart Dries Out Still More* (July 1976). Another play Penny authored is *Who Loves the Dancer* (1976, revised 1985), a full-length play. It was produced by Kuntz at the University of Pittsburgh (1976) and the NFT in New York City (1982) and revised and presented by the NFT again (25 February–13 March 1985) and the Harry De Jury Henry Street Settlement Playhouse under the direction of Canaile Perry. Professor Penny was posthumously inducted into the International Literary Hall of Fame for Writers of African Descent.

PENUMBRA THEATRE. Located in Saint Paul, MN, Penumbra Theatre is one of the longest-running black theaters in the country. It sprang from the wellspring of the black arts movement and the **civil rights movement** and is one of the few theaters coming out of the movement that still survives today. Penumbra was founded in 1976 by **Lou Bellamy**, who obtained a $150,000 Comprehensive Employment Training Act grant to hire a core group of 20 actors. Their earliest performing space was the Martin Luther King Center in St. Paul. Today they have their own theater, a semithrust stage with a seating capacity of 260 and a yearly budget of $1.8 million. Bellamy became the artistic director, a position he still holds today. He is a graduate of Minnesota State University and also holds an M.A. from the University of Minnesota, where he has been a professor in the Theatre Department for over 20 years.

Penumbra has the singular distinction of being the host theater for the creativity of **August Wilson**. Wilson moved there in 1978 at the urging of fellow poet and director **Claude Purdy**. At Penumbra, Wilson was baptized as a playwright, stumbling along the way, but evolved as one of America's premier writers for the stage. During Wilson's stay at Penumbra, he wrote 3 of his 10-play cycle, including *Ma Rainey's Black Bottom* (1984), *Fences* (1987), and *The Piano Lesson* (1990), the last 2 of which were **Pulitzer Prize** winners. Penumbra is one of a few theaters to have produced all of Wilson's plays and practically every major African American playwright, including the works of **Charles Fuller, Endesha Mae Holland, Amiri Baraka (LeRoi Jones)**, and **Lorraine Hansberry**. The performances and other activities of the theater attract over 40,000 yearly, and an educational outreach program brings another 5,000 students yearly. The theater also sponsors a contest annually to develop aspiring young playwrights. The grand prize winner is granted a full-scale production of his or her play on the Penumbra stage. Penumbra received the 1999 Jujamycn Award for "continued excellence in the American Theatre" in recognition of its outstanding work. The award carried a cash prize of $50,000. In addition, Bellamy received a McKnight Distinguished Artist Award (2006).

PEOPLE'S THEATRE, INC. Founded in Orlando, FL, in June 1999, People's Theatre, Inc., is a nonprofit organization dedicated to community service through the arts. Their goal is to enlighten audiences and to develop motivational programs through theater. People's completed its first season with five productions. Each play carried a message about humanity. These plays were unique given their exposure to several cultures, including the Deaf, Caribbean, and Russian cultures. By the third season, African American and Yoruba cultures were highlighted. People's by then had established an official ticket outlet, website, and new board of directors. In January 2000, People's partnered with the city of Orlando's Community and Youth Department to initiate the Spot Light Workshops, a monthly interactive workshop to aid in the personal development of youths. Topics ranged from vocal/drama games to self-esteem and etiquette. For 2005–6 the season, People's offered *The Meeting: MLK and Malcolm X* (1984) by **Jeff Stetson**, a one-act play depicting a fictional meeting between Dr. Martin Luther King Jr. and Malcolm X. *Two Trains Running* (1992) by **August Wilson** is set in Memphis Lee's diner in a depressed Pittsburgh, PA, neighborhood in 1969. The patrons realize they cannot stop the two trains from running, a continuum of life and death. *School Daze*, adapted from Spike Lee's film of the same name, examines the tensions, issues, and frustrations of middle-class black youth at a southern college campus.

PERKINS, USENI EUGENE. Perkins, a playwright and sociologist, was born in Chicago. He earned a B.S. from George Williams College in 1963 and an M.S. in administration in 1966. He spent over 45 years working with troubled black youth and gangs. Perkins wrote well over 30 plays and several books of poetry and articles. He taught playwriting at Chicago State University, Malcolm X College, and Roosevelt University. His plays were produced at such theaters as eta Creative Arts Foundation, X Bag Players, Kuumba Workshop, and other venues. His landmark play is *The Image Makers*, a satirical look at the blaxploitation films of the 1970s. It ran at eta Creative Arts and was then taken overseas to the Lagos Black Arts Festival. Other plays Perkins wrote are *Turn a Black Cheek* (1965), set during the sit-in demonstrations of the 1960s; *The Legacy of Leadbelly* (1966), about the life and times of the extraordinary blues man know as Leadbelly; *Assassination of a Dream* (1967), portraying a black politician who learns a lesson about black justice; *God Is Black, But He's Dead* (1968), depicting an altercation between a black revolutionary and the black church; *Nothing but a Nigger* (1969), set in pool hall; *Cry of the Black Ghetto* (1970), centered on tensions between a black policeman and his family; *Black Is So Beautiful* (1970), a children's play; *Fred Hampton* (1970), tracking the events leading up to Hampton's death; and *Cinque* (1975), dramatizing the famous *Amistad* mutiny by Cinque in 1839 in which Africans revolted and killed the captain and seized their Spanish ship off the coast of Cuba. Perkins was founder and first president of the Chicago **Black Theatre Alliance** and a member of the **Black Theatre Network**. He was also the recipient of the Monarch Foundation Award and Black Theatre Network Playwright Award.

PERRY, LESLIE DAVID. A playwright and musical writer, Perry was based in the San Francisco Bay area. His plays have been produced at California State University/Hayward and by the Afro-American Studies Department of University of California at Berkeley. Among the plays he authored is *Rats* (1974), a musical drama in two acts. The Afro-American Studies Department at University of California at Berkeley produced it.

PERRY, SHAUNEILLE. A distinguished director, playwright, and educator, Perry has worked in the American theater for over 40 years, primarily as a director. A native of Chicago, she is a cousin of the late playwright **Lorraine Hansberry**. After graduating from Howard University in Washington, DC, she attended the Art Institute of Chicago. Perry was awarded a Fulbright fellowship, which she used to attend the prestigious Royal Academy of Dramatic Arts in London. Thus credentialed, she returned to the United States and embarked on a career during which she has directed over 100 plays at regional and professional theaters here and abroad. They include the American Place Theatre; **Black Spectrum Theatre Company, Inc.**; **Roger Furman** Theatre; Ubu Repertory Theatre; **Negro Ensemble Company**; Bermuda Black Theatre; and the **New Federal Theatre**, where she has directed over 20 productions. She has also taught at several universities and is currently a professor at Lehman College of the City University of New York. Among Perry's directing credits are *Black Girl, In Dahomey, Sty of the Blind Pig, On Striver's Row, Paul Robeson, The Taking of Miss Janie, Music, Magic, Moon on a Rainbow Shawl, Celebration, The Old Settler, Daddy Goodness*, and *Williams and Walker*. Perry is the author of a short story collection and has written six plays, all of which have been produced. Awards for Perry include four **Audience Development Committee Awards**, two Ceba Awards, the Black Rose of Excellence Award from *Encore* magazine, and the **Lloyd Richards** Directing Award from the **North Carolina Black Repertory Theatre**.

PERRY, TYLER. A playwright and producer, Perry was born in New Orleans. He exemplifies the "rags to riches" American dream story with his creation and portrayal of his outrageous, over-the-top female alter ego Madea. The character is a study in conflicting and paradoxical behavior. On one hand, she engages in domestic violence, smokes marijuana, and shoots and cuts people. On the other hand, she reinforces the notion of strength of family, love of family, and family values. Perry's first play, *I Know I've Been Changed*, failed abominably, plunging him into homelessness. Six years after the failure of *Woman, Thou Art Loosed*, he captivated black audiences. He created a structure based on broad satire, black humor, double entendres, familiar and melodramatic characters, bawdy language, gospel songs, sexy male and female leads, and religious overtones. Owing to the success of this show, Perry did not bother to change the structure of his next play and has not wavered since. *Woman, Thou Art Loosed* was equally successful. It is an adaptation of the T. D. Jakes novel of the same name. Both plays eschewed conventional regional theaters, instead playing in rented theaters on the now popular "Urban Circuit," formerly known as the "Chitlin' Circuit." Perry also rendered three of his plays to film, *Diary of a Mad Black Woman* (2002); *Madea's Family Reunion* (2003), which grossed $40 million; and his most recent film, *Why Did I Get Married?* (2007), which opened number one at the box office to more than $21 million (first weekend). Other plays Perry wrote are *I Know I've Been Changed* (1992), which deals with adult survivors of child abuse; *I Can Do Bad All by Myself* (2002); and *Meet the Browns* (2004). According to trade magazines, these ventures have grossed over $100 million for Perry.

PETERS, BROCK (1927–2005). An actor and singer, Peters was a striking character actor of the 20th century known primarily for his resonating bass voice, impeccable diction, and the variety of roles he played both in movies and on the legitimate stage. The roles were a menacing Crown in George Gershwin's opera *Porgy and Bess*, a man falsely accused of rape in the 1962 film *To Kill a Mockingbird* with Gregory Peck, and the ghetto hood in the 1965 film *The Pawnbroker* with Rod Steiger. Peters was a native of New York City and attended New York's Music and Arts High School, where he studied drama and music. He made his professional debut at the age of 16 in a 1943 production of *Porgy and Bess*. By age 18, he had worked both on and off Broadway. Later he found the need for more education and studied both at City College of New York and the University of Chicago. Along the way, Peters developed his own nightclub singing act, which he fell back on between television, film, and radio engagements.

Peters's career spanned some 50 years, during which he made over 150 movie, television, and stage appearances. They include the following: *The Wild Thornberrys*; *Star Trek: Deep Space Nine*; *The Commish*; *The Importance of Being Earnest*; *Othello*; *Cagney and Lacey*; *Murder, She Wrote*; *The Young and the Restless*; *Police Story*; *Baretta*; *Lost in the Stars*; *McCloud*; *Gunsmoke*; *Longstreet*; *Mission Impossible*; *Carmen Jones*; *Unforgivable Blackness: The Rise and Fall of Jack Johnson*; *Roots: The Next Generations*; and *The L-Shaped Room*. Because of his superb diction and voice, Peters made numerous voiceovers that include *Challenge of the Gobots*, *Galtar and the Golden Lance*, *Batman: The Animated Series*, and *Swat Kats: The Radical Squadron*. Among his awards, Peters holds a **Drama Desk Award**, an Outer Critics Circle Award, and a Screen Actors Guild Lifetime Achievement Award. He was inducted into the Black Filmmaker's Hall of Fame.

PETERSON, LOUIS (1922–98). A playwright, actor, screenwriter, television scriptwriter, and pianist, Peterson, the son of a bank employee, was born in Hartford, CT. He received his education at Morehouse College (B.A. in English and sociology, 1944), Yale University School of Drama (1944–45), and New York University (M.A. in drama, 1947). He also studied with Sanford Meisner at the Neighborhood Playhouse School of the Theatre (1948–49), Clifford Odets (playwriting, 1950–51), and Lee Strasberg (acting, 1950–52) at the Actors Studio. Peterson's landmark play, *Take a Giant Step* (1953), is a two-act semiautobiographical coming-of-age play showing the ramifications of urban flight for a black youth. It was selected as best play for the 1953–54 season by the *Bums Mantle Yearbook*. It opened in Philadelphia at the Forrest Theatre (September), where it ran for 16 performances before it opened on Broadway at the Lyceum Theatre (September–November 1953) for 76 performances. The cast featured Louis Gossett in his acting debut, **Frederick O'Neal**, **Frank Wilson**, Dorothy Carver, and **Maxwell Glanville**. *Giant Step* was also produced as a feature film (1960) starring Johnny Nash, **Ruby**

Dee, Frederick O'Neal, **Beah Richards**, and Estelle Hemsley. Thereafter, it was in great demand throughout the country at theaters catering to black audiences. Other pieces that Peterson wrote include *Class of 1958* (1954); *Joey* (1956), a full-length TV drama that was nominated for an Emmy Award (1956); and *Entertain a Ghost* (1962), a play within a play drama in two acts. Peterson was the recipient of the Benjamin Brawley Award at Morehouse College for excellence in English, an Emmy nomination (1956), and a Black Filmmakers Hall of Fame Award as a pioneer in the film industry.

THE PIANO LESSON (**1990**). **August Wilson**'s second **Pulitzer Prize** winner, *The Piano Lesson*, was hailed as one of his finest plays. It is the 4th play of Wilson's epic 10-play cycle. The play premiered at the Yale Repertory Theatre under the direction of Artistic Director **Lloyd Richards** in 1987. After a series of productions traveled around the country, which included rewrites, the play premiered on Broadway on 16 April 1990. The cast included **Charles Dutton, S. Epatha Merkerson**, and **Carl Gordon**. The plot is overlaid with historical and family significance. A brother, Boy Willie, and sister, Berniece, come into conflict over the family piano, which is inscribed with the family history. The brother wants to sell the piano to purchase the land their ancestors worked on all their lives. The sister wants to retain the piano because of its historical significance. *Lesson* was made into a movie in 1995, with Dutton and Gordon reprising their roles, while Alfre Woodard replaced Merkerson in the role of Berniece. In addition to the Pulitzer Prize, the play also won a **Tony Award** and a **Drama Desk Award**.

PINERO, MIGUEL. A Hispanic playwright of part-black heritage, Pinero was based in New York City. He is the winner of a **New York Drama Critics' Circle Award** and an **Obie Award** (1974) for *Short Eyes* (1974), a drama in two acts. A young, white inmate jailed for child molestation is assaulted and killed by the other prisoners. The New York NYSF/Public Theatre produced it (March 1974), and it was mounted by "the Family," a group composed mainly of ex-inmates under the direction of Marvin Felix Camillo. It was also made into a feature film (1977) starring Bruce Davidson. Lewis Harris produced it as a Film League Presentation with musical score by Curtis Mayfield. Pinero and musician-songwriter Curtis Mayfield appeared in supporting roles. Other plays Pinero wrote are *York Sideshow* (1975), a drama in one act that portrays ghetto life among teenagers on the Lower East Side of New York City, produced by the Space Theatre in New York (January 1975); *Straight from the Ghetto* (1976), a full-length musical revue coauthored with **Neil Harris** that combines music, poetry, and drama to provide a picture of street life in New York City's **Harlem**, produced and performed as street theater by "the Family" in New York City (summer 1976) as well as at the Theatre for the New City in New York (January 1977); and *The Sun Always Shines for the Cool* (1976), a full-length drama about a confrontation in a New York bar between two street gangs, produced by the Booth Theatre in New York City (February 1976).

PITCHER, OLIVER. Born in Massachusetts, Pitcher is a playwright, poet, and drama teacher and has acted professionally with college and little theater groups. He studied at Bard College, the Dramatic Workshop of the New School, and the **American Negro Theatre**. He taught black theater at Vassar College in the 1970s. Among his better known plays is *Spring Beginning* (1940s), a full-length poetic drama that was produced by the **115th Street Library Theatre** in **Harlem** during the 1940s and featured **Maxwell Glanville** and **Ruby Dee** in the cast. Thereafter it moved to Broadway for a successful run. *The Daisy* (pre-1975) is an avant-garde symbolic drama in two acts. The playwright explores the psyche of a black man to determine the meaning of his life. *The Meaning of Strings* (pre-1975) is a one-act drama. A puppeteer operating the strings attached to a black man posits the question, Who controls the lives of black people?

PLANT, PHILIP PAUL. Plant, a playwright, was associated with the **Frank Silvera Writers' Workshop** in New York City. His play of note is *Switcheroo* (pre-1975), a fantasy in one act dealing with issues of masculinity. *Different Strokes from Different Folks* (pre-1975) is a domestic drama in one act. A black family is thrust into conflict with issues of sexual and political values.

PLOWSHARES THEATRE COMPANY. In 1989, Gary Anderson founded Plowshares Theatre Company with Michael Garza. Established on the ideal of diversity in artistic expression, the two men formed the company to provide challenging opportunities for local artists. The name of the theater company is synonymous with its goal of "breaking new ground." Through a city arts grant and the good graces of friends and family who donated funds, Plowshares began with a production of the South African satire *Woza Albert!* in a small storefront theater in downtown Detroit. It received high praise by Lawrence DeVine, critic for the *Detroit Free Press*. Three years later, when Garza left the company, Anderson focused the cultural mission on African American theater. Since then, Plowshares has served thousands of theater lovers and those who appreciate black culture. The productions have received critical and public acclaim for giving patrons memorable experiences dealing with the joys, strengths, and the character that is the **black experience**.

A landmark moment came in 1994, with the founding of the New Voices Play Development Program. The program was designed to nurture and promote new plays by emerging and established African American writers. Now in its ninth year, New Voices has cultivated four plays for Plowshares—*Harriet Tubman Loved Somebody*; *Passages*; *Full Circle*, which received a Kennedy Center Award for new American plays; and *The Black White Man* by **OyamO**, which takes place in the heart of colonialism, an intentionally foggy area where good hearts buy into bad-hearted schemes. Evidence of their artistic quality can be seen in their reviews. In the last 12 years, the theater company has consistently received high acclaim.

POITIER, SIDNEY. With over five decades of work in the field of entertainment, Poitier has established himself as an actor extraordinaire. He has made over 50 films, directed 8 films, and had 6 television appearances. He was the first black actor to win an **Academy Award**, and he won a Screen Actors Guild Lifetime Achievement Award and Honorary Academy Award from the Academy of Motion Picture Arts and Sciences. Poitier is a native of Cat Island in the Bahamas. He was born the son of a poor potato farmer. With little formal education, he was sent to live with his brother in Miami, FL, but soon moved to New York City. His existence there was hand to mouth, and he worked mostly as a dishwasher. Answering an ad from the **American Negro Theatre (ANT)**, he was turned down because of his heavy Bahamian accent. **Frederick O'Neal** advised him to lose the accent if he was serious about the theater. Poitier did this by listening to the radio constantly and repeating the words over and over. He was accepted the second time around and trained assiduously with ANT in stagecraft, diction, and choreography. He made his stage debut as Harry Belafonte's understudy in *Days of Our Youth*. This led to a bit part in a Broadway production of *Lysistrata*. Poitier made his first appearance in films in Darryl F. Zanuck's *No Way Out* (1950). Other roles followed with *In The Heat of the Night*; *Blackboard Jungle*; *Lilies of the Field*; *The Defiant Ones*; *Porgy and Bess*; *To Sir, with Love*; *The Slender Thread*; *Guess Who's Coming to Dinner?*; **A Raisin in the Sun**; *They Call Me Mister Tibbs*; *Buck and the Preacher*; *Uptown*; *Saturday Night*; *The Jackal*; and *A Piece of the Action*. Poitier returned to the stage in a brilliant performance of Walter Lee in the 1959 groundbreaking production of **Lorraine Hansberry**'s *A Raisin in the Sun*. He parlayed that performance into one groundbreaking film after another, which culminated in numerous awards. He has received an Emmy Award, an American Film Institute Award, a British Academy of Film and Television Arts Award, a Berlin International Film Festival Award, a Cecil B. De Mille Award, a Golden Globe Award, a San Sebastian Award, and a star on Hollywood's Walk of Fame.

POLE, CHARLES (JAMAL DAVID). A playwright, lyricist, and producer, Pole was founder and chief administrator of the Everlasting Life Company in the Bronx. His goal was to promote and produce unknown talented artists in theater and other arts. His plays of note are *Super Nigger Right around the Corner* (1973), which was produced at St. Theresa's Church in New York (September 1973) and Taft United Methodist Church and Community Center in New York (December 1973), and *Forty Years-Later* (pre-1976), a domestic drama in three acts about a black family that has constant arguments and disagreements.

PORTER, REGINA M. A playwright and educator, Porter is a native of Savannah, GA. She graduated from the Tisch School of the Arts and taught at New York University. Her plays have been produced at Horizon Theatre, Playwrights Horizons, Vassar College, the Wooly Mammoth, and other theaters. Among the plays Porter has written are

A Classic Misunderstanding, Man, Woman, Dinosaur (1992); *Tripping through the Car House* (1996); and *Negro Dance Lessons* (2002). Porter received the Roger L. Stevens Award and the Doris Duke Charitable Foundation Award.

POWER, WILL. Power is an actor, rapper, and playwright. Black theater has long dealt with a wide swath of genres, and the 21st century brings yet another in the development of hip-hop theater, where Power has emerged as the primary pioneer. His birth name is William Wylie, and he was born in New York but raised on the mean streets of the Fillmore District in San Francisco. He grew up in the age of rap, break dancing, and hip hop and soon developed into a very successful rapper, making some four albums and appearing on television and in movies. He has appeared in over 30 states and 60 cities in the United States and the world, both performing and giving lectures and demonstrations. Over the years, he developed a signature style of combining rhymed lyrics, original music with a DJ, and complex choreography to tell stories of intergenerational culture, violence, HIV, homelessness, and a host of other themes related to issues that are endemic in today's society. This manifested itself with his first effort of hip-hop theater, the 2001 production of *The Gathering*, presenting a journey to the all-male sanctuaries of the pool hall, tavern, basketball court, and barbershop where black men gather and exchange the dreams, heartbreak, joys, and broken promises of their lives. Other hip-hop theater pieces by Power include the *Flow*, over the course of which Power becomes seven distinct characters, including a homeless man, a Native American, a teenage girl, and a high school teacher who are secretly chosen to pass on vital, ancient truths, and *The Seven*, based upon the Greek play *Seven against Thebes* by Aeschylus, but in Power's adaptation, the king is now an abusive father and the two sons are engaged in gang warfare in the present day. Power received a 2005 commission from the Joyce Foundation to write a play for the Children's Theatre of Minneapolis titled *Cipher*. It is the story of a volunteer soldier going to Afghanistan with his PlayStation in hand. Power has been the recipient of the New York Foundation for the Arts fellowship (2004), **Black Theatre Network** Trailblazer Award (2005), Lucille Lortel Award (2006), and Theatre Communications Group Peter Zeisler Memorial Award (2006).

PRETTYMAN, KATHLEEN COLLINS (1942–88). A playwright, novelist, and filmmaker, Collins was a native of Jersey City, NJ. She earned her B.A. from Skidmore College before she ventured overseas, where she studied French literature and film, coming away with both her M.A. and Ph.D. from the Middlebury Graduate School in Paris. Upon returning to the United States, she began work at City College of New York, where she was a professor in cinema for 15 years. She wrote almost an equal number of plays and films during her lifetime but is best remembered for being the first African American woman to write and direct a feature film, *Losing Ground* (1982). She also directed two other films, *The Cruz Brothers* and *Miss Malloy*, in 1980, and a documentary, *Gouldtown: A Mulatto Settlement*, in 1986.

Two of the six plays Collins wrote are regularly produced by black theaters across the country and grace the pages of several anthologies. Her plays include *In the Midnight Hour* (1980), depicting an upper-class black family that feels threatened by the **civil rights movement**. *Brothers* (1982) is about blacks with white blood who fear they will be discovered. The American Place Theatre produced these two plays. Collins also wrote *Remembrances*, *Only the Sky Is Free*, *Where Is Love*, and *The Reading*. She received a New York State Council on the Arts grant (1980), American Film Institute grant (1981), and National Endowment for the Arts grant.

PRICE, ROBERT EARL. A playwright and poet, Price has taken a roundabout route to the world of theater. After graduating from Clark Atlanta University, he traveled to California, where he attended the American Film Institute. Years of work in film were highlighted in being principal writer for the CBS TV series *Palmerstown* with Alex Haley. He returned to Atlanta in 1985 and in 1988 began a fruitful relationship with Seven Stages Theatre as playwright-in-residence, where he works as of this writing. During the 2004–5 academic year, he served in a position at nearby Oglethorpe University. Price's plays often explore the road taken by such musical personalities as Robert Johnson, Charlie Parker, and Thelonius Monk. This is often reflected in the titles of the plays he writes, including *Hush: Composing Blind Tom Williams*; *Come on in My Kitchen*; *Blue Monk*; *Black Cat Bones for Seven Sons*; *Yardbirds Vamp*; and *Manchild in the Promised Land*, an adaptation of the novel by Claude Brown. Price has also written three volumes of poetry, *Blues Blood, Wise Blood,* and *Blood Elegy,* and a book, *Bloodlines,* that includes poetry and short stories. His work has appeared in several black magazines. Some of the awards and honors Price has earned are the Bronze Jubilee Award, National Endowment for the Arts/Theatre Communications Group Theatre Residency Award/7 Stages Theatre (2004), American Film Institute William Wyler Award, Broadside Press Award, and Georgia Poetry Circuit Tour Award.

PROTEST THEME. During the early decades of the 20th century, a major theme among African American writers was protest against lynching, the evils of **slavery**, racial discrimination, poverty, inadequate education, and blacks in the military. These issues created uncertainty and instability within the black family and retarded social advancement. In the 1920s, the National Association for the Advancement for Colored People (NAACP) waged a nationwide campaign against lynching in its monthly publication, *Crisis* magazine, that conducted investigations and published articles and editorials assailing lynching. Each week, the organization flew a flag from its **Harlem** office with information stating how many blacks had been hanged down South. The NAACP also sponsored **Angelina Weld Grimké**'s play on the subject, *Rachel* (1916), a 1925 *Crisis* prize winner. The play is set in Chicago in the home of the Loving family. It opens on the 10th anniversary of the lynching of the father and son down South by a white mob. The mother had reluctantly withheld this secret from the other two children because she did not want them to bear this burden and to grow up hating whites. The play shows how once she tells them about this terrible tragedy, this event disrupts their lives in regard to the issues of racial discrimination, education, marriage, color stratification, and social injustice. In 1927, Paul Green's (white) antilynching play *In Abraham's Bosom* won the **Pulitzer Prize** in drama, bringing to the forefront one of the most important issues at that time.

William Wells Brown's semiautobiographical play *The Escape; or, A Leap for Freedom: Life in the South* (1856) is important historically as the first play by an African American to protest in dramatic form the evils of slavery in America; it is also the first play to be published in the United States by a black dramatist. The work is a five-act melodrama mixed with minstrel elements satirizing the institution of slavery on a Mississippi plantation during the antebellum period of the South. It comments on the inhumane treatment of slaves by their plantation owners and the slaves' indomitable will to escape.

In *A Raisin in the Sun* (1959), **Lorraine Hansberry** protests racial discrimination in housing that violated the law of restricted covenant that confined blacks to ghettos and limited accessibility and social integration. A representative of the white citizens' council offers the Younger family twice the amount of money the mother had paid for their new home in an all-white neighborhood to not move in. They refuse the offer.

Mary Burrill's *They That Sit in Darkness* is a protest against the poverty cycle perpetuated among lower-income blacks and one that raised a lot of controversy. A bright young black woman receives a scholarship to attend Tuskegee Institute in Alabama but has to forego her education to take care of the family after the mother dies giving birth to her eighth child. This issue of women's reproductive rights (an issue that was not settled until 1965) was important at the time in that this mother, like many other impoverished black women, had been denied information about birth control as a means of alleviating the poverty cycle.

Ted Ward's *Big White Fog* (1938) is a protest against educational systems in the United States. Victor, a college-educated father, and his brother-in-law Dan are unable to find work suitable to the training in agriculture they received at Tuskegee Institute; one works as a porter and the other as a bricklayer. Les, the son, is awarded a college scholarship, but the offer is withdrawn when the selection committee discovers he is black. These factors have a ripple effect on the family, in particular the daughter, who drops out of school because she does not see education as a viable alternative for her. In this play, Ward is making a commentary on why so many blacks are dissuaded from pursuing education as a means of social advancement.

Charles Fuller's Pulitzer Prize–winning drama *A Soldier's Play* is a protest against the inequitable treatment of blacks in the armed services. A black captain investigates the death of a black sergeant at a segregated U.S. military base during World War II. They are also assigned to serve whites in the military and are the first to be sent to the front lines and killed. This issue was resolved after World War II in 1946, when President Harry S. Truman desegregated the U.S. military. Ward's *Big White Fog* is also a protest against the treatment of black soldiers at home. Percy, a World War I soldier, returns home to America from France only to be stripped of his uniform, spat upon, and limited to working as a porter; he resorts to alcoholism as a psychological escape. This issue was crucial to black soldiers who were unable to find employment when they returned home from the war and did not experience the same honor and respect white soldiers received. In her play *Mine Eyes Have Seen* (1918), **Alice Dunbar-Nelson** raises the question as to whether a black soldier who fought in a segregated military in World War I should be loyal to a nation that denies him social acceptance at home.

PROVIDENCE BLACK REPERTORY THEATRE (PBRT). Based in Providence, RI, the PBRT began in 1996 in a small fourth-floor loft that formerly housed a printing shop. Donald W. King pursued his dream of starting a theater. He produced Athol Fugard's *The Island*, a searing look at prison life. With a seating capacity of less than 200 in a less than ideal location from the start, King began planning for a bigger theater. He wanted a theater large enough to raise the earned income necessary to sustain the company. He continued producing plays; making social and political contacts; meeting the movers and shakers; and building a politically shrewd, well-connected board. They made the decision to begin raising funds to purchase and renovate a building to house the theater. It dovetailed with the city's wish to revitalize a centrally located neighborhood in downtown Providence. City, state, and federal funds and gifts from corporations like America Insurance and the *Providence Journal* combined with such fund raisers as **Ossie Davis**, **Ruby Dee**, and B. B. King. They coalesced to raise the necessary $4 million to make the theater a reality. Today it is housed in a brand new building in downtown Providence and has become the cultural hub of downtown Providence.

The theater has thrived with the mounting of three main-stage productions every year and three readings of new American plays. There is a café/bar on the first floor of the theater that features poetry readings and jazz weekly. The PBRT has also launched a series of educational programs in city schools. In addition, they collaborate with the famed **Rites and Reason Theatre** at Brown University and other colleges in an M.F.A. Program. Some of the plays the PBRT presented were *Yellowman* by **Dael Orlandersmith**, *The Colored Museum* by **George C. Wolfe**, *The Mojo and the Sayso* by **Aishah Rahman**, and *The Piano Lesson* by **August Wilson**. In addition, they produced plays by Harold Pinter, Maria Irene Fornes, and Federico Garcia Lorca. King continues as artistic director, but he has added another title as executive director into the mix. Under his leadership, the theater has prospered.

PULITZER PRIZE AWARDS. Founded in 1917, this prestigious annual award was named after Hungarian-born Joseph Pulitzer (1847–1911). He garnered a reputation as an innovative American journalist and newspaper publisher of the *New York World* and *St. Post-Dispatch* and crusader against private and public corruption. Pulitzer made a $2 million endowment in his will to establish a School of Journalism at Columbia University. An amount of $500,000 was to be applied to prizes and scholarships for excellence in literature, drama, poetry, music, and photography. It was administered by a 19-member board of leading editors or newspaper publishers, the president of Columbia University, and persons of distinction who were not journalists or editors. Among the African American playwrights to receive the award in drama, **Charles Gordone** was the first to win for *No Place to Be Somebody* in 1970. Thereafter **Charles Fuller** won for *A Soldier's Play* in 1982, **August Wilson** for *Fences* in 1987 and *The Piano Lesson* in 1990, and **Suzan-Lori Parks** for *Topdog/Underdog* in 2002—the first black female recipient.

PURDY, CLAUDE. Purdy is an independent director who has worked at regional theaters across the country. In the industry, he is credited with influencing **August Wilson** in becoming a playwright and providing a comfortable, creative environment to make it happen—the theater. He has directed plays at the American Conservatory Theatre in San Francisco; Cleveland Playhouse; Arizona Repertory Theatre; Intiman Theatre in Seattle; Tyrone Guthrie Theatre in Minneapolis; GeVa Theatre in Rochester, NY; Alabama Shakespeare Festival; and

Penumbra Theatre in Saint Paul, MN, among others. A graduate of Southern University, Purdy studied with Philip Glass, Joanne Akailaitis, and Lee Bruer. Abroad, he worked and studied at the American Theatre in Paris, France, and the University of Ibadan in Nigeria with John Pepper Clark and Wole Soyinka. He was also a playwright-in-residence for 10 years at the Penumbra Theatre, where he specialized in works of the African American canon. Purdy has directed most of Wilson's plays, including *Fences, Jitney, Joe Turner's Come and Gone*, and *Ma Rainey's Black Bottom*. His awards include the **New York Drama Critics' Circle Award** and a Theatre Communications Group Award.

PURLIE **(1970).** This is a two-act musical version of **Ossie Davis's** best-known play *Purlie Victorious* (1961), a satire on black and white stereotypes in the South. In it, a black preacher has to outwit a plantation owner to get his church back. *Purlie* opened at the Broadway Theatre (15 March 1970) under the direction of Philip Rose with book by Davis, Rose, and Peter Udell; composition by Gary Geld; and lyrics by Udell. It enjoyed great success, running for 688 performances. The star-laden cast featured Cleavon Little (Purlie), Melba Moore (Lutibelle), Linda Hopkins (church soloist), **Novella Nelson** (Missy), Sherman Hemsley (Gitlow), C. David Colson (Charlie), Helen Martin (Idella), and John Heffernan (Ol' Cap'n). Subsequently, *Purlie* was moved to the Winter Garden Theatre (15 December 1970), then to the American National Theatre and Academy Theatre, where it closed (7 November 1971). Thereafter Rose took *Purlie* on a national tour (20 November 1971–May 1972) to the Shubert Theatre in Philadelphia. He returned the show to Broadway (27 December 1972–7 January 1973) for 14 performances and 2 reviews before he continued the national tour. A later production by the Repertory Company of Virginia Museum Theatre opened in Richmond, VA (8 November 1974) under the direction of Albert B. Reyes, with choreography by Nat Horne. Little and Moore both received a **Tony Award** and **New York Drama Desk Critics' Award**, and the play received *Variety's* Drama Critics' Poll. Moore also won a Theatre World Award.

PURLIE VICTORIOUS **(1961).** This comedy by **Ossie Davis** satirizes racial stereotypes of the old South. It opened at the height of the **civil**

rights movement on 28 September 1961 at the Cort Theatre on Broadway. The cast featured Davis in the title role, with **Ruby Dee** and Godfrey Cambridge in supporting roles. The play was a success, running some 261 performances. The thinly contrived plot line of reclaiming a family inheritance was a vehicle for Davis to poke fun at some of the racial attitudes of the South, including an old plantation owner and his faithful "darky." It was a welcome relief from many of the plays of that period that espoused hatred, violence, and black nationalism. In 1963, the play was adapted into the film *Gone Are the Days*, with Davis writing the screenplay and most of the original cast reprising their roles. In 1970, the play was also made into the musical *Purlie*. It opened on 15 March 1970 and played through 6 November 1971, running for 688 performances. The musical won two **Tony Awards**, the Featured Actor Award, the Theatre World Award, and the **Drama Desk Award**.

– R –

RACHEL **(1916).** This full-length play by **Angelina Weld Grimké** addresses one of the most pressing issues at the turn of the century—lynching. A sensitive young black teacher whose greatest love is for children is traumatized by the discovery of a lynching 10 years earlier and by the hostile racial attitudes against young black children, especially the darker ones. She is faced with a dilemma as to whether she should marry and bring children into this hostile environment. The Drama Committee of the National Association for the Advancement of Colored People first produced *Rachel* in Washington, DC (March 1916), and a year later in Boston and New York City.

A RAISIN IN THE SUN **(1959). Lorraine Hansberry**'s prize-winning play was the catalyst that propelled the black arts movement and in the process became an American classic. It focuses on a poor black family's search for the American dream as they confront issues of manhood, nationalism, racism, abortion, values, religion, and identity while wrestling with the notion of moving into an all-white neighborhood in Chicago. Hansberry drew the subject matter from her life experience. Her father filed a suit against the city of Chicago for the restrictive housing covenant law. Subsequently, he had to take the case to the U.S. Supreme Court before he won his case against the city. *A Raisin in the Sun* played New Haven, CT; Chicago; and Philadelphia prior to opening in New York in 1959 at the Ethel Barrymore Theatre, where it ran for 530 performances. Overnight it became a raging success, propelled by dynamic performances from **Sydney Poitier**, **Diana Sands**, **Ruby Dee**, **Ivan Dixon**, and **Claudia McNeil**. The play won a **New York Drama Critics' Circle Award** and four **Tony Awards** for best play, director, actor, and actress. In 1961, it was made into a movie, with Poitier, Sands, and McNeil reprising their stage roles.

RAHMAN, AISHAH (VIRGINIA HUGHES). A playwright and educator, Rahman is known for her avant-garde dramatic style. She was born and raised as a foster child in **Harlem** and began writing plays in the sixth grade while attending P.S. 184 High School. Rahman pursued a political science degree at Howard University (B.S., 1968). It took her another 17 years, but she earned an M.A. in playwriting and dramatic writing from Goddard College (1985). She taught at Nassau Community College in New York for 10 years and at Amherst College in New York. She also headed the Henry Street Settlements Playwriting Program at the **New Federal Theatre** for five years. In addition, she was founder and editor of *NuMuse*, an annual journal of new plays, and cofounder of the Blackberry Production Company. Since 1992, she served on the faculty at Brown University as a professor of creative writing.

Rahman's career as a playwright began with *Lady Day: A Musical Tragedy* (1972). It is a full-length musical tragedy centering on the life and times of legendary jazz singer Billie Holiday. Rahman wrote the book for the musical and **Archie Shepp** the music. The Chelsea Theatre in Brooklyn produced it (17 October–November 1972) for 34 performances under the direction of **Paul Carter Harrison**. Like *Lady Day*, many of Rahman's plays deal with the lives of African American cultural icons, such as jazz musician Charlie Parker in *Unfinished Women Cry in No Man's Land While a Bird Dies in a Gilded Cage* (1977), a play in 12 scenes set in the hide-a-wee home for unwed mothers who must decide whether to keep their babies or give them up for adoption on the same day that Parker (known as "bird") dies. The show opened at the New York Shakespeare Festival/Public Theatre in June 1977. It also toured a production around New York City under the direction of Bill Duke. It received the **Audience Development Committee (Audelco) Award** (1976). *Tales of Madame Zora* (1986) is a full-length blues musical on the life of **Zora Neale Hurston**, the black folklorist and novelist of the Harlem Renaissance. The Ensemble Studio produced it in New York City (February–March 1986) under **Glenda Dickerson**'s direction. *The Opera of Marie Laveau* (1989, later renamed *Anybody Seen Marie Laveau?*) is about the life of voodoo queen Marie Laveau.

Rahman's other representative pieces include *The Jukebox* (1974), a drama in one act about the problems of high school integration; *The Mama, A Folk's Tale* (1974), a drama in one act based on the relationship between George Jackson, a political prisoner, and his mother; *Portrait of a Blues Lady* (1974), a memory play in one act about a great blues singer contemplating a comeback; *The Lady and the Tramp* (1976), a drama in one act exploring how a black man and woman feel alienated by society; *The Transcendental Blues* (1976), a drama in one act that was a companion piece to the author's *The Lady and the Tramp* about a middle-aged woman whose young lover abandons her, which was produced by the Frederick Douglass Creative Arts Centre in New York (August 1976); and *In Men's Eyes* (1976), a 90-minute TV drama about a black high school principal who commits suicide during a school integration crisis. Other plays Rahman authored are *The Mojo and the Sayso* (1987); *Only in America* (1993); and *Chewed Water* (2001), her memoir. Rahman's works have received little attention in mainstream American theater venues because her plays are often regarded as "underground classics." Still, these works have enjoyed wide popularity off Broadway, at regional theaters, and at college/university venues, such as the Brooklyn Academy of Music, **Joseph Papp**'s NYSF/Public Theatre, the Manhattan Theatre Club, the **St. Louis Black Repertory Theatre**, **La MaMa Experimental Theatre Club**, and Hartford Stage. Rahman has received fellowships from the New York Foundation of the Arts and the Rockefeller Foundation, a Theatre Communications Group collaborative grant for artists, the Doris Abramson Playwriting Award for *Mojo and the Sayso*, and three Audelco Awards.

RANDOLPH, JEREMY. A playwright, director, composer, and literary agent, Randolph resided in New York City. He cofounded with Georgia Nicholas the Theatre of the Incentive, the Nicholas Literary Agency, and Rannick-Amuru Press (also known as Rannick Press and Amuru Press). Among the plays Randolph wrote are *Cartouche* (1970), a semimusical drama in three acts with book, music, and lyrics by Randolph, Jerry Stevenson, and Richard Bone, respectively, which was produced at Cami Hall (formerly Judson Hall) in New York City for two performances (November 1970), and *Tribute to Sojourner Truth* (1979), about the American Civil War activist, coauthored with **June Jordan** and produced (1979) at the New York Shakespeare Festival/Public Theatre under the direction of **Ntozake Shange.**

RASHAD, PHYLICIA ALLEN-. Actor, director, producer, Rashad is one of the most well known actresses on the planet thanks to an eight-year run as Claire Huxtable, Bill Cosby's wife on NBC TV's *The Cosby Show.* She has been equally prominent on the American stage. In 2004, she became the first African American actress to win the Tony Award as Best Actress for her performance as Lena Younger in the Broadway revival of *A Raisin in the Sun.* She repeated the feat in 2005 for her Broadway performance as Aunt Ester in August Wilson's *Gem of the Ocean.*

Overall, Rashad has appeared on Broadway eight times. She was one of the few woman to direct an August Wilson play, *Gem of the Ocean* for the Seattle Repertory Theatre in 2007.

Rashad was born as Phylicia Allen in Houston Texas. Rashad is her married name. A gifted family, her parents moved to Mexico to escape American racism. Her father was a dentist, her mother a writer who was once nominated for a Pulitzer Prize, her brother a jazz musician, and her sister, Debbie Allen, a world-renowned dancer and choreographer. Rashad received a B.F.A. (magna cum laude) in theater from Howard University. Her early work was in theater, where she appeared both On and Off-Broadway. She performed for the **Negro Ensemble Company**, New York Shakespeare Festival, Roundabout Theatre Company, Arena Stage, the NYST/Public Theatre, Center Theatre Group, and many others. She has appeared in such disparate stage efforts as *Zooman and the Sign*, *The Cherry Orchard*,

Into the Woods, The Wiz, Jelly's Last Jam, Media, Dreamgirls, Sons Fathers of Sons, Cymbeline, and *Blue.*

On television, she has appeared in more than 70 productions either as an actress, a producer, or herself. They include *Cosby; Murder, She Wrote; The Old Settler; Once Upon Time When We Were Colored; The Love Boat; The Kennedy Center Honor; The Rosie O'Donnell Show; Bob Hope's High Flying Birthday; One Life to Live; Santa Barbara; Bill Cosby Salutes Alvin Ailey;* and numerous appearences on the annual Tony Awards show celebrating excellence in the American theater.

Rashad made her ninth appearance on Broadway in 2008 in a star-studded, all-black production of Tennessee Williams play, *Cat on a Hot Tin Roof.* Rashad played Big Momma opposite **James Earl Jones** as Big Daddy.

Rashad is a member of the Screen Actors Guild, American Federation of Television, and Actors Equity Association. She is also a board member of the Alliance Theatre in Atlanta.

REDMOND, EUGENE B. A poet, publisher, critic, and teacher, Redmond has written and adapted a number of poetic works for the stage. He was born in Saint Louis, MO, and reared in East Saint Louis, IL. He attended Southern Illinois University (B.A. in English literature, 1964) and Washington University (M.A., 1966). His poetry and writings have appeared in numerous black publications, and he has edited the works of the late Henry Dumas (1974). Redmond has taught at institutions of higher education—as a visiting lecturer in Afro-American literature at Webster College (summer 1968), poet-in-residence and director of language arts workshops at Southern Illinois University (1968–69), writer-in-residence and lecturer in Afro-American studies at Oberlin College (1969–70), English professor and poet-in-residence with the Ethnic Studies Department at California State University at Sacramento (1970), and writer-in-residence at Southern University in Baton Rouge, LA (summers of 1971 and 1972). Redmond consulted numerous public, private, and community institutions and educational programs.

Redmond's representative plays include *The Face of the Deep* (1971), a full-length poetic ritual. It utilizes song, dance, music, and the works of several black poets and singers to extol the black mystique of endurance, strength, and power. It was produced at California State University in Sacramento (winter 1971) and at Southern University in Baton Rouge (summer 1971) under the author's direction. *9 Poets with the Blues* (also produced as *Poets with the Blues*, 1971) is a full-length poetic ritual exploring the concept of blues through the work of nine poets. It was produced at California State University in Sacramento (May 1971) and performed at several other Northern California sites during spring and summer of that year under the author's direction. *River of Bones* (1972) is a full-length poetic ritual combining drums, music, and dance to capture the roots of black tradition. California State University at Sacramento produced it (late fall 1972). *The Night John Henry Was Born* (1972) is a full-length poetic ritual that incorporates the work of several black poets interspersed with choral interludes. It celebrates the legend of John Henry, the black folk hero, as a symbol of the struggles and endurance of black people. It was produced at Southern University, Baton Rouge (summer 1972), and at Cliff Top, WV, during the second annual John Henry Memorial Blues and Gospel Jubilee (summer 1974). *Will I Still Be Here Tomorrow?* (1973) is a surrealistic ritualistic eulogy with music about a 15-year-old who was killed but speaks from the afterworld about what he could have been. It was produced at California State University at Sacramento and on KVOR-TV (spring and summer 1973). **Frank Silvera Writers' Workshop** gave it a public reading at the Martinique Theatre in New York (May 1975). *Music and I Have Come at Last* (1974) is a full-length theatrical collage adaptation on the prose and poetry of the late Henry Dumas. California State University at Sacramento produced it (1974) with the Sons/Ancestors Players. *There's a Wiretap in My Soup; or, Quit Bugging Me* (1974) is a morality play with music in one act, satirizing the Watergate scandal. It was produced in Miller's Park, Sacramento, before 4,000 people during the Juneteenth celebration (June 1974) and commissioned by the Sacramento Area Black Caucus. It received several academic, literary, community service, and performance awards.

REDWOOD, JOHN HENRY (1943–2003). An actor and playwright, Redwood was a towering presence in the world of black theater, both physically and professionally as a gifted actor, director, and playwright. He died at age 60 but not before establishing his credentials as an actor of both stage and screen and also writing some of the most provocative theater of the 20th century. His Broadway credits include *Guys and Dolls* and **The Piano Lesson**. Other plays he performed in across the regional theater circuit include *Macbeth*, *A Lesson before Dying*, and *One Flew over the Cuckoo's Nest*. His movie credits include *Mr. Holland's Opus*, *Passion Fish*, and *Boys and Girls*.

Redwood's most successful play is *The Old Settler* (1998). Leslie Uggams starred in the comedy set in 1940s **Harlem** about two aging churchgoing sisters, one of whom has decided to become "settled" and live her life without the intimacy of a male companion. Uggams starred in its 1997 premier. *Settler* became an instant hit, playing at such theaters as the Long Wharf, GeVa Theatre, McCarter Theatre, and other regional entities. *American Theatre* magazine reported it as one of the 10 most produced plays for the 1998–99 and 1999–2000 seasons. The play garnered countless awards, including the Julie Harris Playwright Award, the American Theatre Critics Association Award, and the Beverly Hills Theatre Guild Award. Redwood's other widely produced play is *No Niggers, No Jews, No Dogs!* (2003). Set in 1949 rural Halifax, NC, a black woman whose husband is away frequently is left home alone struggling to raise their daughter and to save her marriage. The play addresses issues of anti-Semitism and racism. Philadelphia Theatre Company coproduced the world premier with Primary Stages in New York. Other plays Redwood wrote are *An Old Soul*, *Mark VIII XXXL*, *A Sunbeam*, *Acted within Proper Departmental Procedure*, *What If You're the One*, and *But I Can't Go Alone*. Redwood was a U.S. Marine and held an M.A. in both religion and history and a Ph.D. in religion. He won an **Audience Development Committee Award** for his play *A Sunbeam* (1986) and received a McDonald's Literary Award for another play, *Acted within Proper Departmental Procedure*. Redwood died of heart disease at his home on Fernon Street in South Philadelphia.

RICHARDS, BEAH (1920–2000). An actor and playwright, Richards was one of the great ladies of American theater. In a career spanning almost 50 years, she played a variety of roles at a time when there were few opportunities for women of color. Richards was born in Vicksburg, MS. She graduated from Dillard University in 1948 and took flight to New York City to begin her acting career. Her first break came in 1953 when she was cast in **Louis Peterson**'s play *Take a Giant Step*, which played off Broadway and then enjoyed a lengthy run on Broadway. Despite her success, other parts were not forthcoming readily. She persevered, however, until she landed roles on television and in plays, such as *The Miracle Worker*, *The Little Foxes*, and *The Amen Corner*. It was *Amen*, produced in 1964 by **Frank Silvera**, that jump-started the second phase of her career. It coincided with the **civil rights movement** and laws that struck down many discriminatory practices.

Richards's career took off, and the records show over 60 movie and television credits to her name, including appearances on *The Cosby Show*; *Murder, She Wrote*; *L.A. Law*; and *The Practice*. She is best remembered as **Sidney Poitier**'s mother in the film *Guess Who's Coming to Dinner* with Katherine Hepburn and Spencer Tracy. An early militant and feminist, Richards used the term *black* in self-description long before the term *Negro* faded into obscurity. As a playwright, she wrote three one-woman plays that she would perform in theaters, the college circuit, or wherever the money would lead. Her plays are *One Is a Crowd*, *A Black Woman Speaks*, and *An Evening with Beah Richards*. Richards was honored with the **Paul Robeson** Pioneer Award, a National Association for the Advancement of Colored People Image Award, the Los Angeles Pan African Film Festival Lifetime Achievement Award, and an Emmy Award for her 2000 role in the episodic TV series *The Practice*. In 2003, actress Lisa Gay Hamilton produced and directed a documentary on the life of Richards titled *A Black Woman Speaks*.

RICHARDS, LLOYD (1919–2006). From the midpoint of the 20th century to the dawn of the 21st century, Richards, a director, administrator, and producer, was a towering giant of the theatrical world—black or white. In a career spanning over six decades, he was head of the Actor Training Program at New York University, dean of the Yale Drama School, artistic director of the Yale Repertory Theatre, and for over 30 years was the first artistic director of the Eugene O'Neill Playwrights Center, its first. He has also been credited with nurturing and launching the mercurial career of the two-time **Pulitzer Prize**–winning playwright **August Wilson**.

Richards was the child of Jamaican immigrants living in Toronto who moved to Detroit when he was 10 years old. After graduation from Wayne State University and a two-year stint in the air force, he moved to New York to embrace a theatrical career. His work with Paul Mann and Morris Carnovsky, in which he embraced the whole canon of classical and contemporary theater, led to many acting roles. His big break came in 1959, when he directed the groundbreaking production of **Lorraine Hansberry**'s *A Raisin in the Sun*. He became the first African American to direct a Broadway show. The play was a major success and established Richards in the forefront of American theatrical directors. Over the years, he directed more than 15 Broadway shows. He subsequently became professor of theater and cinema at Hunter College and head of the Actor Training Program at New York University (1966).

In 1969, Richards was appointed artistic director of the Eugene O'Neill Playwrights Center, a position he held for over 30 years. His reforms at the center were legendary and included room, board, and stipends for playwrights; staged readings with professional actors; the initiation of a European-oriented Dramaturge Program; and pathways to professional productions for promising playwrights. He is credited with discovering such playwrights as John Guare, Wendy Wasserstein, Athol Fugard, Lee Blessing, and August Wilson. His association with Wilson led to Richards directing the first 6 plays of Wilson's epic 10-play canon spanning every decade of the 20th century. He was also a father figure to Wilson. He helped Wilson structure his long poetical texts into leaner vehicles suitable for the stage. The two men developed and refined a producer-sharing process where each new play would be produced at five nonprofit theaters around the country. All of the Wilson and Richard's collaboration of plays were produced on Broadway.

In 1979, Richards was appointed dean of the Yale School of Drama and artistic director of the Yale Repertory Theatre. Richards juggled these two roles with his duties as head of the Eugene O'Neill Center while directing plays on Broadway. He rapidly became one of the more powerful and influential men in the American theater. During his lifetime, Richards served as president of the Theatre Communications Group, the Society of Stage Directors and Choreographers, and the Theatre Development Fund. He also served on the National Endowment for the Arts and the Connecticut Commission on the Arts. Richards's honors and awards are quite lengthy, but a partial list includes the **Tony Award**, National

Medal of Arts, **Audience Development Committee** Pioneer Award, Frederick Douglass Award, Fulbright fellowship, Helen Hayes Award, Dorothy and Lillian Gish Award, **Drama Desk Award**, Outer Critics Circle Award, Pell Award for achievement in the arts, and Actors Equity **Paul Robeson** Award.

RICHARDSON, WILLIS (1889–1977). Richardson was a pioneer playwright and drama anthologist, essayist, poet, and short-story writer. He was best known as the first African American to have a serious dramatic play produced on Broadway, *The Chip Woman's Fortune* (1923). A prolific black playwright of the early 20th century, Richardson has written some 48 plays, more than half of which have been published and included in anthologies and collections. Reportedly, Richardson was born in Wilmington, NC, where his family lived until they were forced to move to Washington, DC, after the Wilmington Riots of 1899. He graduated from the M Street School (later known as Dunbar High School) in Washington, where several of his teachers were important influences on his writing, such as playwright **Mary Burrill** and **Angelina Weld Grimké**, with whom he studied playwriting by correspondence from 1916 to 1918. Richardson was a member of **Georgia Douglas Johnson**'s Washington, DC, literary group the Saturday Nighters and one of the founders of the Washington branch of Dr. **W. E. B. DuBois**'s **Krigwa Players** based in New York City. His earliest plays were published mainly in *Crisis* and *The Brownies' Book*, both magazines affiliated with the National Association for the Advancement of Colored People. He also edited two major drama anthologies and published works of several playwrights.

Many of Richardson's plays deal with the lives of urban blacks and show the influence of the folk tradition of Ridgely Torrence and Paul Green. One of his more recognized plays is *The Deacon's Awakening* (1920), a social problem play in one act about women's suffrage. A church deacon plans to take action against women who attend a Voting Society meeting until he learns his wife and daughter are active members. It was produced in St. Paul, MN (1921). *The Dragon's Tooth* (1921) is a children's fairytale in one act. Children are trying to steal a magic dragon's tooth with the secret of the future written on it. *The Chip Woman's Fortune* (1922), the first serious black one-act play to be produced on Broadway, is a folk drama. An out-of-work store porter in a small southern town believes a street person, an old woman who sells chips and bits of coal, will loan him the money from the fortune she has hidden. The Ethiopian Art Theatre of Chicago (also called the Chicago Folk Theatre) produced it in Chicago (January 1923). It opened on Broadway at the Frazee Theatre (May 1923) for a week. The **Afro-American Studio of Acting and Speech** also produced it in New York City (1973). *Mortgaged* (1924) is a race-propaganda play in one act. Two brothers have different ideologies about race. One wants to contribute to the uplift and advancement of his people; the other wants to exploit them for personal financial gain. It was the first play by an African American playwright produced by the Howard University Players. *Compromise* (1925) is a folk drama in one act about black and white relationships in the Deep South. A young black man who becomes fed up with the compromises black folk have to make in their dealings with whites decides to take matters into his own hands after his sister is impregnated by the son of a white family. The Gilpin Players at **Karamu Repertory Theatre** produced it in Cleveland, OH (February 1925), the first play by a black playwright to be produced by the players. *The Broken Banjo* (1925) is a folk tragedy in one act about a selfish banjo player who murders a man for breaking his banjo. It earned first prize in the *Crisis* Contest Awards (1925). *Banjo* was produced by the Krigwa Players of New York City (August 1925 and May 1926) and the Dixwell (House) Players at Yale University Theatre, New Haven, CT (March 1928), where the author won the Schwab Cup. Various college and university groups also presented the play. It was published in two installments in *Crisis* (February 1926 and March 1926).

Other representative plays Richardson authored are *The Bootblack Lover* (1926); *The King's Dilemma* (1926); *Rooms for Rent* (1926); *Flight of the Natives* (1927); *The Idle Head* (1927); *The Wine Seller* (1927); *The Black Horseman* (1929); *The House of Sham* (1929); *Antonio Maceo* (1935); *In Menelik's Court* (1935); *Attucks, the Martyr* (1935); *The Three Musketeers and the Count of Monte Cristo, Near Calvary* (1935); *Miss or Mrs.* (1941); *The Gypsy's Finger Ring* (1956); *Magic* (1956); *The New Santa Claus* (1956); and *The Visiting Lady* (1967). Richardson won the *Crisis* Contest Awards twice (1925, 1926), as well as the Schwab Cup at Yale University (1928). He retired as a

U.S. civil service clerk in 1954 from U.S. Department of Engraving and Printing. He died in Washington, DC, at age 88.

RIPE AND READY PLAYERS (RRP). This senior citizen theater group was founded by Suzanne Carter, a University of Tennessee theater professor in Chattanooga, TN. Initially the RRP was funded by Senior Neighbors, a social services agency, and Allied Arts of Chattanooga. Carter selected a cast and worked with the eight members to gather material for the senior troupe, ranging in age between 62 and 95. None of them had previous stage experience. She collected information from company members through conversations about life experiences, learning what was important to them, to develop through improvisation 3- to 12-minute scenes with humor combining musical numbers with thought-provoking skits. Carter wrote the stories, composed songs and music for the cast, and played piano for the group. The vignettes deal with issues of the elderly from their past, a mix of improvisation and learned text. They performed at local theaters, conferences, college campuses, public schools, reunions, festivals, and political events. By 1987, the group toured these sites in their own bus. By 1998, they were playing before sold-out audiences at such venues as the Piccolo Spoleto Festival in Charleston, SC. This is truly a diverse group of African Americans and whites, rural and city dwellers, former executives and domestic workers. Because of their background, the troupe was able to adapt each show to its audience without losing its energy and essence.

RITES AND REASON THEATRE (RRT). Back in the late 1960s, student unrest fomented by the **civil rights movement** became a fait accompli. It struck colleges and universities across the land. In 1968, at Brown University, an Ivy League university in existence since 1864, African American students walked out of classes, demanding institutional change, including an African American Studies Program. In 1969, the university hired Charles Brown, an African American with a doctorate from Brown, to become the first chair of the Afro-American Studies Program. Brown in turn hired the distinguished **George Houston Bass** to head the Theatre Department. Bass, with degrees from Fisk University, New York University, and Yale and over 20 plays under his belt, introduced what was to become the research-to-performance method into the curriculum. The method was developed and honed in Group Study Project 21, with 15 undergraduate students. Over time, the group was enlarged to include scholars and playwrights. Specific cultural traditions and rituals were identified and translated into theatrical forms, which in turn were developed into plays. Bass then started the RRT as a vehicle to rehearse and perform plays that evolved from this process. Since then, RRT has developed and produced over 80 new scripts. These range in subject matter from stories of Armenian American women and their families to stories of black soldiers in the Revolutionary War. The RRT evolved into a research-and-development theater dedicated to providing a voice to the disparate cultural values and realities of the African American diaspora. While their mission had been to develop new works for the American stage reflective of the African American experience, over the years, their goal expanded to embrace expressions of other cultural experiences. The program was immensely successful over the years and attracted such writers as **Ray Aranha, Ed Bullins, Ossie Davis, Ruby Dee, P. J. Gibson, OyamO, Adrienne Kennedy, Elmo Terry-Morgan, Ifa Bayeza, Dominic Taylor,** and **J. E. Franklin**. The RRT had been widely supported with grants from the state, the Ford Foundation, Rockefeller Foundation, Nellie Mae Foundation, National Endowment for the Arts, and National Endowment for the Humanities.

***THE RIVER NIGER* (1972). Joseph Walker**'s *The River Niger* was the first play the **Negro Ensemble Company (NEC)** moved to Broadway and toured. The show also garnered accolades for the playwright. Set in **Harlem**, it is a three-act drama on the **black experience**. A frustrated father, a painter and poet who is psychologically devastated because of racial restraints, sacrifices his dreams for his son's aspirations. The NEC first produced it at the St. Marks Playhouse (December 1972–March 1973) for 120 performances before they moved it to the Brooks Atkinson Theatre on Broadway (March–November 1970) for a total of 400 performances. It also toured nationally (1973–74). **Douglas Turner Ward**, Gil Lewis, and Ed Cambridge all played the father at one time or another. Others in the cast were Robin Braxton, Hilda Haynes, Albert LeVeau, Les Roberts, Dean Irby, **Charles Brown, Carl Gordon**, Kim Sullivan,

Charles Grant-Green, and Taurean Blacque. Among the 1975 cast were Cicely Tyson, **James Earl Jones**, Louis Gossett, **Frances Foster**, **Graham Brown**, Grenna Whitaker, Saundra McClain, **Charles Weldon**, and Dean Irby. *Niger* was also adapted as a feature film (1976) by Sidney Beckerman under the direction of Krishna Shah. It was the recipient of the **Drama Desk Award** and the Burns Mantle Theatre Yearbook best play of the season (1972–73). The play was also showered with such awards as the **Tony Award**, **Obie Award**, and **Audience Development Committee Award**, as well as an Obie for actors Douglas Turner Ward and Roxie Roker. Walker was honored with the Drama Desk Award as the most promising playwright of the 1972–73 season for *Niger*.

ROBESON, PAUL (1898–1976). Active between the early 1920s and the late 1960s, Robeson was a celebrated stage and screen actor, singer, **civil rights** activist, and symbol of racial pride and black **manhood**. Born in Princeton, NJ, Robeson was the son of a Presbyterian minister who was a former slave and a school teacher who died when he was nine. Robeson received his education at Lincoln University in Pennsylvania and Rutgers University (B.A., 1919). There he was the debating team champion, class valedictorian, and member of Phi Beta Kappa and excelled in athletics. He lettered all four years in football, receiving all-American honors twice. He continued his education at the Columbia University Law School (L.L.B.) in New York City. During this time, he was in great demand as an athlete and on the American stage. He played professional football briefly and sang in the chorus of *The Plantation Revue*. He was hired for his first acting role in Ridgely Torrence's *Simon the Cyrenian*, sponsored by the Colored Player's Guild of the **Harlem** YWCA (c. 1920) under the direction of Dora Cole Norman (**Bob Cole's** sister). Eugene O'Neill saw this production and cast Robeson in the revival of *The Emperor Jones* in 1925 as Brutus Jones and also as Jim Harris in *All God's Chillun' Got Wings* in 1934. The two shows played in repertory.

Robeson made his Broadway debut in *Taboo* (1922), Mary Hoyt Wiborg's play, opposite Margaret Wycherly, who played the character of a white voodoo queen. The play came under criticism from both black and white audiences. It ran briefly before it was taken to London, where Robeson played opposite the great Flora Robeson. In

1928, he played in the role of Joe in the London production of *Show Boat*, where he first sang "Old Man River," the song with which he became identified throughout his career for changing the offensive lyrics. Concurrently, as Robeson was making his mark onstage, his career in films and as a concert singer was also advancing. Oscar Micheaux, a black filmmaker, cast Robeson to play the dual role of identical twins, one a preacher, the other a con artist, in *Body and Soul* (1924). In the 1930s, he appeared in such talking films as *Emperor Jones* (1933), *Show Boat* (1936), *Sanders of the River* (1935), and *King Solomon's Mines* (1937). Earlier, he was also invited to the Soviet Union in 1934 on a concert tour. There he was introduced to the communist ideology that would cause him to lose his passport and to be banned from performing in concerts for nine years until 1958. Back in the United States in 1943, Robeson's landmark performance on Broadway in Shakespeare's *Othello* opposite the legendary Uta Hagen was described by critics as "stunning and provocative, violent and tender." The show ran for 296 performances, a record for a Shakespearean play on Broadway. Robeson received many awards and honorary degrees. Among them were the Donaldson Award (for *Othello*, 1940), **Spingarn Medal Award** (1945), Academy of Arts and Letters' Gold Medal for best diction in the American theater (1940s), Stalin Peace Prize (1952), College Football Hall of Fame (posthumously, 1955), and the first Actor's Equity Paul Robeson citation (1974). Robeson died in Philadelphia at age 77.

ROBEY THEATRE. In 1994, Danny Glover and fellow actor Bennet Guillory founded Robey Theatre in Los Angeles. The theater was named in honor of the mythic stage and screen actor, singer, and **civil rights** activist **Paul Robeson**, a true renaissance man of the 20th century. The theater was founded to provide opportunity and access to actors and playwrights who have lacked a forum where their work can be developed in collaboration with their peers. Robey is different in that they have not committed themselves to being a yearround, grind-it-out, producing entity. While they originally committed to produce two plays a year, the reality is that by selective design, they have produced only six plays during their first 10 years. Rather, the emphasis focuses on acting workshops under the direction of Guillory and a playwrights' workshop under the direction of veteran playwright Silas Jones, where plays are developed over time and are fully produced only when judged suitable. The acting and playwriting workshops are held on Monday evenings at the Raven Playhouse in North Hollywood. Robey has no venue of its own, but produces plays at various locations in the City of Angels. Robey is also unique in terms of collaborating with other theaters in the production of selected plays. For the production of *Yohen*, they shared collaboration with East West Players, the oldest Asian American theater in America. Robey also shared resources with the Greenway Arts Alliance to mount Levy Lee Simon's epic trilogy *For The Love of Freedom*, a sprawling costume drama of the Haitian revolution with over 30 speaking roles. Other plays Robey produced were *Bee-Luther-Hatchee* by Thomas Gibbons; *Souls on Fire* by Patrick Sheane Duncan; and *The Last Season*, Christopher Moore's searing look at the early days of black baseball. Since the organization does not produce revenue through productions, they have relied on the largesse of Hollywood studios, corporate and individual contributions, and fund raisers for their survival. A large chunk of money is derived each year from a fund raiser titled Discovered Voices. This event features Hollywood celebrity actors doing staged readings of new works developed at Robey in a posh Hollywood setting.

ROGERS, ALVA. Rogers, a multitalented actor, musician, and playwright, is of the new breed of performance artists. She has accomplished much in her short lifetime, performing at various venues across the country, appearing in three movies, and writing five plays and three musicals. A native of Brooklyn, she has been active professionally since 1996. Rogers attended Fiorello LaGuardia High School of Performing Arts; Brown University, where she earned a B.A. in creative writing; and the New York University Tisch School of the Arts, where she earned an M.F.A. Rogers has performed and recorded with the Band of Susans, Elliot Sharp, **Carl Hancock Rux**, and Urban Bush Women and on the compilation album *Live at the Knitting Factory*. Her film credits include *School Daze, Daughters of the Dust*, and *Fresh Kill*. Rogers has also written plays and musicals. They are *Belly: Three Shorts, The Doll Plays, Scooping the Darkness Empty, The Whole Wide World, The Bride Who Became Frightened*

When She Saw Life Open, Mermaids and Sundays (a musical), *Aunt Aida's Hands* (a musical written with Lisa Jones), and *Stained* (another musical written with Lisa Jones). Rogers served as playwright-in-residence at the NYSF/Public Theatre (1993–94). She has been awarded grants and fellowships from the National Endowment for the Arts, the Jim Henson Foundation, the Rockefeller Foundation, and the New York Foundation for the Arts.

ROLLE, ESTHER (1920–98). Rolle was one of the many black actors whose career was launched at the famed **Negro Ensemble Company (NEC)**. She is perhaps best known for her roles in two hit comedies of the 1970s, *Maude* and *Hard Times*. Rolle made over 35 television and movie appearances in vehicles like *Murder, She Wrote*; *A Raisin in the Sun*; *Touched by an Angel*; *The Love Boat*; *I Know Why the Caged Bird Sings*; *The Incredible Hulk*; *Poltergeist: The Legacy*; *Rosewood*; and *The Kid Who Loved Christmas*, to name just a few. Rolle was the 10th born of 18 children of her Caribbean immigrant parents in Pompano Beach, FL. She graduated from Spelman College and moved to New York City, where she was awarded a scholarship to study acting at the New School for Social Research. She found work in some of the seminal black theater productions of the 1960s, such as Jean Genet's *The Blacks*, **James Baldwin**'s *Blues for Mr. Charlie*, and *The Amen Corner*. When the NEC was formed in 1968, **Douglas Turner Ward** selected her as a charter member of the 15-actor ensemble group. She had worked with Ward in his play *Day of Absence* in 1965. In 1972, while performing in **Melvin Van Peebles**'s *Don't Play Us Cheap*, she was seen by producer Norman Lear, who asked her to audition for *Maude*, a TV spin-off from *All in the Family*. The character she created for that series was so popular that it, too, was spun off into a new series titled *Good Times*, which ran for five seasons on CBS. Rolle was nominated for an Emmy for her work on Maya Angelou's *I Know Why the Caged Bird Sings* and won an Emmy for *Summer of My German Soldier*. She is also the recipient of the National Association for the Advancement of Colored People **Civil Rights** Leadership Award.

ROSEMOND, HENRI CHRYSOSTONE. A playwright, Rosemond was Haitian and lived in Brooklyn during the mid-1940s. He used theater as a forum for social protest. A political exile, Rosemond brought serious criticism against President Elie Lescott and the Haitian administration in his play *Haiti Our Neighbor: A Play in One Act and Twelve Scenes* (1944). It is a melodrama of Haitian life about the country's struggle for independence amid political instability, autocracy, bitter poverty and low standards of living, illiteracy, class and color stratification, and voodooism. Rosemond's other plays include *No More* (1931), a satire on the issue of color differences among the islanders; *Black and Conservative* (1966), an autobiography; and *The Witch Hunt* (1948), a satire skit of communism. Rosemond died in New York City at age 82.

ROSS, GARY EARL. A playwright, educator, poet, and fiction writer, Ross is a writing professor at the University of Buffalo Educational Opportunity Center in Buffalo, NY. He wrote several winning novels, including *Wheel of Desire*; *Shimmerville*; and *Dots*, a children's tale. He turned to playwriting in the 21st century. Four of his plays have been produced by the Towne Players; **Ujima Company, Inc.**; and the Tennessee Stage Company. Other plays he authored include *The Best Woman* (2006), set in the not-too-distant future. Marred by war and cultural conflict, two women, a conservative black Republican and liberal white Democrat, face off for the presidency amid the wheeling and dealing after their first debate. *Matter of Intent* (2004) is set in Buffalo in 1960. It depicts Temple Scott, one of the city's three black attorneys defending her first murder case, where a young black maid is charged with killing her white employer. *Picture Perfect* (2003) portrays a criminal psychologist and his mystery-writer wife who find their lives changing after they hang a portrait of them done by a notorious serial killer just before his execution. *Sleepwalker* (2002) is a stage rendering of the classic silent horror film *The Cabinet of Dr. Caligari*. It is a horror tale of a mad zombie who kills for the doctor. Among Ross's honors and awards are a Mystery Writers of America Award, Edgar Award for best mystery play (*Matter of Intent*, 2006), Artvoice/Emmanuel Fried Outstanding New Play Award (*Matter of Intent*, 2005), Buffalo Arts Council/Individual Artist of the Year Award (2003), and Buffalo Writer in Residence Fiction Award (1987 and 1992).

RUSSELL CHARLIE L. A playwright and writer, Russell was born in Monroe, LA, the eldest of two children. (His younger brother is Bill Russell of professional basketball fame.) After attending Santa Rosa Junior College and Oakland Junior College, Russell served with the U.S. Army in the Korean War. He earned a B.S. from the University of San Francisco (1959) and an M.A. in social work from New York University (1966). He studied acting in New York with the Actors Studio, the **National Black Theatre (NBT)**, and the New Dramatists Guild Workshop and privately under **Clarice Taylor** and **Gilbert Moses**. Russell taught as an assistant professor and counselor at institutions of higher education, such as the SEEK Program at City College of New York, Department of Special Programs (1967–74); writer-in-residence and chairman of the NBT's Playwrights Workshop (1969–74); adjunct assistant professor, Livingston College of Rutgers University, NJ, where he taught basic English and creative writing (1972–73); adjunct assistant professor, film scriptwriting at the Visual Arts Department at New York University (1974–75); writer-in-residence at the American Place Theatre (APT, 1977–78); drama instructor at Contra Costa College, San Pablo, CA (1977–82); and executive and artistic director, East Bay Players, a community theatrical group based in Richmond, CA.

Russell was a columnist and fiction editor, and he published articles, short stories, and a novella and directed numerous plays in New York and California. His best-known play is *Five on the Black Hand Side* (original title, *Gladys*), which premiered in 1969. This domestic comedy is in two acts, centering on an old-fashioned domineering husband, a fed-up wife, and three siblings expressing various views of being "black" in the **civil rights** era, and was a rousing success. United Artists produced a film version of the play in 1973, and it won a National Association for the Advancement of Colored People Image Award for best screenplay. It was produced off Broadway at St. Clement's Church in New York City by the APT with members of NBT (December 1969–31 January 1970) for 62 performances. **Barbara Ann Teer** directed a cast of L. Errol Jaye (succeeded by **Maxwell Glanville**), Clarice Taylor, and Theresa Merritt. It was also produced by the Black American Theatre Company of the New Theatre School in Washington, DC (1972–73 season) and by the Kuumba

Workshop of Chicago (1974). Another play Russell wrote was *The Revival!* (subtitled: *Revival! Change! Love! Organize!* 1972), a full-length ritual. A frequently revived and revised ritual, it utilizes music; drama; dance; rap; and the rhythms, fervor, and style of the black church to teach black people to unite, love one another, and appreciate the values and traditions of their heritage. The NBT first produced it in 1969 under Barbara Ann Teer's direction. It remained in repertory until about 1974. Russell received a grant from the Institute of International Education to study African rituals and ceremonies in Nigeria for three months (1973) and a Rockefeller playwright's grant (1977).

RUX, CARL HANCOCK. A playwright, poet, novelist, and performer, Rux is a multidisciplinary writer and one of the most influential artists of the 21st century. Destitute and raised as a foster child, Rux epitomizes the American success story. He put himself through college at Columbia University and wrote plays, poetry, novels, essays, and operas, all too great critical acclaim. At the age of 19, his play *Talk* was produced at the NYSF/Public Theatre and won an **Obie Award** as best off-Broadway production. His works have been performed in the United States at such venues as the Nuyorican Poets Café, **Penumbra Theatre**, **Joseph Papp**'s NYSF/Public Theatre, Lincoln Center, and Mabou Mines and internationally at the Teatro de Beligni, Italy; the Paris Opera; and in Berlin. Among the plays Rux wrote are *Talk* (1990), a multigenerational discussion of the meaning of black art, and *Song of Sad Young Men* (1990), about the AIDS epidemic in the black community. Other plays he wrote include *Chapter and Verse* (1991), *Geneva Cottell* (1991), *Waiting for the Dog to Die* (1991), *Singing in the Womb of Angels* (1992), *Smoke, Lillies and Jades* (2002), Rux originated the title role in the folk opera *The Temptation of St. Anthony* in 2003. The production subsequently toured Germany, Italy, France, the Netherlands, and Spain. He continues to produce CDs of astonishing versatility, including *Music, Rux Revue, Cornbread, Cognac, Collard Green Revolution*, and *Apothecary RX*. In 2005, Rux was chosen to be artist-in-residence at the new multimillion dollar Miami Performing Arts Center. Among the honors and awards Rux has received are the Fresh Poet Award, Bessie Schomburg Award, Village Voice Literary Prize, National Endowment for the Arts (NEA)/Theatre Communications Group playwright-in-residence fellowship, Kitchen Theatre Artist Award, Rockefeller map grant, Creative Capital artist grant, NYFA Gregory Millard fellowship, New York Foundation for the Arts Prize, CalArts Alpert Award in the arts, and the NEA Leadership Initiatives meet-the-composer grant.

– S –

SALAAM, KALAMU YA (VAL FERDINAND). A playwright, poet, author, administrator, fiction writer, and producer, Salaam is a jack of all trades. He attended Carleton College and holds an A.A. in business administration from Delgado Junior College. He has written numerous books of fiction, poetry, and essays. His work has appeared in leading black journals and countless other publications. He was born in New Orleans as Val Ferdinand but changed his name to Kalamu Ya Salaam in 1970 after he became involved in the **civil rights movement** with the **Free Southern Theatre (FST)**. After **Gilbert Moses** left the organization, **Tom Dent** stepped into the void, reorganized the company, and moved the base of operations from Jackson, MS, to New Orleans. Enter Ferdinand, who was primarily a poet but started writing plays that touched on themes of the movement. His early plays were produced by the FST in the late 1960s, and his later plays by Black Arts/South. The following is a listing of his known plays: *The Picket* (1968), about a black man's attempts to show different standards for white and black families set up by a civil rights activist; *Mama* (1968), about a black family member trying desperately to keep the family together; *Black Liberation Army* (1969), about some consciously aware blacks who attempt to educate their siblings of the needs of black people; *Black Love Song #1* (1969), about both the positive and negative images of black life; *The Destruction of the American Stage*, about a white stranger (devil) attempting to corrupt black people and succeeds with some whose consciousness of black unity is undeveloped; and *Homecoming* (1969), about a returning black veteran who is not the same man he was prior to returning home after being subjected to racism in the military. Other plays Salaam wrote are *Happy Birthday Jesus* (1969); *Black Love Song* (1970); *The Quest* (1972); *God Bless the Child* (a musical,

1991); and *The Breath of Life* (1993). Salaam was a Louisiana literature fellow and received the Louisiana Endowment for the Humanities Award and the senior literature fellowship.

SALIMU (NETTIE MCCRAY). A playwright, Salimu was associated with the **New Lafayette Theatre** in New York City. Her play of note is *Growin' into Blackness* (1969), a drama in one act about a black mother objecting to three children wearing naturals (Afros) and dedicating their lives to social uplift of the race.

SANCHEZ, SONIA. Sanchez is a world-class poet, playwright, educator, and novelist of international renown. During a career that has spanned over 40 years, Sanchez has lectured and taught at over 50 colleges both in the United States and abroad. She has written over a dozen books of poetry, eight plays, and several novels. Born in Birmingham, AL, Sanchez graduated from Hunter College in 1955 and did postgraduate work at New York University. Like many others, she found herself swept up in the **civil rights** fervor of the 1960s. She became an avowed militant but came into conflict with some of the male-dominated black leadership of the movement. She believed some preached a philosophy of black unity but relegated women to a secondary status. It was in this context that Sanchez wrote several plays questioning the true intention of black male leadership.

Sister Sonji (1969) and *The Bronx Is Next* (1968) are great examples of that questioning. *Sister* is a semiautobiographical monologue in one act. Sanchez's search for identity as a black woman corresponds with the search by African Americans during the volatile black arts movement of the 1960s dominated by black men. **Concept East Theatre** in Detroit first produced it (December 1970). Thereafter it played at the **Negro Ensemble Company** in St. Mark's Playhouse (January 1971) for two performances and the New York Shakespeare Festival in the Public Theatre Annex (April 1972) for 64 performances on a program of four one-act plays. *Bronx* is a drama in one act addressing the issue of poor housing in **Harlem** and the Bronx. Theatre Black at the University of the Streets produced it (October 1970). *Uh, Huh: But How Do It Free Us?* (1970) is a ritual in three acts dealing with black male–female relationships during their struggle for freedom. *Dirty Hearts* (1971) is a poetic allegory in one act. The game of Dirty Hearts represents race relations in America, whereby white men control the game. The black man gets the Queen of Spades, so he always loses. *I'm Black When I'm Singing, I'm Blue When I Ain't* (1982) was produced by **Jomandi Productions** in Atlanta (April 1982). The show served as Sanchez's M.F.A. thesis at Virginia Commonwealth University (January 1985). A list of other plays Sanchez wrote includes *Black Cats and Uneasy Landings* (1995). During a celebrated career, Sanchez has received many awards and honors. Among them are the American Book Award, National Academy of Arts and Letters Award, National Education Award, Robert Frost Medal, PEN Writing Award, Phyllis Wheatley Award, Pew Charitable Trust fellowship, Lucretia Mott Award, and National Endowment for the Arts fellowship. Sanchez was appointed chairperson of the English Department at Temple University in 1976. She occupied the Nora Carnell Chair until her retirement in 1999.

SANDERS, JOE, JR. An actor, poet, and playwright, Sanders is affiliated with the Experimental Black Actors Guild (X-Bag) in Chicago. He attended the University of Illinois, where he majored in psychology and speech. His play of note is *All Men Are Created* (1972), a full-length dramatization of J. A. Rogers's book *From Superman to Man.* X-Bag produced it in Chicago (1972–73).

SANDS, DIANA (1934–73). Active between the 1950s and 1960s, Sands was a leading actress of stage, screen, and television. A native of New York City, Sands attended the High School of the Performing Arts (1952), graduating with honors and voted best actress of her class. She also studied with Herbert Berghof at the HB Studio and privately with **Lloyd Richards**. Beginning in the early 1950s, she played a variety of roles in off-Broadway productions, such as Juliet in *An Evening with Will Shakespeare* at the Caravan Theatre (1953), a defending angel in *The World of Scholem Aleichem* at the Barbizon Place Theatre (1953), Jenny Hill in *Major Barbara* at the Greenwich Mews Theatre (1954), a dancer in *The Man with the Golden Arm* at the Cherry Lane Theatre (1956), Laura Turman in *A Land beyond the River* at the Greenwich Mews Theatre (1957), and Betty McDonald in *The Egg and I* with the Harlem YMCA Group Jan Hus Theatre

(1958), for which she received the **Obie Award**. Sands debuted on Broadway as Beneatha Younger, the liberated young black woman in **Lorraine Hansberry**'s *A Raisin in the Sun* (1959), which earned her the Outer Circle Critics Award as best supporting actress, a role she reprised in the film version (1961), receiving the International Artist Award. Sands also won the Theatre World Award as Adelaide in the Broadway production of *Tiger, Tiger, Burning Bright* (1963–64). After a promising play and film career, Sands died of cancer at age 39.

SANTIAGO-HUDSON, RUBEN. An actor, director, playwright, and producer, Santiago-Hudson is brash and well educated and has won a **Tony Award**. He let it be known that he seeks to follow in the footsteps of **Lloyd Richards**, **Claude Purdy**, **Marion McClinton**, **Kenny Leon**, and **Phylicia Allen-Rashad** as an advocate and interpreter of the work of the late **August Wilson**. He has already appeared as an actor in 3 plays of the 10-play Wilson canon and is now embarking on a voyage in which he hopes to direct all 10 of Wilson's plays.

Hudson was born in the small upstate town of Lackawanna, NY, in 1956 to interracial parents, one of whom (his mother) was addicted to drugs. He was essentially raised by a nanny who served as a surrogate mother. He attended college on a "disadvantaged" scholarship, which he used to earn a B.A. in theater from the State University of New York at Binghamton and an M.F.A. in theater from Wayne State University in Michigan. His big break as an actor was in **Charles Fuller**'s *A Soldier's Play* with the **Negro Ensemble Company**. His career took off after that. He performed at some of the leading theaters in the country, including the Manhattan Theatre Club, Contemporary Theatre, Mark Taper Forum, American Contemporary Theatre, and the New York Shakespeare Festival Theatre. At this last venue, he enjoyed a stunning success as the lead in *Henry VII*. Hudson made his Broadway debut in 1992 in **George C. Wolfe**'s *Jelly's Last Jam*. He has appeared in over 40 film and television projects, including *American Gangster*, *Michael Hayes*, *Long Island Confidential*, *The West Wing*, *All My Children*, *Their Eyes Were Watching God*, *Devil's Advocate*, and *Coming to America*. Hudson also wrote *Lackawanna Blues*, a one-man autobiographical piece about growing up, which he toured around the country. On the heels of its success, the play was made into a television movie in 2005 starring the inimitable **S. Epatha Merkerson**. His career has produced Tony, Obie, and **Audience Development Committee Awards** for his work onstage and a Humanitas Prize for his screenplay for *Lackawanna Blues*.

SAUTI, INSAN. A playwright, Sauti was based in Norfolk, MA. His representative plays include *The Installment Plan* (1972), a drama in one act that deals with one man's attempt to cope with black prisoner recidivism. *We Must Eat the Black Root* (1984) is a full-length domestic drama about the struggle for survival of a poor black family. Sun People Theatre, Inc., produced it at the African Poetry Theatre in Jamaica, New York (October 1984). *Sun People Turn Ice* (pre-1986) is a full-length dramatic ethnic collage utilizing history and dance. The African Experience in America and Sun People Theatre, Inc., produced it (pre-1986). *Malcolm's Time: A Collaborative Play* (pre-1986) is a full-length drama about Malcolm X.

SCHULTZ, MICHAEL. Schultz is a working director in the Hollywood film industry, however he cut his teeth on the American theater, most notably with the **Negro Ensemble Company (NEC)** in the late 1960s and early 1970s. Schultz was born in Milwaukee, WI, and after high school studied at the University of Wisconsin but earned his degree from Marquette University in 1964. As a student at Princeton University, he directed his first play, Samuel Beckett's *Waiting for Godot*. His work attracted the attention of the newly formed NEC, which hired him to direct its inaugural production, Peter Weiss's story of African colonialism *Song of the Lusitanian Bogey*. Subsequent NEC productions Schultz directed include *Kongi's Harvest*, ***Dream on Monkey Mountain***, and *God Is a (Guess What?)*. Schultz staged a PBS television special of *To Be Young, Gifted, and Black* in 1972, and the success of that production led him from the stage to the soundstages of Hollywood, where he has since prevailed.

Schultz has directed and produced over 100 television episodes and movies since moving to Hollywood. He has directed episodes of *Picket Fences, Sisters, Chicago Hope, The Practice, Buffy, The Vampire Slayer, Touched by an Angel, The Rockford Files, Starsky and Hutch, JAG,* and *Ally McBeal*, to name a few. He has also directed such movies as *Car Wash*, *The Last Dragon*, *Sgt. Pepper's Lonely Hearts Club Band*, *Cooley High*, *Greased Lightning*, *Scavenger Hunt*, and *Which Way Is Up?* Schultz's early work onstage was rewarded with an **Obie Award** and a **Drama Desk Award**, both for outstanding director.

SCOTT, BARRY. An actor, director, playwright, Scott is a native of Nashville, TN, with a B.S. from Tennessee State University. During his early acting career—primarily with the Tennessee Repertory Theatre—he also worked on a one-man show on the life of Martin Luther King. This stemmed from a 16-mm film his father gave him as a child and which he studied over and over. The show *Ain't Got Long to Stay Here* features the main speeches of Dr. King augmented with music and slides. It has been successful wherever presented. Scott is also theater manager at Tennessee State University, where he founded the African American Negro Playwright Theatre, whose avowed mission is to "use theatre arts to develop more responsible and informed citizens in the community." The theater, an arm of the university, presents several productions a year with Scott directing and occasionally bringing in guest directors like **Woodie King Jr.** Scott has written several other plays, including *When I Grow Up, I'm Gonna Get Me Some Big Words* (a children's play); *Lisa's Story*; *An American Slavery Play*; and *Harlem Voices: The Story of the Harlem Renaissance in the Words of Langston Hughes, Countee Cullen, Zora Neale Hurston, Claude McKay*; and *James Weldon Johnson and Others*. Scott is the recipient of an Ingram Fellowship Award.

SCOTT, HAROLD (1935–2006). Scott, an actor, director, and producer, was an all-around man of the theater. He started out as an actor but progressed to directing before becoming a producer. He was perhaps the first African American to assume the mantle of leadership of a white regional theater when he was hired as artistic director of the Cincinnati Playhouse in the Park in 1973. Scott was born in Morristown, NJ. He received his education from Phillips Exeter Academy and Harvard University (A.B., 1957). In a lengthy career spanning four decades, Scott, either performed in, directed, or produced some 12 Broadway productions.

Four years after making his Broadway debut in *The Cool World*, Scott was chosen to be a member of the prestigious Repertory Theatre of Lincoln Center under Elia Kazan and Robert Whitehead. This was big news at the time because it was seen as the first attempt to create a true "national theater." It did not come to pass, but Scott took advantage of the situation and blossomed as an actor. He performed in world classics like *The Changeling, Incident at Vichy, After the Fall*, and *Marco Millions* under directors like Kazan and Jose Quintero. With that quality experience as underpinning, Scott began a career as an independent actor and director that found him performing and directing at theaters throughout the land. These include the Roundabout Theatre, Seattle Repertory Theatre, Repertory Theatre of St. Louis, **Arena Playhouse**, Circle in the Square, Indiana Repertory Theatre, and Atlanta's Alliance Theatre, among others. His Broadway credits include **Richard Wesley**'s *The Mighty Gents*, **Lorraine Hansberry**'s *Les Blancs*, and **Laurence Holder**'s *Paul Robeson*. He has spent the last 20 years as head of the Directing Program at Rutgers University's Mason Gross School of the Arts. Scott is the recipient of an **Obie Award** for his 1958 performance in Jean Genet's *Deathwatch*.

SCOTT, OZ (OSBORNE). Scott is one of the leading stage and film directors of this generation. His rise through the theatrical ranks to the top tier was swift and sudden. Within two years of graduating from New York University's (NYU) Tisch School of the Arts, Scott found himself the director of record for the smash 1976 Broadway production of **Ntozake Shange**'s *For Colored Girls Who Have Considered Suicide When the Rainbow Is Enuf*. The fact that he was chosen to direct *Colored Girls* by the twin theatrical giants of **Woodie King Jr.** and **Joseph Papp** did not go unnoticed. Within a few years of success on the theatrical stage, Scott transitioned to Hollywood, where he found equal rewards as a writer, director, and producer. He has functioned in one or another of these categories in over 100 television episodes, specials, or television movies. They include *CSI: New York, Boston Legal, The Unit, The Practice, Play'd: A Hip Hop Story, Ally McBeal, American Gothic, Chicago Hope, L.A. Law, Dirty Dancing, Hill Street Blues, Kevin Hill, JAG*, and many others.

Scott was born the son of an army chaplain who spent the first 12 years growing up in Germany and Japan. He earned a B.A. from

Antioch College in 1972 and then continued on to receive his M.F.A. in theater from NYU. His apprenticeship was brief. He spent a year with **Arena Playhouse** as head of the Living Stage. The astute Papp then hired him as stage manager for the New York Shakespeare Festival, where he stage-managed such productions as *Merry Wives of Windsor*, *The Taking of Miss Janie*, *Crucificado*, and *The Sun Always Shines for the Cool*. The peripatetic Oz Scott padded his frequent flyer miles when he went to Chicago to direct Ifa Bayeza's new play, *The Ballad of Emmett Till*. It was produced at the Goodman Theatre to rave reviews in the spring of 2008. His next project took him to Atlanta, where he directed Daniel Beatty's new opus, *Resurrection*. The play is being presented in a dual format: a piece for six actors, and the one man format in which Beatty excels. He will tour the country in this format for the next year.

Although Scott now works primarily in television, he maintains a strong presence in the theater community. He is on the board of the Eugene O'Neill Playwrights Conference, where he works in a variety of ways. In 1996, he directed a production of **Marion McClinton**'s *The Old Settler* that toured Russia with both an American and Russian cast. Scott also evaluates new scripts and assists fledgling writers with their work. He was the catalyst who started the Eugene O'Neill Film and Television Screenwriters Conference, which assists writers in transitioning from one medium into another. Scott is the recipient of a Genesis Award, an **Obie Award**, **Drama Desk Award**, a National Association for the Advancement of Colored People Image Award, and the Nancy Susan Reynolds Award.

SCOTT, SERET. Scott's imprint on theater is threefold: as an actor, director, and writer. A Washington, DC, native, Scott's talent has propelled her to the front ranks of American theater, performing or directing at such institutions as the Yale Repertory Theatre, McCarter Theatre, the Long Wharf, **Arena Playhouse**, **Penumbra Theatre**, and the Old Globe Theatre. She has appeared both on and off Broadway, worked as an associate artist at the Old Globe Theatre, and worked for five years at the Sundance Institute Playwrights Laboratory. Though Scott is mostly engaged as a director, she is also a playwright whose works have been produced since the 1970s, such as *The Owl Attack Chronicles*, a one-woman show chronicling her work in the theater. *Funnytime* is a one-act comedy about a married man who makes a full-time commitment to his girlfriend. *Second Line* is a futuristic look at the history of the **civil rights movement**. Her other plays are *Safehouse, No You Didn't*, and *Wine and Cheese*. Scott has received the **Drama Desk Award** for *My Sister, My Sister* (1974) and the Theatre Communications Group/Pew artist residency at Long Wharf Theatre.

SCRUGGS, JAMES. A performance artist and playwright, Scruggs is a graduate of the School of Visual Arts in New York. He has become a prominent artist in the field of performance art, particularly where there is a relationship among live performance, music, and video. His mastery of this technique is shown in his ground-breaking performance piece *Disposable Men*, which premiered at the HERE Arts Center (HAC) in New York. It is a socially transformative work focusing on the history of stereotyping and violence visited on black men. The play is fast becoming a cult classic. Scruggs has written two other pieces, *Thuggish* and *Touchscape*. He is a resident playwright at HAC and has acquired the following awards and honors: the Franklin Furnace grant, Edith Lutyens and Norman Bel Geddes grant, New York Innovative Theatre Award, and New Jersey State Arts Council fellowship.

SEARCH FOR IDENTITY. During the postslavery (*see* SLAVERY THEME) period in the United States, many blacks were scattered throughout the southern countryside, displaced, disoriented, and lacking direction. They migrated to the industrial North to escape a tragic past in search of their identity and the American dream. In **August Wilson**'s *Joe Turner's Come and Gone* (1986), Harold Loomis, captured by the notorious Joe Turner illegally and incarcerated in a southern prison for seven years, has lost his spirituality, his song, and his essence of life. His wife, believing he is dead, leaves their daughter with her mother and goes North. Upon release from prison, Loomis collects his daughter and goes in search of his estranged wife as well as his lost soul. They turn up in a boardinghouse in Pittsburgh, PA, where the daughter is reunited with her mother, after which during an African ritual, Loomis is exorcized of the evil spirits and finds his identity through ancestor worship with the help of Bynum, the conjure man. In **Amiri Baraka**'s **(LeRoi Jones)** imagistic play *Dutchman* (1964), set on a New York subway, Clay is a "wanna be middle-class white man" with an identity crisis. He is sought out, seduced, and then verbally attacked by Lula, a representative of hegemony. Clay finds his identity as an African American warrior and prophet in a telling monologue to Lula about Uncle Toms, blues people, identity, and insanity before Lula kills him with her phallic-like knife. Jones contends if Clay had stayed true to his newfound identity, his death would not have been worthless.

SEATON, SANDRA CELIA. A playwright and educator, Seaton was born in Columbia, TN. She received her B.A. from the University of Illinois in 1971. Later she earned an M.A. in creative writing at Michigan State University. She is a professor of English at Central Michigan University, teaching courses in playwriting, fiction writing, and African American literature. Seaton wrote several plays showing the interrelationship between American and African American history. *The Bridge Party* (1989), her first play, portrays a group of indifferent black females playing bridge while the community is being terrorized. It won the **Theodore Ward** Prize for new African American playwrights. *The Will*, set during the Reconstruction, is about a black family dealing with problems within the family as well as with vigilante "justice." *Do You Like Phillip Roth?* is a portrayal of black college students' involvement in the **civil rights movement** of the 1960s. Seaton's latest play, *From the Diary of Sally Hemmings* (2001), is about Sally Hemmings, the slave mistress of President Thomas Jefferson, and their children. It debuted at the Library of Congress in 2001, where it was well received. The author later changed the play into a one-woman performance piece, *Sally* (2003), that played throughout the country with great success.

SEJOUR, VICTOR (JUAN VICTOR SEJOUR MARCON ET FERRAND, 1817–74). Sejour was a French mulatto actor, playwright, and poet. Born in New Orleans, he was the son of a Creole mother and black father from Santo Domingo. Educated at Saint Barbe Academy, Sejour at age 17 read one of his original poems before the (Creole) Society of Artisans. He had been sent to France to complete his education, where he published his first poem at age 24 in 1841. This heroic poem "Le Retour de Napoléon" (The Return of Napoleon) gave him the recognition to be accepted into literary circles of Paris. He became friends with Emile Augier and Alexandre Dumas père, also a mulatto, who inspired him to act and to write plays. By age 35, he had gained fame as a revered French actor and playwright.

Of the more that 21 plays he wrote, all are in French and most were produced and published in Paris. He wrote no plays about blacks or mulattoes or with an American theme. Only one, *Le Martyre du Coeur* (*The Martyrdom of the Heart*, 1858), includes a black character (a Jamaican). Sejour's best-known play is *Diegarias* (1844), a drama in five acts in heroic verse. It is a revenge play on the theme of anti-Semitism. Set in Spain during the 16th century, Diegarias, a persecuted Jew, hides his ethnicity from his daughter. It was first produced at the Théâtre Français, Paris (July 1844). The New Orleans Theatre in Louisiana produced it (January 1847). The last two plays were scheduled for production at the Gaieté Paris in 1874 but were canceled after Sejour died of tuberculosis at age 57. Sejour was honored with the title chevalier and made a member of the Légion d' Honneur.

SHADOW THEATRE COMPANY (STC). Located in Denver, CO, the STC was organized in 1997 by Jeffrey Nickelson, a professional actor, director, writer, and singer. Nickelson, growing tired of the scuffling life of the actor, decided to start his own theater despite the odds. By all accounts, he has beaten the odds for the company is now in its 11th season, mounted over 40 productions, and attracts more than 20,000 patrons on an annual basis. With a seating capacity of 80, they produce an average of four shows every year. The operating budget for the 2007 fiscal year was $270,000. The theater's avowed goal is to develop cultural awareness through the theater and provide a vehicle of artistic expression that will be nonexclusive to all cultural communities. As executive artistic director, Nickelson has offered a diverse season of plays for the last 10 years.

The STC has presented such African American plays as **Carlyle Brown**'s *The Little Tommy Parker Celebrated Colored Minstrel Show*, Laurence Fishburne's *Riff Raff*, and James Weldon Johnson's *God's Trombones*. In addition, they have offered their share of the

classics with *Macbeth* by Shakespeare, *The Evils of Tobacco* by Anton Chekhov, *Hughie* by Eugene O'Neill, and *Come Back Little
Sheba* by William Inge. The theater is still anchored, however, in the
black experience with plays by **August Wilson, Phillip Hayes
Dean, Suzan-Lori Parks, Pearl Cleage**, and **William Parker**. The
STC has also formed a six-week Summer Residency Program for students. They are taught the rudiments of theater in acting, movement,
dance, and music. The program culminates in a program written by
the students in collaboration with a professional playwright. Each
year, the theater presents a gala black-tie fund raiser to raise half of
their operating budget. Support beyond the box office comes from
donations, grants, and corporate sponsorship.

SHANGE, NTOZAKE (PAULETTE WILLIAMS). A feminist, poet,
playwright, author, dancer, actress, musician, director, and college
teacher, Shange startled the theater world with her "choreopoem," a
unique form she experimented with in *For Colored Girls Who Have
Committed Suicide When the Rainbow Is Enuf*. Shange was born as
Paulette Williams to an upper-middle–class family in Trenton, NJ.
Her father, an air force surgeon, and mother, an educator, entertained
frequently. Their circle of friends included **W. E. B. DuBois, Paul
Robeson**, Miles Davis, and Josephine Baker. In her early childhood,
Shange attended a school where racism turned her inward. She began
writing as a form of creative release.

In 1966, she enrolled in Barnard College, graduating cum laude in
American studies (1970). Her early marriage to a law student broke
up, and she survived several suicide attempts. Seeking a change, she
enrolled in graduate school at the University of Southern California,
eventually graduating with an M.A. in 1973. While there, with the
nation awash in the **civil rights movement**, gay rights, and feminism,
in 1971, she decided to change her "slave name" to an African Zulu
one, Ntozake Shange (pronounced en-to-zah-ki shong-gay). The first
name means "she who comes with her own things," and her surname
means "she who walks like a lion."

Shange taught writing in the Humanities and Women's Studies
Programs at Mills College in Oakland, CA, before she moved to New
York City to pursue her career as a playwright and poet. It was there
her choreopoem *Colored Girls* catapulted her to national acclaim.

Woodie King Jr. produced it at the **New Federal Theatre** for six months and then moved it to Broadway in a collaborative venture with **Joseph Papp**, artistic director of the NYSF/Public Theatre. Thereafter it went on tour. It won several awards, an **Obie** Outer Circle Award, **Tony**, Grammy, and Emmy Award nominations. Shange has written other choreopoems since then, but none have garnered the acclaim, honors, and success of *Colored Girls*.

Some of Shange's other efforts include *A Photograph: Lovers-in-Motion* (original title, *A Photograph: A Still Life in Shadows*, also produced as *A Photograph: A Study of Cruelty*, 1977). It is a play-poem in two acts and concerns a young, strong-willed, ambitious photographer and his relationship with three women who love him and must continuously stroke his ego. His world comes crashing down after he is denied a fellowship and a gallery exhibition that would help catapult his career. *Photograph* was produced at various theaters, such as New York Shakespeare Festival (NYSF)/Public Theatre (January 1977) under its original title, *A Photograph: A Study of Cruelty*, and in a full production at LuEsther Hall (December 1977–22 January 1978) for 60 performances. It was also mounted as *A Photograph: Lovers-in-Motion* by the Equinox Theatre in Houston, TX (November–December 1979). *Where the Mississippi Meets the Amazon* (1977), coauthored with Jessica Hagedorn and Thulani Nkakinda (T. Davis), is a full-length cabaret-style musical composition. Three women, the Satin Sisters, perform their own poetry, dance, and sing along to the jazz band of Teddy and His Sizzling Romancers. NYSF/Public Theatre produced it (December 1977–March 1978).

Spell #7 (1979) is a choreopoem set in a St. Louis bar frequented by black male and female artists and musicians who recite monologues that are jazzlike solos reinforced by dance to capture their emotional state. As the play opens, the ensemble wear grotesque black minstrel masks as a giant minstrel mask oversees the action narrated by an interlocutor. The NYSF/Public Theatre produced it (April–November 1979) under the direction of **Oz Scott**. *Boogie Woogie Landscapes* (1979) is a full-length experimental one-woman theater piece exploring what it means to be black and female. It was produced by the NYSF/Public Theatre as part of the Poetry at the Public Series (1979), by **Frank Silvera Writers' Workshop** (FSWW) at Symphony Space in New York in play form (June 1979), and by the Black Touring Circuit at the Kennedy Center's Terrace Theatre in Washington, DC (June–July 1980). *Mother Courage and Her Children* (1980) is a full-length adaptation from Bertolt Brecht's play of the same title. The setting is changed to post–Civil War America, with Mother Courage as an emancipated slave. The NYSF/Public Theatre produced it (April–June 1980), and it received an Obie Award for outstanding adaptation.

A Daughter's Geography (original title: *Mouths: A Daughter's Geography,* 1981) is a full-length choreopoem. As in *Spell #7*, performers wear grotesque black minstrel masks as a cosmic couple observes the history of a black woman's life from **slavery** to the time of the play through dance. The Kitchen in New York City first produced it as *Mouths: A Daughter's Geography: A Performance Piece* (April 1981). Subsequently, it was produced as *Triptych and Bocas: A Performance Piece* at the Mark Taper Theatre Lab in Los Angeles (March–April 1982) under the direction of Oz Scott and by the Mark Taper Forum as a revised *A Daughter's Geography: A Choreopoem* (July 1983). *The Dancin' Novel: Sassafrass, Cypress, and Indigo* (1982) is in three pieces that infuse music, poetry, and dancing. It is coauthored by Shange with Dianne McIntyre and Rod Rogers and is based on her novella *Sassafrass, Cypress, and Indigo*, which centers on two sisters from Charleston, SC, who relate to the world differently. Sassafrass is in an abusive relationship with her boyfriend, a junky and infrequently employed musician. Cypress is a feminist who has multiple relationships with male friends, but none are her lovers. NYSF/Pubic Theatre produced it (March 1982). *From Okra to Greens* (1978) is a full-length theater piece that was produced at Barnard College in New York (November 1978), at Greenwich Mews Theatre in New York (January 1973), and by the Folger Theatre Group in Washington, DC (February 1974), for 28 performances under the direction of **Harold Scott**.

Shange is also a prolific writer of literature, having written several novels. She continues to write, teach, and perform at educational institutions across the country, including Howard, Florida, Rice, Yale, Villanova, and others. She has performed with many of the greatest jazz artists of this age, such as Max Roach, David Murray, and the Chicago Art Ensemble. Among the many honors Shange has received are fellowships from Guggenheim, Chubb, and the National Endowment for the Arts; two **Audience Development Committee Awards**, and a Los *Angeles Times* Book Review Prize for poetry for *Three Pieces* (1981). She also has two honorary doctorates. She is a member of Dramatists Guild and PEN. Shange is also a recipient of an Outer Critics' Circle Award, Obie Awards (one in 1980 for outstanding adaptation of Bertolt Brecht's *Mother Courage*), Mademoiselle Award (1977) for *Colored Girls* (which was also nominated for a Tony Award and a Grammy Award), FSWW Award (1978), Guggenheim fellowship for writing (1981), Medal of Excellence from Columbia University (1981), New York State Council of the Arts Award (1981), National Endowment for the Arts fellowship for creative writing (1981) for *A Photograph: Lovers-in-Motion* and *Boogie Woogie Landscapes*.

SHAY, MICHELE. A veteran actor, director, and teacher, Shay was born in East Orange, NJ. She earned a B.F.A. in theater at Carnegie Mellon University in Pittsburgh, PA. Shay has made four separate appearances on Broadway, playing classical roles in *A Midsummer Night's Dream* and *Coriolanus* and black roles in *For Colored Girls Who Have Considered Suicide When the Rainbow Is Enuf* and *Home*. She has performed at some of the leading theaters in the country, including the Tyrone Guthrie Theatre, Lincoln Center, Actor's Theatre of Louisville, Seattle Repertory Theatre, Yale Repertory Theatre, American Conservatory Theatre, New York Shakespeare Festival, and **Negro Ensemble Company (NEC)**. Shay has directed a wide variety of plays, such as **Pearl Cleage**'s *Blues for an Alabama Sky*; **Alice Childress**'s *Wedding Band*; and two plays from the **August Wilson** canon, *Joe Turner's Come and Gone* and *Seven Guitars*. Her movie credits include *Manhunter*, *He Got Game*, *Crooklyn*, and *Never Die Alone*. Among her television appearances are *ER*, *Chicago Hope*, *The Cosby Show*, *Miami Vice*, and *Skokie*. Shay has taught acting at Cal Arts University, the American Conservatory Theatre, North Carolina School of the Arts, the University of Michigan and the NEC. She is the recipient of an **Obie Award** Outer Critics' Circle Award, and a National Association for the Advancement of Colored People Image Award.

SHEPP, ARCHIE VERNON. Born in Fort Lauderdale, FL, and raised in Philadelphia, Shepp is known worldwide as a jazz musician of enormous talent and creativity. He is also known as a playwright and educator. His early interest was in theater. He received a B.A. in dramatic literature from Goddard College in 1959. He fell upon difficult times, and he soon found himself playing saxophone in dance bands to make ends meet. Shepp's occasional forays into theater resulted in three plays, two of which were produced at the Chelsea Theatre Center, *The Communist* (1965), *Junebug Graduates Tonight* (1967), and *Lady Day: A Musical Tragedy* (1971). *Junebug* is a jazz allegory in two acts and four scenes. Characters take on symbolic representation with such names as Junebug, White Woman, America, Blackman, the Muslim, Uncle Sam, the Birchite, and the Panther. On the eve of his high school graduation, Junebug, as valedictorian of his class, is plagued with a psychological challenge, whether to become an integrationist, a black separatist, or find his own path. The Church of the Holy Apostles in New York City first produced it (February–March 1967). **Paul Carter Harrison** directed the cast of **Rosalind Cash**, **Glynn Turman**, Minnie Gentry, and Cynthia Belgrave. Howard University produced it in Washington, DC (late 1970s). *Lady Day* is a two-act with music by Shepp and book by **Aishah Rahman** based on the career of the jazz legend Billie Holiday. It was produced first at the Brooklyn Academy of Music (1971) in New York, then at the Chelsea Theatre, Brooklyn (October–November 1972), for 34 performances. Cecilia Norfleet played Billie Holiday under the direction of Harrison. Also in the cast were **Rosetta LeNoire** and **Maxwell Glanville**. For **Amiri Baraka's (LeRoi Jones)** *Slave Ship* (1967), Shepp cocomposed the incidental music with Baraka. Shepp's musical talent, however, took hold and blossomed. Over the next 30 years, he became one of the leading jazz musicians of his time, alongside such artists as Art Blakey, John Coltrane, Dizzy Gillespie, and Miles Davis. His albums often used poetry and other literature to paint an aural picture of American life. He returned to academe in the early 1970s, where he has been an associate professor in the **W. E. B. DuBois** Department of African American Music at Amherst, MA.

SHINE, TED. Born in Baton Rouge, LA, Shine, a playwright, university professor, and editor, grew up in Dallas, TX. He earned a B.A. from Howard University (1953), where **Owen Dodson** and Sterling Brown oversaw the development of his writing. He also attended the

State University of Iowa (M.A., 1958) and the University of California at Santa Barbara (Ph.D., 1973), where he was the company playwright at the Institute of Black Repertory Theatre (summer 1968). For two years (1953–55), Shine was involved with **Karamu Repertory Theatre** in Cleveland, OH. A few years later, he began his career as a professor at Dillard University in New Orleans (1960–61). From there, he moved to Howard University (1961–67) before he accepted a position at Prairie View A&M University in Texas.

Shine's literary output was most prolific. He coedited with **James V. Hatch** the ground-breaking *Black Theatre, USA: An Anthology of 45 Plays by Black American Playwrights* and was a scriptwriter for television. His plays, mostly one-acts, were produced frequently throughout the country. Among them are *Contribution* (1969), a comedy set during the **civil rights movement** of the 1960s. The grandson of an elderly black woman learns a lesson about the contributions of the older generation made in the struggle for social justice when the local sheriff is poisoned. The **Negro Ensemble Company** first produced it off Broadway (March–April 1969) for 32 performances. *Shoes* (1969) is a humorous look at three black youths who try to figure out how to spend the money they earned working during the summer. It was produced at Tambellini's Gate Theatre off Broadway (March 1970) for 16 performances and at the Federal City College Environmental Theatre (1972–73). *Cold Day in August* (1950) is a domestic drama in one act. It is about a young couple whose relationship is tested after they move in with a family member. Shine wrote and produced it as an undergraduate at Howard University. Among the later plays Shine authored are *Baby Cakes* (1981), *Poor Ol' Soul* (1982), *Bats Out of Hell* (1955), *Entourage Royale* (1958), *Rat's Revolt* (1959), *Miss Victoria* (1965), *Jeanne West* (1968), *Riot* (1968), *The Coca-Cola Boys* (1969), *Waiting Room* (1969), *Goin' Berserk* (1983), and *Vestibule* (1983). These plays are mostly one-acts. Shine was the recipient of a Rockefeller scholarship to study at Karamu Repertory Theatre in Cleveland (1953–55) and a Brooks-Hines Award for playwriting from Howard University for his play *Morning, Noon, and Night* (1962).

***SHUFFLE ALONG* (1921).** A musical comedy by composer Eubie Blake and lyricist Noble Sissle and book by Flournoy Miller and

Aubrey Lyles, this work was the most significant achievement in black theater of its time. *Shuffle Along* opened at the Howard Theatre in Washington, DC, in late March (1921) for two weeks. It finally settled at the 63rd Street Theatre in New York City (May 1921). Promoters and theater managers were skeptical at first as to whether white audiences would accept a black musical because no black show had been successful on Broadway in over 12 years. The musical mélange became an instant hit because of the energetic, vivacious, torso-twisting dancers who gave birth to the speed shows that were to characterize black shows thereafter. It also won the distinction of becoming an "actor's" show during its more than its 200 performances. It proved that white audiences would pay to see black musical comedies on Broadway.

Among the cast were Blake (at the piano), Miller (Steve Jenkins), Lyles (Sam Peck), Sissle (Tom Sharper), Paul Floyd (Jim Williams), Lottie Gee (Jessie Williams), Gertrude Saunders (Ruth Floyd), Roger Matthews (Harry Walton), Mattie Wilkes (Mrs. Sam Peck), Lawrence Deas (Jack Penrose), and Adelaide Hall (Jazz Jasmine). The plot centers on Sam and Steve, who run for mayor in Jimtown, USA. If either one wins, he will appoint the other his chief of police. Sam wins with the help of a crooked campaign manager and keeps his promise to appoint Steve as chief of police, but they begin to disagree on petty matters. They resolve their differences in a rousing, humorous 20-minute fight scene. As they fight, their opponent for the mayoral position, Harry Walton, vows to end their corrupt regime, underscored in the song "I'm Just Wild about Harry." Harry wins the next election as well as the girl and runs Sam and Steve out of town. Recording companies marketed every one of the 18 songs from the show. Some of the songs that gave audiences something to talk about were "Love Will Find a Way" by Lottie Gee, "I'm Just Wild about Harry" (which became presidential candidate Harry S. Truman's campaign slogan), "Gypsy Blues," "I'm Cravin' for That Kind of Love," and "Shuffle Along." The landmark production renewed interest in black theatricals by the public and marked a decided turning point in the history of black entertainment in America. It introduced to the Broadway stage a black chorus of partially garbed girls in the style of the white follies. Because of the show's popularity, the entertainment profession witnessed the return of black musical comedies to Broadway on a regular basis.

SILVERA, FRANK ALVIN (1914–70). Silvera was a distinguished actor; producer; and director of stage, screen, and broadcasting. He is unique in theater circles for his ability to portray characters without representing stereotypes. Born in Kingston, Jamaica, Silvera received his education at Boston High School in Massachusetts (1934), Northwestern Law School (1934–35), the Old Vic School in London (1948), and the Actors' Studio in New York City (1950). He honed his craft at the Boston Federal Theatre, at which he appeared in 30 productions (1935–39), and at the New England Repertory Theatre (1939–40). He wrote and directed radio shows while stationed at the Great Lakes Naval Training Station during World War II. His acting credits, however, were numerous. He played in the **American Negro Theatre**'s production of *Anna Lucasta* on Broadway (1945) and in London (1947–48). His play of note is *Just Ten Days* (1937), a full-length melodrama that deals with black poverty and homelessness during the Great Depression of the 1930s. The mobile theater division of the **Harlem** Unit of the New York **Federal Theatre Project** toured the production throughout Harlem for one month to thousands of children (August–September 1937). *See also* FRANK SILVERA WRITERS' WORKSHOP (FSWW).

SIMON, LEVY LEE. Simon is an accomplished actor and playwright. He is well grounded educationally, with a B.A. from Cheyney State College in Pennsylvania and an M.F.A. from the famed Iowa Playwrights Workshop. As an actor, he has appeared on Broadway, **Arena Playhouse**, and other regional theaters across the country. His plays have received staged readings at Victory Gardens Theatre, **La MaMa Experimental Theatre Club**, Stella Adler Workshop, and Denver Theatre Center. His development as a playwright mushroomed when the **Robey Theatre** and the Greenway Arts Alliance agreed to produce his epic trilogy *For the Love of Freedom*, the story of Toussaint L'Ouverture, the leader who freed Haiti from the bondage of Napoleon Bonaparte. The first production of the trilogy, encompassing some 30 odd actors, premiered in 2001, with the final play being produced in 2004. When not acting, Simon has written the following plays: *In the Middle of the Bubbling Tar*; *Caseload*; *God, the Crackhouse, and the Devil*; *The Bow Wow Club*; *Utopia*; *The Junction Limited Midnight Express*; *Pitbulls and Daffodils*; *Fireflies on Fluorescent Sand*; *The*

Stuttering Preacher; and *The Guest at Central Park West*. His most recent play, *The Bow Wow Club*, was presented at the North Carolina Theatre Festival held in Winston– Salem (summer 2007). Simon is the winner of the 1999 Kennedy Center **Lorraine Hansberry** Award for *The Bow Wow Club*.

SIMPLY HEAVENLY (1957). This play is based on **Langston Hughes**'s *Simple Takes a Wife* and other "Simple" stories. It opened at the Playhouse Theatre in New York City (20 August 1957) and ran for 62 performances. The Playhouse Heavenly Company produced it, Hughes wrote the book and lyrics, David Martin composed the music, and Joshua Shelly directed it. Set in Patty's Bar in **Harlem**, it centers on Jess B. Simple (**Melvin Stewart**), who has to raise money to get a divorce and marry his new love, Joyce Lane (Marilyn Berry). The bar is frequented by ordinary, hard-working, lower-income patrons. Simple epitomizes the simple, ordinary man with great insight. Joyce is quiet, cultured, and charming. Boyd is a college dropout and writer. Zarita is a lively barstool girl. Miss Mamie is a hard-working, harsh-talking domestic. **Claudia McNeil**, later to gain fame as Mama in *A Raisin in the Sun*, played Mamie.

SLAVERY THEME. While European immigrants came to the New World to escape oppression, seek a better life, and pursue the American dream, Africans were brought against their will. After 400 years of involuntary servitude, an overriding issue was how to break the psychological chains of slavery and gain full citizenship within that society. This depiction of the cruel and unjust treatment of Africans during and after slavery is prevalent in many plays that show black resistance to this social structure. Three plays exemplify this issue: *Our Lan'* (1948) by **Ted Ward**, *Slave Ship* (1967) by **Amiri Baraka (LeRoi Jones)**, and *Joe Turner's Come and Gone* (1988) by **August Wilson**.

Our Lan, a 2-act drama in 10 scenes, is set off the coast of Georgia after the Civil War during the Reconstruction Era (1863–77). Displaced slaves make their claim to land they consider in a status of a newly conquered territory. Once they get settled in and begin to make a life for themselves, the U.S. military arrives and orders them to vacate the land so it may be returned to the previous owners before the war. They refuse to leave. As the curtain falls, the audience hears a cannon blast. This is an example of how blacks sought compensation after a lifetime of providing free labor and how they were prepared to fight for land they perceived to be theirs. Ward shows their courage in the face of betrayal and raises the question of what to do with ex-slaves who were set free in a society that did not make proper provisions for them educationally or economically.

Slave Ship replicates the journey of African people being brought to America during the early phase of the slave trade. The set was designed as a virtual slave ship. Audiences walked into what approximated the belly of a pitch-black ship that rocked and smelled of urine and feces, and amplified sounds of waves, moans, and wails reverberated throughout the ship. The virtual reality heightened the experience of what African slaves had to endure during the crossing of "the big pond," and it was a testament to their ability to survive.

Joe Turner's Come and Gone is set during the postslavery period. Harold Loomis, a deacon in the church, is subjected to another form of slavery. He is arrested illegally by Joe Turner and sentenced to work on a chain gang for seven years. When Loomis is released, he discovers he has lost his soul and his family has been displaced. The play shows how this new social system disorients individuals.

SMITH, ANNA DEVEARE. A performing artist, educator, and playwright, Smith was born in Baltimore, MD. She attended Beaver College and received her M.F.A. from the American Conservatory Theatre in 1976. She is primarily an educator and has taught at various institutions, including Yale University, the University of Southern California, Carnegie Mellon University, Stanford University, and New York University. She has also enjoyed a secondary career as a playwright as well as an actor. But it is as a playwright that her name appears among the vanguard of leading writers in the theatrical world. Her plays are not structured traditionally in that they are performance pieces that evolve around real events and continually break down the fourth wall that exists between performer and audience. The pieces are based upon recorded interviews with hundreds of people who have been involved with or are knowledgeable of some cataclysmic event. Smith then absorbs the text, speech rhythms, cadences, and eccentricities of the interviewee, memorizes them, and performs them, usually in a one-woman format. She has been known to perform over 50 characters in a single play.

Her breakout performance piece was *Fires in the Mirror*, first performed in 1992 at the NYSF/Public Theatre. It documents the rioting and tension among blacks and Jews in Crown Heights, Brooklyn. The production earned her an **Obie Award**, **Drama Desk Award**, Drama League Award, and **Pulitzer Prize** nomination. Her next significant piece was *Twilight: Los Angeles, 1992*. It was performed in 2000 at the Mark Taper Forum and was based on the Los Angeles riots after the Rodney King beating by 15 policemen captured on videotape. It was unanimously praised and won a **Tony Award** and Obie Award, as well as an Outer Critics' Circle Award and a Drama Desk Award.

Smith has written other plays as well, including *On the Road: A Search for Character* (1982); *Aye, Aye, I'm Integrated* (1984); *On Black Identity and Black Theatre* (1990); *From the Inside Looking In* (1990); *House Arrest, First Edition* (1997); and *Piano* (2000). Smith has also performed in film, most notably in *Philadelphia*, *An American President*, and *The Human Stain*. TV Credits include *The Practice*, *Presidio Med*, and *The West Wing*. Smith has also written two books, *Letters to a Young Artist* and *Talk to Me*. She received a MacArthur Foundation award in 1996 for creating a new form of theater, a blend of theatrical art, social commentary, journalism, and intimate reverie. Later that same year, she became the first artist-in-residence at the Ford Foundation. In 1997, she served as moderator in the great debate between the late **August Wilson** and Robert Brustein.

SMITH, CHARLES. A playwright and educator, Smith is an influential voice in the black theater movement. He is currently head of the M.F.A. Playwriting Program at Ohio University and playwright-in-residence at the Indiana Repertory Theatre, a position he formerly held at Victory Gardens Theatre in Chicago. His plays have been produced both locally and nationally at such institutions as the **New Federal Theatre**, Seattle Repertory Theatre, **Penumbra Theatre**, and **St. Louis Black Repertory Theatre**. Smith was born and raised on Chicago's south side, earned a B.A. from University of Iowa, and graduated with an M.F.A. from the Iowa Playwright's Workshop in 1984. He started out as a member of the New Dramatists in New York but returned to Chicago and assumed a significant role in a burgeoning movement to expand the role of black theater in the Windy City. With at least five functioning black theaters producing plays year-round, Chicago is fast overtaking New York as the destination of choice for aspiring actors and playwrights, and Smith is leading the way with his plays that focus on race, politics, and historical icons like **W. E. B. DuBois**, Alexandre Dumas père, and Denmark Vesey. His 1996 play *Black Star Line*, focusing on the life of Marcus Garvey, was commissioned and produced by the Goodman Theatre and was nominated for the **Pulitzer Prize** in drama. His 2001 play *Pudd'nhead Wilson*, a tale of a white child and a black slave child who are switched at birth, toured over 22 cities across the nation. Among the plays Smith authored are *Cane*, the story of the **Harlem** Renaissance; *Young Richard*, about a young black writer facing the reality of his profession; and *City of Gold*, which addresses the real legacy of Christopher Columbus. Other plays Smith wrote are *Free Man of Color*, *Freefall*, *Golden Leaf Ragtime Blues*, *Jelly Belly*, *Knock Me a Kiss*, *The Sutherland*, *Les Trois Dumas*, and *Sister Carrie*. Smith has also won fellowship awards from the Illinois Arts Council, the Princess Grace Foundation, and the Joyce Foundation.

SMITH, CHARLES "CHUCK." Smith, a native of Chicago, is a journeyman director of long standing whose experience in the American theater is of legendary status. As a youngster, Smith enlisted in the U.S. Marines after high school. He studied theater at Loop College and at Governor's State University, where he received a B.A. in drama. Beginning in the 1960s, Smith worked with the Experimental Black Actors Guild (X-BAG), Kuumba Theatre, eta Creative Arts Foundation, **Ma'at Production Association of Afrikan-Centered Theatre (MPAACT)**, and the Goodman Theatre, where he has held the position of associate director and dramaturge from 1992 to the present.

Along the way, he has mounted plays of distinction at such venues as the Pegasus Players, **Congo Square Theatre Company**, Goodman Theatre, Milwaukee Repertory, **Robey Theatre**, Victory Gardens, Legacy Productions, Alabama Shakespeare Festival, Seattle Repertory Theatre, **New Federal Theatre**, eta, **Black Ensemble Theatre**, MPAACT, New Regal Theatre, Fleetwood-Jourdain Theatre, and Timberlake Playhouse. Among the plays he directed are **James Baldwin**'s *Amen Corner*; **August Wilson**'s *Ma Rainey's Black Bottom*; Charles

Dickens's *A Christmas Carol* (1993–95); **Alonzo Lamont**'s *Vivisections of a Blown Mind*; **Lorraine Hansberry**'s *A Raisin in the Sun*; Athol Fugard, John Koni and Winston Ntoshona's *Siswe Banzi Is Dead*; **Pearl Cleage**'s *Blues for an Alabama Sky*; **Jeff Stetson**'s *The Meeting*; Fugard's *Master Harold . . . and the Boys*; **Samm-Art Williams**'s *Home*; **Steve Carter**'s *Eden* and *Dame Lorraine* (with **Esther Rolle**); *The Last Season*; *Knock Me a Kiss*; *That Apple Don't Shine*; *Dream Maker*; *Drink the Contents of This Vial*; *Fathers and Other Strangers*; *Suspenders*; *The Hooch*; *The Gift Horse*; *The Story*; and *The Graduate*. Smith recently directed **Cheryl L. West**'s *Birdie Blue* at the Seattle Repertory Theatre (November 2007). Smith has directed shows for the NBC teleplay *Crime and Innocence*, the Emmy Award–winning *Fast Break to Glory*, the Emmy-nominated *Suspenders*, the Jefferson Award–winning musical *PO.*

Since 1983, he has been teaching at Columbia College, where he is also a faculty member, and served as facilitator for the **Theodore Ward** Playwriting Award. He also cofounded the esteemed Chicago Theatre Company, where he served as artistic director for four years. Smith is a board member of the League of Chicago Theatres and the African American Arts Alliance of Chicago. Among the numerous awards and accommodations he received are the **Paul Robeson** Award (1982), Award of Merit presented by the **Black Theatre Alliance** of Chicago (1997), *Chicago Tribune* Chicagoan of the Year Award (2001), Independent Reviewers of New England Award for best direction, and Jefferson Award nomination for best direction of *Eden*. He was also inducted into the Chicago State University Gwendolyn Brooks Center's Literary Hall of Fame (2001).

SMITH, J. AUGUSTUS (GUS SMITH, J. A. SMITH, 1891–1950).
An actor, playwright, producer, and director, Smith was born in Gainesville, FL. He began his theatrical career acting in vaudeville and minstrel shows at age 14 and later worked in silent films. Smith was one of the three directors of the **Harlem** Unit of the Works Progress Administration's **Federal Theatre Project**. Two of his plays were produced by this unit during the 1930s. One was *Turpentine* (1936), a 3-act play in 10 scenes coauthored with Peter Morrell. It depicts the mistreatment of black workers in the turpentine southern labor camps in Florida. The other play Smith authored a few

years earlier is *Louisiana* (1933), a folk drama in three acts. The play shows a conflict between Christianity and black voodoo religious beliefs in attempts to save a pastor's daughter.

SMITH, ROGER GUENVEUR. An actor, director, and playwright, Smith is one of the most prolific artists working today and is equally at home as actor, writer, or director. Smith, a native of Berkeley, CA, earned a doctorate from Yale University before studying theater abroad at London's Barbican Center. Since then, he has made over 20 films and a like number of TV appearances in *Murphy Brown, All about the Benjamins, Hamlet, Malcolm X, Incognito, Third Watch, Son of Sam, I Believe in America,* and *He Got Game,* to name just a few. When not working in film, he keeps active as an actor on the American stage, notably as an interpreter of his own work as a playwright. In 1997, Smith's signature solo piece, *The Huey Newton Story,* was developed with composer Marc Anthony Thompson and has been performed at leading theaters across the country. Among the awards it received were the **Obie Award** and an **Audience Development Committee Award**. It was later made into a film by Spike Lee, with Smith in the title role, and won a prestigious Peabody Award. Other plays Smith wrote are *Inside the Creole Mafia,* a play set in New Orleans about two misfits; *Iceland,* about a military strongman being exiled to Iceland; *Frederick Douglass Now,* about the life and times of the famous abolitionist; *Blood and Brains*; and *Christopher Columbus.* Honors, awards, fellowships, and commissions for Smith include the Helen Hayes Award; John Barrymore Award; National Association for the Advancement of Colored People Theatre Award; and Thomas J. Watson fellowship;

SMITH-DAWSON, BEVERLY. A director and playwright, Smith-Dawson was born in Phoenix, AZ, in 1955 and is a graduate of Arizona State University and Yale University, where she received her M.F.A. in directing. Her career has been threefold, split between writing, directing, and teaching. She has worked for the Playwrights Center in Minneapolis and for Arizona State University and is the founder and artistic director of Stormy Weather Production. She was also an assistant director for the 1988 Broadway hit *A Walk in the Woods.* Over the years, she has written a variety of plays that have enjoyed productions at the Black Repertory Group, the NYSF/Public Theatre, the **Lorraine Hansberry Theatre**, Rutgers University, and Playwrights Horizon, among others. Smith-Dawson's plays are *Heat*, about a young woman coming of age after having a mysterious dream; *Family Portrait*, a portrait of a dysfunctional family trying to cope with reality; *Water Torture*, a story about a mother's return from prison that sparks a reenactment of the crime that put her there; *Cover*, a surreal farce in which a casual pickup in a bar is not what it seems to be; *5 Day . . . And before Atomi*; *Dog Catcher*; *The Women*; *Composition*; *Man with the Blue Guitar*; *House of Mirrors*; and *Slow Dancin'*. Honors and awards Smith-Dawson received are the Jerome fellowship (1988–89), Playwright's Center in Minneapolis fellowship, and the A. L. Hughes fellowship (1990).

SNIPES, MARGARET FORD-TAYLOR. Snipes is an actress, director, playwright, and educator. She was known formerly as Margaret Ford and Margaret Taylor. She has played a significant role in the development of black theater for many years. She was born in Detroit and earned her M.F.A. from Kent State University in Ohio. After acting and directing for a few years, she became executive director of the famed **Karamu Repertory Theatre** in Cleveland, OH. During her stewardship, Karamu expanded its budget and programs to include a wide variety of training in the arts. It was at Karamu that Snipes began her writing career. Her 1971 play *Hotel Happiness*, a one-act kinky comedy, became an overnight hit and quickly morphed into a staple of black theaters across the country. Other plays Snipes wrote include *I Want to Fly*, *Will Somebody Please Die?*, *Folklore, Black American Style*, *The Hymie Finkelstein Used Lumber Company* (a musical comedy), and *Sing a Song of Watergate* (a musical). She also wrote a documentary titled *The Second Reconstruction* that was shown on network television. In 2002, Snipes had a featured role in the movie *Antwone Fisher* starring **Denzel Washington**. She has taught theater arts at Cleveland State University, the University of Akron, and Kent State. She is cofounder of the Cleveland Art Theatre at Cleveland State.

A SOLDIER'S PLAY **(1981). Charles L. Fuller's Pulitzer Prize**–winning drama premiered off Broadway at the **Negro Ensemble Com-**

pany (10 November 1981) and ran for a record 468 performances. As a black captain investigates the death of a black sergeant at a military base during World War II, issues surface dealing with black self-hatred, color stratification, and the reality of being black in a segregated military. **Douglas Turner Ward** directed an all-star cast featuring **Adolph Caesar, Denzel Washington, Charles Brown,** and **Samuel L. Jackson.** When the play was adapted into a movie in 1985, the title was changed to *A Soldier's Story.* Fuller wrote the screenplay, and several members of the original cast reprised their roles, namely Caesar and Washington. In addition to the Pulitzer Prize, the play won the **New York Drama Critics' Circle Award.**

SOPHISTICATED LADIES **(1981).** This elaborately staged and costumed song-and-dance show is a musical retrospective of Duke Ellington's hit tunes in two acts. Originally conceived, choreographed, and staged by Donald McKayle, it opened in Washington, DC. Michael Smuin provided additional choreography and made changes in the staging for its debut on Broadway at the Lunt-Fontainne Theatre (1 March 1982), where it ran for 767 performances. Robert S. Berlind, Manheim Fox, Sondra Gilman, Burton Litwin, and Louise Westergaard produced it. Featured actor Hinton Battle received a **Tony Award** for distinguished dancing and Phyllis Hyman won a Theatre World Award. Critics also raved about dancers Gregory Hines and Judith Jameson. In addition, Tony Walton won a Tony Award for outstanding costume designer. Ellington's son, Mercer, conducted the band onstage that played more than 35 of Ellington's songs. Among the hit songs Ellington composed or cocomposed that particularly delighted audiences are "Music Is a Woman," "The Mooche," "It Don't Mean a Thing if It Don't Have That Swing," "Solitude," "Don't Get Around Much Anymore," Caravan," "Rockin' in Rhythm," "In a Sentimental Mood," "I'm Beginning to See the Light," "Satin Doll," "Do Nothing 'til You Hear from Me," "I Got It Bad and That Ain't Good," "Mood Indigo," "Sophisticated Lady," and "Take the 'A' Train."

SPENCE, EULALIE (1894–1981). Born on the island of Nevis in the British West Indies, this pioneer playwright was also a high school teacher and drama director during the 1920s and 1930s. She attended

Wadleigh High School and the Normal Department of the New York Training School for Teachers (1920s). She advanced her education at the College of the City of New York (City College of New York), majoring in English and speech, and at Columbia University, where she studied playwriting under **Pulitzer Prize**–winning playwright Hatcher Hughes. While at Columbia, she was active with the National Ethiopian Art Theatre School (NEATS, c. 1924). Over 10 years later, she earned a B.A. in speech from Teachers College (1937) and an M.A. in speech from Columbia University (1939).

Spence directed the Dunbar Garden Players at St. Mark's Church in New York (late 1920s) and wrote many one-act plays on domestic life. Several were awarded prizes by *Crisis* and *Opportunity* magazines in their annual literary contests. **W. E. B. DuBois's Krigwa Players** Little Negro Theatre (KPLNT) based in New York City produced several of her plays. They include Spence's first play, *Foreign Mail* (1926), a comedy. It received second prize in the *Crisis* Contest Awards (October 1926). *The Hunch* (1927) was a comedy of **Harlem** life about a young woman with two suitors, one of whom informs her that the other suitor is married. She, however, believes that the informer is trying to ruin her chance for happiness. *The Hunch* was awarded second prize in the *Opportunity* Contest Awards (June 1927). The KPLNT produced it in Washington, DC (June 1927), and also produced *Stage and Screen Works: Brothers and Sisters of the Church Council* and *Her* (both 1920s).

Other one-act plays Spence wrote were also produced around the New York City area. *Being Forty* (1924) is about middle-age angst. NEATS produced it at the **Lafayette Theatre** (October 1924) on a double bill with Eloise Bibb Thompson's *Cooped Up* and at the Bank Street Players at the Robert Treat School, Newark, NJ (April 1927). *The Starter: A Comedy of Harlem Life* (1926) is about a couple, one a realist, the other an idealist, wanting to get married but changing their mind after they discuss financial responsibilities. A favorite among amateur groups, it received a third-place tie in the *Opportunity* Contest Awards (June 1927). *The Fool's Errand* (1927) is about the damage that vicious gossiping can cause within the black church. An unmarried woman is rumored to be pregnant because baby clothes are among her belongings. It received the Samuel French Prize. *Undertow* (1927) is a melodrama set in Harlem dealing with a domestic triangle. An altercation ensues among a cheating husband, a dark-skinned wife, and a light-skinned woman who had a child by the husband. *Undertow* and *Hot Stuff* won third prize in the *Crisis* Contest Awards (1927). *Episode* (1928) is a domestic comedy about a husband who is inattentive to his wife. *La Divina Pastora* (1929) is a drama set in Trinidad concerning a blind woman about to be married who seeks a cure for her condition. The Lighthouse Players of the New York Association for the Blind produced it at the Booth Theatre (March 1929). *The Whipping* (1932; also a screenplay, 1934) is a comedy in three acts dramatizing Roy Flannagan's novel. A southern woman gains notoriety for being whipped publicly by the Ku Klux Klan. Paramount Pictures bought the rights for $5,000 in 1934 and produced it under the title *Ready to Love*, starring Ida Lupino and Richard Arlen. The setting was changed to Puritan New England, where the heroine was placed in stocks. Throughout her playwriting career, Spence taught speech and directed the dramatic society at the Eastern District High School in Brooklyn until her retirement. One of her most successful students was director **Joseph Papp** of the New York Shakespeare Festival/Public Theatre. Spence died in Gettysburg, PA, at age 87.

SPINGARN MEDAL AWARDS. This prestigious award was created in 1917 and focuses on the life of persons of African descent who have made significant contributions to various fields. The award is named after Joel Elias Spingarn, a white scholar and chair of the National Association for the Advancement of Colored People, who bequeathed in his will $20,000 for the continuation of the award. Each recipient received a gold medal valued at $100. The award winners in related and other fields who greatly impacted the advancement of African American theater include Harry T. Burleigh (1917, music), **W. E. B. DuBois** (1920, education), **Charles Sidney Gilpin** (1921, performing arts), Roland Hayes (1924, music), James Weldon Johnson (1925, literature), Charles Waddell Chestnutt (1928, literature), Mary McLeod Bethune (1935, education), Walter White (1937, race relations), Marion Anderson (1939, music), Richard Nathaniel White (1941, literature), Asa Philip Randolph (1942, labor relations), **Paul Robeson** (1945, performing arts), Thurgood Marshall (1946, law), Martin Luther King Jr. (1957, religious service), Edward "Duke"

Ellington (1959, music), **Langston Hughes** (1960, literature), Sammy Davis Jr. (1968, performing arts), Gordon A. B. Parks (1972, photography), Alvin Ailey Jr. (1976, performing arts), Rosa Lee Parks (1979, race relations), and Lena Horne (1983, performing arts).

ST. LOUIS BLACK REPERTORY THEATRE (SLBRT). One of the oldest black theaters in the country, the SLBRT, has a history of producing plays of distinction for the black community. Ronald Himes and a group of students at Washington University started the SLBRT in 1976, initially calling themselves the Phoenix Theatre Troupe. The SLBRT mainly subsisted by touring plays in area schools, universities, and other groups. Its first performing space was the sanctuary at the former Greeley Presbyterian Church, which Himes converted into a performing space and named it the 23rd Street Theatre. They grew exponentially over the years. In 1986, Himes secured a union contract with Actors Equity and began paying actors a living wage. During this transitional phase, the theater was renamed the SLBRT.

In 1991, they moved to the more centrally located, 467-seat Grandel Theatre in downtown St. Louis, MO, where they have flourished. They have produced five main-stage productions per year, attracting more than 175,000 people annually. In addition, they have toured productions to universities and schools and served more than 60,000 students each year. Over the years, the theater has grown fiscally to the level of a $1.5 million annual budget. Sixty percent of that is earned income. The other 40 percent comes from different sources, like corporate sponsors, foundations, fund-raising efforts, and contributions. The theater's 26-member board, made up of a cross-section of business leaders and pillars of the community, has embraced this task with relish to the point of finding a specific corporation to underwrite the cost of each main-stage production. They have involved such institutions as the Lila Wallace Foundation, the Ford Foundation, and the Nathan Cummings Foundation and have started the Cornerstone Project, a fund to build cash reserves and establish an endowment for future operation.

The SLBRT has taken the lead in presenting the work of some of the finest playwrights, including Athol Fugard, Tony Kushner, **August Wilson**, **Charles Fuller**, **Langston Hughes**, **Bill Harris**, **Phillip**

Hayes Dean, **Cassandra Medley**, and **Laurence Holder**. They produced such diverse productions as *I'm Not Rappaport*, *The Piano Lesson*, *The Gospel at Colonus*, *Guys and Dolls*, *Gem of the Ocean*, *Relativity*, *Mahalia: A Gospel Musical*, and *The River Niger*. They also instituted a Theatre Intern Program and a Teen Tech Program where young people are introduced to lighting, carpentry, and costuming. In a bold move, Artistic Director Himes established the Woodie Award, named in honor of black theater pioneer **Woodie King Jr.** It is designed to honor outstanding achievement by black theater workers in the fields of acting, directing, technical work, and producing. The SLBRT is not only one of the five oldest extant black theaters, but it has assumed flagship status as a well-rounded, diversified, financially stable institution that is of, by, and for the community in which it resides.

ST. LOUIS WOMAN (1944). This is a musical based on the novel *God Sends Sunday* by **Arna Bontemps**. It opened in New York City at the Martin Beck Theatre (30 March 1956) and ran for 113 performances. Edward Gross produced it, Bontemps and **Countee Cullen** wrote the book, Johnny Mercer wrote the lyrics, Harold Arlen composed the music, and Rouben Mamoulian directed it. It concerns the love affair between L'il Augie (Harold Nicholas), a successful horse jockey, and Della Green (Ruby Hill), who shoots her ex-boyfriend, Bigelow Brown (Rex Ingram), for beating her. Brown, believing Augie had shot him, puts a curse on Augie before he dies. When Augie begins losing races, Della leaves Augie, fearing she has caused him to be jinxed. After a climactic horse-racing scene, Augie's string of losses comes to an end, and he and Della reunite. Nicholas as L'il Augie and Hill as Della Green received praise in the leading roles. Pearl Bailey as Butterfly caught the attention of the critics for her rousing rendition of "Legalize My Name" and "A Woman's Prerogative." Other members of the cast included Juanita Hall (Lila), Souis Sharp (Slim), Elwood Smith (Ragsdale), Merritt Smith (Pembroke), Charles Welch (Jasper), Maude Russell (the hostess), J. Mardo Brown (drum major), Milton J. Williams (Mississippi), Frank Green (Dandy Dave), Joseph Eady (Jackie), Yvonne Coleman (Celestine), Herbert Coleman (Piggie), Lorenzo Fuller (Joshua), Milton Wood (Mr. Hopkins), Creighton Thompson (preacher), and Carrington Lewis (waiter).

STETSON, JEFF. A playwright and screenwriter, Stetson's best-known play is *The Meeting* (1984). It premiered in Los Angeles with **Dick Anthony Williams** and the late **Jason Bernard** playing the protagonists. **Civil rights** leaders Dr. Martin Luther King and Malcolm X meet in a **Harlem** hotel room a week before Malcolm's death. *The Meeting* was frequently produced throughout the country as well as in Asia and Europe, winning Stetson kudos and a host of awards. It was transformed into film, with Stetson writing the screenplay. It aired on American Playhouse in 1989. Other plays Stetson wrote are *Fraternity*, *To Find a Man*, *And the Men Shall Also Gather*, and *Fathers and Other Strangers*. Stetson also found success in the film medium, writing screenplays for *Buffalo Soldiers*, *The Marvin Gaye Story*, *Out of the Ashes*, *Passenger 57*, and *Keep the Faith: The Story of Adam Clayton Powell Jr.* Stetson's first novel, *Blood on the Leaves* (2004), was optioned by Paramount Pictures as a movie starring Jamie Foxx. For many years, Stetson was director of public affairs and relations for the California State University System. The awards Stetson accumulated include the National Association for the Advancement of Colored People Theatre Image Awards, Louis B. Mayer Outstanding Achievement Award in playwriting, and **Theodore Ward** Award for best play playwright/administrator.

STEWART, MELVIN "MEL" (1929–2002). Stewart, a veteran character stage actor and musician of the 20th century, was also prominent in television and the movies. For four decades, Stewart appeared in more than 70 television and movie productions in a variety of roles, but most of them fell solidly in the character-actor genre. Stewart was born in Cleveland, OH. He did not begin acting until the late 1950s, appearing in small parts in films and television. In the 1960s, he landed substantial roles in such plays as **Ossie Davis**'s *Purlie Victorious*. Stewart was also an accomplished musician who played the saxophone and occasionally sat in with the likes of John Coltrane and Charlie Parker, two jazz giants. Acting was his passion, however, and he embarked on a career that found him performing in television series like *East Side, West Side*; *The Smothers Brothers*; *Marcus Welby*; *The Love Boat*; *Benson*; *Little House on the Prairie*; *Matlock*; *Sanford and Son*; *Cheers*; *Police Story*; and *The Bob Newhart Show*. He also had a recurring role as Archie Bunker's neighbor in the smash hit *All in the Family*. Movies he appeared in include *Petulia, Steelyard Blues, Nothing but a Man, The Landlord, Trick Baby, Cry Uncle!, The Death of Ocean View Park, Dead Heat*, and *Made in America*. A man of many interests, Stewart also studied martial arts. He was proficient enough to obtain third-degree black-belt status in Aikido. In his later years, he began teaching theater at San Francisco State University. One of his many unknown students at the time was Danny Glover. He also organized a theater troupe for black actors that he named Bantu for "Black Actors Now Through Unity."

STREATOR, GEORGE. A playwright and journalist, Streator was a business manager and managing editor of *Crisis* magazine (1933–34). Due to ideological differences, he resigned along with **W. E. B. Du Bois**. Streator's landmark plays are *New Courage*, which deals with racial prejudice in New Jersey. A black woman sitting on a New Jersey city bus is being harassed as white passengers idly sit by. *A Sign* (1934) portrays a white clergyman who ignores the lynching of a black man to appease the state's governor and his white congregation. *Cooped Up* (1924) is a domestic drama. A landlady is attracted to a happily married man in her rooming house. She devises a scheme to break up the couple by enlisting the aid of a local Romeo to woo the wife away from the husband. The *Opportunity* Contest Awards (1925) gave it an honorable mention. It was produced by the National Ethiopian Art Players at the **Lafayette Theatre** (October 1924), the Ethiopian Art Players in Chicago (1925), the Intercollegiate Association at the Imperial Elks Auditorium in **Harlem** (May 1926), and the New Negro Art Theatre at the Lincoln Theatre (November 1928).

SULLIVAN, MRS. JOHN. *See* MILLER, MAY (MRS. JOHN SULLIVAN).

SUNDIATA, SEKOU (1948–2007). A performance artist, musician, poet, and playwright, Sundiata was named Robert Franklin Feaste at his birth in East **Harlem**. As a reflection of his emerging black consciousness, he changed his name in the late 1960s to Sundiata, a military ruler in old Mali. Sundiata received his degrees from City College of New York and Columbia University. He taught literature at the Eugene Lang College of the New School for Social Research until his death. He was representative of a new breed of performance artists who combined the elements of poetry, narrative, music, and improvisation to tell a story that changed from performance to performance. His work is described as an exploration of the whole idea of text and noise, cadences, and pauses. He was a preeminent performance artist of the 21st century and won many awards for his work. His performance pieces include *Blessing the Boats*, an autobiographical story of his kidney transplant using a meld of theatrical monologue, griot storytelling, standup comedy, the spoken word, and music. *51st Dream State* was written in 2006 using the same techniques to explore the shifting definition of America and what it means to be a citizen in a deeply complex, conflicted society. *The Circle Unbroken Is a Hard Bop* is a 1993 effort examining the radical politics in the black arts movement of the 1960s. His other pieces include *Udu*, a chronicle of human **slavery** in the 18th century juxtaposed against human slavery in present-day Africa, and *The Mystery of Love*. Honors for Sundiata included a Charles Revson fellowship, a Sundance screenwriting fellowship, a New School Film Institute fellowship, a Bessie Award, and an **Audience Development Committee Award**. Sundiata died on 18 July 2007.

THE SWING MIKADO (1939) AND THE HOT MIKADO (1939). These are both adaptations of Gilbert and Sullivan's (white) operetta *The Mikado* cast with all black actors. After eight months of rehearsal, the **Federal Theatre Project (FTP)** first produced *The Swing Mikado* at the Great Northern Theatre in Chicago (25 September 1938). Director Harry Minturn changed the location from Japan to a coral island in the Pacific. The FTP moved it to the New Yorker Theatre on 54th Street on Broadway (1 May 1939) with great artistic and financial success. The Marolin Corporation produced it with Charles Levy and Gentry Warden providing swing music. The cast included Edward Fraction (the Mikado), Maurice Cooper (Nanki-Poo), Lewis White (Pish-Tush), Herman Greene (Ko-Ko), William Franklin (Poo-Bah), Gladys Boucree (Yum-Yum), Frankie Fambro (Pitti-Sing), Mabel Carter (Peep-Bo), and Mabel Walker (Katisha). Three weeks after *The Swing Mikado* arrived on Broadway, Mike Todd opened *The Hot Mikado* at another Broadway theater, the Broadhurst, starring Bill "Bojangles" Robinson in the role of the Mikado. *The Swing Mikado* was no match for *The Hot Mikado*. Because the FTP rules stipulated that they had to hire primarily unemployed actors, the show could not compete with the lavish costumes and set and with "Bojangles" singing and dancing in the role of the Mikado—all the elements of a legitimate Broadway show. *The Swing Mikado* was forced to close after a three-week run.

– T –

TAYLOR, ANTOINETTE "TONI". A playwright, Taylor is a Louisville, KY, native and graduate of Eastern Kentucky University. Her most successful play is *The Triangle*, about a student in a genealogy class studying the Middle Passage slave trade who discovers a family linkage. Most of her plays were performed at the **Juneteenth Legacy Theatre** in Louisville founded by **Lorna Littleway**. Other plays Taylor wrote are *Miss Amanda's Place*, *And the Next Day They Changed the Water*, *More Than Cooking Going On in This Kitchen*, and *This Land Is Your Land/Can You Hear It?*

TAYLOR, CLARICE. Active since the 1940s, Taylor is an actress and director of stage, screen, and television. Born in Buckingham County, VA, Taylor moved to New York City to study acting at the New Theatre School and the **American Negro Theatre** in **Harlem**. Taylor made her stage debut in the role of Sophie Slow in **Abram Hill**'s *On Striver's Row* (1940). Subsequently, she was cast in *Natural Man* (1941), *Home Is the Hunter* (1945), *The Peacemakers* (1946), *Rain* (1948), and *Skeleton* (1948). Taylor was also associated with two prominent theaters. At the Committee for the Negro in the Arts in Harlem, she performed in *A Medal for Willie* (as the mother, 1950) by **William Branch**, and directed *Gold through the Trees* (1952) by **Alice Childress**. At the Greenwich Mews Theatre, she acted in *Major Barbara* (c. 1953) and in Branch's *In Splendid Error* (1954) and codirected Childress's *Trouble in Mind* (1955). In the late 1960s, Taylor performed at other off-Broadway theaters, such as the **Negro Ensemble Company**, as well as on Broadway. Television audiences of the late 1980s and early 1990s readily recognized Taylor as Grandmother Huxtable on *The Cosby Show* and for her portrayal of Jackie ("Moms") Mabley in the off-Broadway production of Childress's *Moms* (1987), for which she won an **Obie Award** for her performance.

TAYLOR, DOMINIC. A playwright and educator, Taylor was born in Orange, NJ. Taylor received a B.A. in engineering at Brown University (1987). After he was introduced to the work of the famed **Rites and Reason Theatre** Taylor switched his major, and in 1995, he emerged with an M.F.A. in creative writing and hasn't looked back. After being commissioned by the Goodman Theatre in Chicago, Taylor wrote his most successful play, *Wedding Dance*. Produced at the **Crossroads Theatre Company** in New Jersey, it won the first Scott McPherson Award. Other plays he wrote are *Hype Hero, Up City Service(s), Public Transportation, Photo Op, Reflexions in D Minor, It's Your Birthday, Arrythmia,* and *Personal History.* Taylor's plays have been produced across the country at **Joseph Papp**'s NYSF/Public Theatre, the Kennedy Center, Hartford Stage, and Playwright's Horizons. He wrote several screenplays, including *Hit Me on the Hip* and *Memoirs of My Nervous Illness.* Taylor is now associate director at the Penumbra Theatre in St. Paul, MN. Among the awards and honors Taylor has accumulated are the Rockefeller Foundation fellowship, Jerome Foundation Fellowship, Illinois State Arts Council grant, McDowell Foundation fellowship, Theatre Communications Group Award, and United States/Africa Writers fellowship. Taylor was a visiting assistant professor of theatre in the Africana Studies Department at Bard College.

TAYLOR, JACQUELINE "JACKIE." Taylor, a director, actor, playwright, and producer, believes theater can be used as a strong educational tool and motivating force to help remove the blinders of racism. Discouraged by the negative images of black people in the era of blaxploitation films, Taylor founded the **Black Ensemble Theatre (BET)** in 1976. Not only has the BET thrived as an institution in theater-rich Chicago, Taylor has produced over 100 plays and musical biographies. More incredibly, the BET has done so in a fiscally prudent manner, never running a deficit or shutting down.

Born in Chicago, Taylor earned a B.A. in theater from Loyola University in 1973. After working for the Free Street Theatre, Victory Gardens, and the Goodman Theatre, she organized the BET. She had a three-pronged agenda—to create realistic roles for women, to avoid the stereotyping of African Americans, and to bring people of all races together in a communal setting. Initially the audiences were 100 percent black, but over the years, the demographics have changed to 55 percent black, 40 percent Caucasian, and 5 percent other. The bill of fare has changed over the years from such classics as *A Raisin in the Sun*, *Glass Menagerie*, and *Julius Caesar* to musically oriented biographies like *Muddy Waters: The Hoochie Coochie Man*, *Great Women in Gospel*, and *The Nat King Cole Story*. Indeed, musical biographies have become the signature of the BET. Taylor has taken on the role of playwright and has written such plays and musicals as *The Other Cinderella* and *Muddy Waters* (both cowritten with Jimmy Tillman), *Dynamite Divas*, *Sweet Mama Stringbean* (about Ethel Waters), *Ella* (biography of Ella Fitzgerald), *This Is My Play Song* (1978), and *The Jackie Wilson Story* (1999). This last play was such a huge success at the **National Black Theatre Festival** in Winston-Salem, NC, in 2003 that the festival invited Taylor to return the show for an encore engagement in 2005. Taylor served as the artistic director of the Regal Theatre and was vice president of the League of Chicago Theatres. She also worked with troubled students in a Strengthening the School through Theatre Arts Program and was president of the African American Arts Alliance.

TAYLOR, MARGARET. *See* SNIPES, MARGARET FORD-TAYLOR.

TAYLOR, REGINA. An actor and playwright, Taylor was born in Dallas, TX. She earned a B.A. in theater arts from Southern Methodist University in 1981. Taylor is widely known for her role as Lily in the television series *I'll Fly Away*, for which she received a Golden Globe Award and was nominated for an Emmy Award. She has appeared in such films as *Clockers* and *The Negotiator*, as well as in such Shakespearean productions as *Macbeth*, *As You Like It*, and

Romeo and Juliet, for which she was the first black woman to play Juliet on Broadway. Taylor is also a playwright of substance, having written over 10 plays. Her most successful play is *Crowns*, adapted from the book of the same name. It premiered at the McCarter Theatre in 2002 and was an instant success. Subsequently, it played regional theaters throughout the United States at such theaters as the Intiman, Tyrone Guthrie, **St. Louis Black Repertory**, and **Arena Playhouse**, where it broke box-office records running at 99 percent capacity. The play was showered with honors, including four Helen Hayes Awards, a National Association for the Advancement of Colored People Image Award, and seven **Audience Development Committee Awards** for excellence in black theater. Among the other plays Taylor wrote are *A Night in Tunisia*, *Oblide*, *Watermelon Rinds*, *Drowning Crow*, *The Seagull* (an adaptation of Anton Chekhov's play), *Oo-Bla-Dee*, *Between the Lines*, *The Dreams of Sarah Breedlove*, *Jennine's Diary*, *Inside the Belly of the Beast*, and *Behind Every Good Man*. Taylor has been awarded a Distinguished Alumni Award from Southern Methodist University and a Best New Play Award from the American Critics Association for her play *Oo-Bla-Dee*.

TAYLOR, ROBERT "ROB". In the early 1970s, Taylor was an inmate at Riker's Island Prison in New York City. Rather than letting this situation debilitate him, he rechanneled his creative energies into a positive experience. Writing plays gave him a new perspective on life. Taylor collaborated with Cecil Alonzo to write *Somewhere between Us Two* (1972) while in prison. It was a poetic love story in one act. Two pen pals disappointed in each other when they finally meet reassess the qualities that attracted them to each other in the first place. The **Alonzo Players** produced it in Brooklyn at the **Billie Holiday Theatre** (1973) as well as the **Black Theatre Alliance** annual festival in New York (1974). *Strike One Blow* (1973) is a drama in one act coauthored with Alonzo. It is based on psychological challenges the author struggled with as an inmate. It was produced at the Tompkins Square Park Players in New York City and at the Billie Holiday Theatre in Brooklyn (1973).

TEER, BARBARA ANN (1937–2008). A black theater founder, actress, educator, and choreographer, Teer was best known as organizer, producer, director, resident playwright, and executive producer of the acclaimed **National Black Theatre** (NBT, 1968). Born in East St. Louis, IL, Teer was educated at the University of Illinois (B.A. in dance, 1957). She studied drama with Sanford Meisner, Paul Mann, Phillip Burton, and **Lloyd Richards** and dance at Vigmont School of Dance in Berlin and in Paris. She was married to the late comedian Godfrey Cambridge and with him had two children. Teer had a rich and varied theatrical career. She danced with the Alvin Ailey and Louis Johnson Dance Companies and was dance captain on Broadway for Agnes DeMille in the musical *Kwamina*. She taught dance and drama in New York City public schools and founded with **Robert Hooks** the Group Theatre Workshop (1964), which later became the **Negro Ensemble Company**. In addition, she was cultural director of a teenage workshop at the **Harlem** School of the Arts (1967).

As the spiritual force and prime mover behind the NBT, Teer developed and created a black art standard that became the trademark of the NBT. All theatrical presentations, including plays, musicals, rituals, and revivals, adhered to her mandate to raise the level of consciousness, address political issues, educate, illuminate, and entertain. Teer also developed new art forms: "ritualistic revivals" and "blackenings." She created what has been called the "Teer Technology of Soul" as a technique of teaching "God Conscious Art" at the NBT. She toured the NBT to theaters, colleges, and universities throughout the eastern United States, the Caribbean, and Nigeria. Since early 1960s, Teer has performed in film and frequently as a stage actress appearing in New York productions. She coproduced and directed the screenplay *Rise: A Love Song for a Love People* (1975), based on the life of Malcolm X. It received the National Association of Media Women's Black Film Festival Award as best film (1975). Her directing credits include productions at the NBT, including her own dramatic works, off Broadway, and CBS-TV (1973). She was also contributing editor of numerous articles to black theater magazines.

Among the plays Teer wrote are *Tribute to Brother Malcolm* (late 1960s), a historical documentation of Malcolm X's tragic assassination. The NBT Workshop performed it (late 1960s) under Teer's direction. *Organize!* (1969–72) is a full-length ritual coauthored with

Charlie L. Russell that took three years to evolve. In what was to become Teer's trademark, she infused music, chants, and dance and involved audience members to create a warm spiritual experience. *Sojourney into Truth* (also known as *Soul Journey into Truth*, 1975) is a full-length theatrical collage written, directed, and choreographed by Teer. The NBT produced it (1975). Thereafter it toured three West Indian and Caribbean countries. Costumer Larry Le Gaspi was honored with an **Audience Development Committee (Audelco) Award** (1976). Teer was the recipient of numerous awards and citations for her contributions to the theater and the community. Among them were the Vernon Rice/**Drama Desk Award** as best actress (196), the first annual Audelco Recognition Award in theater (1973), International Benin Award (1974), Cultural Arts Service Award from the **Black Spectrum Theatre Company** (1978), Monarch Merit Award from the Special Council for Culture and Art for outstanding contributions to the performing and visual arts (1983), and the National Black Treasure Award presented by the Hamilton Arts Center in Schenectady, NY, for outstanding contribution to black American theater.

TERRELL, VINCENT. A playwright, Terrell was a former artistic director of the Society of Creative Concern in Boston (1969–75). Terrell's plays were produced by the society, including *The Caskets* (1969), a drama in one act that deals with the murders of three civil rights activists—Medgar Evers, Malcolm X, and Martin Luther King Jr.; *Genuine Minstrel Show* (1969), a musical comedy in three acts; *Apollo #19* (1970), a one-act that centers on the relationship between two astronauts during a space flight; *God's a Faggot: A Biblical Confession* (1970); a morality drama in one act that raises conflicting notions about spirituality; *Sarge* (1970), a drama in one act set in a courtroom, where a black soldier is on trial for defecting to the side of the Viet Cong during the Vietnam War; *Several Barrels of Trash* (1970), a morality drama in one act about garbage collectors who find a large sum of money; *Shuttle United States* (1970), a drama in one act advocating a revolutionary solution to America's racial and political problems. *Us* (1971) is a drama in one act. As in his play *Shuttle*, the author offers another radical solution to America's racial problems. *Trotter* (1972) is a historical drama in one act. It portrays the last days in the life of William Monroe Trotter, Boston's militant black leader. Other plays Terrell wrote *Will It Be Like This Tomorrow* (1972); *Trotter Debates* (1973); *An Evening with William Wells Brown* (1974); *From These Shores; or, Good Olde Crispus* (1974); and *Miss Phyllis* (1974).

TERRY-MORGAN, ELMO. A playwright and educator, Terry-Morgan is one of the unsung heroes of black theater. As an associate professor and artistic director of the **Rites and Reason Theatre (RRT)** at Brown University, he continues the research-to-performance method (RPM) pioneered by its founder, **George Houston Bass**. The RPM is a systematic process that organizes teams of artists, scholars, and researchers in the creative development of new plays. Since its inception in 1970, the RRT has developed and produced some 75 widely divergent scripts, and spawned such playwrights as J. E. Franklin, **P. J. Gibson, Dominic Taylor**, and Jake Ann Jones. Terry-Morgan specializes in African American theater, African American folk traditions and expressions, and playwriting. Elmo, as his students call him, earned a B.A. in American history from Brown University and an M.F.A. in playwriting from the University of California at San Diego. He is also a director of plays and a playwright. Some of the plays he has written are *The Fruits of Miss Morning*, *Heart to Heart: Ain't Your Life Worth Saving* (commissioned play), *Spider Weave a Lovely Lie*, *Renaissance*, *Song of Sheba* (a musical), and *Ophelia's Cotillion* (a musical). Terry-Morgan is a member of the **Audience Development Committee**, **Black Theatre Network**, the National Alliance for Musical Theatre, and the Dramatists Guild. He is also an associate director and playwright at the **National Black Theatre** in **Harlem**.

THEATRE OF THE ABSURD. A phrase that gained popularity after Alfred Jarry's (white) production of *Ubu Roi* during the late 1800s. It was an alternative surrealistic theater form that viewed life and theater as being absurd. By the turn of the century, this absurdist style and confrontational stance influenced the works of such playwrights as **Adrienne Kennedy** in *Funnyhouse of a Negro* (1963), *The Rat's Mass* (1966), and *The Owl Answers* (1965). Her objects and characters embrace multiple people and ideas, sometimes simultaneously, creating the effect of nightmares; however as in a dream, behind her kaleidoscopic vision hovers a literal story. *Funnyhouse* is emblematic of the madhouse of racism in America. A biracial woman is torn between the paradoxes of black and white, past and present, flesh and spirit. Shunned by the commercial theater, Kennedy's plays gained popularity in institutions of higher education.

This avant-garde confrontational style also attracted the more radical sector of African American theater, such as **Amiri Baraka's (LeRoi Jones)** *Dutchman* (1964), *The Baptism* (1964), *The Slave* (1962), and *The Toilet* **(1962)** and **Ed Bullins's** *The Electronic Nigger*. Kennedy's *Funnyhouse* and Baraka's *Dutchman* were both honored with **Obie Awards** in 1964 as the best off-Broadway dramas of the season. The contemporary successor to this absurdist style is **Suzan-Lori Parks**, the first African American female playwright to receive the prestigious **Pulitzer Prize**. Although Parks won the grand prize for *Topdog/Underdog* (2003, a nonabsurdist play), the influence of the absurdist style becomes evident in such plays as *The Last Black Man on the Entire Earth*.

THOMAS, VEONA. A director, playwright, storyteller, and entrepreneur, Thomas is the artistic director of Rejoti Productions in Teaneck, NJ. They have been a producing entity for the past 20 years, during which Thomas has usually directed three to four productions each year. A professional storyteller, Thomas has performed in schools, libraries, and senior centers in both New York and New Jersey. She has also written over 30 plays, one of which, *The Diva and the Rapper*, has been very successful. The play explores the generational conflict between an elderly blues singer and a young rapper. Among the plays Thomas has written are *The Head Lady—Madame C. J. Walker*, a dramatization of the life of C. J. Walker; *Tuesday in No Man's Land*, about three women bonding in an abortion clinic; *Nzinga's Children* (1983), which centers on a young woman having to choose whether to marry an unsuccessful black man or a successful white attorney; *A Matter of Conscience* (1985), in which a woman must make a decision between an easy theft and her conscience; and *MLK: A Personal Look* (1985), a one-woman show about the great **civil rights** leader Dr. Martin Luther King. Other plays she wrote are *Couple Wanted, Heaven Sent, The Execution*, and *Follow the Drinking Gourd*. Thomas is the recipient of the Grandmother Winifred Award and Puffin Award.

THOMPSON, GARLAND LEE SR. Born in Muskogee, OK, and raised in the state of Oregon, Thompson is a director, actor, poet, and playwright. He spent a year at the University of Oregon before he was lured to Los Angeles to pursue an acting career. As a member of the touring production of **Charles Gordone**'s play *No Place to Be Somebody*, he ended up in New York City. It was there in 1973, that Thompson, along with actor **Morgan Freeman**, conceived the idea of a playwright's workshop, a place where fledgling writers could work with professional actors and use audience feedback to develop their works. Thus, the **Frank Silvera Writer's Workshop** was born. It still thrives today, with Thompson as the driving force.

As a playwright, Thompson's plays were widely produced at such institutions as Studio West, Open Eye Theatre, the Schomburg Center, and the **Negro Ensemble Company**. *Papa B on the D Train* (1972), a play within a play, is about the New York subway system. *Sisyphus and the Blue Eyed Cyclops* (1970) is an exploration of the thin line between madness and sanity. *The Incarnation of Reverend Good Blacque Dress* (1978) is about a man who exorcises his demons during a surprise visit by an ex-girlfriend. *Tut-Ank-Amen, The Boy King* (1982) is a historical drama. *Jesse and the Games* (1984) is a dramatization of events leading up to Jesse Owens's victory in the 1936 Olympic Games. Thompson received two **Audience Development Committee Awards**.

THOMPSON, TAZEWELL. Thompson is one of the more versatile directors and producers working today, being equally comfortable in plays, musicals, and opera. He is one of the first African Americans to assume the directorship of two white regional theaters. From 1992 to 1995, he was artistic director of Syracuse Stage. The versatility and broad palette of Thompson's play selections led to his appointment in January 2005 as artistic director of the 75-year-old Westport County Playhouse, succeeding Joanne Woodward. He took the job, however, in 2006. He directed more than 60 plays and musicals across the country in venues like the Oregon Shakespeare Festival, Hartford Stage, Indiana Rep, and Goodman Theatre. He has also directed at La Scala, the Paris Opera, Teatro Real, and the Opera Bastille, as well as operas in San Francisco, New York, and

Los Angeles. Thompson has also directed plays at **Arena Playhouse**, Cleveland Playhouse, Virginia Stage Company, Lincoln Center, and a host of other regional theaters. He has directed the works of established masters like Molière, Euripides, Shakespeare, Ibsen, Chekhov, Feydeau, and Shaw, as well as the modern playwrights Arthur Miller, Thornton Wilder, Athol Fugard, Tennessee Williams, Terrence McNally, **Marion McClinton**, and Alan Ayckbourn. His opera productions include *Les Dialogues des Carmélites* and *Porgy and Bess* for the New York City Opera and *Death in Venice* for Glimmerglass Opera.

As a playwright, he is mostly known for *Constant Star*, a play with music about the life of **civil rights** activist Ida Wells Barnett. The play was an instant success, and Thompson has subsequently been commissioned to write plays for the Lincoln Center, South Coast Repertory Theatre, and People's Light and Repertory Company. Thompson was a recipient of the Helen Hayes Award, National Association for the Advancement of Colored People Image Award, Alan Schneider Distinguished Fund Award, and a National Endowment for the Arts/Theatre Communications Group Theatre Residency Award.

THURMAN, WALLACE (1902–34). A major writer during the **Harlem** Renaissance, Thurman was a playwright, novelist, magazine editor, and film scenarist. He was born in Salt Lake City, UT, where he attended the University of Utah (1919–20). Lured by the vibrant literary movement in Harlem, Thurman settled in New York City in 1925. This was after he spent a few years in Los Angeles as a writer for the *Outlet*, a black newspaper. In Harlem, he assumed a position as a reporter and editor of the *Looking Glass*, a short-lived publishing house. His criticism of Alain Locke's *The New Negro* (1925), the breakthrough anthology of black art during the Harlem Renaissance, set him apart from the "talented tenth," as the black literary intelligentsia was called. Thurman also served as editor for the *Messenger*, a radical periodical (1926); as circulation manager for *The World Tomorrow*, a liberal white monthly (1926); and as cofounder of *Fire!*, a controversial magazine that included the works of younger black writers (it only had one issue). He cofounded and published with his own funds *Harlem: A Forum of Negro Life*, which resulted in two publications. Thurman also worked as a ghostwriter (1929) for *True*

Story magazine (and other McFadden publications) and contributed articles to other magazines.

In 1929, Thurman earned critical acclaim for his first novel, *The Blacker the Berry*, and for his Broadway show *Harlem*. *Blacker* was about color stratification among blacks. Thurman, a dark-skinned man, depicted a somewhat autobiographical account of intraracism among dark- and light-complexioned blacks. Thurman cowrote with William Jourdan Rapp his three-act play *Harlem: Cordelia the Crude and Black Belt, A Melodrama of Negro Life in Harlem* (1929). It was taken from Thurman's short story, *Cordelia the Crude, A Harlem Sketch*. A transplanted Harlem family from South Carolina is forced to give "rent parties" to survive while the daughter gets involved with a street hustler. It opened on Broadway (1929) at the Apollo Theatre (not the **Apollo Theatre** in Harlem) and ran for 93 performances with a cast that included Inez Clough as Ma Williams and Lew Payton as Pa Williams. The play moved to the Times Square Theatre on 42nd Street on April 1929 but was closed due to a strike (May 1929). The show was taken on the road by another company. It returned to Broadway at the Times Square Theatre for 16 performances (1929). Thurman also wrote *Jeremiah the Magnificent* (1930). After being hospitalized for six months in the city hospital of New York's Welfare Island, Thurman died at age 32.

TILLMAN, KATHERINE DAVIS. A pioneer playwright, Tillman was among the first African American women to have a play published. Between 1890 and 1910, Davis wrote *Fifty Years of Freedom; or, From Cabin to Congress*. It was about the life of Benjamin Banneker, an early black astronomer, mathematician, scientist, and inventor. *Aunt Betsy's Thanksgiving* (c. 1910) presents a mother who, many years earlier, abandoned her infant daughter, leaving her in the care of the child's grandmother. The mother returns home as a wealthy woman to share her riches with her daughter and the grandmother.

TOLSON, MELVIN BEAUNORUS (1900–66). A playwright, poet, teacher, and politician, Tolson, was born in Moberly, MO. He attended Fisk and Lincoln Universities and earned an M.A. at Columbia University. For 20 years, Tolson taught English at Wiley College in Texas. He became a professor of creative literature at Langston University in Oklahoma, where he directed the Campus Dust Bowl Theatre and served four terms as mayor of Langston. In retirement, in the 1960s, Tolson was lured to Tuskegee Institute in Alabama to assume a post created by the Department of Humanities. He is best known for his wildly poetically satirical look at life in Harlem in his book, *Harlem Gallery* (1965). It is widely hailed as one of the finest pieces of writing extant, and it put Tolson in the top ranks of worldwide wordsmiths.

Tolson was best known as a poet. He received numerous fellowships, prizes, and awards for his poems, which were widely published and anthologized. His playwriting efforts are *The Moses of Beale Street* (pre-1941), a full-length black miracle play with music coauthored with Edward Boatner, and *Black Boy*, a full-length drama adapted from **Richard Wright**'s autobiographical novel.

TONY AWARDS (ANTOINETTE PERRY AWARD). In 1947, the American Theatre Wing's Talk of New York Award (Tony) started a program to celebrate excellence in the theater. It was named in honor of Antoinette Perry, the recently deceased (28 June 1946) actress, director, and producer who was also an active wartime leader of the American Theatre Wing. The Tony Awards debuted with a dinner at the Waldorf Astoria Hotel (6 April 1947) on Easter Sunday. Awards are usually presented in seven categories along with special awards.

African American recipients of the Tony Awards from its inception to 2007 include Harry Belafonte for best supporting or featured actor (*Almanac*, 1954), *A Raisin in the Sun* for best play (1960), Diahann Carroll for best actress in a musical (*No Strings*, 1962), Pearl Bailey for a special award (1968), **James Earl Jones** for best actor in a play (*The Great White Hope*, 1969), and the **Negro Ensemble Company** for a special award (1969). Other recipients are listed according to the decade the award was received.

In the 1970s, Cleavon Little won for best actor in a musical (*Purlie*, 1970), Ben Vereen for best actor in a musical (*Pippin*, 1973), *Raisin* for best musical (1974), *The River Niger* for best play (1974), *The Wiz* for best musical (1975), Ted Ross for best supporting or featured actor in a musical (*The Wiz*, 1975), Dee Dee Bridgewater for best featured or supporting actress in a musical (*The Wiz*, 1975), Geoffrey Holder for best director and best costume designer (*The Wiz*, 1975), Charlie Smalls for best score (music and lyrics, *The Wiz*, 1975), Trazana Beverly for best featured Actress in a play (*For Colored Girls Who Have Considered Suicide When the Rainbow Is Enuf*, 1977), Dolores Hall for best featured actress in a musical (*Your Arms Too Short to Box with God*, 1977), Diana Ross for a special award (1977), and Nell Carter for best featured actress in a Musical (*Ain't Misbehavin'*, 1978).

In the1980s, Lena Horne won a special award (*Lena Horne, The Lady and Her Music*, 1981), and Hinton Battle won for best featured actor in a musical (*Sophisticated Ladies*, 1982); Ben Harney for best actor in a musical (*Dreamgirls*, 1982); Jennifer Holliday for best actress in a musical (*Dreamgirls*, 1982); Cleavant Derricks for best featured actor in a musical (*Dreamgirls*, 1982); Michael Peters for best choreographer (*Dreamgirls*, 1982); Charles "Honi" Coles for best featured actor in a musical (*My One and Only*, 1983); Hinton Battle for best featured actor in a musical (*Tap Dance Kid*, 1984); **Fences** for best play (1987); **Lloyd Richards** for best director (*Fences*, 1987); James Earl Jones for best actor in a play (*Fences*, 1987); **Mary Alice** for best featured actress in a play (*Fences*, 1987); **L. Scott Caldwell** for best featured actress in a play (*Joe Turner's Come and Gone*, 1988); Ruth Brown for best actress in a musical (*Black and Blue*, 1989); Hinton Battle for best featured actor in a musical (*Miss Saigon*, 1991); and Cholly Atkins, Henry LeTang, Frankie Manning, and Fayard Nicholas for best choreographers (*Black and Blue*, 1989).

In the 1990s, Laurence Fishburne won for featured actor in a play (*Two Trains Running*, 1992), Gregory Hines for featured actor in a play (*Jelly's Last Jam*, 1992), the Goodman Theatre of Chicago for a special award (1992), Tonya Pinkins for best featured actress in a musical (*Jelly's Last Jam*, 1992), **George C. Wolfe** for best director of a play (*Angels in America: Millennium Approaches*, 1993), **Jeffrey Wright** for best featured actor in a play (*Angels in America: Perestroika*, 1994), **Ruben Santiago-Hudson** for featured role in a play (*Seven Guitars*, 1996), George C. Wolfe for best director in a musical (*Bring in 'da Noise, Bring in 'da Funk*, 1996), Savion Glover for best choreographer (*Bring in 'da Noise, Bring in 'da Funk*, 1996), Ann Duquesnay for best featured actress in a musical (*Bring in 'da Noise, Bring in 'da Funk*, 1996), **Audra McDonald** for best featured actress in a musical (*Ragtime*, 1998), Donald Holder for best lighting designer (*The Lion King*, 1998), and **Crossroads Theatre Company** for best regional theater (1999).

In the 2000s, Heather Headley won for best actress in a musical (*Aida*, 2000), Viola Davis for best featured actress in a play (*King Hedley II*, 2001), Russell Simmons for best director of a special theatrical event (*Def Poetry Jam on Broadway*, 2003), **Phylicia Allen-Rashad** for best actress in a play (*A Raisin in the Sun*, 2004), Audra McDonald for best featured actress in a play (*A Raisin in the Sun*, 2004), La Chanze for best actress in a musical (*The Color Purple*, 2006), Bill T. Jones for best choreography (*Spring Awakening* 2007), and Alliance Theatre for best regional theater (2007).

TOOMER, JEAN (NATHAN EUGENE TOOMER, 1894–1967). Toomer was a mulatto playwright, poet, short-story writer, essayist, and novelist. He is historically significant as one of the most original and influential talents of the Negro Renaissance in **Harlem**. Born in Washington, DC, of a prestigious family, he was the grandson of P. S. B. Pinchback, the famous black politician of the Reconstruction who served as acting governor and later state senator of Louisiana. Growing up, Toomer never knew much about his father, Nathan Toomer, who deserted his mother, Nina Pinchback Toomer. After high school in 1914, he took up playwriting. He was inspired by the writing style and themes of George Bernard Shaw's plays. His most noted play is *Kabnis* (1923), an experimental drama in one long act and six scenes. It is a semiautobiographical play about a black intellectual from the North. Kabnis accepts a teaching position in the Deep South, where he searches for his identity. Although he makes the pilgrimage to the region that he posits as his ancestral home, he does not identify with other successful blacks or mingle with uneducated blacks who live in that region because of cultural dissimilarities. Failing to find intellectual, religious, or romantic fulfillment, Kabnis gets a revelation from Father John, who lives in a basement. John has not spoken for years. He is the symbol of the archetypal wise old man or spiritual ancestor of the black race who makes a mundane pronouncement. Thoroughly disillusioned by this utterance, Kabnis consoles himself with a night of debauchery and resolves to abandon his intellectual pursuits and begin an apprenticeship as a blacksmith. The play was rejected for production because of its avant-garde style, but during the renaissance of the 1960s, it was reclaimed as a classic by the bourgeoning black aesthetic movement. Other plays Toomer wrote include *The Sacred Factory* (1927) and *The Gallonwerps* (1928). Both are full-length expressionistic dramas. Still other plays he authored are *A Drama of the Southwest* (1935) and *Topsy and Eva* (c. late 1930).

TOPDOG/UNDERDOG (2001). **Suzan-Lori Parks**, best known as a writer of avant-garde plays, adapted the linear format for *Topdog/ Underdog* and became the first African American woman to win the prestigious **Pulitzer Prize** for drama. It is a darkly, sardonic story of two shiftless brothers, Lincoln and Booth, whose obsession with three-card monte, a street card game, affects their lives. The play touches on sibling rivalry, family myth, **slavery**, past and present, and history. The play debuted at **Joseph Papp**'s NYSF/Public Theatre on 22 July 2001. The two-actor play was directed by **George C. Wolfe**, artistic director of the NYSF/Public Theatre in New York City. It featured **Jeffrey Wright** and Don Cheadle as the Booth brothers in a limited run. On 7 April 2002, the play opened to great reviews on Broadway at the Ambassador Theatre, with a cast including Wright and Mos Def, playing some 144 performances through 11 August of that year before closing. The production also received several other major awards—the **Drama Desk Award** as best play, a Theatre World Award for Def, and a **Tony Award** and Drama Desk Award in the outstanding actor category for Wright.

TOWNE STREET THEATRE (TST). The TST was established in 1992 in Los Angeles by the triumvirate of Nancy Cheryl Davis, Nathaniel Bellamy, and Nancy Renee. They had a twofold purpose: to develop and produce new works by Los Angeles playwrights reflective of the **black experience** and to produce a Black Classic Series for works by established African American playwrights that have become a seminal part of black theater. Not too much has been seen of the latter, but they have succeeded admirably in developing and producing the works of new young playwrights like Barbara Morgan, Stan Sellars, Harriett Dickey, and Sherie Bailey. Established playwrights have been represented by productions of **Loften Mitchell**'s

The Phonograph and **Charlie Russell**'s rambunctious comedy *Five on the Black Hand Side.*

The TST is one of only four black theaters in Los Angeles, having been in existence for exactly 15 years now, which portends well for the future. They have produced widely divergent plays, like Bernardo Solano's *Science and the Primitives*, a look at altered states in the jungles of South America, and Barbara White Morgan's *The Dance Begins When the Waltz Goes Backward*, an urban comedy that explores the encounter between an aging, white, savvy television writer and a black intellectual, homeless philosopher. The TST has added two similar additional programs to the mix over the years. One is a film reading series, and the other a stage reading affair. Both are designed to allow aspiring film writers and playwrights to hear their works read by professional actors and others informed by a professional sensibility. Scripts are read and judged by a professional panel of writers before being accepted for a reading. Revenue to support the TST comes from admissions, donations, grants, and corporate support from Toyota Motor Corporation, Northrop Grumman Corporation, Miller Brewing Company, and the Beuth Foundation.

A TRIP TO COONTOWN **(1891).** This is a musical farce by **Bob Cole** and William (Billy) Johnson, with additional music by Willis Accooe. It is the first full-length musical comedy written, performed, directed, and produced by African Americans and one of the first to depart from the minstrel pattern. This landmark production showed producers and theater owners there was an audience for all-black shows.

A Trip to Coontown opened on Broadway at the Third Avenue Theatre (4 April 1898) for eight performances. Its journey to Broadway began at the Proctor's Music Hall in New York City (August 1897), where Cole rehearsed the show. *Coontown* received its tryout in the Catskills in upstate New York and in South Amboy, NJ (27 September 1897). By the end of the year, it had opened at Milner's Eighth Avenue Theatre in New York City but had to close because of the New York Theatrical Syndicate lockout. After touring the Canadian provinces to great success at the Queens Theatre in Montreal, the Victoria Park Theatre in Ottawa, and in Toronto (February 1898), it landed at the Third Avenue Theatre. The plot centers on a naïve old black man who is saved at the last minute from being cheated out of his pension by a con man. The setting in *Coontown* served as a backdrop for several vaudeville specialty acts by Jim Wilson (equilibrist), Lloyd G. Gibbs (the greatest living black tenor), the Freeman Sisters (contortional dancers), and Juvia Roan (the Cuban nightingale). Among the cast were Cole (Willie Wayside, a tramp, played in whiteface), Billy Johnson (Jim Flimflammer, a confidence artist), Silas Green (the grand old man of Coontown), and Bob A. Kelley (Silas Green Jr.). The show closed in 1891 after touring for two seasons.

TURMAN, GLYNN. Turman is an actor, director, and producer. He made his stage debut at the age of 12 when he played young Travis in the ground-breaking 1959 Broadway production of **Lorraine Hansberry**'s *A Raisin in the Sun* with **Sidney Poitier** and **Ruby Dee**. Eleven years after his debut, he performed in *Raisin* again in the 1970 production when he played the lead role of Walter Lee under the direction of theatrical guru **Woodie King Jr.** at the **New Federal Theatre**. A Native New Yorker, Turman studied theater at the Manhattan School of Performing Arts, where he launched a career in theater and show business that extends to this day. He has taught acting for 15 years at the Inner-City Cultural Center in Los Angeles, where **C. Bernard Jackson** presided. There he directed W. B. Burdine's satirical western musical *Deadwood Dick*.

Turman worked onstage and in radio, movies, and television in a varied career that has extended from coast to coast. His career has focused mainly on movies and television, where he has made over 100 appearances in everything from the legendary *Cooley High* to the hit HBO series *The Wire*, in which he has a recurring role. Turman is known as a character actor who works "beneath the radar," in that he is noted for developing steady, workmanlike characters who contribute immeasurably to the script, but afterward one is hard pressed to recall his name. This faceless name recognition works both ways, for when viewers recognize the face, they know they are assured of a fine performance. His current project is touring his one-man autobiographical show titled *Movin' Man*. Though autobiographical in form, *Movin' Man* pays homage to those who helped him along the way, people who are no longer here, like **Ossie Davis**, **Lloyd Richards**, and **Brock Peters**. As Turman says, "I had some great shoulders to stand on—and you'll get to meet those shoulders in *Movin' Man*." He now lives outside of Los Angeles on a ranch. There he established Camp Giddy Up, a free western-style summer camp for inner-city and at-risk children. Turman is also a professional rodeo rider and competes on a national level as his schedule permits. He is the recipient of several National Association for the Advancement of Colored People (NAACP) Image Awards and an NAACP Lifetime Achievement Award. He is also the holder of several awards for his humanitarian work with youth in the community.

TURNER, JOSEPH (1936–87). A playwright, newspaper journalist, and television producer, Turner was born in Phoenix, AZ. His educational credentials include a B.S. in business administration from Loyola University in Chicago and an M.A. in communication, theater, and playwriting from the University of Illinois at Chicago. He is credited with writing at least 12 plays, which includes *A Change Gon' Come* (mid-1980s), exploring the mysterious and surprising death of singer Sam Cooke in a seedy Los Angeles hotel in 1967. It was produced for a lengthy engagement at Excellence through the Arts in Chicago (mid-1980s). *The Family Gathering* (1987) is a full-length drama. It is a passionate and emotionally charged play focusing on the interactions and conflicts of a black southern family after the matriarch becomes critically ill. It was produced at the South Side Community Arts Center in Chicago (June 1987) under the direction of Claudia McCormick (Turner attended a performance on the evening before his death). *The Scheme* (1968) is a drama in one act depicting the moral dilemmas that confronts a black National Guard officer during the 1960s **civil rights** riots.

TURNER, MARY ELIZABETH (BETH). A playwright, actor, editor, publisher, administrator, and educator, Turner was a native of Troy, NY. She is best known as the founder of ***Black Masks*** magazine, a national bimonthly publication that she established in 1984 to chronicle the black performing arts. Turner received her B.A. (magna cum laude; Phi Beta Kappa) from Colby College in 1963, having spent her junior year at the University of Paris in France. She earned her master's in education from New York University in 1966 and shortly thereafter married actor Charles Turner. At his suggestion, she began writing for the stage by enrolling at the famed **Frank Silvera Writers' Workshop** in New York. Between raising two children and working for various institutions of higher learning, she has written over 10 plays, most of which have been produced professionally. Among them are *The Hungering Lion* (1976), a short play about Mali's first emperor; *Crisis at Little Rock* (1977), about the desegregation of Little Rock High School in Arkansas; *Ode to Mariah* (1979), centering on a young girl's struggles against racism and sexism and which was produced at the Henry Street Settlements Family Theatre; *Visions: A Dream for the Bronx* (1980), a musical history in one act about the Bronx; *Gursky and the Fabulous Four* (1980), a comedy about students who outwit drug dealers; *LaMorena* (1981), a play in one act depicting the struggles of an interracial Puerto Rican family; and *Sing on Ms. Griot* (1976), which was produced at Afro American Total Theatre. Turner's plays have also been produced at the **New Federal Theatre (NFT)**, Lincoln Center Library for the Performing Arts, Smithsonian Discovery Theatre, Lehman College, and the Madrona Youth Theatre in Seattle. She has held a variety of positions during her career, including with the **Harlem** Youth Opportunity Unlimited, the Urban League, the Franklin Library, Bloomfield College, NFT, and New York University Tisch School of the Arts, where she worked for 15 years until her retirement in 2005.

Turner received many grants and awards during her career, such as the Hamilton College Travelli scholarship (1961), membership in Phi Sigma Iota French Honor Society (1962), membership in Phi Beta Kappa through the Maine chapter (1963), John Hay Whitney opportunity fellowship (1965), New York State Council on the Arts grant (1974), New Jersey State challenge grant, and Bloomfield College Award (1990). Turner in retirement continues to produce *Black Masks* but is still working for the ultimate prize, a Ph.D.

– U –

UJIMA COMPANY, INC. (BUFFALO, NY). Ujima Company, Inc., was founded in Buffalo, NY, in December 1978 by Lorna C. Hill— the first black woman admitted to Dartmouth College (B.A., 1973).

After graduation, she conceived the idea of the company as a theatrical entity of the now defunct Center for Positive Thought School of Movement and Dance. The notion was to hone a group that in time would develop into a cohesive acting ensemble and professional producing company. The first few years were marked by hard work, hard work, and more hard work, with an occasional performance thrown in to measure progress. In 1981, they established themselves as an independent entity and the following year relocated to the Theatre Loft, where they have been producing plays ever since. Their repertoire of work includes diverse plays by new playwrights, familiar plays from the African American cannon, lesser-known plays, and standard works of Western and contemporary theater. They also offer training in basic, fundamental aspects theater, but the initial thrust was toward new, original works created by the company and by Hill, an accomplished writer herself. One of the most popular of her plays is *Yalla Bitch*, which was produced several times at the theater and also performed at the First International Woman's Playwright Festival in 1986. Another play she developed is *And Bid Him Sing*, a pastiche of Paul Laurence Dunbar's poetry augmented with old-time spirituals. The play is mounted almost annually, alternating the poetry and songs to keep the piece fresh. Other productions mounted over the years include the Oscar Brown musical *It's about That Time*, *Sty of the Blind Pig* by **Phillip Hayes Dean**, *From the Mississippi Delta* by **Endesha Mae Holland**, *Riff Raff* by Laurence Fishburne, *Green Pastures* by Marc Connelly, and *In the Blood*. It continues to be the longest-running and most heralded black arts organization in the western New York State region, as evidenced when they received the Outstanding Arts Organization Award from the Greater Buffalo Chamber of Commerce.

UJIMA THEATRE COMPANY (COLUMBUS, OH). Based in Columbus, OH, Ujima is named after an African term meaning "collective work and responsibility." It is a resurrection of the original Ujima Theatre founded in Pittsburgh, PA, in 1972 by Ron Pitts, **Rob Penny**, and **August Wilson**. Pitts relocated to Columbus in 1991 and organized the new Ujima, of which he is CEO. That same year, he produced the company's first production, ***Black Nativity*** by **Langston Hughes**, a gospel pageant that is a perennial Christmas holiday favorite. The goals of this community-based art organization, articulated by its founder, were to present quality dramatic stage productions that inspire and preserve the contributions of artistic interest to the African American community and the total community at large. Pitts's attempt to capture lightning in a bottle twice got off to a rocky start when he was transferred to another city in a job shuffle. Since his return to Columbus in 2001, he has slowly brought the theater back to life with such productions as *The Meeting* by **Jeff Stetson**, which portrays a hypothetical meeting of Malcolm X and Dr. Martin Luther King, two African American **civil rights** icons. Ujima has produced Rob Penny's *Good Black Don't Crack*; a doo-wop musical from the1960s, 1970s, and 1980s titled *Love and Street Corner Harmony*; *God What Color Is Trouble*, which Pitts coauthored with Dr. Raymond Wise; *Ma Rainey's Black Bottom* by August Wilson; and *Long Time Since Yesterday* by **P. J. Gibson**. Pitts has garnered a lot of community support and has ambitious plans for the theater, including a yearround Theatre Training Program.

UNITY PLAYERS ENSEMBLE THEATRE COMPANY (UPETC). The UPETC has been in existence in Los Angeles since 1997, the brainchild of Spencer Scott, who continues to serve as its producing artistic director. Scott, a University of Southern California graduate and a working actor, model, and speaker, has done something remarkable in Los Angeles by producing 10 consecutive seasons of black theater in a city where that is a rarity, for Los Angeles houses over 200 theater companies, only 4 of which are black, and their production history is sporadic. The UPETC has embraced a formula of producing new plays mixed in with older vehicles, like **N. R. Davidson**'s *El Hajj Malik*, but mostly it has been newer work like Duane Chandler's *The Trees Don't Bleed in Tuskegee*, *Joimanju's Corner* by Nashid Fareed, *COTO: Chocolate on the Outside* by April Turner, *The Queen of Sheba* by **Bill Harris**, and *Angel* by **P. J. Gibson**. They have also encouraged the submission of one-act plays and produce the best of them each year under the umbrella title "A Black Trilogy."

Over their 10-year existence they have called several venues home. First it was the Inglewood Playhouse under the sponsorship of the city of Inglewood. Then it was the Complex Theatre in Hollywood, but in their fifth season, they finally found a permanent home at the historic Stella Adler Theatre on Hollywood Boulevard, where they are now the resident company. The UPETC's existence has been eventful, with the premiering of no fewer than 45 new plays. They have received corporate sponsorship from American Airlines; the Walt Disney Company; Hertz Car Rentals; Northrup Grumman; and local, state, and federal arts councils. They seem to be on their way.

– V –

VAN DYKE, ELIZABETH. Van Dyke is a 30-year veteran of American theater who has steadily risen through the ranks from fledgling actress to accomplished director and playwright. She is a mainstay in the black theater movement and has also performed and directed in American regional theater, as well as abroad in Australia, England, Europe, and Japan. Van Dyke has also appeared on television in such shows as *Law and Order*, *100 Centre Street*, and *Third Watch* and has a recurring role on *All My Children*. Her acting credits include *The River Niger*, *For Colored Girls Who Have Considered Suicide When the Rainbow Is Enuf*, *Macbeth*, *Zora Neale Hurston*, *Checkmates*, and many other plays. Directorial credits include *Pretty Fire*; *The Marian Anderson Story*; *Great Men of Gospel*; *Ti Jean and His Brothers*; *Remembering We Selves: Black Renaissance in Harlem*; and *To Be Young, Gifted and Black*.

Van Dyke is a native New Yorker who holds an M.F.A. from the New York University's Tisch School of the Arts Theatre Program. She also studied abroad with Peter Brooke at the International Theatre Institute in Paris with the courtesy of a Rockefeller grant. She was artistic director of the **Ensemble Theatre**'s Going to the River Project, a program nurturing the development of underserved African American female playwrights in Houston. Van Dyke wrote *Love to All* (1985), in which she pays homage to **Lorraine Hansberry**, author of *A Raisin in the Sun*. *Love* is well documented through the letters and papers of Hansberry. She paints a revealing, incisive portrait of a brilliant woman who died at the tender age of 34. Van Dyke has accumulated the following awards: the Roy Acuff chair of excellence in theatre/Austin Peay State University, Presidents Award/**Black**

Theatre Network, Audience Development Committee (Audelco)
Board of Directors Award, Audelco Award for the play *Zora Neale Hurston*, and the Cable Ace Award.

VAN PEEBLES, MELVIN. An actor, director, and playwright, Peebles was born in Chicago. After graduating from Ohio Wesleyan University and spending four years in the U.S. Air Force, he married and moved to the Netherlands. It was there he added *Van* to his name and began a crossover career between filmmaking and playwriting, although his plays were actually poetry shaped by others into a play format. He wrote over 11 films, a number of unproduced screenplays, 5 plays, and 10 books (5 are published). His filmmaking career began in France with *The Making of a Three Day Pass* (1967). It culminated with his ground-breaking 1970 production of *Sweet Sweetback's Baadasssss Song*, a film generally acknowledged with ushering in the blaxploitation era of filmmaking.

That same year, **Paul Carter Harrison** molded a selection of Van Peebles's poetry into dramatic form for presentation at Sacramento State College. The next year, it was optioned for a Broadway production under the direction of **Gilbert Moses**, whose production of **Amiri Baraka's (LeRoi Jones)** *Slave Ship* had rocked the theatrical world in 1969. Moses used an eight-week summer workshop at **Douglas Q. Barnett's Black Arts/West** in Seattle to mold and shape the poetry into a play with music set in a black ghetto. It opened in the fall of 1971 under the unwieldy title of *Ain't Supposed to Die a Natural Death* and was a marginal financial success. It did, however, win a **Drama Desk Award** and was nominated for seven **Tony Awards**. Van Peebles quickly followed up with a more conventionally structured play, *Don't Play Us Cheap*, adapted from his novel *The Party in Harlem*. A notable achievement for Van Peebles was having two plays running on Broadway at the same time. Other plays he wrote are *Out There by Your Lonesome* (1973), *Waltz of the Stork* (1981), and *Champeen* (1983). Among the honors and awards Van Peebles has received are the French Foreign Legion of Honor (2001), Chicago Underground Foreign Film Lifetime Achievement Award (1999), Acapulco Black Film Festival Award (2000), and the Children's Live-Action Humanitas Prize (1987).

– W –

WALCOTT, DEREK. A playwright and poet, Walcott was awarded the Nobel Prize for literature in 1992. He is a world-class wordsmith whose plays, poetry, and prose have elevated him to the status of nonpareil in the world of arts and letters. He was born on the West Indian island of St. Lucia. He began writing around the time he attended college, graduating from the University of West Indies in 1957. Walcott has taught creative writing at Harvard, Rutgers, and Yale Universities. He presently teaches at Boston University.

During a lengthy career, Walcott has written over 17 volumes of poetry and over 30 plays. He founded the acclaimed Trinidad Theatre Workshop in 1959, a vehicle he used to develop the many plays he wrote. Among them are *Ti Jean and His Brothers* (1958), a West Indian folktale about three brothers; *Pantomime* (1978), a satire of colonial relationships using the metaphor of Robinson Crusoe; and *Dream on Monkey Mountain* (1967), a tale about Makak, a charcoal burner in search of his identity and heritage. *Dream*, his most well-known play, debuted at the Mark Taper Forum in Los Angeles with a cast that included **Ron O'Neal** and **Jason Bernard**. Later, in 1971, Bernard directed the play in an acclaimed production at **Black Arts/West** in Seattle with a cast that included Alexander Conley III, Robert Livingston, and Charles Canada. The prestigious **Negro Ensemble Company** also produced the play in 1971 with the famed **Roscoe Lee Browne** in the role of Makak and O'Neal reprising his role as Corporal Lestrade. Walcott's published poetry includes *Selected Poems* (1964), *The Gulf* (1969), *Another Life* (1973), *The Fortunate Traveler* (1981), *The Bounty* (1997), and *The Prodigal* (2005). Among his awards, Walcott is the recipient of a fellowship from the Rockefeller Foundation, a Royal Society of Literature Award, the Queen's Medal for poetry, and a MacArthur Foundation "genius" award. He is also an honorary member of the American Academy and Institute of Arts and Letters.

WALKER, CELESTE BEDFORD. Walker is a veteran writer out of Houston, TX. She is resident playwright at the **Ensemble Theatre Company** of Houston that was founded by the late George Hawkins in 1976. Walker has written many plays over the years but is best known for *Camp Logan*, a play based on the tragic events of the all-black 24th Infantry in World War I, of which 13 infantrymen ended up being hanged. The play premiered at the **Billie Holiday Theatre** in 1963 and continues to play at other venues around the country to this day. Other plays written by Walker include *Over Forty*, a musical comedy featuring four women over 40; *Distant Voices*, a theatrical collage with music about preserving African American culture; *Freedom Train*, a children's play about the underground railway in Texas; and *Profiles in Black*, a children's play about hidden African American history. Other plays include *Rep Day, Harlem after Hours* (cowritten with Audrey H. Lawson), *Reunion in Bartersville*, and *Fabulous African Fables* (a children's play). Walker was the recipient of the National Association for the Advancement of Colored People Image Award and the Kennedy Center Award.

WALKER, EVAN K. (1937–82). Walker was one of a host of authors who emerged—seemingly out of nowhere—to become one of the cutting-edge playwrights during the black arts movement that began in the 1960s. He was a native Georgian but lived in New York City and Washington, DC, where at least two of his plays were produced at the DC Black Repertory Theatre (DCBRT). Other productions of his plays were also mounted at the **Freedom Theatre (FT)** in Philadelphia, the **Free Southern Theatre (FST)** in New Orleans, and Vantile Whitfield's (*see* MOTOJICHO [VANTILE EMMANUAL WHITFIELD, 1930–2005]) Performing Arts Society in Los Angeles (PASLA). His plays include *The Message* (1960), a satirical comedy in one act about the desire of middle-class blacks to integrate into American society. It was produced by PASLA (1960) and the DCBRT (1973). *East of Jordan* (1969) is a drama in two acts about a black mother in **Harlem** who suppressed family secrets from the past. The FT (1969) produced it, as did the FST during the same year. *Coda* (also known as *Coda for the Blues*, late 1969) is a drama in three acts set in the late 1960s. A black military man returns home to a family wrestling with white oppression during the **civil rights movement**. The DCBRT opened it at the Last Colony Theatre in Washington, DC (December 1972) for 20 performances. *A War for Brutus* (1950) is a drama in three acts about a young black paratrooper's induction into a segregated airborne infantry regiment shortly before the outbreak of the Korean War. Walker received the Conrad Kent Rivers Award for a short story in 1970.

WALKER, JOSEPH A. (1936–2003). Walker, a playwright, actor, director, and educator, was honored with the **Drama Desk Award** as the most promising playwright of the 1972–73 season for *The River Niger* (1972). He was born in Washington, DC, and earned a B.A. in philosophy and drama at Howard University in 1956, where he was active with the Howard Players. He also earned his M.F.A. (1970) and Ph.D. in the Department of Cinema (1970) at Catholic University. Walker has taught in the public schools of Washington, DC, and the City College of New York and was full professor of drama at Howard University, as well as playwright-in-residence at Yale University (1970–71). Walker has performed onstage, in television, and in films. He cofounded with his wife Dorothy Dinroe (Walker) the Demi-Gods, a professional music-dance repertory company. There he served as artistic director, with his wife as musical director.

In 1969, Walker formed an alliance with the **Negro Ensemble Company (NEC)**. It produced four of his plays off Broadway at St. Marks Playhouse (December 1969–February 1970) for 56 performances, with music by Dorothy Dinroe under the direction of **Israel Hicks**. Those plays include *Tribal Harangue One* (1969), a vignette in one act set in a slave dungeon off the coast of West Africa during the 14th or 15th century. An African couple takes the life of their only son to spare him from a life in **slavery**. *Tribal Harangue Two* (1969) is a drama in one act set in Texas. Two lovers, a black man and white woman, conspire to kill her rich stepfather and use his money to aid a black revolutionary. Among the cast members were **Robert Hooks**, David Downing, William Jay, Julius W. Harris, and **Douglas Turner Ward**. *Tribal Harangue Three* (1969) is a vignette in one act set in the future following the black revolution. The father, a leader in the revolution in *Tribal Harangue One*, tries to protect his son from the racial confrontation even though it may cost the father his life. *Harangue* (1969) is a drama in one act set in a Lower East Side bar in New York City. A deranged African American man, believing he is producing a television show, holds the patrons at gunpoint and forces them to reveal whether or not they are virtuous. The cast included Julius W. Harris, William Jay, Linda Carlson, and Douglas Turner

Ward. *Niger* garnered Walker the most accolades as a playwright. Set in **Harlem**, it is a three-act drama about the **black experience**. Walker's other plays include *The Believers: The Black Experience in Song* (1968); *Out of the Ashes: A Minstrel Show* (1974); *Antigone Africanus* (1975), an African adaptation of Sophocles' *Antigone*; and *District Line* (1984), a full-length dramedy. Walker was the recipient of a Guggenheim fellowship to study creative writing for the theater (c. 1974–75).

WALKER, LUCY M. (MARGARET). Walker is a director, playwright, and freelance journalist. She attended elementary school in her hometown of Memphis, TN, and completed her secondary and high school education in Denver, CO. Walker received a B.S. in secondary education from Central State College at Wilberforce, OH, before transferring to the University of Denver to do graduate work in theater. In 1963, Walker founded the **Eden Theatrical Workshop**, Inc., of which she is president.

Walker is active as a playwright. Most of her plays have been one-act social-action dramas that have been produced by the Eden Theatrical Workshop for the Curtis Park Cultural Heritage Program in Denver. They include *It's Only Money* (1970), about a married couple whose furniture is repossessed; *A Dollar a Day Keeps the Doctor Away* (1970), an attack on neighborhood community health services; *We All Pay* (1970), which has to do with a housewife who hears the screams of a women being raped and stabbed but doesn't want to get involved, only to find out that the victim is her daughter; *My Own Man* (1970), about a young man turning 21 who is trying to decide which political party he wants to join; *The Real Estate Man* (1970), centering on a realtor so determined to make a sale that he is insensitive to his clients' needs; *To Cuss or Bus* (1970), a dialectic on the advantages and disadvantages of bussing; *Grades—Plus or Minus* (1970), which presents a dialectic among parents after they put their son on punishment until he improves his school grades; and *Blood, Booze and Booty* (1975), a full-length bicentennial play based on the life of Aunt Clara Brown, who arrived in Denver in 1859. Walker received several honors in Denver, including the Lucy M. Walker Humanitarian Award (1976); Woman of the Year Award (1977); Founder's Award from the Eden Theatrical Workshop (1979); Citizen of the Week by KOA Radio and Capital Federal Savings and Loan Association (1980); and Community Development, Services and Education Award from the Regional Office of the U.S. Office of Human Development Services (1982).

WALKER, PHILLIP E. Walker is performing artist, director, producer, and artistic director of the **African American Drama Company** of San Francisco. Born in Chicago, Walker received his B.A. in theater from Loyola University, M.A. in theater history and criticism from the University of Illinois at Urbana, and M.F.A. in acting from the University of California at Davis. He has taught theater at Lincoln University of Missouri, the University of Illinois, Yuba College in Illinois, the University of California at Davis, and the People's School of Dramatic Arts in San Francisco Company. Walker has performed in more than 100 plays and television and film productions. He found his niche as a performance artist in his piece *Can I Speak for You Brother?* (1978), in which he incorporates dance, poetry, drama, letters, storytelling, speeches, music, and puppetry to focus on nine exceptional African American figures. He traces the plight of **black experiences** beginning with the crossing of the Middle Passage to "tomorrow."

WARD, DOUGLAS TURNER. Ward, an actor, director, and playwright, is a living legend in the world of theater. Although he has achieved much during his lifetime, his cofounding of the **Negro Ensemble Company (NEC)** in 1968 ranks as his greatest achievement. The NEC has spawned over 200 productions within a 35-year period. It has been the incubator of opportunity for such talents as **Denzel Washington, Phylicia Allen-Rashad, Samuel L. Jackson**, Angela Bassett, Giancarlo Esposito, Laurence Fishburne, **Esther Rolle**, Cleavon Little, **Frances Foster**, Sherman Helmsley, David Alan Grier, and Lynn Whitfield. Playwrights like **Paul Carter Harrison, Charles Fuller, Judi Ann Mason, Joseph A. Walker, Phillip Hayes Dean**, J. E. Franklin, Endesha Mae Holland, and **Aishah Rahman** have all found a nurturing environment for the production of their plays. The NEC was the flagship theater for the torrid black arts movement of the halcyon 1960s **civil rights movement**.

Ward was born in Burnside, LA. His education was at Wilberforce University and the University of Michigan. His early life was uneventful, save for his flirtation with extreme left-wing causes. He was a journalist in those days but had a hard time making a living. In 1955, he began studying acting with Paul Mann at the Actor's Workshop in New York, and by 1956, he debuted in Eugene O'Neill's play *The Iceman Cometh*. Later he understudied **Sidney Poitier** in **Lorraine Hansberry**'s 1959 Broadway production of *A Raisin in the Sun*. It was around this time that Ward began writing plays. His first two efforts, *Day of Absence* and *Happy Ending*, were very successful off Broadway.

Ward, a garrulous, outspoken man, began talking about the lack of opportunity for black actors and black theater. This led to an invitation from the *New York Times* to write an op-ed piece on the state of black theater. Ward accepted and threw down the gauntlet when he wrote "If any hope outside of chance individual fortune exists for Negro playwrights as a group, or for that matter, Negro actors or other theater craftsman, the most immediate, pressing, practical, absolutely minimally essential active first step is the development of a permanent Negro company of at least Off-Broadway size and dimension. Not in the future . . . but now!" W. McNeil Lowrey of the Ford Foundation read the article and invited Ward and his associates, actor **Robert Hooks** and theater manager Gerald S. Krone, to meet with him. The Ford Foundation subsequently funded $434,000 to what eventually became the NEC.

Ward and his associates used as a model Bertolt Brecht's famed Berliner Ensemble, a logical choice given Ward's left-wing past. But Ward also wisely included a training component along with a 15-member acting company. From its first production, Peter Weiss's *Song of the Lusitanian Bogey*, the NEC became the envy of the theatrical world. The productions were sharp and crisp, the actors on point, the costuming outrageous, and the lighting brilliant. Not one to equivocate, Ward led the NEC with an iron hand, acting in some plays, directing others, with an eye to the future. But a reliance on "soft money" led to a retrenchment when Ford ceased funding the theater. Ward continued to lead the company through thick and thin for many years. He finally relinquished the artistic directorship of the NEC in late 1987 and is now semiretired.

WARD, THEODORE (TED, 1902–83). Ward was a prolific pioneer playwright who gained recognition for *Big White Fog* (1938) and *Our Lan'* (1941). *Fog*, a successful black play of the 1940s, was one of the best black plays to evolve out of the Works Progress Administration's **Federal Theatre** Negro Unit. It was among the earliest dramas by an African American playwright to be produced on Broadway in 1947. He moved to New York City during the 1940s, where he was one of the founders and executive director of the Negro Playwrights Company. He wrote news and radio scripts for the War Department during World War II. In the 1950s, he returned to Chicago, where he continued to write. He remained relatively quiescent until the mid-1960s, when interest in his work was revived during the new black theater movement of that decade. After a period of inactivity, Ward was chosen as head of the South Side Center of the Performing Arts, Inc., with the Louis Theatre and School of Drama as its locus. Operating under a grant, Ward leased and refurbished a movie house on 35th Street, renaming it the Louis Theatre. He programmed a new version of his 20-year-old play, *Our Lan'*, as the opening production. Since the 1960s, Ward has conducted writing seminars in Chicago and New Orleans, where he was playwright-in-residence at the **Free Southern Theatre**.

Ward has authored 19 plays. His two most popular plays are *Big White Fog* and *Our Lan'*. *Fog* is a historical drama set in Chicago during the height of the Negro Renaissance of the 1920s and the Great Depression of the 1930s. It intertwines issues of Garveyism, capitalism, communism, color stratification, and intraracism to depict an African American family wrestling with the big white fog of oppression. *Fog* was produced by the Negro Unit of the Chicago Federal Theatre at the Great Northern Theatre (April–May 1938) and the Negro Playwrights Company at the Lincoln Theatre in **Harlem** (October–December 1940) for 64 performances under the direction of Powell Lindsay. **Canada Lee** was featured in the cast. *Our Lan'* is also a historical drama in two acts. It is set shortly after the American Civil War and depicts the efforts of newly freed slaves to settle on land off the coast of Georgia. It was the recipient of the Theatre Guild Award (1947). Productions were produced by Associated Playwrights, Inc., at the Henry Street Settlement Playhouse in New York City (February 1947); on Broadway by the Theatre Guild at the

Royal Theatre in New York City (September–November 1947) for 41 performances; and by Ward at the South Side Center of the Performing Arts in Chicago (1968) for a 10-month run.

Other plays Ward authored include *Sick and Tiahd* (alternate title, *Sick and Tired*, 1937), *Falcon of Adowa* (1938), *Even the Dead Arise* (1938), *Deliver the Goods* (1941), *Shout Hallelujah!* (1941), *Of Human Grandeur* (original title, *John Brown*, 1949, revised in 1963), *Throwback* (1951), *Whole Hog or Nothing* (1952), and *Daubers* (1953). Ward was the recipient of numerous awards, including the Zona Gale fellowship and **Audience Development Committee** Outstanding Pioneer Award for his contributions to the growth and development of black theater (1975), Theatre Guild Award for *Our Lan'* (1947), Negro of the Year Award (1947) by the Schomburg Collection of the New York Public Library, Guggenheim Foundation fellowship for creative writing (1947), National Theatre Conference Award (1947–48), Rockefeller Foundation grant (1978), and DuSable Writers' Seminary and Poetry Festival Award (1982). Ward died in Chicago at age 81 after a short illness.

WARD, VAL GRAY. Ward, an actor and producer, was a seminal figure in the world of black theater, both onstage and as founder of Kuumba Theatre in Chicago. She was born in Mound Bayou, MS, America's oldest black town. She moved to Chicago in 1951 and became involved in the arts community. At the height of the black arts movement in 1968, she and her husband, Francis Gray, founded Kuumba Theatre. Most of their plays combined elements from the Christian church and African ritual. She served as director and producer of the organization for over 25 years, during which they produced such gems as *The Amen Corner* and *Five on the Black Hand Side*. She also produced **Useni Eugene Perkins**'s play *The Image Makers*, which was also presented in Lagos, Nigeria, at the 1977 African Arts Festival. Over time, Ward developed her own one-woman shows that she performs at various colleges and universities around the country. They are *I Am a Black Woman* (1966), and *The Life of Harriett Tubman* (1971).

WASHINGTON, CAESAR G. Washington, a playwright, honed his craft with the National Ethiopian Art Theatre in New York City, which grew out of the Ethiopian Art Theatre in Chicago during the 1920s. Washington's two best-known plays are *The Gold Front Stores, Inc.* (1924), and *Candle in the Wind* (1967). His first play, *Front Stores*, is a comedy in three acts about a fraudulent scheme devised by two grocery store owners to swindle a not-too-bright young man out of his money. The National Ethiopian Art Theatre mounted it at the **Lafayette Theatre** in New York City (March 1924) under the direction of Raymond O'Neill (white) featuring Abbie Mitchell and Edna Thomas. *Candle* is a historical drama in four acts chronicling the events leading up to the murder of a black senator from Mississippi during the Reconstruction period in 1875. Productions were mounted by the South Side Center of the Performing Arts, Chicago (1969), and the **Free Southern Theatre** in New Orleans (1978) on a Rockefeller Foundation grant.

WASHINGTON, DENZEL. Touted as one of the finest actors onstage, on screen, and in television, Washington is also a producer and director. He has made well over 100 appearances in movies, television, and the theater. Among them are *The Manchurian Candidate, Training Day, Remember the Titans, The Bone Collector, Man on Fire, The Pelican Brief, Malcolm X, Glory, A Soldier's Story, Mo' Better Blues, Antwone Fischer, The Preacher's Wife, He Got Game, Much Ado about Nothing, St. Elsewhere, Philadelphia, Devil in a Blue Dress,* and *American Gangster.*

Washington was born in Mount Vernon, NY. He enrolled in Fordham University in 1976 as a premedicine major. He dropped out of college due to poor grades but decided to reenroll and become a double major in journalism and drama. He continued to study drama at the American Conservatory Theatre in San Francisco but left prematurely and moved to Los Angeles. Unable to find work, he returned to Mount Vernon. He struggled to find acting parts in New York City until he was cast in **Laurence Holder**'s play *When the Chickens Come Home to Roost*, a play about an imaginary meeting between Martin Luther King and Malcolm X. Washington plunged into the role of Malcolm X and, with the aid of director **Allie Woods**, gave a mesmerizing performance at **Woodie King Jr.**'s Henry Street Theatre on the Lower East Side. His work in *Chickens* helped him to land the role of Private First Class Melvin Peterson in the **Negro Ensem-**

ble Company's production of **Charles Fuller**'s **Pulitzer Prize**–winning *A Soldier's Play*. Washington played the role of Peterson in both the stage and film versions. This solid body of work put him on the A list in Hollywood. Thereafter Washington worked steadily as an actor in film and television but was occasionally lured back to live theater. In 2005, he returned to the stage for a limited run in a NYSF/Public Theatre presentation of Shakespeare's *Julius Caesar*. Among the numerous awards Washington has garnered as an actor, two are historic. He won an Oscar for best supporting actor in the film *Glory* (1989), the first for an African American, and another for *Training Day* (2001) in the leading man category, the second for a black actor—**Sidney Poitier** was the first.

WASHINGTON, VON H. Washington is a multitalented, nationally known performer, director, playwright, and teacher whose attributes have contributed immeasurably to the American theater for over 30 years. He has worked on over 300 productions of stage, screen, and television in various capacities. Washington holds a B.S. and an M.A. from Western Michigan University and a Ph.D. from Wayne State University. He presently teaches at Wayne State University. In the early days of the black arts movement, Washington was involved in the old **Concept East Theatre** in Detroit after **Woodie King Jr.** Washington has written 15 plays, mostly on the twin themes of African American history and the quest for freedom. They have been performed at various theaters and academic institutions across the country. He has either taught, directed, or performed at the Missouri Repertory Theatre, Los Angeles Theatre Center, University of Michigan, Detroit Repertory Theatre, and various other theaters and institutions. Among the plays written by Washington are *The Black American Dream* (1986); *Seven Stops to Freedom* (1996), about the Underground Railroad during **slavery** times; *Down by the Riverside* (1996), depicting the life of Sojourner Truth; and *Rosa Parks: More Than a Woman* (1996), the life story of the woman who spawned the **civil rights movement**. His other plays include *The Children of Herero* (1999), *When Freedom Came* (2002), *Let the Brotha Talk* (1995), and *Looking for a Good Thing* (1998). Washington is a member of Actors Equity, the Screen Actors Guild, and the American Federation of Television and Radio Artists.

WELDON, CHARLES. A journeyman actor, director, and producer, Weldon worked for over 30 years in theater in a variety of roles before being tapped to become the artistic director of the famed **Negro Ensemble Company (NEC)** in 2004. He has appeared in nearly 40 NEC productions, such as *A Soldier's Play*, *The River Niger*, *Colored People's Time*, *Ododo*, and *The Brownsville Raid*. Weldon has also performed in regional theater in productions like *Birdie Blue*, *The Little Tommie Parker Celebrated Colored Minstrel Show*, *King Hedley II*, *Jitney*, and *The Piano Lesson*.

Born in Oklahoma, Weldon moved to New York City at an early age. His career in show business began with the Paradons, a doo-wop rhythm and blues singing group that had mixed success. He made his stage debut in the 1969 Broadway production of *Big Time Buck White* with Muhammad Ali in the cast, and he was in the 1973 production of *The River Niger*. He auditioned for and was accepted by the NEC in 1970, where he has primarily worked except for the odd job regionally or in television and film. In these twin mediums, he has appeared in *Roots: The Next Generations*, *Malcolm X*, *A Woman Called Moses*, *Police Story*, *Law and Order*, *Brewster Place*, *Hoop Soldiers*, *Rooster Cogburn*, and *Dynasty*. Weldon is a cofounder of the Alumni of the NEC. His first two seasons as artistic director were marked by the debuts of two new plays, **Leslie Lee**'s *Blues for a Broken Tongue* and **Jimmy Barden**'s *Offspring*. Weldon received an **Obie Award** for his performance in **Gus Edward**'s *The Offering*.

WESLEY, RICHARD. A playwright and screenwriter, Wesley was born in Newark, NJ. He became interested in writing in the 1950s after witnessing the works of Rod Serling, Paddy Chayefsky, and others during the golden age of television. Upon enrollment at Howard University, he informed **Owen Dodson** that his interest was writing for television and the big screen and that he had no plans to be a playwright. Dodson responded with "Child, if I can teach you to write for the stage, you'll be able to write for anything." Over the next four years, Wesley absorbed the technique of writing for the stage under the direction of Dodson and the estimable **Ted Shine**. He wrote his first play, *Put My Dignity before 307*, as an undergraduate and was a finalist in the Samuel French National Collegiate Playwriting Award.

After graduation in 1967, he was offered a job as editor of *Black Theatre* magazine for the **New Lafayette Theatre** by playwright **Ed Bullins**. It was there that Wesley's talents bloomed as a playwright. He wrote *The Street Corner*; *Black Terror*; *Knock, Knock, Who Dat'*; *Gettin' It Together*; and *Black Terror*. This last play was produced at **Joseph Papp**'s NYSF/Public Theatre and won a **Drama Desk Award**. Wesley went on to write many other plays, including *The Past Is the Past*, *Butterfly*, *The Mighty Gents*, and *Strike Heaven on the Face*.

His screenwriting debut was a huge success with the 1974 comedy *Uptown Saturday Night* with **Sidney Poitier** and Harry Belafonte. It was a box office hit, as was the 1975 sequel, *Let's Do It Again*, with the same actors. His other screenwriting credits include *Fast Forward*, *Mandela and DeKlerk*, *Native Son*, *Bojangles*, *A Piece of the Action*, and *Deacons for Defense*. He has also written a film for children, *The House of Dies Drear*, for PBS and episodes for the TV series *100 Centre St.* and *Fallen Angels*. Though Wesley has succeeded in his quest to write for the screen, he prefers to write for the stage because of the immediacy of theater. Wesley has worked as an adjunct at such educational institutions as Manhattanville College, Wesleyan University, Manhattan Community College, and Rutgers University. He was an associate professor at Tisch School of the Arts at New York University.

WEST, ALLISON. West, a playwright, was active at **Roger Furman**'s **New Heritage Repertory Theatre Company** (NHRTC) and the **National Black Theatre** (NBT) in New York City. His one-act play *Casualties* (1984) is about two women who examine their loves, sorrows, hopes, and scattered joys through the lives of their professional children. It was produced at P. S. W. Studios in New York City (October 1983) under the direction of Sidney Best and by the NBT in association with the NHRTC at the NBT (June–August 1984) under the direction of Andre Robinson. *Lesson Plans* (1984) is a one-act play about two middle-aged teachers whose marriages have recently ended.

WEST, CHERYL L. A playwright, West was born in Chicago. She received her B.A. from the University of Illinois and for many years worked as a social worker before she started writing. Her first play, *Before It Hits Home*, is an exploration of the AIDS epidemic. It was a roaring success. Subsequent plays, such as *Jar the Floor* and *Holiday Heart*, have had equally hard-hitting themes. *Heart*, a redemptive play about a drag queen, premiered on Showtime in 2000, with Ving Rhames in the title role. Her play *Before It Hits Home* has been optioned by Spike Lee, for whom West is writing the original screenplay. Other plays West wrote are *Puddin Pete* (1993); *Play On* (1997), an adaptation of Shakespeare's *Twelfth Night* written with **Sheldon Epps** and music by Duke Ellington and Billy Strayhorn; and *Birdie Blue* (1998). West now lives and works in Seattle. Her plays have been produced at regional theaters across the country and in England. Honors and awards for West include the Susan Smith Blackburn Prize, National Association for the Advancement of Colored People Playwriting Award, Helen Hayes Award, **Audience Development Committee Award**, and MacArthur Foundation Award.

WHITE, EDGAR MONK NKOSI. A playwright, White was born in the West Indies island of Montserrat in 1947. He migrated to New York in 1952, living in Spanish **Harlem**. He joined a seminary at an early age but dropped out. After graduation from Theodore Roosevelt High School, he attended City College of New York, New York University, and the Yale School of Drama. Within two years, he was expelled by Dean Robert Brustein for performing with a Yale Black Players troupe. Early on, he had met **Langston Hughes**, who championed his work. At the young age of 20, **Joseph Papp** produced his first play, *The Mummers*, at the NYSF/Public Theatre, as well as six more plays during the 1970s and 1980s. The Eugene O'Neil Center, the **Negro Ensemble Company (NEC)**, and the **La MaMa Experimental Theatre Club** also produced his plays.

White traveled to London in the 1980s to see a production of his play *Masada*. This international city also produced two of his other plays, *The Nine Nights* and *Lament for Rastafari* (1971). By this time, White's plays were becoming increasingly more militant and political in tone, especially in regard to colonialism. While in exile, White changed his middle name to Nkosi, reflecting his kinship to the motherland, Africa. His plays were also produced throughout Europe, Africa, and even Asia. White returned to the United States in

1989, completing his divinity school training as an ordained minister. He became a minister at the Cathedral of Saint John the Divine Church. Production of his plays continued apace with **Roger Furman** at **New Heritage Repertory Theatre Company**, producing *Trinity* and *Like Them That Dream*. His *I, Marcus Garvey* became a huge success when it was produced at the Ward Theatre in Jamaica. Taking time from his writing for the stage, White wrote his first novel, *The Rising*, in 1990. In 1993, in conjunction with La MaMa, he wrote a blues opera about the Scottsboro boys, *Ghosts: Live from Galilee, The Scottsboro Boys*. It was a thinly disguised version of an earlier play, *The Burghers of Calais*, directed by George Ferencz and with music by Genji Ito.

Over the years, White performed as a musician and also wrote musical compositions. He has been an adjunct professor of creative writing, playwriting, and humanities at City College of New York and has also taught writing at the NEC. White is a prolific writer, having written over 40 plays, many of which have been produced both here and abroad. In his varied career, White has developed his own unique writing style incorporating several different techniques. His early plays are written in a traditional realist manner. But over the years, elements of the theater of the absurd, commedia dell'arte, and English medieval plays have colored his efforts.

Two of White's more popular plays include *The Life and Times of J. Walter Smintheus* (1971), an allegorical play in one act. It shows the pitfalls and tragedy of a black man with an identity crisis. It was produced by the American National Theatre and Academy Matinee Theatre at the Theatre De Lys in New York City (February 1971) and off Broadway by the New York Shakespeare Festival/Public Theatre at the Other Stage (April 1971) for 38 performances. *The Crucificado* (1971) is a modern allegory in 25 scenes. A black man trying to escape an oppressive and unjust environment through drugs and sex murders his white father. It was produced by the Urban Arts Corps in New York City (June 1972) and the Frederick Douglass Creative Arts Center in New York (March 1978). Some of White's other plays are *The Mummer's Play* (1965), *The Cathedral at Chartres* (also known as *The Figures at Chartres*, 1968), *The Wonderful Years* (1969), *Seigismundo's Tricycle: A Dialogue of Self and Soul* (1971), *Les Femmes Noires* (*The Black Ladies*, 1974), and *The Pygmies and the*

Pyramid (1976). White was a member of the Authors Guild of New York. His honors and awards include a Rockefeller grant for playwrights, and a New York State Council grant.

WHITE, JAMES E., III. White is a playwright. Among the plays he garnered a reputation for is *The Defense* (1976), a fantasy in 23 scenes with music composed by White himself. A guard in a New York housing project dreams he has died. In the afterlife, he conducts a defense of his life. It was produced by the National Playwrights Conference of the Eugene O'Neill Theatre Center in the Amphitheater at Waterford, CT (July 1976), for two performances. It was also produced by the **New Federal Theatre** at the Henry Street Settlement in New York City (November 1976). Both productions were directed by Dennis Scott. *Trinity—The Long and Cheerful Road to Slavery* (1982) is a trilogy of short plays. Set in postcolonial times, it depicts the consequence of colonialism on West Indian blacks. Other plays by White are *La Gente* (*The People*, 1973), *Ode to Charlie Parker* (1973), *Offering for Nightworld* (1973), *Masada* (a South African ritual, 1979), and *Like Them That Dream: Children of Ogun* (1983).

WHITE, JOSEPH. A playwright, White was born in Philadelphia in 1933. He has a degree in journalism and has worked as a newspaper columnist for the *Newark News* and has also worked for the radio station WNJR. White rose to prominence during the **civil rights movement** when, during a seven-year period, he wrote four plays that became staples in the repertoire of many emerging black theaters. With black theaters being created almost every week, there was a tremendous demand for plays, but the older authors, such as **Langston Hughes**, **Owen Dodson**, and **Alice Childress**, did not echo the revolutionary militant stance theaters wanted to send. White's plays were militant but also laced with humor, irony, and understanding— often absent from plays of that era. White's plays initially played in some of the most militant theaters, like **Amiri Baraka**'s **(LeRoi Jones)** Spirit House, **Black Arts Repertory Theatre School**, and Kuumba House, but their elegance showed, and they quickly became the staple of almost every leading black theater in the country. Among the plays White wrote are *The Blue Boy in Black* (1963), *The*

Leader (1968), *Ol Judge Mose Is Dead* (1968), and *The Hustle* (1970). In 1963, White received a grant from the New York State Council on the Arts and a John Hay Whitney Award.

WHITEHEAD, MARYLENE. Whitehead is a Chicago-based playwright who holds a degree from Columbia College in that city. She is a faculty member at Northeastern Illinois University and teaches playwriting at **Jackie Taylor**'s eta Creative Arts Foundation. She has written several plays, and her musical *This Far by Faith* has been exceptionally successful. Other plays she wrote are *A House Divided, The Forbidden Place, J Day* (a musical), *Born Rich*, and *Why Don't You Tell Us Who You Are?* Whitehead's plays have been produced at eta Creative Arts and other venues.

WHITFIELD, VANTILE EMMANUEL. *See* MOTOJICHO (VANTILE EMMANUAL WHITFIELD).

WILKS, TALVIN. A well-traveled director, playwright, and dramaturge, Wilks's work has carried him from **Crossroads Theatre Company (CTC)** in New Jersey to Seattle, where he joined the now-defunct Group Theatre. He is best known for his surrealistic look at an African American man's search for identity in such plays as *Tod, The Boy Toy*, which premiered at the CTC in 1990. He has also directed *The Love Space Demands, The Shaneequa Chronicles*, and *Yellow Eye*. His record as a dramaturge is extensive, highlighted by his ongoing work with Ping Chong in *Undesirable Elements* in Seattle and Saravejo, Bosnia-Herzegovina. He has worked at the NYSF/Public Theatre, **St. Louis Black Repertory Theatre**, and **Ensemble Theatre**, as well as in France, Rome, and Scotland. Wilks also wrote *Bread of Heaven* (1994), presenting 30 years of a family redefining itself; *The Trial of Uncle S/M, The Life in Between; The Last Oppression Drama; An American Triptych*; and *Occasional Grace*. Wilks is a member of Spin Lab. From 2002 to 2004, he was an associate professor at the University of Massachusetts at Amherst. He also served as interim artistic director of the New World Theatre.

WILLIAMS, DICK ANTHONY. Born in Chicago, Williams made major contributions to the field of African American theater as an actor, director, and producer during his 30 years onstage, in television, and in film. His New York City stage debut was in the title role of *Big Time Buck White* at the Village South Theatre (1968). Among the numerous plays Williams performed in are *Nigger Nightmare* (New York Shakespeare Festival/NYSF/Public Theatre, 1971), *Ain't Supposed to Die a Natural Death* (Ethel Barrymore Theatre in New York City, 1971), *Jamimma* (Henry Street Playhouse in New York City, 1972), *What the Wine Sellers Buy* (**New Federal Theatre** in New York City, 1973), *Black Picture Show* (Vivian Beaumont Theatre in New York City, 1975), *We Interrupt This Program* (Ambassador Theatre in New York City, 1975), *The Poison Tree* (Ambassador Theatre in New York City, 1976), and *The Pig Pen* (American Place Theatre in New York City, 1970). Williams coproduced (with **Woodie King Jr.**) *Black Girl* (Theatre de Lys in New York City, 1971), directed *In New England Winter* (Henry Street Playhouse in New York City, 1971), and produced *A Recent Killing* (New Federal Theatre in New York City, 1973). This extensive theatrical background served him well as he transitioned into film and television, in which his credits are numerous. On Broadway, Williams won the **Drama Desk Award** for outstanding performance in *What the Wine Sellers Buy* (1974) and a nomination for outstanding featured actor in a play for *Black Picture Show* (1975). He also earned consecutive **Tony Award** nominations as best supporting or featured actor (dramatic) for *What the Wine Sellers Buy* (1974) and for *Black Picture Show* (1975).

WILLIAMS, JAYE AUSTIN. Williams has functioned in the theater world for several years and in many ways, equally adept at acting, directing, dramaturgy, and playwriting. Since earning a B.S. from Skidmore College in 1978, Williams has honed her craft at the Cherry Lane Theatre, the Manhattan Theatre Club, Sundance Theatre Lab, and other venues. She has directed at **Karamu Repertory Theatre Company**, the Hangar Theatre, and the Long Wharf Theatre and has functioned as a dramaturge at various theaters across the country. She has used this experience to her advantage in crafting her own plays, which include *American Dreams*, an adaptation from the book *New Work Now by Sapphire*, and *A Not So Quiet Nocturne*, about an African American deaf woman living with AIDS. Her other plays are

Passion Play, *If One Could Fly*, *Suburbs*, *Ascent of the Muse*, and *Girth*. Williams is also the author of the novel *Jasmine* (2005). Her honors and awards are playwright fellow at Manhattan Theatre Club (1997–98), National Endowment for the Arts/Theatre Communications Group director fellowship (1999–2000), and artist-in-residence at Tribecca Performing Arts Center (2000–2).

WILLIAMS, PAULETTE. *See* SHANGE, NTOZAKE (PAULETTE WILLIAMS).

WILLIAMS, SAMM-ART. An actor and playwright, Williams was born in Burgaw, NC. He was encouraged at an early age by his mother to write plays. She was a high school English teacher and drama director who cast him in the plays she directed. Williams received his B.A. from Morgan State College in Baltimore, MD (1968). He majored in political science and had wanted to become a **civil rights** lawyer, however the lure of theater won out. He moved to Philadelphia and joined the **Freedom Theatre**, where he gained acting experience.

In 1974, Williams went to New York City, where he joined the Playwrights Workshop of the celebrated **Negro Ensemble Company (NEC)**. He performed in several productions, and the NEC produced two of his earliest plays in the Season-within-a-Season productions. His signature play is *Home* (1979), a full-length drama about a young black North Carolina farmer who, like the prodigal son, leaves home for the good life up North. He becomes absorbed in the underbelly of the city only to return home to his roots as a better and more enlightened person. *Home* was produced off Broadway by the NEC at St. Marks Playhouse (December 1979–February 1980) for 82 performances and on Broadway at the Cort Theatre (May 1980) for an additional 279 performances under the direction of Dean Irby. Cast members included **Charles Brown** (nominated for a **Tony Award**), **L. Scott Caldwell**, and **Michele Shay**. Subsequent productions of *Home* were mounted throughout the country. It was nominated for a Tony Award and won the John Gassner Playwriting Medallion for the most provocative new play by an American, as well as an **Audience Development Committee Award** for best play of 1980.

In 2007, the new NEC welcomed back alumnus Williams with a production of his new plays, *The Waiting Room*, at the 45th Street Theatre in New York City. It is a dramedy set in a hospital waiting room where strange things happen when friends and relatives gather around a loved one who appears to be at death's door. It was directed by **Charles Weldon**, an NEC member since 1970 and a veteran of stage and screen, who was selected as the new artistic director. Other play Williams authored include *Welcome to Black River* (1974), *The Coming* (1974), *Do unto Others* (1974), *A Love Play* (1976), *The Sixteenth Round II* (original title, *The Pathetique*, 1980), *Friends* (1980), *Kamilia* (1975), and *The Last Caravan* (a musical, mid-1970s).

WILLIAMS-LAWRENCE, VALERIE J. A playwright Williams-Lawrence was born and reared in Gulfport, MS, and received her education at Dillard University in New Orleans. The mother of three boys, Williams-Lawrence has been employed as human resources manager for Mellon Bank in Pittsburgh, PA, since 1968. Her representative plays include *Royal Relations* (1983), a full-length play. It is a satirical look at upper-middle–class black families. **Kuntu Repertory Theatre** at the University of Pittsburgh gave two staged readings of the play (1983). *Magnolia Aid Society* (1984) is a full-length drama dealing with struggle, love, and hope in a traditional black environment.

WILLIAMS-WITHERSPOON, KAMMIKA. Professor Williams-Witherspoon, an associate professor of theater at Temple University, is a playwright, poet, anthropologist, and educator. She earned a B.A., M.A., M.F.A., and Ph.D. and has written 6 books of poetry and over 20 plays, with 10 being produced professionally. To the theatergoing public, however, she is largely unknown. A native of Darby, PA, she has had a divided career, using her journalism degree at Howard University (1980) to work as a newspaper reporter, television editor, and magazine writer. As a writer, she has concentrated on poetry and playwriting. Among the plays she wrote are *Nappy Truths*; *What Price: Unity*; *Dog Days: The Killing of Octavio Catto*; *Gumbo*; *From Brillo Pads to Feminine Pads*; *Where Were You in 1965?*; *Brown Ices: Chocolate Drops and We the People*; *Common Folk*; and *Survival Strategies: A Tale of Faith, We the People*. Williams-Witherspoon was the recipient of the American Poetry Center Award, Lila Wallace creative arts fellowship, Women's International League Peace and Freedom Award, Theatre Association fellowship, Pew Charitable Trust playwright exchange, and **Penumbra Theatre Award** (1993, 1997).

WILSON, AUGUST (1945–2005). A playwright extraordinaire, Wilson ushered in the 21st century with *Radio Golf,* as the last installment of an unprecedented 10-play cycle chronicling the **black experience** for each decade of the 20th century. It was an achievement that is unmatched in the annals of black theater. Among his awards, he received two **Pulitzer Prizes** and seven **New York Drama Critics' Circle Awards.** *Fences* alone won four **Tony Awards** and grossed over $11 million—a Broadway record for a nonmusical.

Wilson was born in Pittsburgh, PA, one of six children of a biracial relationship. Wilson's mother, Daisy Wilson, was an African American cleaning woman who, according to Wilson, influenced his warrior spirit. His father, Frederick August Kittel, a German immigrant, lived with the family only a short time. At age 15, Wilson dropped out of the predominantly white parochial Gladstone Vocational High School after a teacher accused him of plagiarizing a 20-page paper he wrote on Napoleon. Wilson could have very easily become another black dropout statistic, but his determination and quest for knowledge led him to the Carnegie Library. There he studied and read everything of interest to him, in particular anthropology; theology; and works by Ralph Ellison, **Richard Wright, Arna Bontemps,** and **Langston Hughes.** He even memorized the dictionary. Also during this time, Wilson became intrigued by the poetry of black nationalist writer **Amiri Baraka (LeRoi Jones).** He bought a typewriter for $20 in 1965 to pursue his interest in writing poetry.

In 1968, Wilson cofounded Black Horizons Theatre with **Rob Penny,** a playwright and professor at the University of Pittsburgh. The first two plays they produced were by Baraka and **Ed Bullins.** In 1977, **Claude Purdy,** a long-time friend, invited Wilson to come to Saint Paul, MN. There Wilson met **Marion McClinton,** who would become Wilson's primary director after **Lloyd Richards**'s health began to deteriorate (by then, Lloyd had directed 6 of Wilson's plays in the 10-play cycle). Purdy encouraged Wilson to try his hand at playwriting, and he began writing *Jitney* after he received a fellowship from the Playwrights Center in Minneapolis. Purdy also suggested to Wilson that he submit scripts to the Eugene O'Neill Playwright Center in Waterford, CT, which he did. Wilson's *Ma Rainey's Black Bottom* was one of the scripts that eventually caught the eye of director Richards in 1981, and he gave it a staged reading. *Ma Rainey* premiered at the Yale Repertory Theatre before it opened on Broadway in 1984, where it won the New York Drama Critics' Circle Award for best play. It was at the Eugene O'Neill Theatre that Wilson first met actor **Charles S. Dutton**, who later played Levee Green in *Ma Rainey* to great acclaim. Dutton's overbearing personality and nonstop energy exploded on the Broadway stage, and he so affected Wilson's creative juices that he constructed the character of Boy Willie in *The Piano Lesson* after Dutton, a role he also played on Broadway.

Wilson's relationship with Lloyd was fortuitous. Wilson was self-educated with a gift of language and characterization but a novice in the theater world. Richards, the dean and artistic director of the Yale Repertory Theatre, was a theater veteran. In 1959, he had directed the pioneering Broadway production of **Lorraine Hansberry**'s *A Raisin in the Sun*—the first black director to do so. The play readings at the Eugene O'Neill Center brought Richards and Wilson together in a professional working relationship that was almost familial, like father and son—the father Wilson never had. Richards, some 20 years his senior, was able to harness Wilson's poetry into theatrical shape. Lloyd also introduced Wilson to Ben Mordecai, a Broadway producer who eventually produced most of Wilson's plays. This format of reading and developing Wilson's plays through the workshop process helped him to shape and focus his plays and to evolve as a playwright of exceptional talent. Together, Wilson, Lloyd, and Mordecai had formed a dynamic theatrical team that was of financial advantage to all three. Richards directed the first 6 plays of Wilson's epic 10-play cycle, and Mordecai was involved in all of them, which played on Broadway.

After 14 years and a mercurial ride of theatrical success, the Wilson–Richards–Mordecai partnership was cut short due to Richards's failing health. In 1999, Wilson called upon his old friend McClinton to direct *King Hedley II*. The transition was almost seamless. Wilson by then had moved to Seattle, where he finished writing the last three plays of the cycle. Wilson died on 2 October 2005, a few months shy of seeing the last play he wrote of the cycle, *Radio Golf*. Ironically, all three theatrical giants, Mordecai, Wilson, and Richards, died within a year of one another.

Wilson's 10-play cycle, as they were written, includes *Ma Rainey's Black Bottom* (1984). It was set in 1927 in a recording studio during a frigid winter in Chicago. Ma Rainey and her fellow musicians combat their white manager, an opportunistic record producer, and themselves, as Ma tries to preserve the legacy of the gut-bucket blues she made so popular in the South. This is the only play in Wilson's 10-play cycle that Wilson sets outside the Hill District of his hometown, Pittsburgh. *Fences* (1987), set in 1957, deals with issues of father and son, dreams deferred, infidelity and betrayal, denial, and how these issues affect relationships. It was first presented at the National Playwrights Conference (1983). From there it moved to the Yale Repertory Theatre in New Haven (April–May 1985). Richards directed a stellar cast of **James Earl Jones**, **Mary Alice**, **Charles Brown**, Courtney Vance, **Ray Aranha**, Russell Costen, Crystal Coleman, and LaJara Henderson. It opened on Broadway to critical applause at the 46th Street Theatre (March 1987) under Richards's direction, with James Earl Jones and Mary Alice retaining the role of the central characters. It won the Pulitzer Prize for drama in April 1987, four Tony Awards for best play, best director, best performance by a leading actor for Jones, and best performance by a featured actress for Alice. *Joe Turner's Come and Gone* (1988) is set in 1911. It is about Herald Loomis, who had been captured illegally by a bounty hunter and worked on a chain gang for seven years. Upon his release, he collects his daughter and turns up in a boardinghouse looking for his missing wife. It was first produced on the **Arena Playhouse** at the Yale Repertory Theatre (October 1987). Five months later, it opened on Broadway at the Ethel Barrymore Theatre (March 1988) with Delroy Lindo as Loomis and Angela Basset as Martha Pentecost. *The Piano Lesson* (1990) is set in 1936. A brother and sister fight over whether to sell a rare piano that is emblematic of the family history. *Two Trains Running* (1992) is set in 1969 in a dilapidated restaurant scheduled for demolition. A recently released convict joins the displaced dreamers, who hunger for a new life. *Jitney* (1982) is set in 1977. In it, a gypsy cab company is scheduled to be demolished as the owner and his son clash over their shared history. *Seven Guitars* (1996), set in 1948, tells the story of the final days of a Pittsburgh blues guitarist and how and why he died. *King Hedley II* (1999) is set in 1985. Hedley returns to his old neighborhood to find everything changed and tries to reestablish himself. *Gem of the Ocean* (2004) is set in 1904. Former slaves and men born into freedom meet in the home of Aunt Ester, a central figure in the Hill District. *Radio Golf* (2005) is set in 1990. Two real estate entrepreneurs have to decide between opportunity and tradition as the home of the historical black matriarch, Aunt Ester, is scheduled for demolition. Early plays written by Wilson include *The Janitor, Recycle, Malcolm X, The Coldest Day of the Year, The Homecoming,* and the musical satire *Black Bart and the Sacred Hills.* Over the years, with the success of his plays, Wilson achieved one honor after another. He garnered the Guggenheim and Rockefeller fellowships, Heinz Award, Great Britain's Olivier Award, Presidential National Humanities Award; and an election to the Academy of Arts and Letters and the Academy of Humanities.

After Wilson announced his terminal illness, Rocco Landesman, President of the Jujamcyn Theatre Group and a producer of Wilson's plays, announced on 2 September 2005 that the former Virginia Theatre would be renamed the August Wilson Theatre. The theater was named formally the August Wilson Theatre in ceremonies held on 16 October 2005. This marks the first time a Broadway theater has been named for an African American. Also, Wilson's hometown of Pittsburgh renamed the former African American Culture Center of Greater Pittsburgh the August Wilson Center for African American Culture. Tributes poured in from all over the world, including one held at the Intiman Theatre in Seattle highlighted by a moving, emotional speech by novelist/professor Charles Johnson. This was followed by the Seattle Repertory Theatre's all-out tribute to Wilson in February 2006. They presented scenes from all 10 of the Wilson canon, performed by a who's-who list of professional actors who had achieved prominence by appearing in Wilson's plays. Among them were Anthony Chisholm, **Stephen McKinley Henderson**, Keith Randolph Smith, **Ruben Santiago-Hudson**, John Earl Jelks, Rocky Carroll, Derrick Sanders, Cynthia Jones, and **Charlayne Woodard**. It was truly a night of remembrance, and while there were other tributes around the country, it would be hard to imagine any of them exceeding what happened on 13 February 2006. Even by 2007, it was still difficult to measure the impact of Wilson's death.

Wilson was also awarded honorary degrees from the New School University, Columbia University, University of Pittsburgh, University of Washington, State University of New York, Old Westbury, Howard University, Yale University, Hamilton College, DePaul University, University of Minnesota, Seattle University, Manhattanville College, Boston University, Cal State Northridge, MaCalester College, Clarion College, Lincoln University, Amherst College, Hamline University, Rutgers University, University of Hartford, Dartmouth College, Morgan State University, Carnegie Mellon University, City University of New York, Princeton University, Washington University of St. Louis, and Carnegie Library of Pittsburgh (high school diploma), at which Wilson said he had returned the book he had "borrowed."

WILSON, FRANK H. (1886–1956). Active between the 1910s and 1940s, Wilson was a pioneer playwright, actor, and singer in regional and Broadway stage and films. His play *Meek Mose* (1928), a social drama, was the third play by an African American to be produced on Broadway and the first by a black production company. A native of New York City, after World War I, he studied theater at the American Academy of Dramatic Art at Carnegie Hall under Franklin H. Sargent and later Anne Wolter. In 1908 at age 22, he joined a vaudeville troupe, Carolina Comedy Four, for three years. Shortly thereafter, as a mail carrier, he began writing short plays about his life experiences. During the mid-1910s, he found an outlet for his passion in **Harlem** with the Lincoln Players, a group he organized at the Lincoln Theatre. There he wrote, directed, and performed in his own plays, *The Flash*, *The Prison of Life*, *Colored America*, *Race Pride*, *The Good Sister Jones*, *Roseanna*, *Happy Southern Folk*, *Back Home*, and *The Frisco Kid*. Later, he joined the Lafayette Players at the **Lafayette Theatre**, playing his first role there in *The Deep Purple*. He also produced his own plays at the Lafayette, including *The Heartbreakers* (1921), with Edna Thomas and Lionel Monagas; *Pa Williams' Gal* (1923), featuring **Rose McClendon** and Richard B. Harrison; and *A Train North*, a play the players produced at the Harlem YMCA Little

Theatre on a double bill with *Heartbreakers* in 1923. Wilson also founded the **Aldridge Players** (1926) at the YMCA, which mounted three of his one-act plays, *Flies*, *Color Worship*, and *Sugar Cane*—the first-prize winner of the *Opportunity* Contest Awards (1926). In 1928, *Meek Mose* opened on Broadway for one week. The Works Division of the New York Department of Public Welfare presented it under the revised title *Brother Mose* throughout New York City on the Park Circuit and at Central Park. Wilson's last and best-known play, *Walk Together, Chillun*, a social drama with black spirituals, was the first production of the New York Negro Unit of the Works Progress Administration's **Federal Theatre Project** at the Lafayette Theatre in 1936.

In 1925, Wilson made his professional debut as a stage actor in a supporting role with the Provincetown Players in Greenwich Village, New York City, in the original stage production of *The Emperor Jones*. It starred **Charles Gilpin** and later **Paul Robeson**, whom he played opposite in the 1933 film version. A year before, Wilson had appeared with Robeson in the premier of *All God's Chillun Got Wings* (1924). In 1926, he played a supporting role and later the lead in *In Abraham's Bosom*. Owing to the recognition he garnered in these plays as a leading black actor, he landed roles in several off-Broadway and Broadway plays, such as *Justice* (1920), *Porgy* (1927), *Roll Sweet Chariot* (1930), *Blood Stream* (1932), *They Shall Not Die* (1934), *Memphis Bound* (1945), *Anna Lucasta* (1946), and *Take a Giant Step* (1953). Wilson also independently produced such all-black films as *Paradise in Harlem* (1939), *Murder on Lenox Avenue* (1941), and *Sunday Sinners* (1941).

WILSON, TRACY SCOTT. A playwright, Wilson is from Newark, NJ. She obtained her B.A. from Rutgers in 1989 and M.A. in English literature from Temple University in 1995. After receiving 28 rejection letters for her novel *I Don't Know Why the Caged Bird Won't Shut Up*, she enrolled in a playwriting course. Wilson became immersed in theater, reading over 100 plays at the Lincoln Center library. The next year, 1998, she won the prized Van Lier playwriting fellowship from the New York Theatre Workshop. In 2003, her play *The Story* was presented at the NYSF/Public Theatre in a joint venture with the Long Wharf Theatre. It is based on a real-life incident of an incendiary view of racial politics, journalistic malfeasance, and murder. Critics raved, and the play was produced all over the country in such theaters as the **Ensemble Theatre** in Houston, TX; the Tyrone Guthrie in Minneapolis; and Goodman in Chicago. Wilson is among a cadre of young, black female playwrights who dominate the black theater landscape thus far in the 21st century. Among the plays she has written are *Exhibit #9*, *Leader of the People*, *The Good Negro*, *Fairy Tale*, *A Small World* (10-minute play), *Order My Steps, A Musical*, and *Sista Style*. Wilson has been recognized with several distinctive and prestigious awards, including Jerome Foundation grant, Helen Merrill emerging playwright grant, AT&T onstage grant, Giles writing fellowship, Kesselring playwriting fellowship, and the Van Lier playwriting fellowship (twice).

WIMBERLY, BRIDGETTE. Wimberly is an emerging playwright of the 21st century. She is a native of Cleveland who resides in New York and works in the field of medicine. Her biggest success has been *Saint Lucy's Eyes*, which was developed from a working exercise when she was enrolled in the Lincoln Center Playwrights Laboratory. It was subsequently chosen by the late Wendy Wasserstein in 1999 for the Women's Mentors Project at the famed Cherry Lane Theatre in New York. For over a year, Wasserstein served as a dramaturge and mentor to Wimberly as she rewrote and polished the play. Cherry Lane produced it off Broadway in 2001 in a successful run. The play has since become a staple in the regional theater circuit. It takes place in Memphis, TN, one day before the assassination of Dr. Martin Luther King Jr. and centers on an elderly woman abortionist called Grandma. The role was created by **Ruby Dee**, and it has quickly become a signature role. Other plays Wimberly wrote include *Forest City*, *The Mark*, and *Separation of Blood*, the last play being an exploration of the life of Charles Drew, a pioneer in the field of blood transplants. Wimberly's plays have been produced at the **St. Louis Black Repertory Theatre**, Cleveland Playhouse, Alliance Theatre, and the **Ensemble Theatre**, among others. Wimberly is a member of Dramatists Guild and is on the board of Cherry Lane Theatre. She has won a New York Foundation for the Arts fellowship, Van Lier fellowship at Manhattan Theatre Club, and a Sloan Foundation grant.

WINDE, BEATRICE (1924–2004). Born in Chicago, Winde was an actress and vocalist who enjoyed a long, illustrious career in the American theater, as well as in film and television. She is perhaps best known for her role as the forlorn lover in **Melvin Van Peebles's** 1971 Broadway production of *Ain't Supposed to Die a Natural Death*, for which she received a **Tony Award** nomination. Winde was a graduate of the Chicago Music Conservatory. She sang with several groups in Chicago and also as a soloist in a church choir before embarking on a career in the theater. She studied at the Yale School of Music and Juilliard.

Though she occasionally played lead roles, Winde was basically a character actor who relished finding the "spine" of the character and then embellishing it in a richly detailed, nuanced characterization. Sometimes she would render conversationally, "When I find the spine, it's mine, honey!" During her lengthy career, Winde appeared at the Jean Cocteau Repertory Theatre, Manhattan Theatre Club, the **Negro Ensemble Company (NEC)**, Playwrights Horizons, Seattle Repertory Theatre, Signature Theatre Company, A Contemporary Theatre, the NYSF/Public Theatre, and many others. She has appeared in *A Lesson before Dying*, *The Young Man from Atlanta*, *Dreaming Emmit*, *In White America*, *One Last Look*, and numerous productions at the NEC. Winde also made over 30 film and television appearances in such vehicles as *The Sopranos*, *Jefferson in Paris*, *The Taking of Pelham One Two Three*, *The Cosby Show*, *The Autobiography of Miss Jane Pittman*, *NYPD Blue*, *Malcolm X*, *The Doctors*, and *Mickey Blue Eyes*, to name a few. Winde died two days short of her 80th birthday. She is the recipient of an **Audience Development Committee Award**, a Theatre World Award, and a Living Legend Award from the **National Black Theatre Festival**.

WOLFE, ELTON (CLYDE). Playwright Wolfe was formerly associated with Aldridge Players/West (AP/W) in San Francisco. He received a Ph.D. in theater from Stanford University (1977). His plays of note include *Men Wear Mustaches* (1968), a domestic drama in one act. After a woman deserts her husband, she has second thoughts and tries to get back together with him, but it is too late. *The Big Shot* (1969) is a comedy in one act. A young chauffeur visits his mother in his employer's Rolls Royce. He plays the part of a wealthy man after he finds out his mother had told everyone he rich. *The After Party*

(1970) is a comedy in one act. Two young men have a dialogue about "black" and "Negro" attitudes.

WOLFE, GEORGE C. A director, playwright, and producer, the mercurial Wolfe was a dominating force on the American theatrical landscape in the 1990s. In 1992, he held two positions as artistic director and producing manager of the New York Shakespeare Festival (NYSF)/Public Theatre, succeeding the late **Joseph Papp**. By decade's end, he had won two **Tony Awards** for his musicals *Jelly's Last Jam* (1991) and *Bring in 'da Noise, Bring in 'da Funk* (1996) and directed Tony Kushner's *Angels in America*, which not only won a Tony but the **Pulitzer Prize** as well. All three productions had lengthy Broadway runs and were successful financially.

Wolfe was born in Frankfort, KY, in 1954, and began writing plays at the age of eight or nine. His attendance at Kentucky State College was short lived. He transferred to Pomona College, where he earned a B.A. in theater (1976). While in California, he worked with **C. Bernard Jackson** at the Inner-City Cultural Center and picked up additional theater experience. He moved to New York City in 1979 and enrolled at New York University, where he earned an M.F.A. in dramatic writing and musical theater. He began teaching at City College of New York and the Richard Allen Center. It was also in New York where he worked with **James V. Hatch** at the Hatch-Billops Archival Center. During the 1990s and into the 21st century, Wolfe directed some 11 Broadway hits, including *Topdog/Underdog*, *Elaine Stritch at Liberty*, *Twilight: Los Angeles*, and *Caroline or Change*.

His first success as a playwright is *The Colored Museum* (1986), which premiered at **Crossroads Theatre Company** in New Brunswick, New Jersey (March 1986), under the direction of Lee Richardson. This satire explored the myths and contradictions inherent in the African American community. It was an instant hit and soon became a staple in the repertoire of black theaters across the country. It is a lampoon of the **black experience** comprised of a series of 12 museum exhibits that come to life, revealing the myths and madness of stereotypes of black culture. Among the subjects hilariously and mercilessly satirized are Afro wigs, Josephine Baker, *A Raisin in the Sun*, black song-and-dance musicals, *Ebony* magazine, and many other

aspects of the black heritage. In New York City, the NYSF/Public Theatre produced it at the Susan Stein Shiva Theatre (October 1986) with
the same director as the premiere and with a cast that featured Loretta
Devine, Tommy Hollis, Reggie Montgomery, Vickilyn Reynolds, and
Danitra Vance. It won the 1986 Dramatists Guild Award. Other plays
Wolfe penned include *Up for Grabs* (1975), *Block Party* (play of
black life with music, 1976), *Queenie Pie: An Evening of Vintage
Ellington* (a full-length musical, 1986), *Harlem Song* (a Broadway-
style musical illustrating the history of **Harlem**, 2002), *The Wild
Party* (2000), *Blackout: A Play* (1990), *Spunk* (1989), *Paradise*
(1985), *Back Alley Tales* (1979), *Tribal Rites* (1978), and *The Block
Party* (1976). After 12 successful years, Wolfe left the NYSF/Public
Theatre to seek opportunities in film, though he continues to work in
theater. His latest effort was directing Bertolt Brecht's *Mother
Courage* for the NYSF/Public Theatre's annual Theatre in the Park
series in Central Park in the summer of 2006.

He is the recipient of a CBS/Foundation of the Dramatists Guild
Playwriting Award for *The Colored Museum* (1986) and grants from
the Rockefeller Foundation, the National Endowment for the Arts, and
the National Institute for Musical Theatre. Wolfe's honors and awards
include the **New York Drama Critics' Circle Award**, **Drama Desk
Award**, **Obie Award**, and Tony Awards.

WOMEN'S ISSUES. During the early decades of the 1920s and 1930s,
pioneer African American female playwrights, such as **Angelina
Weld Grimké**, Ruth Gaines-Shelton, **Myrtle Smith Livingston**, **Alice Dunbar-Nelson**, **Eulalie Spence**, and **Marita Bonner**, established black theater traditions. Their primary concern was the well-
being of the black community. They explored issues that were
different from those of their black male counterparts and that impacted the lives of black people—the military, children, lynching, the
sanctity of family, the absent father, **miscegenation**, marriage,
racism, the disparity between religious ideology and practice, and the
depiction of heroes and heroines. In the 1970s, during the early stages
of the women and feminist movement, contemporary black female
dramatists like **Adrienne Kennedy, Ntozake Shange, Alice Childress, Anna Deveare Smith, Sonia Sanchez, Aishah Rahman**, and

Suzan-Lori Parks built upon the themes and subject matter of their predecessors. They also broadened the landscape to explore the experience of being black and female while relating historical, social, political, theoretical, and cultural issues to their works. In *For Colored Girls Who Have Considered Suicide When the Rainbow Is Enuf* (1977), Ntozake Shange examines the theme of black male–black female relationships told from a feminist perspective and of women struggling to survive. It is a drama of self-celebration, utilizing poetry, dance, color symbolism, and intimate personal experiences that explore the many facets of a black woman's psyche. It is performed by seven black women. Each is distinguished by a color of the rainbow— Lady in Brown, Lady in Yellow, Lady in Red, Lady in Green, Lady in Purple, Lady in Blue, and Lady in Orange. It sparked wails of protest from both sides of the gender divide, but the richness of its prose could not be denied. Sonia Sanchez's play *Sister Sonji* (1969) is a semiautobiographical monologue in one act. Her plea is for equal representation for women within the black arts movement of the 1960s that was dominated by black men. Alice Childress's *Wedding Band: A Love/Hate Story in Black and White* (1973) is about the denial of women's rights in the South after the Reconstruction. She challenges the laws that prohibit marriage between blacks and whites, divorce (even within the race), and property rights, as well as unwritten laws that limit upward mobility. In *Sally's Rape* (1989), an audience interactive piece by Robby McCauley, the subject matter comes from the title. The printed text is a dialogue scenario of what evolved out of the performances at the Kitchen in Soho, Lincoln Center, Studio Museum of **Harlem**, and the Davis Center at City College of New York (all in New York) City. The participants were comprised of three groups— two women, one black (Robbie), one white (Jeannine), and the audience, whom the women take on a historical journey through time. The audience is subdivided into groups of three. They serve as performers, witnesses, and chorus members who speak out against the inhuman atrocities that violate women's bodies.

WOODARD CHARLAYNE. An actress and playwright, Woodard was born in 1955 in Albany, NY. She graduated from the Goodman School of Theatre of DePaul University in Chicago with an M.F.A. in

1977 and promptly set off for New York City. Within two weeks, she won a role in the Broadway production of the Fats Waller musical *Ain't Misbehavin'* with Nell Carter. She won a **Drama Desk Award** and received a nomination for her performance. The musical was a huge success and ran on Broadway for three years. After she appeared in the 1982 film of the same name, she was cast into the real world of fledgling actors trying to make a living. She was marginally successful, appearing in films like *Hair* and *One Good Cop* and the TV drama *Days of Our Lives*. But she also learned the reality that all actors endure dry spells and inactivity. She determined that there are few roles for black female actors and made a conscious decision to rectify the situation.

Woodard wrote three one-woman plays. The first two, *Pretty Fire* (1995) and *Neat* (1997), mirror real-life childhood experiences of growing up in Albany. *In Real Life* (2000) tells her story of trying to become an actor in New York. All these pieces were done in collaboration with and directed by Dan Sullivan, a veteran Broadway director and former artistic director of the Seattle Repertory Theatre. Sullivan started the New Playwrights Program at the theater where Woodard first applied, and the two have worked together seamlessly to realize the full potential in her plays, which have been very successful. During this period, Woodard's career has expanded exponentially, with TV roles in *Chicago Hope, Boomtown, Frasier,* and *Law and Order.* She also appeared on and off Broadway in such plays as *In the Blood, The Caucasian Chalk Circle, King Henry IV, Part I,* and *Twelfth Night.* Woodard's latest play *Flight* was commissioned by the CTG (CTG stands for the Center Theatre Group of La La Land). It premiered at the new Kirk Douglas Theatre in Los Angeles (January 2005). Unlike her other plays, this was her first ensemble piece, featuring six actors weaving stories of African folktales. Another solo piece *The Night Watcher* premiered in July of 2008 at the La Jolla Playhouse. Woodard's awards include the Los Angeles Drama Critics' Circle Award for best play for *Pretty Fire,* National Association for the Advancement of Colored People Theatre Award for best play and best actress for *Pretty Fire* (1992), an **Obie Award** for performance of *In the Blood* (1999), and a Theatre Communications Group/Pew Charitable Trust National Theatre Artist Residency Program fellowship with the Mark Taper Forum.

WOODS, ALLIE, JR. A native of Houston, TX, Woods is an award-winning director and actor of over 200 productions nationally and internationally. He received his theatrical training at Texas Southern and Tennessee State University. Woods moved to New York City in 1967 to join the prestigious **Negro Ensemble Company (NEC)** as a founding member. Woods has directed productions off Broadway at both the NEC Playwrights/Directors Units and the Actors Studio, as well as at the New York Shakespeare Festival, Brooklyn Academy of Music, and **La MaMa Experimental Theatre Club.** He also codirected the *Black Quartet* production that was later taken on an Eastern and Los Angeles tour, and he staged the American premiere of **Ed Bullins**'s *The Gentleman Caller.* It was at the **New Federal Theatre** where Woods received his greatest recognition and praise as a director for **Laurence Holder**'s *When the Chickens Came Home to Roost,* starring **Denzel Washington** in his award-winning stage portrayal of Malcolm X. Outside of New York City, Woods has directed productions at A Contemporary Theatre, **Black/Arts West**, and the University of Washington Department of Theatre in Seattle; the **Ensemble Theatre** in Houston, TX; and internationally at the La Venice Biennial in Italy. Wood's most recent directing project was **August Wilson**'s *Gem of the Ocean* at the Ensemble Theatre that opened in January 2008.

As an actor, Woods has performed on Broadway in *Mule Bone* (1991) and *The Little Foxes* (1997) and off Broadway in *The Forbidden City, Ma Rainey's Black Bottom, Day of Absence, Kongi's Harvest,* and *Daddy Goodness.* He has worked at regional theaters around the country, such as the Alley Theatre; Actor's Theatre of Louisville; Alabama Shakespeare Festival; Center Stage in Baltimore, MD; Denver Center Theatre Company; Pittsburgh Public Theatre; George Street Playhouse; Dayton, Ohio's Human Race Theatre Company; and Stages Repertory of Houston, TX. Recently at the Seattle Repertory Theatre, he portrayed Ely in Wilson's *Gem of the Ocean* directed by **Phylicia Allen-Rashad**. Woods also acted on the international stages at the Royal Shakespeare Company/World Theatre Season, the Barbican Center, Bristol Old Vic, and the Festival of Pearth and Adelaide in Australia. On the silver screen he can be seen in *Girl Fight, 13 Conversations about One Thing,* and *Bellclair Times.* His television credits include the *Law and Order* franchise,

One Life to Live, Six Degrees, and *Day of Absence* (PBS). Among his awards, Woods was honored with the **Audience Development Committee** Recognition Award in black theater as best director for *When the Chickens Came Home to Roost,* which won dramatic production of the year. He also received the Trailblazer Award by the Beverly Hollywood Chapter of the National Association for the Advancement of Colored People. In August 2008, Woods received Houston's Ensemble Theatre 2008 Giorgee Award (named after founder George Wayne Hawkins) as Best Director for August Wilson's *Gem of the Ocean.*

WRIGHT, CHARLES RANDOLPH. A director, playwright, and actor, Wright was born in York, SC. He graduated with honors from Duke University in 1978. He traveled abroad and studied acting with the Royal Shakespeare Company in London and studied dance at the Alvin Ailey School in New York City. His early work as an actor was with regional theater and TV appearances in such shows as *Melrose Place, Hill Street Blues,* and *Falcon Crest.* He was also in the original cast of the 1981 hit musical *Dreamgirls.* In 2000, Wright's direction of *Guys and Dolls* at **Arena Playhouse** broke all box-office records for the theater's 50-year history. It was chosen by the Loesser estate for a national tour to celebrate the musical's 50th anniversary. Other plays he wrote are *Cuttin' Up* (2005), an adaptation from the novel by Craig Marberry about life inside of a black barbershop, and *Blue,* a semiautobiographical look at three generations of a black middle-class family. Wright also cowrote several plays, including the hit musical *Me and Mrs. Jones,* which broke box-office records at the Prince Music Theatre in Philadelphia. Among the honors and awards Wright received are the National Association for the Advancement of Colored People Image Award, Helen Hayes Award, **Audience Development Committee Award**, Theatre Communications Group/Pew Charitable Trust residency grant at the American Conservatory Theatre, Robbie Award, and the Ovation Award.

WRIGHT, DAMON (1950–98). A playwright and journalist, Wright was born in Long Beach, CA. He attended Stanford University, graduating with a degree in English (1972). He began his career in New York City as an administrator for Dance Visions, Inc. After working for over 10 years with the *New York Times*, he decided to pursue his interest in theater. He became active in the New York Theatre Laboratory for playwrights. Wright died prematurely but not before writing six plays, two of which have achieved some prominence. *The Quadroon Ball: An American Tragedy* focuses on the free colored society that thrived from the 18th century up to the Civil War. Wright wrote *Mr. Baldwin Goes to Heaven* after he attended **James Baldwin**'s memorial. Wright's plays have been performed at the Lincoln Center Theatre Directors Lab, the New Theatre, and the Adelaide Institute Center for Performing Arts in Australia. Wright's other plays include *A Struggle to the End*, *Little Black Sambo*, *Testimony*, and *The Murderous Power of Prayer*.

WRIGHT, JAY. A playwright and poet, Wright was born and raised in Albuquerque, NM. After serving in the U.S. Army, he earned his B.A. from the University of California at Berkeley. He studied at Union Theological Seminary with the intention of becoming a priest but abandoned that idea and went back to school. He received his M.A. from Rutgers University in 1966. His background in religion, however, never left him, as evidenced in his plays that reflect his deep religious convictions. Two examples are *Balloons*, a one-act comedy in which a Christian finds himself in conflict with today's society, and *The Adoration of Fire*, a mythical drama with religious overtones. Other plays Wright wrote include *Love's Equation*, *The Death and Return of Paul Batusta*, *The Unfinished Saint*, *A Sacred Impurity: The Dead's First Invention*, *The Hunt and Double Night of the Wood*, *Homage to Anthony Braxton*, *The Crossing*, *The Doors*, and *The Final Celebration*. Wright has written three volumes of poetry. His poetry has been published in *The Nation*, *Hiram Poets Review*, *Yale Review*, and *Black World*.

WRIGHT, JEFFREY. Wright is an accomplished actor both onstage and in films. Born in the mid 1960s in Washington, DC, he was raised by his mother after his father died when he was a baby. Wright enrolled in Amherst College with the intention of following in his mother's footsteps and becoming a lawyer, but he was sidetracked after he took an acting class. In 1987, upon receiving his B.A., he cancelled plans to attend law school and set his sights on being an actor. After a brief stint at New York University's Tisch School of the Arts, he transferred to the Yale Repertory Theatre Program and thereafter at the **Arena Playhouse** in Washington, DC. Among the plays he appeared in at these venues were *Search and Destroy*, *Juno and the Paycock*, and *She Stoops to Conquer*. Wright also appeared in *Othello* at the New York Shakespeare Festival/Public Theatre in 1991. His break came in 1993, when he was cast in Tony Kushner's award-winning play *Angels in America: Perestroika*—winning a **Tony Award**, **Drama Desk Award**, and Outer Critics Circle Award for his performance. Three years later, he was cast as the avant-garde graffiti artist in the film *Basquiat*. This exposure to a newer, wider audience was a boost to his career. Wright has divided his time since then between the stage, television, and film. His credits in films include *Casino Royale*, *Syriana*, *The Manchurian Candidate*, and *Hamlet*. In this last movie, he played the gravedigger opposite Ethan Hawke as Hamlet. Other movies include a remake of *Shaft*, Woody Allen's *Celebrity*, *Ride with the Devil*, and *Broken Flowers*. Wright returned to the stage in 2001 to perform in **Suzan-Lori Park**'s *Topdog/Underdog* at the NYSF/Public Theatre. He reprised the role the next year on Broadway when the play won the **Pulitzer Prize** for drama. His appearances on television have been in *Homicide: Life on the Street*, *Boycott*, *Lackawanna Blues*, a reprise of *Angels of America*, and *Young Indiana Jones and the Mystery of the Blues*. During his brief career thus far, Wright has won acclaim with an Emmy, Golden Globe, American Film Institute, Black Reel (twice), San Diego Film Critics, and Toronto Film Critics Awards.

WRIGHT, RICHARD (1909–60). Wright was a playwright, novelist, short-story writer, radio scriptwriter, essayist, and autobiographer. Born on a plantation near Natchez, MS, Wright, at age six, and his sickly mother were abandoned by his father. They moved from town to town, living with any relative who would take them. He even spent time in an orphanage. The family settled in Jackson, where Wright graduated from the 9th grade at age 15. Within a few years, he was awakened to the harsh reality of black and white race relations in the Deep South. By age 17, he fled to Memphis, TN, to avoid going to jail for petty criminal activities. There he was inspired to be a writer after reading the works of H. L. Mencken, Sinclair Lewis, and

Theodore Dreiser. Two years later, he moved to Chicago, where he worked at menial jobs until he secured a position at the Chicago post office as a clerk. All the while, he continued writing and reading. After losing his job during the Great Depression (1930s), he joined the Communist Party. He remained a member for 10 years until 1935, when he became disillusioned with the ideology of the party, about which he later wrote in *The God That Failed* (1950).

Wright's writing talents by that time were becoming recognized. He was hired as a writer for the Works Progress Administration's Federal Writers Project, the Federal Negro Theatre, and the white Federal Experimental Theatre. By 1937, he was getting his works published in such leftist periodicals as *Daily Worker* and *New Masses*. A year later, his first important book was published, *Uncle Tom's Children*, a collection of short stories that won him a $500 prize. His later books include *The Outsider* (1953); *Black Power* (1954); *The Color Curtain* (1956); *White Man, Listen!* (1957); and *The Long Dream* (1958). In 1946, Wright, his wife Ellen, whom he married in 1940, and their five-year-old daughter moved to Paris, where he lived as an expatriate until his death. He died of a heart attack in Paris in 1960 at the age of 51. Two of his works were published posthumously, *Eight Men* (1961), a collection of stories, and *Lawd Today* (1963), a novel.

In 1940, Wright and Paul Green adapted *Native Son* (1941) into a 10-scene protest drama. Set in the rat-infested black ghetto of South Side Chicago, it depicts how an oppressive and restrictive environment shaped the actions of Bigger Thomas, a rebellious black youth. Orson Welles and John Houseman produced it as a Mercury Production at the St. James Theatre in New York City (March–June 1941) for 114 performances under Welles's direction. The cast included **Canada Lee** (Bigger Thomas), Anne Burr (Mary Dolton), and Evelyn Ellis (Bigger's mother). Welles took a trim-downed version of the show on tour before returning it for a second run in New York, this time at the Majestic Theatre (October–January 1943) for 84 performances. Lee reprised the role of Bigger. Thereafter, the show was produced at theaters in and around New York City. Later it was made into two films (1951 and 1978). The early version with Wright playing Bigger was not well received. Cinecom International Films produced the later rendition with a degree of success. Among the cast were Victor Love (Bigger), Elizabeth McGovern (Mary Dolton),

Geraldine Page (Mary's mother), Oprah Winfrey (Bigger's mother), Matt Dillon (Jan), and Caroll Baker. Other plays Wright authored are *Fire and Cloud* (1941), a radio play in one-act; *The Long Dream* (1960), a drama in three acts; and *Daddy Goodness* (1968), a comedy in three acts. Among the honors and awards Wright received were the Guggenheim fellowship in creative writing (1939) and a **Spingarn Medal** from the National Association for the Advancement of Colored People. *Native Son* was a Book-of-the-Month Club selection (1941), the first book by a black author to achieve this distinction.

– X –

X, MARIAN WARRINGTON. A playwright, Marian X is a native of Trenton, NJ. She received her education from Morgan State University, where she earned a B.A. in English. After marriage and raising two children, she continued her schooling at Villanova University, where she attained an M.A. in theater. Marian X also studied at the **Frank Silvera Writers' Workshop** and **Crossroad Theatre Company**'s innovative "New Play Rites" series, in which her play *Wet Carpets* was chosen as its premiere production in 1988. This marked the beginning of a new voice on the American theatrical scene, joining **Ntozake Shange**, **Suzan-Lori Parks**, and **Lynn Nottage** in the growing vanguard of outstanding black female playwrights. Among the plays Marian X wrote are *Dream Variation* (1986), a drama in black and white about a man who escapes his roots to find success and returns home to rescue a child and recapture his humanity, which Kuumba Theatre Company produced at the Theatre Center; *Wet Carpets* (1987), a comedy with music about the midlife crises of three women raised as sisters; *The Mayor's Wife* (1990), which used the Philadelphia's MOVE tragedy as background for a woman to examine the politics of love; *Warrior Stance or Sex, A Comedy* (1992), an allegorical tale about contemporary family life on planet Earth in a place due south of the Caucasoid Ridge, which was produced at the **Penumbra Theatre**, **Freedom Theatre**, and **National Black Theatre Festival**; and *The Screened-In Porch* (1994), about two women who reunite after 35 years with disastrous results, which was produced at the Horizon Theatre, **St. Louis Black Repertory Theatre**, and Florida A&M. Marian X's plays have also been produced at the **Oakland Ensemble Theatre** and District One in Cape Town, South Africa. She is a member of the Dramatists Guild, Sangoma, the **Black Theatre Network**, and Working Title Playwrights. Among her honors and awards are the Theatre Communications Group playwriting residency, Pew Charitable Trust fellowship, Kennedy Center Playwriting Award, Pennsylvania Council on the Arts Award, Independence Foundation fellowship, Playwright's Exchange Philadelphia residency, and New Professional Theatre Playwriting Award.

X, MARVIN (MARVIN E. JACKMON). Marvin X was born in Fowler, CA, in 1944. He received an associate's degree from Merritt College in 1964. Later he earned a B.A. and M.A. from San Francisco State University. Marvin X was one of the leading foot voices and philosophers in the emerging black arts movement of the **civil rights** Era. He wrote plays, poems, and essays, and along with **Larry Neal**, **Amiri Baraka (LeRoi Jones)**, **Ed Bullins**, **Tom Dent**, and others, he became a spokesperson for the movement, outlining short- and long-term goals and objectives. Marvin X was perhaps best known for his play *Flowers for the Trashman*, a play about a black intellectual dealing with education in a white-controlled culture. Other plays he wrote include *Come Next Summer*, *The Black Bird*, *The Resurrection of the Dead*, *In the Name of Love*, *The Trial*, and *One Day in the Life*. Marvin X continues to work as a teacher, lecturer, and producer. He has taught at many institutions, such as Mills College, Fresno State, Laney, Merritt, San Francisco State University, the University of Nevada, and the University of California at Berkeley. He received a writing fellowships from Columbia University and the National Endowment for the Arts and a planning grant from the National Endowment for the Humanities. He has also written a book, *In the Crazy House Called America* (2003).

– Y –

YOUNG, CLARENCE, III. Young was born in Dayton, OH. He served in the U.S. Air Force from 1961 to 1965 and earned his B.A. in 1979 from Capitol University. He was the director and resident playwright of Theatre West in Dayton. Young is known to have written three plays. *Perry's Mission* (1969) shows how the white man divides the black community. *The System* (1973) is a musical psychodrama about America and the black man. *Black Love* (1975) is about removing the barriers to love. Aside from presentations at Theatre West, Young's plays have received productions at the **Negro Ensemble Company** and Spelman College.

YOUNGBLOOD, SHAY. A playwright and educator, Youngblood was born in Columbus, GA. She was orphaned when her mother died and was raised by relatives. She began writing at an early age after the local library had become her second home. After receiving her B.A. from Clark-Atlanta University in 1981, she began working. She attained her M.F.A. in 1993 from Brown University. Youngblood is in the tide of black female writers who have risen to the forefront in African American literature during the 1990s and into the 21st century. She has not restricted herself to one genre but has written fiction, short stories, plays, poetry, and screenplays and produced and directed two short videos. She is perhaps best known for her play *Shakin' the Mess Out of Misery*, which premiered at Atlanta's Horizon Theatre in 1988. It has since been optioned by **Sidney Poitier**, with Youngblood writing the screenplay. Other plays Youngblood wrote are *Communism Killed My Dog* (1991), *Talking Bones* (1992), *Square Blues* (1992), *Black Power Barbie* (1992), *Amazing Grace* (1995), and *There Are Many Houses in My Tribe* (1996).

Youngblood's achievements in the field of fiction are even more impressive, starting with *Big Momma Stories* in 1989 and followed by two novels, *Soul Kiss* in 1997 and *Black Girl in Paris* in 2000. She has also written stories, essays, poems, and commentaries that appeared in publications across the land. Youngblood has been teaching creative writing for many years at such institutions as Wheaton College, Brown University, Spelman University, Emory, Columbia, and the New School for Social Research in New York. Among the awards she has won are the Hollywood National Association for the Advancement of Colored People Theatre Award for best playwright (1991), Kennedy Center **Lorraine Hansberry** Playwriting Award for *Talking Bones* (1993), Edward Albee Honoree Award and Paul Green

National Theatre Award for *Square Blues* (1992), and Pushcart Prize for her story *Born with Religion* (1986).

***YOUR ARMS TOO SHORT TO BOX WITH GOD* (1976).** This gospel musical based on the Book of Matthew is about the last days of Christ. The composer and lyricist was Alex Bradford, with additional songs provided by Micki Grant. It opened at the Lyceum Theatre in New York City on 22 December 1977 and ran for 429 performances. **Vinnette Carroll** developed the show at the Urban Arts Corps for the Festival of Two Worlds in Spoleto, Italy, in 1976. It was produced by Frankie Hewitt and the Shubert Organization and directed by Carroll. The show marked Carroll's return to Broadway as well as the return of two cast members, Alex Bradford and Grant from her first musical, ***Don't Bother Me, I Can't Cope*.** The singing of William Hardy Jr., Salome Bey, Clinton Derricks-Carroll, and Delores Hall particularly caught the eye of the critics. Hall received a **Tony Award** for her electrifying singing talents. After the lengthy Broadway run, this play visited 66 cities throughout the United States and then returned to the Ambassador Theatre on Broadway in 1980.

Bibliography

CONTENTS

HISTORICAL STUDIES

Abramson, Doris. *Negro Playwrights in the American Theatre, 1925–1959.* New York: Columbia University Press, 1969.

Birdoff, Harry. *The World's Greatest Hit: Uncle Tom's Cabin.* New York: S. F. Vanni, 1947.

Bond, Frederick W. *The Negro and the Drama: The Direct and Indirect Contribution Which the American Negro Has Made to Drama and the Legitimate Stage, with the Underlying Conditions Responsible.* Washington, DC: Associated Publishers, 1940 (Repr., McGrath, 1969).

Bontempts, Arna, ed. *The Harlem Renaissance Remembered.* New York: Dodd, Mead, 1972.

Burton, Jennifer. *Zora Neale Hurston, Eulalie Spence, Marita Bonner and Others: The Prize Plays and Other One-Acts.* New York: G. K. Hall, 1996.

Callow, Simon. *Orson Welles: The Road to Xanadu.* New York: Penguin Books, 1996.

Craig, E. Quita. *Black Drama of the Federal Theatre Era: Beyond the Formal Horizons.* Boston: University of Massachusetts Press, 1980.

Cruse, Harold. *The Crisis of the Negro Intellectual.* New York: William Morrow, 1967.

Cullen, Rosemary L. *The Civil War in American Drama before 1900: Catalog of an Exhibition, November 1982.* Providence, RI: Brown University Press, 1982.

Curtis, Susan. *The First Black Actors on the Great White Way.* Columbia: The University of Missouri Press, 1998.

Dennis, Ethel. *The Black People of America: Illustrated History.* New York: McGraw-Hill, 1970.

Dent, Thomas C., Richard Schechner, and Gilbert Moses, eds. *The Free Southern Theater by the Free Southern Theater.* Indianapolis: Bobbs-Merril, 1969.

Elkins, Marilyn. *August Wilson: A Casebook.* New York: Garland, 2000.

Epstein, Helen. *Joe Papp: An American Life.* New York: DaCapo Press, 1996.

Fabre, Genevieve. *Drumbeats, Masks and Metaphor: Contemporary Afro-American Theatre.* Washington, DC: Howard University Press, 1983.

Flanagan, Hallie. *Arena: The History of the Federal Theatre.* New York: Duell, Sloan, and Pearce, 1940.

Flanagan, Hallie (Hallie Ferguson Flanagan Davis). *Arena: The History of the Federal Theatre.* New York: Benjamin Blom, 1965.

Fletcher, Tom. *100 Years of the Negro in Show Business.* New York: Burdge and Company, 1954.

Flowers, H. D., II. *Blacks in American Theatre History: Images, Realities.* Potential. Blacksburg, VA: Bellwether Press, 1992.

Fraden, Rena. *Blueprints for a Black Federal Theatre, 1935–1939.* Cambridge: Cambridge University Press, 1994.

Gottschild, Brenda Dixon. *Digging the Africanist Presence in American Performance: Dance and Other Contexts.* Westport, CT: Greenwood, 1996.

Haskins, James. *Black Theater in America.* New York: Crowell, 1982.

Hatch, James V., and Errol G. Hill. *A History of African American Theatre.* New York: Cambridge University Press, 2003.

Hatch, James V., Errol G. Hill, and Ted Shine, eds. *Black Theatre USA: Plays by African Americans.* Rev. ed. New York: Free Press, 1996.

Hay, Samuel. *African American Theatre: An Historical and Critical Analysis.* New York: Cambridge University Press, 1994.

Hill, Anthony D. *Pages from the Harlem Renaissance: A Chronicle of Performance.* New York: Peter Lang, 1966.

Hill, Errol G. *Shakespeare in Sable: A History of Black Shakespearean Actors.* Amherst: University of Massachusetts Press, 1984.

———. *The Theatre of Black Americans.* 2 vols. 1980. Repr. one volume. New York: Applause Theatre Books, 1987.

Holmes, Dwight Oliver Wendell. *The Evolution of the Negro College*. New York: AMS Press, 1970.

Huggins, Nathan Irvin. *Harlem Renaissance*. New York: Oxford University Press, 2007.

Hughes, Langston, and Milton Meltzer. *Black Magic: A Pictorial History of Black Entertainers in America*. New York: Bonanza Books, 1968.

Hughes, Langston, Milton Meltzer, Harris, Middleton A., Morris Levitt, Roger Furman, and Ernest Smith. *The Black Book*. New York: Random House, 1974.

———. *A Pictorial History of the Negro in America*. New York: Crown, 1968.

Hutchinson, George. *The Harlem Renaissance in Black and White*. Cambridge, MA: Harvard University Press, 1995.

Johnson, Helen A. *Black Americans on Stage*. New York: Amstead-Johnson Foundation, 1982.

Johnson, James Weldon. *Black Manhattan*. New York: Alfred A. Knopf, 1930.

Jones, Phillip, and Everett L. Jones. *The Negro Cowboys*, New York: Dodd, Mead, 1965.

Jones, Rhodessa. *Let's Get It On: The Politics of Black Performance*. Seattle: Bay Press, 1995.

Katz, William Loren. *The Black West*. New York: Anchor Press/Doubleday, 1971.

King, Woodie, Jr. *Black Theatre: Present Condition*. New York: Publishing Center for Cultural Resources, 1981.

Krasner, David. *A Beautiful Pageant African American Theatre Drama and Performance in the Harlem Renaissance, 1910–1927*. New York: Palgrave MacMillan, 2004.

———. *Resistance, Parody, and Double Consciousness in African American Theatre, 1895–1910*. New York: St. Martin's Press, 1997.

Little, Stuart. *Enter: Joseph Papp*. New York: Coward, McCann, and Geohegan, 1974.

Locke, Alain. *The New Negro: An Interpretation*. New York: Arno Press and the *New York Times*, 1968.

McMillan, Felecia Piggot. *The North Carolina Black Repertory Company: 25 Marvtastic Years*. Greensboro, NC: Open Hand, 2005.

Mitchell, Loften. *Black Drama: The Story of the American Negro in the Theatre*. New York: Hawthorn, 1967.

O'Connor, John, and Lorraine Brown, eds. *Free, Adult, Uncensored: The Living History of the Federal Theatre Project*. Washington, DC: New Republic Books, 1978.

Odell, George C. D. *Annals of the New York Stage, 1882–1885*. Vol. 12. New York: AMS Press, 1970.

Oliver, Clinton F., and Stephanie Sills, eds. *Contemporary Black Drama*. New York: Scribner's, 1971.

Poland, Albert, and Bruce Mailman, eds. *The Off-Off Broadway Book: The Plays, People, and Theatre*. Indianapolis: Bobbs-Merrill, 1972.

Sampson, Henry T. *The Ghost Walks: A Chronological History of Blacks in Show Business, 1865–1910*. Metuchen, NJ: Scarecrow Press, 1988.

Sanders, Leslie. *The Development of Black Theatre in America: From Shadows to Selves*. Baton Rouge: Louisiana State University Press, 1998.

Shannon, Sandra G., *August Wilson's Fences: A Reference Guide*. Westport, CT: Greenwood Press, 2003.

———. *The Dramatic Vision of August Wilson*. Washington, DC: Howard University Press, 1995.

Shannon, Sandra G. and Dana Williams, eds. *August Wilson and Black Aesthetics*. New York: Palgrave MacMillan, 2004.

Thompson, George A., Jr. *Documentary History of the African Theater*. Chicago: Northwestern University Press, 1998.

Toll, Robert C. *Blacking Up: The Minstrel Show in Nineteenth-Century America*. Oxford: Oxford University Press, 1974.

Turner, Darwin T. *Black Drama in America*. Greenwich, CT: Fawcett Premier Books, 1971.

Watson, Steven. *The Harlem Renaissance*. New York, Pantheon Books, 1995.

William, Mance. *Black Theatre in the 1960s and 1970s: A Historical-Critical Analysis of the Movement*. Westport, CT: Greenwood, 1985.

Wilson, Garff B. *Three Hundred Years of American Drama and Theatre*. 2nd ed. Englewood Cliffs. NJ: Prentice-Hall, 1982.

PLAYWRIGHTS

Arata, Esther Spring. *More Black American Playwrights: A Bibliography*. Metuchen, NJ: Scarecrow Press, 1978.

Arata, Esther Spring, and Nicholas John Rotoli. *Black American Playwrights, 1800 to the Present: A Bibliography*. Metuchen, NJ: Scarecrow Press, 1976.

Couch, William, Jr. *New Black Playwrights*. Baton Rouge: Louisiana State University Press, 1968.

Hatch, James V. *Sorrow Is the Only Faithful One: The Life of Owen Dodson*. Urbana: University of Illinois Press, 1993.

Hatch, James V., and Omanii Abdullah, eds. *Black Playwrights, 1823–1977: An Annotated Bibliography of Plays*. New York: R. R. Bowker, 1977.

Peterson, Bernard L. *Contemporary Black American Playwrights and Their Plays: A Biographical Directory and Dramatic Index*. New York: Greenwood Press, 1988.

———. *Early Black American Playwrights and Dramatic Writers: A Biographical Directory and Catalogue of Plays, Films and Broadcasting Scripts*. New York: Greenwood Press, 1990.

Williams, Dana A. *Contemporary African American Female Playwrights: An Annotated Bibliography*. Westport, CT: Greenwood Press, 1998.

AUTOBIOGRAPHIES AND BIOGRAPHIES

Benston, Kimberly W. *Baraka: The Renegade and the Mask*. New Haven, CT: Yale University Press, 1976.

Bernard, Emily. *Remember Me to Harlem: The Letters of Langston Hughes and Carl Van Vechten*. New York: Alfred A. Knopf, 2001.

Bryer, Jackson R., and Mary C. Hartig. *Conversations with August Wilson*. Jackson: University Press of Mississippi, 2006.

Carter, Steven R. *Hansberry's Drama: Commitment and Complexity*. Urbana: University of Illinois Press, 1991.

Charter, Ann. *Nobody: The Story of Bert Williams*. New York: Macmillan, 1970.

Davis, Ossie, and Ruby Dee. *With Ossie and Ruby: In This Life Together*. New York: Perennial, 2004.

Editors of *Freedomways*. *Paul Robeson: The Great Forerunner*. New York: International, 1998.

Fabre, Michel. *The Unfinished Quest of Richard Wright*. New York: William Morrow, 1973.

Gilliam, Dorothy Butler. *Paul Robeson: All American*. Washington, DC: New Republic Book Company, 1978.

Hatch, James V. *Sorrow Is the Only Faithful One: The Life of Owen Dodson*. Urbana: University of Illinois Press, 1993.

Horn, Barbara Lee. *Joseph Papp: A Bio-Bibliography*. Westport, CT: Greenwood Press, 1992.

Marshall, Herbert, and Mildred Stock. *Ira Aldridge: The Negro Tragedian*. Washington, DC: Howard University Press, 1993.

Mitchell, Loften. *Voices of the Black Theatre*. Clifton, NJ: James T. White, 1975.

Neal, Lester A. *Ntozake Shange: A Critical Study of the Plays*. New York: Garland, 1995.

O'Daniel, Therman B., ed. *James Baldwin: A Critical Evaluation*. Washington, DC: Howard University Press, 1977.

Rowland, Mabel, ed. *Bert Williams: Son of Laughter: A Symposium of Tribute to the Man and His Work, by His Friends and Associates*. Westport, CT: Negro University Press, 1969.

Sollors, Werner. *Amiri Baraka/LeRoi Jones: The Quest for a "Populist Modernism."* New York: Columbia University Press.

Wright, Ellen, and Michel Fabre, eds. *Richard Wright Reader.* New York: Da Capo Press, 1978.

CRITICISM, ANALYSIS, AND THEORY

Abramson, Doris E. *Negro Playwrights in the American Theatre: 1925–1959.* New York: Columbia University Press, 1969.

Bassett, John E. *Harlem in Review: Critical Reactions to Black American Writers, 1917.* London: Associated University Presses, 1992.

Cruse, Harold. *The Crisis of the Negro Intellectual.* New York: William Morrow, 1987.

Elam, Harry J., and David Krasner. *African American Performance and Theater History: A Critical Reader.* New York: Oxford University Press, 2001.

Gayle, Addison, Jr. *The Black Aesthetic.* Garden City, NJ: Anchor Books, 1971.

Hill, Errol. *The Theatre of Black Americans: A Collection of Critical Essays.* New York: Applause, 1987.

Krasner, David. *A Beautiful Pageant: African American Theatre, Drama, and Performance in the Harlem Renaissance, 1910–1927.* New York: Palgrave MacMillian, 2002.

———. *Resistance, Parody, and Double Consciousness in African American Theatre, 1895–1910,* New York: St. Martin's Press.

Mahar, William J. *Behind the Burnt Cork Mask: Early Blackface Minstrelsy an Antebellum American Popular Culture.* Urbana: University of Illinois Press, 1999.

Molette, Carlton W., and Barbara J. Molette. *Black Theatre: Premise and Presentation.* Bristol, IN: Wyndham Hall Press, 1986.

Shannon, Sandra G. *The Dramatic Vision of August Wilson.* Washington, DC: Howard University Press, 1995.

Stewart, Jeffrey C., ed. *The Critical Temper of Alain Locke: A Selection of His Essays on Art and Culture.* New York: Garland, 1983.

ANTHOLOGIES

Branch, William B., ed. *Black Thunder: An Anthology of Contemporary African American Drama.* New York: Penguin, 1992.

———. *Crosswinds: An Anthology of Black Dramatists in the Diaspora.* Bloomington: Indiana University Press, 1993.

Elam, Harry J., Jr. *The Past as Present in the Drama of August Wilson.* Ann Arbor: University of Michigan Press, 2006

Elam, Harry J., Jr., and Robert Alexander. *Colored Contradictions: An Anthology of Contemporary African-American Plays.* New York: Penguin, 1996.

Hamalian, Leo, and James V. Hatch. *The Roots of African American Drama: An Anthology of Early Plays, 1858–1938.* Detroit: Wayne State University Press.

Hatch, James V., and Ted Shine, eds. *Black Theatre USA: Forty-five Plays by African Americans.* New York: Free Press, 1996.

Hill, Errol. *Black Heroes: 7 Plays.* New York: Applause Theatre Book, 1989.

King, Woodie, Jr. *New Plays for the Black Theatre.* Chicago: Third World Press, 1989.

Mitchell, Angelyn. *Within the Circle: An Anthology of African American Literary Criticism from the Harlem Renaissance to the Present.* Durham, NC: Duke University Press, 1994.

Nadel, Alan. *May All Your Fences Have Gates: Essays on the Drama of August Wilson.* Iowa City: University of Iowa Press, 1994.

Oliver, Clinton F., and Stephanie Sills. *Contemporary Black Drama: From A Raisin in the Sun to No Place to Be Somebody.* New York: Charles Schribner's Sons, 1971.

Ostrow, Eileen Joyce. *Center Stage: An Anthology of 21 Contemporary Black-American Plays.* Oakland, CA: Sea Urchin Press, 1981.

Patterson, Lindsay, ed. *Anthology of the American Negro in the Theatre: A Critical Approach.* New York: Publishers Company, 1968.

———. *Black Theater: A 20th Century Collection of the Work of Its Best Playwrights.* New York: New American Library, 1971.

Perkins, Kathy A., and Judith L. Stephens. *Strange Fruit: Plays on Lynching by American Women.* Bloomington: Indiana University Press, 1998.

Perkins, Kathy A., Judith L. Stephens, and Roberto Uno, eds. *Contemporary Plays by Women of Color.* New York: Routledge, 1966.

Rampersad, Arnold. *The Life of Langston Hughes, Volume 1.* New York: Oxford University Press, 1986.

———. *The Life of Langston Hughes, Volume 2.* New York: Oxford University Press, 1988.

Richardson, Willis, and May Miller, eds. *Negro History in Thirteen Plays.* Washington, DC: Associated Publishers, 1935.

Sell, Mike, ed. *Ed. Bullins: Twelve Plays and Selected Writings.* Ann Arbor: University of Michigan Press, 2006.

Shannon, Sandra. *August Wilson and Black Aesthetics.* New York: Palgrave Macmillian, 2004.

ARTICLES

Abramson, Doris E. "Review of *The Escape; or, A Leap for Freedom*." *Educational Theatre Journal* 24 (1972): 190–91.

Ackamoor, Idris. "Black Performance Art at the Turn of the Century: A Personal History; Cultural Odyssey." *Black Theatre News* 8 (Spring 1998): 3, 13–14.

Anderson, Addell Austin. "The Ethiopian Art Theatre." *Theatre Survey* 33 (November 1992).

Anderson, Garland. "How I Became a Playwright." In *Anthology of the American Negro in the Theatre*, comp. Lindsay Patterson. Washington, DC: Publishers Company, 1967.

Brown, Lorraine. "Library of Congress Takes Back Federal Theatre Project Archive." *New Federal One* 19 (October 1994): 3.

Brustein, Robert. "The Lessons of *The Piano Lesson*." *New Republic* 202 (22 May 1990).

Castleberry, Bill. "Black Theatre Alliance Closes Down." *Uptown* (Summer 1981): 34.

Ceynowa, Andrzej. "Black Theaters . . . 1961–1982." *Black American Literature Forum* 17 (Summer 1983): 84–93.

Childress, Alice. "For a Negro Theatre." *Masses and Mainstream* (February 1952): 61–65.

Clarke, Breena. "Minnesota's Penumbra Theatre Moves into the Light." *Black Masks* 7 (August/September 1991): 6–8, 19.

Coleman, Mike. "What Is Black Theatre?" Interview with Amiri Baraka. *Black World* 20 (April 1971): 6, 32–36.

Colman, Stephen. "Crossroads Marks the Spot." *Black Masks* 7 (August/September 1991): 5–6.

Constantinidis, Stratos, ed. "American Theatre and the African Diaspora: What Is a Black Play?" *Text and Presentation*: *Journal of the Comparative Drama Conference* 24 (April 2003): 161–91.

"Detroit's Plowshares: A New Home for a Bold Theatre." *Black Theatre News* 6 (Fall 1997): 1.

Edmonds, Randolph S. "The Negro Little Theater Movement." *Negro History Bulletin* (January 1949): 82–84.

Fraden, Rena. "The Cloudy History of *Big White Fog*: The Federal Theatre Project, 1938." *American Studies* 29 (Spring 1988): 1, 5–27.

Gates, Henry Louis, Jr. "The Chitlin' Circuit." *New Yorker* 3 (February 1997): 44–55.

Grimké, Angelina Weld. "*Rachel* the Play of the Month, the Reason and Synopsis by the Author." *Competitor* 1 (January 1920): 51.

Hatch, James V. Interview with Winona Lee Fletcher, 8 May 1995. *Artist and Influence* 14 (1995); 107–18.

Hay, Samuel A. "The Death of Black Educational Theatre, 94, Stirs Huge Controversy." *Black Theatre News* 9 (Fall 1998): 27–28.

Martin, Sister Kathryn, S. P. "On Black Theatre of Revolution." *Today's Speech* (1972).

Morris, Eileen. "Theatre's Duality, Art and Industry." In *Black Theatre's Unprecedented Times* (pp. 93–94), ed. Hely Manuel Perez. Gainesville, FL: Black Theatre Network, 1999.

Oliver, Edith. "The Theatre Off-Broadway." *New Yorker* (11 February 1978).

Pawley, Thomas D. "The First Black Playwrights." *Black World* 21 (April 1972): 16–25.

Tanner, Jo. "Classical Black Theatre: Federal Theatre's All-Black 'Voodoo Macbeth.'" *American Drama and Theatre* 7 (Winter 1995): 1, 52.

Tooks, Kim. "Kia Corthron: Staying on Track." *Black Masks* 13 (May/June 1998): 1, 5–6.

Wallace, Michele. Interview with Abram Hill, 19 January 1974. *Artist and Influence* 19 (2000): 120.

DICTIONARIES, DIRECTORIES, REFERENCE WORKS, GUIDES, AND SOURCEBOOKS

Bean, Annemarie. *Sourcebook of African American Performance: Plays, People, Movements.* New York: Routledge, 1999.

Bergman, Peter M. *The Negro in America.* New York: A Mentor Book, 1969.

Bordman, Gerald. *American Musical Theatre: A Chronicle.* Oxford: Oxford University Press, 1978.

Carter, Steven R. *Hansberry's Drama: Commitment and Complexity.* Urbana: University of Illinois Press, 1991.

Edwards, Gus. *Advice to a Young Black Actor: Conversations with Douglas Turner Ward.* Portsmouth, NH: Heinemann, 2004.

Gray, John. *Black Theatre and Performance: A Pan-African Bibliography.* New York: Greenwood Press, 1990.

Hartnoll, Phyllis, ed. *The Oxford Companion to the Theatre.* 3rd ed. New York: Oxford University Press, 1870.

Hatch, James V. *Black Image on the American Stage: A Bibliography of Plays and Musicals 1770–1970.* New York: Drama Book Specialists, 1970.

Hatch, James V., and Leo Hamalian, eds. *The Roots of African American Drama: An Anthology of Early Plays, 1858–1938.* Detroit: Wayne State University Press, 1991.

——, eds. *Lost Plays of the Harlem Renaissance, 1920–1940.* Detroit: Wayne State University Press, 1996.

Harris, Trudier, and Thadious M. Davis, eds, *Afro-American Writers before the Harlem Renaissance.* Detroit: Gale Research, 1986.

Kellner, Bruce. *Harlem Renaissance: A Historical Dictionary for the Era.* Westport, CT: Greenwood Press, 1984.

Mapp, Edward. *Directory of Blacks in the Performing Arts.* Metuchen, NJ: Scarecrow Press, 1978.

National Committee on Cultural Diversity in the Performing Arts with the American Theatre Association. *Black Theatre Directory.* Washington, DC: John F. Kennedy Center for the Performing Arts, 1981.

Peterson, Bernard L. *A Century of Musicals in Black and White: An Encyclopedia of Musical Stage "Works by, about, or involving African Americans."* Westport, CT: Greenwood Press, 1993.

——. *Profiles of African American Stage Performers and Theatre People, 1816–1960.* Westport, CT: Greenwood Press, 2001.

——. *The African American Theatre Dictionary: A Comprehensive Guide to Early Black Theatre Organizations, Theatres, and Performance Groups.* Westport, CT: Greenwood Press, 1897.

Sampson, Henry T. *Blacks in Blackface: A Source Book on Early Black Musical Shows.* Metuchen, NJ: Scarecrow Press, 1980.

——. *The Ghost Walks: A Chronological History of Blacks in Show Business, 1865–1910.* Metuchen, NJ: Scarecrow Press, 1988.

Shannon, Sandra G. *August Wilson's* Fences*: A Reference Guide.* Westport, CT: Greenwood Press, 2003.

Woll, Allen. *Dictionary of the Black Theatre: Broadway, Off-Broadway and Selected Harlem Theatre.* Westport, CT: Greenwood Press, 1983.

DISSERTATIONS, PAMPHLETS, UNPUBLISHED PAPERS, AND PRESENTATIONS

Anderson, Addell Austin. "Pioneering Black Authored Dramas: 1924–27." Ph.D. dissertation, Michigan State University, 1986.

Belcher, Fannin Saffore, Jr. "The Place of the Negro in the Evolution of the American Theatre, 1762–1940." Ph.D. dissertation, Yale University, 1940.

Bullins, Ed., ed. *The Drama Review* 12, no.4 (Summer 1968).

Lewis, Barbara. "From Slavery to Segregation: On the Lynching Trial." Ph.D. dissertation, City University of New York, 2000.

Miller, Henry. "Art or Propaganda? A Historical and Critical Analysis of African American Theoretical Approaches to Drama, 1900–1975." Ph.D. dissertation, City University of New York, 2002.

Monroe, John Gilbert. "A Record of the Black Theatre in New York City: 1920–29." Ph.D. dissertation, University of Texas at Austin, 1980.

Nadler, Paul. "American Theatre and the Civil Rights Movement, 1945–1965." Ph.D. dissertation, City University of New York, 1996.

Perez, Manuel, and Victor Walker II, eds. *Black Theatre's Unprecedented Times: The Tribute of the Black Theatre Network to the Summits of 1998 and the African Grove Institute for the Arts.* A special publication of BTNews, 1998.

Silver, Reuben. "A History of the Karamu Theatre of Karamu House, 1915–1960." Ph.D. dissertation, The Ohio State University, 1961.

Thompson, Mary Francesca. "The Lafayette Players 1915–1932." Ph.D. dissertation, University of Michigan, 1972.

Vactor, Vanita. "A History of the Chicago Federal Theatre Project Negro Project Negro Unit: 1935–1939." Ph.D. dissertation, New York University, 1998.

Wilkerson, Margaret B. Wilkerson, and Veve A. Clark, eds. *The Black Scholar: Journal of Black Studies and Research* 10, no. 10 (July/August 1979).

Williams, Kathy Ervin. "Concept East Theatre: 1962–1976." Unpublished paper, National Conference on African American Theatre, 1987.

Wilson, August. "The Ground upon Which I Stand." Keynote address at Theater Communications Group, Princeton University, 26 June 1996.

INTERVIEWS

Edwards, Gus. *Advice to a Young Black Actor: Conversations with Douglas Turner Ward.* Portsmouth, NH: Heineman, 2004.

Hatch, James V. "Interview with Beth Turner." *Artist and Influence.* Vol. 24. New York: Hatch-Billops Collection, 2005, 163–73.

Hatch, James V. Interview with Douglas Q. Barnett, 1 October 1997. *Artist and Influence* 17 (1998): 1–27.

Jackson, Deliah. "Sirens, Sweethearts, and Showgirls of the Stage and Silver Screen." Interview with Edna Mae Harris and Vivian Harris, 4 February 1991. *Artist and Influence* 10 (1991): 75.

Lewis, Barbara. Interview with Woodie King Jr., 14 February 1999. *Artist and Influence* 18 (1999): 55–68.

Parks, Suzan-Lori. "Elements of Style." In *The America Play and Other Works.* New York: Theatre Communications Group, 1995.

Sellar, Tom. Interview with Suzan-Lori Parks. *Theatre Forum* 9 (Summer 1996): 37–39.

Wallace, Michele. Interview with Abram Hill, 19 January 1974. *Artist and Influence* 19 (2000): 120.

INTERNET RESOURCES

2007 African American Theatre Festival. www.theatermania.com/content/show .cfm/section/synopsis/show/130103.

African-American Theatre on the Web—Part 3. www.suite101.com/article.cfm/ 240/5589.

African Company/African Grove Theatre. www.blackpast.org/?q=aah/african company-african-grove-theatre.

American Theater Guide: African Americans in the American Theatre. www .answers.com/topic/african-americans-in-the-american-theatre.

Amiri Baraka: Poet, Playwright, Activist. www.amiribaraka.com.

The Great Black Way: African American Theater Producer Woodie King, Jr. www.findarticles.com/p/articles/mi_m1546/is_2_15/ai_62024114.

HistoryLink.org: The Online Encyclopedia of Washington State History. www .historylink.org/results.cfm?searchfield=topics&keyword=Ethnic%20 Communities.

New England Entertainment Digest—Online. www.jacneed.com/African _American_Theatre.html.

Onnaday: Donna Bennett. www.onnadaydonna.blogspot.com/2007/05/ schomburg-collection.html.

UrbanMecca.com. www.urbanmecca.com/search/search.php/search:cat/category.

Urban Reviews. www.msoyonline.com/african-american-web-portal/black -entertainment-theatre.htm.

Yale Library Research Workshop: African-American Theater. www.library.yale .edu/humanities/theater/instruction/afamtheater.html.

Young African American Poets: A Celebration of New Writing Poetry Readings by Evie Shockly, Douglas Kearney, and Amaud Jamal Johnson. www .beineckejwj.wordpress.com.

NEWSPAPERS AND PERIODICALS

African American Review
American Visions
Atlanta Constitution
Atlanta Journal and Constitution
Berkeley (California) Calendar
Black Liberator
Black Masks
Black Theatre

Chicago Defender
Chicago Inter-Ocean
Colored American Magazine
Crisis
Denver Exchange
Drama
Frederick Douglass' Paper (continuation of *North Star*)
Freedomways
Freeman (Indianapolis)
Indianapolis Freeman
Los Angeles Eagle
Los Angeles Herald Examiner
Los Angeles Times
Louisville (Kentucky) *Courier-Journal*
Messenger
Nation
National Advocate
Negro Handbook
Negro Heritage
Negro Year Book: An Annual Encyclopedia of the Negro
New York Age
New York American
New York Amsterdam News
New York Freeman
New York Globe
New York Herald
New York Times
Opportunity
Philadelphia Inquirer
Phylon: The Atlanta University Review of Race and Culture
Theatre Forum
Variety
Village Voice
Washington (DC) *Bee*
Washington (DC) *Post*
Yale Alumni Magazine

About the Authors

Dr. Anthony D. Hill is a writer, director, administrator, and associate professor of drama in the Department of Theatre at the Ohio State University. His work has concentrated extensively on previously marginalized theatre practices, African American and American theatre history, and performance theory and criticism. He recently developed and implemented upper-division undergraduate seminars on the life and works of August Wilson. He is featured in *Who's Who in Black Columbus* (2006 ed.). His book *Pages from the Harlem Renaissance: A Chronicle of Performance* (1996) is now in its second edition. His essays have appeared in such journals as *Text and Presentation, Journal of the Comparative Drama Conference*; *Black Studies: Current Issues, Enduring Questions*; and *African American Review* (formerly *Black American Literature Forum*). He contributed several historical articles to Dr. Quintard Taylor's *Pursuing the Past in the Twenty-first Century* on the World Wide Web and a book review in *The Journal of the Southern Central Modern Language Association* and was contributing editor for *History of the Theatre* (9th ed.), *Theatre Studies*, and *Elimu*.

Hill received advanced degrees in theatre at the University of Washington (B.A.) and Queens College (M.A.) and in performance studies at New York University (Ph.D.). He has taught at Vassar College, University of California at Santa Barbara, and the Ohio State University. He has been active professionally at the National Black Theatre Network Conference, the National Black Theatre Festival in Winston-Salem, NC, the National Conference of African American Theatre, the American Theatre of Higher Education, and other theatre organizations.

Douglas Q. Barnett is a writer, theatre administrator, play director, and producer. In 1968, he founded Black Arts/West (BA/W) in Seattle. During his five-year tenure as founding director of BA/W (1968–73), Barnett produced nearly 50 plays and recruited reputable directors from New York City to direct plays at the theatre. A significant number of students at BA/W have become professionals and have performed on Broadway, in regional theatres, on television, and in dance companies. Because of its success, BA/W has become a nationally acclaimed entity across the United States. A highlight of Barnett's career after he left BA/W was serving as company manager for the national tour (1973–74) of Joseph A. Walker's Tony award-winning play *The River Niger*, produced by the Negro Ensemble Company. He has also worked for the Seattle Arts Commission and GeVa Theatre in Rochester, NY.

Barnett has directed and written plays at BA/W, including *Da Minstrel Show* and *Days of Thunder, Nights of Violence*, and arranged, edited, and directed productions of African American poetry—a particular passion. He has also authored articles for the *Seattle Times*, the *Seattle Post Intelligencer*, *Negro Digest*, *Black World*, and *Historylink.org*, an online repository of Pacific Northwest history. Barnett has acted in over 30 productions with five different companies, including BA/W, A Contemporary Theatre, the Ensemble Theatre, and the Seattle Repertory Theatre. In 2007, the National Black Theatre Network (BTN) honored Barnett with the Pioneer Theatre Award at the historic North Carolina A&T in Greensborough, NC, with BTN president Dr. Sandra G. Shannon and Woodie King Jr. presiding.